Computing Concepts
with Java Essentials

3rd Edition

Cay Horstmann

San Jose State University

John Wiley & Sons, Inc.

ACQUISITIONS EDITOR: Paul Crockett

EDITORIAL ASSISTANT: Susannah Barr

MARKETING MANAGER: Katherine Hepburn

SENIOR PRODUCTION EDITOR: Valerie Vargas

PRODUCTION SERVICES MANAGER: Jeanine Furino

SENIOR DESIGNER: Harry Nolan

COVER DESIGN: Susan Cyr

PHOTO EDITOR: Lisa Gee

PRODUCTION MANAGEMENT SERVICES: Publication Services

This book was set in 10.5/12 Adobe Caslon Regular by Publication Services and printed and bound by RR Donnelley & Sons Company. The cover was printed by The Lehigh Press, Inc.

This book is printed on acid-free paper ∞

ISBN 0-471-24371-x (cloth : alk. paper)

Printed in the United States of America

10 9 8 7 6 5 4 3 2 1

Preface

This book is an introductory text in computer science, focusing on programming principles and practices. Why should you choose this book for your first course in computer science? Here are the key reasons:

- I take a point of view that goes beyond language syntax and focuses on computer science concepts.

- I stress the object-oriented paradigm, starting with the first example—an object-oriented version of the traditional "Hello, World" program.

- I motivate students to master the practical aspects of programming, with lots of useful tips and a chapter on testing and debugging.

- I present a carefully selected subset of the Java library that is accessible to beginners and rich enough to create interesting programs.

- I use the standard Java language, library, and tools—not a specialized "training wheels" environment.

The Use of Java

This book is based on the Java programming language. I chose Java for four reasons:

- Object orientation

- Safety

- Simplicity

- Breadth of the standard library

At this point, the object-oriented point of view is the predominant paradigm for software design. I strongly believe that object orientation enables students to spend more time on the design of their programs and less time coding and debugging. In this book, I start out with objects and classes early. Students learn how to manipulate objects and build simple classes in Chapter 2.

I rarely use static methods other than `main`. As a result, students think in terms of objects from the outset—they don't have to spend the second half of the course unlearning bad habits developed in the first half.

When designing classes, I strictly separate the classes from the test driver programs. (In fact, if you use an environment such as BlueJ, then you don't need the test driver programs at all. This book doesn't require that you use BlueJ or any other particular environment, but it works very well with BlueJ. Give it a try and you too may become a convert—my students were delighted when they were able to interact with their objects in an intuitive fashion.)

Another notable aspect of this book is that I cover interfaces before subclasses. This has a great advantage: Students see the power of polymorphism before having to worry about technicalities of extending classes.

Of course, there are many object-oriented programming languages besides Java. In principle, one can teach object-oriented programming using the C++ language. However, Java has a fundamental advantage over C++, namely its safety. Students can—and do—make an amazing number of errors when using C++, many of which lead to mysterious and irreproducible program behavior. When using C++, an instructor must spend a great deal of class time on safe programming habits, or students will end up with a well-deserved lack of confidence in their creations—hardly an ideal situation for a beginning course.

Another major advantage of Java is its simplicity. Although it is not a reasonable goal to cover all constructs of Java in the first course, instructors can master all of the syntax and semantics of the Java language and can answer student questions with complete confidence. In contrast, the C++ language is so complex that very few people can truthfully state that they understand all features of the language. Even though I have used C++ extensively for over a dozen years, I regularly get stumped by freshmen who show me a particularly baffling compiler error message. Simplicity is important, especially for a foundational course. It is not a good practice to choose as a foundational tool a programming language that students and instructors cannot master with confidence.

Finally, the standard Java library has sufficient breadth that it can be used for most courses in a computer science curriculum. Graphics, user interface construction, database access, multithreading, and network programming are all part of the standard library. Thus, the skills that students learn in the beginning course will serve them well throughout the curriculum. Again, C++ falls notably short in this regard. There are no standard toolkits for any of the above-mentioned programming domains in C++. The Java library subset that this book covers enables students to handle a wide variety of common programming tasks.

A Tour of the Book

The book can be naturally grouped into three parts. Figure 1 shows the dependencies among the chapters.

Part A

Chapters 1 through 8 cover the fundamentals of object-based programming: objects, methods, classes, variables, number types, strings, and control structures. Students learn how to build very simple classes in Chapter 2. Chapter 7 takes up the subject of class design in a more systematic fashion.

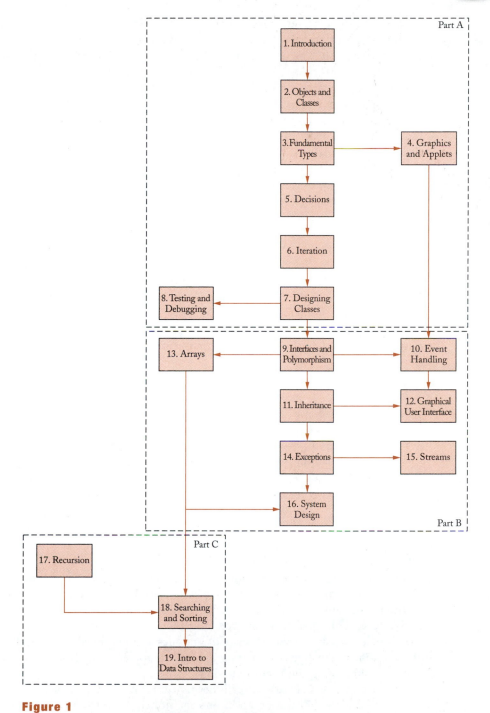

Figure 1

Chapter Dependencies

Starting with Chapter 7, I use a very small subset of the UML notation—just class diagrams and four arrow types for dependency, realization of interfaces, inheritance, and directed association. That small subset is useful for visualizing the relationships between classes, but it minimizes issues that beginners find complex, such as when to choose association, aggregation, or attributes.

I cover graphics very early, in Chapter 4, because many students enjoy writing programs that create drawings, and because rectangles, ellipses, and lines are good examples of objects. I use the "2D graphics" classes in the `java.awt.geom` package throughout, not the outdated procedural methods in the `Graphics` class. Calling `g.drawRect(x,y,w,h)` is *not* object-oriented. Manipulating geometric objects is both object-oriented and fun for the students. I use applets because students can program them with very little technical knowledge.

However, coverage of graphics is entirely optional. All material has been carefully presented so that you can skip all chapters that cover graphics and graphical user interfaces.

Chapter 8 covers testing and debugging, a subject that is unfortunately given short shrift in many textbooks.

As explained in Chapter 3, you can either use the `JOptionPane` class to read input from a dialog box (even in a console program), or you can use a `BufferedReader`. The latter forces you to tag the `main` method with `throws IOException`, which I used to find unacceptable until I reorganized all programs so that the `main` method is just a "throwaway" test driver class. I don't find it problematic if methods in a test driver class throw exceptions. (By the end of the first semester, students will know how to catch exceptions.)

Part B

Chapters 9 through 16 cover inheritance, arrays, exceptions, streams and, optionally, graphical user interface (GUI) programming.

The discussion of inheritance is split into two chapters. Chapter 9 covers interfaces and polymorphism, whereas Chapter 11 covers inheritance. Introducing interfaces before inheritance pays off in several ways. Students immediately see polymorphism before getting bogged down with superclass construction. It becomes possible to discuss event-driven programming at an early stage. Students are naturally led to local inner classes for event handlers, a more robust technique than the "opportunistic" realization of event interfaces that one still finds in older textbooks.

GUI programming is split into two chapters. Chapter 10 covers event-driven programming, relying just on the notion of an interface introduced in Chapter 9. Chapter 12 covers GUI components and their layout. This chapter requires some knowledge of inheritance (extending frames and panels and invoking `super.paintComponent`). It is possible to cover both of these chapters together, either before or after Chapter 11.

Again, let me stress that coverage of graphics and graphical user interfaces is entirely optional. One alternative is to cover graphics and applets (which are quite simple to program) and skip GUIs and event handling.

I cover arrays and streams after inheritance. From an object-oriented point of view, inheritance is a crucial concept, and I find that it helps to introduce it as early as possible. However, if you prefer to cover arrays and streams earlier, you can simply switch the chapters without incurring any problems.

I prefer to cover array lists first before covering arrays. In my experience, students find the `get`/`set` syntax perfectly natural and have surprisingly little attachment to the `[]` operator. They aren't even overly bothered by the cast required when using the `get` method. By using array lists, you avoid the unpleasantness of partially filled arrays altogether—it is no wonder that most professional programmers use array lists (or vectors) all the time and rarely resort to arrays. Of course, you need arrays for numbers, but lists of numbers aren't all that common in object-oriented programs.

I highly recommend covering object streams and serialization, especially if the course involves significant programming projects. In my experience, students are delighted when they discover that they can store the entire state of their application with a single `writeObject` call and retrieve it again just as easily.

Part C

Chapters 17 through 19 contain an introduction to algorithms and data structures, covering recursion, sorting and searching, linked lists, binary trees, and hash tables. These topics are probably outside the scope of a one-semester course.

When discussing recursion, I find that the object-oriented point of view is very helpful. In my introductory examples, an object that solves a problem recursively constructs another object of the same class that solves a simpler problem. Having the other object do the simpler job is much more plausible to students than having a function call itself.

I place the data structures into the context of the standard Java collections library. However, a detailed discussion of the implementation of data structures is beyond the scope of this book.

Appendices

Appendix A1 contains a style guide for use with this book. I have found it highly beneficial to require a consistent style for all assignments. If this style guide conflicts with instructor sentiment or local customs, it can be modified. The style guide is available in electronic form for this purpose. Other appendices contain an overview over the parts of the standard library that this book covers, as well as a table of the Latin-1 subset of Unicode and a glossary.

The Pedagogical Structure

The beginning of each chapter has the customary overview of chapter objectives and motivational introduction. Throughout each chapter, margin notes show the places at which new concepts are introduced. The notes are summarized at the end of the chapter.

> To help students locate key concepts easily, margin notes show the place at which new concepts are introduced.

Throughout the chapters, there are five sets of notes to help your students, namely those entitled "Common Errors", "Productivity Hints", "Quality Tips", "Advanced Topics", and "Random Facts". These notes are specially marked so that they don't interrupt the flow of the main material. I expect that most instructors cover only a few of these notes in class and assign others for home reading. Some notes are quite short; others extend over a page. I decided to give each note the space that is needed for a full and convincing explanation, rather than attempting to fit them into one-paragraph "tips".

- **Common Errors** describe the kinds of errors that students often make, with an explanation of why the errors occur, and what to do about them. Most students quickly discover the Common Errors sections and read them on their own.

- **Quality Tips** explain good programming practices. Since most of them require an initial investment of effort, these notes carefully motivate the reason behind the advice, and explain why the effort will be repaid later.

- **Productivity Hints** teach students how to use their tools more effectively. Many beginning students put little thought into their use of computers and software. They are often unfamiliar with tricks of the trade such as keyboard shortcuts, global search and replace, or automation of common tasks with scripts.

- **Advanced Topics** cover nonessential or more difficult material. Some of these topics introduce alternative syntactical constructions that are not necessarily technically advanced. In many cases, the book uses one particular language construct but explains alternatives as Advanced Topics. Instructors and students should feel free to use those constructs in their own programs if they prefer them. It has, however, been my experience that many students are grateful for the "keep it simple" approach, because it greatly reduces the number of gratuitous decisions they have to make.

- **Random Facts** provide historical and social information on computing, as required to fulfill the "historical and social context" requirements of the ACM curriculum guidelines, as well as capsule reviews of advanced computer science topics. Many students will read the Random Facts on their own while pretending to follow the lecture.

- New to this edition is a set of **HOWTO** sections, inspired by the Linux HOWTO guides. These sections are intended to answer the common student question: "Now what do I do?", by giving step-by-step instructions for common tasks.

Web Resources

Additional resources are found on the book's web site at http://www.wiley.com/college/horstmann. These resources include:

- Solutions to selected exercises (accessible to students)
- Solutions to all exercises (for instructors only)
- A test bank
- A laboratory manual
- A list of frequently asked questions
- Help with common compilers
- Presentation slides for lectures
- Discussion boards for instructors and students
- Source code for all examples in the book

- The programming style guide in electronic form, so you can modify it to suit local preferences

- A "crash course in C++" that takes students rapidly from the material covered in this book to C++ programming

Acknowledgments

Many thanks to Paul Crockett, Bill Zobrist, Katherine Hepburn, and Lisa Gee at John Wiley & Sons and Jerome Colburn, Lori Martinsek, and the team at Publication Services for their hard work and support for this book project.

I am very grateful to the many individuals who reviewed the manuscript, made valuable suggestions and brought an embarrassingly large number of errors and omissions to my attention. They include:

Sven Anderson, University of North Dakota, Robert Burton, Brigham Young University, Bruce Ellinbogen, University of Michigan-Dearborn, John Franco, University of Cincinnati, Rick Giles, Acadia University, John Gray, University of Hartford, Joann Houlihan, John Hopkins University, Richard Kick, Hinsdale Central High School, Michael Kölling, University of Southern Denmark, Miroslaw Majewski, Zayed University, Blaine Mayfield, Oklahoma State University, Hugh McGuire, University of California-Santa Barbara, Jim Miller, Bradley University, Jim Miller, University of Kansas, Don Needham, US Naval Academy, Ben Nystin, University of Colorado at Colorado Springs, Hugh O'Brien, University of California-Santa Barbara, Kathleen O'Brien, West Valley College, Richard Pattis, Carnegie Mellon University, Pete Peterson, Texas A&M University, Sarah Pham, SGI, Stuart Reges, University of Arizona, Jim Roberts, Carnegie Mellon University, John Rose, University of South Carolina-Columbia, Kenneth Slonneger, University of Iowa, and Monica Sweck, University of Florida.

Finally, as always, my gratitude goes to my family—Hui-Chen, Thomas and Nina—for their never-ending encouragement and patience.

Contents

Introduction

1.1   What Is a Computer?

You have probably used a computer for work or fun. Many people use computers for everyday tasks such as balancing a checkbook or writing a term paper. Computers are good for such tasks. They can handle repetitive chores, such as totaling up numbers or placing words on a page, without getting bored or exhausted. More importantly, the computer presents you with the checkbook or the term paper on the screen and lets you fix up mistakes easily. Computers also make good game machines because they can play sequences of sounds and pictures, involving the human user in the process.

> A computer must be programmed to perform tasks. Different tasks require different programs.

What makes all this possible is not just the computer. The computer must be *programmed* to perform these tasks. A computer itself is a machine that stores data (numbers, words, pictures), interacts with devices (the monitor screen, the sound system, the printer), and executes programs. Programs are sequences of instructions and decisions that the computer carries out to achieve a task. One program balances checkbooks; a different program, perhaps designed and constructed by a different company, processes words; and a third program, probably from yet another company, plays a game.

> A computer program executes a sequence of very basic operations in rapid succession.

Today's computer programs are so sophisticated that it is hard to believe that they are all composed of extremely primitive operations. A typical operation may be one of the following:

- Put a red dot onto this screen position.
- Send the letter A to the printer.
- Get a number from this location in memory.
- Add up these two numbers.
- If this value is negative, continue the program at that instruction.

Only because a program contains a huge number of such operations, and because the computer can execute them at great speed, does the computer user have the illusion of smooth interaction.

The flexibility of a computer is quite an amazing phenomenon. The same machine can balance your checkbook, print your term paper, and play a game. In contrast, other machines carry out a much narrower range of tasks; a car drives, and a toaster toasts. Computers can carry out a wide range of tasks because they execute different programs, each of which directs the computer to work on a specific task.

1.2   What Is Programming?

> Programmers develop computer programs to make computers perform new tasks.

A computer program tells a computer, in minute detail, the sequence of steps that are needed to fulfill a task. The act of designing and implementing these programs is called computer programming. As you work through this book, you will learn how to program a computer—that is, how to direct the computer to execute tasks.

To use a computer you do not need to do any programming. When you write a term paper with a word processor, that software package has been programmed by the manufacturer and is ready for you to use. That is only to be expected—you can drive a car without being a mechanic and toast bread without being an electrician. Many people who use computers every day in their careers never need to do any programming.

Of course, a professional computer scientist or software engineer does a great deal of programming. You are reading this introductory computer science book, so your career goal may well be to become such a professional. Programming is not the only skill required of a computer scientist or software engineer; indeed, programming is not the only skill required to create successful computer programs. Nevertheless, the activity of programming is an important part of computer science. It is also a fascinating and pleasurable activity that continues to attract and motivate students. The discipline of computer science is particularly fortunate that it can make such an interesting activity the foundation of the learning path.

Writing a computer game with motion and sound effects or a word processor that supports fancy fonts and pictures is a complex task that requires a team of many highly skilled programmers. Your first programming efforts will be more mundane. The concepts and skills you learn in this book form an important foundation, and you should not be disappointed if your first programs do not rival the sophisticated software that is familiar to you. Actually, you will find that there is an immense thrill even in simple programming tasks. It is an amazing experience to see the computer precisely and quickly carry out a task that would take you hours of drudgery, to make small changes in a program that lead to immediate improvements, and to see the computer become an extension of your mental powers.

1.3   The Anatomy of a Computer

To understand the programming process, you need to have a rudimentary understanding of the building blocks that make up a computer. We will look at a personal computer. Larger computers have faster, larger, or more powerful components, but they have fundamentally the same design.

> At the heart of the computer lies the central processing unit (CPU).

At the heart of the computer lies the *central processing unit* (CPU) (see Figure 1). It consists of a single *chip* (integrated circuit) or a small number of chips. A computer chip is a component with a plastic or metal housing, metal connectors, and inside wiring made principally from silicon. For a CPU chip, the inside wiring is enormously complicated. For example, the Pentium III chip (a popular CPU for personal computers at the time of this writing) contains over 28 million structural elements called *transistors*—the elements that enable electrical signals to control other electrical signals, making automatic computing possible. The CPU performs program control, arithmetic, and data movement. That is, the CPU locates and executes the program instructions; it carries out arithmetic operations such as addition, subtraction, multiplication, and division; it fetches data from external memory or devices or stores data back. All data must travel through the CPU whenever it is moved from one location to another. (There are a few technical exceptions to this rule; some devices can interact directly with memory.)

Figure 1

Central Processing Unit

> Data and programs are stored in primary storage (memory) and secondary storage (such as a hard disk).

The computer keeps data and programs in *storage*. There are two kinds of storage. *Primary storage*, also called *random-access memory* (*RAM*) or simply *memory*, is fast but expensive; it is made from memory chips (see Figure 2). Primary storage has two disadvantages. It is comparatively expensive, and it loses all its data when the power is turned off. *Secondary storage*, usually a *hard disk* (see Figure 3), provides less expensive storage that persists without electricity. A hard disk consists of rotating platters, which are coated with a magnetic material, and read/write heads, which can detect and change

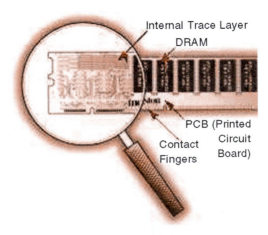

Figure 2

A Memory Module with Memory Chips

Figure 3

A Hard Disk

the patterns of varying magnetic flux on the platters. This is essentially the same recording and playback process that is used in audio or video tapes.

Some computers are self-contained units, whereas others are interconnected through *networks*. Home computers are usually intermittently connected to the Internet via a modem. The computers in your computer lab are probably permanently connected to a local area network. Through the network cabling, the computer can read programs from central storage locations or send data to other computers. For the user of a networked computer, it may not even be obvious which data reside on the computer itself and which are transmitted through the network.

Most computers have *removable storage* devices that can access data or programs on media such as floppy disks, tapes, or compact discs (CDs).

The most common use for a floppy disk is to move data from one computer to another; you can copy data from your home computer and bring the disk to school to continue working with it. Now that network connections have become commonplace, some computer manufacturers have discontinued the use of floppy disk drives, because email or a network-based file-sharing service can transport data between networked computers much more quickly and easily.

Compact discs originally served as read-only memories (CD-ROMs), which, like a commercial audio CD, could only be "played back" to bring the data on them into memory, but more and more new computers support CDs that a personal computer user can record (CD-Rs) or even overwrite with new data (CD-RWs).

Figure 4

A Motherboard

To interact with a human user, a computer requires other peripheral devices. The computer transmits information to the user through a display screen, loudspeakers, and printers. The user can enter information and directions to the computer by using a keyboard or a pointing device such as a mouse.

The CPU, the RAM, and the electronics controlling the hard disk and other devices are interconnected through a set of electrical lines called a *bus*. Data travel along the bus from the system memory and peripheral devices to the CPU and back. Figure 4 shows a *motherboard*, which contains the CPU, the RAM, and *card slots*, through which cards that control peripheral devices connect to the bus.

▼ **Random Fact** 1.1

The ENIAC and the Dawn of Computing

The ENIAC (*e*lectronic *n*umerical *i*ntegrator *a*nd *c*omputer) was the first usable electronic computer. It was designed by J. Presper Eckert and John Mauchly at the University of Pennsylvania and was completed in 1946. Instead of transistors, which were not invented until two years after it was built, the ENIAC contained about 18,000 *vacuum tubes* in many cabinets housed in a large room (see Figure 5). Vacuum tubes burned out at the rate of several tubes per day. An attendant with a shopping cart full of tubes con-

Figure 5

The ENIAC

stantly made the rounds and replaced defective ones. The computer was programmed by connecting wires on panels. Each wiring configuration would set up the computer for a particular problem. To have the computer work on a different problem, the wires had to be replugged.

Work on the ENIAC was supported by the U.S. Navy, which was interested in computations of ballistic tables that would give the trajectory of a projectile, depending on the wind resistance, initial velocity, and atmospheric conditions. To compute the trajectories, one must find the numerical solutions of certain differential equations; hence the name "numerical integrator". Before machines like ENIAC were developed, humans did this kind of work, and until the 1950s the word "computer" referred to these people. The ENIAC was later used for peaceful purposes such as the tabulation of U.S. census data.

Figure 6 gives a schematic overview of the architecture of a computer. Program instructions and data (such as text, numbers, audio, or video) are stored on the hard disk, on a CD, or elsewhere on the network. When a program is started, it is brought into memory, from which the CPU can read it. The CPU reads the program an instruction at a time. As directed by these instructions, the CPU reads data, modifies them, and writes them back to

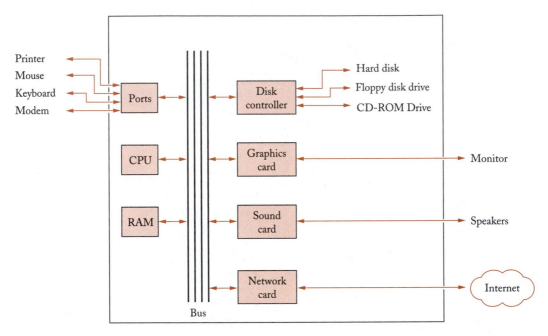

Figure 6

Schematic Diagram of a Computer

> The CPU reads machine instructions from memory. The instructions direct it to communicate with memory, secondary storage, and peripheral devices.

RAM or to secondary storage. Some program instructions will cause the CPU to place dots on the display screen or to vibrate the speaker. As these actions happen many times over and at great speed, the human user will perceive images and sound. Similarly, the CPU can send instructions to a printer to mark the paper with patterns of closely spaced dots, which a human recognizes as text characters and pictures. Some program instructions read user input from the keyboard or mouse. The program analyzes the nature of these inputs and then executes the next appropriate instructions.

1.4 Translating Human-Readable Programs to Machine Code

> Generally, machine code depends on the CPU type. However, the instruction set of the Java virtual machine (JVM) can be executed on many CPUs.

On the most basic level, computer instructions are extremely primitive. The processor executes *machine instructions*. CPUs from different vendors, such as the Intel Pentium or the Sun SPARC, have different sets of machine instructions. To enable Java applications to run on multiple CPUs without modification, most Java programs contain machine instructions for a so-called "Java virtual machine" (JVM), an idealized CPU that is then simulated by a program run on the actual CPU. The difference between actual and virtual machine instructions is not important to us—all you need to know is that machine instructions are very simple and can be executed very quickly.

A typical sequence of machine instructions is

1. Load the contents of memory location 40.
2. Load the value 100.
3. If the first value is greater than the second value, continue with the instruction that is stored in memory location 240.

Actually, machine instructions are encoded as numbers so that they can be stored in memory. On the Java virtual machine, this sequence of instruction is encoded as the sequence of numbers

```
21 40 16 100 163 240
```

Because machine instructions are encoded as numbers, it is difficult to write programs in machine code.

On a processor such as a Pentium or SPARC, the encoding would be quite different.

When the virtual machine fetches this sequence of numbers, it decodes them and executes the associated sequence of commands.

How can you communicate the command sequence to the computer?

The simplest method is to place the actual numbers into the computer memory. This is, in fact, how the very earliest computers worked. However, a long program is composed of thousands of individual commands, and it is tedious and error-prone to look up the numeric codes for all commands and place the codes manually into memory. As we said before, computers are really good at automating tedious and error-prone activities, and it did not take long for computer programmers to realize that the computers themselves could be harnessed to help in the programming process.

The first step was to assign short names to the commands. For example, `iload` denotes "integer load", `bipush` means "push integer constant", and `if_icmpgt` means "if integers compare greater". Using these commands, the instruction sequence becomes

```
iload 40
bipush 100
if_icmpgt 240
```

Assembly language makes it easier to generate machine instructions by translating mnemonics and symbolic names.

That is a lot easier to read for humans. To get the instruction sequences accepted by the computer, though, the names must be translated into the machine codes. Early computers used a computer program called an *assembler* to carry out these translations. An assembler takes the sequence of characters such as `iload`, translates it into the command code 21, and carries out similar operations on the other commands. Assemblers have another feature: They can give names to *memory locations* as well as to instructions. Our program sequence might have checked that some interest rate was greater than 100 percent, and the interest rate was stored in memory location 40. It is usually not important where a value is stored; any available memory location will do. When symbolic names are used instead of memory addresses, the program gets even easier to read:

```
iload       intRate
bipush      100
if_icmpgt   intError
```

It is the job of the assembler program to find suitable numeric addresses for the symbolic names and to put those addresses into the generated code sequence.

Assembler instructions were a major advance over programming with raw machine instructions, but they suffer from two problems: It still takes a great many instructions to achieve even the simplest goals, and the exact instruction sequence differs from one processor to another.

> High-level languages let you describe tasks at a higher conceptual level than machine code.

In the mid-1950s, *high-level* programming languages began to appear. In these languages, the programmer expresses the idea behind the task that needs to be performed, and a special computer program, called a *compiler,* translates the high-level description into machine instructions for a particular processor.

For example, in Java, the high-level programming language that you will use in this book, you might give the following instruction:

```
if (intRate > 100)
    System.out.print("Interest rate error");
```

This means, "If the interest rate is over 100, display an error message." It is then the job of the compiler program to look at the sequence of characters `if (intRate > 100)` and translate that into

```
21 40 16 100 163 240
```

> A compiler translates programs written in a high-level language into machine code.

Compilers are quite sophisticated programs. They have to translate logical statements, such as the `if`, into sequences of computations, tests, and jumps, and they must find memory locations for *variables*—items of information identified by symbolic names—like `intRate`. In this course, we will generally take the existence of a compiler for granted. If you decide to become a professional computer scientist, you may well learn more about compiler-writing techniques later in your studies.

1.5   Programming Languages

> Each programming language has its own set of rules for forming instructions. Compilers enforce these rules strictly.

High-level programming languages are independent of specific computer architecture, but they are human creations. As such, they follow certain conventions. To ease the translation process, those conventions are much stricter than they are for human languages. When you talk to another person, and you scramble or omit a word or two, your conversation partner will usually still understand what you have to say. Compilers are less forgiving. For example, if you omit the quotation mark close to the end of the instruction,

```
if (intRate > 100)
  System.out.print("Interest rate error);
```

the Java compiler will get quite confused and complain that it cannot translate an instruction containing this error. That is actually a good thing. If the compiler were to try to guess what you did wrong and tried to fix it, it might not guess your intentions correctly. In that case, the resulting program would do the wrong thing—quite possibly with disastrous effects, if that program controlled a device on whose functions someone's well-being depends. When a compiler reads programming instructions in a programming language, it will translate them into machine code only if the input follows the language conventions exactly.

Just as there are many human languages, there are many programming languages. Consider the instruction

```
if (intRate > 100)
  System.out.print("Interest rate error");
```

This is how you must express a decision in Java. Java is a very popular programming language, and it is the one we use in this book. But in Pascal (another programming language that was in common use in the 1970s and 1980s) the same instruction would be written as

```
if intRate > 100 then write('Interest rate error');
```

In this case, the differences between the Java and Pascal versions are slight. For other constructions, there will be far more substantial differences. Compilers are language-specific. The Java compiler will translate only Java code, whereas a Pascal compiler will reject anything but legal Pascal code. For example, if a Java compiler reads the instruction `if intRate > 100 then ...`, it will complain, because the condition of the `if` statement isn't surrounded by parentheses () and the compiler doesn't expect the word `then`. The choice of the layout for a language construct like the `if` statement is somewhat arbitrary, and the designers of different languages choose different tradeoffs among readability, easy translation, and consistency with other languages.

1.6   The Java Programming Language

In 1991, a group led by James Gosling and Patrick Naughton at Sun Microsystems designed a language that they code-named "Green" for use in consumer devices such as intelligent television "set-top" boxes. The language was designed to be simple and architecture-neutral, so that it could be executed on a variety of hardware. No customer was ever found for this technology.

> Java was originally designed for programming consumer devices, but it was first successfully used to write Internet applets.

Gosling recounts that in 1994 the team realized, "We could write a really cool browser. It was one of the few things in the client/server mainstream that needed some of the weird things we'd done: architecture neutral, real-time, reliable, secure." The HotJava browser, which was shown to an enthusiastic crowd at the SunWorld exhibition in 1995, had one unique property: It could download programs, called *applets,* from the web and run them. Applets, written in the language now called Java, let web developers provide a variety of animation and interaction that can greatly extend the capabilities of a web page (see Figure 7). Since 1996, both Netscape and Microsoft have supported Java in their browsers.

Java has grown at a phenomenal rate. Programmers have embraced the language because it is simpler than its closest rival, C++. In addition to the programming language itself, Java has a rich *library* that makes it possible to write portable programs that can

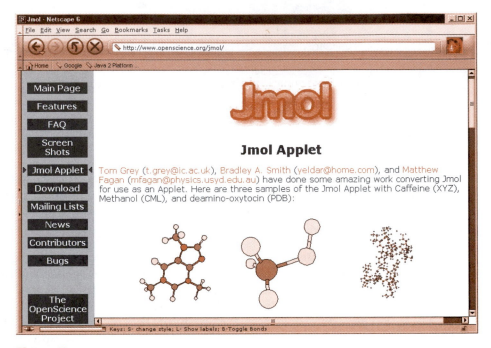

Figure 7

An Applet for Visualizing Molecules (`http://www.openscience.com/jmol`)

bypass proprietary operating systems—a feature that was eagerly sought by those who wanted to be independent of those proprietary systems and was bitterly fought by their vendors.

Some of the early expectations that were placed on the Java language were overly optimistic, and the slogan "write once, run anywhere" turned into "write once, debug everywhere" for the early adopters of Java, who had to deal with less-than-perfect implementations. Since then, Java has come a long way. The Java 2 language and library, released in 1998, has brought a much greater level of stability to Java development. A "micro edition" and an "enterprise edition" of the Java library make Java programmers at home on hardware ranging from the smallest embedded devices to the largest Internet servers.

> Java was designed to be safe and portable, benefitting both Internet users and students.

Because Java was designed for the Internet, it has two attributes that make it very suitable for beginners: safety and portability. If you visit a web page that contains applets, those applets automatically start running. It is important that you can trust that applets are inherently safe. If an applet could do something evil, such as damaging data or reading personal information on your computer, then you would be in real danger every time you browsed the Web—an unscrupulous designer might put up a web page containing dangerous code that would execute on your machine as soon as you visited the page. The Java language has an assortment of security features that guarantee that no evil applets can run on your computer. As an added benefit, these features also help you to learn the language faster. The Java virtual machine can catch many kinds of beginners' mistakes and report them accurately. (In contrast, many beginners' mistakes in the C language merely produce programs that act in random and confusing ways.) The other benefit of Java is portability. The same Java program will run, without change, on Windows, UNIX, Linux, or the Macintosh. This too is a requirement for applets. When you visit a web page, the web server that serves up the page contents has no idea what computer you are using to browse the Web. It simply returns you the portable code that was generated by the Java compiler. The virtual machine on your computer executes that portable code. Again, there is a benefit for the student. You do not have to learn how to write programs for different computers' operating systems.

At this time, Java has already established itself as one of the most important languages for general-purpose programming as well as for computer science instruction. However, although Java is a good language for beginners, it is not perfect, for two reasons.

Because Java was not specifically designed for students, no thought was given to make it really simple to write basic programs. A certain amount of technical machinery is necessary in Java to write even the simplest programs. To understand what this technical machinery does, you need to know something about programming. This is not a problem for a professional programmer with prior experience in another programming language, but not having a linear learning path is a drawback for the student. As you learn how to program in Java, there will be times when you will be asked to be satisfied with a preliminary explanation and wait for complete details in a later chapter.

> Java has a very large library. Focus on learning those parts of the library that you need for your programming projects.

Furthermore, you cannot hope to learn all of Java in one semester. The Java language itself is relatively simple, but Java contains a vast set of *library packages* that are necessary to write useful programs. There are packages for graphics, user interface design, cryptography, networking, sound, database storage, and many other purposes. Even expert Java programmers do not know the contents of all of the packages—they just use those that they need for particular projects. Using this book, you should expect to learn a good deal about the Java language and about the most important packages. Keep in mind that the central goal of this book is not to make you memorize Java minutiae, but to teach you how to think about programming.

1.7   Becoming Familiar with Your Computer

> Set aside some time to become familiar with the computer system and the Java compiler that you will use for your class work.

You may be taking your first programming course as you read this book, and you may well be doing your work on an unfamiliar computer system. You should spend some time making yourself familiar with the computer. Because computer systems vary widely, this book can only give an outline of the steps you need to follow. Using a new and unfamiliar computer system can be frustrating, especially if you are on your own. Look for training courses that your campus offers, or just ask a friend to give you a brief tour.

Step 1. Log In

If you use your own home computer, you probably don't need to worry about this step. Computers in a lab, however, are usually not open to everyone. Access is usually restricted

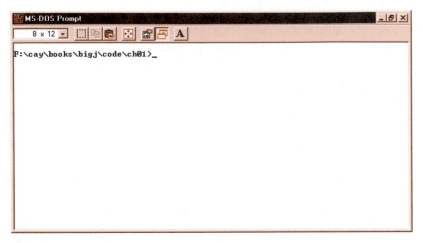

Figure 8

A Shell Window

to those who have paid the necessary fees, and often each student account has permissions and restrictions that enable the student to do class work but not mess up the system for others. You will need an account name or number and a password to gain access to such a system.

Step 2. Locate the Java Compiler

Computer systems differ greatly in this regard. On some systems you must open a *shell window* (see Figure 8) and type commands to launch the compiler. Other systems have an *integrated development environment* in which you can write and test your programs (see Figure 9). Many university labs have information sheets and tutorials that walk you through the tools that are installed in the lab. The companion web site for this book (reference [1] at the end of this chapter) contains instructions for several popular compilers.

Step 3. Understand Files and Folders

As a programmer, you will write Java programs, try them out, and improve them. You will be provided a place in secondary storage to store them, and you need to find out where that place is. Information in secondary storage is kept in *files*. A file is a collection of items of information that are kept together, such as the text of a word processing document or the instructions of a Java program. Files have names, and the rules for legal names differ from one system to another. Some systems allow spaces in file names; others don't. Some distinguish between upper- and lowercase letters; others don't. Most Java compilers require that Java files end in an *extension* .java; for example, Test.java. Java file names cannot contain spaces, and the distinction between upper- and lowercase letters is important.

   Files are stored in *folders* or *directories*. These file containers can be *nested*. That is, a folder can contain not only files but also other folders, which themselves can contain

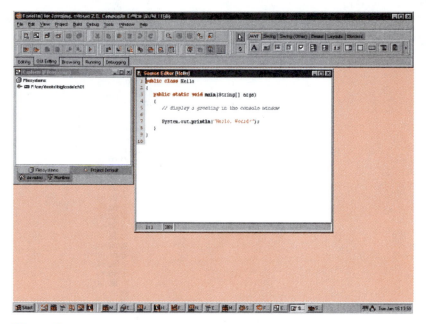

Figure 9

An Integrated Development Environment

more files and folders (see Figure 10). This hierarchy can be quite large, especially on networked computers, where some of the files may be on your local disk, others elsewhere on the network. While you need not be concerned with every branch of the hierarchy, you should familiarize yourself with your local environment. Different systems have different ways of showing files and directories. Some use a graphical display and let you move around by clicking the mouse on folder icons. In other systems, you must enter commands to visit or inspect different locations.

Step 4. Write a Simple Program

In the next section, we will introduce a very simple program. You will need to learn how to type it in, how to run it, and how to fix mistakes.

Step 5. Save Your Work

You will spend many hours typing Java program code and improving it. The resulting program files have some value, and you should treat them as you would other important property. A conscientious safety strategy is particularly important for computer files. They are more fragile than paper documents or other more tangible objects. It is easy to delete a file by accident, and occasionally files are lost because of a computer malfunction. Unless you kept another copy, you must then retype the contents. Because you probably won't remember the entire file, you will likely find yourself spending almost as much time again as you did to enter and improve it in the first place. This costs time, and it may cause you to miss deadlines. It is therefore crucially important that you learn how

Figure 10

Nested Folders

to safeguard files and that you get in the habit of doing so *before* disaster strikes. You can make safety or *backup* copies of files by saving copies on a floppy, into another folder, or to a different computer on your local area network or the Internet.

Productivity Hint   1.1

Backup Copies

Backing up on floppy disks is the easiest and most convenient method for most people. Another increasingly popular form of backup is Internet file storage. Here are a few pointers to keep in mind.

> Develop a strategy for keeping backup copies of your work before disaster strikes.

- *Back up often.* Backing up a file takes only a few seconds, and you will hate yourself if you have to spend many hours recreating work that you could have saved easily. Back up your work once every thirty minutes, and every time before you test one of your programs.

- *Rotate backups.* Use more than one floppy disk for backups, and rotate them. That is, first back up onto the first floppy disk and put it aside. Then back up onto the second floppy disk. Then use the third, and then go back to the first. That way you always have three recent backups. Even if one of the floppy disks has a defect, you can use one of the others.

▼

▼

- *Back up source files only.* The compiler translates the files that you write into files consisting of machine code. There is no need to back up the machine code files, since you can recreate them easily by running the compiler again. Focus your backup activity on those files that represent your effort. That way your backup disks won't fill up with files that you don't need.

▼

- *Pay attention to the backup direction.* Backing up involves copying files from one place to another. It is important that you do this right—that is, copy from your work location to the backup location. If you do it the wrong way, you will over-write a newer file with an older version.

▼

▼

- *Check your backups once in a while.* Double-check that your backups are where you think they are. There is nothing more frustrating than to find out that the backups are not there when you need them. This is particularly true if you use a backup program that stores files on an unfamiliar device (such as data tape) or in a compressed format.

▼

- *Relax, then restore.* When you lose a file and need to restore it from backup, you are likely to be in an unhappy, nervous state. Take a deep breath and think through the recovery process before you start. It is not uncommon for an agitated computer user to wipe out the last backup when trying to restore a damaged file.

▼

1.8   Compiling a Simple Program

You are now ready to write and run your first Java program. The traditional choice for the very first program in a new programming language is a program that displays a simple greeting: "Hello, World!". Let us follow that tradition. Here is the "Hello, World!" program in Java.

File Hello.java

```
1 public class Hello
2 {
3     public static void main(String[] args)
4     {
5         // display a greeting in the console window
6
7         System.out.println("Hello, World!");
8     }
9 }
```

We will examine this program in a minute. For now, you should make a new program file and call it `Hello.java`. Enter the program instructions and compile and run the program, following the procedure that is appropriate for your compiler.

> Java is case-sensitive. You must be careful about distinguishing between upper- and lowercase letters.

    Java is *case-sensitive*. You must enter upper- and lowercase letters exactly as they appear in the program listing. You cannot type `MAIN` or `PrintLn`. If you are not careful, you will run into problems—see Common Error 1.1.

On the other hand, Java has *free-form layout*. You can use any number of spaces and line breaks to separate words. You can cram as many words as possible into each line,

```
public class Hello{public static void main(String[]
args){// display a greeting in the console window
System.out.println("Hello, World!");}}
```

You can even write every word and symbol on a separate line,

```
public
class
Hello
{
public
static
void
main
(
. . .
```

> Lay out your programs so that they are easy to read.

However, good taste dictates that you lay out your programs in a readable fashion. Chapters 2 and 3 contain recommendations for good layout.

When you run the program, the message

```
Hello, World!
```

> Classes are the fundamental building blocks of Java programs.

will appear somewhere on the screen (see Figures 11 and 12). The exact location depends on your programming environment.

Now that you have seen the program working, it is time to understand its makeup. The first line,

```
public class Hello
```

> Each class contains definitions of methods. Each method contains a sequence of instructions.

starts a new *class*. Classes are a fundamental concept in Java, and you will begin to study them in Chapter 2. In Java, every program consists of one or more classes.

The keyword `public` denotes that the class is usable by the "public". You will later encounter `private` features, which are not.

At this point, you should simply regard the

```
public class ClassName
{
    . . .
}
```

as a necessary part of the "plumbing" that is required to write any Java program. In Java, every source file can contain at most one public class, and the name of the public class must match the name of the file containing the class. For example, the class `Hello` *must be* contained in a file Hello.java. It is very important that the names *and the capitalization* match exactly. You can get strange error messages if you call the class `HELLO` or the file `hello.java`.

Running the `Hello` Program in a Console Window

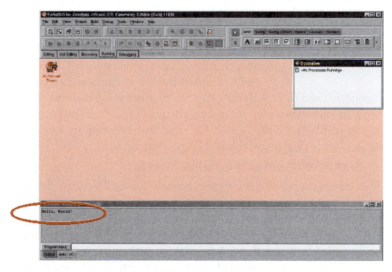

Running the `Hello` Program in an Integrated Development Environment

The construction

```
public static void main(String[] args)
{
}
```

defines a *method* called `main`. A method contains a collection of programming instructions that describe how to carry out a particular task. Every Java application must have a `main` method. Most Java programs contain other methods besides `main`, and you will see in Chapter 2 how to write other methods.

> Every Java application contains a class with a main method. When the application starts, the instructions in the main method are executed.

The *parameter* `String[] args` is a required part of the `main` method. (It contains *command line arguments*, which we will not discuss until Chapter 16.) The keyword `static` indicates that the `main` method does not operate on an *object*. (As you will see in Chapter 2, most methods in Java do operate on objects, and `static` methods are not common in large Java programs. Nevertheless, `main` must always be `static`, because it starts running before the program can create objects.)

At this time, simply consider

```
public class ClassName
{
    public static void main(String[] args)
    {
        . . .
    }
}
```

as yet another part of the "plumbing". Our first program has all instructions inside the `main` method of a class.

> Use comments to help human readers understand your program.

The first line inside the `main` method is a *comment*

```
// display a greeting in the console window
```

This comment is purely for the benefit of the human reader, to explain in more detail what the next statement does. Any text enclosed between `//` and the end of the line is completely ignored by the compiler. Comments are used to explain the program to other programmers or to yourself.

The instructions or *statements* in the *body* of the `main` method—that is, the statements inside the curly braces {}—are executed one by one. Each statement ends in a semicolon `;`. Our method has a single statement:

```
System.out.println("Hello, World!");
```

This statement prints a line of text, namely "Hello, World!". However, there are many places where a program can send that string: to a window, to a file, or to a networked computer on the other side of the world. You need to specify that the destination for the string is the *standard output*—that is, a console window. The console window is represented in Java by an object called `out`. Just as you needed to place the `main` method in a `Hello` class, the designers of the Java library needed to place the `out` object into a class. They placed it in the `System` class, which contains useful objects and methods to access system resources. To use the `out` object in the `System` class, you must refer to it as `System.out`.

> You call a method by specifying an object, the method name, and the method parameters.

To use an object such as `System.out`, you specify what you want to do to it. In this case, you want to print a line of text. The `println` method carries out this task. You do not have to implement this method—the programmers who wrote the Java library already did that for us—but you do need to *call* the method.

Whenever you call a method in Java, you need to specify three items:

1. The object that you want to use (in this case, `System.out`)
2. The name of the method you want to use (in this case, `println`)
3. A pair of parentheses, containing any other information the method needs (in this case, `("Hello, World!")`)

Note that the two periods in `System.out.println` have different meanings. The first period means "locate the `out` object in the `System` class". The second period means "apply the `println` method to that object".

Syntax 1.1: Method Call

object.methodName (*parameters*)

Example:

```
System.out.println("Hello, Dave!");
```

Purpose:

To invoke a method on an object and supply any additional parameters

---

A sequence of characters enclosed in quotation marks

```
"Hello, World!"
```

is called a *string.* You must enclose the contents of the string inside quotation marks so that the compiler knows you literally mean `"Hello, World!"`. There is a reason for this requirement. Suppose you need to print the word *main.* By enclosing it in quotation marks, `"main"`, the compiler knows you mean the sequence of characters m a i n, not the method named `main`. The rule is simply that you must enclose all text strings in quotation marks, so that the compiler considers them plain text and does not try to interpret them as program instructions.

> A string is a sequence of characters enclosed in quotation marks.

You can also print numerical values. For example, the statement

```
System.out.println(3 + 4);
```

displays the number 7.

The `println` method prints a string or a number and then starts a new line. For example, the sequence of statements

```
System.out.println("Hello");
System.out.println("World!");
```

prints two lines of text:

```
Hello
World!
```

There is a second method, called `print`, that you can use to print an item without starting a new line afterward. For example, the output of the two statements

```
System.out.print("00");
System.out.println(3 + 4);
```

is the single line

```
007
```

⊗ Common Error 1.1

Omitting Semicolons

In Java every statement must end in a semicolon. Forgetting to type a semicolon is a common error. It confuses the compiler, because the compiler uses the semicolon to find where one statement ends and the next one starts. The compiler does not use line breaks or closing braces to recognize the end of statements. For example, the compiler considers

```
System.out.println("Hello")
System.out.println("World!");
```

a single statement, as if you had written

```
System.out.println("Hello") System.out.println("World!");
```

Then it doesn't understand that statement, because it does not expect the word `System` following the closing parenthesis after `"Hello"`. The remedy is simple. Scan every statement for a terminating semicolon, just as you would check that every English sentence ends in a period.

Advanced Topic 1.1

Alternative Comment Syntax

In Java there are two methods for writing comments. You already learned that the compiler ignores anything that you type between `//` and the end of the current line. The compiler also ignores any text between a `/*` and `*/`.

```
/* A simple Java program */
```

The `//` comment is easier to type if the comment is only a single line long. If you have a comment that is longer than a line, then the `/* . . . */` comment is simpler:

```
/*
This is a simple Java program that you can use to try out
your compiler and interpreter.
*/
```

It would be somewhat tedious to add the `//` at the beginning of each line and to move them around whenever the text of the comment changes.

In this book, we use `//` for comments that will never grow beyond a line, and `/* . . . */` for longer comments. If you prefer, you can always use the `//` style. The readers of your code will be grateful for *any* comments, no matter which style you use.

▼ **AT** ▼ **Advanced Topic**   **1.2**

Escape Sequences

Suppose you want to display a string containing quotation marks, such as

```
Hello, "World"!
```

You can't use

```
System.out.println("Hello, "World"!");
```

As soon as the compiler reads `"Hello, "`, it thinks the string is finished, and then it gets all confused about `World` followed by two quotation marks. A human would probably realize that the second and third quotation marks were supposed to be part of the string, but compilers have a one-track mind. If a simple analysis of the input doesn't make sense to them, they just refuse to go on, and they report an error. Well, how do you then display quotation marks on the screen? You precede the quotation marks inside the string with a *backslash* character. Inside a string, the sequence `\"` denotes a literal quote, not the end of a string. The correct display statement is therefore

```
System.out.println("Hello, \"World\"!");
```

The backslash character is used as an *escape* character, and the character sequence `\"` is called an escape sequence. The backslash does not denote itself; instead, it is used to encode other characters that would otherwise be difficult to include in a string.

Now, what do you do if you actually want to print a backslash (for example, to specify a Windows file name)? You must enter two `\\` in a row, like this:

```
System.out.println(
    "The secret message is in C:\\Temp\\Secret.txt");
```

This statement prints

```
The secret message is in C:\Temp\Secret.txt
```

Another escape sequence occasionally used is `\n`, which denotes a *newline* or line feed character. Printing a newline character causes the start of a new line on the display. For example, the statement

```
System.out.print("*\n**\n***\n");
```

prints the characters

```
*
**
***
```

on three separate lines. Of course, you could have achieved the same effect with three separate calls to `println`.

Finally, escape sequences are useful for including international characters in a string. For example, suppose you want to print "All the way to San José!", with an accented letter é. If you use a U.S. keyboard, you may not have a key to generate that letter. Java uses

▼ the *Unicode* encoding scheme to denote international characters. For example, the é character has Unicode encoding 00E9. You can include that character inside a string by writing \u, followed by its Unicode encoding:

▼
```
System.out.println("All the way to San Jos\u00E9!");
```

▼ You can look up the codes for the U.S. English and Western European characters in Appendix A3, and codes for thousands of characters in reference [2].

1.9   Errors

Experiment a little with the Hello program. What happens if you make a typing error such as

```
System.ouch.println("Hello, World!");
System.out.println("Hello, World!);
System.out.println("Hell, World!");
```

> A syntax error is a violation of the rules of the programming language. The compiler detects syntax errors.

In the first case, the compiler will complain. It will say that it has no clue what you mean by ouch. The exact wording of the error message is dependent on the compiler, but it might be something like "Undefined symbol ouch". This is a *compile-time error* or *syntax error*. Something is wrong according to the language rules, and the compiler finds it. When the compiler finds one or more errors, it refuses to translate the program to Java virtual machine instructions, and as a consequence you have no program that you can run. You must fix the error and compile again. In fact, the compiler is quite picky, and it is common to go through several rounds of fixing compile-time errors before compilation succeeds for the first time.

If the compiler finds an error, it will not simply stop and give up. It will try to report as many errors as it can find, so you can fix them all at once. Sometimes, however, one error throws it off track. This is likely to happen with the error in the second line. Because the closing quotation mark is missing, the compiler will think that the); characters are still part of the string. In such cases, it is common for the compiler to emit bogus error reports for neighboring lines. You should fix only those error messages that make sense to you and then recompile.

The error in the third line is of a different kind. The program will compile and run, but its output will be wrong. It will print

```
Hell, World!
```

> A logic error causes a program to take an action that the programmer did not intend. You must test your programs to find logic errors.

This is a *run-time error* or *logic error*. The program is syntactically correct and does something, but it doesn't do what it is supposed to do. The compiler cannot find the error. You, the programmer, must flush out this type of error. Run the program, and carefully look at its output.

During program development, errors are unavoidable. Once a program is longer than a few lines, it requires superhuman concentration to enter it correctly without slipping up once. You will find yourself omitting semicolons or quotes more often than you would like, but the compiler will track down these problems for you.

Logic errors are more troublesome. The compiler will not find them—in fact, the compiler will cheerfully translate any program as long as its syntax is correct—but the resulting program will do something wrong. It is the responsibility of the program author to test the program and find any logic errors. Testing programs is an important topic that you will encounter many times in this book. Another important aspect of good craftsmanship is *defensive programming:* structuring programs and development processes in such a way that an error in one place of a program does not trigger a disastrous response.

The error examples that you saw so far were not difficult to diagnose or fix, but as you learn more sophisticated programming techniques, there will also be much more room for error. It is an uncomfortable fact that locating all errors in a program is very difficult. Even if you can observe that a program exhibits faulty behavior, it may not at all be obvious what part of the program caused it and how you can fix it. Special software tools (so-called *debuggers*) let you trace through a program to find *bugs*—that is, logic errors. In this course you will learn how to use a debugger effectively.

Note that all these errors are different from the kind of errors that you are likely to make in calculations. If you total up a column of numbers, you may miss a minus sign or accidentally drop a carry, perhaps because you are bored or tired. Computers do not make these kinds of errors. When a computer adds up numbers, it will get the correct answer. Admittedly, computers can make overflow or roundoff errors, just as pocket calculators do when you ask them to perform computations whose result falls outside their numeric range. An overflow error occurs if the result of a computation is very large or very small. For example, most computers and pocket calculators overflow when you try to compute 10^{1000}. A roundoff error occurs when a value cannot be represented precisely. For example, 1/3 may be stored in the computer as 0.3333333, a value that is close to, but not exactly equal to, 1/3. If you compute $1 - (3 \times 1/3)$, you may obtain 0.0000001, not 0, as a result of the roundoff error. We will consider such errors logic errors, because the programmer should have chosen a more appropriate calculation scheme that handles overflow or roundoff correctly.

You will learn a three-part error management strategy in this book. First, you will learn about common errors and how to avoid them. Then you will learn defensive programming strategies to minimize the likelihood and impact of errors. Finally, you will learn debugging strategies to flush out those errors that remain.

Common Error 1.2

Misspelling Words

If you accidentally misspell a word, then strange things may happen, and it may not always be completely obvious from the error messages what went wrong. Here is a good example of how simple spelling errors can cause trouble:

```
public class Hello
{
```

```
public static void Main(String[] args)
{
    System.out.println("Hello, World!");
}
}
```

This class defines a method called `Main`. The compiler will not consider this to be the same as the `main` method, because `Main` starts with an uppercase letter and the Java language is *case-sensitive*. Upper- and lowercase letters are considered to be completely different from each other, and to the compiler `Main` is no better match for `main` than `rain`. The compiler will cheerfully compile your `Main` method, but when the Java interpreter reads the compiled file, it will complain about the missing `main` method and refuse to run the program. Of course, the message "missing main method" should give you a clue where to look for the error.

If you get an error message that seems to indicate that the compiler is on the wrong track, it is a good idea to check for spelling and capitalization. All Java keywords use only lowercase letters. Names of classes usually start with an uppercase letter, names of methods and variables with a lowercase letter. If you misspell the name of a symbol (for example, `ouch` instead of `out`), the compiler will complain about an "undefined symbol". That error message is usually a good clue that you made a spelling error.

1.10   The Compilation Process

Some Java development environments are very convenient to use. You just enter the code in one window, click on a button to compile, and click on another button to execute your program. Error messages show up in a second window, and the program runs in a third window. With such an environment you are completely shielded from the details of the compilation process. On other systems you must carry out every step manually, by typing commands such as

```
edit Hello.java
javac Hello.java
java Hello
```

into a shell window.

No matter which compilation environment you use, you begin your activity by typing in the program statements. The program that you use for entering and modifying the program text is called an *editor*. Remember to *save* your work to disk frequently, because otherwise the text editor stores the text only in the computer's memory. If something goes wrong with the computer and you

> An editor is a program for entering and modifying text, such as a Java program.

need to restart it, the contents of the primary memory (including your program text) are lost, but anything stored on a hard disk or floppy disk is permanent even if you need to restart the computer.

> The Java compiler translates source code into instructions for the Java virtual machine, called bytecode.

When you compile your program, the compiler translates the Java *source code* (that is, the statements that you wrote) into *bytecode*, which consists of virtual machine instructions and some other pieces of information on how to load the program into memory prior to execution. The bytecode for a program is stored in a separate file, with extension `.class`. For example, the bytecode for the Hello program will be stored in a file `Hello.class`. However, the compiler produces a class file only after you have corrected all syntax errors.

The class file contains the translation of only the instructions that you wrote. That is not enough actually to run the program. To display a string on a window, quite a bit of low-level activity is necessary. The authors of the `System` and `PrintStream` classes (which define the `out` object and the `println` method) have implemented all necessary actions and placed the required bytecode into a *library*. A library is a collection of code that has been programmed and translated by someone else, ready for you to use in your program. (More complicated programs are built from more than one class file and more than one library.)

The *Java interpreter* loads the bytecode of the program that you wrote, starts your program, and loads the necessary library files as they are required.

The steps of compiling and running your program are outlined in Figure 13.

> The Java interpreter runs a program, loading the necessary bytecode from class files and library files.

Your programming activity centers around these steps. You start in the editor, writing the source file. You compile the program and look at the error messages. You go back to the editor and fix the syntax errors. When the compiler succeeds, you run your program. If you find an error, you can run the debugger to execute it a line at a time. Once you find the cause of the error, you go back to the editor and fix it. You compile and run again to see whether the error has gone away. If not, you go back to the editor. This is called the *edit–compile–test loop* (see Figure 14). You will spend a substantial amount of time in this loop whenever you work on programming assignments.

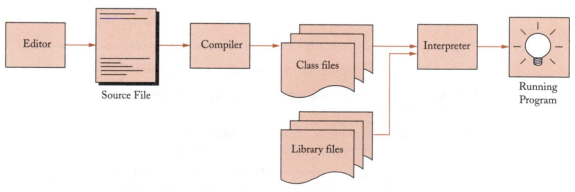

Figure 13

From Source Code to Running Program

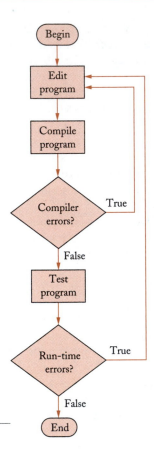

Figure 14

The Edit-Compile-Test Loop

Chapter Summary

1. A computer must be programmed to perform tasks. Different tasks require different programs.

2. A computer program executes a sequence of very basic operations in rapid succession.

3. Programmers develop computer programs to make computers perform new tasks.

4. At the heart of the computer lies the central processing unit (CPU).

5. Data and programs are stored in primary storage (memory) and secondary storage (such as a hard disk).

6. The CPU reads machine instructions from memory. The instructions direct it to communicate with memory, secondary storage, and peripheral devices.

7. Generally, machine code depends on the CPU type. However, the instruction set of the Java virtual machine (JVM) can be executed on many CPUs.

8. Because machine instructions are encoded as numbers, it is difficult to write programs in machine code.

9. Assembly language makes it easier to generate machine instructions by translating mnemonics and symbolic names.

10. High-level languages let you describe tasks at a higher conceptual level than machine code.

11. A compiler translates programs written in a high-level language into machine code.

12. Each programming language has its own set of rules for forming instructions. Compilers enforce these rules strictly.

13. Java was originally designed for programming consumer devices, but it was first successfully used to write Internet applets.

14. Java was designed to be safe and portable, benefitting both Internet users and students.

15. Java has a very large library. Focus on learning those parts of the library that you need for your programming projects.

16. Set aside some time to become familiar with the computer system and the Java compiler that you will use for your class work.

17. Develop a strategy for keeping backup copies of your work before disaster strikes.

18. Java is case-sensitive. You must be careful about distinguishing between upper- and lowercase letters.

19. Lay out your programs so that they are easy to read.

20. Classes are the fundamental building blocks of Java programs.

21. Each class contains definitions of methods. Each method contains a sequence of instructions.

22. Every Java application contains a class with a `main` method. When the application starts, the instructions in the `main` method are executed.

23. Use comments to help human readers understand your program.

24. You call a method by specifying an object, the method name, and the method parameters.

25. A string is a sequence of characters enclosed in quotation marks.

26. A syntax error is a violation of the rules of the programming language. The compiler detects syntax errors.

27. A logic error causes a program to take an action that the programmer did not intend. You must test your programs to find logic errors.

28. An editor is a program for entering and modifying text, such as a Java program.

29. The Java compiler translates source code into instructions for the Java virtual machine, called bytecode.

30. The Java interpreter runs a program, loading the necessary bytecode from class files and library files.

Further Reading

[1] http://www.horstmann.com/bigjava/help/compilers.html Instructions for using several popular Java compilers.

[2] http://www.unicode.org/ The web site of the Unicode Consortium. It contains character tables that show the Unicode values of characters from many scripts.

CLASSES, OBJECTS, AND METHODS INTRODUCED IN THIS CHAPTER

Here is a list of all classes, methods, static variables, and constants introduced in this chapter. Turn to the documentation in Appendix A3 for more information.

```
java.io.PrintStream
    print
    println
java.lang.String
    length
java.lang.System
    out
```

REVIEW EXERCISES

Exercise R1.1. Explain the difference between using a computer program and programming a computer.

Exercise R1.2. What distinguishes a computer from a typical household appliance?

Exercise R1.3. Rank the storage devices that can be part of a computer system by (*a*) speed, (*b*) cost, and (*c*) storage capacity.

Exercise R1.4. What is the Java virtual machine?

Exercise R1.5. What is an applet?

Exercise R1.6. Explain two benefits of higher-level programming languages over assembler code.

Exercise R1.7. List the programming languages mentioned in this chapter.

Exercise R1.8. What is an integrated programming environment?

Exercise R1.9. What is a console window?

Exercise R1.10. Describe *exactly* what steps you would take to back up your work after you have typed in the `Hello.java` program.

Exercise R1.11. On your own computer or on your lab computer, find the exact location (folder or directory name) of

- The sample file `Hello.java`, which you wrote with the editor
- The Java interpreter `java.exe`
- The library file `rt.jar` that contains the runtime library

Exercise R1.12. Explain the special role of the \ escape character in Java character strings.

Exercise R1.13. Write three versions of the `Hello.java` program that have different syntax errors. Write a version that has a logic error.

Exercise R1.14. How do you discover syntax errors? How do you discover logic errors?

Programming Exercises

Exercise P1.1. Write a program that displays your name inside a box on the console screen, like this:

```
+----+
|Dave|
+----+
```

Do your best to approximate lines with characters like | - +.

Exercise P1.2. Write a program that prints a face, using text characters, hopefully better looking than this one:

```
 /////
 | o o |
(|  ^  |)
 | \_/ |
 -----
```

Use *comments* to indicate when you print the hair, ears, mouth, and so on.

Exercise P1.3. Write a program that prints a Christmas tree:

Remember to use escape sequences to print the \ and " characters.

Exercise P1.4. Write a program that prints a staircase:

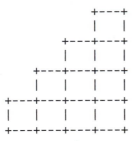

Exercise P1.5. Write a program that computes the sum of the first ten positive integers, $1 + 2 + \cdots + 10$. *Hint:* Write a program of the form

```
public class Sum10
{
   public static void main(String[] args)
   {
      System.out.println(          );
   }
}
```

Exercise P1.6. Write a program that computes the sum of the reciprocals $1/1 + 1/2 + \cdots + 1/10$. This is harder than it sounds. Try writing the program, and check the result. The program's result isn't likely to be correct. Then write the numbers as *floating-point* numbers, `1.0, 2.0, ..., 10.0`, and run the program again. Can you explain the difference in the results? We will explore this phenomenon in Chapter 3.

Chapter 2

An Introduction to Objects and Classes

CHAPTER GOALS

- To understand the concepts of classes and objects
- ▶ To realize the difference between objects and object references
- ▶ To become familiar with the process of implementing classes
- ▶ To be able to implement simple methods
- ▶ To understand the purpose and use of constructors
- ▶ To understand how to access instance fields and local variables
- ▶ To appreciate the importance of documentation comments

Most useful programs don't just manipulate numbers and strings. Instead, they deal with data items that are more complex and that more closely represent entities in the real world. Examples of these data items include bank accounts, employee records, and graphical shapes.

The Java language is ideally suited for designing and manipulating such data items, or *objects*. In Java, you define *classes* that describe the behavior of these objects. In this chapter, you will learn how to define classes that describe objects with very simple behavior. As you learn more about Java programming in subsequent chapters, you will be able to implement classes whose objects carry out more sophisticated actions.

CHAPTER CONTENTS

2.1   Using and Constructing Objects

Objects and classes are central concepts for Java programming. It will take you some time to master these concepts fully, but since every Java program uses at least a couple of objects and classes, it is a good idea to have a basic understanding of these concepts right away.

> Objects are entities in your program that you manipulate by invoking methods.

An *object* is an entity that you can manipulate in your program, generally by calling *methods*. For example, you saw in Chapter 1 that `System.out` refers to an object, and you saw how to manipulate it by calling the `println` method. (Actually, several different methods are available, all called `println`: one for printing strings, one for printing integers, one for printing floating-point numbers, and so on; the reason is discussed in Section 2.8.) When you call the `println` method, some activities occur inside the object, and the ultimate effect is that the object causes text to appear in the console window.

> The public interface of a class specifies what you can do with its objects. The hidden implementation describes how these actions are carried out.

You should think of the object as a "black box" with a public *interface* (the methods you can call) and a hidden *implementation* (the code and data that are necessary to make these methods work).

Different objects support different sets of methods. For example, you can apply the `println` method to the `System.out` object, but not to the string object `"Hello, World!"`. That is, it would be an error to call

```
"Hello, World!".println(); // This method call is an error
```

The reason is simple. The System.out and "Hello, World!" objects belong to different *classes*. The System.out object is an object of the class PrintStream, but the "Hello, World!" object is an object of class String. You can apply the println method to *any* object of the PrintStream class, but the String class does not support the println method. The String class supports a good number of other methods; you will see many of them in Chapter 3. For example, the length method counts the number of characters in a string. You can apply that method to any object of type String. Thus,

```
"Hello, World!".length() // This method call is OK
```

is a correct method call—it computes the number of characters in the string object "Hello, World!" and returns the result, 13. (The quotation marks are not counted.) You can verify that the length method does return the length of a String object by writing a short test program

```java
public class LengthTest
{
    public static void main(String[] args)
    {
        System.out.println("Hello, World!".length());
    }
}
```

Every object belongs to a class. The class defines the methods for the objects. Thus, the PrintStream class defines the print and println methods. The String class defines the length method and many other methods.

> Classes are factories for objects. You construct a new object of a class with the new operator.

The System.out object is created automatically when a Java program loads the System class. String objects are created when you specify a string enclosed in quotation marks. However, in most Java programs, you want to create more objects.

To see how to create new objects, let us turn to another class: the Rectangle class in the Java class library. Objects of type Rectangle describe rectangular shapes—see Figure 1.

Note that a Rectangle object isn't a rectangular shape—it is a set of numbers that describe the rectangle (see Figure 2). Each rectangle is described by the *x*- and *y*-coordinates of its top left corner, its width, and its height. To make a new rectangle, you

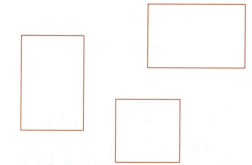

Figure 1

Rectangular Shapes

Figure 2

A Rectangle Object

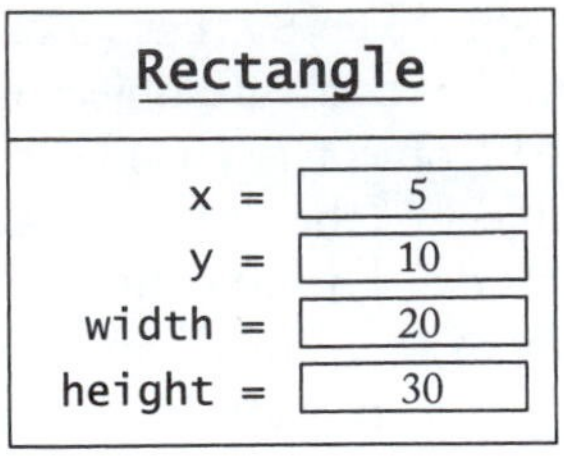

need to specify these four values. For example, you can make a new rectangle with top left corner at (5, 10), width 20, and height 30 as follows:

```
new Rectangle(5, 10, 20, 30)
```

The new operator causes the creation of an object of type Rectangle. The process of creating a new object is called *construction*. The four values 5, 10, 20, and 30 are called the *construction parameters*. Different classes will require different construction parameters. For example, to construct a Rectangle object, you supply four numbers that describe the position and size of the rectangle. To construct a Car object, you might supply the model name and year.

Actually, some classes let you construct objects in multiple ways. For example, you can also obtain a Rectangle object by supplying no construction parameters at all (but you must still supply the parentheses):

```
new Rectangle()
```

This constructs a (rather useless) rectangle with top left corner at the origin (0, 0), width 0, and height 0.

To construct any object, you do the following:

1. Use the new operator.
2. Give the name of the class.
3. Supply construction parameters (if any) inside parentheses.

What can you do with a Rectangle object? Not much, for now. In Chapter 4, you will learn how to display rectangles and other shapes in a window. You can pass a rectangle object to the System.out.println or print method, which just prints a description of the rectangle object onto the console window:

```
public class RectangleTest
{
    public static void main(String[] args)
    {
        System.out.println(new Rectangle(5, 10, 20, 30));
    }
}
```

This program prints the line

```
java.awt.Rectangle[x=5,y=10,width=20,height=30]
```

More specifically, this program creates an object of type Rectangle, then passes that object to the println method. Afterward, that object is no longer used.

Syntax 2.1: Object Construction

new *ClassName* (*parameters*)

Example:

```
new Rectangle(5, 10, 20, 30)
new Car("BMW 540ti", 2004)
```

Purpose:

To construct a new object, initialize it with the construction parameters, and return a reference to the constructed object

---

2.2   Object Variables

You store object locations in object variables.

Of course, usually you want to do something more to an object than just create it, print it, and forget it. To remember an object, you need to hold it in an *object variable*. As was mentioned in Chapter 1, a variable is an item of information in memory whose location is identified by a symbolic name. An object variable is a container that stores the location of an object.

In Java, every variable has a particular *type* that identifies what kind of information it can contain. You create a variable by giving its type followed by a name for the variable. For example,

```
Rectangle cerealBox;
```

This statement defines an object variable, `cerealBox`. The type of this variable is `Rectangle`. That is, after the `cerealBox` variable has been defined by the preceding statement, thereafter in the program it must always contain the location of a `Rectangle` object, never a `Car` or `String` object.

Figure 3
      cerealBox = [   ]

An Uninitialized Object Variable

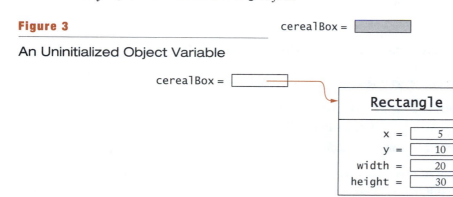

Figure 4

An Object Variable Containing an Object Reference

You can choose any variable names you like, provided you follow a few simple rules.

- Names can be made up of letters, digits, and the underscore (_) character. They cannot start with a digit, though.

- You cannot use other symbols such as ? or % in variable names.

- Spaces are not permitted inside names, either.

- Furthermore, you cannot use *reserved words* such as `public` as names; these words are reserved exclusively for their special Java meanings.

- Variable names are also *case-sensitive;* that is, `cerealBox` and `Cerealbox` are *different* names.

> All object variables must be initialized before you access them.

Look again at the declaration of the `cerealBox` variable. So far, the variable is not *initialized*—it doesn't yet contain any object location at all (see Figure 3). You need to set `cerealBox` to an object location. How do you get an object location? The `new` operator creates a new object and returns its location. Use that value to initialize the variable.

```
Rectangle cerealBox = new Rectangle(5, 10, 20, 30);
```

> An object reference describes the location of an object.

You may wonder what happens if you leave the `cerealBox` variable uninitialized. See Common Error 2.1 for an answer. Figure 4 shows the result.

An object location is also often called an object *reference.* When a variable contains the location of an object, we say that it *refers* to an object. For example, `cerealBox` refers to the `Rectangle` object that the `new` operator constructed.

> Multiple object variables can contain references to the same object.

It is very important that you remember that the `cerealBox` variable *does not contain* the object. It *refers to* the object. You can have two object variables refer to the same object:

```
Rectangle r = cerealBox;
```

Now you can access the same `Rectangle` object both as `cerealBox` and as `r`, as shown in Figure 5.

Usually, your programs use objects in the following ways:

1. Construct an object with the `new` operator.
2. Store the object reference in an object variable.
3. Call methods on the object variable.

The `Rectangle` class has over 50 methods, some useful, some less so. To give you a flavor of manipulating `Rectangle` objects, let us look at a method of the `Rectangle` class. The `translate` method *moves* a rectangle by a certain distance in the *x*- and *y*-directions. For example,

```
cerealBox.translate(15, 25);
```

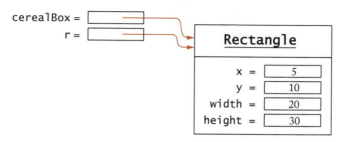

Figure 5

Two Object Variables Referring to the Same Object

moves the rectangle by 15 units in the *x*-direction and 25 units in the *y*-direction. Moving a rectangle doesn't change its width or height, but it changes the top left corner. The code fragment

```
Rectangle cerealBox = new Rectangle(5, 10, 20, 30);
cerealBox.translate(15, 25);
System.out.println(cerealBox);
```

prints

```
java.awt.Rectangle[x=20,y=35,width=20,height=30]
```

Let's turn this code fragment into a complete program. As with the `Hello` program, you need to carry out three steps:

1. Invent a new class, say `MoveTest`.
2. Supply a `main` method.
3. Place instructions inside the `main` method.

> Java classes are grouped into packages. If you use a class from another package (other than the `java.lang` package), you must import the class.

For this program, you need to carry out another step in addition to those: You need to *import* the `Rectangle` class from a *package*. A package is a collection of classes with a related purpose. All classes in the standard library are contained in packages. The `Rectangle` class belongs to the package `java.awt` (where `awt` is an abbreviation for "Abstract Windowing Toolkit"), which contains many classes for drawing windows and graphical shapes.

To use the `Rectangle` class from the `java.awt` package, simply place the following line at the top of your program:

```
import java.awt.Rectangle;
```

Why didn't you have to import the `System` and `String` classes that were used in the `Hello` program? The reason is that the `System` and `String` classes are in the `java.lang` package, and all classes from this package are automatically imported, so you never need to import them yourself.

Thus, the complete program is:

File MoveTest.java

```
1  import java.awt.Rectangle;
2
3  public class MoveTest
4  {
5     public static void main(String[] args)
6     {
7        Rectangle cerealBox = new Rectangle(5, 10, 20, 30);
8
9        // move the rectangle
10       cerealBox.translate(15, 25);
11
12       // print the moved rectangle
13       System.out.println(cerealBox);
14    }
15 }
```

Syntax 2.2: Variable Definition

TypeName variableName;
TypeName variableName = *expression*;

Example:

```
Rectangle cerealBox;
String name = "Dave";
```

Purpose:

To define a new variable of a particular type and optionally supply an initial value

---

Syntax 2.3: Importing a Class from a Package

import *packageName.ClassName*;

Example:

```
import java.awt.Rectangle;
```

Purpose:

To import a class from a package for use in a program

⊗ Common Error 2.1

Forgetting to Initialize Variables

You just learned how to store an object reference in a variable so that you can manipulate the object in your program. This is a very common step, and it can lead to one of the most common programming errors—using a variable that you forgot to initialize.

Suppose your program contains the lines

```
Rectangle cerealBox;
cerealBox.translate(15, 25);
```

Now you have a variable `cerealBox`. An object variable is a container for an object reference. But you haven't put anything into the variable—it is not initialized. Thus, there is no rectangle to translate.

The compiler spots these problems. If you make this mistake, the compiler will complain that you are trying to use an uninitialized variable.

The remedy is to initialize the variable. You can initialize a variable with any object reference, either a reference to a new object or an existing object.

```
// initialize with new object reference
Rectangle cerealBox = new Rectangle(5, 10, 20, 30);
// initialize with existing object reference
Rectangle cerealBox = anotherRectangle;
```

Advanced Topic 2.1

Importing Classes

You have seen the simplest and clearest method for importing classes from packages. Simply use an `import` statement that names the package and class for each class that you want to import. For example,

```
import java.awt.Rectangle;
import java.awt.Point;
```

There is a shortcut that many programmers find convenient. You can import *all* classes from a package name with the construct

```
import packagename.*;
```

For example, the statement

```
import java.awt.*;
```

imports all classes from the `java.awt` package. This is less trouble to type, but we won't use this style in this book, for a simple reason. If a program imports multiple packages

▼ and you encounter an unfamiliar class name, then you have to look up all of those packages to find the class. For example, suppose you see a program that imports

▼
```
import java.awt.*;
import java.io.*;
```

Furthermore, suppose you see a class name Image. You would not know whether the Image class is in the java.awt package or the java.io package. Why do you care in which package it is? You need to know if you want to use the class in your own programs.

Note that you cannot import multiple packages with a single import statement. For example,

▼
```
import java.*.*; // Error
```

is a syntax error.

You can avoid all import statements by using the *full* name (both package name and class name) whenever you use a class. For example,

▼
```
java.awt.Rectangle cerealBox =
    new java.awt.Rectangle(5, 10, 20, 30);
```

That is pretty tedious, and you won't find many programmers doing it.

2.3 Defining a Class

In this section, you will learn how to define your own classes. Recall that a class defines the methods that you can apply to its objects. We will start with a very simple class that contains a single method.

```
public class Greeter
{
   public String sayHello()
   {
      String message = "Hello, World!";
      return message;
   }
}
```

A method definition contains the following parts:

- An *access specifier* (such as public)
- The *return type* of the method (such as String)
- The name of the method (such as sayHello)
- A list of the *parameters* of the method, enclosed in parentheses (the sayHello method has no parameters)
- The *body* of the method: a sequence of statements enclosed in braces

The access specifier controls which other methods can call this method. Most methods should be declared as public. That way, all other methods in your program can call them.

A method definition specifies the method name, parameters, and the statements for carrying out the method's actions.

(Occasionally, it can be useful to have methods that are not so widely callable—turn to Chapter 11 for more information on this issue.)

The return type is the type of the value that the method returns to its caller. The `sayHello` method returns an object of type `String` (namely, the string `"Hello, World!"`).

Some methods just execute some statements without returning a value. Those methods are tagged with a return type of `void`.

Many methods depend on other information. For example, the `translate` method of the `Rectangle` class needs to know how far you want to move the rectangle horizontally and vertically. These items are called the *parameters* of the method. Each parameter is a variable, with a type and a name. Parameter variables are separated by commas. For example, the implementors of the Java library defined the `translate` method like this:

```java
public class Rectangle
{   . . .
    public void translate(int x, int y)
    {
        method body
    }
    . . .
}
```

Syntax 2.4: Method Implementation

```java
public class ClassName
{

    . . .

    accessSpecifier returnType methodName(parameterType parameterName,   ... )
    {
        method body
    }
    . . .
}
```

Example:

```java
public class Greeter
{
    public String sayHello()
    {
        String message = "Hello, World!";
        return message;
    }
}
```

Purpose:

To define the behavior of a method

The method body contains the statements that the method executes. The `sayHello` method body, for example, contains two statements. The first statement initializes a `String` variable with a `String` object:

```
String message = "Hello, World!";
```

> Use the `return` statement to specify the value that a method returns to its caller.

The second statement is a special statement that terminates the method. When the `return` statement is executed, the method exits. If the method has a return type other than `void`, then the `return` statement must contain a *return value*, namely the value that the method sends back to its caller. The `sayHello` method returns the object reference stored in `message`—that is, a reference to the `"Hello, World!"` string object.

Now you have seen how to define a class that contains a method. In the next section, you will see what you can do with the class.

Syntax 2.5: The `return` Statement

```
return expression;
```

or

```
return;
```

Example:

```
return message;
```

Purpose:

To specify the value that a method returns, and exit the method immediately. The return value becomes the value of the method call expression.

2.4   Testing a Class

In the preceding section, you saw the definition of a simple `Greeter` class. What can you do with it? Of course, you can compile the file `Greeter.java`. However, you can't *execute* the resulting `Greeter.class` file. It doesn't contain a `main` method. That is normal—most classes don't contain a `main` method.

> To test a class, use an environment for interactive testing, or write a second class to execute test instructions.

To do something with your class, you have two choices. Some development environments, such as the excellent BlueJ program, let you create objects of a class and call methods on those objects. Figure 6 shows the result of creating an object of the `Greeter` class and invoking the `sayHello` method. The dialog box contains the return value of the method.

Alternatively, if you don't have a development environment that lets you test a class interactively, you can write a *test class*. A test class is a class with a `main` method that contains statements to test another class. A test class typically carries out the following steps:

1. Construct one or more objects of the class that is being tested.
2. Invoke one or more methods.
3. Print out one or more results.

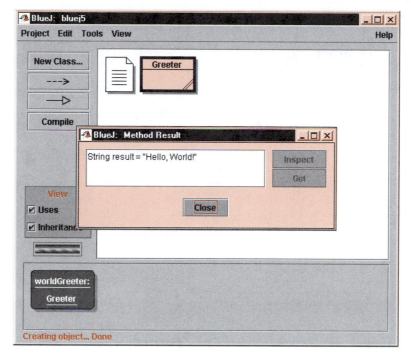

Figure 6

Testing a Class in the BlueJ Environment

The `RectangleTest` class in Section 2.1 is a good example of a test class. That class tests the `Rectangle` class—a class in the Java library.

Here is a class to test the `Greeter` class. The `main` method constructs an object of type `Greeter`, invokes the `sayHello` method, and displays the result on the console.

```
public class GreeterTest
{
    public static void main(String[] args)
    {
        Greeter worldGreeter = new Greeter();
        System.out.println(worldGreeter.sayHello());
    }
}
```

To produce a program, you need to combine these two classes. The details for building the program depend on your compiler and development environment. In most environments, you need to carry out these steps:

1. Make a new subfolder for your program.

2. Make two files, one for each class.

3. Compile both files.

4. Run the test program.

For example, if you use the Java SDK command line tools, the steps are like this:

```
mkdir greeter
cd greeter
edit Greeter.java
edit GreeterTest.java
javac Greeter.java
javac GreeterTest.java
java GreeterTest
```

Many students are surprised that such a simple program contains two classes. However, this is normal. The two classes have entirely different purposes. The `Greeter` class (which we will make more interesting in the next section) describes objects that can utter greetings. The `GreeterTest` class runs a test that puts a `Greeter` object through its paces. The `GreeterTest` program is necessary only if your development environment does not have a facility for interactive testing.

Productivity Hint 2.1

Using the Command Line Effectively

If your programming environment lets you accomplish all routine tasks with menus and dialog boxes, you can skip this note. However, if you need to invoke the editor, the compiler, the linker, and the program to test manually, then it is well worth learning about *command line editing*.

Most operating systems (UNIX, DOS, OS/2) have a *command line interface* to interact with the computer. (In Windows, you can use the DOS command line interface by double-clicking the "MS-DOS Prompt" icon, or, if that icon doesn't appear on your "Programs" menu, clicking "Run..." and typing `command.com`.) You launch commands at a *prompt*. The command is executed, and on completion you get another prompt.

When you develop a program, you find yourself executing the same commands over and over. Wouldn't it be nice if you didn't have to type beastly commands like

```
javac MyProg.java
```

more than once? Or if you could fix a mistake rather than having to retype the command in its entirety? Many command line interfaces have an option to do just that, but they don't always make it obvious. If you use Windows, you need to install a program called `doskey`. If you use UNIX, some shells let you cycle through your old commands. If your default configuration does not have that feature, ask how you can change to a better shell, such as `bash` or `tcsh`.

Once you have your shell configured properly, you can use the up and down arrow keys to recall old commands and the left and right arrow keys to edit lines. You can also perform *command completion*. For example, to reissue the same `javac` command, type `javac` and press F8 (Windows) or type `!javac` (UNIX).

2.5   Instance Fields

Right now, our `Greeter` class isn't very interesting, because all objects act in the same way. Suppose you construct two objects:

```
Greeter greeter1 = new Greeter();
Greeter greeter2 = new Greeter();
```

> An object uses instance fields to store its state—the data that it needs to execute its methods.

Then both `greeter1` and `greeter2` return exactly the same result when you invoke the `sayHello` method. Let's modify the `Greeter` class so that one object can return the message `"Hello, World!"` and another can return `"Hello, Dave!"`.

To achieve this purpose, each `Greeter` object must store *state*. The state of an object is the set of values that determine how an object reacts to method calls. In the case of our improved `Greeter` object, the state is the name that we want to use in the greeting, such as `"World"` or `"Dave"`.

An object stores its state in one or more variables called *instance fields*. You declare the instance fields for an object in the class.

```
public class Greeter
{
    . . .
    private String name;
}
```

An instance field declaration consists of the following parts:

- An *access specifier* (usually `private`)
- The *type* of the variable (such as `String`)
- The name of the variable (such as `name`)

> Each object of a class has its own set of instance fields.

Each object of a class has its own set of instance fields. For example, if `worldGreeter` and `daveGreeter` are two objects of the `Greeter` class, then each object has its own `name` field, called `worldGreeter.name` and `daveGreeter.name` (see Figure 7).

> Encapsulation is the process of hiding object data and providing methods for data access.

Instance fields are generally declared with the access specifier `private`. That specifier means that they can be accessed only by the methods of the *same class*, not by any other method. In particular, the `name` variable can be accessed only by the `sayHello` method.

> You should declare all instance fields as private.

In other words, if the instance fields are declared private, then all data access must occur through the public methods. Thus, the instance fields of an object are effectively hidden from the programmer who uses a class. They are of concern only to the programmer who implements the class. The process of hiding the data and providing methods for data access is called *encapsulation*. Although it is theoretically possible in Java to leave instance fields public, that is very uncommon in practice. We will always make all instance fields private in this book.

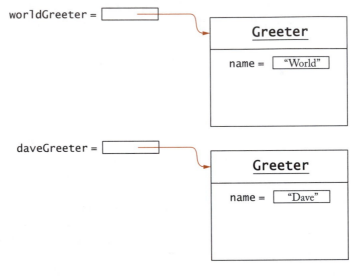

Figure 7

Instance Fields

For example, because the `name` instance field is private, you cannot access the instance field in methods of another class:

```
public class GreeterTest
{
    public static void main(String[] args)
    {
        . . .
        System.out.println(daveGreeter.name); // ERROR
    }
}
```

Only the `sayHello` method can access the private `name` variable. If we later add other methods to the `Greeter` class, such as a `sayGoodbye` method, then those methods can access the private instance field as well.

Here is the implementation of the `sayHello` method of the improved `Greeter` class.

```
public String sayHello()
{
    String message = "Hello, " + name + "!";
    return message;
}
```

The + symbol denotes *string concatenation*, an operation that forms a new string by putting shorter strings together one after another.

This method computes a string `message` by combining three strings: `"Hello, "`, the string stored in the `name` instance field, and the string consisting of an exclamation point "!". If the `name` variable refers to the string `"Dave"`, then the resulting string is `"Hello, Dave!"`.

Note that this method uses two separate object variables: the *local variable* `message` and the instance field `name`. A local variable belongs to an individual method, and you can use it only in the method in which you declare it. An instance field belongs to an object, and you can use it in all methods of its class.

Syntax 2.6: Instance Field Declaration

accessSpecifier `class` *ClassName*
```
{
    . . .
    accessSpecifier fieldType fieldName;
    . . .
}
```

Example:
```
public class Greeter
{
    . . .
    private String name;
    . . .
}
```

Purpose:

To define a field that is present in every object of a class

2.6   Constructors

> Constructors contain instructions to initialize objects. The constructor name is always the same as the class name.

To complete the improved `Greeter` class, we need to be able to construct objects with different values for the `name` instance field. We want to specify the name when constructing the object:

```
Greeter worldGreeter = new Greeter("World");
Greeter daveGreeter = new Greeter("Dave");
```

To accomplish this, we need to supply a *constructor* in the class definition. A constructor specifies how an object should be initialized. In our example, we have one construction parameter—a string describing the name. Here is the code for the constructor.

```
public Greeter(String aName)
{
    name = aName;
}
```

A constructor always has the same name as the class of the objects it constructs. Similar to methods, constructors are generally declared as `public` to enable any code in a program to construct new objects of the class. Unlike methods, though, constructors do not have return types.

> The new operator invokes the constructor.

The `new` operator invokes the constructor:

```
new Greeter("Dave")
```

This expression constructs a new object whose `name` instance field is set to the string `"Dave"`.

Constructors are not methods. You cannot invoke a constructor on an existing object. For example, the call

```
worldGreeter.Greeter("Harry"); // Error
```

is illegal. You can use a constructor only in combination with the `new` operator.

Here is the complete code for the enhanced `Greeter` class.

File Greeter.java

```
1  public class Greeter
2  {
3      public Greeter(String aName)
4      {
5          name = aName;
6      }
7
8      public String sayHello()
9      {
10         String message = "Hello, " + name + "!";
11         return message;
12     }
13
14     private String name;
15 }
```

Here is a test class that you can use to confirm that the `Greeter` class works correctly.

File GreeterTest.java

```
1  public class GreeterTest
2  {
3      public static void main(String[] args)
4      {
5          Greeter worldGreeter = new Greeter("World");
6          System.out.println(worldGreeter.sayHello());
7
8          Greeter daveGreeter = new Greeter("Dave");
9          System.out.println(daveGreeter.sayHello());
10     }
11 }
```

Syntax 2.7: Constructor Implementation

accessSpecifier `class` *ClassName*
```
{
    . . .
    accessSpecifier  ClassName(parameterType  parameterName,  . . .)
    {
        constructor implementation
    }
    . . .
}
```

Example:
```
public class Greeter
{
    . . .
    public Greeter(String aName)
    {
        name = aName;
    }
    . . .
}
```

Purpose:

To define the behavior of a constructor, which is used to initialize the instance fields of newly created objects

---

2.7 ## Designing the Public Interface of a Class

The purpose of the `Greeter` class was to show you the mechanics of defining classes, methods, instance fields, and constructors. Frankly, that class was not very useful. In this section we will create a more interesting class that describes the behavior of a *bank account*. More importantly, we will go through the thought process that is required when you design a new class.

Before you start programming, you need to understand how the objects of your class behave. Consider what kind of operations you can carry out with a bank account. You can

- Deposit money
- Withdraw money
- Get the current balance

In Java, these operations are expressed as method calls. Let's suppose the variable `harrysChecking` contains a reference to an object of type `BankAccount`. You'll want to be able to call methods such as the following:

```
harrysChecking.deposit(2000);
harrysChecking.withdraw(500);
System.out.println(harrysChecking.getBalance());
```

That is, the `BankAccount` class should define three methods:

- `deposit`

- `withdraw`

- `getBalance`

Next, you need to determine the parameters and return types of these methods. As you can see from the code samples, the `deposit` and `withdraw` methods receive a number (the dollar amount) and return no values. The `getBalance` method has no parameter and returns a number.

Java has several number types—you will learn about them in the next chapter. The most flexible number type is called `double`, which stands for "double precision floating-point number". Think of a number in `double` format as any number that can appear in the display panel of a calculator, such as `250`, `6.75`, or `-0.333333333`.

Now that you know that you can use the `double` type for numbers, you can write down the methods of the `BankAccount` class:

```
public void deposit(double amount)
public void withdraw(double amount)
public double getBalance()
```

Now let's do the same for the constructors of the class. How do we want to construct a bank account? It seems reasonable that a call

```
BankAccount harrysChecking = new BankAccount();
```

should construct a new bank account with a zero balance. What if we want to start out with another balance? A second constructor would be useful that sets the balance to an initial value:

```
BankAccount harrysChecking = new BankAccount(5000);
```

That gives us two constructors:

```
public BankAccount()
public BankAccount(double initialBalance)
```

The compiler figures out which constructor to call by looking at the parameters. For example, if you call

```
new BankAccount()
```

then the compiler picks the first constructor. If you call

```
new BankAccount(5000)
```

then the compiler picks the second constructor. But if you call

```
new BankAccount("lotsa moolah")
```

> Overloaded methods are methods with the same name but different parameter types.

then the compiler generates an error message—for this class there is no constructor that takes a parameter of type `String`.

You may think that it is strange to have two constructors that have the same name and that differ only in the parameter type. (The first constructor has no parameters; the second one has one parameter, a number.) If a name is used to denote more than one constructor or method, that name is *overloaded*. See Advanced Topic 2.2 for more information on name overloading. Name overloading is common in Java, especially for constructors. After all, we have no choice what to call the constructor. The name of a constructor must be identical to the name of the class.

The constructors and methods of a class form the *public interface* of the class. These are the operations that any code in your program can access to create and manipulate `BankAccount` objects. Here is a complete listing of the public interface of the `BankAccount` class:

```
public BankAccount()
public BankAccount(double initialBalance)
public void deposit(double amount)
public void withdraw(double amount)
public double getBalance()
```

The behavior of our `BankAccount` class is simple, but it lets you carry out all of the important operations that commonly occur with bank accounts. For example, here is how you can transfer an amount from one bank account to another:

```
// transfer from one account to another
double transferAmount = 500;
momsSavings.withdraw(transferAmount);
harrysChecking.deposit(transferAmount);
```

And here is how you can add interest to a savings account:

```
double interestRate = 5; // 5% interest
double interestAmount =
    momsSavings.getBalance() * interestRate / 100;
momsSavings.deposit(interestAmount);
```

> Abstraction is the process of finding the essential feature set for a class.

As you can see, you can use objects of the `BankAccount` class to carry out meaningful tasks, without knowing how the `BankAccount` objects store their data or how the `BankAccount` methods do their work. This is an important aspect of object-oriented programming. The process of determining the feature set for a class is called *abstraction*.

Think about how an abstract painting strips away extraneous details and tries to represent only the essential features of an object. When you design the public interface of a class, you also need to find what operations are essential to manipulate objects in your program.

▼ Advanced Topic   2.2

Overloading

When the same name is used for more than one method or constructor, the name is *overloaded*. This is particularly common for constructors, because all constructors must have the same name—the name of the class. In Java you can overload methods and constructors, provided the parameter types are different. For example, the `PrintStream` class defines many methods, all called `println`, to print various number types and to print objects:

```
class PrintStream
{
```

```
    public void println(String s) { . . . }
    public void println(double a) { . . . }
    . . .

}
```

When the `println` method is called,

```
system.out.println(x);
```

the compiler looks at the type of `x`. If `x` is a `String` value, the first method is called. If `x` is a `double` value, the second method is called. If `x` does not match the parameter type of any of the methods, the compiler generates an error.

For overloading purposes, the type of the *return value* does not matter. You cannot have two methods with identical names and parameter types but different return values.

2.8   Commenting the Public Interface

> Use documentation comments to describe the classes and public methods of your programs.

When you define classes and methods, you should get into the habit of thoroughly *commenting* their behavior. In Java there is a very useful standard form for *documentation comments*. If you use this form in your classes, a program called `javadoc` can automatically generate a neat set of HTML pages that describe them. (See Productivity Hint 2.2 for a description of this utility.)

A documentation comment starts with a `/**`, a special comment delimiter used by the `javadoc` utility. Then you describe the method's *purpose*. Then, for each method parameter, you supply a line that starts with `@param`, followed by the parameter name and a short explanation. Finally, you supply a line that starts with `@return`, describing the return value. You omit the `@param` tag for methods that have no parameters, and you omit the `@return` tag for methods whose return type is `void`.

The `javadoc` utility copies the *first* sentence of each comment to a summary table. Therefore, it is best to write that first sentence with some care. It should start with an uppercase letter and end with a period. It does not have to be a grammatically complete sentence, but it should be meaningful when it is pulled out of the comment and displayed in a summary.

Here are two typical examples.

```
/**
    Withdraws money from the bank account.
    @param the amount to withdraw
*/
public void withdraw(double amount)
{
    implementation—filled in later
}
/**
    Gets the current balance of the bank account.
    @return the current balance
*/
public double getBalance()
{
    implementation—filled in later
}
```

The comments you have just seen explain individual *methods*. You should also supply a brief comment for each *class,* explaining its purpose. The comment syntax for class comments is very simple: Just place the documentation comment above the class.

```
/**
    A bank account has a balance that can be changed by
    deposits and withdrawals.
*/
public class BankAccount
{
    . . .

}
```

Your first reaction may well be "Whoa! Am I supposed to write all this stuff?" These comments do seem pretty repetitive. But you should still take the time to write them, even if it feels silly at times. There are three reasons.

First, the `javadoc` utility will format your comments into a neat set of documents that you can view in a web browser. It makes good use of the seemingly repetitive phrases. The first sentence of the comment is used for a *summary table* of all methods of your class (see Figure 8). The `@param` and `@return` comments are neatly formatted in the detail description of each method (see Figure 9). If you omit any of the comments, then `javadoc` generates documents that look strangely empty.

Next, it is actually easy to spend more time pondering whether a comment is too trivial to write than it takes just to write it. In practical programming, very simple methods are rare. It is harmless to have a trivial method overcommented, whereas a complicated method without

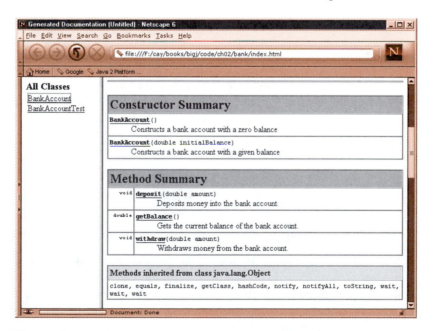

Figure 8

A Method Summary Generated by `javadoc`

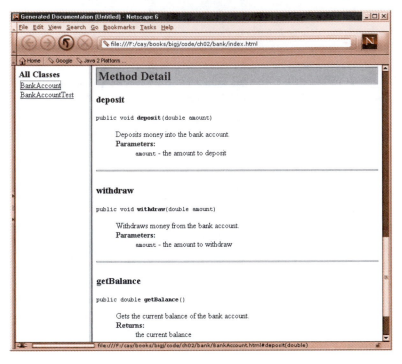

Figure 9

Method Details Generated by `javadoc`

> Provide documentation comments for every class, every method, every parameter, and every return value.

any comment can cause real grief to future maintenance programmers. According to the standard Java documentation style, *every* class, *every* method, *every* parameter, and *every* return value should have a comment.

Finally, it is always a good idea to write the method comment *first*, before writing the method code. This is an excellent test to see that you firmly understand what you need to program. If you can't explain what a class or method does, you aren't ready to implement it.

Productivity Hint   2.2

The `javadoc` Utility

You should always insert documentation comments in your code, whether or not you use `javadoc` to produce HTML documentation. But most people find the HTML documentation convenient, so it is worth learning how to run `javadoc`.

From a command shell, you invoke the `javadoc` utility with the command

```
javadoc MyClass.java
```

or

```
javadoc *.java
```

The `javadoc` utility then produces files `MyClass.html` in HTML format, which you can inspect in a browser. If you know HTML (see Chapter 4), you can embed HTML tags into the comments to specify fonts or add images. Perhaps most importantly, `javadoc` automatically provides *hyperlinks* to other classes and methods.

You can actually run `javadoc` before implementing any methods. Just leave all the method bodies empty. Don't run the compiler—it would complain about missing return values. Simply run `javadoc` on your file to generate the documentation for the public interface that you are about to implement.

The `javadoc` tool is wonderful because it does one thing right: It lets you put the documentation *together with your code*. That way, when you update your programs, you can see right away which documentation needs to be updated. Hopefully, you will update it right then and there. Afterward, run `javadoc` again and get updated information that is both timely and nicely formatted.

Productivity Hint 2.3

Keyboard Shortcuts for Mouse Operations

Programmers spend a lot of time with the keyboard and the mouse. Programs and documentation are many pages long and require a lot of typing. The constant switching among the editor, compiler, and debugger takes up quite a few mouse clicks. The designers of programs such as a Java integrated development environment have added some features to make your work easier, but it is up to you to discover them.

Just about every program has a user interface with menus and dialog boxes. Click on a menu and click on a submenu to select a task. Click on each field in a dialog box, fill in the requested answer, and click on the OK button. These are great user interfaces for the beginner, because they are easy to master, but they are terrible user interfaces for the regular user. The constant switching between the keyboard and the mouse slows you down. You need to move a hand off the keyboard, locate the mouse, move the mouse, click the mouse, and move the hand back onto the keyboard. For that reason, most user interfaces have *keyboard shortcuts:* combinations of keystrokes that allow you to achieve the same tasks without having to switch to the mouse at all.

All Microsoft Windows applications use the following conventions:

- The Alt key plus the underlined letter in a menu name (such as the F in "<u>F</u>ile") pulls down that menu. Inside a menu, just type the underlined character in the name of a submenu to activate it. For example, Alt+F followed by O selects "<u>F</u>ile" "<u>O</u>pen". Once your fingers know about this combination, you can open files faster than the fastest mouse artist.

- Inside dialog boxes, the Tab key is important; it moves from one option to the next. The arrow keys move within an option. The Enter key accepts the entire dialog, and Esc cancels it.

- In a program with multiple windows, Ctrl+Tab usually toggles through the windows managed by that program, for example between the source and error window.

▼
- Alt+Tab toggles between applications, letting you toggle quickly between, for example, the text editor and a command shell window.

▼
- Hold down the Shift key and press the arrow keys to highlight text. Then use Ctrl+X to cut the text, Ctrl+C to copy it, and Ctrl+V to paste it. These keys are easy to remember. The V looks like an insertion mark that an editor would use to insert text. The X should remind you of crossing out text. The C is just the first letter in "Copy". (OK, so it is also the first letter in "Cut"—no mnemonic rule is perfect.) You find these reminders in the Edit menu of most text editors.

▼

Of course, the mouse has its use in text processing: to locate or select text that is on the same screen but far away from the cursor.

▼

Take a little bit of time to learn about the keyboard shortcuts that the designers of your programs provided for you, and the time investment will be repaid many times during your programming career. When you blaze through your work in the computer lab with keyboard shortcuts, you may find yourself surrounded by amazed onlookers who whisper, "I didn't know you could do *that.*"

▼

2.9 Specifying the Implementation of a Class

Now that you understand the public interface of the `BankAccount` class, let's provide the implementation. As you already know, you need to supply a class with these ingredients:

```
public class BankAccount
{
    constructors
    methods
    fields
}
```

We have seen which constructors and methods we need. Let us turn to the instance fields. The instance fields are used to store the object state. In the case of our simple bank account objects, the state is the current balance of the bank account. (A more complex bank account might have a richer state—perhaps the current balance together with the interest rate paid, the date for mailing out the next statement, and so on.) For now, a single instance field suffices:

```
public class BankAccount
{
    . . .
    private double balance;
}
```

Note that the instance field is declared with the access specifier `private`. That means, the bank balance can be accessed only by the constructors and methods of the *same class*—namely, `deposit`, `withdraw`, and `getBalance`—and not by any constructor or method of another class. How the state of a bank account is maintained is a private implementation detail of the class. Recall that the practice of hiding the implementation details and providing methods for data access is called encapsulation.

The BankAccount class is so simple that it is not obvious what benefit you gain from the encapsulation. After all, you can always find out the current balance by calling the getBalance method. You can set the balance to any value by calling deposit with an appropriate amount.

The primary benefit of the encapsulation mechanism is the guarantee that an object cannot accidentally be put into an incorrect state. For example, suppose you want to make sure that a bank account is never overdrawn. You can simply implement the withdraw method so that it refuses to carry out a withdrawal that would result in a negative balance. (You will need to wait until Chapter 5 to see how to implement that protection.) On the other hand, if any code could freely modify the balance instance field of a BankAccount object, then it would be an easy matter to store a negative number in the variable.

Now that you know what methods you need, and how the object state is represented, it is an easy matter to implement each of the methods. For example, here is the deposit method:

```java
public void deposit(double amount)
{
    double newBalance = balance + amount;
    balance = newBalance;
}
```

Here is the constructor with no parameters.

```java
public BankAccount()
{
    balance = 0;
}
```

You will find the complete BankAccount class, with the implementations of all methods, at the end of this section.

If your development environment lets you construct objects interactively, then you can test this class immediately. Figures 10 and 11 show how to test the class in BlueJ. Otherwise, you need to supply a test class. The BankAccountTest class at the end of this section constructs a bank account, deposits and withdraws some money, and prints the remaining balance.

File BankAccount.java

```java
1  /**
2      A bank account has a balance that can be changed by
3      deposits and withdrawals.
4  */
5  public class BankAccount
6  {
7      /**
8          Constructs a bank account with a zero balance.
9      */
10     public BankAccount()
11     {
12         balance = 0;
```

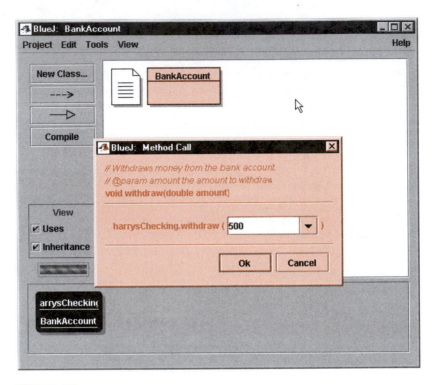

Figure 10

Calling the `withdraw` Method in BlueJ

```
13      }
14
15      /**
16          Constructs a bank account with a given balance.
17          @param initialBalance  the initial balance
18      */
19      public BankAccount(double initialBalance)
20      {
21          balance = initialBalance;
22      }
23
24      /**
25          Deposits money into the bank account.
26          @param amount  the amount to deposit
27      */
28      public void deposit(double amount)
29      {
30          double newBalance = balance + amount;
31          balance = newBalance;
32      }
33
34      /**
```

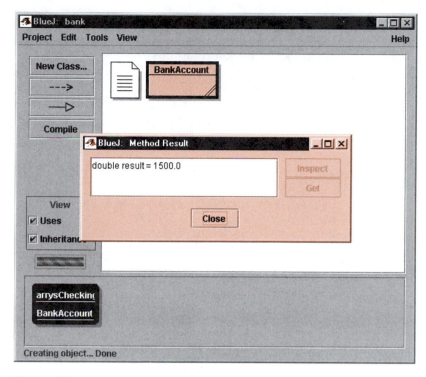

Figure 11

The Return Value of the `getBalance` Method in BlueJ

```
35          Withdraws money from the bank account.
36          @param amount  the amount to withdraw
37       */
38       public void withdraw(double amount)
39       {
40          double newBalance = balance - amount;
41          balance = newBalance;
42       }
43
44       /**
45          Gets the current balance of the bank account.
46          @return  the current balance
47       */
48       public double getBalance()
49       {
50          return balance;
51       }
52
53       private double balance;
54    }
```

File BankAccountTest.java

```
1  /**
2      A class to test the BankAccount class.
3  */
4  public class BankAccountTest
5  {
6      /**
7          Tests the methods of the BankAccount class.
8          @param args not used
9      */
10     public static void main(String[] args)
11     {
12        BankAccount harrysChecking = new BankAccount();
13        harrysChecking.deposit(2000);
14        harrysChecking.withdraw(500);
15        System.out.println(harrysChecking.getBalance());
16     }
17 }
```

⊗ Common Error 2.2

Trying to Reset an Object by Calling a Constructor

The constructor is invoked only when an object is first created. You cannot call the constructor to reset an object:

```
BankAccount harrysChecking = new BankAccount();
harrysChecking.withdraw(500);
harrysChecking.BankAccount(); // Error—can't reconstruct object
```

The constructor sets a *new* account object to a zero balance, but you cannot invoke a constructor on an *existing* object. The remedy is simple: Make a new object and overwrite the current one.

```
harrysChecking = new BankAccount(); // OK
```

? HOWTO 2.1

Designing and Implementing a Class

This is the first of several "HOWTO" sections in this book. Users of the Linux operating system have HOWTO guides that give answers to the common questions "How do I get started?" and "What do I do next?" in solving a variety of problems. Similarly, the HOWTO sections in this book give you step-by-step procedures for carrying out specific tasks.

You will often be asked to design and implement a class. For example, a homework assignment might ask you to design a Car class.

▼   **Step 1** Find out what you are asked to do with an object of the class

For example, suppose you are asked to implement a Car class. You won't have to model
▼   every feature of a real car—there are too many. The assignment should tell you *which*
aspects of a car your class should simulate. Make a list, in plain English, of the operations
that an object of your class should carry out, such as this one:

▼   • Add gas to gas tank.
            • Drive a certain distance.
            • Check the amount of gas left in the tank.

▼   **Step 2** Find names for the methods

Come up with method names and apply them to a sample object, like this:

```
Car myBeemer = new Car(. . .);
myBeemer.addGas(20);
myBeemer.drive(100);
myBeemer.getGas();
```

Step 3 Document the public interface

▼   Here is the documentation, with comments that describe the class and its methods:

```
/**
    A car can drive and consume fuel.
*/
public class Car
{
    /**
        Adds gas to the tank.
        @param amount  the amount of fuel to add
    */
    public void addGas(double amount)
    {
    }

    /**
        Drives a certain amount, consuming gas.
        @param distance  the distance driven
    */
    public void drive(double distance)
    {
    }

    /**
        Gets the amount of gas left in the tank.
        @return  the amount of gas
    */
    public double getGas()
    {
    }
}
```

▼ **Step 4** Determine instance variables

Ask yourself what information an object needs to store to do its job. Remember, the methods can be called in any order! The object needs to have enough internal memory to be able to process every method, using just its instance fields and the method parameters. Go through each method, perhaps starting with a simple one or an interesting one, and ask yourself what you need to carry out the method's task. Make instance fields to store the information that the method needs.

In the car example, we need to know (or compute) the amount of gas in the tank—the `getGas` method asks for it. It makes sense for a `Car` object to store it:

```
public class Car
{
   . . .
   private double gas;
}
```

Then the `addGas` method simply adds to that value. The `drive` method must reduce the gas in the tank. By how much? That depends on the fuel efficiency of the car. If you drive 100 miles, and the car can drive 20 miles per gallon, then 5 gallons are consumed. We don't get the efficiency as part of the `drive` method, so the car must store it:

```
public class Car
{
   . . .
   private double gas;
   private double efficiency;
}
```

▼ **Step 5** Determine constructors

Ask yourself what you need to construct an object. Often, you can just set all fields to 0 or a constant value. Sometimes, you need some essential information. Then you need to set that information in a constructor. Sometimes you will want two constructors: one that sets all fields to a default and one that sets them to user-supplied values. Design constructors as needed.

In the case of the car example, we can start out with an empty gas tank, but we need the efficiency of the car. There is no good default for it, so it should be a construction parameter. It is common to prefix construction parameter names with "a" or "an" so that you don't conflict with instance variable names.

```
/**
   Constructs a car with a given fuel efficiency.
   @param anEfficiency the fuel efficiency of the car
*/
public Car(double anEfficiency)
{
}
```

▼ **Step 6** Implement methods

Implement the methods and constructors in your class, one at a time, starting with the easiest ones. If you find that you have trouble with the implementation, you may need to go back to a previous step. Maybe your set of methods from steps 1 through 3 wasn't good? Maybe you didn't have the right instance fields? It is common for a beginner to run into a couple of problems that require backtracking.

Compile your class and fix any compiler errors.

Step 7 Test your class

Write a short test program and run it. The test program can just carry out the method calls that you found in step 2.

```
public class CarTest
{
   public static void main(String[] args)
   {
      Car myBeemer = new Car(20); // 20 miles per gallon
      myBeemer.addGas(20);
      myBeemer.drive(100);
      double gasLeft = myBeemer.getGas();
      System.out.println(gasLeft);
   }
}
```

Alternatively, if you use a program that lets you test objects interactively, such as BlueJ, construct an object and apply the method calls (see Figure 12).

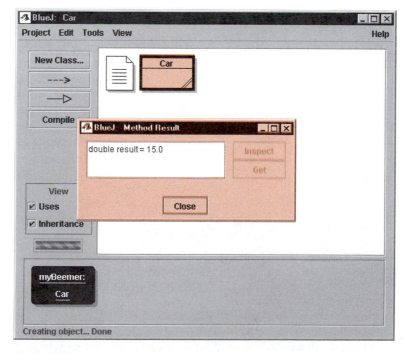

Figure 12

Testing a Class with BlueJ

2.10 Variable Types

You have seen three different types of variables in this chapter:

1. Instance fields, such as the `balance` variable of the `BankAccount` class
2. Local variables, such as the `newBalance` variable of the `deposit` method
3. Parameter variables, such as the `amount` variable of the `deposit` method

> Instance fields belong to an object. Parameter variables and local variables belong to a method—they die when the method exits.

These variables are similar—they all hold a value of a particular type. But they have a couple of important differences. The first difference is their *lifetime*.

An instance field belongs to an object. Each object has its own copy of each instance field. For example, if you have two `BankAccount` objects (say, `harrysChecking` and `momsSavings`), then each of them has its own `balance` field. When an object is constructed, its instance fields are created. They stay alive until no method uses the object any longer.

Local and parameter variables belong to a method. When the method starts, these variables come to life. When the method exits, they die. For example, if you call

```
harrysChecking.deposit(500);
```

then a parameter variable called `amount` is created and initialized with the parameter value, 500. When the method returns, that variable dies. When you make another method call,

```
momsSavings.deposit(1000);
```

a different parameter variable, also called `amount`, is created. It too dies at the end of the method. The same holds for the local variable `newBalance`. When the `deposit` method reaches the line

```
double newBalance = balance + amount;
```

the variable comes to life and is initialized with the sum of the object's balance and the deposit amount. The lifetime of that variable extends to the end of the method. However, the `deposit` method has a lasting effect. Its next line,

```
balance = newBalance;
```

> Instance fields are initialized to a default value, but you must initialize local variables.

sets the `balance` instance field, and that variable lives beyond the end of the `deposit` method, as long as the `BankAccount` object is in use.

The second major difference between instance and local variables is *initialization*.

You must initialize all local variables. If you don't initialize a local variable, the compiler complains when you try to use it.

Parameter variables are initialized with the values that are supplied in the method call.

Instance fields are initialized with a default value if you don't explicitly set them in a constructor. Instance fields that are numbers are initialized to 0. Object references are set to a special value called `null`. If an object reference is `null`, then it refers to no object at all. We will discuss the `null` value in greater detail in Section 5.2. Inadvertent initialization with 0 or `null` is a common cause of errors. Therefore, it is a matter of good style to initialize *every* instance field explicitly in every constructor.

▼ ⊗ **Common Error**   **2.3**

Forgetting to Initialize Object References in a Constructor

Just as it is a common error to forget to initialize a local variable, it is easy to forget about instance fields. Every constructor needs to ensure that all instance fields are set to appropriate values.

If you do not initialize an instance field, the Java compiler will initialize it for you. Numbers are initialized with 0, but object references—such as string variables—are set to the `null` reference.

Of course, 0 is often a convenient default for numbers. However, `null` is hardly ever a convenient default for objects. Consider this "lazy" constructor for the `Greeter` class:

```java
public class Greeter
{
    public Greeter() {} // do nothing
    . . .
    private String name;
}
```

The `name` field is set to a `null` reference. When you call `sayHello`, it will return `"Hello, null!"`.

If you forget to initialize a *local* variable in a *method*, the compiler flags this as an error, and you must fix it before the program runs. If you make the same mistake with an *instance* field, the compiler provides a default initialization, and the error becomes apparent only when the program runs.

To avoid this problem, make it a habit to initialize every instance field in every constructor.

2.11   Explicit and Implicit Method Parameters

Have a look at a particular invocation of the `deposit` method:

```java
momsSavings.deposit(500);
```

Now look again at the code of the `deposit` method:

```java
public void deposit(double amount)
{
    double newBalance = balance + amount;
    balance = newBalance;
}
```

The parameter variable `amount` is set to 500 when the `deposit` method starts. But what does `balance` mean exactly? After all, our program may have multiple `BankAccount` objects, and *each of them* has its own balance.

> The implicit parameter of a method is the object on which the method is invoked. The `this` reference denotes the implicit parameter.

Of course, since we deposit the money into `momsSavings`, `balance` must mean `momsSavings.balance`. In general, when you refer to an instance field inside a method, it means the instance field of the object on which the method was called.

Thus, the call to the `deposit` method depends on two values: the object to which `momsSavings` refers, and the value `500`. The `amount` parameter inside the parentheses is called an *explicit* parameter, because it is explicitly named in the method definition. However, the reference to the bank account object is not explicit in the method definition—it is called the *implicit parameter* of the method.

If you need to, you can access the implicit parameter—the object on which the method is called—with the keyword `this`. For example, in the preceding method invocation, `this` was set to `momsSavings` and `amount` to 500.

Every method has one implicit parameter. You don't give the implicit parameter a name. It is always called `this`. (There is one exception to the rule that every method has an implicit parameter: `static` methods do not. We will discuss them in Chapter 7.) In contrast, methods can have any number of explicit parameters, which you can name any way you like, or no explicit parameter at all.

Next, look again closely at the implementation of the `deposit` method. The statement

```
double newBalance = balance + amount;
```

actually means

```
double newBalance = this.balance + amount;
```

> Use of an instance field name in a method denotes the instance field of the implicit parameter.

When you refer to an instance field in a method, the compiler automatically applies it to the `this` parameter. Some programmers actually prefer to manually insert the `this` parameter before every instance field because they find it makes the code clearer. Here is an example:

```
public void deposit(double amount)
{
    double newBalance = this.balance + amount;
    this.balance = newBalance;
}
```

You may want to try it out and see if you like that style.

⊗ Common Error 2.4

Trying to Call a Method Without an Implicit Parameter

Suppose your `main` method contains the instruction

```
withdraw(30); // Error
```

The compiler will not know which account to access to withdraw the money. You need to supply an object reference of type `BankAccount`:

```
BankAccount harrysChecking = new BankAccount();
harrysChecking.withdraw(30);
```

However, there is one situation in which it is legitimate to invoke a method without, seemingly, an implicit parameter. Consider the following modification to the `BankAccount` class. Add a method to apply the monthly account fee:

```
class BankAccount
{  . . .
   public void monthlyFee()
   {
      withdraw(10); // withdraw $10 from this account
   }
}
```

That means to withdraw from the *same* account object that is carrying out the `monthlyFee` operation. In other words, the implicit parameter of the `withdraw` method is the (invisible) implicit parameter of the `monthlyFee` method.

If you find it confusing to have an invisible parameter, you can always use the `this` parameter to make the method easier to read:

```
class BankAccount
{  . . .
   public void monthlyFee()
   {
      this.withdraw(10); // withdraw $10 from this account
   }
}
```

▼ ⚑ Advanced Topic 2.3

Calling One Constructor from Another

Consider the `BankAccount` class. It has two constructors: a constructor without parameters to initialize the balance with zero, and another constructor to supply an initial balance. Rather than explicitly setting the balance to zero, one constructor can call another constructor of the same class instead. There is a shorthand notation to achieve this result:

```
class BankAccount
{
   public BankAccount (double initialBalance)
   {
      balance = initialBalance;
   }

   public BankAccount()
   {
      this(0);
   }
   . . .
}
```

The command `this(0);` means "Call another constructor of this class and supply the value 0." Such a constructor call can occur only *as the first line in another constructor.*

This syntax is a minor convenience. We will not use it in this book. Actually, the use of the keyword `this` is a little confusing. Normally, `this` denotes a reference to the implicit parameter, but if `this` is followed by parentheses, it denotes a call to another constructor of this class.

Random Fact   2.1

Mainframes—When Dinosaurs Ruled the Earth

When the International Business Machines Corporation, a successful manufacturer of punched-card equipment for tabulating data, first turned its attention to designing computers in the early 1950s, its planners assumed that there was a market for perhaps 50 such devices, for installation by the government, the military, and a few of the country's largest corporations. Instead, they sold about 1,500 machines of their System 650 model and went on to build and sell more powerful computers.

The so-called *mainframe* computers of the 1950s, 1960s, and 1970s were huge. They filled up whole rooms, which had to be climate-controlled to protect the delicate equipment (see Figure 13). Today, because of miniaturization technology, even mainframes are getting smaller, but they are still very expensive. (At the time of this writing, the cost for a midrange IBM 3090 is approximately 4 million dollars.)

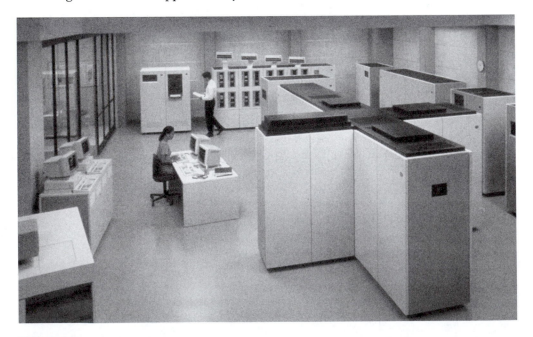

Figure 13

A Mainframe Computer

▼ These huge and expensive systems were an immediate success when they first appeared, because they replaced many roomfuls of even more expensive employees, who had previously performed the tasks by hand. Few of these computers do any exciting

▼ computations. They keep mundane information, such as billing records or airline reservations; they just keep lots of them.

▼ IBM was not the first company to build mainframe computers; that honor belongs to the Univac Corporation. However, IBM soon became the major player, partially because of technical excellence and attention to customer needs and partially because it exploited its strengths and structured its products and services in a way that made it difficult for

▼ customers to mix them with those of other vendors. In the 1960s, IBM's competitors, the so-called "Seven Dwarfs"—GE, RCA, Univac, Honeywell, Burroughs, Control Data, and NCR—fell on hard times. Some went out of the computer business alto-

▼ gether, while others tried unsuccessfully to combine their strengths by merging their computer operations. It was generally predicted that they would eventually all fail. It was in this atmosphere that the U.S. government brought an antitrust suit against IBM in

▼ 1969. The suit went to trial in 1975 and dragged on until 1982, when the Reagan Administration abandoned it, declaring it "without merit".

Of course, by then the computing landscape had changed completely. Just as the

▼ dinosaurs gave way to smaller, nimbler creatures, three new waves of computers had appeared: the minicomputers, workstations, and microcomputers, all engineered by new companies, not the Seven Dwarfs. Today, the importance of mainframes in the market-

▼ place has diminished, and IBM, while still a large and resourceful company, no longer dominates the computer market.

Mainframes are still in use today for two reasons. They still excel at handling large

▼ data volumes. More importantly, the programs that control the business data have been refined over the last 20 or more years, fixing one problem at a time. Moving these programs to less expensive computers, with different languages and operating systems,

▼ is difficult and error-prone. Sun Microsystems, a leading manufacturer of workstations, was eager to prove that its mainframe system could be "downsized" and replaced by its own equipment. Sun eventually succeeded, but it took over five years—far longer

▼ than it expected.

CHAPTER SUMMARY

1. Objects are entities in your program that you manipulate by invoking methods.

2. The public interface of a class specifies what you can do with its objects. The hidden implementation describes how these actions are carried out.

3. Classes are factories for objects. You construct a new object of a class with the new operator.

4. You store object locations in object variables.

5. All object variables must be initialized before you access them.

6. An object reference describes the location of an object.

7. Multiple object variables can contain references to the same object.

8. Java classes are grouped into packages. If you use a class from another package (other than the `java.lang` package), you must import the class.

9. A method definition specifies the method name, parameters, and the statements for carrying out the method's actions.

10. Use the `return` statement to specify the value that a method returns to its caller.

11. To test a class, use an environment for interactive testing, or write a second class to execute test instructions.

12. An object uses instance fields to store its state—the data that it needs to execute its methods.

13. Each object of a class has its own set of instance fields.

14. Encapsulation is the process of hiding object data and providing methods for data access.

15. You should declare all instance fields as private.

16. Constructors contain instructions to initialize objects. The constructor name is always the same as the class name.

17. The `new` operator invokes the constructor.

18. Overloaded methods are methods with the same name but different parameter types.

19. Abstraction is the process of finding the essential feature set for a class.

20. Use documentation comments to describe the classes and public methods of your programs.

21. Provide documentation comments for every class, every method, every parameter, and every return value.

22. Instance fields belong to an object. Parameter variables and local variables belong to a method—they die when the method exits.

23. Instance fields are initialized to a default value, but you must initialize local variables.

24. The implicit parameter of a method is the object on which the method is invoked. The `this` reference denotes the implicit parameter.

25. Use of an instance field name in a method denotes the instance field of the implicit parameter.

REVIEW EXERCISES

Exercise R2.1. Explain the difference between an object and an object reference.

Exercise R2.2. Explain the difference between an object and an object variable.

Exercise R2.3. Explain the difference between an object and a class.

Exercise R2.4. Explain the difference between a constructor and a method.

Exercise R2.5. Give the Java code for an *object* of class `BankAccount` and for an *object variable* of class `BankAccount`.

Exercise R2.6. Explain the difference between an instance field and a local variable.

Exercise R2.7. Explain the difference between a local variable and a parameter variable.

Exercise R2.8. Explain the difference between

```
new BankAccount(5000);
```

and

```
BankAccount b = new BankAccount(5000);
```

Exercise R2.9. Explain the difference between

```
BankAccount b;
```

and

```
BankAccount b = new BankAccount(5000);
```

Exercise R2.10. What are the construction parameters for a `BankAccount` object?

Exercise R2.11. Give Java code to construct the following objects:

- A rectangle with center (100, 100) and all side lengths equal to 50
- A greeter who will say `"Hello, Mars!"`
- A bank account with a balance of $5000

Create just objects, not object variables.

Exercise R2.12. Repeat the preceding exercise, but now define object variables that are initialized with the required objects.

Exercise R2.13. Find the errors in the following statements:

```
Rectangle r = (5, 10, 15, 20);

double x = BankAccount(10000).getBalance();

BankAccount b;
b.deposit(10000);

b = new BankAccount(10000);
b.add("one million bucks");
```

Exercise R2.14. Describe all constructors of the `BankAccount` class. List all methods that can be used to change a `BankAccount` object. List all methods that don't change the `BankAccount` object.

Exercise R2.15. What is the value of b after the following operations?

```
BankAccount b = new BankAccount(10);
b.deposit(5000);
b.withdraw(b.getBalance() / 2);
```

Exercise R2.16. If b1 and b2 store objects of class BankAccount, consider the following instructions.

```
b1.deposit(b2.getBalance());
b2.deposit(b1.getBalance());
```

Are the balances of b1 and b2 now identical? Explain.

Exercise R2.17. What is the this reference?

Exercise R2.18. What does the following method do? Give an example of how you can call the method.

```
public class BankAccount
{
   public void mystery(BankAccount that, double amount)
   {
      this.balance = this.balance - amount;
      that.balance = that.balance + amount;
   }
   . . . // other bank account methods
}
```

PROGRAMMING EXERCISES

Exercise P2.1. Write a program that constructs a Rectangle object, prints it, and then translates and prints it three more times, so that, if the rectangles were drawn, they would form one large rectangle:

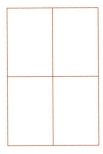

Exercise P2.2. The intersection method computes the *intersection* of two rectangles—that is, the rectangle that is formed by two overlapping rectangles:

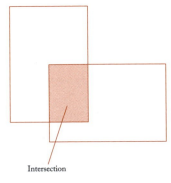

Intersection

You call this method as follows:

```
Rectangle r3 = r1.intersection(r2);
```

Write a program that constructs two rectangle objects, prints them, and then prints the rectangle object that describes the intersection. What happens when the rectangles do not overlap?

Exercise P2.3. Add a method `sayGoodbye` to the `Greeter` class.

Exercise P2.4. Add a method `refuseHelp` to the `Greeter` class. It should return a string such as `"I am sorry, Dave. I am afraid I can't do that."`

Exercise P2.5. Write a program that constructs a bank account, deposits $1000, withdraws $500, withdraws another $400, and then prints the remaining balance.

Exercise P2.6. Add a method

```
void addInterest(double rate)
```

to the `BankAccount` class that adds interest at the given rate. For example, after the statements

```
BankAccount momsSavings = new BankAccount(1000);
momsSavings.addInterest(10); // 10% interest
```

the balance in `momsSavings` is $1,100.

Exercise P2.7. Write a class `SavingsAccount` that is similar to the `BankAccount` class, except that it has an added instance variable `interest`. Supply a constructor that sets both the initial balance and the interest rate. Supply a method `addInterest` (with no explicit parameter) that adds interest to the account. Write a program that constructs a savings account with an initial balance of $1,000 and interest rate 10%. Then apply the `addInterest` method five times and print the resulting balance.

Exercise P2.8. Implement a class `Employee`. An employee has a name (a string) and a salary (a `double`). Write a default constructor, a constructor with two parameters (name and salary), and methods to return the name and salary. Write a small program that tests your class.

Exercise P2.9. Enhance the class in the preceding exercise by adding a method `raiseSalary` (double byPercent) that raises the employee's salary by a certain percentage. Sample usage:

```
Employee harry = new Employee("Hacker, Harry", 55000);
harry.raiseSalary(10); // Harry gets a 10% raise
```

Exercise P2.10. Implement a class `Car` with the following properties. A car has a certain fuel efficiency (measured in miles/gallon or liters/km—pick one) and a certain amount of fuel in the gas tank. The efficiency is specified in the constructor, and the initial fuel level is 0. Supply a method `drive` that simulates driving the car for a certain distance, reducing the fuel level in the gas tank, and methods `getGas`, returning the current fuel level, and `addGas`, to tank up. Sample usage:

```
Car myBeemer = new Car(29); // 29 miles per gallon
myBeemer.addGas(20); // tank 20 gallons
myBeemer.drive(100); // drive 100 miles
System.out.println(myBeemer.getGas());
// print fuel remaining
```

Exercise P2.11. Implement a class `Student`. For the purpose of this exercise, a student has a name and a total quiz score. Supply an appropriate constructor and methods `getName()`, `addQuiz(int score)`, `getTotalScore()`, and `getAverageScore()`. To compute the latter, you also need to store the *number of quizzes* that the student took.

Exercise P2.12. Implement a class `Product`. A product has a name and a price, for example `new Product("Toaster", 29.95)`. Supply methods `getName()`, `getPrice()`, and `setPrice()`. Write in a program that makes two products, prints the name and price, reduces their prices by $5.00, and then prints them again.

Exercise P2.13. Implement a class `Circle` that has methods `getArea()` and `getPerimeter()`. In the constructor, supply the radius of the circle.

Exercise P2.14. Implement a class `Square` that has methods `getArea()` and `getPerimeter()`. In the constructor, supply the width of the square.

Exercise P2.15. Implement a class `SodaCan` with methods `getSurfaceArea()` and `getVolume()`. In the constructor, supply the height and radius of the can.

Exercise P2.16. Implement a class `RoachPopulation` that simulates the growth of a roach population. The constructor takes the size of the initial roach population. The `wait` method simulates a period in which the population doubles. The `spray` method simulates spraying with insecticide, which reduces the population by 10%. The `getRoaches` method returns the current number of roaches. Implement the class and a test program that simulates a kitchen that starts out with 10 roaches. Wait, spray, print the roach count. Repeat three times.

Exercise P2.17. Implement a class `RabbitPopulation` that simulates the growth of a rabbit population. The rules are as follows: Start with one pair of rabbits. Rabbits are able to mate at the age of one month. A month later, each female produces another pair of rabbits. Assume that rabbits never die and that the female always produces one new pair (one male, one female) every month from the second month on. Implement a method `wait` that waits for one month, and a method `getPairs` that prints the current number of rabbit pairs. Write a test program that shows the growth of the rabbit population for ten months. *Hint:* Keep one instance field for the newborn rabbit pairs and another one for the rabbit pairs that are at least one month old.

Fundamental Data Types

To understand integer and floating-point numbers

▶ To recognize the limitations of the `int` and `double` types and the overflow and roundoff errors that can result

▶ To write arithmetic expressions in Java

▶ To use the `String` type to define and manipulate character strings

▶ To learn about the `char` data type

▶ To learn how to read program input

▶ To understand the copy behavior of primitive types and object references

This chapter teaches how to manipulate numbers and character strings in Java. The goal of this chapter is to gain a firm understanding of the fundamental Java data types.

3.1   Number Types

In this chapter, we will use a `Purse` class to demonstrate several important concepts. We won't yet reveal the implementation of the purse, but here is the public interface:

```
public class Purse
{
   /**
      Constructs an empty purse.
   */
   public Purse()
   {
      // implementation
   }

   /**
      Add nickels to the purse.
      @param count the number of nickels to add
   */
   public void addNickels(int count)
   {
      // implementation
   }

   /**
      Add dimes to the purse.
      @param count the number of dimes to add
```

```
*/
public void addDimes(int count)
{
    // implementation
}

/**
    Add quarters to the purse.
    @param count the number of quarters to add
*/
public void addQuarters(int count)
{
    // implementation
}

/**
    Get the total value of the coins in the purse.
    @return the sum of all coin values
*/
public double getTotal()
{
    // implementation
}

    // private instance variables
}
```

Read through the public interface and ask yourself whether you can figure out how to use `Purse` objects. You should find this straightforward. There is a constructor to make a new, empty purse:

```
Purse myPurse = new Purse();
```

You can add nickels, dimes, and quarters. (For simplicity, we don't bother with pennies, half dollars, or dollar coins.)

```
myPurse.addNickels(3);
myPurse.addDimes(1);
myPurse.addQuarters(2);
```

Now you can ask the purse object about the total value of the coins in the purse:

```
double totalValue = myPurse.getTotal(); // returns 0.75
```

> The `int` type denotes integers: numbers without fractional parts.

If you look closely at the methods to add coins, you will see an unfamiliar data type. The `count` parameter has type `int`, which denotes an *integer* type. An integer is a number without a fractional part. For example, 3 is an integer, but 0.05 is not. The number zero and negative numbers are integers. Thus, the `int` type is more restrictive than the `double` type that you saw in Chapter 2.

Why have both integer and floating-point number types? Your calculator doesn't have a separate integer type. It uses floating-point numbers for all calculations. Why don't we just use the `double` type for the coin counts?

There are two reasons for having a separate integer type: one philosophical and one pragmatic. In terms of philosophy, when we think about real purses and modern American coins, we recognize that there can be only a whole number of nickels, say, in a purse. If we were to saw a nickel in half, the halves would be worthless, and dropping one of them into a purse would not increase the amount of money in the purse. By specifying that the number of nickels is an integer, we make that observation into an explicit assumption in our model. The program would have worked just as well with floating-point numbers to count the coins, but it is generally a good idea to choose programming solutions that document one's intentions. Pragmatically speaking, integers are more efficient than floating-point numbers. They take less storage space, are processed faster on some platforms, and don't cause rounding errors.

Now let's start implementing the `Purse` class. Any `Purse` object can be described by the number of nickels, dimes, and quarters that the purse currently contains. Thus, we use three instance variables to represent the state of a `Purse` object:

```java
public class Purse
{
    . . .
    private int nickels;
    private int dimes;
    private int quarters;
}
```

Now we can implement the `getTotal` method simply:

```java
public double getTotal()
{
    return nickels * 0.05 + dimes * 0.1 + quarters * 0.25;
}
```

In Java, multiplication is denoted by an asterisk *, not a raised dot · or a cross ×, because there are no keys for these symbols on most keyboards. For example, $d \cdot 10$ is written as `d * 10`. Do not write commas or spaces in numbers in Java. For example, 10,150.75 must be entered as `10150.75`. To write numbers in exponential notation in Java, use E n instead of "$\times 10^n$". For example, 5.0×10^{-3} is written as `5.0E-3`.

The `getTotal` method computes the value of the expression

```java
nickels * 0.05 + dimes * 0.1 + quarters * 0.25
```

That value is a floating-point number, because multiplying an integer (such as `nickels`) by a floating-point number (such as `0.05`) yields a floating-point number. The `return` statement returns the computed value as the method result, and the method exits.

Quality Tip 3.1

Choose Descriptive Variable Names

In algebra, variable names are usually just one letter long, such as p or A, maybe with a subscript such as p_1. You might be tempted to save yourself a lot of typing by using shorter variable names in your Java programs as well:

```
public class Purse
{
    . . .
    private int n;
    private int d;
    private int q;
}
```

Compare this with the previous one, though. Which one is easier to read? There is no comparison. Just reading `nickels` is a lot less trouble than reading n and then *figuring out* that it must mean "nickels".

In practical programming, descriptive variable names are particularly important when programs are written by more than one person. It may be obvious to *you* that n must stand for nickels, but is it obvious to the person who needs to update your code years later, long after you were promoted (or laid off)? For that matter, will you remember yourself what n means when you look at the code six months from now?

Of course, you could use comments:

```
public class Purse
{
    . . .
    private int n; // nickels
    private int d; // dimes
    private int q; // quarters
}
```

That makes the definitions pretty clear. But in the `getTotal` method, you'd still have a rather cryptic computation `n * 0.05 + d * 0.1 + q * 0.25`. Descriptive variable names are a better choice, because they make your code easy to read without requiring comments.

Advanced Topic   3.1

Numeric Ranges and Precisions

Unfortunately, `int` and `double` values do suffer from one problem: They cannot represent arbitrarily large integer or floating-point numbers. Integers have a range of −2,147,483,648 (about −2 billion) to +2,147,483,647 (about 2 billion). See Advanced Topic 3.4 for an explanation of these values. If you need to refer to these boundaries in your program, use the constants `Integer.MIN_VALUE` and `Integer.MAX_VALUE`, which are defined in a class called `Integer`. If you want to represent the world population, you can't use an `int`. Double-precision floating-point numbers are somewhat less limited; they can go up to more than 10^{300}. However, `double` floating-point numbers suffer from a different problem: *precision*. They store only about 15 significant digits. Suppose your customers might find the price of three hundred trillion dollars ($300,000,000,000,000) for your product a bit excessive, so you want to reduce it by five cents to a more reasonable-looking $299,999,999,999,999.95. Try running the following program:

```
class AdvancedTopic3_1
{
```

```
public static void main(String[] args)
{
    double originalPrice = 3E14;
    double discountedPrice = originalPrice - 0.05;
    double discount = originalPrice - discountedPrice;
        // should be 0.05;
    System.out.println(discount);
        // prints 0.0625;
}
}
```

The program prints out `0.0625`, not `0.05`. It is off by more than a penny!

For most of the programming projects in this book, the limited range and precision of `int` and `double` are acceptable. Just bear in mind that overflows or loss of precision can occur.

AT Advanced Topic   3.2

Other Number Types

If `int` and `double` are not sufficient for your computational needs, there are other data types to which you can turn. When the range of integers is not sufficient, the simplest remedy is to use the `long` type. *Long integers* have a range from −9,223,372,036,854,775,808 to +9,223,372,036,854,775,807.

To specify a long integer constant, you need to append the letter L after the number value. For example,

```
long price = 300000000000000L;
```

There is also an integer type `short` with shorter-than-normal integers, having a range of −32,768 to 32,767. Finally, there is a type `byte` with a range of −128 to 127.

The `double` type can represent about 15 decimal digits. There is a second floating-point type, called `float`, whose values take half the storage space. Computations involving `float` execute a bit faster than those involving `double`, but the precision of `float` values—about 7 decimal digits—is insufficient for many programs. However, some graphics routines require you to use `float` values.

By the way, the name "floating-point" comes from the fact that the numbers are represented in the computer as a sequence of the significant digits and an indication of the position of the decimal point. For example, the numbers 250, 2.5, 0.25, and 0.025 all have the same decimal digits: 25. When a floating-point number is multiplied or divided by 10, only the position of the decimal point changes; it "floats". This representation corresponds to numbers written in "exponential" or "scientific" notation, such as 2.5×10^2. (Actually, internally the numbers are represented in base 2, as binary numbers, but the principle is the same. See Advanced Topic 3.4 for more information on binary numbers.) Sometimes `float` values are called "single-precision", and of course `double` values are "double-precision" floating-point numbers.

If you want to compute with really large numbers, you can use *big number objects*. Big number objects are objects of the `BigInteger` and `BigDecimal` classes in the `java.math` package. Unlike the number types such as `int` or `double`, big number objects have essentially no limits on their size and precision. However, computations with big number objects are much slower than those that involve number types. Perhaps more importantly, you can't use the familiar arithmetic operators (+ - * /) with them. Instead, you have to use methods called `add`, `subtract`, `multiply`, and `divide`. Here is an example of how to create two big numbers and how to multiply them.

```
BigInteger a = new BigInteger("123456789");
BigInteger b = new BigInteger("987654321");
BigInteger c = a.multiply(b);
System.out.println(c); // prints 121932631112635269
```

Random Fact   3.1

The Pentium Floating-Point Bug

In 1994, Intel Corporation released what was then its most powerful processor, the first of the Pentium series. Unlike previous generations of Intel's processors, the Pentium had a very fast floating-point unit. Intel's goal was to compete aggressively with the makers of higher-end processors for engineering workstations. The Pentium was an immediate huge success.

In the summer of 1994, Dr. Thomas Nicely of Lynchburg College in Virginia ran an extensive set of computations to analyze the sums of reciprocals of certain sequences of prime numbers. The results were not always what his theory predicted, even after he took into account the inevitable roundoff errors. Then Dr. Nicely noted that the same program did produce the correct results when run on the slower 486 processor, which preceded the Pentium in Intel's lineup. This should not have happened. The optimal roundoff behavior of floating-point calculations has been standardized by the Institute of Electrical and Electronics Engineers (IEEE), and Intel claimed to adhere to the IEEE standard in both the 486 and the Pentium processors. Upon further checking, Dr. Nicely discovered that indeed there was a very small set of numbers for which the product of two numbers was computed differently on the two processors. For example,

$$4,195,835 - ((4,195,835 / 3,145,727) \times 3,145,727)$$

is mathematically equal to 0, and it did compute as 0 on a 486 processor. On a Pentium processor, however, the result was 256.

As it turned out, Intel had independently discovered the bug in its testing and had started to produce chips that fixed it. (Subsequent versions of the Pentium, such as the Pentium III and IV, are free of the problem.) The bug was caused by an error in a table that was used to speed up the floating-point multiplication algorithm of the processor. Intel determined that the problem was exceedingly rare. They claimed that under normal use a typical consumer would only notice the problem once every 27,000 years. Unfortunately for Intel, Dr. Nicely had not been a normal user.

Now Intel had a real problem on its hands. It figured that replacing all the Pentium processors that it had already sold would cost it a great deal of money. Intel already had more orders for the chip than it could produce, and it would be particularly galling to have to give out the scarce chips as free replacements instead of selling them. Intel's management decided to punt on the issue and initially offered to replace the processors only for those customers who could prove that their work required absolute precision in mathematical calculations. Naturally, that did not go over well with the hundreds of thousands of customers who had paid retail prices of $700 and more for a Pentium chip and did not want to live with the nagging feeling that perhaps, one day, their income tax program would produce a faulty return.

Ultimately, Intel had to cave in to public demand and replaced all defective chips, at a cost of about 475 million dollars.

What do you think? Intel claims that the probability of the bug occurring in any calculation is extremely small—smaller than many chances you take every day, such as driving to work in an automobile. Indeed, many users had used their Pentium computers for many months without reporting any ill effects, and the computations that Professor Nicely was doing are hardly examples of typical user needs. As a result of its public relations blunder, Intel ended up paying a large amount of money. Undoubtedly, some of that money was added to chip prices and thus actually paid by Intel's customers. Also, a large number of processors, whose manufacture consumed energy and caused some environmental impact, were destroyed without benefiting anyone. Could Intel have been justified in wanting to replace only the processors of those users who could reasonably be expected to suffer an impact from the problem?

Suppose that, instead of stonewalling, Intel had offered you the choice of a free replacement processor or a $200 rebate. What would you have done? Would you have replaced your faulty chip, or would you have taken your chance and pocketed the money?

3.2   Assignment

Here is the constructor of the Purse class:

```
public Purse()
{
   nickels = 0;
   dimes = 0;
   quarters = 0;
}
```

The = operator is called the *assignment* operator. On the left, you need a variable name. The right-hand side can be a single value or an expression. The assignment operator sets the variable to the given value. So far, that's straightforward. But now let's look at a more interesting use of the assignment operator, in the addNickels method.

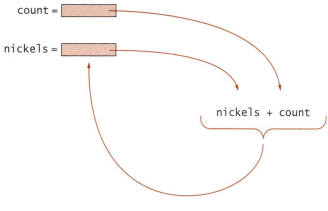

Figure 1

Assignment

```
public void addNickels(int count)
{
   nickels = nickels + count;
}
```

It means, "Compute the value of the expression `nickels + count`, *and place the result again into the variable* `nickels`." (See Figure 1.)

The = sign doesn't mean that the left-hand side is *equal* to the right-hand side but that the right-hand-side value is copied into the left-hand-side variable. You should not confuse this *assignment operation* with the = used in algebra to denote *equality*. The assignment operator is an instruction to do something, namely place a value into a variable. The mathematical equality states the fact that two values are equal. For example, in Java it is perfectly legal to write

```
nickels = nickels + 1;
```

It means to look up the value stored in the variable `nickels`, to add 1 to it, and to stuff the sum back into `nickels`. (See Figure 2.) The net effect of executing this

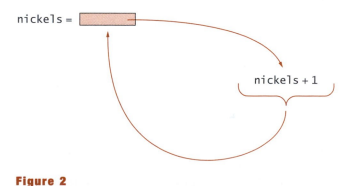

Figure 2

Incrementing a Variable

> Assignment to a variable is not the same as mathematical equality.

statement is to increment `nickels` by 1. Of course, in mathematics it would make no sense to write that $n = n + 1$; no integer can equal itself plus 1.

The concepts of assignment and equality have no relationship with each other, and it is a bit unfortunate that the Java language (following C and C++) uses = to denote assignment. Other programming languages use a symbol such as <- or :=, which avoids the confusion.

> The ++ and -- operators increment and decrement a variable.

Consider once more the statement `nickels = nickels + 1`. This statement increments the `nickels` variable. For example, if `nickels` was 3 before execution of the statement, it is set to 4 afterwards. This increment operation is so common when writing programs that there is a special shorthand for it, namely

```
nickels++;
```

This statement has exactly the same effect—namely, to add 1 to `nickels`—but it is easier to type. As you might have guessed, there is also a decrement operator --. The statement

```
nickels--;
```

subtracts 1 from `nickels`.

▼ **Ⓐ Advanced Topic**   **3.3**

Combining Assignment and Arithmetic

▼ In Java you can combine arithmetic and assignment. For example, the instruction

```
nickels += count;
```

▼ is a shortcut for

```
nickels = nickels + count;
```

▼ Similarly,

```
nickels *= 2;
```

▼ is another way of writing

```
nickels = nickels * 2;
```

▼ Many programmers find this a convenient shortcut. If you like it, go ahead and use it in your own code. For simplicity, we won't use it in this book, though.

Productivity Hint 3.1

Avoid Unstable Layout

You should arrange program code and comments so that the program is easy to read. For example, you should not cram all statements on a single line, and you should make sure that braces { } line up.

However, you should be careful when you embark on beautification efforts. Some programmers like to line up the = signs in a series of assignments, like this:

```
nickels  = 0;
dimes    = 0;
quarters = 0;
```

This looks very neat, but the layout is not *stable*. Suppose you add a line like the one at the bottom of this:

```
nickels  = 0;
dimes    = 0;
quarters = 0;
halfDollars = 0;
```

Oops, now the = signs no longer line up, and you have the extra work of lining them up *again*.

Here is another example. Suppose you have a comment that goes over multiple lines:

```
// In this test class, we compute the value of a set of coins.
// We add a number of nickels, dimes, and quarters
// to a purse. We then get and display the total value.
```

When the program is extended to work for half-dollar coins as well, you must modify the comment to reflect that change.

```
// In this test class, we compute the value of a set of coins.
// We add a number of nickels, dimes, quarters, and
half-dollars // to a purse. We then get and display the total
value.
```

Now you need to rearrange the // to fix up the comment. This scheme is a *disincentive* to keep comments up to date. Don't do it. Instead, for comments that are longer than one line, use the /* . . . */ style for comments, and block off the entire comment like this:

```
/*
    In this test class, we compute the value of a set of coins.
    We add a number of nickels, dimes, and quarters
    to a purse. We then get and display the total value.
*/
```

You may not care about these issues. Perhaps you plan to beautify your program just before it is finished, when you are about to turn in your homework. That is not a

▼

▼ particularly useful approach. In practice, programs are never finished. They are continuously improved and updated. It is better to develop the habit of laying out your programs well from the start and keeping them legible at all times. As a consequence, you should avoid layout schemes that are hard to maintain.

3.3 Constants

Consider once again the `getTotal` method, paying attention to whether it is easy to understand the code.

```java
public double getTotal()
{
    return nickels * 0.05 + dimes * 0.1 + quarters * 0.25;
}
```

Most of the code is self-documenting. However, the three numeric quantities, 0.05, 0.1, and 0.25, are included in the arithmetic expression without any explanation. Of course, in this case, you know that the value of a nickel is five cents, which explains the 0.05, and so on. However, the next person who needs to maintain this code may live in another country and may not know that a nickel is worth five cents.

Thus, it is a good idea to use symbolic names for *all* values, even those that appear obvious. Here is a clearer version of the computation of the total:

```java
double nickelValue = 0.05;
double dimeValue = 0.1;
double quarterValue = 0.25;
return nickels * nickelValue
    + dimes * dimeValue
    + quarters * quarterValue;
```

> A `final` variable is a constant. Once its value has been set, it cannot be changed.

There is another improvement we can make. There is a difference between the `nickels` and `nickelValue` variables. The `nickels` variable can truly vary over the life of the program, as more coins are added to the purse. But `nickelValue` is *always* 0.05. It is a *constant*. In Java, constants are identified with the keyword `final`. A variable tagged as `final` can never change after it has been set. If you try to change the value of a `final` variable, the compiler will report an error and your program will not compile.

> Use named constants to make your programs easier to read and maintain.

Many programmers use all-uppercase names for constants (`final` variables), such as `NICKEL_VALUE`. That way, it is easy to distinguish between variables (with mostly lowercase letters) and constants. We will follow this convention in this book. However, this rule is a matter of good style, not a requirement of the Java language. The compiler will not complain if you give a `final` variable a name with lowercase letters.

Here is the improved version of the `getTotal` method:

```java
public double getTotal()
{
    final double NICKEL_VALUE = 0.05;
    final double DIME_VALUE = 0.1;
    final double QUARTER_VALUE = 0.25;
    return nickels * NICKEL_VALUE
        + dimes * DIME_VALUE
        + quarters * QUARTER_VALUE;
}
```

In this example, the constants are needed only inside one method of the class. Frequently, a constant value is needed in several methods. Then you need to declare it together with the instance variables of the class and tag it as `static final`. The meaning of the keyword `static` will be explained in Chapter 6.

```java
public class Purse
{
    // methods
    . . .

    // constants
    private static final double NICKEL_VALUE = 0.05;
    private static final double DIME_VALUE = 0.1;
    private static final double QUARTER_VALUE = 0.25;

    // instance variables
    private int nickels;
    private int dimes;
    private int quarters;
}
```

Here we defined the constants to be `private` because we didn't think they were of interest to users of the `Purse` class. However, it is also possible to declare constants as `public`:

```java
public static final double NICKEL_VALUE = 0.05;
```

Then methods of other classes can access the constant as `Purse.NICKEL_VALUE`.

The `Math` class from the standard library defines a couple of useful constants:

```java
public class Math
{
    . . .
    public static final double E = 2.7182818284590452354;
    public static final double PI = 3.14159265358979323846;
}
```

You can refer to these constants as `Math.PI` and `Math.E` in any of your methods. For example,

```java
double circumference = Math.PI * diameter;
```

Syntax 3.1: Constant Definition

In a method:

final *typeName* *variableName* = *expression*;

In a class:

accessSpecifier static final *typeName* *variableName* = *expression*;

Example:

```
final double NICKEL_VALUE = 0.05;
public static final double LITERS_PER_GALLON = 3.785;
```

Purpose:

To define a constant of a particular type

File Purse.java

```
1  /**
2      A purse computes the total value of a collection of coins.
3  */
4  public class Purse
5  {
6     /**
7         Constructs an empty purse.
8     */
9     public Purse()
10    {
11       nickels = 0;
12       dimes = 0;
13       quarters = 0;
14    }
15
16    /**
17        Add nickels to the purse.
18        @param count the number of nickels to add
19    */
20    public void addNickels(int count)
21    {
22       nickels = nickels + count;
23    }
24    /**
25        Add dimes to the purse.
26        @param count the number of dimes to add
```

```
27    */
28    public void addDimes(int count)
29    {
30       dimes = dimes + count;
31    }
32
33    /**
34       Add quarters to the purse.
35       @param count the number of quarters to add
36    */
37    public void addQuarters(int count)
38    {
39       quarters = quarters + count;
40    }
41
42    /**
43       Get the total value of the coins in the purse.
44       @return the sum of all coin values
45    */
46    public double getTotal()
47    {
48       return nickels * NICKEL_VALUE
49          + dimes * DIME_VALUE + quarters * QUARTER_VALUE;
50    }
51
52    private static final double NICKEL_VALUE = 0.05;
53    private static final double DIME_VALUE = 0.1;
54    private static final double QUARTER_VALUE = 0.25;
55
56    private int nickels;
57    private int dimes;
58    private int quarters;
59 }
```

File PurseTest.java

```
1  /**
2     This program tests the Purse class.
3  */
4  public class PurseTest
5  {
6     public static void main(String[] args)
7     {
8        Purse myPurse = new Purse();
9
10       myPurse.addNickels(3);
11       myPurse.addDimes(1);
12       myPurse.addQuarters(2);
13       double totalValue = myPurse.getTotal();
```

```
14        System.out.print("The total is ");
15        System.out.println(totalValue);
16    }
17 }
```

Quality Tip   3.2

Do Not Use Magic Numbers

A *magic number* is a numeric constant that appears in your code without explanation. For example, consider the following scary example that actually occurs in the Java library source:

```
h = 31 * h + ch;
```

Why 31? The number of days in January? One less than the number of bits in an integer? Actually, this code computes a "hash code" from a string—a number that is derived from the characters in such a way that different strings are likely to yield different hash codes. The value 31 turns out to scramble the character values nicely.

You should use a named constant instead:

```
final int HASH_MULTIPLIER = 31;
h = HASH_MULTIPLIER * h + ch;
```

You should *never* use magic numbers in your code. Any number that is not completely self-explanatory should be declared as a named constant. Even the most reasonable cosmic constant is going to change one day. You think there are 365 days in a year? Your customers on Mars are going to be pretty unhappy about your silly prejudice. Make a constant

```
final int DAYS_PER_YEAR = 365;
```

By the way, the device

```
final int THREE_HUNDRED_AND_SIXTY_FIVE = 365;
```

is counterproductive and frowned upon.

3.4   Arithmetic and Mathematical Functions

You already saw how to add, subtract, and multiply values. Division is indicated with a /, not a fraction bar. For example,

$$\frac{a + b}{2}$$

becomes

```
(a + b) / 2
```

Parentheses are used just as in algebra: to indicate in which order the subexpressions should be computed. For example, in the expression (a + b) / 2, the sum a + b is computed first, and then the sum is divided by 2. In contrast, in the expression

```
a + b / 2
```

3.4 Arithmetic and Mathematical Functions

only b is divided by 2, and then the sum of a and b / 2 is formed. Just as in regular algebraic notation, multiplication and division *bind more strongly* than addition and subtraction. For example, in the expression a + b / 2, the / is carried out first, even though the + operation occurs further to the left.

> If both arguments of the / operator are integers, the result is an integer and the remainder is discarded.

Division works as you would expect, as long as at least one of the numbers involved is a floating-point number. That is,

```
7.0 / 4.0
7 / 4.0
7.0 / 4
```

all yield 1.75. However, if *both* numbers are integers, then the result of the division is always an integer, with the remainder discarded. That is,

```
7 / 4
```

evaluates to 1, because 7 divided by 4 is 1 with a remainder of 3 (which is discarded). This can be a source of subtle programming errors—see Common Error 3.1.

If you are interested only in the remainder of an integer division, use the % operator:

```
7 % 4
```

> The % operator computes the remainder of a division.

is 3, the remainder of the integer division of 7 by 4. The % symbol has no analog in algebra. It was chosen because it looks similar to /, and the remainder operation is related to division.

Here is a typical use for the integer / and % operations. Suppose you want to know the value of the coins in a purse in dollars and cents. You can compute the value as an integer, denominated in cents, and then compute the whole dollar amount and the remaining change:

```
final int PENNIES_PER_NICKEL = 5;
final int PENNIES_PER_DIME = 10;
final int PENNIES_PER_QUARTER = 25;
final int PENNIES_PER_DOLLAR = 100;

// compute total value in pennies

int total = nickels * PENNIES_PER_NICKEL
   + dimes * PENNIES_PER_DIME
   + quarters * PENNIES_PER_QUARTER;

// use integer division to convert to dollars, cents

int dollars = total / PENNIES_PER_DOLLAR;
int cents = total % PENNIES_PER_DOLLAR;
```

For example, if total is 243, then dollars is set to 2 and cents to 43.

To take the square root of a number, you use the Math.sqrt method. For example, $\sqrt{x}$ is written as Math.sqrt(x). To compute x^n, you write Math.pow(x, n). However, to compute x^2 it is significantly more efficient simply to compute x * x.

⊗ **Common Error**   **3.1**

Integer Division

It is unfortunate that Java uses the same symbol, namely /, for both integer and floating-point division. These are really quite different operations. It is a common error to use integer division by accident. Consider this program segment that computes the average of three integers.

```
int s1 = 5; // score of test 1
int s2 = 6; // score of test 2
int s3 = 3; // score of test 3
double average = (s1 + s2 + s3) / 3;   // Error
System.out.print("Your average score is ");
System.out.println(average);
```

What could be wrong with that? Of course, the average of s1, s2, and s3 is

$$\frac{s_1 + s_2 + s_3}{3}$$

Here, however, the / does not mean division in the mathematical sense. It denotes integer division, because the values s1 + s2 + s3 and 3 are both integers. For example, if the scores add up to 14, the average is computed to be 4, the result of the integer division of 14 by 3. That integer 4 is then moved into the floating-point variable average. The remedy is to make the numerator or denominator into a floating-point number:

```
double total = s1 + s2 + s3;
double average = total / 3;
```

or

```
double average = (s1 + s2 + s3) / 3.0;
```

> The Math class contains methods sqrt and pow to compute square roots and powers.

As you can see, the visual effect of the /, Math.sqrt, and Math.pow notations is to flatten out mathematical terms. In algebra, you use fractions, superscripts for exponents, and radical signs for roots to arrange expressions in a compact two-dimensional form. In Java, you have to write all expressions in a linear arrangement. For example, the subexpression

$$\frac{-b + \sqrt{b^2 - 4ac}}{2a}$$

of the quadratic formula becomes

```
(-b + Math.sqrt(b * b - 4 * a * c)) / (2 * a)
```

Figure 3 shows how to analyze such an expression. With complicated expressions like these, it is not always easy to keep the parentheses (...) matched—see Common Error 3.2.

Table 1 shows additional methods of the Math class. Inputs and outputs are floating-point numbers.

Figure 3

Analyzing an Expression

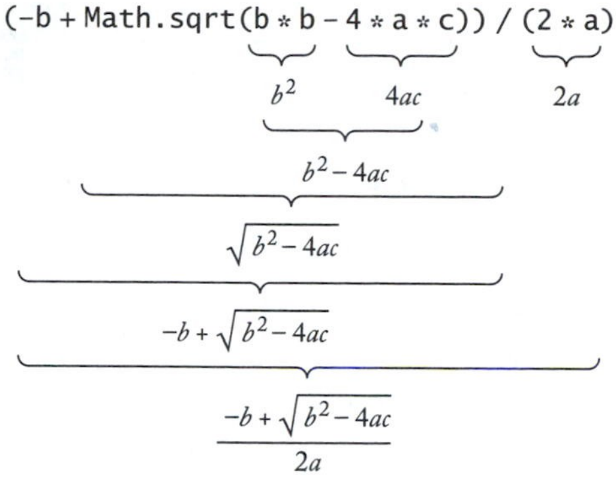
(-b + Math.sqrt(b * b - 4 * a * c)) / (2 * a)
b^2
$4ac$
$2a$
$b^2 - 4ac$
$\sqrt{b^2 - 4ac}$
$-b + \sqrt{b^2 - 4ac}$
$\frac{-b + \sqrt{b^2 - 4ac}}{2a}$

Function	Returns
`Math.sqrt(x)`	Square root of x (≥ 0)
`Math.pow(x, y)`	x^y ($x > 0$, or $x = 0$ and $y > 0$, or $x < 0$ and y is an integer)
`Math.sin(x)`	Sine of x (x in radians)
`Math.cos(x)`	Cosine of x
`Math.tan(x)`	Tangent of x
`Math.asin(x)`	Arc sine ($\sin^{-1} x \in [-\pi/2, \pi/2]$, $x \in [-1,1]$)
`Math.acos(x)`	Arc cosine ($\cos^{-1} x \in [0,\pi]$, $x \in [-1,1]$)
`Math.atan(x)`	Arc tangent ($\tan^{-1} x \in (-\pi/2, \pi/2)$)
`Math.atan2(y, x)`	Arc tangent ($\tan^{-1}(y/x) \in [-\pi/2,\pi/2]$, x may be 0
`Math.toRadians(x)`	Convert x radians to degrees (i.e., returns $x \cdot 180/\pi$)
`Math.toDegrees(x)`	Convert x degrees to radians (i.e., returns $x \cdot \pi/180$)
`Math.exp(x)`	e^x
`Math.log(x)`	Natural log ($\ln(x)$, $x > 0$)
`Math.round(x)`	Closest integer to x (as a `long`)
`Math.ceil(x)`	Smallest integer $\geq x$ (as a `double`)
`Math.floor(x)`	Largest integer $\leq x$ (as a `double`)
`Math.abs(x)`	Absolute value $\|x\|$

Table 1

Mathematical Methods

⊗ Common Error   3.2

Unbalanced Parentheses

Consider the expression

```
1.5 * ((-(b - Math.sqrt(b * b - 4 * a * c)) / (2 * a))
```

What is wrong with it? Count the parentheses. There are five opening parentheses (and four closing parentheses). The parentheses are *unbalanced*. This kind of typing error is very common with complicated expressions. Now consider this expression.

```
1.5 * (Math.sqrt(b * b - 4 * a * c))) - ((b / (2 * a))
```

This expression has five opening parentheses (and five closing parentheses), but it is still not correct. In the middle of the expression,

```
1.5 * (Math.sqrt(b * b - 4 * a * c))) - ((b / (2 * a))
```

there are only two opening parentheses (but three closing parentheses), which is an error. In the middle of an expression, the count of opening parentheses (must be greater than or equal to the count of closing parentheses), and at the end of the expression the two counts must be the same.

Here is a simple trick to make the counting easier without using pencil and paper. It is difficult for the brain to keep two counts simultaneously, so keep only one count when scanning the expression. Start with 1 at the first opening parenthesis; add 1 whenever you see an opening parenthesis; and subtract 1 whenever you see a closing parenthesis. Say the numbers aloud as you scan the expression. If the count ever drops below zero, or if it is not zero at the end, the parentheses are unbalanced. For example, when scanning the previous expression, you would mutter

```
1.5 * (Math.sqrt(b * b - 4 * a * c) )  ) - ((b / (2 * a))
        1          2                 1 0 -1
```

and you would find the error.

⟳ Productivity Hint   3.2

On-Line Help

The Java library has hundreds of classes and thousands of methods. It is neither necessary nor useful trying to memorize them. Instead, you should become familiar with using the on-line documentation. You can download the documentation from http://java.sun.com/j2se/1.3/docs.html. Install the documentation set and point your browser to your Java installation directory /docs/api/index.html. Alternatively, you can browse http://java.sun.com/j2se/1.3/docs/api/index.html. For example, if you are not sure how the pow method works, or cannot remember whether it was called pow or power, the on-line help

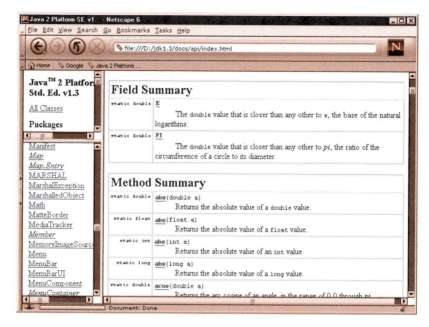

Figure 4

On-Line Help

can give you the answer quickly. Click on the Math class in the class window on the left, and look at the method summary in the main window (see Figure 4).

If you use javadoc to document your own classes, then this documentation format will look extremely familiar to you. The programmers who implement the Java library use javadoc themselves. They too document every class, every method, every parameter, and every return value, and then use javadoc to extract the documentation in HTML format.

 **Quality Tip**   **3.3**

White Space

The compiler does not care whether you write your entire program onto a single line or place every symbol onto a separate line. The human reader, though, cares very much. You should use blank lines to group your code visually into sections. For example, you can signal to the reader that an output prompt and the corresponding input statement belong together by inserting a blank line before and after the group. You will find many examples in the source code listings in this book.

White space inside expressions is also important. It is easier to read

```
x1 = (-b + Math.sqrt(b * b - 4 * a * c)) / (2 * a);
```

than

```
X1=(-b+Math.sqrt(b*b-4*a*c))/(2*a);
```

Simply put spaces around all operators + - * / % =. However, don't put a space after a *unary* minus: a - used to negate a single quantity, as in -b. That way, it can be easily distinguished from a *binary* minus, as in a - b. Don't put spaces between a method name and the parentheses, but do put a space after every Java keyword. That makes it easy to see that the sqrt in Math.sqrt(x) is a method name, whereas the if in if (x > 0)... is a keyword.

Quality Tip   3.4

Factor Out Common Code

Suppose you want to find both solutions of the quadratic equation $ax^2 + bx + c = 0$. The quadratic formula tells us that the solutions are

$$x_{1,2} = \frac{-b \pm \sqrt{b^2 - 4ac}}{2a}$$

In Java, there is no analog to the $\pm$ operation, which indicates how to obtain two solutions simultaneously. Both solutions must be computed separately:

```
x1 = (-b + Math.sqrt(b * b - 4 * a * c)) / (2 * a);
x2 = (-b - Math.sqrt(b * b - 4 * a * c)) / (2 * a);
```

This approach has two problems. First, the computation of Math.sqrt(b * b - 4 * a * c) is carried out twice, which wastes time. Second, whenever the same code is replicated, the possibility of a typing error increases. The remedy is to *factor out* the common code:

```
double root = Math.sqrt(b * b - 4 * a * c);
x1 = (-b + root) / (2 * a);
x2 = (-b - root) / (2 * a);
```

You could go even further and factor out the computation of 2 * a, but the gain from factoring out very simple computations is too small to warrant the effort.

3.5   Calling Static Methods

In the preceding section, you encountered the Math class, which contains a collection of helpful methods for carrying out mathematical computations.

There is one important difference between the methods of the Math class, such as the sqrt method, and the methods that you have seen so far (such as getTotal or println). The `getTotal` and `println` methods, as you have seen, operate on an object such as `myPurse` or `System.out`. In contrast, the `sqrt` method does not operate on any object. That is, you don't call

```
double x = 4;
double root = x.sqrt(); // Error
```

> A `static` method does not operate on an object.

The reason is that, in Java, numbers are not objects, so you can never invoke a method on a number. Instead, you pass a number as an explicit parameter to a method, enclosing the number in parentheses after the method name. For example, the number value `x` can be a parameter of the `Math.sqrt` method: `Math.sqrt(x)`.

This call makes it appear as if the `sqrt` method is applied to an object called `Math`, because `Math` precedes `sqrt` just as `myPurse` precedes `getTotal` in a method call `myPurse.getTotal()`. However, `Math` is a class, not an object. A method such as `Math.round` that does not operate on any object is called a *static* method. (The term "static" is a historical holdover from C and C++ that has nothing to do with the usual meaning of the word.) Static methods do not operate on objects, but they are still defined inside classes. You must specify the class to which the `sqrt` method belongs—hence the call is `Math.sqrt(x)`.

How can you tell whether `Math` is a class or an object? All classes in the Java library start with an uppercase letter (such as `System`). Objects and methods start with a lowercase letter (such as `out` and `println`). You can tell objects and methods apart because method calls are followed by parentheses. Therefore, `System.out.println()` denotes a call of the `println` method on the `out` object inside the `System` class. On the other hand, `Math.sqrt(x)` denotes a call to the `sqrt` method inside the `Math` class. This use of upper- and lowercase letters is merely a *convention*, not a rule of the Java language. It is, however, a convention that the authors of the Java class libraries follow consistently. You should do the same in your programs. If you give names to objects or methods that start with an uppercase letter, you will likely confuse your fellow programmers. Therefore, we strongly recommend that you follow the standard naming convention.

Syntax 3.2: Static Method Call

ClassName.*methodName*(*parameters*)

Example:

```
Math.sqrt(4)
```

Purpose:

To invoke a static method (a method that does not operate on an object) and supply its parameters

3.6   Type Conversion

When you make an assignment of an expression into a variable, the *types* of the variable and the expression must be compatible. For example, it is an error to assign

```
double total = "a lot"; // Error
```

because `total` is a floating-point variable and `"a lot"` is a string. It is, however, legal to store an integer expression in a `double` variable:

```
int dollars = 2;
double total = dollars; // OK
```

In Java, you cannot assign a floating-point expression to an integer variable.

```
double total = . . .;
int dollars = total; // Error
```

You must convert the floating-point value to integer with a *cast*:

```
int dollars = (int)total;
```

> You use a cast (*typeName*) to convert a value to a different type.

The cast (`int`) converts the floating-point value `total` to an integer. The effect of the cast is to discard the fractional part. For example, if `total` is 13.75, then `dollars` is set to 13. If you want to convert the value of a floating-point expression to an integer, you need to enclose the expression in parentheses to ensure that it is computed first:

```
int pennies = (int)(total * 100);
```

This is different from the expression

```
int pennies = (int)total * 100;
```

In the second expression, `total` is *first* converted to an integer, and then the resulting integer is multiplied by 100. For example, if `total` is 13.75, then the first expression computes `total * 100`, or 1375, and then converts that value to the integer 1375. In the second expression, `total` is first cast to the integer 13, and then the integer is multiplied by 100, yielding 1300. Normally, you will want to apply the integer conversion *after* all other computations, so that your computations use the full precision of their input values. That means you should enclose your computation in parentheses and apply the cast to the expression in parentheses.

There is a good reason why you must use a cast in Java when you convert a floating-point number to an integer: The conversion *loses information*. You must confirm that you agree to that information loss. Java is quite strict about this. You must use a cast whenever there is the possibility of information loss. A cast always has the form (*typeName*), for example (`int`) or (`float`).

Actually, simply using an (`int`) cast to convert a floating-point number to an integer is not always a good idea. Consider the following example:

```
double price = 44.95;
int dollars = (int)price; // sets dollars to 44
```

What did you want to achieve? Did you want to get the number of dollars in the price? Then dropping the fractional part is the right thing to do. Or did you want to get the approximate dollar amount? Then you really want to *round up* when the fractional part is 0.5 or larger.

One way to round to the nearest integer is to add 0.5, then cast to an integer:

```
double price = 44.95;
int dollars = (int)(price + 0.5); // OK for positive values
System.out.print("The price is approximately $")
System.out.println(dollars); // prints 45
```

> Use the `Math.round` method to round a floating-point number to the nearest integer.

Adding 0.5 and casting to the `int` type works, because it turns all values that are between 44.50 and 45.4999 . . . into 45.

Actually, there is a better way. Simply adding 0.5 works fine for positive numbers, but it doesn't work correctly for negative numbers. Instead, use the `Math.round` method in the standard Java library. It works for both positive and negative numbers. However, that method returns a `long` integer, because large floating-point numbers cannot be stored in an `int`. You need to cast the return value to an `int`:

```
int dollars = (int)Math.round(price); // better
```

Syntax 3.3: Cast

(*typeName*) *expression*

Example:

```
(int)(x + 0.5)
(int)Math.round(100 * f)
```

Purpose:

To convert an expression to a different type

? HOWTO   **3.1**

Carrying Out Computations

Many programming problems require that you use mathematical formulas to compute values. It is not always obvious how to turn a problem statement into a sequence of mathematical formulas and, ultimately, statements in the Java programming language.

Step 1 Understand the problem: What are the inputs? What are the desired outputs?

For example, suppose you are asked to simulate a postage stamp vending machine. A customer inserts money into the vending machine. Then the customer pushes a "First class stamps" button. The vending machine gives out as many first-class stamps as the customer paid for. (A first-class stamp cost 34 cents at the time this book was written.) Finally, the customer pushes a "Penny stamps" button. The machine gives the change in penny (1-cent) stamps.

In this problem, there is one input:

- The amount of money the customer inserts

There are two desired outputs:

- The number of first-class stamps that the machine returns
- The number of penny stamps that the machine returns

Step 2 Work out examples by hand

This is a very important step. If you can't compute a couple of solutions by hand, it's unlikely that you'll be able to write a program that automates the computation.

Let's assume that a first-class stamp costs 34 cents and the customer inserts $1.00. That's enough for two stamps (68 cents) but not enough for three stamps ($1.02). Therefore, the machine returns 2 first-class stamps and 32 penny stamps.

Step 3 Find mathematical equations that compute the answers

Given an amount of money and the price of a first-class stamp, how can you compute how many first-class stamps can be purchased with the money? Clearly, the answer is related to the quotient

$$\frac{\text{amount of money}}{\text{price of first-class stamp}}$$

For example, suppose the customer paid $1.00. Use a pocket calculator to compute the quotient: $1.00/$0.34 ≈ 2.9412.

How do you get "2 stamps" out of 2.9412? It's the integer part. By discarding the fractional part, you get the number of whole stamps that the customer has purchased.

In mathematical notation,

$$\text{number of first-class stamps} = \left\lfloor \frac{\text{money}}{\text{price of first-class stamp}} \right\rfloor$$

where $\lfloor x \rfloor$ denotes the largest integer $\leq x$. That function is sometimes called the "floor function".

You now know how to compute the number of stamps that are given out when the customer pushes the "First-class stamps" button. When the customer gets the stamps, the amount of money is reduced by the value of the stamps purchased. For example, if the customer gets two stamps, the remaining money is $0.32. It is the difference between $1.00 and 2 · $0.34. Here is the general formula:

remaining money = money − number of first-class stamps · price of first-class stamp

How many penny stamps does the remaining money buy? That's easy. If $0.32 is left, the customer gets 32 stamps. In general, the number of penny stamps is

number of penny stamps = 100 · remaining money

Step 4 Turn the mathematical equations into Java statements

In Java, you can compute the integer part of a nonnegative floating-point value by applying an (`int`) cast. Therefore, you can compute the number of first-class stamps with the following statement:

```
firstClassStamps =
    (int)(money / FIRST_CLASS_STAMP_PRICE);
money = money -
    firstClassStamps * FIRST_CLASS_STAMP_PRICE;
```

Finally, the number of penny stamps is

```
pennyStamps = 100 * money;
```

That's not quite right, though. The value of `pennyStamps` should be an integer, but the right hand side is a floating-point number. Therefore, the correct statement is

```
pennyStamps = (int)Math.round(100 * money);
```

Step 5 Build a class that carries out your computations

HOWTO 2.1 explains how to develop a class by finding methods and instance variables. In our case, we can find three methods:

- `void insert(double amount)`
- `int giveFirstClassStamps()`
- `int givePennyStamps()`

The state of a vending machine can be described by the amount of money that the customer has available for purchases. Therefore, we supply one instance variable, `money`.

Here is the implementation:

```
public class StampMachine
{
    public StampMachine()
    {
        money = 0;
    }

    public void insert(double amount)
    {
        money = money + amount;
    }

    public int giveFirstClassStamps()
    {
        int firstClassStamps =
            (int)(money / FIRST_CLASS_STAMP_PRICE);
        money = money -
            firstClassStamps * FIRST_CLASS_STAMP_PRICE;
```

```
        return firstClassStamps;
    }

    public int givePennyStamps()
    {
        int pennyStamps = (int)Math.round(100 * money);
        money = 0;
        return pennyStamps;
    }

    private double money;
    private static final double FIRST_CLASS_STAMP_PRICE =
        0.34;
}
```

Step 6 Test your class

Run a test program (or use BlueJ) to verify that the values that your class computes are the same values that you computed by hand. In our example, try the statements

```
StampMachine machine = new StampMachine();
machine.insert(1);
System.out.println("First class stamps: " +
    machine.giveFirstClassStamps());
System.out.println("Penny stamps: " +
    machine.givePennyStamps());
```

Check that the result is

```
First class stamps: 2
Penny stamps: 32
```

⊗ Common Error   3.3

Roundoff Errors

Roundoff errors are a fact of life when calculating with floating-point numbers. You probably have encountered that phenomenon yourself with manual calculations. If you calculate 1/3 to two decimal places, you get 0.33. Multiplying again by 3, you obtain 0.99, not 1.00.

In the processor hardware, numbers are represented in the binary number system, not in decimal. You still get roundoff errors when binary digits are lost. They just may crop up at different places than you might expect. Here is an example:

```
double f = 4.35;
int n = (int)(100 * f);
System.out.println(n); // prints 434!
```

Of course, one hundred times 4.35 is 435, but the program prints 434.

▼   Computers represent numbers in the binary system (see Advanced Topic 3.4). In the binary system, there is no exact representation for 4.35, just as there is no exact representation for 1/3 in the decimal system. The representation used by the computer is just a

▼   little less than 4.35, so 100 times that value is just a little less than 435. When a floating-point value is converted to an integer, the entire fractional part is discarded, even if it is almost 1. As a result, the integer 434 is stored in n. Remedy: Use Math.round to convert

▼   floating-point numbers to integers:

```
int n = (int)Math.round(100 * f);
```

▼   Note that the wrong result of the first computation is *not* caused by lack of precision. The problem lies with the wrong choice of rounding method. Dropping the fractional part, no matter how close it may be to 1, is not a good rounding method.

▼   **AT**   **Advanced Topic**   **3.4**

Binary Numbers

▼   You are familiar with *decimal* numbers, which use the digits 0, 1, 2, . . . , 9. Each digit has a place value of 1, 10, 100 = 10^2, 1000 = 10^3, and so on. For example,

▼ $$435 = 4 \cdot 10^2 + 3 \cdot 10^1 + 5 \cdot 10^0$$

Fractional digits have place values with negative powers of ten: $0.1 = 10^{-1}$,

▼ $0.01 = 10^{-2}$, and so on. For example,

$$4.35 = 4 \cdot 10^0 + 3 \cdot 10^{-1} + 5 \cdot 10^{-2}$$

▼   Computers use *binary* numbers instead, which have just two digits (0 and 1) and place values that are powers of 2. Binary numbers are easier for computers to manipulate, because it is easier to build logic circuits that differentiate between "off" and "on" than it

▼   would be to build circuits that can accurately tell ten different voltage levels apart.

It is easy to transform a binary number into a decimal number. Just compute the powers of two that correspond to ones in the binary number. For example,

▼ $$1101 \text{ binary} = 1 \cdot 2^3 + 1 \cdot 2^2 + 0 \cdot 2^1 + 1 \cdot 2^0 = 8 + 4 + 1 = 13$$

Fractional binary numbers use negative powers of two. For example,

▼ $$1.101 \text{ binary} = 1 \cdot 2^0 + 1 \cdot 2^{-1} + 0 \cdot 2^{-2} + 1 \cdot 2^{-3} = 1 + 0.5 + 0.125 = 1.625$$

Converting decimal numbers to binary numbers is a little trickier. Here is an algo-

▼   rithm that converts a decimal integer into its binary equivalent: Keep dividing the integer by 2, keeping track of the remainders. Stop when the number is 0. Then write the remainders as a binary number, starting with the *last* one. For example,

▼ $100 \div 2 = 50$ remainder 0
$50 \div 2 = 25$ remainder 0
$25 \div 2 = 12$ remainder 1
▼ $12 \div 2 = 6$ remainder 0

$6 \div 2 = 3$ remainder 0
$3 \div 2 = 1$ remainder 1
$1 \div 2 = 0$ remainder 1

Therefore, 100 in decimal is 1100100 in binary.

To convert a fractional number <1 to its binary format, keep multiplying by 2. If the result is >1, subtract 1. Stop when the number is 0. Then use the digits before the decimal points as the binary digits of the fractional part, starting with the *first* one. For example,

$0.35 \cdot 2 = 0.7$
$0.7 \cdot 2 = 1.4$
$0.4 \cdot 2 = 0.8$
$0.8 \cdot 2 = 1.6$
$0.6 \cdot 2 = 1.2$
$0.2 \cdot 2 = 0.4$

Here the pattern repeats. That is, the binary representation of 0.35 is 0.01 0110 0110 0110 ...

To convert any floating-point number into binary, convert the whole part and the fractional part separately. For example, 4.35 is 100.01 0110 0110 0110 ... in binary.

You don't actually need to know about binary numbers to program in Java, but at times it can be helpful to understand a little about them. For example, knowing that an `int` is represented as a 32-bit binary number explains why the largest integer that you can represent in Java is 0111 1111 1111 1111 1111 1111 1111 1111 binary = 2,147,483,647 decimal. (The first bit is the sign bit. It is off for positive values.)

To convert an integer into its binary representation, you can use the static `toString` method of the `Integer` class. The call `Integer.toString(n, 2)` returns a string with the binary digits of the integer n. Conversely, you can convert a string containing binary digits into an integer with the call `Integer.parseInt(digitString, 2)`. In both of these method calls, the second parameter denotes the base of the number system. It can be any number between 0 and 36. You can use these two methods to convert between decimal and binary *integers*. However, the Java library has no convenient method to do the same for floating-point numbers.

Now you can see why we had to fight with a roundoff error when computing 100 times 4.35 in Common Error 3.3. If you actually carry out the long multiplication, you get:

```
1 1 0 0 1 0 0 * 1 0 0.0 1|0 1 1 0|0 1 1 0|0 1 1 0 ...

1 0 0.0 1|0 1 1 0|0 1 1 0|0 1 1 0 ...
 1 0 0.0 1|0 1 1 0|0 1 1 0|0 1 1 ...
 0
  0
    1 0 0.0 1|0 1 1 0|0 1 1 0 ...
     0
      0

1 1 0 1 1 0 0 1 0.1 1 1 1 1 1 1 1 ...
```

▼

That is, the result is 434, followed by an infinite number of 1s. The fractional part of the product is the binary equivalent of an infinite decimal fraction 0.999999 . . . , which is equal to 1. But the CPU can store only a finite number of 1s, and it discards them all when converting the result to an integer.

▼

3.7   Strings

Next to numbers, *strings* are the most important data type that most programs use. A string is a sequence of characters, such as `"Hello, World!"`. In Java, strings are enclosed in quotation marks, which are not themselves part of the string. Note that, unlike numbers, strings are objects. (You can tell that `String` is a class name because it starts with an uppercase letter. The basic types `int` and `double` start with a lowercase letter.)

> A string is a sequence of characters. Strings are objects of the `String` class.

The number of characters in a string is called the *length* of the string. For example, the length of `"Hello, World!"` is 13. You can compute the length of a string with the `length` method.

```
int n = message.length();
```

A string of length zero, containing no characters, is called the *empty string* and is written as `""`.

You already saw in Chapter 2 how to put strings together to form a longer string.

```
String name = "Dave";
String message = "Hello, " + name;
```

> Strings can be concatenated, that is, put end to end to yield a new longer string. String concatenation is denoted by the + operator.

The + operator concatenates two strings. The concatenation operator in Java is very powerful. If *one of the expressions*, either to the left or the right of a + operator, is a string, then the other one is automatically forced to become a string as well, and both strings are concatenated.

For example, consider this code:

```
String a = "Agent";
int n = 7;
String bond = a + n;
```

> Whenever one of the arguments of the + operator is a string, the other argument is converted to a string.

Since `a` is a string, `n` is converted from the integer 7 to the string `"7"`. Then the two strings `"Agent"` and `"7"` are concatenated to form the string `"Agent7"`.

This concatenation is very useful to reduce the number of `System.out.print` instructions. For example, you can combine

```
System.out.print("The total is ");
System.out.println(total);
```

to the single call

```
System.out.println("The total is " + total);
```

If a string contains the digits of a number, you use the `Integer.parseInt` or `Double.parseDouble` method to obtain the number value.

The concatenation `"The total is " + total` computes a single string that consists of the string `"The total is "`, followed by the string equivalent of the number `total`.

Sometimes you have a string that contains a number, usually from user input. For example, suppose that the string variable `input` has the value `"19"`. To get the integer value 19, you use the static `parseInt` method of the `Integer` class.

```
int count = Integer.parseInt(input);
   // count is the integer 19
```

To convert a string containing floating-point digits to its floating-point value, use the static `parseDouble` method of the `Double` class. For example, suppose `input` is the string `"3.95"`.

```
double price = Double.parseDouble(input);
   // price is the floating-point number 3.95
```

The `toUpperCase` and `toLowerCase` methods make strings with only upper- or lower-case characters. For example,

```
String greeting = "Hello";
System.out.println(greeting.toUpperCase());
System.out.println(greeting.toLowerCase());
```

This code segment prints HELLO and hello. Note that the `toUpperCase` and `toLowerCase` methods do not change the original `String` object `greeting`. They return new `String` objects that contain the uppercased and lowercased versions of the original string. In fact, *no* `String` methods modify the string object on which they operate. For that reason, strings are called *immutable* objects.

The `substring` computes substrings of a string. The call

```
s.substring(start, pastEnd)
```

Use the `substring` method to extract a part of a string.

returns a string that is made up from the characters in the string `s`, starting at character `start`, and containing all characters up to, but not including, the character `pastEnd`. Here is an example:

```
String greeting = "Hello, World!";
String sub = greeting.substring(0, 4);
   // sub is "Hell"
```

String positions are counted starting with 0.

The `substring` operation makes a string that consists of four characters taken from the string `greeting`. A curious aspect of the `substring` operation is the numbering of the starting and ending positions. Starting position 0 means "start at the beginning of the string". For technical reasons that used to be important but are no longer relevant, Java string position numbers start at 0. The first string position is labeled 0, the second one 1, and so on. For example, Figure 5 shows the position numbers in the `greeting` string.

The position number of the last character (12 for the string `"Hello, World!"`) is always 1 less than the length of the string.

Figure 5

String Positions

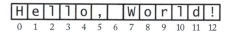

Figure 6

Extracting a Substring

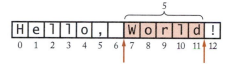

Let us figure out how to extract the substring `"World"`. Count characters starting at 0, not 1. You find that W, the 8th character, has position number 7. The first character that you *don't* want, !, is the character at position 12 (see Figure 6). Therefore, the appropriate substring command is

```
String w = greeting.substring(7, 12);
```

It is curious that you must specify the position of the first character that you do want and then the first character that you don't want. There is one advantage to this setup. You can easily compute the *length* of the substring: it is `pastEnd - start`. For example, the string `"World"` has length $12 - 7 = 5$.

If you omit the second parameter of the `substring` method, then all characters from the starting position to the end of the string are copied. For example,

```
String tail = greeting.substring(7);
    // copies all characters from position 7 on
```

sets `tail` to the string `"World!"`.

▼ ⒶⓉ **Advanced Topic**   **3.5**

Formatting Numbers

▼
The default format for printing numbers is not always what you would like. For example, consider the following code segment:

▼
```
int quarters = 2;
int dollars = 3;
double total = dollars + quarters * 0.25; // price is 3.5
final double TAX_RATE = 8.5; // tax rate in percent
double tax = total * TAX_RATE / 100; // tax is 0.2975
System.out.println("Total: $" + total);
System.out.println("Tax:   $" + tax);
```
▼
The output is

```
Total: $3.5
Tax:   $0.2975
```

You may prefer the numbers to be printed with two digits after the decimal point, like this:

```
Total: $3.50
Tax:   $0.30
```

You can achieve this with the `NumberFormat` class in the `java.text` package. First, you must use the static method `getNumberInstance` to obtain a `NumberFormat` object. Then you set the maximum number of fraction digits to 2:

```
NumberFormat formatter =
    NumberFormat.getNumberInstance();
formatter.setMaximumFractionDigits(2);
```

Then the numbers are rounded to two digits. For example, 0.2875 will be converted to the string `"0.29"`. On the other hand, 0.2975 will be converted to `"0.3"`, not `"0.30"`. If you want trailing zeroes, you *also* have to set the minimum number of fraction digits to 2:

```
formatter.setMinimumFractionDigits(2);
```

Then you use the `format` method of that object. The result is a string that you can print.

```
formatter.format(tax)
```

returns the string `"0.30"`. The statement

```
System.out.println("Tax:    $" + formatter.format(tax));
```

rounds the value of `tax` to two digits after the decimal point and prints: `Tax:  $0.30`.

The "number instance" formatter is useful because it lets you print numbers with as many fraction digits as desired. If you just want to print a currency value, the `getCurrencyInstance` method of the `NumberFormat` class produces a more convenient formatter. The "currency instance" formatter generates currency value strings, with the local currency symbol (such as $ in the United States) and the appropriate number of digits after the decimal point (for example, two digits in the United States).

```
NumberFormat formatter = NumberFormat.getCurrencyInstance();
System.out.print(formatter.format(tax));
    // prints "$0.30"
```

3.8   Reading Input

The Java programs that you have constructed so far have constructed objects, called methods, printed results, and exited. They were not interactive and took no user input. In this section, you will learn one method for reading user input.

The `JOptionPane` class has a static method `showInputDialog` that displays an input dialog (see Figure 7). The user can type any string into the input field and click the "OK" button. Then the `showInputDialog` method returns the string that the user entered. You should capture the user input in a string variable. For example,

> The `JOptionPane` `.showInputDialog` method prompts the user for an input string.

```
String input =
    JOptionPane.showInputDialog("How many nickels do you have?");
```

Figure 7

An Input Dialog

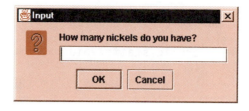

Often you want the input as a number, not a string. Use the `Integer.parseInt` and `Double.parseDouble` methods to convert the string to a number:

```
int count = Integer.parseInt(input);
```

If the user doesn't type in a number, then the `parseInt` method *throws an exception*. An exception is a way for a method to indicate an error condition. You will see in Chapter 15 how to handle exceptions. Until then, we will simply rely on the default mechanism for exception handling. That mechanism terminates the program with an error message.

```
Exception in thread "main"
java.lang.NumberFormatException: x
        at java.lang.Integer.parseInt(Unknown Source)
        at java.lang.Integer.parseInt(Unknown Source)
        at InputTest.main(InputTest.java:10)
```

That doesn't make your programs very user-friendly. You will simply have to wait until Chapter 15 to make your programs bulletproof. In the meantime, you should assume that the user is cooperative and types in an actual number when you prompt for one. Since the users of your first programs are likely to be just yourself, your instructor, and your grader, that should not be a problem.

> You must call `System.exit(0)` to exit a program that has a graphical user interface.

Finally, whenever you call `JOptionPane.showInputDialog` in your programs, you need to add a line

```
System.exit(0)
```

to the end of your `main` method. The `showInputDialog` method starts a user interface *thread* to handle user input. When the `main` method reaches the end, that thread is still running, and your program won't exit automatically. To force the program to exit, you need to call the `exit` method of the `System` class. The parameter of the `exit` method is the status code of the program. A code of 0 denotes successful completion; you can use nonzero status codes to denote various error conditions.

Here is an example of a test class that takes user input. This class tests the `Purse` class and lets the user supply the numbers of nickels, dimes, and quarters.

File InputTest.java

```
1  import javax.swing.JOptionPane;
2
3  /**
4      This program tests input from an input dialog.
```

```
 5  */
 6  public class InputTest
 7  {
 8     public static void main(String[] args)
 9     {
10        Purse myPurse = new Purse();
11
12        String input = JOptionPane.showInputDialog(
13           "How many nickels do you have?");
14        int count = Integer.parseInt(input);
15        myPurse.addNickels(count);
16
17        input = JOptionPane.showInputDialog(
18           "How many dimes do you have?");
19        count = Integer.parseInt(input);
20        myPurse.addDimes(count);
21
22        input = JOptionPane.showInputDialog(
23           "How many quarters do you have?");
24        count = Integer.parseInt(input);
25        myPurse.addQuarters(count);
26
27        double totalValue = myPurse.getTotal();
28        System.out.println("The total is " + totalValue);
29
30        System.exit(0);
31     }
32  }
```

Admittedly, the program is not very elegant. It pops up three dialog boxes to collect input and then displays the output in the console window. You will learn in Chapter 12 how to write programs with more sophisticated graphical user interfaces.

▼ Productivity Hint   3.3

Reading Exception Reports

▼ You will often have programs that terminate and display an error message such as

```
Exception in thread "main" java.lang.NumberFormatException: x
        at java.lang.Integer.parseInt(Unknown Source)
        at java.lang.Integer.parseInt(Unknown Source)
        at InputTest.main(InputTest.java:10)
```

▼ An amazing number of students simply give up at that point, saying "it didn't work", or "my program died", without ever reading the error message. Admittedly, the format of the exception report is not very friendly. But it is actually easy to decipher it.

▼   When you have a close look at the error message, you will notice two pieces of useful information:

▼   1. The name of the exception, such as `NumberFormatException`

     2. The line number of the code that contained the statement that caused the exception, such as `InputTest.java:10`

▼   The name of the exception is always in the first line of the report, and it ends in `Exception`. If you get a `NumberFormatException`, then there was a problem with the format of some number. That is useful information.

▼   The line number of the offending code is a little harder to determine. The exception report contains the entire *stack trace*—that is, the names of all methods that were pending when the exception hit. The first line of the stack trace is the method that actually gener-

▼   ated the exception. The last line of the stack trace is a line in `main`. Often, the exception was thrown by a method that is in the standard library. Look for the first line in *your code* that appears in the exception report. For example, skip the lines that refer to

▼   `java.lang.Integer.parseInt(Unknown Source)`.

     Once you have the line number in your code, open up the file, go to that line, and look at it! In the great majority of cases, knowing the name of the exception and the line that

▼   caused it makes it completely obvious what went wrong, and you can easily fix your error.

▼   **AT** **Advanced Topic**   **3.6**

Reading Console Input

▼   You just saw how to read input from an input dialog. Admittedly, it is a bit strange to have dialogs pop up for every input. Some programmers prefer to read the input from

▼   the console window. Console input has one great advantage. As you will see in Chapter 6, you can put all your input strings into a file and redirect the console input to read from a file. That's a great help for program testing. However, console input is somewhat cum-

▼   bersome to program. This note explains the details.

     Console input reads from the `System.in` object. However, unlike `System.out`, which was ready-made for printing numbers and strings, `System.in` can only read *bytes*.

▼   Keyboard input consists of characters. To get a reader for characters, you have to turn `System.in` into an `InputStreamReader` object, like this:

▼   ```
     InputStreamReader reader =
         newInputStreamReader(System.in);
     ```

     | Wrap `System.in` inside a `BufferedReader` to read input from the console window. | An input stream reader can read characters, but it can't read a whole string at a time. That makes it pretty inconvenient—you wouldn't want to piece together every input line from its individual characters. To overcome this limitation, you can turn an input stream reader into a `BufferedReader` object: |
     | --- | --- |

▼    ```
     BufferedReader console =
         new BufferedReader(reader);
     ```

▼

If you like, you can combine the two constructors:

```
BufferedReader console = new BufferedReader(
    new InputStreamReader(System.in));
```

▼

Now you use the `readLine` method to read an input line, like this:

▼

```
System.out.println(
    "How many nickels do you have?");
String input = console.readLine();
int count = Integer.parseInt(input);
```

▼

> When calling the `readLine` method of the `BufferedReader` class, you must tag the calling methods with `throws IOException`.

There is one remaining problem. When there is a problem with reading input, the `readLine` method generates an exception, just as the `parseInt` method does when you give it a string that isn't an integer. However, the `readLine` method generates an `IOException`, which is a *checked exception*, a more severe kind of exception than the `NumberFormatException` that the `parseInt` method generates. The Java compiler insists that you take one of two steps when you call a method that can throw a checked exception.

▼

1. Handle the exception. You will see how to do that in Chapter 15

2. Acknowledge that you are not handling the exception. Then you have to indicate that your method can cause a checked exception because it calls another method that can cause that exception. You do that by tagging your method with a `throws` specifier, like this:

```
public static void main(String[] args) throws IOException
```

or

```
public void readInput(BufferedReader reader) throws IOException
```

There is no shame associated with acknowledging that your method might throw a checked exception—it is just "truth in advertising". Of course, in a professional program, you do need to handle all exceptions somewhere, and the `main` method won't throw any exceptions. You'll have to wait for Chapter 15 for the details.

Following this note is another version of the test program for the `Purse` class, this time reading input from the console. Figure 8 shows a typical program run.

File ConsoleInputTest.java

```
1  import java.io.BufferedReader;
2  import java.io.InputStreamReader;
3  import java.io.IOException;
4
5  /**
6     This program tests input from a console window.
7  */
```

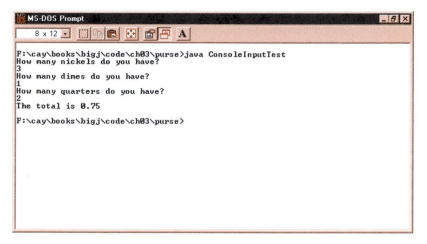

Figure 8

Reading Input from the Console

```
 8  public class ConsoleInputTest
 9  {
10     public static void main(String[] args) throws IOException
11     {
12        Purse myPurse = new Purse();
13
14
15        BufferedReader console = new BufferedReader(
16           new InputStreamReader(System.in));
17        System.out.println(
18           "How many nickels do you have?");
19        String input = console.readLine();
20        int count = Integer.parseInt(input);
21        myPurse.addNickels(count);
22
23        System.out.println("How many dimes do you have?");
24        input = console.readLine();
25        count = Integer.parseInt(input);
26        myPurse.addDimes(count);
27
28        System.out.println(
29           "How many quarters do you have?");
30        input = console.readLine();
31        count = Integer.parseInt(input);
32        myPurse.addQuarters(count);
33
34        double totalValue = myPurse.getTotal();
35        System.out.println("The total is " + totalValue);
```

```
36
37          System.exit(0);
38      }
39  }
```

3.9   Characters

> A char value denotes a single character. Character constants are enclosed in single quotes.

Strings are composed of individual characters. Characters are values of the char type. A variable of type char can hold a single character.

Character constants look like string constants, except that character constants are delimited by single quotes: `'H'` is a character, `"H"` is a string containing a single character. You can use escape sequences (see Advanced Topic 1.1) inside character constants. For example, `'\n'` is the newline character, and `'\u00E9'` is the character é. You can find the values of the character constants that are used in Western European languages in Appendix A3.

Characters have numeric values. For example, if you look at Appendix A3, you can see that the character `'H'` is actually encoded as the number 72.

The charAt method of the String class returns a character from a string. As with the substring method, the positions in the string are counted starting at 0. For example, the statement

```
String greeting = "Hello";
char ch = greeting.charAt(0);
```

sets ch to the character `'H'`.

Random Fact   3.2

International Alphabets

The English alphabet is pretty simple: upper- and lowercase *a* to *z*. Other European languages have accent marks and special characters. For example, German has three *umlaut* characters (ä, ö, ü) and a double-s character (ß). These are not optional frills; you couldn't write a page of German text without using these characters a few times. German computer keyboards have keys for these characters (see Figure 9).

This poses a problem for computer users and designers. The American standard character encoding (called ASCII, for American Standard Code for Information Interchange) specifies 128 codes: 52 upper- and lowercase characters, 10 digits, 32 typographical symbols, and 34 control characters (such as space, newline, and 32 others for controlling printers and other devices). The umlaut and double-s are not among them. Some German data processing systems replace seldom-used ASCII characters with German letters: [\ ] { | } ~ are replaced with Ä Ö Ü ä ö ü ß.

Figure 9

German Keyboard

Most people can live without those ASCII characters, but programmers using Java definitely cannot. Other encoding schemes take advantage of the fact that one byte can encode 256 different characters, but only 128 are standardized by ASCII. Unfortunately, there are multiple incompatible standards for using the remaining 128 characters, such as those used by the Windows and Macintosh operating systems, resulting in a certain amount of aggravation among European computer users and their American email correspondents.

Many countries don't use the Roman script at all. Russian, Greek, Hebrew, Arabic, and Thai letters, to name just a few, have completely different shapes (see Figure 10). To complicate matters, scripts like Hebrew and Arabic are written from right to left instead of from left to right, and many of these scripts have characters that stack above or below other characters, as those marked with a dotted circle in Figure 10 do in Thai. Each of these alphabets has between 30 and 100 letters, and the countries using them have established encoding standards for them.

The situation is much more dramatic in languages that use the Chinese script: the Chinese dialects, Japanese, and Korean. The Chinese script is not alphabetic but *ideographic*—a character represents an idea or thing rather than a single sound. (See Figure 11; can you identify the characters for soup, chicken, and wonton?) Most words are made up of one, two, or three of these ideographic characters. Over 50,000 ideographs are known, of which about 20,000 are in active use. Therefore, two bytes are needed to encode them. China, Taiwan, Japan, and Korea have incompatible encoding standards for them. (Japanese and Korean writing use a mixture of native syllabic and Chinese ideographic characters.)

The inconsistencies among character encodings have been a major nuisance for international electronic communication and for software manufacturers vying for a global market. Between 1988 and 1991 a consortium of hardware and software manufacturers developed a uniform 16-bit encoding scheme called *Unicode* that is capable of encoding text in essentially all written languages of the world (see reference [1]). About 39,000 characters have been given codes, including 21,000 Chinese ideographs. A 16-bit code

	จ	ภ	ะ	เ	๐		เ◌
ก	ฑ	ม	◌ั	แ	๑		แ◌
ข	ฒ	ย	า	โ	๒		โ◌
ฃ	ณ	ร	◌ำ	ใ	๓		ใ◌
ค	ด	ฤ	◌ิ	ไ	๔		ไ◌
ฅ	ต	ล	◌ี	ำ	๕		
ฆ	ถ	ฦ	◌ึ	ๅ	๖		
ง	ท	ว	◌ื	๎	๗		
จ	ธ	ศ	◌ุ	◌่	๘		
ฉ	น	ษ	◌ู	◌๊	๙		
ช	บ	ส	◌.	◌๋	๚		
ซ	ป	ห		◌์	๛		
ฌ	ผ	ฬ		◌๊			
ญ	ฝ	อ		◌ํ			
ฎ	พ	ฮ		๏			
ฏ	ฟ	ฯ					

Figure 10

The Thai Alphabet

CLASSIC SOUPS

			Sm.	Lg.
清燉雞湯	57.	House Chicken Soup (Chicken, Celery, Potato, Onion, Carrot)	1.50	2.75
雞飯湯	58.	Chicken Rice Soup	1.85	3.25
雞麵湯	59.	Chicken Noodle Soup	1.85	3.25
廣東雲吞	60.	Cantonese Wonton Soup	1.50	2.75
蕃茄蛋湯	61.	Tomato Clear Egg Drop Soup	1.65	2.95
雲吞湯	62.	Regular Wonton Soup	1.10	2.10
酸辣湯	63.	Hot & Sour Soup	1.10	2.10
蛋花湯	64.	Egg Drop Soup	1.10	2.10
雲蛋湯	65.	Egg Drop Wonton Mix	1.10	2.10
豆腐菜湯	66.	Tofu Vegetable Soup	NA	3.50
雞玉米湯	67.	Chicken Corn Cream Soup	NA	3.50
蟹肉玉米湯	68.	Crab Meat Corn Cream Soup	NA	3.50
海鮮湯	69.	Seafood Soup	NA	3.50

Figure 11

A Menu with Chinese Characters

can incorporate 65,000 codes, so there is ample space for expansion. Future versions of the standard will be able to encode such scripts as Egyptian hieroglyphs and the ancient script used on the island of Java.

All Unicode characters can be stored in Java strings, but which ones can actually be displayed depends on your computer system.

3.10 Comparing Primitive Types and Objects

> Number variables hold values. Object variables hold references.

In Java, every value is either a primitive type or an object reference. Primitive types are numbers (such as `int`, `double`, `char`, and the other number types listed in Advanced Topic 3.2) and the `boolean` type that you will encounter in Chapter 5. There is an important difference between primitive types and objects in Java. Primitive type variables hold values, but object variables don't hold objects—they hold references to objects. You can see the difference when you make a copy of a variable. When you copy a primitive type value, the original and the copy of the number are independent values. But when you copy an object reference, both the original and the copy are references to the same object.

> A copy of an object reference is another reference to the same object.

Consider the following code, which copies a number and then adds an amount to the copy (see Figure 12):

```
double balance1 = 1000;
double balance2 = balance1; // see Figure 12
balance2 = balance2 + 500;
```

Now the variable `balance1` contains the value 1000, and `balance2` contains 1500.

Figure 12

Copying Numbers

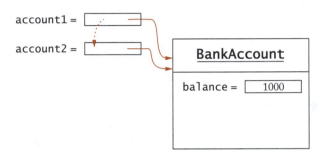

Figure 13

Copying Object References

Now consider the seemingly analogous code with BankAccount objects.

```
BankAccount account1 = new BankAccount(1000);
BankAccount account2 = account1; // see Figure 13
account2.deposit(500);
```

Unlike the preceding code, now *both* account1 and account2 have a balance of $1500.

What can you do if you actually need to make a true copy of an object—that is, a new object whose state is identical to an existing object? As you will see in Chapter 13, you can define a clone method for your classes to make such a copy. But in the meantime, you will simply have to construct a new object:

```
BankAccount account2 = new
    BankAccount(account1.getBalance());
```

Strings are objects; therefore, if you copy a String variable, you get two references to the same string object. However, unlike bank accounts, strings are *immutable*. None of the methods of the String class change the state of a String object. Thus, there is no problem in sharing string references.

CHAPTER SUMMARY

1. The int type denotes integers: numbers without fractional part.

2. Assignment to a variable is not the same as mathematical equality.

3. The ++ and -- operators increment and decrement a variable.

4. A final variable is a constant. Once its value has been set, it cannot be changed.

5. Use named constants to make your programs easier to read and maintain.

6. If both arguments of the / operator are integers, the result is an integer and the remainder is discarded.

7. The % operator computes the remainder of a division.

8. The `Math` class contains methods `sqrt` and `pow` to compute square roots and powers.

9. A `static` method does not operate on an object.

10. You use a cast (*typeName*) to convert a value to a different type.

11. Use the `Math.round` method to round a floating-point number to the nearest integer.

12. A string is a sequence of characters. Strings are objects of the `String` class.

13. Strings can be concatenated, that is, put end to end to yield a new longer string. String concatenation is denoted by the + operator.

14. Whenever one of the arguments of the + operator is a string, the other argument is converted to a string.

15. If a string contains the digits of a number, you use the `Integer.parseInt` or `Double.parseDouble` method to obtain the number value.

16. Use the `substring` method to extract a part of a string.

17. String positions are counted starting with 0.

18. The `JOptionPane.showInputDialog` method prompts the user for an input string.

19. You must call `System.exit(0)` to exit a program that has a graphical user interface.

20. Wrap `System.in` inside a `BufferedReader` to read input from the console window.

21. When calling the `readLine` method of the `BufferedReader` class, you must tag the calling methods with `throws IOException`.

22. A `char` value denotes a single character. Character constants are enclosed in single quotes.

23. Number variables hold values. Object variables hold references.

24. A copy of an object reference is another reference to the same object.

Further Reading

[1] http://www.unicode.org/ The web site of the Unicode consortium. It contains character tables that show the Unicode values of characters from many scripts.

Classes, Objects, and Methods Introduced in This Chapter

```
java.io.BufferedReader
    readLine
java.io.InputStreamReader
java.lang.Double
    parseDouble
    toString
java.lang.Integer
    parseInt
    toString
    MAX_VALUE
    MIN_VALUE
java.lang.Math
    E
    PI
    abs
    acos
    asin
    atan
    atan2
    ceil
    cos
    exp
    floor
    log
    max
    min
    pow
    round
    sin
    sqrt
    tan
    toDegrees
    toRadians
java.lang.String
    length
    substring
    toLowerCase
    toUpperCase
java.lang.System
    exit
    in
java.math.BigDecimal
    add
    divide
    multiply
    subtract
```

```
java.math.BigInteger
   add
   divide
   multiply
   subtract
java.text.NumberFormat
   format
   getCurrencyInstance
   getNumberInstance
   setMaximumFractionDigits
   setMinimumFractionDigits
javax.swing.JOptionPane
   showInputDialog
```

REVIEW EXERCISES

Exercise R3.1. Write the following mathematical expressions in Java.

$$s = s_0 + v_0 t + \frac{1}{2} g t^2$$

$$G = 4\pi^2 \frac{a^3}{P^2(m_1 + m_2)}$$

$$FV = PV \cdot \left(1 + \frac{INT}{100}\right)^{YRS}$$

$$c = \sqrt{a^2 + b^2 - 2ab\cos\gamma}$$

Exercise R3.2. Write the following Java expressions in mathematical notation.

```
dm = m * ((Math.sqrt(1 + v / c) / Math.sqrt(1 - v / c)) - 1);
volume = Math.PI * r * r * h;
volume = 4 * Math.PI * Math.pow(r, 3) / 3;
p = Math.atan2(z, Math.sqrt(x * x + y * y));
```

Exercise R3.3. What is wrong with this version of the quadratic formula?

```
x1 = (-b - Math.sqrt(b * b - 4 * a * c)) / 2 * a;
x2 = (-b + Math.sqrt(b * b - 4 * a * c)) / 2 * a;
```

Exercise R3.4. Give an example of integer overflow. Would the same example work correctly if you used floating-point? Give an example of a floating-point roundoff error. Would the same example work correctly if you used integers? For this exercise, you should assume that the values are represented in a sufficiently small unit, such as cents instead of dollars, so that the values don't have a fractional part.

Exercise R3.5. Write a test program that executes the following code:

```
Purse myPurse = new Purse();
myPurse.addNickels(3);
```

```
myPurse.addDimes(2);
myPurse.addQuarters(1);
System.out.println(myPurse.getTotal());
```

The program prints the total as `0.6000000000000001`. Explain why. Give a recommendation to improve the program so that users will not be confused.

Exercise R3.6. Let n be an integer and x a floating-point number. Explain the difference between

```
n = (int)x;
```

and

```
n = (int)Math.round(x);
```

Exercise R3.7. Let n be an integer and x a floating-point number. Explain the difference between

```
n = (int)(x + 0.5);
```

and

```
n = (int)Math.round(x);
```

For what values of x do they give the same result? For what values of x do they give different results?

Exercise R3.8. Explain the differences between 2, 2.0, '2', "2", and "2.0".

Exercise R3.9. Explain what each of the following two program segments computes:

```
x = 2;
y = x + x;
```

and

```
s = "2";
t = s + s;
```

Exercise R3.10. Uninitialized variables can be a serious problem. Should you *always* initialize every variable with zero? Explain the advantages and disadvantages of such a strategy.

Exercise R3.11. True or false? (x is an `int` and s is a `String`)

- `Integer.parseInt("" + x)` is the same as x
- `"" + Integer.parseInt(s)` is the same as s
- `s.substring(0, s.length())` is the same as s

Exercise R3.12. How do you get the first character of a string? The last character? How do you *remove* the first character? The last character?

Exercise R3.13. How do you get the last digit of an integer? The first digit? That is, if n is 23456, how do you find out that the first digit is 2 and the last digit is 6? Do not convert the number to a string. *Hint:* `%`, `Math.log`.

Exercise R3.14. This chapter contains several recommendations regarding variables and constants that make programs easier to read and maintain. Summarize these recommendations.

Exercise R3.15. What is a `final` variable? Can you define a `final` variable without supplying its value? (Try it out.)

Exercise R3.16. What are the values of the following expressions? In each line, assume that

```
double x = 2.5;
double y = -1.5;
int m = 18;
int n = 4;
String s = "Hello";
String t = "World";
```

- `x + n * y - (x + n) * y`

- `m / n + m % n`

- `5 * x - n / 5`

- `Math.sqrt(Math.sqrt(n))`

- `(int)Math.round(x)`

- `(int)Math.round(x) + (int)Math.round(y)`

- `s + t`

- `s + n`

- `1 - (1 - (1 - (1 - (1 - n))))`

- `s.substring(1, 3)`

- `s.length() + t.length()`

Exercise R3.17. Explain the similarities and differences between copying numbers and copying object references.

Exercise R3.18. What are the values of a, b, c, and d after these statements?

```
double a = 1;
double b = a;
a++;
Purse p = new Purse();
Purse q = p;
p.addNickels(5);
double c = p.getTotal();
double d = q.getTotal();
```

Exercise R3.19. When you copy a `BankAccount` reference, the original and the copy share the same object. That can be significant because you can modify the state of the object through either of the references. Explain why this is not a problem for `String` references.

PROGRAMMING EXERCISES

Exercise P3.1. Enhance the `Purse` class by adding methods `addPennies` and `addDollars`.

Exercise P3.2. Add methods `getDollars` and `getCents` to the `Purse` class. The `get-Dollars` method should return the number of whole dollars in the purse, as an integer. The `getCents` method should return the number of cents, as an integer. For example, if the total value of the coins in the purse is $2.14, `getDollars` returns 2 and `getCents` returns 14.

Exercise P3.3. Write a program that prints the values

1

10

100

1000

10000

100000

1000000

10000000

100000000

1000000000

10000000000

100000000000

Implement a class

```
public class PowerGenerator
{
    /**
        Constructs a power generator.
        @param aFactor  the number that will be multiplied by itself
    */
    public PowerGenerator(int aFactor) { . . . }
    /**
        Computes the next power.
    */
    public double nextPower() { . . . }
    . . .
}
```

Then supply a test class `PowerGeneratorTest` that calls `System.out.println(myGenerator.nextPower())` twelve times.

Exercise P3.4. Write a program that prompts the user for two integers and then prints

- The sum
- The difference
- The product
- The average

- The distance (absolute value of the difference)
- The maximum (the larger of the two)
- The minimum (the smaller of the two)

Implement a class

```
public class Pair
{
    /**
        Constructs a pair.
        @param aFirst the first value of the pair
        @param aSecond the second value of the pair
    */
    public Pair(double aFirst, double aSecond) { . . . }
    /**
        Computes the sum of the values of this pair.
        @return the sum of the first and second values
    */
    public double getSum() { . . . }
    . . .
}
```

Then implement a class `PairTest` that reads in two numbers (using either a `JOption-Pane` or a `BufferedReader`), constructs a `Pair` object, invokes its methods, and prints the results.

Exercise P3.5. Write a program that reads in four integers and prints their sum and average. Define a class `DataSet` with methods

```
void addValue(int x)
int getSum()
double getAverage()
```

Hint: Keep track of the sum and the count of the values. Then write a test program `DataSetTest` that reads four numbers and calls `addValue` four times.

Exercise P3.6. Write a program that reads in four integers and prints the largest and smallest value that the user entered. Use a class `DataSet` with methods

- `void addValue(int x)`
- `int getLargest()`
- `int getSmallest()`

Keep track of the smallest and largest value that you've seen so far. Then use the `Math.min` and `Math.max` methods to update it in the `addValue` method. What should you use as initial values? *Hint:* `Integer.MIN_VALUE`, `Integer.MAX_VALUE`.

Write a test program `DataSetTest` that reads four numbers and calls `addValue` four times.

Exercise P3.7. Write a program that prompts the user for a measurement in meters and then converts it into miles, feet, and inches. Use a class

```
public class Converter
{
```

```java
/**
    Constructs a converter that can convert between two units.
    @param aConversionFactor the factor with which to multiply
    to convert to the target unit
*/
public Converter(double aConversionFactor) { . . . }
/**
    Converts from a source measurement to a target measurement.
    @param fromMeasurement the measurement
    @return the input value converted to the target unit
*/
public double convertTo(double fromMeasurement) { . . . }
}
```

Then construct three instances, such as

```java
final double MILE_TO_KM = 0.621;
Converter metersToMiles = new Converter(1000 * MILE_TO_KM);
```

Exercise P3.8. Write a program that prompts the user for a radius and then prints

- The area and circumference of the circle with that radius
- The volume and surface area of the sphere with that radius

Define classes `Circle` and `Sphere`.

Exercise P3.9. Implement a class `SodaCan` whose constructor receives the height and diameter of the soda can. Supply methods `getVolume` and `getSurfaceArea`. Supply a `SodaCanTest` class that tests your class.

Exercise P3.10. Write a program that asks the user for the length of the sides of a square. Then print

- The area and perimeter of the square
- The length of the diagonal (use the Pythagorean theorem)

Define a class `Square`.

Exercise P3.11. *Giving change.* Implement a program that directs a cashier how to give change. The program has two inputs: the amount due and the amount received from the customer. Compute the difference, and compute the dollars, quarters, dimes, nickels, and pennies that the customer should receive in return.

First transform the difference into an integer balance, denominated in pennies. Then compute the whole dollar amount. Subtract it from the balance. Compute the number of quarters needed. Repeat for dimes and nickels. Display the remaining pennies.

Define a class `Cashier` with methods

- `setAmountDue`
- `receive`
- `returnDollars`
- `returnQuarters`

- `returnDimes`
- `returnNickels`
- `returnPennies`

For example,

```
Cashier harry = new Cashier();
harry.setAmountDue(9.37);
harry.receive(10);
double quarters = harry.returnQuarters(); // returns 2
double dimes = harry.returnDimes(); // returns 1
double nickels = harry.returnNickels(); // returns 0
double pennies = harry.returnPennies(); // returns 3
```

Exercise P3.12. Write a program that reads in an integer and breaks it into a sequence of individual digits in reverse order. For example, the input 16384 is displayed as

```
4
8
3
6
1
```

You may assume that the input has no more than five digits and is not negative.

Define a class `DigitExtractor`:

```
public class DigitExtractor
{
    /**
        Constructs a digit extractor that gets the digits
        of an integer in reverse order.
        @param anInteger  the integer to break up into digits
    */
    public DigitExtractor(int anInteger) { . . . }
    /**
        Returns the next digit to be extracted.
        @return  the next digit
    */
    public double nextDigit() { . . . }
}
```

Then call `System.out.println(myExtractor.nextDigit())` five times.

Exercise P3.13. Implement a class `QuadraticEquation` whose constructor receives the coefficients a, b, c of the quadratic equation $ax^2 + bx + c = 0$. Supply methods `getSolution1` and `getSolution2` that get the solutions, using the quadratic formula. Write a test class `QuadraticEquationTest` that prompts the user for the values of a, b, and c, constructs a `QuadraticEquation` object, and prints the two solutions.

Exercise P3.14. Write a program that reads two times in military format (0900, 1730) and prints the number of hours and minutes between the two times. Here is a sample run. User input is in color.

```
Please enter the first time: 0900
Please enter the second time: 1730
8 hours 30 minutes
```

Extra credit if you can deal with the case where the first time is later than the second time:

```
Please enter the first time: 1730
Please enter the second time: 0900
15 hours 30 minutes
```

Implement a class `TimeInterval` whose constructor takes two military times. The class should have two methods `getHours` and `metMinutes`.

Exercise P3.15. *Writing large letters.* A large letter H can be produced like this:

```
*   *
*   *
*****
*   *
*   *
```

Define a class `LetterH` with a method

```
String getLetter()
{
    return "*   *\n*   *\n*****\n*   *\n*   *\n";
}
```

Do the same for the letters E, L, and O. Then write the message

```
H
E
L
L
O
```

in large letters.

Exercise P3.16. Write a program that transforms numbers 1, 2, 3, . . . , 12 into the corresponding month names January, February, March, . . . , December. *Hint:* Make a very long string "January February March. . .", in which you add spaces such that each month name has *the same length*. Then use `substring` to extract the month you want. Implement a class `Month` whose constructor parameter is the month number and whose `getName` method returns the month name.

Exercise P3.17. Write a program to compute the date of Easter Sunday. Easter Sunday is the first Sunday after the first full moon of Spring. Use this algorithm, invented by the mathematician Carl Friedrich Gauss in 1800:

1. Let y be the year (such as 1800 or 2001)
2. Divide y by 19 and call the remainder a. Ignore the quotient.
3. Divide y by 100 to get a quotient b and a remainder c
4. Divide b by 4 to get a quotient d and a remainder e
5. Divide 8 * b + 13 by 25 to get a quotient g. Ignore the remainder.

6. Divide $19 * a + b - d - g + 15$ by 30 to get a remainder h. Ignore the quotient.
7. Divide c by 4 to get a quotient j and a remainder k
8. Divide $a + 11 * h$ by 319 to get a quotient m. Ignore the remainder.
9. Divide $2 * e + 2 * j - k - h + m + 32$ by 7 to get a remainder r. Ignore the quotient.
10. Divide $h - m + r + 90$ by 25 to get a quotient n. Ignore the remainder.
11. Divide $h - m + r + n + 19$ by 32 to get a remainder p. Ignore the quotient.

Then Easter falls on day p of month n. For example, if y is 2001:

```
a = 6
b = 20
c = 1
d = 5, e = 0
g = 6
h = 18
j = 0, k = 1
m = 0
r = 6
n = 4
p = 15
```

Therefore, in 2001, Easter Sunday fell on April 15. Write a class Year with methods getEasterSundayMonth and getEasterSundayDay.

Applets and Graphics

There are three kinds of Java programs that you will learn to write: *console applications*, *graphical applications*, and *applets*. Console applications run in a single, usually rather plain-looking terminal window (see Figure 1). Applications with a graphical user interface use one or more windows filled with *user interface components* such as buttons, text input fields, and menus (see Figure 2). *Applets* are similar to applications with a graphical user interface, but they run *inside a web browser*.

Console programs are simpler to write than programs with a graphical user interface, and we will continue to use console programs frequently in this book to learn about fundamental concepts. Graphical user interface programs can show more interesting output, however, and are often more fun to develop. In this chapter you will learn how to write simple applets that display graphical shapes.

CHAPTER CONTENTS

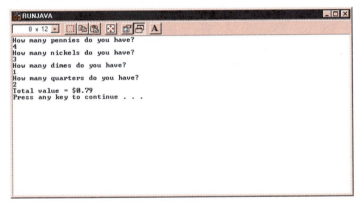

Figure 1

A Console Application

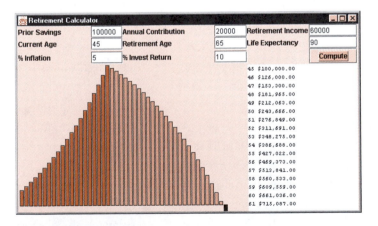

Figure 2

A Graphical Application

4.1   Why Applets?

> There are three types of Java programs: *console applications, applets,* and *graphics applications.*

The World Wide Web makes a huge amount of information available to anyone with a web browser. When you use a web browser, you connect to a *web server,* which sends web pages and images to your browser (see Figure 3). Because the web pages and images have standard formats, your web browser can display them. To retrieve the daily news or your bank balance, you don't have to be at home, in front of your own computer. You can use a browser at school or in an airport terminal or Web café anywhere in the world. This ubiquitous access to information is one reason why the World Wide Web is so hugely popular.

> Applets are programs that run inside a web browser.

Applets are programs that run inside a web browser. The code for an applet is stored on a web server and downloaded into the browser whenever you access a web page that contains the applet. That has one big advantage: You don't have to be at your own computer to run a program that is implemented as an applet. There is also an obvious disadvantage: You have to wait for the applet code to download into the browser, which can take a long time if you have a slow Internet connection. For that reason, complex applets are rare in web pages with a wide audience. Applets work very nicely, however, over a fast connection. For example, employees in a company often have a fast local area network connection. Then the company can deploy applets for schedule planning, health benefit access, product catalog lookup, and so on, and gain a big cost savings over the traditional process of developing corporate applications to be rolled out on the desktop of every user. When the program application changed, a system administrator had to make sure that every desktop was updated—a real hassle. When an applet changes, on the other hand, the code needs to be updated in one location: on the web server.

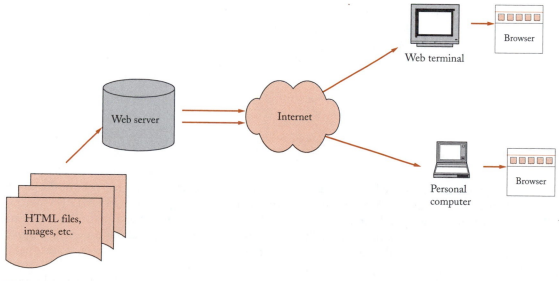

Figure 3

Web Browsers Accessing a Web Server

Web browser programs run on PCs, Macintoshes, UNIX workstations, and special web devices. For this reason, it is important that the applet code be able to execute on multiple platforms. Most traditional programs (such as word processors, computer games, and browsers) are written for a single platform, or perhaps written twice, for the two most popular platforms. Applets, on the other hand, are delivered as Java bytecode. Any computer or device that can execute Java bytecode can execute the applet.

> The applet security mechanisms let you safely execute applets on your computer.

Whenever you run a program on your computer, you run a risk that the program might do some kind of damage either because it is poorly written or because it is outright malicious. A poorly written program might accidentally corrupt or erase some of your files. A virus program might do the same intentionally. In the old days, before computers were networked, you had to install every program yourself, and it was a relatively easy matter to check for viruses on the floppy disks that you used to add new programs or data to your computer. Nowadays, programs can come from anywhere—from another machine on a local area network, as email attachments, or as code that is included in a web page. Code that is part of a web page is particularly troublesome, because it starts running immediately when the browser loads the page. It would be an easy matter for a malicious person to set up a web page with enticing content, have many people visit the page, and attempt to infect each visitor with a virus. The designers of Java anticipated this problem and came up with two safeguards: Java applets can run at specified *security privileges*, and they can be *signed*. If you allow a machine language program to run, there is no control over what it can do, and it can create many kinds of problems. In contrast, the Java virtual machine can limit the actions of an applet. By default, an applet runs in a *sandbox*, where it can display information and get user input, but it can't read or touch anything else on the user's computer. You can give an applet more privileges, such as the ability to read and write local files, if you notify your browser that the applet is *trusted*. An applet can carry a *certificate* with a *signature* from an authentication firm such as VeriSign, which tells you where the applet originated. If the applet comes from a source you trust, such as a vendor who has delivered quality code to you in the past, you can tell the browser that you trust it. Signatures are not limited to applets; some browsers support certificates for machine language code.

4.2   A Brief Introduction to HTML

Applets are embedded inside web pages, so you need to know a few facts about the structure of web pages. A web page is written in a language called HTML (Hypertext Markup Language). Like Java code, HTML code is made up of text that follows certain strict rules. When a browser reads a web page, the browser *interprets* the code and *renders* the page, displaying characters, fonts, paragraphs, tables, and images.

> Web pages are written in HTML, using tags to format text and include images.

HTML files are made up of text and *tags* that tell the browser how to render the text. Nowadays, there are dozens of HTML tags. Fortunately, you need only a few to get started. Most HTML tags come in pairs consisting of an opening tag and a closing tag, and each pair applies to the text between the two tags. Here is a typical example of a tag pair:

```
Java is an <i>object-oriented</i> programming language.
```

The tag pair `<i>` `</i>` directs the browser to display the text inside the tags as *italics:* Java is an *object-oriented* programming language.

The closing tag is just like the opening tag, but it is prefixed by a slash (/). For example, bold-faced text is delimited by `<b>` `</b>`, and a paragraph is delimited by the tag pair `<p>` `</p>`.

```
<p><b>Java</b> is an <i>object-oriented</i>
programming language.</p>
```

The result is the paragraph

Java is an *object-oriented* programming language.

Another common construct is a bulleted list.

Java is

- object-oriented

- safe

- platform-independent

Here is the HTML code to display it:

```
<p>Java is</p>
<ul><li>object-oriented</li>
<li>safe</li>
<li>platform-independent</li></ul>
```

Each item in the list is delimited by `<li>` `</li>` (for "list item"), and the whole list is surrounded by `<ul>` `</ul>` (for "unnumbered list").

As in Java code, you can freely use white space (spaces and line breaks) in HTML code to make it easier to read. For example, you can lay out the code for a list as follows:

```
<p>Java is</p>
<ul>
    <li>object-oriented</li>
    <li>safe</li>
    <li>platform-independent</li>
</ul>
```

The browser ignores the white space.

If you omit a tag (such as a `</li>`), most browsers will try to guess the missing tags—sometimes with differing results. It is always best to include all tags.

You can include images in your web pages with the `img` tag. In its simplest form, an image tag has the form

```
<img src="hamster.jpeg" />
```

This code tells the browser to load and display the image that is stored in the file hamster.jpeg. This is a slightly different type of tag. Rather than text inside a tag pair `<img>` `</img>`, the img tag uses an *attribute* to specify a file name. Attributes have names and values. For example, the src attribute has the value "hamster.jpeg". It is considered polite to use several additional attributes with the img tag, namely the *image size* and an *alternate description:*

```
<img src="hamster.jpeg" width="640" height="480"
alt="A photo of Harry, the Horrible Hamster" />
```

These additional attributes help the browser lay out the page and display a temporary description while gathering the data for the image (or if the browser cannot display images, such as a voice browser for blind users). Users with slow network connections really appreciate this extra effort.

Because there is no closing </img> tag, we put a slash / before the closing >. This is not a requirement of HTML, but it is a requirement of the emerging XHTML standard, the XML-based successor to HTML. See [1] for more information on XHTML.

The most important tag in web pages is the <a> </a> tag pair, which makes the enclosed text into a *link* to another file. The links between web pages are what makes the Web into, well, a web. The browser displays a link in a special way (for example, underlined text in blue color). Here is the code for a typical link:

```
<a href="http://java.sun.com">Java</a> is an object-oriented
programming language.
```

When the viewer of the web page clicks on the word <u>Java</u>, the browser loads the web page located at java.sun.com. (The value of the href attribute is a *Universal Resource Locator (URL)*, which tells the browser where to go. The prefix http:, for *Hypertext Transfer Protocol*, tells the browser to fetch the file as a web page. Other protocols allow different actions, such as ftp: to download a file, mailto: to send email to a user, and file: to view a local HTML file.)

> To run an applet, you need an HTML page with the applet tag.

Finally, the applet tag includes an applet in a web page. To display an applet, you need first to write and compile a Java file to generate the applet code—you will see how in the next section. Then you tell the browser how to find the code for the applet and how much screen space to reserve for the applet. Here is an example:

```
<applet code="HamsterApplet.class" width="400" height="300">An
animation of Harry, the Horrible Hamster</applet>
```

The text between the <applet> and </applet> tags is only displayed in lieu of the actual applet by browsers that can't run Java applets.

You have noticed that tags are enclosed in angle brackets (less-than and greater-than signs). What if you want to show an angle bracket on a web page? HTML provides the notations < and > produce the < and > symbols, respectively. Other codes of this kind produce symbols such as accented letters. The & (ampersand) symbol introduces these codes; to get that symbol itself, use &.

You may already have created web pages with a web editor that works like a word processor, giving you a WYSIWYG (what you see is what you get) view of your web page. But the tags are still there, and you can see them when you load the HTML file into a text editor. If you are comfortable using a WYSIWYG web editor, and if your editor can insert applet tags, you don't need to memorize HTML tags at all. But many programmers and professional web designers prefer to work directly with the tags at least some of the time, because it gives them more control over their pages.

 **Random Fact** **4.1**

The Evolution of the Internet

Home computers and laptops are usually self-contained units with no permanent connection to other computers. Office and lab computers, however, are usually connected with each other and with larger computers: so-called *servers*. A server can store application programs and make them available on all computers on the network. Servers can also store data, such as schedules and mail messages, that everyone can retrieve. Networks that connect the computers in one building are called local area networks, or LANs.

Other networks connect computers in geographically dispersed locations. Such networks are called *wide area networks* or WANs. The most prominent wide area network is the *Internet*. At the time of this writing, the Internet is in a phase of explosive growth. Nobody knows for certain how many users have access to the Internet, but the user population is estimated in the hundreds of millions. The Internet grew out of the ARPAnet, a network of computers at universities that was funded by the Advanced Research Planning Agency of the U.S. Department of Defense. The original motivation behind the creation of the network was the desire to run programs on remote computers. Using remote execution, a researcher at one institution would be able to access an underutilized computer at a different site. It quickly became apparent, though, that remote execution was not what the network was actually used for. Instead, the "killer application" was *electronic mail:* the transfer of messages between computer users at different locations. To this day, electronic mail is one of the most compelling applications of the Internet.

Over time, more and more *information* became available on the Internet. The information was created by researchers and hobbyists and made freely available to anyone, either out of the goodness of their hearts or for self-promotion. For example, the *GNU* (GNU's Not UNIX) project is producing a set of high-quality operating system utilities and program development tools that can be used freely by anyone (ftp://prep.ai.mit.edu/pub/gnu), and Project Gutenberg makes available the text of important classical books, whose copyright has expired, in computer-readable form (http://www.gutenberg.org).

The first interfaces to retrieve this information were clumsy and hard to use. All that changed with the appearance of the *World Wide Web* (WWW). The World Wide Web brought two major advances to Internet information. The information could contain *graphics* and *fonts*—a great improvement over the older text-only format—and it became possible to embed *links* to other information pages. Using a *browser* such as Netscape or Internet Explorer, surfing the Web becomes easy and fun (Figure 4).

Figure 4

A Web Browser

A Simple Applet

In our first applet we will simply draw a couple of rectangles (see Figure 5). You'll soon see how to produce more interesting drawings. The purpose of this applet is to show you the basic outline of an applet that creates a drawing.

This applet will be implemented in a single class `RectangleApplet`. To run this applet, you need an HTML file with an `applet` tag. Here is the simplest possible file to display the applet:

File RectangleApplet.html

```
1  <applet code="RectangleApplet.class" width="300" height="300">
2  </applet>
```

Or you can proudly explain your creation, by adding text and more HTML tags:

File RectangleAppletExplained.html

```
1  <p>Here is my <i>first applet</i>:</p>
2  <applet code="RectangleApplet.class" width="300" height="300">
3  </applet>
```

Figure 5

The Rectangle Applet in the Applet Viewer

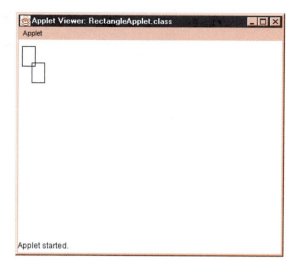

An HTML file can have multiple applets. For example, you can place all your homework solutions into a single HTML file.

You can give the HTML file any name you like. It is easiest to give the HTML file the same name as the applet. But some development environments already generate an HTML file with the same name as your project to hold your project notes; then you must give the HTML file containing your applet a different name.

> You view applets with the applet viewer or a Java-enabled browser.

To run the applet, you have two choices. You can use the *applet viewer*, a program that is included with the Java Software Development Kit from Sun Microsystems. You simply start the applet viewer, giving it the name of the HTML file that contains your applets:

```
appletviewer RectangleApplet.html
```

The applet viewer brings up one window for each applet in the HTML file. It ignores all other HTML tags. Figure 5 shows the applet inside the applet viewer.

> Your applet class needs to extend the Applet class.

You can also show the applet inside any Java 2–enabled web browser such as Netscape 6 (or later) or Opera. Figure 6 shows the applet running in a browser. As you can see, both the text and the applet are displayed.

An applet is programmed as a class, like any other program in Java. However, the class is declared `public`, and it *extends* `Applet`. That means that our rectangle applet *inherits* the behavior of the `Applet` class. We will discuss inheritance in Chapter 11.

```
public class RectangleApplet extends Applet
{
    public void paint(Graphics g)
    {
        . . .
    }
}
```

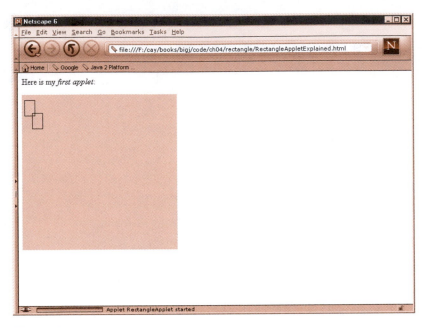

Figure 6

The Rectangle Applet in a Browser

> You draw graphical shapes in an applet by placing the drawing code inside the `paint` method. The `paint` method is called whenever the applet needs to be refreshed.

Unlike applications, applets don't have a `main` method. The web browser (or applet viewer) is responsible for starting up the Java virtual machine, for loading the applet code, and for starting the applet. This applet implements only one method: `paint`. There are other methods that you *may* implement; see Advanced Topic 4.3.

The window manager calls the `paint` method whenever the surface of the applet needs to be filled in. Of course, when the applet is shown for the first time, its contents need to be painted. If the user visits another web page and then goes back to the web page containing the applet, the surface must be painted again, and the window manager calls the `paint` method once more. Thus, you must put all drawing instructions inside the `paint` method, and you must be aware that the window manager can call the `paint` method many times.

> The `Graphics2D` class stores the graphics state (such as the current color) and has methods to draw shapes. You need to cast the `Graphics` parameter of the `paint` method to `Graphics2D` to use these methods.

The `paint` method receives an object of type `Graphics`. The `Graphics` object stores the *graphics state:* the current color, font, and so on, that are used for the drawing operations. For the drawing programs that we explore in this book, we always convert the `Graphics` object to an object of the `Graphics2D` class:

```
public class RectangleApplet extends Applet
{
    public void paint(Graphics g)
```

```
    {
        // recover Graphics2D
        Graphics2D g2 = (Graphics2D)g;
        . . .
    }
}
```

To understand why, you need to know a little about the history of these classes. The `Graphics` class was included with the first version of Java. It is suitable for very basic drawings, but it does not use an object-oriented approach. After some time, programmers clamored for a more powerful graphics package, and the designers of Java created the `Graphics2D` class. They did not want to inconvenience those programmers who had produced programs that used simple graphics, so they did not change the **paint** method. Instead, they made the `Graphics2D` class extend the `Graphics` class, a process that will be discussed in Chapter 9. Whenever the window manager calls the **paint** method, it actually passes a parameter of type `Graphics2D`. Programs with simple graphics needs do not need to know about this, but if you want to use the more sophisticated 2D graphics methods, you recover the `Graphics2D` reference by using a cast as discussed in Chapter 3.

You use the `draw` method of the `Graphics2D` class to draw shapes such as rectangles, ellipses, line segments, polygons, and arcs. Here we draw a rectangle:

```
public class RectangleApplet extends Applet
{
    public void paint(Graphics g)
    {
        . . .

        Rectangle cerealBox = new Rectangle(5, 10, 20, 30);
        g2.draw(cerealBox);
        . . .
    }
}
```

The `Graphics`, `Graphics2D`, and `Rectangle` classes are part of the `java.awt` package. As was mentioned in Chapter 1, the acronym AWT stands for Abstract Windowing Toolkit. This is the original user interface toolkit that Sun supplied for Java. It defines many classes for graphics programming, a mechanism for event handling, and a set of user interface components. In this chapter, we focus on the graphics classes of the AWT.

Here is the complete applet for displaying the rectangle shapes.

File RectangleApplet.java

```
1  import java.applet.Applet;
2  import java.awt.Graphics;
3  import java.awt.Graphics2D;
4  import java.awt.Rectangle;
5
6  /**
7      An applet that draws two rectangles.
```

```
 8   */
 9   public class RectangleApplet extends Applet
10   {
11      public void paint(Graphics g)
12      {
13         // recover Graphics2D
14
15         Graphics2D g2 = (Graphics2D)g;
16
17         // construct a rectangle and draw it
18
19         Rectangle cerealBox = new Rectangle(5, 10, 20, 30);
20         g2.draw(cerealBox);
21
22         // move rectangle 15 units sideways and 25 units down
23
24         cerealBox.translate(15, 25);
25
26         // draw moved rectangle
27
28         g2.draw(cerealBox);
29      }
30   }
```

Advanced Topic 4.1

The Java Runtime Environment and Java Plug-ins

You can run applets inside the applet viewer program, but applets are meant to be executed inside a browser. The first versions of browser programs that supported Java contained a built-in Java virtual machine to execute the downloaded Java applets. That turned out not to be a good idea. New versions of Java appeared rapidly, and the browser manufacturers were unable to keep up. Also, browser manufacturers made minor changes to the Java implementations, causing compatibility problems.

In 1998, Sun Microsystems, the company that invented the Java language, realized that it is best to separate the browser and the virtual machine. Sun now packages the virtual machine as the "Java Runtime Environment", which is to be installed in a standard place on each computer that supports Java. Browser manufacturers are encouraged to use the Java Runtime Environment, not their own Java implementation, to execute applets. That way, users can update their Java implementations and browsers separately. If your browser uses this approach, then it will be able to execute your Java applets without problems. As of this writing, Netscape 6 and Opera work in this way.

However, Microsoft's Internet Explorer browser does not currently support a modern version of the Java virtual machine. To solve this problem, Sun Microsystems provided a second tool, the "Java Plug-in". The Java Plug-in uses the Microsoft ActiveX component

▼ architecture to add Java support to Internet Explorer. If you want to display your applets inside Internet Explorer, you need to download the Java Plug-in from http://java.sun.com/products/plugin/index.html.

▼ Unfortunately, the HTML required to activate the browser extension is quite a bit more arcane than the simple `applet` tag. Sun has developed a program, the "Java Plug-in

▼ HTML Converter", that can translate HTML pages containing `applet` tags to HTML pages with the appropriate tags to launch the Java Plug-in. You can download the converter from http://java.sun.com/products/plugin/1.3/converter.html.

4.4 Graphical Shapes

In Section 4.3 you learned how to write an applet that draws rectangles. In this section you will learn how to draw other shapes: ellipses and lines. With these graphical elements you can draw quite a few interesting pictures.

> The `Rectangle2D.Double`, `Ellipse2D.Double`, and `Line2D.Double` classes describe graphical shapes.

To draw an ellipse, you specify its *bounding box* (see Figure 7) in the same way that you would specify a rectangle, namely by the *x*- and *y*-coordinates of the top-left corner and the width and height of the box.

However, there is no simple `Ellipse` class that you can use. Instead, you must use one of the two classes `Ellipse2D.Float` and `Ellipse2D.Double`, depending on whether you want to store the ellipse coordinates as `float` or as `double` values. Since `double` values are more convenient to use than `float` values in Java, we will always use the `Ellipse2D.Double` class. Here is how you construct an ellipse:

```
Ellipse2D.Double easterEgg = new Ellipse2D.Double(5, 10, 15, 20);
```

The class name `Ellipse2D.Double` looks different from the class names that you have encountered up to now. It consists of two class names `Ellipse2D` and `Double` separated by a period (.). This indicates that `Ellipse2D.Double` is a so-called *inner* class inside `Ellipse2D`. When constructing and using ellipses, you don't actually need to worry about the fact that `Ellipse2D.Double` is an inner class—just think of it as a class with a long name. However, in the `import` statement at the top of your program, you must be careful that you import only the *outer* class:

```
import java.awt.geom.Ellipse2D;
```

You may wonder why an ellipse would want to store its size as `double` values when the screen coordinates are measured in pixels. As you'll see later in this chapter, working with pixel coordinates can be cumbersome. It is often a good idea to switch to different units, and then it can be handy to use floating-point coordinates. (Note that the `Rectangle` class uses integer coordinates, so you will need to use a separate class called `Rectangle2D.Double` whenever you use rectangles with floating-point coordinates.)

Drawing an ellipse is easy: You use exactly the same `draw` method of the `Graphics2D` class that you used for drawing rectangles.

```
g2.draw(easterEgg);
```

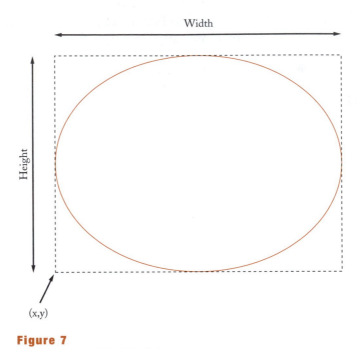

Figure 7

An Ellipse and Its Bounding Box

To draw a circle, simply set the width and height to the same value:

```
Ellipse2D.Double circle =
    new Ellipse2D.Double(x, y, diameter, diameter);
g2.draw(circle);
```

Notice that (x, y) is the top-left corner of the bounding box, *not* the center of the circle.

To draw a line, you use an object of the `Line2D.Double` class. You construct a line by specifying its two end points. You can do this in two ways. You can simply give the *x*- and *y*-coordinates of both end points:

```
Line2D.Double segment = new Line2D.Double(x1, y1, x2, y2);
```

Or you can specify each endpoint as an object of the `Point2D.Double` class:

```
Point2D.Double from = new Point2D.Double(x1, y1);
Point2D.Double to = new Point2D.Double(x2, y2);

Line2D.Double segment = new Line2D.Double(from, to);
```

The latter is more object-oriented, and it is also often more useful, in particular if the point objects can be reused elsewhere in the same drawing.

To draw thicker lines, supply a different *stroke* object to the `Graphics2D` parameter. For example, to get lines that are 4 pixels thick, you call

```
g2.setStroke(new BasicStroke(4.0F));
```

All shapes that you draw after making that call will be drawn with thicker lines.

4.5   Colors

When you first start drawing, all shapes are drawn with a black pen. To change the color, you need to supply an object of type `Color`. Java uses the *RGB color model*. That is, you specify a color by the amounts of the *primary colors*—red, green, and blue—that make up the color. The amounts are given as `float` values, which you must identify by a suffix F. They vary from `0.0F` (primary color not present) to `1.0F` (maximum amount present). For example,

```
Color magenta = new Color(1.0F, 0.0F, 1.0F);
```

When you set a new color in the graphics context, it is used for subsequent drawing operations.

constructs a `Color` object with maximum red, no green, and maximum blue, yielding a bright purple color called magenta.

For your convenience, a variety of colors have been predefined in the `Color` class. Table 1 shows those predefined colors and their RGB values. For example, `Color.pink` has been predefined to be the same color as `new Color(1.0F, 0.7F, 0.7F)`.

Color	RGB Value
`Color.black`	`0.0F, 0.0F, 0.0F`
`Color.blue`	`0.0F, 0.0F, 1.0F`
`Color.cyan`	`0.0F, 1.0F, 1.0F`
`Color.gray`	`0.5F, 0.5F, 0.5F`
`Color.darkGray`	`0.25F, 0.25F, 0.25F`
`Color.lightGray`	`0.75F, 0.75F, 0.75F`
`Color.green`	`0.0F, 1.0F, 0.0F`
`Color.magenta`	`1.0F, 0.0F, 1.0F`
`Color.orange`	`1.0F, 0.8F, 0.0F`
`Color.pink`	`1.0F, 0.7F, 0.7F`
`Color.red`	`1.0F, 0.0F, 0.0F`
`Color.white`	`1.0F, 1.0F, 1.0F`
`Color.yellow`	`1.0F, 1.0F, 0.0F`

Table 1

Predefined Colors and Their RGB Values

Once you have an object of type `Color`, you can change the *current color* of the `Graphics2D` object with the `setColor` method. For example, the following code draws a rectangle in black, then switches the color to red, and draws the next rectangle in red:

```
public void paint(Graphics g)
{
    Graphics2D g2 = (Graphics2D)g;

    Rectangle cerealBox = new Rectangle(5, 10, 20, 30);
    g2.draw(cerealBox); // draws in black

    cerealBox.translate(15, 25); // move rectangle

    g2.setColor(Color.red); // set current color to red
    g2.draw(cerealBox); // draws in red
}
```

If you want to color the inside of the shape, you use the `fill` method instead of the `draw` method. For example,

```
g2.fill(cerealBox);
```

fills the inside of the rectangle with the current color.

4.6 Fonts

> The `drawString` method of the `Graphics2D` class draws a string, starting at its basepoint.

You often want to put text inside a drawing, for example to label some of the parts. You use the `drawString` method of the `Graphics2D` class to draw a string anywhere in a window. You must specify the string and the *x*- and *y*-coordinates of the *basepoint* of the first character in the string (see Figure 8). For example,

```
g2.drawString("Applet", 50, 100);
```

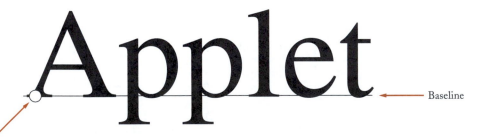

Baseline

Basepoint

Basepoint and Baseline

> A font is described by its face name, style, and point size.

You can select different fonts. The procedure is similar to setting the drawing color. You create a `Font` object and call the `setFont` method of the `Graphics2D` class. To construct a `Font` object, you specify

- The font face name
- The *style* (one of `Font.PLAIN`, `Font.BOLD`, `Font.ITALIC`, or `Font.BOLD + Font.ITALIC`)
- The point size

The font face name is either one of the five *logical face names* in Table 2 or a *typeface name*, the name of a typeface that is available on your computer, such as "Times Roman" or "Helvetica". "Times Roman" and "Helvetica" are the names of popular typefaces that were designed many years ago and are in very widespread use today. These fonts differ in the shapes of their letters. The most visible difference is that the characters of the Times Roman font are composed of strokes with small cross segments at the ends, called *serifs*. The characters of the Helvetica font do not have serifs (see Figure 9). A typeface such as Helvetica is called a *sans-serif* font. It is generally believed that the serifs help make text easier to read. In

Name	Sample	Description
`Serif`	The quick brown fox	A serif-style font such as Times Roman
`SansSerif`	The quick brown fox	A sans-serif font such as Helvetica
`Monospaced`	The quick brown fox	A font in which all characters have the same width, such as Courier
`Dialog`	**The quick brown fox**	A screen font suitable for labels in dialogs
`DialogInput`	The quick brown fox	A screen font suitable for user input in text field

Table 2

Logical Font Names

Helvetica

Times Roman

Figure 9

Common Fonts

Courier

fact, the Times Roman font was designed specifically for the London *Times* newspaper, to be easy to read on newsprint paper. Most books (including this one) use a serif typeface for the body text. Sans-serif typefaces are appropriate for headlines, figure labels, and so on. Many other typefaces have been designed over the centuries, with and without serifs. For example, Garamond is another popular serif-style typeface. A third kind of typeface that you will commonly see is Courier, a font that was originally designed for typewriters.

The design of a good typeface requires artistic judgment and substantial experience. However, in the United States, the shapes of letters are considered industrial design that cannot be protected by copyright. For that reason, typeface designers protect their rights by trademarking the *names* of the fonts. For example, the names "Times Roman" and "Helvetica" are trademarks of the Linotype Corporation. Although other companies can create lookalike fonts (just as certain companies create imitations of famous perfumes), they have to give them different names. That's why you find fonts with names such as "Times New Roman" or "Arial". That makes it bit of a bother to select fonts by their names, especially if you don't know what fonts are available on a particular computer. For that reason, we will specify fonts by their *logical* face names. Java recognizes five logical font names (see Table 2) that are mapped to fonts that exist on every computer system. For example, if you request the "SansSerif" font, then the Java font mapper will go and search for the best general-purpose sans-serif font available. On a computer running the Windows operating system, you will get the "Arial" font. On a Macintosh, you will get "Helvetica".

To create a font, you must specify the *point size:* the height of the font in the typesetter's unit called *points.* The height of a font is measured from the top of the *ascender* (the top part of letters such as *b* and *l*) to the bottom of the *descender* (the bottom part of letters such as *g* and *p*). There are 72 points per inch. For example, a 12-point font has a height of $1/6$ inch. Actually, the point size of a font is only an approximate measure, and you can't necessarily be sure that two fonts with the same point size have matching character sizes. The actual sizes will in any case depend on the size and resolution of your monitor screen. Without getting into fine points of typography, it is best if you simply remember a few typical point sizes: 8 point ("small"), 12 point ("medium"), 18 point ("large"), and 36 point ("huge").

Here is how you can write "Applet" in huge pink letters:

```
final int HUGE_SIZE = 36;
String message = "Applet";
Font hugeFont = new Font("Serif", Font.BOLD, HUGE_SIZE);
g2.setFont(hugeFont);
g2.setColor(Color.pink);
g2.drawString(message, 50, 100);
```

The *x*- and *y*-positions in the `drawString` method can be specified either as `int` or as `float`.

▼ **AT** Advanced Topic 4.2

Accurate Positioning of Text

▼

When drawing strings on the screen, you usually need to position them accurately. For example, if you want to draw two lines of text, one below the other, then you need to

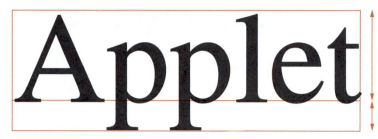

Ascent

Descent

Figure 10

Text Layout Measurements

know the distance between the two basepoints. Of course, the size of a string depends on the shapes of the letters, which in turn depends on the font face and point size. You will need to know a few typographical measurements (see Figure 10):

- The *ascent* of a font is the height of the largest letter above the baseline.

- The *descent* of a font is the depth below the baseline of the letter with the lowest descender.

These values describe the *vertical* extent of strings. The *horizontal* extent depends on the individual letters in a string. In a `monospaced` font, all letters have the same width. Monospaced fonts are still used for computer programs, but for plain text they are as outdated as the typewriter. In a *proportionally spaced font*, different letters have different widths. For example, the letter *l* is much narrower than the letter *m*.

To measure the size of a string, you need to construct a `FontRenderContext` object, which you obtain from the `Graphics2D` object by calling `getFontRenderContext`. A font render context is an object that knows how to transform letter shapes (which are described as curves) into pixels. In general, a "context" object is usually an object that has some specialized knowledge how to carry out complex tasks. You don't have to worry how the context object works; you just create it and pass it along as required. The `Graphics2D` object is another example of a context object—many people call it a "graphics context".

To get the size of a string, you call the `getStringBounds` method of the `Font` class. For example,

```
String message = "Applet";
FontRenderContext context = g2.getFontRenderContext();
Rectangle2D bounds = hugeFont.getStringBounds(message, context);
```

The returned rectangle is positioned so that the origin (0, 0) falls on the basepoint (see Figure 8). Therefore, you can get the ascent, descent, height, and width as

```
double yMessageAscent = -bounds.getY();
double yMessageDescent = bounds.getHeight() + bounds.getY();
double yMessageHeight = bounds.getHeight();
double xMessageWidth = bounds.getWidth();
```

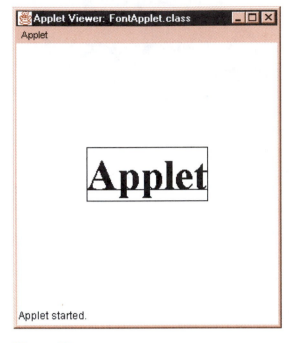

Figure 11

The Font Applet Displays a Centered String

The following program uses these measurements to center a string precisely in the middle of the applet window (see Figure 11). To center the string, you need to know the size of the applet. (The user might have resized it, so you can't simply use the values of width and height in the HTML file.) The getWidth and getHeight methods return the applet size in pixels. To center the string horizontally, think of the amount of blank space that you have available. The width of the applet window is getWidth(). The width of the string is xMessageWidth. Therefore, the blank space is the difference,

```
getWidth() - xMessageWidth
```

Half of that blank space should be distributed on either side. Therefore, the string should start at

```
double xLeft = (getWidth() - xMessageWidth) / 2;
```

For the same reason, the top of the string is at

```
double yTop = (getHeight() - yMessageHeight) / 2;
```

But the drawString method needs the basepoint of the string. You get to the baseposition by adding the ascent:

```
double yBase = yTop + yMessageAscent;
```

Following this note is the complete program. When you run it in the applet viewer, try resizing the applet window and observe that the string always stays centered.

File FontApplet.java

```
1  import java.applet.Applet;
2  import java.awt.Font;
3  import java.awt.Graphics;
4  import java.awt.Graphics2D;
5  import java.awt.font.FontRenderContext;
6  import java.awt.geom.Line2D;
7  import java.awt.geom.Rectangle2D;
8
9  /**
10     This applet draws a string that is centered in the
11     applet window.
12  */
13 public class FontApplet extends Applet
14 {
15    public void paint(Graphics g)
16    {
17       Graphics2D g2 = (Graphics2D)g;
18
19       // select the font into the graphics context
20
21       final int HUGE_SIZE = 48;
22       Font hugeFont =
23          new Font("Serif", Font.BOLD, HUGE_SIZE);
24       g2.setFont(hugeFont);
25
26       String message = "Applet";
27
28       // measure the string
29
30       FontRenderContext context =
31          g2.getFontRenderContext();
32       Rectangle2D bounds =
33          hugeFont.getStringBounds(message, context);
34
35       double yMessageAscent = -bounds.getY();
36       double yMessageDescent =
37          bounds.getHeight() + bounds.getY();
38       double yMessageHeight = bounds.getHeight();
39       double xMessageWidth = bounds.getWidth();
40
41       // center the message in the window
42
43       double xLeft = (getWidth() - xMessageWidth) / 2;
44       double yTop = (getHeight() - yMessageHeight) / 2;
45       double yBase = yTop + yMessageAscent;
46
47       g2.drawString(message, (float)xLeft, (float)yBase);
48       // draw bounding rectangle
49
```

```
50      g2.draw(new Rectangle2D.Double(xLeft, yTop,
51          xMessageWidth, yMessageHeight));
52
53      // draw base line
54      g2.draw(new Line2D.Double(xLeft, yBase,
55          xLeft + xMessageWidth, yBase));
56   }
57 }
```

4.7   Drawing Complex Shapes

> It is a good idea to make a class for each complex graphical shape.

The next program shows how you can put shapes together to draw a simple figure of a car—see Figure 12. It is a good idea to make a separate class for each complex shape that you want to draw. For example, the program at the end of this section defines a Car class.

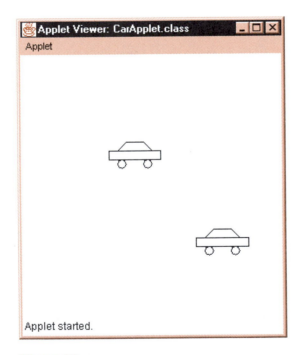

Figure 12

The Car Applet Draws Two Car Shapes

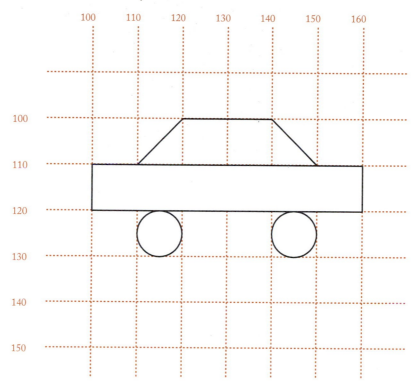

Figure 13

Using Graph Paper to Find Shape Coordinates

```
class Car
{
    . . .
    public void draw(Graphics2D g2)
    {
        // drawing instructions
        . . .
    }
}
```

> To figure out how to draw a complex shape, make a sketch on graph paper.

The coordinates of the car parts seem a bit arbitrary. To come up with suitable values, you want to draw the image on graph paper and read off the coordinates—see Figure 13.

Here is the program. Unfortunately, in programs such as these it is difficult to avoid the "magic numbers" for the coordinates of the various shapes.

File CarApplet.java

```
1 import java.applet.Applet;
2 import java.awt.Graphics;
3 import java.awt.Graphics2D;
```

```
 4  /**
 5      This applet draws two car shapes.
 6  */
 7  public class CarApplet extends Applet
 8  {
 9      public void paint(Graphics g)
10      {
11          Graphics2D g2 = (Graphics2D)g;
12
13          Car car1 = new Car(100, 100);
14          Car car2 = new Car(200, 200);
15
16          car1.draw(g2);
17          car2.draw(g2);
18      }
19  }
```

File Car.java

```
 1  import java.awt.Graphics2D;
 2  import java.awt.geom.Ellipse2D;
 3  import java.awt.geom.Line2D;
 4  import java.awt.geom.Point2D;
 5  import java.awt.geom.Rectangle2D;
 6
 7  /**
 8      A car shape that can be positioned anywhere on the screen.
 9  */
10  public class Car
11  {
12      /**
13          Constructs a car with a given top left corner.
14          @param x  the x-coordinate of the top left corner
15          @param y  the y-coordinate of the top left corner
16      */
17      public Car(double x, double y)
18      {
19          xLeft = x;
20          yTop = y;
21      }
22
23      /**
24          Draws the car.
25          @param g2  the graphics context
26      */
27      public void draw(Graphics2D g2)
28      {
29          Rectangle2D.Double body  = new
```

```
30            Rectangle2D.Double(xLeft, yTop + 10, 60, 10);
31        Ellipse2D.Double frontTire  = new
32            Ellipse2D.Double(xLeft + 10, yTop + 20, 10, 10);
33        Ellipse2D.Double rearTire = new
34            Ellipse2D.Double(xLeft + 40, yTop + 20, 10, 10);
35
36        // the bottom of the windshield
37        Point2D.Double r1
38            = new Point2D.Double(xLeft + 10, yTop + 10);
39        // the front of the roof
40        Point2D.Double r2
41            = new Point2D.Double(xLeft + 20, yTop);
42        // the rear of the roof
43        Point2D.Double r3
44            = new Point2D.Double(xLeft + 40, yTop);
45        // the bottom of the rear window
46        Point2D.Double r4
47            = new Point2D.Double(xLeft + 50, yTop + 10);
48
49        Line2D.Double frontWindshield
50            = new Line2D.Double(r1, r2);
51        Line2D.Double roofTop
52            = new Line2D.Double(r2, r3);
53        Line2D.Double rearWindow
54            = new Line2D.Double(r3, r4);
55
56        g2.draw(body);
57        g2.draw(frontTire);
58        g2.draw(rearTire);
59        g2.draw(frontWindshield);
60        g2.draw(roofTop);
61        g2.draw(rearWindow);
62    }
63
64    private double xLeft;
65    private double yTop;
66 }
```

? HOWTO   **4.1**

Drawing Graphical Shapes

You can program applets that display a wide variety of graphical shapes. These instructions give you a step-by-step procedure how to decompose a drawing into parts and implement a program that produces the drawing.

Step 1 Determine the shapes that you need for the drawing

You can use the following shapes:

- Squares and rectangles
- Circles and ellipses
- Lines

You can draw the outlines of these shapes in any color, or you can fill the insides of these shapes with any color.

You can also use text to label parts of your drawing.

For example, many national flag designs consist of three equally wide sections of different colors, side by side:

You could draw such a flag using three rectangles. But if the middle rectangle is white, as it is, for example, in the flag of Italy (green, white, red), it is easier and looks better just to draw two lines on the top and bottom of the middle portion:

Two lines

Two rectangles

Step 2 Find the coordinates for the shapes

You now need to find the exact positions for the geometric shapes.

- For rectangles, you need the x- and y-position of the top left corner, the width, and height.
- For ellipses, you need the top left corner, width, and height of the bounding rectangle.

- For lines, you need the x- and y-positions of the starting point and the end point.

- For text, you need the x- and y-positions of the basepoint.

A typical size for an applet is 300 by 300 pixels. You may not want the flag crammed all the way to the top, so perhaps the upper left corner of the flag should be at the point (100, 100).

Many flags, such as the flag of Italy, have a width : height ratio of 3 : 2. (You can often find exact proportions for a particular flag by doing a bit of Internet research on one of several Flags of the World sites.) For example, if you make the flag 90 pixels wide, then it should be 60 pixels tall. (Why not make it 100 pixels wide? Then the height would be $100 \cdot 2 / 3 \approx 67$, which seems more awkward.)

Now you can compute the coordinates of all the important points of the shape:

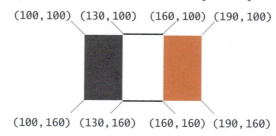

```
(100,100)  (130,100)   (160,100)  (190,100)
```

```
(100,160)  (130,160)   (160,160)  (190,160)
```

Step 3   Write Java statements to draw the shapes

In our example, there are two rectangles and two lines:

```java
Rectangle2D.Double leftRectangle
   = new Rectangle2D.Double(100, 100, 30, 60);
Rectangle2D.Double rightRectangle
   = new Rectangle2D.Double(160, 100, 30, 60);
Line2D.Double topLine
   = new Line2D.Double(130, 100, 160, 100);
Line2D.Double bottomLine
   = new Line2D.Double(130, 160, 160, 160);
```

If you are more ambitious, then you can express the coordinates in terms of a few variables. In the case of the flag, we have arbitrarily chosen the top left corner and the width. All other coordinates follow from those choices. If you decide to follow the ambitious approach, then the rectangles and lines are determined as follows:

```java
Rectangle2D.Double leftRectangle
   = new Rectangle2D.Double(xLeft, yTop,
      width / 3, width * 2 / 3);
Rectangle2D.Double rightRectangle
   = new Rectangle2D.Double(xLeft + width / 3, yTop,
      width / 3, width * 2 / 3);
Line2D.Double topLine
   = new Line2D.Double(xLeft + width / 3, yTop,
      xLeft + width * 2 / 3, yTop);
```

```
Line2D.Double bottomLine
   = new Line2D.Double(
       xLeft + width / 3, yTop + width * 2 / 3,
       xLeft + width * 2 / 3, yTop + width * 2 / 3);
```

Now you need to fill the rectangles and draw the lines. For the flag of Italy, the left rectangle is green and the right rectangle is red. Remember to switch colors before the filling and drawing operations:

```
g2.setColor(Color.green);
g2.fill(leftRectangle);
g2.setColor(Color.red);
g2.fill(rightRectangle);
g2.setColor(Color.black);
g2.draw(topLine);
g2.draw(bottomLine);
```

Step 4 Combine the drawing statements with the applet "plumbing"

The simplest form of the "plumbing" looks like this:

```
public class MyApplet extends Applet
{
   public void paint(Graphics g)
   {
      Graphics2D g2 = (Graphics2D)g;
      // your drawing code goes here
         . . .
   }
}
```

In our example, you can simply add all shapes and drawing instructions inside the `paint` method:

```
public class ItalianFlagApplet extends Applet
{
   public void paint(Graphics g)
   {
      Graphics2D g2 = (Graphics2D)g;
      Rectangle2D.Double leftRectangle
         = new Rectangle2D.Double(100, 100, 30, 60);
         . . .
      g2.setColor(Color.green);
      g2.fill(leftRectangle);
         . . .
   }
}
```

That approach is acceptable for simple drawings, but it is not very object-oriented. After all, a flag is an object. It is better to make a separate class for the flag. Then you can draw different flags at different positions and sizes. Specify the sizes in a constructor and supply a **draw** method:

```
public class ItalianFlag
{
    public ItalianFlag(double x, double y, double aWidth)
    {
        xLeft = x;
        yTop = y;
        width = aWidth;
    }

    public void draw(Graphics2D g2)
    {
        Rectangle2D.Double leftRectangle
            = new Rectangle2D.Double(xLeft, yTop,
                width / 3, width * 2 / 3);
        . . .
        g2.setColor(Color.green);
        g2.fill(leftRectangle);
        . . .
    }

    private double xLeft;
    private double yTop;
    private double width;
}
```

You still need a separate class for the applet, but it is very simple:

```
public class ItalianFlagApplet extends Applet
{
    public void paint(Graphics g)
    {
        Graphics2D g2 = (Graphics2D)g;
        ItalianFlag flag = new ItalianFlag(100, 100, 90);
        flag.draw(g2);
    }
}
```

You may wish to modify this code to make the flag fit comfortably in the applet area even if the applet is not 300 by 300. Use the applet `getWidth()` and `getHeight()` methods to find the actual size of the applet window, and use these dimensions to compute the constructor parameters, similar to what was done for text in Advanced Topic 4.2.

Step 5 Write the HTML file for the applet

To show an applet in the applet viewer or a Java 2-enabled browser, you need an HTML file that specifies the name of the applet class and the desired width and height of the applet. Here is a minimal HTML file for the Italian flag applet:

```
<applet code="ItalianFlagApplet.class"
    width="300" height="300"></applet>
```

▼ If you like, you can add more HTML code around the `applet` tag to describe your applet. The description shows up when you view the HTML file in a browser, but the applet viewer displays only the applet.

▼ **Random Fact** 4.2

Computer Graphics

▼ Generating and manipulating visual images are among the most exciting applications of the computer. We distinguish different kinds of graphics.

▼ *Diagrams, such as numeric charts or maps, are artifacts that convey information to the viewer* (see Figure 14). They do not directly depict anything that occurs in the natural world but are a tool for visualizing information.

▼ *Scenes* are computer-generated images that attempt to depict images of the real or an imagined world (see Figure 15). It turns out to be quite challenging to render light and shadows accurately. Special effort must be taken so that the images do not look overly

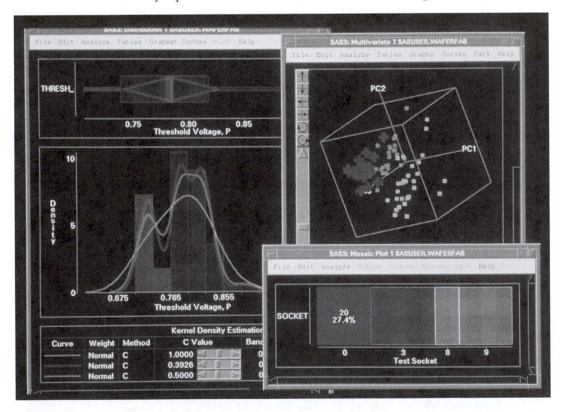

Figure 14

Diagrams

Scene

neat and simple; clouds, rocks, leaves, and dust in the real world have a complex and some-what random appearance. The degree of realism in these images is constantly improving.

Manipulated images are photographs or film footage of actual events that have been converted to digital form and edited by the computer (see Figure 16). For example, film

Manipulated Image

▼

sequences of the movie *Apollo 13* were produced by starting from actual images and changing the perspective, showing the launch of the rocket from a more dramatic viewpoint.

▼

Computer graphics is one of the most challenging fields in computer science. It requires processing of massive amounts of information at very high speed. New algorithms are constantly invented for this purpose. Displaying an overlapping set of three-dimensional objects with curved boundaries requires advanced mathematical tools. Realistic modeling of textures

▼

and biological entities requires extensive knowledge of mathematics, physics, and biology.

4.8   Reading Text Input

The applets that you have seen so far are quite nice for drawing, but they aren't interactive—you can't change the positions of the shapes that are drawn on the screen. Interactive input in a graphical program turns out to be more complex than in a console program. In a console program, the programmer dictates the control flow and forces the user to enter input in a predetermined order. A graphical program, however, generally makes available to the program user a large number of controls (buttons, input fields, scroll bars, and so on), which users can manipulate in any order they please. Therefore, the program must be prepared to process input from multiple sources in random order. You will learn how to do that in Chapter 10.

In the meantime, we will simply read input with the `JOptionPane.showInputDialog` method that you saw in Chapter 3.

You should place any calls to the `showInputDialog` method into the applet constructor, not the `paint` method. That way, the user is prompted for input once, when the applet is first displayed. (If you place the calls to `showInputDialog` inside the `paint` method, then you are prompted for new input every time the applet is repainted.) To get another chance to supply input, select "Reload" or "Refresh" from the browser or applet viewer menu.

If you put the call to `showInputDialog` inside the applet constructor, then your applet needs to remember the user input in one or more instance fields and refer to these variables in the `paint` method. The following program is an example. It prompts the user for red, green, and blue values, and then fills a rectangle with the color that the user specified. For example, if you enter 1.0, 0.7, 0.7, then the rectangle is filled with pink color.

File ColorApplet.java

```
1  import java.applet.Applet;
2  import java.awt.Color;
3  import java.awt.Graphics;
4  import java.awt.Graphics2D;
5  import java.awt.Rectangle;
6  import javax.swing.JOptionPane;
7
8  /**
9      An applet that lets a user choose a color by specifying
10     the fractions of red, green, and blue.
11  */
12  public class ColorApplet extends Applet
13  {
```

```
14      public ColorApplet()
15      {
16         String input;
17         // ask the user for red, green, blue values
18
19         input = JOptionPane.showInputDialog("red:");
20         float red = Float.parseFloat(input);
21
22         input = JOptionPane.showInputDialog("green:");
23         float green = Float.parseFloat(input);
24
25         input = JOptionPane.showInputDialog("blue:");
26         float blue = Float.parseFloat(input);
27
28         fillColor = new Color(red, green, blue);
29      }
30
31      public void paint(Graphics g)
32      {
33         Graphics2D g2 = (Graphics2D)g;
34
35         // select color into graphics context
36
37         g2.setColor(fillColor);
38
39         // construct and fill a square whose center is
40         // the center of the window
41
42         Rectangle square = new Rectangle(
43            (getWidth() - SQUARE_LENGTH) / 2,
44            (getHeight() - SQUARE_LENGTH) / 2,
45            SQUARE_LENGTH,
46            SQUARE_LENGTH);
47
48         g2.fill(square);
49      }
50
51      private static final int SQUARE_LENGTH = 100;
52
53      private Color fillColor;
54   }
```

When you run this program, you will note that the input dialog has a label identifying it as an "applet window" (see Figure 17). That is an applet security feature. It would be an easy matter for a cracker to write an applet that pops up a dialog "Your password has expired. Please reenter your password." and then sends the input back to the web server. If you should happen to visit the web page containing that applet, you might be confused and reenter the password to your computer account, giving it to the cracker. The window label tips you off that it is an applet, and not your operating system, that displays the dialog. All windows that pop up from an applet have this warning label.

Figure 17

Applet Dialog with Warning Label

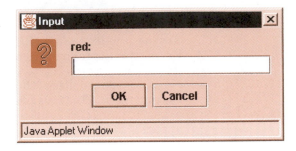

While the input dialog window is on the screen, the user is not allowed to do anything in the browser except type input and click on the OK or Cancel button. This kind of dialog is called a *modal dialog*. A sequence of modal input dialogs can be frustrating to the user, so it is not really a good user interface design. However, it is easy to program, and it makes sense for you to use it until you learn how to gather input in a more professional way—the topic of Chapter 12.

Advanced Topic 4.3

Applet Parameters

You have seen how to use the `showInputDialog` method of the `JOptionPane` class to supply user input to an applet. Another way of supplying input is sometimes useful: Use the `param` tag in the HTML page that loads the applet. The `param` tag has the form

```
<param name="..." value="..." />
```

You place one or more `param` tags between the `<applet>` and `</applet>` tags, like this:

```
<applet code="ColorApplet.class" width="300" height="300">
<param name="Red" value="1.0" />
<param name="Green" value="0.7" />
<param name="Blue" value="0.7" />
</applet>
```

The applet can read these values with the `getParameter` method. For example, when the `ColorApplet` is loaded with the HTML tags given above, then `getParameter("Blue")` returns the string `"0.7"`. Of course, you then need to convert the string into a number.

You cannot call the `getParameter` method in the applet constructor. When the applet is first constructed, the parameters are not yet ready. Instead, you can read them either in the `paint` method or in a special `init` method. The applet viewer or browser calls the `init` method after the constructor but before the first call to `paint`.

```
public class ColorApplet extends Applet
{
    public void init()
```

▼
```
        {
            float r = Float.parseFloat(getParameter("Red"));
            float g = Float.parseFloat(getParameter("Green"));
            float b = Float.parseFloat(getParameter("Blue"));
            fillColor = new Color(r, g, b);
        }
```

▼
```
        public void paint(Graphics g)
        {
            . . .
        }
```

▼
```
        private Color fillColor;
    }
```

Now you can change the color values simply by editing the HTML page.

Comparing Visual and Numerical Information

The next example shows how one can look at the same problem both visually and numerically. You want to figure out the intersection between a circle and a line. The circle has radius 100 and center (100, 100). Ask the user to specify the position of a vertical line. Then draw the circle, the line, and the intersection points (see Figure 18). Label them to display the exact locations.

Exactly where do the two shapes intersect? We need a bit of mathematics. The equation of a circle with radius r and center point (a, b) is

$$(x - a)^2 + (y - b)^2 = r^2$$

If you know x, then you can solve for y:

$$(y - b)^2 = r^2 - (x - a)^2$$

or

$$y - b = \pm\sqrt{r^2 - (x - a)^2}$$

hence

$$y = b \pm \sqrt{r^2 - (x - a)^2}$$

That is easy to compute in Java:

```
        double root = Math.sqrt(r * r - (x - a) * (x - a));
        double y1 = b + root;
        double y2 = b - root;
```

But how do you know that you did both the math and the programming right?

Figure 18

Intersection of a Line and a Circle

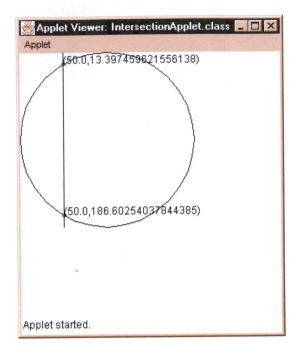

If your program is correct, these two points will show up right on top of the actual intersections in the picture. If not, the two points will be at the wrong place.

If you look at Figure 18, you will see that the results match perfectly, which gives us confidence that everything is correct. See Quality Tip 4.1 for more information on verifying that this program works correctly.

Here is the complete program.

File IntersectionApplet.java

```
1  import java.applet.Applet;
2  import java.awt.Graphics;
3  import java.awt.Graphics2D;
4  import java.awt.geom.Ellipse2D;
5  import java.awt.geom.Line2D;
6  import javax.swing.JOptionPane;
7
8  /**
9      An applet that computes and draws the intersection points
10     of a circle and a line.
11  */
12  public class IntersectionApplet extends Applet
13  {
14     public IntersectionApplet()
15     {
```

```
16        String input
17            = JOptionPane.showInputDialog("x:");
18        x = Integer.parseInt(input);
19      }
20
21    public void paint(Graphics g)
22    {
23        Graphics2D g2 = (Graphics2D)g;
24
25        double r = 100;  // the radius of the circle
26
27        // draw the circle
28
29        Ellipse2D.Double circle  = new
30            Ellipse2D.Double(0, 0, 2 * RADIUS, 2 * RADIUS);
31        g2.draw(circle);
32
33        // draw the vertical line
34
35        Line2D.Double line
36            = new Line2D.Double(x, 0, x, 2 * RADIUS);
37        g2.draw(line);
38
39        // compute the intersection points
40
41        double a = RADIUS;
42        double b = RADIUS;
43
44        double root =
45            Math.sqrt(RADIUS * RADIUS - (x - a) * (x - a));
46        double y1 = b + root;
47        double y2 = b - root;
48
49        // draw the intersection points
50
51        LabeledPoint p1 = new LabeledPoint(x, y1);
52        LabeledPoint p2 = new LabeledPoint(x, y2);
53
54        p1.draw(g2);
55        p2.draw(g2);
56    }
57
58    private static final double RADIUS = 100;
59    private double x;
60 }
```

File LabeledPoint.java

```
1 import java.awt.Graphics2D;
2 import java.awt.geom.Ellipse2D;
```

```
 3  /**
 4      A point with a label showing the point's coordinates.
 5  */
 6  public class LabeledPoint
 7  {
 8      /**
 9          Construct a labeled point.
10          @param anX the x-coordinate
11          @param aY the y-coordinate
12      */
13      public LabeledPoint(double anX, double aY)
14      {
15          x = anX;
16          y = aY;
17      }
18
19      /**
20          Draws the point as a small circle with a coordinate label.
21          @param g2 the graphics context
22      */
23      public void draw(Graphics2D g2)
24      {
25          // draw a small circle centered around (x, y)
26
27          Ellipse2D.Double circle = new Ellipse2D.Double(
28                  x - SMALL_CIRCLE_RADIUS,
29                  y - SMALL_CIRCLE_RADIUS,
30                  2 * SMALL_CIRCLE_RADIUS,
31                  2 * SMALL_CIRCLE_RADIUS);
32
33          g2.draw(circle);
34
35          // draw the label
36
37          String label = "(" + x + "," + y + ")";
38
39          g2.drawString(label, (float)x, (float)y);
40      }
41
42      private static final double SMALL_CIRCLE_RADIUS = 2;
43
44      private double x;
45      private double y;
46  }
```

At this point you should be careful to specify only lines that intersect the circle. If the line doesn't meet the circle, then the program will attempt to compute a square root of a negative number, and a math error will occur. We have not yet discussed how to implement a test to protect against this situation. That will be the topic of the next chapter.

▼ ▶ Quality Tip   **4.1**

Calculate Sample Data Manually

> You should calculate test cases by hand to double-check that your program computes the correct answers.

It is usually difficult or impossible to prove that a given program functions correctly in all cases. For gaining confidence in the correctness of a program, or for understanding why it does not function as it should, manually calculated sample data are invaluable. If the program arrives at the same results as the manual calculation, our confidence in it is strengthened. If the manual results differ from the program results, we have a starting point for the debugging process.

Surprisingly, many programmers are reluctant to perform any manual calculations as soon as a program carries out the slightest bit of algebra. Their math phobia kicks in, and they irrationally hope that they can avoid the algebra and beat the program into submission by random tinkering, such as rearranging the + and − signs. Random tinkering is always a great time sink, but it rarely leads to useful results.

It is much smarter to look for test cases that are representative and easy to compute. In our example, let us look for three easy cases that we can compute by hand and then compare against program runs.

First, let the vertical line pass through the center of the circle. That is, x is 100. Then we expect the distance between the center and the intersection point to be the same as the radius of the circle. Now `root = Math.sqrt(100 * 100 - 0 * 0)`, which is 100. Therefore, y1 is 0 and y2 is 200. Those are indeed the top and bottom points on the circle. Now, that wasn't so hard.

Next, let the line touch the circle on the right. Then x is 200 and `root = Math .sqrt(100 * 100 - 100 * 100)`, which is 0. Therefore, y1 and y2 are both equal to 100, and indeed (200, 100) is the rightmost point of the circle. That also was pretty easy.

The first two cases were *boundary cases* of the problem. A program may work correctly for several special cases but still fail for more typical input values. Therefore we must come up with an intermediate test case, even if it means a bit more computation. Let us pick a simple value for x, say x = 50. Then `root = Math.sqrt(100 * 100 - 50 * 50) =` `Math.sqrt(7500)`. Using a calculator, you get approximately 86.6025. That yields y1 = 100 − 86.6025 = 13.3975 and y2 = 100 + 86.6025 = 186.6025. So what? Run the program and enter 50. First, you will find that the program also computes the same x- and y-values that you computed by hand. That is good—it confirms that you probably typed in the formulas correctly, and the intersection points really do fall on the right place.

4.10   Coordinate Transformations

By default, the `draw` method of the `Graphics2D` class uses *pixels* to measure screen locations. A pixel (short for "picture element") is a dot on the screen. For example, the point (50, 100) is 50 pixels to the right and 100 pixels down from the top left corner of the panel. This default coordinate system is fine for simple test programs, but it is

Figure 19

Plotting Temperature Data

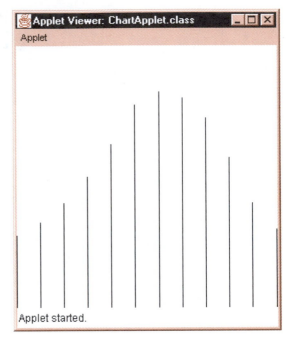

tedious when dealing with real-world data. For example, suppose you want to show a chart plotting the average temperature (degrees Celsius) in Phoenix, Arizona, for every month of the year (see Figure 19). The temperature ranges from 11 degrees Celsius in January to 33 degrees Celsius in July (see Table 3).

Here, the x-values range from 1 to 12 and the y-values range from 11 to 33. The applet pixel coordinates range from 0 to `getWidth()` - 1 and 0 to `getHeight()` - 1. If the width and height of the applet are 300 pixels each, then we can't just use pixel coordinates for the data, or the graph would only occupy a tiny area of the window.

> Pixel coordinates are not useful for real-world data sets. Pick convenient user coordinates and convert to pixels.

In such a situation, you need to define *user coordinates* that makes sense for your particular application and then transform them to pixel coordinates. Suppose the application coordinates range from x_{min} to x_{max} and y_{min} to y_{max}. Then you can transform user coordinates to pixel coordinates, by using the following equations:

$$x_{pixel} = (x_{user} - x_{min}) \cdot (\text{width} - 1) / (x_{max} - x_{min})$$

$$y_{pixel} = (y_{user} - y_{min}) \cdot (\text{height} - 1) / (y_{max} - y_{min})$$

To see that these equations make sense, plug in $x_{user} = x_{min}$ and $x_{user} = x_{max}$ and check that you get $x_{pixel} = 0$ and $x_{pixel} = \text{width} - 1$. Do the same for the y values.

Note that for the y-coordinates, the roles for y_{min} and y_{max} are reversed. In Java, y-coordinates increase when moving down, whereas in mathematics, they increase when moving up. That is, y_{max} corresponds to pixel 0 and y_{min} to pixel height -1.

Let's apply this to our temperature chart. The month range is

$$x_{min} = 1, x_{max} = 12$$

Table 3

Average Temperatures in Phoenix, Arizona

Month	Temperature
January	11
February	13
March	16
April	20
May	25
June	31
July	33
August	32
September	29
October	23
November	16
December	12

We'll choose a temperature range

$$y_{\min} = 0, y_{\max} = 50$$

We draw each data point as a line from (month, 0) to (month, temperature) in user coordinates. Here is how you compute the pixel coordinates.

```
final double XMIN = 1;
final double XMAX = 12;
final double YMIN = 0;
final double YMAX = 50;

double xpixel = (month - XMIN) * (getWidth() - 1) /
   (XMAX - XMIN);
double y1pixel = getHeight() - 1; // 0 in user coordinates
double y2pixel = (temperature - YMAX)
   * (getHeight() - 1) / (YMIN - YMAX);

Line2D.Double bar =
   new Line2D.Double(xpixel, y1pixel, xpixel, y2pixel);
```

This approach works, but it is tedious and can make your code hard to read. It is better to write a couple of simple helper methods for the coordinate transformation.

```
public class Phoenix extends Applet
{
   . . .
   public double xpixel(double xuser)
   {
      return
         (xuser - XMIN) * (getWidth() - 1) / (XMAX - XMIN);
   }

   public double ypixel(double yuser)
   {
      return
         (yuser - YMAX) * (getHeight() - 1) / (YMIN - YMAX);
   }

   private static final double XMIN = 1;
   private static final double XMAX = 12;
   private static final double YMIN = 0;
   private static final double YMAX = 50;
}
```

Now you can compute pixel coordinates conveniently:

```
Line2D.Double stick = new Line2D.Double(
   xpixel(month), ypixel(0),
   xpixel(month), ypixel(temperature));
```

Advanced Topic 4.4 shows another solution that is even more elegant.

Here is the complete program for drawing the temperature bar chart. Figure 18 shows the output.

File ChartApplet.java

```
1  import java.applet.Applet;
2  import java.awt.Graphics;
3  import java.awt.Graphics2D;
4  import java.awt.geom.Line2D;
5
6  /**
7     This applet draws a chart of the average monthly
8     temperatures in Phoenix, AZ.
9  */
10 public class ChartApplet extends Applet
11 {
12    public void paint(Graphics g)
13    {
14       Graphics2D g2 = (Graphics2D)g;
15
16       month = 1;
```

```
17        drawBar(g2, JAN_TEMP);
18        drawBar(g2, FEB_TEMP);
19        drawBar(g2, MAR_TEMP);
20        drawBar(g2, APR_TEMP);
21        drawBar(g2, MAY_TEMP);
22        drawBar(g2, JUN_TEMP);
23        drawBar(g2, JUL_TEMP);
24        drawBar(g2, AUG_TEMP);
25        drawBar(g2, SEP_TEMP);
26        drawBar(g2, OCT_TEMP);
27        drawBar(g2, NOV_TEMP);
28        drawBar(g2, DEC_TEMP);
29     }
30
31     /**
32        Draws a bar for the current month and increments
33        the month.
34        @param g2 the graphics context
35        @param temperature the temperature for the month
36     */
37     public void drawBar(Graphics2D g2, int temperature)
38     {
39        Line2D.Double bar
40           = new Line2D.Double(xpixel(month), ypixel(0),
41              xpixel(month), ypixel(temperature));
42
43        g2.draw(bar);
44
45        month++;
46     }
47
48     /**
49        Converts from user coordinates to pixel coordinates.
50        @param xuser an x value in user coordinates
51        @return the corresponding value in pixel coordinates
52     */
53     public double xpixel(double xuser)
54     {
55        return
56           (xuser - XMIN) * (getWidth() - 1) /
57           (XMAX - XMIN);
58     }
59
60     /**
61        Converts from user coordinates to pixel coordinates.
62        @param yuser a y-value in user coordinates
63        @return the corresponding value in pixel coordinates
64     */
65     public double ypixel(double yuser)
66     {
```

```
67        return
68            (yuser - YMAX) * (getHeight() - 1) /
69            (YMIN - YMAX);
70    }
71
72    private static final int JAN_TEMP = 11;
73    private static final int FEB_TEMP = 13;
74    private static final int MAR_TEMP = 16;
75    private static final int APR_TEMP = 20;
76    private static final int MAY_TEMP = 25;
77    private static final int JUN_TEMP = 31;
78    private static final int JUL_TEMP = 33;
79    private static final int AUG_TEMP = 32;
80    private static final int SEP_TEMP = 29;
81    private static final int OCT_TEMP = 23;
82    private static final int NOV_TEMP = 16;
83    private static final int DEC_TEMP = 12;
84
85    private static final double XMIN = 1;
86    private static final double XMAX = 12;
87    private static final double YMIN = 0;
88    private static final double YMAX = 40;
89
90    private int month;
91 }
```

▼ AT Advanced Topic   4.4

Let the Graphics Context Transform the Coordinates

You can change the coordinate system of the graphics context. At the beginning of the
paint method, insert the following two calls:

```
double xscale = (getWidth() - 1.0) / (XMAX - XMIN);
double yscale = (getHeight() - 1.0) / (YMIN - YMAX);
g2.scale(xscale, yscale);
g2.translate(-XMIN, -YMAX);
g2.setStroke(new BasicStroke(0));
```

Now the graphics context translates user coordinates to pixels, leaving the programmer
to focus on more important issues. You simply draw objects in user coordinates, such as

```
Line2D.Double rect =
    new Line2D.Double(month, 0, month, temperature);
```

The call to setStroke is necessary to set the line thickness. The default drawing operation draws lines of width 1 in user coordinates, which would result in lines that are much

▼ too fat. A stroke with thickness zero is always drawn one pixel wide. Font size is also specified in user coordinates. If your drawing contains fonts, you need to divide the point size by `Math.max(xscale, -yscale)`.

▼ The program after this note shows how the chart applet is implemented with graphics context transformations. Note that the `xpixel` and `ypixel` methods are no longer required.

File ChartApplet.java

```java
1  import java.applet.Applet;
2  import java.awt.BasicStroke;
3  import java.awt.Graphics;
4  import java.awt.Graphics2D;
5  import java.awt.geom.Line2D;
6
7  /**
8      This applet draws a chart of the average monthly
9      temperatures in Phoenix, AZ.
10 */
11 public class ChartApplet extends Applet
12 {
13    public void paint(Graphics g)
14    {
15       Graphics2D g2 = (Graphics2D)g;
16
17       double xscale =
18          (getWidth() - 1.0) / (XMAX - XMIN);
19       double yscale =
20          (getHeight() - 1.0) / (YMIN - YMAX);
21       g2.scale(xscale, yscale);
22       g2.translate(-XMIN, -YMAX);
23       g2.setStroke(new BasicStroke(0));
24
25       month = 1;
26
27       drawBar(g2, JAN_TEMP);
28       drawBar(g2, FEB_TEMP);
29       drawBar(g2, MAR_TEMP);
30       drawBar(g2, APR_TEMP);
31       drawBar(g2, MAY_TEMP);
32       drawBar(g2, JUN_TEMP);
33       drawBar(g2, JUL_TEMP);
34       drawBar(g2, AUG_TEMP);
35       drawBar(g2, SEP_TEMP);
36       drawBar(g2, OCT_TEMP);
37       drawBar(g2, NOV_TEMP);
38       drawBar(g2, DEC_TEMP);
39    }
```

```
40    /**
41       Draws a bar for the current month and increments
42       the month.
43       @param g2 the graphics context
44       @param temperature the temperature for the month
45    */
46    public void drawBar(Graphics2D g2, int temperature)
47    {
48       Line2D.Double bar = new
49          Line2D.Double(month, 0, month, temperature);
50
51       g2.draw(bar);
52
53       month++;
54    }
55
56    private static final int JAN_TEMP = 11;
57    private static final int FEB_TEMP = 13;
58    private static final int MAR_TEMP = 16;
59    private static final int APR_TEMP = 20;
60    private static final int MAY_TEMP = 25;
61    private static final int JUN_TEMP = 31;
62    private static final int JUL_TEMP = 33;
63    private static final int AUG_TEMP = 32;
64    private static final int SEP_TEMP = 29;
65    private static final int OCT_TEMP = 23;
66    private static final int NOV_TEMP = 16;
67    private static final int DEC_TEMP = 12;
68
69    private static final double XMIN = 1;
70    private static final double XMAX = 12;
71    private static final double YMIN = 0;
72    private static final double YMAX = 40;
73
74    private int month;
75 }
```

Productivity Hint 4.1

Choose Convenient Units for Drawing

Whenever you deal with real-world data, you should use units that are matched to the data. Figure out which range of x- and y-coordinates is most appropriate for the program data. For example, suppose you want to display a tic-tac-toe board (see Figure 20) that is supposed to fill the entire applet.

▼   **Figure 20**

▼   A Tic-Tac-Toe Board

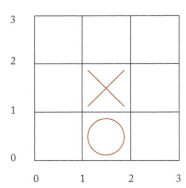

Of course, you could labor mightily and figure out where the lines are in relation to the default pixel coordinate system. Or you can simply set your own units with both *x* and *y* going from 0 to 3.

```
g2.draw(new Line2D.Double(
    xpixel(0), ypixel(1), xpixel(3), ypixel(1)));
g2.draw(new Line2D.Double(
    xpixel(0), ypixel(2), xpixel(3), ypixel(2)));
g2.draw(new Line2D.Double(
    xpixel(2), ypixel(0), xpixel(1), ypixel(3)));
g2.draw(new Line2D.Double(
    xpixel(2), ypixel(0), xpixel(2), ypixel(3)));
```

Some people have horrible memories about coordinate transformations from their high-school geometry class and have taken a vow never to think about coordinates again for the remainder of their lives. If you are among them, you should reconsider. If pixel coordinates are a poor match for your drawing, you may end up spending a lot of time fussing with coordinates to get the drawing right. Pick the right coordinate system and use the standard conversion functions (or, even better, let the graphics context do them, as described in Advanced Topic 4.4). Then all the horrible algebra is done automatically for you, so you don't have to program it by hand.

CHAPTER SUMMARY

1. There are three types of Java programs: *console applications*, *applets*, and *graphics applications*.

2. Applets are programs that run inside a web browser.

3. The applet security mechanisms let you execute applets safely on your computer.

4. Web pages are written in HTML, using tags to format text and include images.

5. To run an applet, you need an HTML page with the `applet` tag.

6. You view applets with the applet viewer or a Java-enabled browser.

7. Your applet class needs to extend the `Applet` class.

8. You draw graphical shapes in an applet by placing the drawing code inside the `paint` method. The `paint` method is called whenever the applet needs to be refreshed.

9. The `Graphics2D` class stores the graphics state (such as the current color) and has methods to draw shapes. You need to cast the `Graphics` parameter of the `paint` method to `Graphics2D` to use these methods.

10. The `Rectangle2D.Double`, `Ellipse2D.Double`, and `Line2D.Double` classes describe graphical shapes.

11. When you set a new color in the graphics context, it is used for subsequent drawing operations.

12. The `drawString` method of the `Graphics2D` class draws a string, starting at its basepoint.

13. A font is described by its face name, style, and point size.

14. It is a good idea to make a class for each complex graphical shape.

15. To figure out how to draw a complex shape, make a sketch on graph paper.

16. An applet can obtain input by displaying a `JOptionPane` in its constructor.

17. You should calculate test cases by hand to double-check that your application computes the correct answer.

18. Pixel coordinates are not useful for real-world data sets. Pick convenient user coordinates and convert to pixels.

References

[1] For details about the XHTML standard, see http://www.w3.org/MarkUp/.

CLASSES, OBJECTS, AND METHODS INTRODUCED IN THIS CHAPTER

```
java.applet.Applet
    getHeight
    getWidth
    init
    paint
java.awt.BasicStroke
java.awt.Color
java.awt.Font
```

```
      getStringBounds
java.awt.Graphics
java.awt.Graphics2D
   draw
   drawString
   fill
   getFontRenderContext
   getParameter
   scale
   setColor
   setFont
   setStroke
   translate
java.awt.font.FontRenderContext
java.awt.geom.Ellipse2D.Double
java.awt.geom.Line2D.Double
   getX1
   getX2
   getY1
   getY2
   setLine
java.awt.geom.Point2D.Double
   getX
   getY
   setLocation
java.awt.geom.Rectangle2D.Double
java.awt.geom.RectangularShape
   getCenterX
   getCenterY
   getMaxX
   getMaxY
   getMinX
   getMinY
   getWidth
   getHeight
   setFrameFromDiagonal
java.lang.Float
   parseFloat
javax.swing.JOptionPane
   showInputDialog
```

REVIEW EXERCISES

Exercise R4.1. What is the difference between an applet and an application?

Exercise R4.2. What is the difference between a browser and the applet viewer?

Exercise R4.3. Why do you need an HTML page to run an applet?

Exercise R4.4. Who calls the `paint` method of an applet? When does the call to the `paint` method occur?

Exercise R4.5. Why does the parameter of the `paint` method have type `Graphics` and not `Graphics2D`?

Exercise R4.6. What is the purpose of a graphics context?

Exercise R4.7. How do you specify a text color?

Exercise R4.8. What is the difference between a font and a font face?

Exercise R4.9. What is the difference between a monospaced font and a proportionally spaced font?

Exercise R4.10. What are serifs?

Exercise R4.11. What is a logical font?

Exercise R4.12. How do you determine the pixel dimensions of a string in a particular font?

Exercise R4.13. Which classes are used in this chapter for drawing graphical shapes?

Exercise R4.14. What are the three different classes for specifying rectangles in the Java library?

Exercise R4.15. You want to plot a bar chart showing the grade distribution of all students in your class (where A = 4.0, F = 0). What coordinate system would you choose to make the plotting as simple as possible?

Exercise R4.16. Let e be any ellipse. Write Java code to plot the ellipse e and another ellipse of the same size that touches e. *Hint:* You need to look up the accessors that tell you the dimensions of an ellipse.

Exercise R4.17. Write Java instructions to display the letters X and T in a graphics window, by plotting line segments.

Exercise R4.18. Introduce an error in the program `Intersect.java`, by computing `double root = Math.sqrt(r * r + (x - a) * (x - a));`. Run the program. What happens to the intersection points?

Exercise R4.19. Suppose you run the `Intersect` program and give a value of 30 for the *x*-position of the vertical line. Without actually running the program, determine what values you will obtain for the intersection points.

PROGRAMMING EXERCISES

Exercise P4.1. Write a graphics program that draws your name in red, centered inside a blue rectangle.

Exercise P4.2. Write a graphics program that draws your name four times, in a large serif font, in plain, bold, italic, and bold italic. The names should be stacked on top of each other, with equal distance between them. Each of them should be centered horizontally, and the entire stack should be centered vertically.

Exercise P4.3. Write a graphics program that draws twelve strings, one each for the 12 standard colors besides `Color.white`, each in its own color.

Exercise P4.4. Write a graphics program that prompts the user to enter a radius. Draw a circle with that radius.

Exercise P4.5. Write a program that draws two solid circles: one in pink and one in purple. Use a standard color for one of them and a custom color for the other.

Exercise P4.6. Draw a "bull's eye"—a set of concentric rings in alternating black and white colors. *Hint:* Fill a black circle, then fill a smaller white circle on top, and so on.

Exercise P4.7. Write a program that fills the applet window with a large ellipse, filled with your favorite color, that touches the window boundaries. The ellipse should resize itself when you resize the window.

Exercise P4.8. Write a program that draws the picture of a house. It could be as simple as the accompanying figure, or if you like, make it more elaborate (3-D, skyscraper, marble columns in the entryway, whatever).

Implement a class `House` and supply a method `draw(Graphics2D g2)` that draws the house.

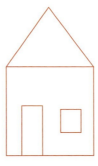

Exercise P4.9. Extend Exercise 4.8 by allowing the user to specify houses of different sizes in the `House` constructor. Then populate your screen with a few houses of different sizes.

Exercise P4.10. Write a program to plot the following face.

Exercise P4.11. Write a program to plot the string "HELLO", using just lines and circles. Do not call `drawString`, and do not use `System.out`. Make classes `LetterH`, `LetterE`, `LetterL` and `LetterO`.

Exercise P4.12. *Plotting a data set.* Make a bar chart to plot the following data set:

Bridge Name	Longest Span (ft)
Golden Gate	4,200
Brooklyn	1,595
Delaware Memorial	2,150
Mackinac	3,800

Make the bars horizontal for easier labeling. *Hint:* Set the window coordinates to 5,000 in the *x*-direction and 4 in the *y*-direction.

Exercise P4.13. Write a graphics program that displays the values of Exercise 4.11 as a *pie chart.* Just draw a circle and the edges of the pie slices. You don't have to color the slices. (If you want to color them, look at the online API documentation for the `Arc2D` class.)

Exercise P4.14. Write a program that displays the Olympic rings.

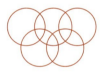

Color the rings in the Olympic colors.

Exercise P4.15. Write a graphics program that draws a clock face with a time that the user enters in a text field. (The user must enter the time in the format `hh:mm`, for example `09:45`.)

Hint: You need to find out the angles of the hour hand and the minute hand. The angle of the minute hand is easy: The minute hand travels 360 degrees in 60 minutes. The angle of the hour hand is harder; it travels 360 degrees in 12 × 60 minutes.

Design a class `Clock` and supply a method `draw(Graphics2D g2)` that draws the clock.

Exercise P4.16. Change the `CarApplet` program to make the cars appear twice the size of the original example.

Exercise P4.17. Change the `CarApplet` program to make the cars appear in different colors. Each `Car` object should store its own color.

Exercise P4.18. Design a class `Truck` whose constructor takes the top left corner point of the truck. Supply a method `draw(Graphics2D g2)` that draws the truck. Then populate your screen with a few cars and trucks.

Decisions

To be able to implement decisions using if statements

▶ To understand how to group statements into blocks

▶ To learn how to compare integers, floating-point numbers, strings, and objects

▶ To recognize the correct ordering of decisions in multiple branches

▶ To program conditions using Boolean operators and variables

The programs we have seen so far were able to do fast computations and render graphs, but they were very inflexible. Except for variations in the input, they worked the same way with every program run. One of the essential features of nontrivial computer programs is the ability to make decisions and to carry out different actions, depending on the nature of the inputs. The goal of this chapter is to learn how to program simple and complex decisions.

5.1 The if Statement

Consider the bank account class of Chapter 3. The withdraw method allows you to withdraw as much money from the account as you like. The balance just moves ever further into the negatives. That is not a realistic model for a bank account. Let's implement the withdraw method so that you cannot withdraw more money than you have in the account. That is, the withdraw method must make a *decision:* whether to allow the withdrawal or not.

> The if statement lets a program carry out different actions depending on the outcome of a condition.

The if statement is used to implement a decision. The if statement has two parts: a *test* and a *body*. If the test succeeds, the body of the statement is executed. The body of the if statement consists of a statement:

```
if (amount <= balance)
    balance = balance - amount;
```

The assignment statement is carried out only when the amount to be withdrawn is less than or equal to the balance. (See Figure 1.)

Let us make the withdraw method of the BankAccount even more realistic. Most banks not only disallow withdrawals that exceed your account balance; they also—adding insult to injury—charge you a penalty for every attempt to do so.

You can't simply program that by providing two complementary if statements:

```
if (amount <= balance)
    balance = balance - amount;
if (amount > balance) // NO
    balance = balance - OVERDRAFT_PENALTY;
```

There are two problems with this approach. First, if you need to modify the condition amount <= balance for some reason, you must remember to update the condition

Figure 1

Flowchart for an if Statement

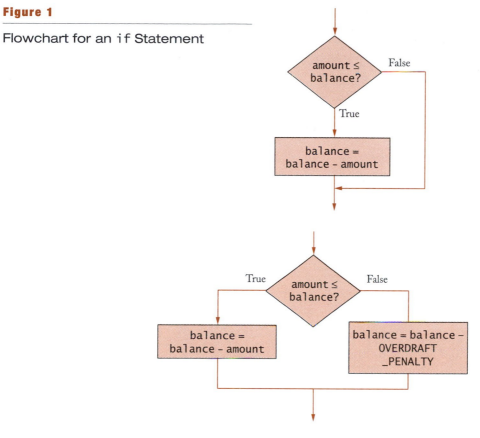

Figure 2

Flowchart for an if/else Statement

amount > balance as well. If you do not, the logic of the program will no longer be correct. More importantly, if you modify the value of balance in the body of the first if statement (as in this example), then the second condition uses the new value.

To implement a choice between alternatives, use the if/else statement:

```
if (amount <= balance)
    balance = balance - amount;
else
    balance = balance - OVERDRAFT_PENALTY;
```

> A block statement groups together several statements.

Now there is only one condition. If it is satisfied, the first statement is executed. Otherwise, the second is executed. The flowchart in Figure 2 gives a graphical representation of the branching behavior.

Quite often, however, the body of the if statement consists of multiple statements that must be executed in sequence whenever the test is successful. These statements must be grouped together to form a *block statement* by enclosing them in braces { }. Here is an example.

```
if (amount <= balance)
{
    double newBalance = balance - amount;
    balance = newBalance;
}
```

Syntax 5.1: The if Statement

```
if (condition)
    statement
```

```
if (condition)
    statement
else
    statement
```

Example:

```
if (amount <= balance)
    balance = balance - amount;
```

```
if (amount <= balance)
    balance = balance - amount;
else
    balance = balance - OVERDRAFT_PENALTY;
```

Purpose:

To execute a statement when a condition is true or false

Syntax 5.2: Block Statement

```
{
    statement
    statement
    . . .
}
```

Example:

```
{
    double newBalance = balance - amount;
    balance = newBalance;
}
```

Purpose:

To group several statements together to form a single statement

A statement such as

```
balance = balance - amount;
```

is called a *simple statement*. A conditional statement such as

```
if (x >= 0) y = x;
```

is called a *compound statement*. In Chapter 6, you will encounter loop statements; they too are compound statements.

The body of an if statement or the else alternative must be a statement—that is, a simple statement, a compound statement (such as another if statement), or a block statement.

Advanced Topic   5.1

The Selection Operator

Java has a selection operator of the form

test ?   *value1* :   *value2*

The value of that expression is either *value1* if the test passes or *value2* if it fails. For example, we can compute the absolute value as

```
y = x >= 0 ? x : -x;
```

which is a convenient shorthand for

```
if (x >= 0)
    y = x;
else
    y = -x;
```

The selection operator is similar to the if/else statement, but it works on a different syntactical level. The selection operator combines *expressions* and yields another expression. The if/else statement combines statements and yields another statement.

Expressions have values. For example, balance + amount is an expression, as is x >= 0 ? x : -x. Any expression can be made into a statement by adding a semicolon. For example, y = x is an expression (with value x), but y = x; is a statement. Statements do not have values. Since if/else forms a statement and does not have a value, you cannot write

```
y = if (x > 0) x; else -x; // Error
```

We don't use the selection operator in this book, but it is a convenient and legitimate construct that you will find in many Java programs.

Quality Tip   5.1

Brace Layout

The compiler doesn't care where you place braces, but we strongly recommend that you follow a simple rule: *Line up* { and }.

```
if (amount <= balance)
{
   double newBalance = balance - amount;
   balance = newBalance;
}
```

This scheme makes it easy to spot matching braces.

Some programmers put the opening brace on the same line as the if:

```
if (amount <= balance) {
   double newBalance = balance - amount;
   balance = newBalance;
}
```

That saves a line of code, but it makes it harder to match the braces.

It is important that you pick a layout scheme and stick with it consistently. Which scheme you choose may depend on your personal preference or a coding style guide that you need to follow.

Productivity Hint 5.1

Indentation and Tabs

When writing Java programs, you use *indentation to indicate nesting levels:*

```
public class BankAccount
{
|  . . .
|  public void withdraw(double amount)
|  {
|  |  if (amount <= balance)
|  |  {
|  |  |  double newBalance = balance - amount;
|  |  |  balance = newBalance;
|  |  }
|  }
|  . . .
}
0  1  2  3
```
Indentation level

How many spaces should you use per indentation level? Some programmers use eight spaces per level, but that isn't a good choice:

```
public class BankAccount
{

        . . .
        public void withdraw(double amount)
        {
                if (amount <= balance)
                {
```

```
                            double newBalance =
                                   balance - amount;
                            balance = newBalance;
                     }
              }
               . . .
       }
```

It crowds the code too much to the right side of the screen. As a consequence, long expressions frequently must be broken into separate lines. More common values are two, three, or four spaces per indentation level.

How do you move the cursor from the leftmost column to the appropriate indentation level? A perfectly reasonable strategy is to hit the space bar a sufficient number of times. However, many programmers use the Tab key instead. A tab moves the cursor to the next tab stop. By default, there are tab stops every eight columns, but most editors let you change that value; you should find out how to set your editor's tab stops to, say, every three columns.

Some editors actually help you out with an *autoindent* feature. They automatically insert as many tabs or spaces as the preceding line had, because the new line is quite likely to belong to the same logical indentation level. If it isn't, you must add or remove a tab, but that is still faster than tabbing all the way from the left margin.

As nice as tabs are for data entry, they have one disadvantage: They can mess up printouts. If you send a file with tabs to a printer, the printer may either ignore the tabs altogether or set tab stops every eight columns. It is therefore best to save and print your files with spaces instead of tabs. Most editors have settings that convert tabs to spaces before you save or print a file.

5.2 Comparing Values

5.2.1 Relational Operators

Every `if` statement performs a test. In many cases, the test compares two values. For example, in the previous example we tested `amount <= balance`. Comparison operators such as `<=` are called *relational operators*. Java has six relational operators:

Java	Math Notation	Description
>	$>$	Greater than
>=	$\geq$	Greater than or equal
<	$<$	Less than
<=	$\leq$	Less than or equal
==	$=$	Equal
!=	$\neq$	Not equal

> Relational operators compare values. The == operator tests for equality.

As you can see, only two Java relational operators (> and <) look as you would expect from the mathematical notation. Computer keyboards do not have keys for ≥, ≤, or ≠ , but the >=, <=, and != operators are easy to remember because they look similar.

The == operator is initially confusing to most newcomers to Java. In Java, the = symbol already has a meaning, namely assignment. The == operator denotes equality testing:

```
a = 5; // assign 5 to a
if (a == 5) ... //   test whether a equals 5
```

You will have to remember to use == for equality testing and to use = for assignment.

5.2.2 — Comparing Floating-Point Numbers

Floating-point numbers have only a limited precision, and calculations can introduce roundoff errors. For example, the following code multiplies the square root of 2 by itself and then subtracts 2.

```
double r = Math.sqrt(2);
double d = r * r - 2;
if (d == 0)
   System.out.println("sqrt(2) squared minus 2 is 0");
else
   System.out.println(
      "sqrt(2) squared minus 2 is not 0 but " +  d);
```

Even though the laws of mathematics tell us that equals 0, this program fragment prints

```
sqrt(2) squared minus 2 is not 0 but 4.440892098500626E-16
```

> When comparing floating-point numbers, don't test for equality. Instead, check whether they are *close enough*.

Unfortunately, such roundoff errors are unavoidable. It plainly does not make sense in most circumstances to compare floating-point numbers exactly. Instead, we should test whether they are *close enough*.

To test whether a number x is close to zero, you can test whether the absolute value $|x|$ (that is, the number with its sign removed) is less than a very small threshold number. That threshold value is often called ε (the Greek letter epsilon). It is common to set ε to 10^{-14} when testing `double` numbers.

In Java, we program the test as follows: x is close to 0 if

```
Math.abs(x) <= EPSILON
```

where we define

```
final double EPSILON = 1E-14;
```

Similarly, you can test whether two numbers are close to each other by checking whether their difference is close to 0.

$$|x - y| \le \varepsilon$$

However, this is not always good enough. Suppose x and y are rather large, say a few billion each. Then they could be the same, except for a roundoff error, even if their difference was quite a bit larger than 10^{-14}. To overcome this problem, you need to divide by the magnitude of the numbers before comparing how close they are. Here is the formula: x and y are close enough if

$$\frac{|x - y|}{\max(|x|, |y|)} \leq \varepsilon$$

In Java, the code for this test is

```
Math.abs(x-y) / Math.max(Math.abs(x), Math.abs(y))
    <= EPSILON;
```

For this test to work, both x and y must be nonzero. If one of the values is zero, you lose the magnitude information. Then all you can do is test whether the absolute value of the other number is at most ε.

5.2.3 — Comparing Strings

> Do not use the == operator to compare strings. Use the equals method instead.

To test whether two strings are equal to each other, you must use the method called `equals`:

```
if (string1.equals(string2)) ...
```

Do not use the == operator to compare strings! The expression

```
if (string1 == string2) // not useful
```

has an unrelated meaning. It tests whether the two string variables refer to the *identical* string object. You can have strings with identical contents stored in different objects, so this test never makes sense in actual programming; see Common Error 5.1.

In Java, letter case matters. For example, "Harry" and "HARRY" are not the same string. To ignore the letter case, use the `equalsIgnoreCase` method:

```
if (string1.equalsIgnoreCase(string2)) ...
```

> The compareTo method compares strings in dictionary order.

If two strings are not identical to each other, you still may want to know the relationship between them. The `compareTo` method compares strings in dictionary order. If

```
string1.compareTo(string2) < 0
```

then the string `string1` comes before the string `string2` in the dictionary. For example, this is the case if `string1` is "Harry", and `string2` is "Hell". If

```
string1.compareTo(string2) > 0
```

then `string1` comes after `string2` in dictionary order. Finally, if

```
string1.compareTo(string2) == 0
```

then `string1` and `string2` are equal.

Actually, the "dictionary" ordering used by Java is slightly different from that of a normal dictionary. Java is case-sensitive and sorts characters by putting numbers first, then uppercase characters, then lowercase characters. For example, 1 comes before B, which comes before a. The space character comes before all other characters.

Figure 3

Lexicographic Comparison

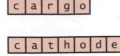

Let us investigate the comparison process closely. When Java compares two strings, corresponding letters are compared until one of the strings ends or the first difference is encountered. If one of the strings ends, the longer string is considered the later one. If a character mismatch is found, the characters are compared to determine which string comes later in the dictionary sequence. This process is called *lexicographic* comparison. For example, let's compare "car" with "cargo". The first three letters match, and we reach the end of the first string. Therefore "car" comes before "cargo" in the lexicographic ordering. Now compare "cathode" with "cargo". The first two letters match. In the third character position, t comes after r, so the string "cathode" comes after "cargo" in lexicographic ordering. (See Figure 3.)

⊗ Common Error   5.1

Using == to Compare Strings

It is an extremely common error in Java to write == when `equals` is intended. This is particularly true for strings. If you write

```
if (nickname == "Rob")
```

then the test succeeds only if the variable `nickname` refers to the exact same string object as the string constant "Rob". For efficiency, Java makes only one string object for every string constant. Therefore, the following test will pass:

```
String nickname = "Rob";
...
if (nickname == "Rob") // test is true
```

However, if the string with the letters R o b has been assembled in some other way, then the test will fail:

```
String name = "Robert";
String nickname = name.substring(0, 3);
...
if (nickname == "Rob") // test is false
```

This is a particularly distressing situation: The wrong code will sometimes do the right thing, sometimes the wrong thing. Since string objects are always constructed by the compiler, you never have an interest in whether two string objects are shared. You must remember never to use == to compare strings. Always use `equals` or `compareTo` to compare strings.

5.2.4 — Comparing Objects

If you compare two object references with the == operator, you test whether the references refer to the same *object*. Here is an example:

```
Rectangle cerealBox = new Rectangle(5, 10, 20, 30);
Rectangle r = cerealBox;
Rectangle oatmealBox = new Rectangle(5, 10, 20, 30);
```

The comparison

```
cerealBox == r
```

is true. Both object variables refer to the same object. But the comparison

```
cerealBox == oatmealBox
```

> The == operator tests whether two object references are identical. To compare the contents of objects, you need to use the equals method.

is false. The two object variables refer to *different* objects (see Figure 4). It does not matter that the objects have identical contents.

You can use the equals method to test whether two rectangles have the same *contents*, that is, whether they have the same upper left corner and the same width and height. For example, the test

```
cerealBox.equals(oatmealBox)
```

is true.

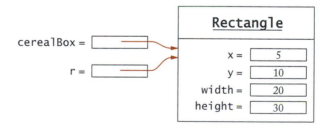

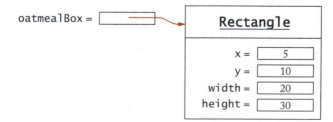

Figure 4

Comparing Object References

However, you must be careful when using the `equals` method. It works correctly only if the implementors of the class have defined it. The `Rectangle` class has an `equals` method that is suitable for comparing rectangles.

For your own classes, you need to supply an appropriate `equals` method. You will learn how to do that in Chapter 9. Until that point, you should not use the `equals` method to compare objects of your own classes.

5.2.5 — Testing for `null`

An object reference can have the special value `null` if it refers to no object at all. You use the `==` operator (and not `equals`) to test whether an object reference is a `null` reference:

```
if (account == null) . . .
    // account is a null reference
```

> The null reference refers to no object.

Frequently, methods return `null` if they are not able to return a valid object. For example, the `showInputDialog` method of the `JOptionPane` class returns `null` if the user hits the "Cancel" button of the input dialog.

```
String input = JOptionPane.showInputDialog(
    "How many nickels do you have?");
if (input == null) . . .
    // user canceled dialog
```

Note that the `null` reference is *not the same* as the empty string `""`. The empty string is a valid string of length 0, whereas a `null` indicates that a string variable refers to no string at all. For example, the `showInputDialog` method returns an empty string if the user leaves the input field of an input dialog blank and hits the "Ok" button.

▼

Quality Tip   5.2

Avoid Conditions with Side Effects

▼

In Java, it is legal to nest assignment statements inside test conditions:

```
if ((d = b * b - 4 * a * c) >= 0) r = Math.sqrt(d);
```

▼   It is legal to use the decrement operator inside other expressions:

```
if (n-- > 0)  ...
```

▼   These are bad programming practices, because they mix a test with another activity. The other activity (setting the variable d, decrementing n) is called a *side effect* of the test.

As you will see in Advanced Topic 6.2, conditions with side effects can occasionally
▼   be helpful to simplify *loops*. For `if` statements they should always be avoided.

5.3 Multiple Alternatives

5.3.1 — Sequences of Comparisons

> Multiple conditions can be combined to evaluate complex decisions. The correct arrangement depends on the logic of the problem to be solved.

The following program asks for a value describing the magnitude of an earthquake on the Richter scale and prints a description of the likely impact of the quake. The Richter scale is a measurement for the strength of an earthquake. Every step in the scale, for example from 6.0 to 7.0, signifies a tenfold increase in the strength of the quake. The 1989 Loma Prieta earthquake that damaged the Bay Bridge in San Francisco and destroyed many buildings in several Bay Area cities registered 7.1 on the Richter scale.

File Earthquake.java

```
 1  /**
 2      A class that describes the effects of an earthquake.
 3  */
 4  public class Earthquake
 5  {
 6      /**
 7          Constructs an Earthquake object.
 8          @param magnitude the magnitude on the Richter scale
 9      */
10      public Earthquake(double magnitude)
11      {
12          richter = magnitude;
13      }
14
15      /**
16          Gets a description of the effect of the earthquake.
17          @return the description of the effect
18      */
19      public String getDescription()
20      {
21          String r;
22          if (richter >= 8.0)
23              r = "Most structures fall";
24          else if (richter >= 7.0)
25              r = "Many buildings destroyed";
26          else if (richter >= 6.0)
27              r = "Many buildings considerably damaged;"
28                  + "some collapse";
29          else if (richter >= 4.5)
30              r = "Damage to poorly constructed buildings";
31          else if (richter >= 3.5)
32              r = "Felt by many people, no destruction";
```

```
33          else if (richter >= 0)
34             r = "Generally not felt by people";
35          else
36             r = "Negative numbers are not valid";
37          return r;
38       }
39
40       private double richter;
41    }
```

File EarthquakeTest.java

```
1  import javax.swing.JOptionPane;
2
3  /**
4      A class to test the Earthquake class.
5  */
6  public class EarthquakeTest
7  {
8     public static void main(String[] args)
9     {
10        String input = JOptionPane.showInputDialog(
11           "Enter a magnitude on the Richter scale:");
12        double magnitude = Double.parseDouble(input);
13        Earthquake quake = new Earthquake(magnitude);
14        System.out.println(quake.getDescription());
15        System.exit(0);
16     }
17  }
```

Here we must sort the conditions and test against the largest cutoff first. Suppose we reverse the order of tests:

```
if (richter >= 0) // Tests in wrong order
   r = "Generally not felt by people";
else if (richter >= 3.5)
   r = "Felt by many people, no destruction";
else if (richter >= 4.5)
   r = "Damage to poorly constructed buildings";
else if (richter >= 6.0)
   r = "Many buildings considerably damaged;"
      + "some collapse";
else if (richter >= 7.0)
   r = "Many buildings destroyed";
else if (richter >= 8.0)
   r = "Most structures fall";
```

This does not work. All positive values of richter fall into the first case, and the other tests will never be attempted.

In this example, it is also important that we use an if/else/else test, not just multiple independent if statements. Consider this sequence of independent tests:

```
if (richter >= 8.0) // Didn't use else
   r = "Most structures fall";
if (richter >= 7.0)
   r = "Many buildings destroyed";
if (richter >= 6.0)
   r = "Many buildings considerably damaged;"
      + "some collapse";
if (richter >= 4.5)
   r = "Damage to poorly constructed buildings";
if (richter >= 3.5)
   r = "Felt by many people, no destruction";
if (richter >= 0)
   r = "Generally not felt by people";
```

Now the alternatives are no longer exclusive. If richter is 6.0, then the last *four* tests all match, and r is set four times.

Advanced Topic 5.2

The switch Statement

A sequence of if/else/else that compares a *single integer value* against several *constant* alternatives can be implemented as a switch statement. For example,

```
int digit;
. . .
switch (digit)
{
   case 1: System.out.print("one"); break;
   case 2: System.out.print("two"); break;
   case 3: System.out.print("three"); break;
   case 4: System.out.print("four"); break;
   case 5: System.out.print("five"); break;
   case 6: System.out.print("six"); break;
   case 7: System.out.print("seven"); break;
   case 8: System.out.print("eight"); break;
   case 9: System.out.print("nine"); break;
   default: System.out.print("error"); break;
}
```

This is a shortcut for

```
int digit;
. . .
if (digit == 1) System.out.print("one");
else if (digit == 2) System.out.print("two");
else if (digit == 3) System.out.print("three");
else if (digit == 4) System.out.print("four");
else if (digit == 5) System.out.print("five");
```

```
else if (digit == 6) System.out.print("six");
else if (digit == 7) System.out.print("seven");
else if (digit == 8) System.out.print("eight");
else if (digit == 9) System.out.print("nine");
else System.out.print("error");
```

Using the `switch` statement has one advantage. It is obvious that all branches test the *same* value, namely `digit`.

The `switch` statement can be applied only in narrow circumstances. The test cases must be constants, and they must be integers or characters. You cannot use a `switch` to branch on floating-point or string values. For example, the following is an error:

```
switch (name)
{
   case "one": ... break; // Error
   ...
}
```

Note how every branch of the switch was terminated by a `break` instruction. If the `break` is missing, execution *falls through* to the next branch, and so on, until finally a `break` or the end of the `switch` is reached. For example, consider the following `switch` statement:

```
switch (digit)
{
   case 1: System.out.print("one"); // oops—no break
   case 2: System.out.print("two"); break;
   . . .
}
```

If `digit` has the value 1, then the statement after the `case 1:` label is executed. Since there is no `break`, the statement after the `case 2:` label is executed as well. The program prints "onetwo".

There are a few cases in which this fall-through behavior is actually useful, but they are very rare. Peter van der Linden [1, p. 38] describes an analysis of the `switch` statements in the Sun C compiler front end. Of the 244 `switch` statements, each of which had an average of 7 cases, only 3 percent used the fall-through behavior. That is, the default—falling through to the next case unless stopped by a `break`—was *wrong 97 percent of the time*. Forgetting to type the `break` is an exceedingly common error, yielding wrong code.

We leave it to you to use the `switch` statement for your own programs or not. At any rate, you need to have a reading knowledge of `switch` in case you find it in the code of other programmers.

Productivity Hint 5.2

Copy and Paste in the Editor

When you see code like

```
if (richter >= 8.0)
   r = "Most structures fall";
else if (richter >= 7.0)
```

```
       r = "Many buildings destroyed";
   else if (richter >= 6.0)
       r = "Many buildings considerably damaged;"
           + "some collapse";
   else if (richter >= 4.5)
       r = "Damage to poorly constructed buildings";
   else if (richter >= 3.5)
       r = "Felt by many people, no destruction";
```

you should think "copy and paste".

Make a template

```
   else if (richter >= )
       r = "";
```

and copy it. That is usually done by highlighting with the mouse and then selecting Edit and then Copy from the menu bar. (If you follow Productivity Hint 3.1, you are smart and use the keyboard. Hit Shift+End to highlight the entire line, then Ctrl+C to copy it. Then paste it (Ctrl+V) multiple times and fill the text into the copy. Of course, your editor may use different commands, but the concept is the same.)

The ability to copy and paste is always useful when you have code from an example or another project that is similar to your current needs. To copy, paste, and modify is faster than to type everything from scratch. You are also less likely to make typing errors.

Random Fact   5.1

Minicomputers and Workstations

Within 20 years after the first computers became operational, they had become indispensable for organizing the customer and financial data of every major corporation in America. Corporate data processing required a centralized computer installation and high staffing levels to ensure the round-the-clock availability of the data. These installations were enormously expensive, but they were vital to running a modern business. Major universities and large research institutions could also afford the installation of these expensive computers, but many scientific and engineering organizations and corporate divisions could not.

In the mid-1960s, when integrated circuits first became available, the cost of computers could be brought down for users who did not require as high a level of support and services (or data storage volume) as corporate data processing installations. Such users included scientists and engineers who had the expertise to operate computers. (At that time, to "operate" a computer did not just mean to turn it on. Computers came with little off-the-shelf software, and most tasks had to be programmed by the computer users.) In 1965 Digital Equipment Corporation introduced the PDP-8 *minicomputer*, housed in a single cabinet (see Figure 5) and thus small enough for departmental use. In 1978, the first 32-bit minicomputer, the VAX, was released, also by DEC. Other companies, such as Data General, brought out competing designs; the book [2] contains a fascinating description of the engineering work at Data General to bring out a machine that could compete with the VAX. Minicomputers were not just used for engineering applications, however. System integration companies would buy these machines, supply software, and resell them to smaller

Figure 5

An Early Minicomputer

companies for business data processing. Minicomputers such as IBM's successful AS/400 line are still in use today, but they face stiff competition from workstations and personal computers, which are much less expensive and have increasingly powerful software.

In the early 1980s, engineering users became increasingly disenchanted with having to share computers with other users. Computers did divide up their attention among multiple users who were currently logged on, a process known as *time sharing*. However, graphical terminals were becoming available, and the fast processing of graphics was more than could be done in the allotted time slices. The technology had again advanced to the point where an entire computer could be put into a box that would fit on a desk. A new breed of manufacturers, such as Sun Microsystems, started producing *workstations* (Figure 6). These computers are used by individuals with high computing demands—for example, electronic-circuit designers, aerospace engineers, and, more recently, cartoon artists. Workstations typically run an operating system called *UNIX*. Although each workstation manufacturer had its own brand of UNIX, with slight differences in each version, it became economical for software manufacturers to produce programs that could run on several hardware platforms. This was aided by the fact that most workstation manufacturers standardized on the *X Window system* for displaying graphics.

Not all workstation manufacturers were successful. The book [3] tells the story of NeXT, a company that tried to build a workstation and failed, losing over $250 million of its investors' money in the process.

Nowadays workstations are used mainly for two distinct purposes: as fast graphics processors and as *servers* to store data such as electronic mail, sales information, or web pages.

Figure 6

A Workstation

— Nested Branches

In the United States, taxpayers pay federal income tax at different rates depending on their incomes and marital status. There are two main tax schedules: one for single taxpayers and one for married taxpayers "filing jointly", meaning that the married taxpayers add their incomes together and pay taxes on the total. (In fact, there are two other schedules, "head of household" and "married filing separately", which we will ignore for simplicity.) Table 1 gives the tax rate computations for each of the filing categories, using the values for the 1992 federal tax return. (We're using the 1992 tax rate schedule in this illustration because of its simplicity. Legislation in 1993 increased the number of rates in each status and added more complicated rules. By the time that you read this, the tax laws may well have become even more complex.)

Now let us compute the taxes due, given a filing status and an income figure. The key point is that there are two *levels* of decision making. First, we must branch on the filing status. Then, for each filing status, we must have another branch on income level.

File TaxReturn.java

```
 1  /**
 2      A tax return of a taxpayer in 1992.
 3  */
 4  class TaxReturn
 5  {
 6      /**
```

If your filing status is Single

If the taxable income is over	But not over	The tax is	Of the amount over
$0	$21,450	15%	$0
$21,450	$51,900	$3,217.50 + 28%	$21,450
$51,900		$11,743.50 + 31%	$51,900

If your filing status is Married filing jointly

If the taxable income is over	But not over	The tax is	Of the amount over
$0	$35,800	15%	$0
$35,800	$86,500	$5,370.00 + 28%	$35,800
$86,500		$19,566.00 + 31%	$86,500

Table 1

Federal Tax Rate Schedule (1992)

```
7          Constructs a TaxReturn object for a given income and
8          marital status.
9          @param anIncome the taxpayer income
10         @param aStatus either SINGLE or MARRIED
11     */
12     public TaxReturn(double anIncome, int aStatus)
13     {
14         income = anIncome;
15         status = aStatus;
16     }
17
18     public double getTax()
19     {
20         double tax = 0;
21
22         if (status == SINGLE)
23         {
24            if (income <= SINGLE_CUTOFF1)
25               tax = RATE1 * income;
26            else if (income <= SINGLE_CUTOFF2)
27               tax = SINGLE_BASE2
28                  + RATE2 * (income - SINGLE_CUTOFF1);
29            else
30               tax = SINGLE_BASE3
31                  + RATE3 * (income - SINGLE_CUTOFF2);
32         }
```

```
33          else
34          {
35             if (income <= MARRIED_CUTOFF1)
36                tax = RATE1 * income;
37             else if (income <= MARRIED_CUTOFF2)
38                tax = MARRIED_BASE2
39                   + RATE2 * (income - MARRIED_CUTOFF1);
40             else
41                tax = MARRIED_BASE3
42                   + RATE3 * (income - MARRIED_CUTOFF2);
43          }
44
45          return tax;
46       }
47
48       public static final int SINGLE = 1;
49       public static final int MARRIED = 2;
50
51       private static final double RATE1 = 0.15;
52       private static final double RATE2 = 0.28;
53       private static final double RATE3 = 0.31;
54
55       private static final double SINGLE_CUTOFF1 = 21450;
56       private static final double SINGLE_CUTOFF2 = 51900;
57
58       private static final double SINGLE_BASE2 = 3217.50;
59       private static final double SINGLE_BASE3 = 11743.50;
60       private static final double MARRIED_CUTOFF1 = 35800;
61       private static final double MARRIED_CUTOFF2 = 86500;
62
63       private static final double MARRIED_BASE2 = 5370;
64       private static final double MARRIED_BASE3 = 19566;
65
66       private double income;
67       private int status;
68  }
```

File TaxReturnTest.java

```
1  import javax.swing.JOptionPane;
2
3  /**
4      A class to test the TaxReturn class.
5  */
6  public class TaxReturnTest
7  {
8     public static void main(String[] args)
9     {
10        String input = JOptionPane.showInputDialog(
11           "Please enter your income:");
12        double income = Double.parseDouble(input);
13
```

```
14        input = JOptionPane.showInputDialog(
15            "Please enter S (single) or M (married)");
16        int status = 0;
17
18        if (input.equalsIgnoreCase("S"))
19            status = TaxReturn.SINGLE;
20        else if (input.equalsIgnoreCase("M"))
21            status = TaxReturn.MARRIED;
22        else
23        {
24            System.out.println("Bad input.");
25            System.exit(0);
26        }
27
28        TaxReturn aTaxReturn =
29            new TaxReturn(income, status);
30
31        System.out.println("The tax is "
32            + aTaxReturn.getTax());
33
34        System.exit(0);
35     }
36 }
```

The two-level decision process is reflected in two levels of if statements. We say that the income test is *nested* inside the test for filing status. (See Figure 7 for a flowchart.)

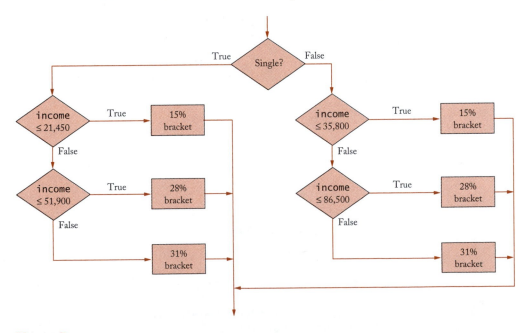

Figure 7

Income Tax Computation Using 1992 Schedule

Quality Tip 5.3

Prepare Test Cases Ahead of Time

Let us consider how we can test the tax computation program. Of course, we cannot try out all possible inputs of filing status and income level. Even if we could, there would be no point in trying them all. If the program correctly computes one or two tax amounts in a given bracket, then we have a good reason to believe that all amounts within that bracket will be correct. We want to aim for complete *coverage* of all cases.

There are two possibilities for the filing status and three tax brackets for each status. That makes six test cases. Then we want to test a handful of *error conditions*, such as a negative income. That makes seven test cases. For the first six, we need to compute manually what answer we expect. For the remaining one, we need to know what error reports we expect. We write down the test cases and then start coding.

Should you really test seven inputs for this simple program? You certainly should. Furthermore, if you find an error in the program that wasn't covered by one of the test cases, make another test case and add it to your collection. After you fix the known mistakes, *run all test cases again*. Experience has shown that the cases that you just tried to fix are probably working now, but that errors that you fixed two or three iterations ago have a good chance of coming back! If you find that an error keeps coming back, that is usually a reliable sign that you did not fully understand some subtle interaction between features of your program.

It is always a good idea to design test cases *before* starting to code. There are two reasons for this. Working through the test cases gives you a better understanding of the algorithm that you are about to program. Furthermore, it has been noted that programmers instinctively shy away from testing fragile parts of their code. That seems hard to believe, but you will often make that observation about your own work. Watch someone else test your program. There will be times when that person enters input that makes you very nervous because you are not sure that your program can handle it, and you never dared to test it yourself. This is a well-known phenomenon, and making the test plan before writing the code offers some protection.

Productivity Hint 5.3

Make a Schedule and Make Time for Unexpected Problems

Commercial software is notorious for being delivered later than promised. For example, Microsoft originally promised that the successor to its Windows 3 operating system would be available early in 1994, then late in 1994, then in March 1995; it finally was released in August 1995. Some of the early promises might not have been realistic. It was in Microsoft's interest to let prospective customers expect the imminent availability of the product. Had customers known the actual delivery date, they might have switched to a different product in the meantime. Undeniably, though, Microsoft had not anticipated the full complexity of the tasks it had set itself to solve.

Microsoft can delay the delivery of its product, but it is likely that you cannot. As a student or a programmer, you are expected to manage your time wisely and to finish your assignments on time. You can probably do simple programming exercises the night before the due date, but an assignment that looks twice as hard may well take four times as long, because more things can go wrong. You should therefore make a schedule whenever you start a programming project.

First, estimate realistically how much time it will take you to

- Design the program logic

- Develop test cases

- Type the program in and fix syntax errors

- Test and debug the program

For example, for the income tax program I might estimate 30 minutes for the design, because it is mostly done; 30 minutes for developing test cases; one hour for data entry and fixing syntax errors; and 2 hours for testing and debugging. That is a total of 4 hours. If I work 2 hours a day on this project, it will take me two days.

Then think of things that can go wrong. Your computer might break down. The lab might be crowded. You might be stumped by a problem with the computer system. (That is a particularly important concern for beginners. It is *very* common to lose a day over a trivial problem just because it takes time to track down a person who knows the "magic" command to overcome it.) As a rule of thumb, *double* the time of your estimate. That is, you should start four days, not two days, before the due date. If nothing goes wrong, great; you have the program done two days early. When the inevitable problem occurs, you have a cushion of time that protects you from embarrassment and failure.

Common Error 5.2

The Dangling else Problem

When an if statement is nested inside another if statement, the following error may occur.

```
if (richter >= 0)
    if (richter <= 4)
        System.out.println("The earthquake is harmless");
else // Pitfall!
    System.out.println("Negative value not allowed");
```

The indentation level seems to suggest that the `else` is grouped with the test `richter >= 0`. Unfortunately, that is not the case. The compiler ignores all indentation and follows the rule that an `else` always belongs to the closest `if`. That is, the code is actually

```
if (richter >= 0)
    if (richter <= 4)
        System.out.println("The earthquake is harmless");
    else // Pitfall!
        System.out.println("Negative value not allowed");
```

That isn't what we want. We want to group the `else` with the first `if`. For that, we must use braces.

```
if (richter >= 0)
{
    if (richter <= 4)
        System.out.println("The earthquake is harmless");
}
else
    System.out.println("Negative value not allowed");
```

To avoid having to think about the pairing of the `else`, we recommend that you *always* use a set of braces when the body of an `if` contains another `if`. In the following example, the braces are not strictly necessary, but they help clarify the code:

```
if (richter >= 0)
{
    if (richter <= 4)
        System.out.println("The earthquake is harmless");
    else
        System.out.println("Damage may occur");
}
```

The ambiguous `else` is called a *dangling* `else`, and it is enough of a syntactical blemish that some programming language designers developed an improved syntax that avoids it altogether. For example, Algol 68 uses the construction

`if` *condition* `then` *statement* `else` *statement* `fi`;

The `else` part is optional, but since the end of the `if` statement is clearly marked, the grouping is unambiguous if there are two `if`s and only one `else`. Here are the two possible cases:

`if` *c1* `then if` *c2* `then` *s1* `else` *s2* `fi fi`;

`if` *c1* `then if` *c2* `then` *s1* `fi else` *s2* `fi`;

By the way, `fi` is just `if` backwards. Other languages use `endif`, which has the same purpose but is less fun.

5.4   Using Boolean Expressions

5.4.1 — The boolean Type

> The boolean type has two values: true and false.

In Java, an expression such as amount < 1000 has a value, just as the expression amount + 1000 has a value. The value of a relational expression is either true or false. For example, if amount is 500, then the value of amount < 1000 is true. Try it out: The program fragment

```
double amount = 0;
System.out.println(amount < 1000);
```

prints true. The values true and false are not numbers, nor are they objects of a class. They belong to a separate type, called boolean. The Boolean type is named after the mathematician George Boole (1815–1864), a pioneer in the study of logic.

5.4.2 — Predicate Methods

> A predicate method returns a Boolean value.

A *predicate method* is a method that returns a boolean value. Here is an example of a predicate method:

```
public class BankAccount
{
```

```
        public boolean isOverdrawn()
        {
            return balance < 0;
        }
    }
```

You can use the return value of the method as the condition of an `if` statement:

```
    if (harrysChecking.isOverdrawn()) . . .
```

There are several useful static predicate methods in the `Character` class:

```
isDigit
isLetter
isUpperCase
isLowerCase
```

that let you test whether a character is a digit, a letter, an uppercase letter, or a lowercase letter:

```
    if (Character.isUpperCase(ch)) . . .
```

It is a common convention to give a prefix "`is`" to the name of a predicate method.

5.4.3 — The Boolean Operators

> You can form complex tests with the Boolean operators `&&` (and), `||` (or) and `!` (not).

Suppose you want to find whether `amount` is between 0 and 1000. Then two conditions have to be true: `amount` must be greater than 0, *and* it must be less than 1000. In Java you use the `&&` operator to represent the *and* to combine test conditions. That is, you can write the test as follows:

```
    if (0 < amount && amount < 1000) . . .
```

The `&&` operator combines several tests into a new test that passes only when all conditions are true. An operator that combines test conditions is called a *logical* operator.

The `||` (*or*) logical operator also combines two or more conditions. The resulting test succeeds if at least one of the conditions is true. For example, here is a test to check whether the string `input` is a "S" or "M":

```
    if (input.equals("S") || input.equals("M")) . . .
```

Figure 8 shows flowcharts for these examples.

Sometimes you need to *invert* a condition with the `!` (*not*) logical operator. For example, we may want to carry out a certain action only if two strings are *not* equal:

```
    if (!input.equals("S")) . . .
```

The `!` operator takes a single condition and evaluates to `true` if that condition is false and to `false` if the condition is true.

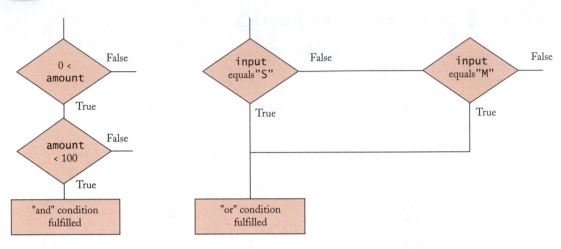

Figure 8

Flowcharts for && and || Combinations

Here is a summary of the three logical operations:

A	B	A && B
true	true	true
true	false	false
false	*Any*	false

A	B	A ‖ B
true	*Any*	true
false	true	true
false	false	false

A	!A
true	false
false	true

⊗ Common Error 5.3

Multiple Relational Operators

Consider the expression

```
if (0 < amount < 1000) ... // Error
```

This looks just like the mathematical notation for "amount is between 0 and 1000". But in Java, it is a syntax error.

Let us dissect the condition. The first half, 0 < amount, is a test with outcome true or false. The outcome of that test (true or false) is then compared against 1000. This seems to make no sense. Can one compare truth values and numbers? Is true larger than 1000 or not? In Java, you cannot. The Java compiler rejects this statement.

Instead, use && to combine two separate tests:

```
if (0 < amount && amount < 1000) ...
```

Another common error, along the same lines, is to write

```
if (ch == 'S' || 'M') ... // Error
```

to test whether ch is 'S' or 'M'. Again, the Java compiler flags this construct as an error. You cannot apply the || operator to characters. You need to write two Boolean expressions and join them with the || operator:

```
if (ch == 'S' || ch == 'M') ...
```

⊗ Common Error 5.4

Confusing && and || Conditions

It is a surprisingly common error to confuse *and* and *or* conditions. A value lies between 0 and 100 if it is at least 0 *and* at most 100. It lies outside that range if it is less than 0 *or* greater than 100. There is no golden rule; you just have to think carefully.

Often the *and* or *or* is clearly stated, and then it isn't too hard to implement it. Sometimes, though, the wording isn't as explicit. It is quite common that the individual conditions are nicely set apart in a bulleted list, but with little indication how they should be combined. The instructions for the 1992 tax return say that you can claim single filing status if any one of the following is true:

- You were never married.

- You were legally separated or divorced on December 31, 1992.

- You were widowed before January 1, 1992, and did not remarry in 1992.

Since the test passes if *any one* of the conditions is true, you must combine the conditions with *or*. Elsewhere, the same instructions state that you may use the more advantageous status of married filing jointly if all five of the following conditions are true:

- Your spouse died in 1990 or 1991 and you did not remarry in 1992.

- You have a child whom you can claim as dependent.

- That child lived in your home for all of 1992.

- You paid over half the cost of keeping up your home for this child.

- You filed (or could have filed) a joint return with your spouse the year he or she died.

Because *all* of the conditions must be true for the test to pass, you must combine them with an *and*.

Advanced Topic 5.3

Lazy Evaluation of Boolean Operators

The **&&** and **||** operators in Java are computed using *lazy* (or *short circuit*) evaluation. In other words, logical expressions are evaluated from left to right, and evaluation stops as soon as the truth value is determined. When an *and* is evaluated and the first condition is false, then the second condition is skipped—no matter what it is, the combined condition must be false. When an *or* is evaluated and the first condition is true, the second condition is not evaluated, because it does not matter what the outcome of the second test is. Here is an example:

```
if (input != null && Integer.parseInt(input) > 0) . . .
```

If `input` is `null`, then the first condition is false, and thus the combined statement is false, no matter what the outcome of the second test is. The second test is never evaluated if `input` is `null`, and there is no danger of parsing a `null` string (which would cause an exception).

If you do need to evaluate both conditions, then use the **&** and **|** operators. When evaluated with Boolean arguments, these operators always evaluate both arguments.

5.4.4 — De Morgan's Law

> De Morgan's law shows how to simplify expressions in which a ! operator is applied to terms joined by the && or || operator.

In the preceding section, we programmed a test to see whether `amount` was between 0 and 1000. Let's find out whether the opposite is true:

```
if (!(0 < amount && amount < 1000)) . . .
```

This test is a little bit complicated, and you have to think carefully through the logic. "When it is *not* true that 0 < `amount` and `amount` < 1000 . . ." Huh? It is not true that some people won't be confused by this code.

The computer doesn't care, but humans generally have a hard time comprehending logical conditions with *not* operators applied to *and/or* expressions. De Morgan's law, named after the logician Augustus de Morgan (1806–1871), can be used to simplify these Boolean expressions. De Morgan's law has two forms: one for the negation of an *and* expression and one for the negation of an *or* expression:

```
!(A && B) is the same as !A || !B
```

```
!(A || B) is the same as !A && !B
```

Pay particular attention to the fact that the *and* and *or* operators are *reversed* by moving the *not* inwards. For example, the negation of "the input is S or the input is M",

```
!(input.equals("S") || input.equals("M"))
```

is "the input is not S *and* the input is not M":

```
!input.equals("S") && !input.equals("M")
```

Let us apply the law to the negation of "the amount is between 0 and 1000":

```
!(0 < amount && amount < 1000)
```

is equivalent to

```
!(0 < amount) || !(amount < 1000)
```

which can be further simplified to

```
0 >= amount || amount >= 1000
```

Note that the opposite of `<` is `>=`, not `>`!

5.4.5 — Using Boolean Variables

> You can store the outcome of a condition in a Boolean variable.

You can use a Boolean variable if you know that there are only two possible values. Have another look at the tax program in Section 5.3.2. The marital status is either single or married. Instead of using an integer, you can use a variable of type `boolean`:

```
private boolean married;
```

The advantage is that you can't accidentally store a third value in the variable.

Then you can use the Boolean variable in a test:

```
if (married)
    . . .
else
    . . .
```

Sometimes Boolean variables are called *flags* because they can have just two states: "up" and "down".

It pays to think carefully about the naming of Boolean variables. In our example, it would not be a good idea to give the name `maritalStatus` to the Boolean variable.

What does it mean that the marital status is `true`? With a name like `married` there is no ambiguity; if `married` is `true`, the taxpayer is married.

By the way, it is considered gauche to write a test such as

```
if (married == true) ... // Don't
```

Just use the simpler test

```
if (married) ...
```

In Chapter 6 we will use Boolean variables to control complex loops.

Random Fact   5.2

Artificial Intelligence

When one uses a sophisticated computer program such as a tax preparation package, one is bound to attribute some intelligence to the computer. The computer asks sensible questions and makes computations that we find a mental challenge. After all, if doing our taxes were easy, we wouldn't need a computer to do it for us.

As programmers, however, we know that all this apparent intelligence is an illusion. Human programmers have carefully "coached" the software in all possible scenarios, and it simply replays the actions and decisions that were programmed into it.

Would it be possible to write computer programs that are genuinely intelligent in some sense? From the earliest days of computing, there was a sense that the human brain might be nothing but an immense computer, and that it might well be feasible to program computers to imitate some processes of human thought. Serious research into *artificial intelligence* (*AI*) began in the mid-1950s, and the first twenty years brought some impressive successes. Programs that play chess—surely an activity that appears to require remarkable intellectual powers—have become so good that they now routinely beat all but the best human players. In 1975 an *expert-system* program called Mycin gained fame for being better in diagnosing meningitis in patients than the average physician. *Theorem-proving* programs produced logically correct mathematical proofs. *Optical character recognition* software can read pages from a scanner, recognize the character shapes (including those that are blurred or smudged), and reconstruct the original document text, even restoring fonts and layout.

However, there were serious setbacks as well. From the very outset, one of the stated goals of the AI community was to produce software that could translate text from one language to another, for example from English to Russian. That undertaking proved to be enormously complicated. Human language appears to be much more subtle and interwoven with the human experience than had originally been thought. Even the grammar-checking programs that come with many word processors today are more a gimmick than a useful tool, and analyzing grammar is just the first step in translating sentences.

From 1982 to 1992, the Japanese government embarked on a massive research project, funded at over 50 billion Japanese yen. It was known as the *Fifth-Generation Project*. Its goal was to develop new hard- and software to greatly improve the performance

▼

▼

▼

▼

▼

▼

▼

▼

▼

▼

▼

▼

▼

of expert systems. At its outset, the project created great fear in other countries that the Japanese computer industry was about to become the undisputed leader in the field. However, the end results were disappointing and did little to bring artificial intelligence applications to market.

One reason that artificial intelligence programs have not performed as well as it was hoped seems to be that they simply don't know as much as humans do. In the early 1990s, Douglas Lenat and his colleagues decided to do something about it and initiated the CYC project (from en*cyc*lopedia), an effort to codify the implicit assumptions that underly human speech and writing. The team members started out analyzing news articles and asked themselves what unmentioned facts are necessary to actually understand the sentences. For example, consider the sentence "Last fall she enrolled in Michigan State." The reader automatically realizes that "fall" is not related to falling down in this context, but refers to the season. While there is a State of Michigan, here Michigan State denotes the university. A priori, a computer program has none of this knowledge. The goal of the CYC project was to extract and store the requisite facts—that is, (1) people enroll in universities; (2) Michigan is a state; (3) a state X is likely to have a university named X State University, often abbreviated as X *State*; (4) most people enroll in a university in the fall. In 1995, the project had codified about 100,000 common-sense concepts and about a million facts of knowledge relating them. Even this massive amount of data has not proven sufficient for useful applications.

Successful artificial intelligence programs, such as chess-playing programs, do not actually imitate human thinking. They are just very fast in exploring many scenarios and have been tuned to recognize those cases that do not warrant further investigation. *Neural networks* are interesting exceptions: coarse simulations of the neuron cells in animal and human brains. Suitably interconnected cells appear to be able to "learn". For example, if a network of cells is presented with letter shapes, it can be trained to identify them. After a lengthy training period, the network can recognize letters, even if they are slanted, distorted, or smudged.

When artificial intelligence programs are successful, they can raise serious ethical issues. There are now programs that can scan résumés, select those that look promising, and show only those to a human for further analysis. How would you feel if you knew that your résumé had been rejected by a computer, perhaps on a technicality, and that you never had a chance to be interviewed? When computers are used for credit analysis, and the analysis software has been designed to deny credit systematically to certain groups of people (say, all applicants with certain ZIP codes), is that illegal discrimination? What if the software has not been designed in this fashion, but a neural network has "discovered" a pattern from historical data? These are troubling questions, especially because those that are harmed by such processes have little recourse.

CHAPTER SUMMARY

1. The if statement lets a program carry out different actions depending on the outcome of a condition.

2. A block statement groups together several statements.

3. Relational operators compare values. The == operator tests for equality.

4. When comparing floating-point numbers, don't test for equality. Instead, check whether they are *close enough*.

5. Do not use the == operator to compare strings. Use the `equals` method instead.

6. The `compareTo` method compares strings in dictionary order.

7. The == operator tests whether two object references are identical. To compare the contents of objects, you need to use the `equals` method.

8. The `null` reference refers to no object.

9. Multiple conditions can be combined to evaluate complex decisions. The correct arrangement depends on the logic of the problem to be solved.

10. The `boolean` type has two values: `true` and `false`.

11. A predicate method returns a Boolean value.

12. You can form complex tests with the Boolean operators **&&** (and), **||** (or), and **!** (not).

13. De Morgan's law shows how to simplify expressions in which a **!** operator is applied to terms joined by the **&&** or **||** operator.

14. You can store the outcome of a condition in a Boolean variable.

Further Reading

[1] Peter van der Linden, *Expert C Programming*, Prentice-Hall, 1994.
[2] Tracy Kidder, *The Soul of a New Machine*, Little, Brown and Co., 1981.
[3] Randall E. Stross, *Steven Jobs and the NeXT Big Thing*, Atheneum, 1993.
[4] William H. Press et al., *Numerical Recipes in C*, Cambridge, 1988.

CLASSES, OBJECTS, AND METHODS INTRODUCED IN THIS CHAPTER

```
java.lang.Character
    isDigit
    isLetter
    isUpperCase
    isLowerCase
java.lang.Object
    equals
java.lang.String
    equalsIgnoreCase
    compareTo
```

REVIEW EXERCISES

Exercise R5.1. Find the errors in the following `if` statements.

```
• if quarters > 0 then System.out.println(quarters + " quarters");
• if (1 + x > Math.pow(x, Math.sqrt(2)) y = y + x;
• if (x = 1) y++; else if (x = 2) y = y + 2;
• if (x && y == 0) { x = 1; y = 1; }
• if (1 <= x <= 10)
    System.out.println(x);
• if (s != "nickels" || s != "pennies"
    || s != "dimes" || s != "quarters")
    System.out.print("Input error!");
• if (input.equalsIgnoreCase("N") || "NO")
    return;
• int x = Integer.parseInt(input);
• if (x != null) y = y + x;
• language = "English";
  if (country.equals("US"))
    if (state.equals("PR")) language = "Spanish";
  else if (country.equals("China"))
    language = "Chinese";
```

Exercise R5.2. Explain the following terms, and give an example for each construct:

- Expression
- Condition
- Statement
- Simple statement
- Compound statement
- Block

Exercise R5.3. Explain the difference between an `if/else /else` statement and nested `if` statements. Give an example for each.

Exercise R5.4. Give an example for an `if/else /else` statement where the order of the tests does not matter. Give an example where the order of the tests matters.

Exercise R5.5. Of the following pairs of strings, which comes first in lexicographic order?

```
• "Tom", "Dick"
• "Tom", "Tomato"
• "church", "Churchill"
• "car manufacturer", "carburetor"
• "Harry", "hairy"
• "C++", " Car"
```

- "Tom", "Tom"
- "Car", "Carl"
- "car", "bar"

Exercise R5.6. Complete the following truth table by finding the truth values of the Boolean expressions for all combinations of the Boolean inputs p, q, and r.

p	q	r	(p && q) || !r	!(p && (q || !r))
false	false	false		
false	false	true		
false	true	false		
...				
5 more combinations				
...				

Exercise R5.7. Before you implement any complex algorithm, it is a good idea to understand and analyze it. The purpose of this exercise is to gain a better understanding of the tax computation algorithm of Section 5.3.2.

Some people object to the fact that the tax rates increase with higher incomes, claiming that certain taxpayers are then better off *not* to work hard and get a raise, since they would then have to pay a higher tax rate and actually end up with less money after taxes. Can you find such an income level, and if not, why not?

Another feature of the tax code is the *marriage penalty*. Under certain circumstances, a married couple pays higher taxes than the sum of what the two partners would pay if they both were single. Find examples for such income levels.

Exercise R5.8. True or false? *A* && *B* is the same as *B* && *A* for any Boolean conditions *A* and *B*.

Exercise R5.9. Explain the difference between

```
s = 0;
if (x > 0) s++;
if (y > 0) s++;
```

and

```
s = 0;
if (x > 0) s++;
else if (y > 0) s++;
```

Exercise R5.10. Use De Morgan's law to simplify the following Boolean expressions.

- !(x > 0 && y > 0)
- !(x != 0 || y != 0)

- `!(country.equals("US") && !state.equals("HI")
      && !state.equals("AK"))`

- `!(x % 4 != 0 || !(x % 100 == 0 && x % 400 == 0))`

Exercise R5.11. Make up another Java code example that shows the dangling-`else` problem, using the following statement. A student with a GPA of at least 1.5, but less than 2, is on probation. With less than 1.5, the student is failing.

Exercise R5.12. Explain the difference between the `==` operator and the `equals` method when comparing strings.

Exercise R5.13. Explain the difference between the tests

```
r == s
```

and

```
r.equals(s)
```

where both `r` and `s` are of type `Rectangle`.

Exercise R5.14. What is wrong with this test to see whether `r` is `null`? What happens when this code runs?

```
Rectangle r;
. . .
if (r.equals(null))
    r = new Rectangle(5, 10, 20, 30);
```

Exercise R5.15. Explain how the lexicographic ordering of strings differs from the ordering of words in a dictionary or telephone book. *Hint:* Consider strings like `IBM`, `wiley.com`, `Century 21`, `While-U-Wait`, `7-11`.

Exercise R5.16. Write Java code to test whether two objects of type `Line2D.Double` represent the same line when displayed on the graphics screen. *Do not* use `a.equals(b)`.

```
Line2D.Double a;
Line2D.Double b;

if (your condition goes here)
    g2.drawString("They look the same!", x, y);
```

Hint: If `p` and `q` are points, then `Line2D.Double(p, q)` and `Line2D.Double(q, p)` look the same.

Exercise R5.17. Explain why it is more difficult to compare floating-point numbers than integers. Write Java code to test whether an integer `n` equals 10 and whether a floating-point number `x` equals 10.

Exercise R5.18. Give an example for two floating-point numbers `x` and `y` such that `Math.abs(x - y)` is larger than 1000, but `x` and `y` are still identical except for a round-off error.

Exercise R5.19. Give a set of test cases for the tax program in Section 5.3.2. Compute the expected results manually.

Exercise R5.20. Consider the following test to see whether a point falls inside a rectangle.

```
Point2D.Double p = . . .
Rectangle2D.Double r = . . .
boolean xInside = false;
if (r.getX() <= p.getX() &&
      p.getX() <= r.getX() + r.getWidth())
   xInside = true;
boolean yInside = false;
if (r.getY() <= p.getY() && p.getY() <= r.getY())
   yInside = true;
if (xInside && yInside)
   g2.drawString("p is inside the rectangle.",
      p.getX(), p.getY());
```

Rewrite this code to eliminate the explicit `true` and `false` values, by setting `xInside` and `yInside` to the values of Boolean expressions.

PROGRAMMING EXERCISES

Exercise P5.1. Write a program that prints all real solutions to the quadratic equation $ax^2 + bx + c = 0$. Read in a, b, c and use the quadratic formula. If the *discriminant* $b^2 - 4ac$ is negative, display a message stating that there are no real solutions.

Implement a class `QuadraticEquation` whose constructor receives the coefficients `a`, `b`, `c` of the quadratic equation. Supply methods `getSolution1` and `getSolution2` that get the solutions, using the quadratic formula. Supply a method

```
boolean hasSolutions()
```

that returns `false` if the discriminant is negative.

Exercise P5.2. Write a program that takes user input describing a playing card in the following shorthand notation:

Notation	Meaning
A	Ace
2...10	Card values
J	Jack
Q	Queen
K	King
D	Diamonds
H	Hearts
S	Spades
C	Clubs

Your program should print the full description of the card. For example,

```
Enter the card notation:
QS
Queen of spades
```

Implement a class `Card` whose constructor takes the card letters and whose `get-Description` method returns a description of the card.

Exercise P5.3. As in the `IntersectionApplet` program of Chapter 4, compute and plot the intersection of a line and a circle. However, if the line and the circle do not intersect, do not plot the intersection points but display a message instead.

Exercise P5.4. Write a program that reads in three floating-point numbers and prints the three inputs in sorted order. For example:

```
Please enter three numbers:
4
9
2.5
The inputs in sorted order are
2.5
4
9
```

Exercise P5.5. Write a program that draws a circle with radius 100 and center (110, 120). Ask the user to specify the *x*- and *y*-coordinates of a point. If the point lies inside the circle, then show a message "Congratulations." Otherwise, show a message "You missed." In your excercise, define a class `Circle` and a method `boolean isInside( Point2D.Double p)`.

Exercise P5.6. Write a graphics program that asks the user to specify the radii of two circles. The first circle has center (100, 200), and the second circle has center (200, 100). Draw the circles. If they intersect, then display a message "Circles intersect." Otherwise, display "Circles don't intersect." *Hint:* Compute the distance between the centers and compare it to the radii. Your program should draw nothing if the user enters a negative radius. In your excercise, define a class `Circle` and a method `boolean intersects( Circle other)`.

Exercise P5.7. Write a program that prints the question "Do you want to continue?" and reads a user input. If the user input is "Y", "Yes", "OK", "Sure", or "Why not?", print out "OK". If the user input is "N" or "No", then print out "Terminating." Otherwise, print "Bad input." The case of the user input should not matter. For example, "y" or "yes" are also valid inputs. Write a class `InputChecker` for this purpose.

Exercise P5.8. Write a program that translates a letter grade into a number grade. Letter grades are A B C D F, possibly followed by + or -. Their numeric values are 4, 3, 2, 1, and 0. There is no F+ or F-. A + increases the numeric value by 0.3, a - decreases it by 0.3. However, an A+ has value 4.0.

```
Enter a letter grade:
B-
The numeric value is 2.7.
```

Use a class `Grade` with a method `getNumericGrade`.

Exercise P5.9. Write a program that translates a number between 0 and 4 into the closest letter grade. For example, the number 2.8 (which might have been the average of several grades) would be converted to B-. Break ties in favor of the better grade; for example, 2.85 should be a B.

Use a class `Grade` with a method `getLetterGrade`.

Exercise P5.10. Write a program that reads in four strings and prints the lexicographically smallest and largest one:

```
Enter three strings:
Charlie
Able
Delta
Baker
The lexicographic minimum is Able
The lexicographic maximum is Delta
```

Hint: Use a class that keeps track of the current maximum and minimum.

Exercise P5.11. If you look at the tax tables in Section 5.3.2, you will note that the percentages 15%, 28%, and 31% are identical for both single and married taxpayers, but the cutoffs for the tax brackets are different. Married people get to pay 15% on their first $35,800, then pay 28% on the next $50,700, and 31% on the remainder. Single people pay 15% on their first $21,450, then pay 28% on the next $30,450, and 31% of the remainder. Write a `TaxReturn` class with the following logic. Set variables `cutoff1` and `cutoff2` that depend on the marital status. Then have a single formula that computes the tax, depending on the incomes and the cutoffs. Verify that your results are identical to that of the `TaxReturn` class in this chapter.

Exercise P5.12. A year with 366 days is called a leap year. A year is a leap year if it is divisible by 4 (for example, 1980). However, since the introduction of the Gregorian calendar on October 15, 1582, a year is not a leap year if it is divisible by 100 (for example, 1900); however, it is a leap year if it is divisible by 400 (for example, 2000). Write a program that asks the user for a year and computes whether that year is a leap year. Implement a class `Year` with a predicate method `boolean isLeapYear()`.

Exercise P5.13. Write a program that asks the user to enter a month (1 = January, 2 = February, and so on) and then prints the number of days of the month. For February, print "28 days".

```
Enter a month:
5
30 days
```

Implement a class `Month` with a method `int getDays()`.

Exercise P5.14. Write a program that reads in two floating-point numbers and tests whether they are the same when rounded to two decimal places. Here are two sample runs.

```
Enter two floating-point numbers:
2.0
1.99998
They are the same when rounded to two decimal places.


Enter two floating-point numbers:
2.0
1.98999
They are different.
```

Exercise P5.15. Enhance the `BankAccount` class of Chapter 3 by

- Rejecting negative amounts in the `deposit` and `withdraw` methods
- Rejecting withdrawals that would result in a negative balance

Exercise P5.16. Write a program that reads in the name and hourly wage of an employee. Then ask how many hours the employee worked in the past week. Be sure to accept fractional hours. Compute the pay. Any overtime work (over 40 hours per week) is paid at 150 percent of the regular wage. Solve this problem by implementing a class `Paycheck`.

Exercise P5.17. Write a unit conversion program using the conversion factors of Appendix A7. Ask the users the unit from which they want to convert and the unit to which they want to convert. Legal units are in, ft, mi, mm, cm, m, km. *Hint:* Define seven objects of a class `UnitConverter` that convert from and to meters. (ml, l, g, kg, mm, cm, m, km).

```
Convert from?
in
Convert to?
mm
Value?
10
10 in = 254 mm
```

Exercise P5.18. Implement a *combination lock* class. A combination lock has a dial with 26 positions labeled A ... Z. The dial needs to be set three times. If it is set to the correct combination, the lock can be opened. When the lock is closed again, the combination can be entered again. If a user sets the dial more than three times, the last three settings determine whether the lock can be opened. Support the following interface:

```
public class CombinationLock
{
    /**
        Constructs a lock with a given combination.
        @param aCombination the combination; a string
        with three uppercase letters A ... Z
```

```
*/
public CombinationLock(String aCombination) { . . . }

/**
    Set the dial to a position.
    @param aPosition a string consisting of a single uppercase
    letter A . . . Z
*/
void setPosition(String aPosition) { . . . }

/**
    Try unlocking the lock.
*/
void unlock() { . . . }

/**
    Check whether the lock is unlocked.
    @return true if the lock is currently open.
*/
boolean isOpen() { . . . }

/**
    Close the lock.
*/
void lock() { . . . }
}
```

Chapter 6

Iteration

CHAPTER GOALS

To be able to program loops with the while, for, and do statements

▶ To avoid infinite loops and off-by-one errors

▶ To understand nested loops

▶ To learn how to process input

▶ To implement simulations

CHAPTER CONTENTS

6.1 while Loops

In this chapter you will learn how to write programs that repeatedly execute one or more statements. We will illustrate these concepts by looking at typical investment situations. Consider a bank account with an initial balance of $10,000 that earns 5% interest. The interest is computed at the end of every year on the current balance and then deposited into the bank account. For example, after the first year, you earned $500 (5% of $10,000). The interest gets added to your bank account. Next year, the interest is $525 (5% of $10,500), and your balance is $11,025. Table 1 shows how the balance grows in the first five years:

Year	Balance
0	$10,000.00
1	$10,500.00
2	$11,025.00
3	$11,576.25
4	$12,155.06
5	$12,762.82

Table 1

Growth of an Investment

> A while statement executes a block of code repeatedly. A termination condition controls how often the loop is executed.

How many years does it take for the balance to reach $20,000? Of course, it won't take longer than 20 years, because at least $500 is added to the bank account each year. But it may take less than 20 years, because interest is computed on increasingly larger balances.

In Java, the while statement implements such a repetition. The code

```
while (condition)
    statement
```

keeps executing the statement while the condition is true. Most commonly, the statement is a block statement, that is, a set of statements delimited by { ... }.

In our case, we want to know when the bank account has reached a particular balance. While the balance is less, we keep adding interest and incrementing the year counter:

```
while (balance < targetBalance)
{
    years++;
    double interest = balance * rate / 100;
    balance = balance + interest;
}
```

Here is the program that solves our investment problem:

File Investment.java

```
1  /**
2      A class to monitor the growth of an investment that
3      accumulates interest at a fixed annual rate.
4  */
5  public class Investment
6  {
7      /**
8          Constructs an Investment object from a starting balance and
9          interest rate.
10         @param aBalance  the starting balance
11         @param aRate  the interest rate in percent
12     */
13     public Investment(double aBalance, double aRate)
14     {
15         balance = aBalance;
16         rate = aRate;
17         years = 0;
18     }
19
20     /**
21         Keeps accumulating interest until a target balance has
22         been reached.
23         @param targetBalance  the desired balance
24     */
25     public void waitForBalance(double targetBalance)
26     {
27         while (balance < targetBalance)
28         {
29             years++;
30             double interest = balance * rate / 100;
31             balance = balance + interest;
32         }
33     }
34
35     /**
36         Gets the current investment balance.
37         @return  the current balance
38     */
39     public double getBalance()
40     {
41         return balance;
42     }
43
44     /**
45         Gets the number of years this investment has accumulated
46         interest.
47         @return  the number of years since the start of the investment
```

```
48      */
49      public int getYears()
50      {
51         return years;
52      }
53
54      private double balance;
55      private double rate;
56      private int years;
57   }
```

File InvestmentTest.java

```
1   /**
2       This program computes how long it takes for an investment
3       to double.
4   */
5   public class InvestmentTest
6   {
7      public static void main(String[] args)
8      {
9         final double INITIAL_BALANCE = 10000;
10        final double RATE = 5;
11        Investment invest =
12           new Investment(INITIAL_BALANCE, RATE);
13        invest.waitForBalance(2 * INITIAL_BALANCE);
14        int years = invest.getYears();
15        System.out.println("The investment doubled after "
16           + years + " years");
17     }
18  }
```

A `while` statement is often called a *loop*. If you draw a flowchart, you will see that the control loops backward to the test after every iteration (see Figure 1).

The following loop,

```
while (true)
{
    body
}
```

executes the *body* over and over, without ever terminating. Whoa! Why would you want that? The program would never stop. There are two reasons. Some programs indeed never stop; the software controlling an automated teller machine, a telephone switch, or a microwave oven doesn't ever stop (at least not until the device is turned off). Our programs aren't usually of that kind, but even if you can't terminate the loop, you can exit from the method that contains it. This can be helpful when the termination test naturally falls into the middle of the loop (see Advanced Topic 6.5).

Figure 1

Flowchart of a while Loop

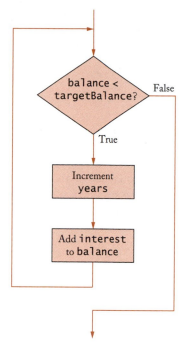

Syntax 6.1: The while Statement

while (*condition*)
 statement

Example:

```
while (balance < targetBalance)
{
    years++;
    double interest = balance * rate / 100;
    balance = balance + interest;
}
```

Purpose:

To execute a statement while a condition is true

⊗ **Common Error** 6.1

Infinite Loops

The most annoying loop error is an infinite loop: a loop that runs forever and can be stopped only by killing the program or restarting the computer. If there are output statements in the loop, then reams and reams of output flash by on the screen. Otherwise, the program just sits there and *hangs*, seeming to do nothing. On some systems you can kill a hanging program by hitting Ctrl+Break or Ctrl+C. On others, you can close the window in which the program runs.

A common reason for infinite loops is forgetting to advance the variable that controls the loop:

```
int years = 0;
while (years < 20)
{
    double interest = balance * rate / 100;
    balance = balance + interest;
}
```

Here the programmer forgot to add a `years++` command in the loop. As a result, the value of `years` always stays 0, and the loop never comes to an end.

Another common reason for an infinite loop is accidentally incrementing a counter that should be decremented (or vice versa). Consider this example:

```
int years = 20;
while (years > 0)
{
    years++; // Oops, should have been years--
    double interest = balance * rate / 100;
    balance = balance + interest;
}
```

The `years` variable really should have been decremented, not incremented. This is a common error, because incrementing counters is so much more common than decrementing that your fingers may type the `++` on autopilot. As a consequence, `years` is always larger than 0, and the loop never terminates. (Actually, eventually `years` will exceed the largest representable positive integer and *wrap around* to a negative number. Then the loop exits—of course, that takes a long time, and the result is completely wrong.)

⊗ **Common Error** 6.2

Off-by-1 Errors

Consider our computation of the number of years that are required to double an investment:

```
int years = 0;
while (balance < targetBalance)
{
    years++;
    double interest = balance * rate / 100;
    balance = balance + interest;
}
System.out.println(
    "The investment reached the target after "
    + years + " years.");
```

Should `years` start at 0 or at 1? Should you test for `balance < 2 * initialBalance` or for `balance <= 2 * initialBalance`? It is easy to be *off by 1* in these expressions.

> An off-by-one error is a common error when programming loops. Think through simple test cases to avoid this type of error.

Some people try to solve off-by-1 errors by randomly inserting + 1 or – 1 until the program seems to work. That is, of course, a terrible strategy. It can take a long time to compile and test all the various possibilities. Expending a small amount of mental effort is a real time saver.

Fortunately, off-by-1 errors are easy to avoid, simply by thinking through a couple of test cases and using the information from the test cases to come up with a rationale for your decisions.

Should `years` start at 0 or at 1? Look at a scenario with simple values: an initial balance of $100 and an interest rate of 50%. After year 1, the balance is $150, and after year 2 it is $225, or over $200. So the investment doubled after 2 years. The loop executed two times, incrementing `years` each time. Hence `years` must start at 0, not at 1.

In other words, the `balance` variable denotes the balance *after* the end of the year. At the outset, the `balance` variable contains the balance after year 0 and not after year 1.

Next, should you use a < or <= comparison in the test? That is harder to figure out, because it is rare for the balance to be exactly twice the initial balance. Of course, there is one case when this happens, namely when the interest is 100%. The loop executes once. Now `years` is 1, and `balance` is exactly equal to 2 * `initialBalance`. Has the investment doubled after one year? It has. Therefore, the loop should *not* execute again. If the test condition is `balance < 2 * initialBalance`, the loop stops, as it should. If the test condition had been `balance <= 2 * initialBalance`, the loop would have executed once more.

In other words, you keep adding interest while the balance *has not yet doubled*.

 Advanced Topic   **6.1**

do **Loops**

Sometimes you want to execute the body of a loop at least once and perform the loop test after the body was executed. The do loop serves that purpose:

```
do
    statement
while (condition);
```

The *statement* is executed while the *condition* is true. The condition is tested after the statement is executed, so the statement is executed at least once.

For example, suppose you want to make sure that a user enters a positive number. As long as the user enters a negative number or zero, just keep prompting for a correct input. In this situation, a do loop makes sense, because you need to get a user input before you can test it.

```
double value;
do
{
    String input = JOptionPane.showInputDialog(
        "Please enter a positive number");
    value = Double.parseDouble(input);
}
while (value <= 0);
```

See Figure 2 for a flowchart.

Figure 2

Flowchart of a do Loop

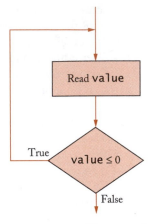

In practice, this situation is not very common. You can always replace a do loop with a while loop, by introducing a boolean control variable.

```
boolean done = false;
while (!done)
{
    String input = JOptionPane.showInputDialog(
        "Please enter a positive number");
    value = Double.parseDouble(input);
    if (value > 0) done = true;
}
```

Random Fact 6.1

Spaghetti Code

In this chapter we are using flowcharts to illustrate the behavior of the loop statements. It used to be common to draw flowcharts for every method, on the theory that flowcharts were easier to read and write than the actual code (especially in the days of machine-language and assembler programming). Nowadays, flowcharts are no longer routinely used for program development and documentation.

Flowcharts have one fatal flaw. Although it is possible to express the while and do loops with flowcharts, it is also possible to draw flowcharts that cannot be programmed with loops. Consider the chart in Figure 3. The top of the flowchart is simply a statement

```
years = 1;
```

The lower part is a do loop:

```
do
{
    years++;
    double interest = balance * rate / 100;
    balance = balance + interest;
}
while (balance < targetBalance);
```

Figure 3

Spaghetti Code

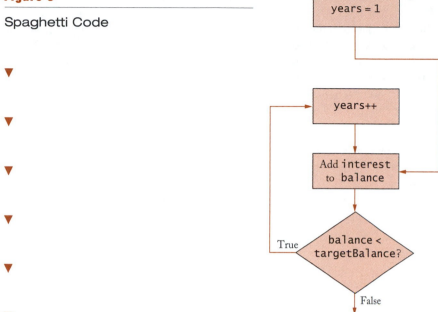

But how can you join these two parts? According to the flowchart, you are supposed to jump from the first statement into the middle of the loop, skipping the first statement.

```
years = 1;
goto a; // not an actual Java statement
do
{
    years++;
    a:

    double interest = balance * rate / 100;
    balance = balance + interest;
}
while (balance < targetBalance);
```

In fact, why even bother with the do loop? Here is a faithful interpretation of the flowchart:

```
years = 1;
goto a; // not an actual Java statement
b:
years++;
a:
double interest = balance * rate / 100;
balance = balance + interest;
if (balance < targetBalance) goto b;
```

This *nonlinear* control flow turns out to be extremely hard to read and understand if you have more than one or two goto statements. Because the lines denoting the goto

▼   statements weave back and forth in complex flowcharts, the resulting code is named *spaghetti code.*

▼   In 1968 the influential computer scientist Edsger Dijkstra wrote a famous note, entitled "Goto Statements Considered Harmful" [1], in which he argued for the use of loops instead of unstructured jumps. Initially, many programmers who had been using `goto` for years were mortally insulted and promptly dug out examples in which the use of `goto` does lead to clearer or faster code. Some languages offer weaker forms of `goto` that are less harmful, such as the `break` statement in Java, discussed in Advanced Topic 6.5. Nowadays, most computer scientists accept Dijkstra's argument and fight bigger battles than optimal loop design.

▼

6.2   for Loops

Far and away the most common loop has the form

```
i = start;
while (i <= end)
{
    . . .
    i++;
}
```

Because this loop is so common, there is a special form for it that emphasizes the pattern:

```
for (i = start; i <= end; i++)
{
    . . .
}
```

You can also *declare* the loop counter variable inside the `for` loop header. That convenient shorthand restricts the use of the variable to the body of the loop (as will be discussed further in Advanced Topic 6.2).

```
for (int i = start; i <= end; i++)
{
    . . .
}
```

> You use a for loop when a variable runs from a starting to an ending value with a constant increment or decrement.

Let us use this loop to find out the size of our $10,000 investment if 5% interest is compounded for 20 years. Of course, the balance will be larger than $20,000, because at least $500 is added every year. You may be surprised to find out just how much larger the balance is.

In our loop, we let i go from 1 to n, the number of years for which we want to compound interest.

```
for (int i = 1; i <= n; i++)
{
    double interest = balance * rate / 100;
    balance = balance + interest;
}
```

Figure 4 shows the corresponding flowchart.

Figure 4

Flowchart of a for Loop

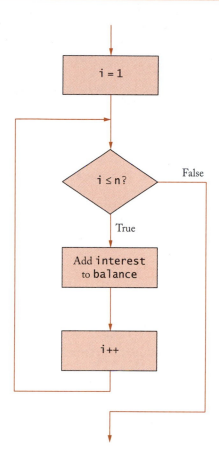

File Investment.java

```
 1  /**
 2      A class to monitor the growth of an investment that
 3      accumulates interest at a fixed annual rate.
 4  */
 5  public class Investment
 6  {
 7     /**
 8         Constructs an Investment object from a starting balance and
 9         interest rate.
10         @param aBalance the starting balance
11         @param aRate the interest rate in percent
12     */
13     public Investment(double aBalance, double aRate)
14     {
15        balance = aBalance;
16        rate = aRate;
```

```
17          years = 0;
18       }
19
20       /**
21          Keeps accumulating interest until a target balance has
22          been reached.
23          @param targetBalance the desired balance
24       */
25       public void waitForBalance(double targetBalance)
26       {
27          while (balance < targetBalance)
28          {
29             years++;
30             double interest = balance * rate / 100;
31             balance = balance + interest;
32          }
33       }
34
35       /**
36          Keeps accumulating interest for a given number of years.
37          @param n the number of years
38       */
39       public void waitYears(int n)
40       {
41          for (int i = 1; i <= n; i++)
42          {
43             double interest = balance * rate / 100;
44             balance = balance + interest;
45          }
46          years = years + n;
47       }
48
49       /**
50          Gets the current investment balance.
51          @return the current balance
52       */
53       public double getBalance()
54       {
55          return balance;
56       }
57
58       /**
59          Gets the number of years this investment has accumulated
60          interest.
61          @return the number of years since the start of the investment
62       */
63       public int getYears()
64       {
65          return years;
66       }
```

```
67
68     private double balance;
69     private double rate;
70     private int years;
71  }
```

File InvestmentTest.java

```
1  /**
2       This program computes how much an investment grows in
3       a given number of years.
4  */
5  public class InvestmentTest
6  {
7     public static void main(String[] args)
8     {
9        final double INITIAL_BALANCE = 10000;
10       final double RATE = 5;
11       final int YEARS = 20;
12       Investment invest =
13          new Investment(INITIAL_BALANCE, RATE);
14       invest.waitYears(YEARS);
15       double balance = invest.getBalance();
16       System.out.println("The balance after " + YEARS +
17          " years is " + balance);
18    }
19 }
```

Syntax 6.2: The for Statement

```
for (initialization; condition; update)
   statement
```

Example:
```
for (i = 1; i <= n; i++)
{
   double interest = balance * rate / 100;
   balance = balance + interest;
}
```

Purpose:

To execute an initialization, then keep executing a statement and updating an expression while a condition is true

---

The three slots in the for header can contain any three expressions. You can count down instead of up:

```
for (years = n; years > 0; years--)
```

The increment or decrement need not be in steps of 1:

```
for (x = -10; x <= 10; x = x + 0.5) . . .
```

It is possible—but a sign of unbelievably bad taste—to put unrelated conditions into the loop:

```
for (rate = 5; years-- > 0; System.out.println(balance))
    . . . // Bad taste
```

We won't even begin to decipher what that might mean. You should stick with `for` loops that initialize, test, and update a single variable.

Quality Tip 6.1

Use for **Loops for Their Intended Purpose Only**

A `for` loop is an *idiom* for a `while` loop of a particular form. A counter runs from the start to the end, with a constant increment:

```
for (set counter to start; test whether counter at end;
        update counter by increment)
{   . . .
    // counter, start, end, increment not changed here
}
```

If your loop doesn't match this pattern, don't use the `for` construction. The compiler won't prevent you from writing idiotic `for` loops:

```
// bad style—unrelated header expressions
for (System.out.println("Inputs:");
        (x = Double.parseDouble(console.readLine())) > 0;
        sum = sum + x)
    count++;

for (int i = 1; i <= years; i++)
{
    // bad style—modifies counter
    if (balance >= targetBalance)
        i = years + 1;
    else
    {
        double interest = balance * rate / 100;
        balance = balance + interest;
    }
}
```

These loops will work, but they are plainly bad style. Use a `while` loop for iterations that do not fit into the `for` pattern.

▼ AT Advanced Topic   6.2 ▶

Scope of Variables Defined in a for Loop Header

As mentioned, it is legal in Java to declare a variable in the header of a for loop. Here is the most common form of this syntax:

```
for (int i = 1; i <= n; i++)
{
    . . .
}

// i  no longer defined here
```

The scope of the variables extends to the end of the for loop. Therefore, i is no longer defined after the loop ends. If you need to use the value of the variable beyond the end of the loop, then you need to define it outside the loop. In this loop, you don't need the value of i—you know it is years + 1 when the loop is finished. (Actually, that is not quite true—it is possible to break out of a loop before its end; see Advanced Topic 6.5). When you have two or more exit conditions, though, you may still need the variable. For example, consider the loop

```
for (i = 1; balance < targetBalance && i <= n; i++)
{
    . . .
}
```

You want the balance to reach the target, but you are willing to wait only a certain number of years. If the balance doubles sooner, you may want to know the value of i. Therefore, in this case, it is not appropriate to define the variable in the loop header.

Note that the variables named i in the following pair of for loops are independent:

```
for (int i = 1; i <= 10; i++)
        System.out.println(i * i);
for (int i = 1; i <= 10; i++) // declares a new variable i
        System.out.println(i * i * i);
```

In the loop header, you can declare multiple variables, as long as they are of the same type, and you can include multiple update expressions, separated by commas:

```
for (int i = 0, j = 10; i <= 10; i++, j--)
{
    . . .
}
```

However, many people find it confusing if a for loop controls more than one variable. I recommend that you not use this form of the for statement (see Quality Tip 6.1). Instead, make the for loop control a single counter, and update the other variable explicitly:

```
int j = 10;
```

```
for (int i = 0; i <= 10; i++)
{
    . . .
    j--;
}
```

⊗ Common Error   6.3

Forgetting a Semicolon

It occasionally happens that all the work of a loop is already done in the loop header. Suppose you ignored Quality Tip 6.1. Then you could write the investment doubling loop as follows:

```
for (years = 1;
    (balance = balance + balance * rate / 100)
        < targetBalance;
    years++)
    ;
return years;
```

The body of the `for` loop is completely empty, containing just one empty statement terminated by a semicolon.

If you do run into a loop without a body, it is important that you really make sure the semicolon is not forgotten. If the semicolon is accidentally omitted, then the next line becomes part of the loop statement!

```
for (years = 1;
    (balance = balance + balance * rate / 100)
        < targetBalance;
    years++)
return years;
```

To make the semicolon really stand out, place it on a line all by itself, as shown in the first example.

⊗ Common Error   6.4

A Semicolon Too Many

What does the following loop print?

```
sum = 0;
for (i = 1; i <= 10; i++);
    sum = sum + i;
System.out.println(sum);
```

Of course, this loop is supposed to compute $1 + 2 + \cdots + 10 = 55$. But actually, the print statement prints 11!

Why 11? Have another look. Did you spot the semicolon at the end of the `for` loop? This loop really is a loop with an empty body.

```
for (i = 1; i <= 10; i++)
    ;
```

The loop does nothing ten times, and when it is finished, sum is still 0 and i is 11. Then the statement

```
sum = sum + i;
```

is executed, and sum is 11. The statement was indented, which fools the human reader. But the compiler pays no attention to indentation.

Of course, the semicolon at the end of the statement was a typing error. Someone's fingers were so used to typing a semicolon at the end of every line that a semicolon was added to the for loop by accident. The result was a loop with an empty body.

Quality Tip   6.2

Don't Use != to Test the End of a Range

Here is a loop with a hidden danger:

```
for (i = 1; i != n; i++)
{
    . . .
}
```

The test i != n is a poor idea. What would happen if n happened to be negative? Then the test i != n is never false, because i starts at 1 and increases with every step.

The remedy is simple. Test

```
for (i = 1; i <= n; i++) . . .
```

For floating-point values, there is another reason not to use !=: Because of roundoff errors, the exact termination point may never be reached.

Of course, you would never write

```
for (rate = 5; rate != 10; rate = rate + 0.3333333) . . .
```

because it is highly unlikely that rate would match 10 exactly after 15 steps. But the same problem may happen for the harmless-looking

```
for (rate = 5; rate != 10; rate = rate + 0.1) . . .
```

The number 0.1 is exactly representable in the decimal system, but the computer represents floating-point numbers in binary. There is a slight error in any finite binary representation of 1/10, just as there is a slight error in a decimal representation 0.3333333 of 1/3. Maybe rate is exactly 10 after 50 steps; maybe it is off by a tiny amount. There is no point in taking chances. Just use < instead of !=:

```
for (rate = 5; rate < 10; rate = rate + 0.1) . . .
```

6.3   **Nested Loops**

Suppose you need to print the following triangle shape:

```
[]
[][]
[][][]
[][][][]
[][][][][]
[][][][][][]
[][][][][][][]
```

The basic idea is simple. You have to generate a number of rows:

```
for (int i = 1; i <= width; i++)
{
    // make triangle row
    . . .
}
```

> Loops can be nested. A typical example for nested loops is printing a table with rows and columns.

How do you make a triangle row? Use another loop to concatenate the squares [] for that row. Then add a newline at the end of the row. The ith row has i symbols, so the loop counter goes from 1 to i.

```
for (int j = 1; j <= i; j++)
    r = r + "[]";
r = r + "\n";
```

Putting both loops together yields two *nested loops*:

```
String r = "";
for (int i = 1; i <= width; i++)
{
    // make triangle row
    for (int j = 1; j <= i; j++)
        r = r + "[]";
    r = r + "\n";
}
return r;
```

Here is the complete program:

File Triangle.java

```
1  /**
2      This class describes triangle objects that can be displayed
3      as shapes like this:
4      []
5      [][]
6      [][][]
```

```java
 7  */
 8  public class Triangle
 9  {
10     /**
11         Constructs a triangle.
12         @param aWidth  the number of [] in the last row of the triangle
13     */
14     public Triangle(int aWidth)
15     {
16        width = aWidth;
17     }
18
19     /**
20         Computes a string representing the triangle.
21         @return  a string consisting of [] and newline characters
22     */
23     public String toString()
24     {
25        String r = "";
26        for (int i = 1; i <= width; i++)
27        {
28           // make triangle row
29           for (int j = 1; j <= i; j++)
30              r = r + "[]";
31           r = r + "\n";
32        }
33        return r;
34     }
35     private int width;
36  }
```

File TriangleTest.java

```java
 1  /**
 2      This program tests the Triangle class.
 3  */
 4  public class TriangleTest
 5  {
 6     public static void main(String[] args)
 7     {
 8        Triangle small = new Triangle(3);
 9        System.out.println(small.toString());
10
11        Triangle large = new Triangle(15);
12        System.out.println(large.toString());
13     }
14  }
```

Advanced Topic 6.3

String Buffers

It is somewhat inefficient to form a string by concatenating many small strings. Each intermediate string is a new object that is only used once. The `StringBuffer` class offers a more efficient way. Start with an empty string buffer, then keep calling the `append` method to add characters to the end of the string buffer. When you are done, call the `toString` method to obtain the string whose characters are stored in the string buffer.

```
StringBuffer r = new StringBuffer();
for (int i = 1; i <= width; i++)
{
   // make triangle row
   for (int j = 1; j <= i; j++)
      r.append("[]");
   r.append("\n");
}
return r.toString();
```

To keep our programs as simple as possible, we will not use string buffers in this book. However, for "real-world" programs it is a good idea to use a string buffer whenever you build up a long string from many individual pieces.

6.4 Processing Input

6.4.1 Reading a Set of Values

Suppose you want to process a set of values, for example a set of measurements, to compute some property, such as the average of the values or the largest value. For reading input, you can use the `showInputDialog` method of the `JOptionPane` class or the `readLine` method of the `BufferedReader` class (see Advanced Topic 3.6).

This loop reads through input data:

```
boolean done = false;
while (!done)
{
   String input = read input;
   if (end of input indicated)
      done = true;
   else
   {
      process input
   }
}
```

> Processing input is complicated by the fact that checking for the end of input occurs in the middle of the loop.

This loop is a little different from the ones you saw before, because the test condition is a variable `done`. That variable stays `false` until you reach the end of the input data; then it is set to `true`. The next time the loop starts at the top, `done` is `true`, and the loop exits.

There is a reason for using a variable. The test for loop termination occurs in the *middle* of the loop, not at the top or the bottom. You must first try to read input before you can test whether you have reached the end of input. In Java, there isn't a ready-made control structure for the pattern "do work, then test, then do more work". Therefore, we use a combination of a `while` loop and a `boolean` variable. This pattern is sometimes called "loop and a half". Some programmers find it clumsy to introduce a control variable for such a loop. Advanced Topic 6.5 shows a few alternatives.

Let's write a program that analyzes a set of values. To decouple the input handling from the computation of the average and the maximum, we'll introduce a class `DataSet`. You add values to a `DataSet` object with the `add` method. The `getAverage` method returns the average of all added data and the `getMaximum` method returns the largest.

File DataSet.java

```
 1  /**
 2      Computes the average of a set of data values.
 3  */
 4  public class DataSet
 5  {
 6      /**
 7          Constructs an empty data set.
 8      */
 9      public DataSet()
10      {
11          sum = 0;
12          count = 0;
13          maximum = 0;
14      }
15
16      /**
17          Adds a data value to the data set.
18          @param x a data value
19      */
20      public void add(double x)
21      {
22          sum = sum + x;
23          if (count == 0 || maximum < x) maximum = x;
24          count++;
25      }
26
27      /**
28          Gets the average of the added data.
29          @return the average or 0 if no data have been added
```

```
30      */
31      public double getAverage()
32      {
33          if (count == 0) return 0;
34          else return sum / count;
35      }
36
37      /**
38          Gets the largest of the added data.
39          @return the maximum or 0 if no data have been added
40      */
41      public double getMaximum()
42      {
43          return maximum;
44      }
45
46      private double sum;
47      private double maximum;
48      private int count;
49  }
```

We use JOptionPane input dialogs to collect the inputs. The **showInputDialog** method returns null if the user clicks the "Cancel" button of the dialog. Thus, we can ask the user to keep entering numbers, or to click on "Cancel" to end the input.

You read the input as a string, but you want to interpret it as a number. Therefore, you must use the Integer.parseInt or Double.parseDouble method to convert the input data from a string to a number. Here is the program to compute the average of a set of input data.

File InputTest.java

```
1   import javax.swing.JOptionPane;
2
3   /**
4       This program computes the average and maximum of a set
5       of input values.
6   */
7   public class InputTest
8   {
9       public static void main(String[] args)
10      {
11          DataSet data = new DataSet();
12
13          boolean done = false;
14          while (!done)
15          {
16              String input = JOptionPane.showInputDialog(
17                  "Enter value, Cancel to quit");
18              if (input == null)
19                  done = true;
20              else
```

```
21            {
22                double x = Double.parseDouble(input);
23                data.add(x);
24            }
25        }
26
27        System.out.println("Average = " +
28            data.getAverage());
29        System.out.println("Maximum = " +
30            data.getMaximum());
31    }
32 }
```

This program pops up a set of input dialogs, which makes for rather tedious data entry. Advanced Topic 6.6 shows you how to read the data from the console window instead. For even more efficient input, use Productivity Hint 6.1 to read data from a file.

▼ **AT Advanced Topic   6.4**

The "Loop and a Half" Problem

When reading data from input, we always used to use a loop like the following, which is somewhat unsightly:

```
boolean done = false;
while (!done)
{
   String input = JOptionPane.showInputDialog(
      "Enter value, Cancel to quit");
   if (input == null)
      done = true;
   else
   {
      process data
   }
}
```

The true test for loop termination is in the middle of the loop, not at the top. This is called a "loop and a half", because one must go halfway into the loop before knowing whether one needs to terminate.

Some programmers dislike the introduction of an additional Boolean variable for loop control. Two Java language features can be used to alleviate the "loop and a half" problem. I don't think either is a superior solution, but both approaches are fairly common, so it is worth knowing about them when reading other people's code.

You can combine an assignment and a test in the loop condition:

```
while ((input = JOptionPane.showInputDialog(
         "Enter value, Cancel to quit")) != null)
```

```
{
    process data
}
```

The expression (input = JOptionPane.showInputDialog("Enter value, Cancel to quit")) != null means, "First read a line; then test whether the end of the input has been reached." This is an expression with a side effect. The primary purpose of the expression is to serve as a test for the while loop, but it also actually does some work—namely, reading the input and storing it in the variable input. In general, it is always a bad idea to use side effects, because they make a program hard to read and maintain. In this case, however, that practice is somewhat seductive, because it eliminates the control variable done, which also makes the code hard to read and maintain.

The other solution is to exit the loop from the middle, either by a return statement or by a break statement (see Advanced Topic 6.5). Here is an example. This loop reads input data, and the method containing the loop returns value when the end of input is encountered.

```
while (true)
{
    String input = JOptionPane.showInputDialog(
        "Enter value, Cancel to quit");
    if (input == null) // leave loop in the middle
        return data;
    double x = Double.parseDouble(input);
    data.add(x);
}
```

Advanced Topic 6.5

The break and continue Statements

You already encountered the break statement in Advanced Topic 5.2, where it was used to exit a switch statement. In addition to breaking out of a switch statement, a break statement can also be used to exit a while, for, or do loop. For example, the break statement in the following loop terminates the loop when the end of input is reached.

```
while (true)
{
    String input = JOptionPane.showInputDialog(
        "Enter value, Cancel to quit");
    if (input == null) // leave loop in the middle
        break;
    double x = Double.parseDouble(input);
    data.add(x);
}
```

▼ In general, a `break` is a very poor way of exiting a loop. In 1990, a misused `break` caused
an AT&T 4ESS telephone switch to fail, and the failure propagated through the entire
U.S. network, rendering it nearly unusable for about nine hours. A programmer had used
▼ a `break` to terminate an `if` statement. Unfortunately, `break` cannot be used with `if`, so
the program execution broke out of the enclosing `switch` statement, skipping some variable initializations and running into chaos [2, p. 38]. Using `break` statements also makes
▼ it difficult to use *correctness proof* techniques (see Advanced Topic 6.8).

However, when faced with the bother of introducing a separate loop control variable,
some programmers find that `break` statements are beneficial in the "loop and a half"
▼ case. This issue is often the topic of heated (and quite unproductive) debate. In this
book, we won't use the `break` statement, and we leave it to you to decide whether you
like to use it in your own programs.

▼ In Java, there is a second form of the `break` statement that is used to break out of a
nested statement. The statement `break` *label*; immediately jumps to the *end* of the statement that is tagged with a label. Any statement (including `if` and block statements) can
▼ be tagged with a label—the syntax is

label: *statement*

▼ The labeled `break` statement was invented to break out of a set of nested loops.

```
outerloop:
while (outer loop condition)
{  . . .
    while (inner loop condition)
    {  . . .
        if (something really bad happened)
            break outerloop;
    }
}
```
jumps here if something really bad happened

Naturally, this situation is quite rare. We recommend that you try to introduce additional
▼ methods instead of using complicated nested loops.

Finally, there is another `goto`-like statement, the `continue` statement, which jumps
to the end of the *current iteration* of the loop. Here is a possible use for this statement:

```
do
{
    input = JOptionPane.showInputDialog(
        "Enter value, Cancel to quit");
    if (input == null) continue; // jump to the end of the loop body
    double x = Double.parseDouble(input);
    data.add(x);
    // continue statement jumps here
}
while (input != null);
```

▼ By using the `continue` statement, you don't need to place the remainder of the loop
code inside an `else` clause. This is a minor benefit. Few programmers use this statement.

▼ ⫶AT⫶ **Advanced Topic** **6.6**

Reading Data from the Console

In Advanced Topic 3.6, you saw how to use a `BufferedReader` to read input from the console window. It is easier to enter a large quantity of data in the console window than it is to type the data into a sequence of input dialogs. More importantly, Productivity Hint 6.1 shows how console input can be *redirected* to read from a file. That is a true time saver that is impossible to achieve with input dialogs.

Recall from Advanced Topic 3.6 that you need to turn `System.in` into a `BufferedReader` as follows:

```
BufferedReader console = new BufferedReader(
    new InputStreamReader(System.in));
```

You use the `readLine` method to read a line of input. The `readLine` method returns `null` at the end of input.

Since `readLine` throws an `IOException`, you need to tag the method in which you call `readLine` with a `throws IOException` specifier.

Here is the `InputTest` program, rewritten to read from the console. The changes are in color.

```
public class InputTest
{
    public static void main(String[] args)
        throws IOException
    {
        BufferedReader console = new BufferedReader(
            new InputStreamReader(System.in));
        DataSet data = new DataSet();

        System.out.println(
            "Enter value, close input to quit");
        boolean done = false;
        while (!done)
        {
            String input = console.readLine();
            if (input == null)
                done = true;
            else
            {
                double x = Double.parseDouble(input);
                data.add(x);
            }
        }

        System.out.println(
            "Average = " + data.getAverage());
```

```
        System.out.println(
            "Maximum = " + data.getMaximum());
    }
}
```

To supply data to the program, you type the input data, a line at a time. When you are done typing, you must indicate to the operating system that all console input for this program has been supplied. The mechanism for this differs from one operating system to another. For example, in DOS you type Ctrl+Z, whereas on UNIX you type Ctrl+D, to indicate the end of console input. This special keystroke combination is a signal to the *operating system* (and not to Java) to close console input. The `System.in` stream never sees this special character. Instead, it just senses that console input has been closed. The `readLine` method returns a `null` string (and not a string containing a control character) at the end of input.

Of course, typing a long set of numbers at the console is tedious and error-prone. Productivity Hint 6.1 shows you how you can prepare the input data in a file and use input redirection to have the `System.in` stream read the characters from that file. In that case you do not terminate the file with a control character, because the operating system knows the size of the file and therefore knows where it ends. But the operating system, not being clairvoyant, cannot know the end of keyboard input—hence the need for the special control character. (Some ancient versions of DOS did terminate text files on disk with a Ctrl+Z, and you will still find some "experts" who tell you that all files have a special end-of-file character at the end. This is plainly not the case—the operating system uses the size of a disk file to determine its end.)

Productivity Hint   6.1

Redirection of Input and Output

> Use input redirection to avoid repetitive typing during testing. Use output redirection to save your program output in a file.

It is tedious to test programs by typing data in for every test run. Testing is far easier if the program reads its input from a *file*. You can then prepare the file once and reuse it for many tests. The command line interfaces of most operating systems provide a way to link a file to the input of a program, as if all the characters in the file had actually been typed by a user. If you type

```
java Average < data.txt
```

the `Average` program is executed. Its input instructions no longer expect input from the keyboard. The `readLine` method gets the input from the file `data.txt`.

This mechanism works for any program that reads its input from the standard input stream `System.in`. By default, the standard input is tied to the keyboard, but it can be tied to any file by specifying *input redirection* on the command line.

If you have always launched your program from the integrated environment, you need to find out whether your environment supports input redirection. If it does not, you need to learn how to open a command window (often called a *shell*) and launch the program in the command window by typing its name and redirection instructions.

▼ You can also redirect output. In this program, that is not terribly useful. If you run

```
java Average < data.txt > output.txt
```

▼ the file `output.txt` contains two lines ("Enter value, close input to quit" and something like "Average = . . ."). However, redirecting output is obviously useful for programs that produce lots of it. You can print the file containing the output or edit it before you turn it in for grading.

6.4.2 String Tokenization

In the last examples, input data were provided a line at a time. However, sometimes it is convenient to have an input line that contains *several* items of input data. Suppose an input line contains two numbers:

```
5.5 10000
```

You can't convert the string `"5.5 10000"` to a number, because the parsing method would complain that this string is not a legal number and throw an exception. Instead, you need to break the input line into a sequence of strings, each of which represents a separate input item. There is a special class, the `StringTokenizer`, that can break up a string into items or, as they are sometimes called, *tokens*. By default, the string tokenizer uses white space (spaces, tabs, and newlines) as delimiters. For example, the string `"5.5 10000"` will be decomposed into two tokens: `"5.5"` and `"10000"`. The delimiting white space is discarded.

> You can break a line into words by using a `StringTokenizer`.

Here is how you break up a string. Construct a `StringTokenizer` object and supply the string to be broken up in the constructor:

```
StringTokenizer tokenizer = new StringTokenizer(input);
```

Then keep calling the `nextToken` method to get the next token.

However, if the entire string has been consumed and there are no more tokens, the `nextToken` method is a bit hostile and throws an exception rather than returning a `null` string. Therefore, you need to call the `hasMoreTokens` method to ensure that there still are tokens to be processed. The following loop traverses all tokens in a string:

```
while (tokenizer.hasMoreTokens())
{
    String token = tokenizer.nextToken();
    do something with token
}
```

If you want to use another separator, such as a comma, to separate the individual values, then you can specify the separator as a second argument when you construct the `StringTokenizer` object:

```
StringTokenizer tokenizer =
    new StringTokenizer(input, ",");
```

If you use this option, you should make sure that there are no extra white spaces in the input file between the commas and your tokens; otherwise the white spaces will be included in the tokens.

Here is a program that computes the average and the maximum of input values that are all specified on a single line. Naturally, that is a reasonable option only for a small data set.

File InputTest.java

```java
1  import java.util.StringTokenizer;
2  import javax.swing.JOptionPane;
3
4  /**
5      This program computes the average and maximum of a set
6      of input values that are entered on a single line.
7  */
8  public class InputTest
9  {
10     public static void main(String[] args)
11     {
12        DataSet data = new DataSet();
13
14        String input =
15           JOptionPane.showInputDialog("Enter values:");
16        StringTokenizer tokenizer =
17           new StringTokenizer(input);
18        while (tokenizer.hasMoreTokens())
19        {
20           String token = tokenizer.nextToken();
21
22           double x = Double.parseDouble(token);
23           data.add(x);
24        }
25
26        System.out.println("Average = " +
27           data.getAverage());
28        System.out.println("Maximum = " +
29           data.getMaximum());
30     }
31  }
```

6.4.3 — Traversing the Characters in a String

> You can access the individual characters of a string with the charAt method.

In the last section, you learned how to decompose a string into tokens. Sometimes, you need to go further and analyze the individual characters of a string. The charAt method of the String class returns an individual character as a value of the char type. Recall from Chapter 3 that string positions are counted starting from 0. That is, the parameter i in the call s.charAt(i) must be a value between 0 and s.length() - 1.

Therefore, the general pattern to traverse all characters in a string is

```java
for (int i = 0; i < s.length(); i++)
{
   char ch = s.charAt(i);
   do something with ch
}
```

Suppose you want to count the number of vowels in a string. The following loop carries out that task.

```
int vowelCount = 0;
String vowels = "aeiouy";
for (int i = 0; i < s.length(); i++)
{
    char ch = Character.toLowerCase(s.charAt(i));
    if (vowels.indexOf(ch) >= 0)
        vowelCount++;
}
```

Here we use the `indexOf` method of the string class. The call

```
s.indexOf(ch)
```

returns the position of the first occurrence of the character `ch` in the string `s`, or −1 if `ch` doesn't occur in `s`. For example, `"Mississippi".indexOf('s')` is 2.

Quality Tip 6.3

Symmetric and Asymmetric Bounds

It is easy to write a loop with i going from 1 to n:

```
for (i = 1; i <= n; i++) . . .
```

The values for i are bounded by the relation $1 \leq i \leq n$. Because there are $\leq$ comparisons on both bounds, the bounds are called *symmetric*.

When traversing the characters in a string, the bounds are *asymmetric*.

```
for (i = 0; i < s.length(); i++) . . .
```

The values for i are bounded by $0 \leq i < s.length()$, with a $\leq$ comparison to the left and a $<$ comparison to the right. That is appropriate, because `s.length()` is not a valid position.

It is not a good idea to force symmetry artificially:

```
for (i = 0; i <= s.length() - 1; i++) . . .
```

> Make a choice between symmetric and asymmetric bounds for each `for` loop.

That is more difficult to read and understand.

For every loop, consider which form is most natural according to the needs of the problem, and use that.

Quality Tip 6.4

Count Iterations

Finding the correct lower and upper bounds for an iteration can be confusing. Should I start at 0? Should I use `<= b` or `< b` as a termination condition?

Counting the number of iterations is a very useful device for better understanding a loop. Counting is easier for loops with asymmetric bounds. The loop

```
for (i = a; i < b; i++) . . .
```

is executed b - a times. For example, the loop traversing the characters in a string,

```
for (i = 0; i < s.length(); i++) . . .
```

runs `s.length()` times. That makes perfect sense, because there are `s.length()` characters in a string.

The loop with symmetric bounds,

```
for (i = a; i <= b; i++)
```

is executed b - a + 1 times. That "+ 1" is the source of many programming errors. For example,

```
for (x = 0; x <= 10; x++)
```

runs 11 times. Maybe that is what you want; if not, start at 1 or use < 10.

One way to visualize this "+1" error is to think of the posts and sections of a fence. Suppose the fence has ten sections (=). How many posts (|) does it have?

$$|=|=|=|=|=|=|=|=|=|=|$$

> Count the number of iterations of a for loop to check that your loop is correct.

A fence with ten sections has *eleven* posts. Each section has one post to the left, *and* there is one more post after the last section. Forgetting to count the last iteration of a "<=" loop is often called a "fence post error".

If the increment is a value c other than 1, then the counts are

$$(b - a) / c \qquad \text{for the asymmetric loop}$$

$$(b - a) / c + 1 \quad \text{for the symmetric loop}$$

For example, the loop `for (i = 10; i <= 40; i += 5)` executes $(40 - 10)/5 + 1 = 7$ times.

HOWTO 6.1

Implementing Loops

You write a loop because your program needs to repeat an action multiple times. As you have seen in this chapter, there are several loop types, and it isn't always obvious how to structure loop statements. This HOWTO walks you through the thought process that is involved when programming a loop.

Step 1 List the work that needs to be done in every step of the loop body

For example, suppose you need to read in input values in gallons and convert them to liters, until the end of input is reached. Then the operations are:

- Read input.

- Convert the input to liters.

- Print out the response.

Suppose you need to scan through the characters of a string and count the vowels. Then the operations are:

- Get the next character.

- If it's a vowel, increase a counter.

Step 2 Find out how often the loop is repeated

Typical answers might be:

- Ten times

- Once for each character in the string

- Until the end of input is reached

- While the balance is less than the target balance

If a loop is executed for a definite number of times, a `for` loop is usually appropriate. The first two loops lead to `for` loops, such as

```
for (int i = 1; i <= 10; i++) . . .
for (int i = 0; i < str.length(); i++) . . .
```

The other two loops need to be implemented as `while` loops—you don't know how many times the loop body is going to be repeated.

Step 3 With a `while` loop, find out where you can determine that the loop is finished

There are three possibilities:

- Before entering the loop

- In the middle of the loop

- At the end of the loop

For example, if you execute a loop while the balance is less than the target balance, you can check for that condition at the beginning of the loop. If the balance is less than the target balance, you enter the loop. If not, you are done. In such a case, your loop has the form

```
while (condition)
{
    do work
}
```

However, checking for input requires that you first *read* the input. That means, you'll need to enter the loop, read the input, and then decide whether you want to go any further. Then your loop has the form

```
boolean done = false;
while (!done)
```

```
{
    do the work needed to check the condition
    if (condition)
        done = true;
    else
    {
        do more work
    }
}
```

This loop structure is sometimes called a "loop and a half".

Finally, if you know whether you need to go on after you have gone through the loop once, then you use a **do/while** loop:

```
do
{
    do work
}
while (condition)
```

However, these loops are very rare in practice.

Step 4 Implement the loop by putting the operations from Step 1 into the loop body

When you write a **for** loop, you usually use the loop index inside the loop body. For example, "get the next character" is implemented as the statement

```
char ch = str.charAt(i);
```

Step 5 Double-check your variable initializations

If you use a Boolean variable **done**, make sure it is initialized to **false**. If you accumulate a result in a **sum** or **count** variable, make sure that you set it to 0 before entering the loop for the first time.

Step 6 Check for off-by-one errors

Consider the simplest possible scenarios:

- If you read input, what happens if there is no input at all? Exactly one input?

- If you look through the characters of a string, what happens if the string is empty? If it has one character in it?

- If you accumulate values until some target has been reached, what happens if the target is 0? A negative value?

Manually walk through every instruction in the loop, including all initializations. Carefully check all conditions, paying attention to the difference between comparisons such as < and <=. Check that the loop is not traversed at all, or only once, and that the final result is what you expect.

If you write a **for** loop, check to see whether your bounds should be symmetric or asymmetric (see Quality Tip 6.3) and count the number of iterations (see Quality Tip 6.4).

▼ 𝐀𝐓 Advanced Topic   6.7

Pipes

In many operating systems, output of one program can become the input of another program. Here is a simple program that writes each word of the input file onto a separate line:

File Split.java

```
 1 import java.io.BufferedReader;
 2 import java.io.InputStreamReader;
 3 import java.io.IOException;
 4 import java.util.StringTokenizer;
 5
 6 /**
 7    This program splits the lines read from System.in into
 8    individual words.
 9 */
10 public class Split
11 {
12    public static void main(String[] args)
13       throws IOException
14    {
15       BufferedReader console = new BufferedReader(
16          new InputStreamReader(System.in));
17       boolean done = false;
18       while (!done)
19       {
20          String inputLine = console.readLine();
21          if (inputLine == null)
22             done = true;
23          else
24          {
25             // break input line into words
26
27             StringTokenizer tokenizer =
28                new StringTokenizer(inputLine);
29             while (tokenizer.hasMoreTokens())
30             {
31                // print each word
32                String word = tokenizer.nextToken();
33                System.out.println(word);
34             }
35          }
36       }
37    }
38 }
```

▼   Then

```
java Split < article.txt
```

▼   lists the words in the file article.txt, one on each line. That isn't too exciting, but it
becomes useful when combined with another program: *sort*. You don't yet know how to
write a program that sorts strings, but most operating systems have a sort program. A

▼   sorted list of the words in a file would be quite useful—for example, for making an index.
You can save the unsorted words in a temporary file:

```
java Split < article.txt > temp.txt
sort < temp.txt > sorted.txt
```

▼   Now the sorted words are in the file sorted.txt.
Because this operation is so common, there is a command line shorthand for it.

▼

```
java Split < article.txt | sort > sorted.txt
```

The split program runs first, reading input from article.txt. Its output becomes the input
of the sort program. The output of `sort` is saved in the file sorted.txt. The | operator

▼   instructs the operating system to construct a *pipe* that links the output of the first program to the input of the second.
The file sorted.txt has one blemish. It is likely to contain runs of repeated words, like

▼

```
a
a
a
an
an
anteater
asia
```

This is easy to fix with another program that removes *adjacent* duplicates. Removing
duplicates in arbitrary positions is quite hard, but adjacent duplicates are easy to handle:

▼

File Unique.java

```
1   import java.io.BufferedReader;
2   import java.io.InputStreamReader;
3   import java.io.IOException;
4
5   /**
6       This program removes adjacent duplicate lines from
7       the input read from System.in.
8   */
9   public class Unique
10  {
11      public static void main(String[] args)
12          throws IOException
13      {
14          BufferedReader console = new BufferedReader(
15              new InputStreamReader(System.in));
16
17          String lastLine = "";
18
```

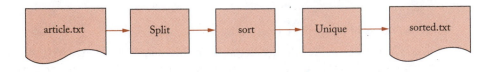

Figure 5

A Series of Pipes

```
19        boolean done = false;
20
21        while(!done)
22        {
23            String inputLine = console.readLine();
24            if (inputLine == null)
25                done = true;
26            else if (!inputLine.equals(lastLine))
27            {
28                // it's a different line from its predecessor
29                System.out.println(inputLine);
30                lastLine = inputLine;
31            }
32        }
33    }
34 }
```

The sorted word list, with duplicates removed, is obtained as the series of pipes (see Figure 5).

```
java Split < article.txt | sort | java Unique >
sorted.txt
```

Redirection and pipes make it possible to combine simple programs to do useful work. This approach was pioneered in the UNIX operating system, which comes with dozens of commands that perform common tasks and are designed to be combined with each other.

6.5   Random Numbers and Simulations

> In a simulation, you repeatedly generate random numbers and use them to simulate an activity.

In a simulation you generate random events and evaluate their outcomes. Here is a typical problem that can be decided by running a simulation: the *Buffon needle experiment*, devised by Comte Georges-Louis Leclerc de Buffon (1707–1788), a French naturalist. On each *try*, a needle of length 1 inch is dropped onto paper that is ruled with lines 2 inches apart. If the needle drops onto a line, count it as a hit. Buffon conjectured that the quotient *tries/hits* approximates π. (See Figure 6.)

Now, how can you run this experiment in the computer? You don't actually want to build a robot that drops needles on paper. The Random class of the Java library implements

Figure 6

The Buffon Needle Experiment

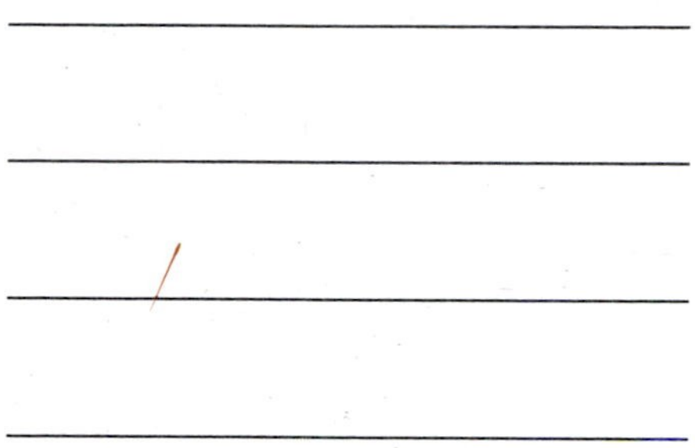

a *random number generator,* which produces numbers that appear to be completely random. To generate random numbers, you construct an object of the **Random** class, and then apply one of the following methods:

Method	Returns
`nextInt(n)`	A random integer between the integers 0 (inclusive) and **n** (exclusive)
`nextDouble()`	A random floating-point number between 0 (inclusive) and **n** (exclusive)

For example, you can simulate the cast of a die as follows:

```
Random generator = new Random();
int d = 1 + generator.nextInt(6);
```

The call `generator.nextInt(6)` gives you a random number between 0 and 5 (inclusive). Add 1 to obtain a number between 1 and 6.

To give you a feeling for the random numbers, run the following program a few times:

File Die.java

```
 1  import java.util.Random;
 2
 3  /**
 4      This class models a die that, when cast, lands on a random
 5      face.
 6  */
 7  public class Die
 8  {
 9     /**
10         Constructs a die with a given number of sides.
11         @param s the number of sides, e.g. 6 for a normal die
12     */
13     public Die(int s)
14     {
15        sides = s;
16        generator = new Random();
17     }
18
```

```
19   /**
20       Simulates a throw of the die.
21       @return  the face of the die
22   */
23   public int cast()
24   {
25       return 1 + generator.nextInt(sides);
26   }
27
28
29   private Random generator;
30   private int sides;
31 }
```

File DieTest.java

```
1  /**
2      This program simulates casting a die ten times.
3  */
4  public class DieTest
5  {
6     public static void main(String[] args)
7     {
8        Die d = new Die(6);
9        final int TRIES = 10;
10       for (int i = 1; i <= TRIES; i++)
11       {
12          int n = d.cast();
13          System.out.print(n + " ");
14       }
15       System.out.println();
16    }
17 }
```

Here are a few typical program runs.

```
6 5 6 3 2 6 3 4 4 1
3 2 2 1 6 5 3 4 1 2
4 1 3 2 6 2 4 3 3 5
```

As you can see, this program produces a different stream of simulated die casts every time it is run. Actually, the numbers are not completely random. They are drawn from very long sequences of numbers that don't repeat for a long time. These sequences are actually computed from fairly simple formulas; they just behave like random numbers. For that reason, they are often called *pseudorandom* numbers. How to generate good sequences of numbers that behave like truly random sequences is an important and well-studied problem in computer science. We won't investigate this issue further, though; we'll just use the random numbers produced by the Random class.

To run the Buffon needle experiment, we have to work a little harder. When you throw a die, it has to come up with one of six faces. When throwing a needle, however, there are many possible outcomes. You must generate *two* random numbers: one to

Figure 7

When Does the Needle Fall on a Line?

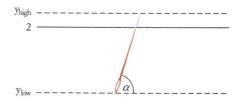

describe the starting position and one to describe the angle of the needle with the *x*-axis. Then you need to test whether the needle touches a grid line. Stop after 10,000 tries.

Let us agree to generate the *lower* point of the needle. Its *x*-coordinate is irrelevant, and you may assume its *y*-coordinate y_{low} to be any random number between 0 and 2. However, because it can be a random *floating-point* number, we use the `nextDouble` method of the `Random` class. It returns a random floating-point number between 0 and 1. Multiply by 2 to get a random number between 0 and 2.

The angle α between the needle and the *x*-axis can be any value between 0 degrees and 180 degrees. The upper end of the needle has *y*-coordinate

$$y_{high} = y_{low} + \sin(\alpha)$$

The needle is a hit if y_{high} is at least 2. See Figure 7.

Here is the program to carry out the simulation of the needle experiment.

File Needle.java

```
 1 import java.util.Random;
 2
 3 /**
 4     This class simulates a needle in the Buffon needle experiment.
 5 */
 6 public class Needle
 7 {
 8     /**
 9         Constructs a needle.
10     */
11     public Needle()
12     {
13         hits = 0;
14         generator = new Random();
15     }
16
17     /**
18         Drops the needle on the grid of lines and
```

```
19        remembers whether the needle hit a line.
20     */
21     public void drop()
22     {
23         double ylow = 2 * generator.nextDouble();
24         double angle = 180 * generator.nextDouble();
25
26         // compute high point of needle
27
28         double yhigh = ylow
29             + Math.sin(Math.toRadians(angle));
30         if (yhigh >= 2) hits++;
31         tries++;
32     }
33
34     /**
35         Gets the number of times the needle hit a line.
36         @return the hit count
37     */
38     public int getHits()
39     {
40         return hits;
41     }
42
43     /**
44         Gets the total number of times the needle was dropped.
45         @return the try count
46     */
47     public int getTries()
48     {
49         return tries;
50     }
51
52     private Random generator;
53     private int hits;
54     private int tries;
55 }
```

File NeedleTest.java

```
1  public class NeedleTest
2  {
3     public static void main(String[] args)
4     {
5        Needle n = new Needle();
6        final int TRIES1 = 10000;
7        final int TRIES2 = 100000;
8
9        for (int i = 1; i <= TRIES1; i++)
10           n.drop();
11        System.out.println("Tries / Hits = "
```

```
12                 + (double)n.getTries() / n.getHits());
13
14         for (int i = TRIES1 + 1; i <= TRIES2; i++)
15            n.drop();
16         System.out.println("Tries / Hits = "
17                 + (double)n.getTries() / n.getHits());
18      }
19 }
```

On one computer I obtained the result 3.10 when running 10,000 iterations and 3.1429 when running 100,000 iterations.

The point of this program is *not* to compute π—there are far more efficient ways for that purpose. Rather, the point is to show how a physical experiment can be simulated on the computer. Buffon had to drop the needle physically thousands of times and record the results, which must have been a rather dull activity. You can have the computer execute the experiment quickly and accurately.

Simulations are very common computer applications. Many simulations use essentially the same pattern as the code of this example: In a loop, a large number of sample values are generated, and the values of certain observations are recorded for each sample. When the simulation is completed, the averages, or other statistics of interest from the observed values are printed out.

A typical example of a simulation is the modeling of customer queues at a bank or a supermarket. Rather than observing real customers, one simulates their arrival and their transactions at the teller window or checkout stand in the computer. One can try out different staffing or building layout patterns in the computer simply by making changes in the program. In the real world, making many such changes and measuring their effect would be impossible, or at least very expensive.

Advanced Topic   6.8

Loop Invariants

Consider the task of computing a^n, where a is a floating-point number and n is a positive integer. Of course, you can multiply $a \cdot a \cdot \cdots \cdot a$, n times, but if n is large, you'll end up doing a lot of multiplications. The following loop computes a^n in far fewer steps:

```
double a = . . .;
int n = . . .;
double r = 1;
double b = a;
int i = n;
while (i > 0)
{
   if (i % 2 == 0) // n is even
   {
      b = b * b;
      i = i / 2;
   }
```

```
        else
        {
            r = r * b;
            i--
        }
    }
// now r equals a to the nth power
```

Consider the case n = 100. The method performs the following steps.

b	i	r
a	100	1
a^2	50	
a^4	25	
	24	a^4
a^8	12	
a^{16}	6	
a^{32}	3	
	2	a^{36}
a^{64}	1	
	0	a^{100}

Amazingly enough, the algorithm yields exactly a^{100}. Do you understand why? Are you convinced it will work for all values of n? Here is a clever argument to show that the method always computes the correct result. We will demonstrate that whenever the program reaches the top of the while loop, it is true that

$$r \cdot b^i \ = \ a^n \tag{I}$$

Certainly, it is true the first time around, because b == a and i == n. Suppose that (I) holds at the beginning of the loop. We label the values of r, b, and i as "old" when entering the loop, as "new" when exiting the loop. We assume that upon entry

$$r_{old} \cdot b_{old}^{i_{old}} \ = \ a^n$$

In the loop we have to distinguish two cases: i_{old} even and i_{old} odd. If i_{old} is even, the loop performs the following transformations:

$$r_{new} \ = \ r_{old}$$

$$b_{new} \ = \ b_{old}^2$$

$$i_{new} \ = \ i_{old} / 2$$

Therefore,

$$r_{new} \cdot b_{new}^{i_{new}} = r_{old} \cdot b_{old}^{2 \cdot i_{old}/2}$$

$$= r_{old} \cdot b_{old}^{i_{old}}$$

$$= a^n$$

On the other hand, if i_{old} is odd, then

$$r_{new} = r_{old} \cdot a_{old}$$

$$b_{new} = b_{old}$$

$$i_{new} = i_{old} - 1$$

Therefore,

$$r_{new} \cdot b_{new}^{i_{new}} = r_{old} \cdot b_{old} \cdot b_{old}^{i_{old} - 1}$$

$$= r_{old} \cdot b_{old}^{i_{old}}$$

$$= a^n$$

In either case, the new values for r, b, and i fulfill the *loop invariant* (I). So what? When the loop finally exits, (I) holds again:

$$r \cdot b^i = a^n$$

Furthermore, we know that $i = 0$, because the loop is terminating. But because $i = 0$, $r \cdot b^i = r \cdot b^0 = r$. Hence $r = a^n$, and the method really does compute the nth power of a.

This technique is quite useful, because it can explain an algorithm that is not at all obvious. The condition (I) is called a loop invariant because it is true when the loop is entered, at the top of each pass, and when the loop is exited. If a loop invariant is chosen skillfully, you may be able to deduce correctness of a computation. See [3] for another nice example.

Random Fact   6.2

Correctness Proofs

In Advanced Topic 6.7 we introduced the technique of loop invariants. If you skipped that note, have a glance at it now. That technique can be used to prove rigorously that a loop computes exactly the value that it is supposed to compute. Such a proof is far more valuable than any testing. No matter how many test cases you try, you always worry whether another case that you haven't tried yet might show a bug. A proof settles the correctness for *all possible inputs*.

For some time, programmers were very hopeful that proof techniques such as loop invariants would greatly reduce the need of testing. You would prove that each simple method is correct, and then put the proven components together and prove that they work together as they should. Once it is proved that main works correctly, no testing is required at all! Some researchers were so excited about these techniques that they tried to

▼ omit the programming step altogether. The designer would write down the program requirements, using the notation of formal logic. An automatic prover would prove that such a program could be written and generate the program as part of its proof.

▼ Unfortunately, in practice these methods never worked very well. The logical notation to describe program behavior is complex. Even simple scenarios require many formulas. It is easy enough to express the idea that a method is supposed to compute a^n, but

▼ the logical formulas describing all methods in a program that controls an airplane, for instance, would fill many pages. These formulas are created by humans, and humans make errors when they deal with difficult and tedious tasks. Experiments showed that

▼ instead of buggy programs, programmers wrote buggy logic specifications and buggy program proofs.

Van der Linden [2, p. 287], gives some examples of complicated proofs that are much

▼ harder to verify than the programs they are trying to prove.

Program proof techniques are valuable for proving the correctness of individual methods that make computations in nonobvious ways. At this time, though, there is no

▼ hope to prove any but the most trivial programs correct in such a way that the specification and the proof can be trusted more than the program. There is hope that correctness proofs will become more applicable to real-life programming situations in the future. At

▼ this point, however, engineering and management are at least as important as mathematics and logic for the successful completion of large software projects.

CHAPTER SUMMARY

1. A `while` statement executes a block of code repeatedly. A termination condition controls how often the loop is executed.

2. An off-by-one error is a common error when programming loops. Think through simple test cases to avoid this type of error.

3. You use a `for` loop when a variable runs from a starting to an ending value with a constant increment or decrement.

4. Loops can be nested. A typical example for nested loops is printing a table with rows and columns.

5. Processing input is complicated by the fact that checking for the end of input occurs in the middle of the loop.

6. Use input redirection to avoid repetitive typing during testing. Use output redirection to save your program output in a file.

7. You can break a line into words by using a `StringTokenizer`.

8. You can access the individual characters of a string with the `charAt` method.

9. Make a choice between symmetric and asymmetric bounds for each `for` loop.

10. Count the number of iterations of a `for` loop to check that your loop is correct.

11. In a simulation, you repeatedly generate random numbers and use them to simulate an activity.

Further Reading

[1] E. W. Dijkstra, "Goto Statements Considered Harmful", *Communications of the ACM*, vol. 11, no. 3 (March 1968), pp. 147–148.
[2] Peter van der Linden, *Expert C Programming*, Prentice-Hall, 1994.
[3] Jon Bentley, *Programming Pearls*, Addison-Wesley, 1986, Chapter 4, "Writing Correct Programs".
[4] Kai Lai Chung, *Elementary Probability Theory with Stochastic Processes*, Undergraduate Texts in Mathematics, Springer-Verlag, 1974.
[5] Rudolf Flesch, *How to Write Plain English*, Barnes & Noble Books, 1979.

CLASSES, OBJECTS, AND METHODS INTRODUCED IN THIS CHAPTER

```
java.lang.String
    indexOf
java.util.Random
    nextDouble
    nextInt
java.util.StringTokenizer
    countTokens
    hasMoreTokens
    nextToken
```

REVIEW EXERCISES

Exercise R6.1. Which loop statements does Java support? Give simple rules when to use each loop type.

Exercise R6.2. What does the following code print?

```
for (int i = 0; i < 10; i++)
{
    for (int j = 0; j < 10; j++)
        System.out.print(i * j % 10);
    System.out.println();
}
```

Exercise R6.3. How often do the following loops execute? Assume that i is an integer variable that is not changed in the loop body.

- `for (i = 1; i <= 10; i++) ...`
- `for (i = 0; i < 10; i++) ...`

- `for (i = 10; i > 0; i-) ...`
- `for (i = -10; i <= 10; i++) ...`
- `for (i = 10; i >= 0; i++) ...`
- `for (i = -10; i <= 10; i = i + 2) ...`
- `for (i = -10; i <= 10; i = i + 3) ...`

Exercise R6.4. Rewrite the following `for` loop into a `while` loop.

```
int s = 0;
for (int i = 1; i <= 10; i++) s = s + i;
```

Exercise R6.5. Rewrite the following `do` loop into a `while` loop.

```
int n = 1;
double x = 0;
double s;
do
{
    s = 1.0 / (n * n);
    x = x + s;
    n++;
}
while (s > 0.01);
```

Exercise R6.6. What is an infinite loop? On your computer, how can you terminate a program that executes an infinite loop?

Exercise R6.7. There are two ways to supply input to `System.in`. Describe both methods. Explain how the "end of input" is signaled in both cases.

Exercise R6.8. In UNIX and Windows, there is no special "end of file" character stored in a file. Verify that statement by producing a file with known character count—for example, a file consisting of the following three lines

```
Hello
cruel
world
```

Then look at the directory listing. How many characters does the file contain? Remember to count the newline characters. (In DOS, you may be surprised that the count is not what you expect. DOS text files store each newline as a two-character sequence. The input readers and output streams automatically translate between this carriage return/line feed sequence used by files and the `'\n'` character used by Java programs, so you don't need to worry about it.) Why does this prove that there is no "end of file" character? Why do you nevertheless need to type Ctrl+D/Ctrl+Z to end console input?

Exercise R6.9. Show how to use a string tokenizer to break up the string `"Hello, cruel world!"` into tokens. What are the resulting tokens?

Exercise R6.10. How do you break up the string `"Hello, cruel world!"` into characters? What are the resulting characters?

Exercise R6.11. What is a "loop and a half"? Give three strategies to implement the following "loop and a half":

```
loop
{
    read name of bridge
    if not OK, exit loop
    read length of bridge in feet
    if not OK, exit loop
    convert length to meters
    print bridge data
}
```

Use a Boolean variable, a `break` statement, and a method with multiple `return` statements. Which of these three approaches do you find clearest?

Exercise R6.12. Give a strategy for reading input of the form

     name of bridge   length of bridge

Here the name of the bridge can be a single word ("Brooklyn") or consist of several words ("Golden Gate"). The length is a floating-point number. Unlike the preceding exercise, the entire input is provided on a single line.

Exercise R6.13. Sometimes students write programs with instructions such as "Enter data, 0 to quit" and exit the data entry loop when the user enters the number 0. (Such a value is called a sentinel value.) Explain why that is usually a poor idea.

Exercise R6.14. How would you use a random number generator to simulate the drawing of a playing card?

Exercise R6.15. What is an "off by one" error? Give an example from your own programming experience.

Exercise R6.16. Give an example of a `for` loop in which symmetric bounds are more natural. Give an example of a `for` loop in which asymmetric bounds are more natural.

Exercise R6.17. What are nested loops? Give an example where a nested loop is typically used.

Programming Exercises

Exercise P6.1. *Currency conversion.* Write a program that asks the user to enter today's exchange rate between U.S. dollars and the Euro. Then the program reads U.S. dollar values and converts each to Euro values. Stop when the user hits the "Cancel" button of the input dialog (or when the user closes input if you read from `System.in`).

Exercise P6.2. *Random walk.* Simulate the wandering of an intoxicated person in a square street grid. Draw a grid of 10 streets horizontally and 10 streets vertically. Represent the simulated drunkard by a dot, placed in the middle of the grid to start. For 100 times, have the simulated drunkard randomly pick a direction (east, west, north, south), move one block in the chosen direction, and redraw the dot. After the iterations, display the distance that the drunkard has covered. (One might expect that on average the person might not get anywhere because the moves to different directions cancel another out in the long run, but in fact it can be shown that with probability 1 the person eventually moves outside any finite region. See, for example, [4], Chapter 8, for more details.) Use classes for the grid and the drunkard.

Exercise P6.3. *Projectile flight.* Suppose a cannonball is propelled vertically into the air with a starting velocity v_0. Any calculus book will tell us that the position of the ball after t seconds is $s(t) = -0.5 \cdot g \cdot t^2 + v_0 \cdot t$, where $g = 9.81$ m/sec^2 is the gravitational force of the earth. No calculus book ever mentions why someone would want to carry out such an obviously dangerous experiment, so we will do it in the safety of the computer.

In fact, we will confirm the theorem from calculus by a simulation. In our simulation, we will consider how the ball moves in very short time intervals Δt. In a short time interval the velocity v is nearly constant, and we can compute the distance the ball moves as $\Delta s = v \cdot \Delta t$. In our program, we will simply set

```
double deltaT = 0.01;
```

and update the position by

```
s = s + v * deltaT;
```

The velocity changes constantly—in fact, it is reduced by the gravitational force of the earth. In a short time interval, v decreases by $g \cdot \Delta t$, and we must keep the velocity updated as

```
v = v - g * deltaT;
```

In the next iteration the new velocity is used to update the distance.

Now run the simulation until the cannonball falls back onto the earth. Get the initial velocity as an input (100 m/sec is a good value). Update the position and velocity 100 times per second, but print out the position only every full second. Also print out the values from the exact formula $s(t) = -0.5 \cdot g \cdot t^2 + v_0 \cdot t$ for comparison. Use a class `Cannonball`.

What is the benefit of this kind of simulation when an exact formula is available? Well, the formula from the calculus book is *not* exact. Actually, the gravitational force diminishes the further the cannonball is away from the surface of the earth. This complicates the algebra sufficiently that it is not possible to give an exact formula for the actual motion, but the computer simulation can simply be extended to apply a variable gravitational force. For cannonballs, the calculus-book formula is actually good enough, but computers are necessary to compute accurate trajectories for higher-flying objects such as ballistic missiles.

Exercise P6.4. Most cannonballs are not shot upright but at an angle. If the starting velocity has magnitude v and the starting angle is α, then the velocity is actually a vector with components $v_x = v \cdot \cos(\alpha)$, $v_y = v \cdot \sin(\alpha)$. In the x-direction the velocity does not change. In the y-direction the gravitational force takes its toll. Repeat the simulation from the previous exercise, but update the x and y components of the location and the velocity separately. Every full second, plot the location of the cannonball on the graphics display. Repeat until the cannonball has reached the earth again. Again, use a class `Cannonball`.

This kind of problem is of historical interest. The first computers were designed to carry out just such ballistic calculations, taking into account the diminishing gravity for high-flying projectiles and wind speeds.

Exercise P6.5. The *Fibonacci sequence* is defined by the following rule. The first two values in the sequence are 1 and 1. Every subsequent value is the sum of the two values preceding it. For example, the third value is $1 + 1 = 2$, the fourth value is $1 + 2 = 3$, and the fifth is $2 + 3 = 5$. If f_n denotes the nth value in the Fibonacci sequence, then

$$f_1 = 1$$
$$f_2 = 1$$
$$f_n = f_{n-1} + f_{n-2} \text{ if } n > 2$$

Write a program that prompts the user for n and prints the nth value in the Fibonacci sequence. Use a class `FibonacciGenerator` with a method `nextNumber`.

Hint: There is no need to store all values for f_n. You only need the last two values to compute the next one in the series:

```
fold1 = 1;
fold2 = 1;
fnew = fold1 + fold2;
```

After that, discard `fold2`, which is no longer needed, and set `fold2` to `fold1` and `fold1` to `fnew`.

Exercise P6.6. Write a program that draws a *bar chart* from a data set. The program should be a graphics applet that prompts the user for the values, all to be entered into a single option dialog, separated by spaces (for example, 40 60 50). Assume all values are between 0 and 100. Then draw a bar chart like this:

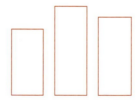

Exercise P6.7. *Mean and standard deviation.* Write a program that reads a set of floating-point data values from the input. When the end of file is reached, print out the count of the values, the average, and the standard deviation. The average of a data set $x_1, \ldots, x_n$ is

$$\bar{x} = \frac{\sum x_i}{n}$$

where $\sum x_i = x_1 + \cdots + x_n$ is the sum of the input values. The standard deviation is

$$S = \sqrt{\frac{\sum (x_i - \bar{x})^2}{n - 1}}$$

However, that formula is not suitable for our task. By the time you have computed the mean, the individual x_i are long gone. Until you know how to save these values, use the numerically less stable formula

$$S = \sqrt{\frac{\sum x_i^2 - \left(\sum x_i\right)^2 / n}{n - 1}}$$

You can compute this quantity by keeping track of the count, the sum, and the sum of squares in the `DataSet` class as you process the input values.

Exercise P6.8. Write a graphical applet that prompts a user to enter a number n and that draws n circles with random center and random radius.

Exercise P6.9. *Flesch Readability Index.* The following index [5] was invented by Flesch as a simple tool to gauge the legibility of a document without linguistic analysis.

- Count all words in the file. A *word* is any sequence of characters delimited by white space, whether or not it is an actual English word.

- Count all syllables in each word. To make this simple, use the following rules: Each *group* of adjacent vowels (a,e,i,o,u,y) counts as one syllable (for example, the "ea" in "real" contributes one syllable, but the "e..a" in "regal" count as two syllables). However, an "e" at the end of a word doesn't count as a syllable. Also, each word has at least one syllable, even if the previous rules give a count of 0.

- Count all sentences. A sentence is ended by a period, colon, semicolon, question mark, or exclamation mark.

- The index is computed by

$$\text{Index} = 206.835$$
$$- 84.6 \times (\text{Number of syllables} / \text{Number of words})$$
$$- 1.015 \times (\text{Number of words} / \text{Number of sentences})$$

rounded to the nearest integer.

This index is a number, usually between 0 and 100, indicating how difficult the text is to read. Some examples for random material for various publications are

Comics	95
Consumer ads	82
Sports Illustrated	65
Time	57
New York Times	39
Auto insurance policy	10
Internal Revenue Code	−6

Translated into educational levels, the indices are

91–100	5th grader
81–90	6th grader
71–80	7th grader
66–70	8th grader
61–66	9th grader
51–60	High school student
31–50	College student
0–30	College graduate
Less than 0	Law school graduate

The purpose of the index is to force authors to rewrite their text until the index is high enough. This is achieved by reducing the length of sentences and by removing long words. For example, the sentence

> The following index was invented by Flesch as a simple tool to estimate the legibility of a document without linguistic analysis.

can be rewritten as

> Flesch invented an index to check whether a text is easy to read. To compute the index, you need not look at the meaning of the words.

His book [5] contains delightful examples of translating government regulations into "plain English".

Your program should read a text file in, compute the legibility index, and print out the equivalent educational level. Use classes `Word` and `Document`.

Exercise P6.10. *Factoring of integers.* Write a program that asks the user for an integer and then prints out all its factors. For example, when the user enters 150, the program should print

```
2
3
5
5
```

Use a class `FactorGenerator` with methods `nextFactor` and `hasMoreFactors`.

Exercise P6.11. *Prime numbers.* Write a program that prompts the user for an integer and then prints out all prime numbers up to that integer. For example, when the user enters 20, the program should print

```
2
3
5
7
11
13
17
19
```

Recall that a number is a prime number if it is not divisible by any number except 1 and itself.

Use a class `PrimeGenerator` with a method `nextPrime`.

Exercise P6.12. The *Heron method* is a method for computing square roots that was known to the ancient Greeks. If x is a guess for the value $\sqrt{a}$, then the average of x and a/x is a better guess.

Implement a class `RootApproximator` that starts with an initial guess of 1 and whose `nextGuess` method produces a sequence of increasingly better guesses. Supply a method `hasMoreGuesses` that returns `false` if two successive guesses are sufficiently close to each other. Then test your class like this:

```
RootApproximator r = new RootApproximator(n);
while (r.hasMoreGuesses())
    System.out.println(r.nextGuess());
```

Exercise P6.13. The best known iterative method for computing the *roots* of a function f (that is, the x-values for which $f(x)$ is 0) is *Newton–Raphson approximation*. To find the zero of a function whose derivative is also known, compute

$$x_{\text{new}} = x_{\text{old}} - f(x_{\text{old}})/f'(x_{\text{old}}).$$

For this exercise, write a program to compute nth roots of floating-point numbers. Prompt the user for a and n, then obtain $\sqrt[n]{a}$ by computing a zero of the function $f(x) = x^n - a$. Follow the approach of the preceding exercise.

Exercise P6.14. The value of e^x can be computed as the power series

$$e^x = \sum_{n=0}^{\infty} \frac{x^n}{n!}$$

where $n! = 1 \cdot 2 \cdot 3 \cdot \cdots \cdot n$.

Write a program that computes e^x using this formula. Of course, you can't compute an infinite sum. Just keep adding values until an individual summand (term) is less than a certain threshold. At each step, you need to compute the new term and add it to the total. Update these terms as follows:

```
term = term * x / n;
```

Follow the approach of the preceding two exercises, by implementing a class `ExpApproximator`.

Exercise P6.15. Write a graphical applet that displays a checkerboard with 64 squares, alternating white and black.

Exercise P6.16. *The game of Nim.* This is a well-known game with a number of variants. We will consider the following variant, which has an interesting winning strategy. Two players alternately take marbles from a pile. In each move, a player chooses how many marbles to take. The player must take at least one but at most half of the marbles. Then the other player takes a turn. The player who takes the last marble loses.

Write a program in which the computer plays against a human opponent. Generate a random integer between 10 and 100 to denote the initial size of the pile. Generate a random integer between 0 and 1 to decide whether the computer or the human takes the first turn. Generate a random integer between 0 and 1 to decide whether the computer plays *smart* or *stupid*. In stupid mode, the computer simply takes a random legal value (between 1 and $n/2$) from the pile whenever it has a turn. In smart mode the computer takes off enough marbles to make the size of the pile a power of two minus 1—that is, 3, 7, 15, 31, or 63. That is always a legal move, except if the size of the pile is currently one less than a power of 2. In that case, the computer makes a random legal move.

Note that the computer cannot be beaten in smart mode when it has the first move, unless the pile size happens to be 15, 31, or 63. Of course, a human player who has the first turn and knows the winning strategy can win against the computer.

Exercise P6.17. Program the following simulation: Darts are thrown at random points onto the square with corners (1,1) and (−1,−1). If the dart lands inside the unit circle (that is, the circle with center (0,0) and radius 1), it is a hit. Otherwise it is a miss. Run this simulation and use it to determine an approximate value for π. Explain why this is a better method for estimating π than the Buffon needle program.

Exercise P6.18. It is easy and fun to draw graphs of curves with the Java graphics library. Simply draw a hundred line segments joining the points $(x, f(x))$ and $(x + d, f(x + d))$, where x ranges from x_{min} to x_{max} and $d = (x_{max} - x_{min})/100$. Draw the curve $f(x) = x^3/100 - x + 10$, where x ranges from -10 to 10 in this fashion.

Exercise P6.19. Draw a picture of the "four-leaved rose" whose equation in polar coordinates is $r = \cos(2\theta)$. Let θ go from 0 to 2π in 100 steps. Each time, compute r and then compute the (x,y) coordinates from the polar coordinates by using the formula

$$x = r\cos\theta, \quad y = r\sin\theta$$

You can get extra credit if you can vary the number of petals.

Exercise P6.20. The series of pipes in Advanced Topic 6.7 has one final problem: The output file contains upper- and lowercase versions of the same word, such as "The" and "the". Modify the procedure, either by changing one of the programs or, in the true spirit of piping, by writing another short program and adding it to the series.

Designing Classes

To learn how to choose appropriate classes to implement

▶ **To understand** the concepts of cohesion and coupling

▶ **To minimize** the use of side effects

▶ **To document** the responsibilities of methods and their callers with preconditions and postconditions

▶ **To understand** the difference between instance methods and static methods

▶ **To introduce** the concept of static fields

▶ **To understand** the scope rules for local variables and instance fields

▶ **To learn** about packages

In this chapter you will learn more about designing classes. First, we will discuss the process of discovering classes and defining methods. Next, we will discuss how the concepts of pre- and postconditions enable you to specify, implement, and invoke methods correctly. You will also learn about several more technical issues, such as static methods and variables. Finally, you will see how to use packages to organize your classes.

CHAPTER CONTENTS

7.1 Choosing Classes

You have used a good number of classes in the preceding chapters and probably designed a few classes yourself as part of your programming assignments. Designing a class can be a challenge—it is not always easy to tell how to start or whether the result is of good quality.

Students who have prior experience with programming in another programming language are used to programming *functions*. A function carries out an action. In object-oriented programming, the actions appear as methods. Each method, however, belongs to a class. Classes are collections of objects, and objects are not actions—they are entities.

So you have to start the programming activity by identifying objects and the classes to which they belong.

> A class should represent a single concept from the problem domain, such as business, science, or mathematics.

Remember the rule of thumb from Chapter 2: Class names should be nouns, and method names should be verbs.

What makes a good class? Most importantly, a class should *represent a single concept*. Some of the classes that you have seen represent concepts from mathematics:

- Point
- Rectangle
- Ellipse

Other classes are abstractions of real-life entities.

- BankAccount
- Purse

For these classes, the properties of a typical object are easy to understand. A `Rectangle` object has a width and height. Given a `BankAccount` object, you can deposit and withdraw money. Generally, concepts from the part of the universe that our program concerns, such as science, business, or a game, make good classes. The name for such a class should be a noun that describes the concept. Some of the standard Java class names are a bit strange, such as `Ellipse2D.Double`, but you can choose better names for your own classes.

Another useful category of classes can be described as *actors*. Objects of an actor class does some kind of work for you. Examples of actors are the `StringTokenizer` class of Chapter 6 and the `Random` class in Chapter 4. A `StringTokenizer` object breaks up strings. A `Random` object generates random numbers. It is a good idea to choose class names for actors that end in "-er" or "-or". (A better name for the `Random` class might be `RandomNumberGenerator`.)

Very occasionally, a class has no objects, but it contains a collection of related static methods and constants. The `Math` class is a typical example. Such a class is called a *utility class*.

Finally, you have seen classes with just a `main` method. Their sole purpose is to start a program. From a design perspective, these are somewhat degenerate examples of classes.

What might not be a good class? If you can't tell from the class name what an object of the class is supposed to do, then you are probably not on the right track. For example, your homework assignment might ask you to write a program that prints paychecks. Suppose you start by trying to design a class `PaycheckProgram`. What would an object of this class do? An object of this class would have to do everything that the homework needs to do. That doesn't simplify anything. A better class would be `Paycheck`. Then your program can manipulate one or more `Paycheck` objects.

Another common mistake, particularly by students who are used to writing programs that consist of functions, is to turn an action into a class. For example, if your homework assignment is to compute a paycheck, you may consider writing a `ComputePaycheck` class. But can you visualize a "ComputePaycheck" object? The fact that "ComputePaycheck" isn't a noun tips you off that you are on the wrong track. On the other hand, a `Paycheck` class makes intuitive sense. The word "paycheck" is a noun. You can visualize a paycheck object. You can then think about useful methods of the `Paycheck` class, such as `compute`, that help you solve the assignment.

7.2   Cohesion and Coupling

> The public interface of a class is cohesive if all of its features are related to the concept that the class represents.

In this section you will learn a couple of useful criteria for analyzing the quality of the public interface of a class.

A class should represent a single concept. The public methods and constants that the public interface exposes should be *cohesive*. That is, all interface features should be closely related to the single concept that the class represents.

If you find that the public interface of a class refers to multiple concepts, then that is a good sign that it may be time to use separate classes instead. Consider, for example, the public interface of the `Purse` class in Chapter 3:

```
public class Purse
{
```

```java
    public Purse() { . . . }
    public void addNickels(int count)  { . . . }
    public void addDimes(int count)  { . . . }
    public void addQuarters(int count)  { . . . }
    public double getTotal()  { . . . }
    public static final double NICKEL_VALUE = 0.05;
    public static final double DIME_VALUE = 0.1;
    public static final double QUARTER_VALUE = 0.25;
    . . .
}
```

There are really two concepts here: a purse that holds coins and computes their total, and the values of individual coins. It would make more sense to have a separate `Coin` class and have coins responsible for knowing their values.

```java
public class Coin
{
    public Coin(double aValue, String aName) { . . . }
    public double getValue() { . . . }
    . . .
}
```

Then the `Purse` class can be simplified:

```java
public Purse
{
    public Purse() { . . . }
    public void add(Coin aCoin) { . . . }
    public double getTotal()  { . . . }
    . . .
}
```

This is clearly a better solution, because it separates the responsibilities of the purse and the coins. The only reason we didn't follow this approach in Chapter 3 was to keep the `Purse` example simple.

> A class depends on another class if it uses objects of that other class.

Many classes need other classes to do their job. For example, the restructured `Purse` class now depends on the `Coin` class to determine the total value of the coins in the purse.

To visualize relationships such as dependence between classes, programmers draw class diagrams. In this book, we use the UML ("Unified Modeling Language") notation for objects and classes. UML is a notation for object-oriented analysis and design invented by Grady Booch, Ivar Jacobson, and James Rumbaugh, three leading researchers in object-oriented software development. The UML notation distinguishes between *object diagrams* and class diagrams. In an object diagram the class names are <u>underlined</u>; in a class diagram the class names are not underlined. In a class diagram, you denote dependency by a dashed line with a >-shaped open arrow tip that points to the dependent class. Figure 1 shows a class diagram that indicates that the `Purse` class depends on the `Coin` class.

Note that the `Coin` class does *not* depend on the `Purse` class. Coins have no idea that they are being collected in purses, and they can carry out their work without ever calling any method in the `Purse` class.

Figure 1

Dependency Relationship between the
Purse and Coin Classes

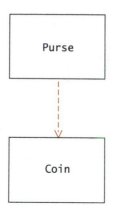

> It is a good practice to
> minimize the coupling (i.e.,
> dependency) between classes.

If many classes of a program depend on each other, then we say that the *coupling* between classes is high. Conversely, if there are few dependencies between classes, then we say that the coupling is low (see Figure 2).

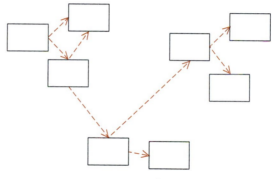

Low coupling

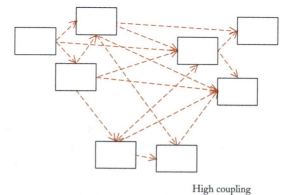

High coupling

Figure 2

High and Low Coupling between Classes

Why does coupling matter? If the `Coin` class changes in the next release of the program, all the classes that depend on it may be affected. If the change is drastic, the coupled classes must all be updated. Furthermore, if we would like to use a class in another program, we have to take with it all the classes on which it depends. Thus, we want to remove unnecessary coupling between classes.

Quality Tip 7.1

Consistency

In this section you learned of two criteria to analyze the quality of the public interface of a class. You should maximize cohesion and remove unnecessary coupling. There is another criterion that we would like you to pay attention to—consistency. When you have a set of methods, follow a consistent scheme for their names and parameters. This is simply a sign of good craftsmanship.

Sadly, you can find any number of inconsistencies in the standard library. Here is an example. To show an input dialog, you call

```
JOptionPane.showInputDialog(promptString)
```

To show a message dialog, you call

```
JOptionPane.showMessageDialog(null, messageString)
```

What's the `null` parameter? It turns out that the `showMessageDialog` method needs a parameter to specify the parent window, or `null` if no parent window is required. But the `showInputDialog` method requires no parent window. Why the inconsistency? There is no reason. It would have been an easy matter to supply a `showMessageDialog` method that exactly mirrors the `showInputDialog` method.

Inconsistencies such as these are not a fatal flaw, but they are an annoyance, particularly because they can be so easily avoided.

7.3 Accessor and Mutator Methods

> An accessor method does not change the state of its implicit parameter. A mutator method can change the state.

In this section we introduce a useful terminology for the methods of a class. A method that accesses an object and returns some information about it, without changing the object, is called an *accessor* method. In contrast, a method whose purpose is to modify the state of an object is called a *mutator* method. For example, in the `BankAccount` class, `getBalance` is an accessor method, because getting the account balance does not change the account. In contrast, the `deposit` and `withdraw` methods are mutator methods.

As a rule of thumb, it is a good idea for mutators to have return type `void`. This is not a rule of the Java language, but just a recommendation to make it easy to differentiate between mutators and accessors. The `BankAccount` methods follow this recommendation. The `getBalance` method returns the current balance without changing it. The `deposit` and `withdraw` methods change the object state, and they have return type `void`.

> An immutable class has no mutator methods.

You can call an accessor method as many times as you like—you always get the same answer, and it does not change the state of your object. That is clearly a desirable property, because it makes the behavior of such a method very predictable. Some classes have been designed to have only accessor methods and no mutator methods at all. Such classes are called *immutable*. An example is the `String` class. Once a string has been constructed, its contents never change. No method in the `String` class can modify the contents of a string. For example, the `substring` method does not remove characters from the original string. Instead, it constructs a *new* string that contains the substring characters.

An immutable class has a major advantage: It is safe to give out references to its objects freely. If no method can change the object's value, then no code can modify the object at an unexpected time. In contrast, if you give out a `BankAccount` reference to any other method, you have to be aware that the state of your object may change—the other method can call the `deposit` and `withdraw` methods on the reference that you gave it.

7.4   Side Effects

> A side effect of a method is any externally observable behavior outside the implicit parameter. You should minimize side effects.

We have classified methods as accessors or mutators depending on what effect they have on their implicit parameters. If a method modifies some outside value other than its implicit parameter, we call that modification a *side effect*. A side effect of a method is *any kind of observable behavior* outside the object.

Here is an example of a method whose side effect is the updating of an explicit parameter:

```
public class BankAccount
{
   /**
      Transfers money from this account to another account.
      @param amount the amount of money to transfer
      @param other the account into which to transfer the money
   */
   public void transfer(double amount, BankAccount other)
   {
      balance = balance - amount;
      other.balance = other.balance + amount;
   }
   . . .
}
```

As a rule of thumb, updating an explicit parameter can be surprising to programmers, and it is best to avoid it whenever possible.

Note that a method can update only *object* parameters. Primitive type parameters are safe—a method can never change them. See Common Error 7.1 for more information.

Another example of a side effect is output. Consider how we have always printed a bank balance:

```
System.out.println("The balance is now $" +
   momsSavings.getBalance());
```

Why don't we simply have a `printBalance` method?

```
public void printBalance() // not recommended
{
   System.out.println("The balance is now $" + balance);
}
```

That would be more convenient when you actually want to print the value. But, of course, there are cases when you want the value for some other purpose. Thus, you can't simply drop the `getBalance` method in favor of `printBalance`.

More importantly, the `printBalance` method forces strong assumptions on the `BankAccount` class.

- The message is in English—you assume that the user of your software reads English. The majority of people on the planet don't.

- You rely on `System.out`. A method that relies on `System.out` won't work in an embedded system, such as the computer inside an automatic teller machine.

A method with a side effect introduces additional dependencies, thus violating the rule of minimizing the coupling of the classes. For example, the `printBalance` method couples the `BankAccount` class with the `System` and `PrintStream` classes. It is best to decouple input/output from the actual work of your classes.

One particularly reprehensible practice is printing error messages inside methods. You should never do that:

```
public void deposit(double amount)
{
   if (amount < 0)
      System.out.println("Bad value of amount");
      // bad style
   else
      balance = balance + amount;
}
```

You will learn in Section 7.5 and in Chapter 14 how a method can use *exceptions* to indicate problems.

Quality Tip   7.2

Minimize Side Effects

In an ideal world, all methods would be accessors that simply return an answer without changing any value at all. (In fact, programs that are written in so-called *functional* programming languages, such as Scheme and ML, come close to this ideal.) Of course, in an object-oriented programming language, we use objects to remember state changes. Therefore, a method that just changes the state of its implicit parameter is certainly acceptable. A method that does anything else is said to have a side effect, as described in Section 7.4. Although side effects cannot be completely eliminated, they can be the cause of surprises and problems and should be minimized. Here is a classification of method behavior.

- *Best:* Accessor methods with no changes to any explicit parameters—no side effects. Example: `getBalance`.

- *Good:* Mutator methods with no changes to any explicit parameters—no side effects: Example: `withdraw`.

- *Fair:* Methods that change an explicit parameter. Example: `transfer`.

- *Poor:* Methods that change a static field of another class such as `System.out`. (See Section 7.6 for more information on static fields.)

Common Error   7.1

Trying to Modify Primitive Type Parameters

> In Java, a method can never change parameters of primitive type.

Methods can't update parameters of primitive type (numbers and `boolean`). To illustrate this point, let us try to write a method that updates a number parameter:

```
public class BankAccount
{
    /**
        Transfers money from this account and tries to add it to a balance.
        @param amount the amount of money to transfer
        @param otherBalance balance to add the amount to
    */
    void transfer(double amount, double otherBalance)
    {
```

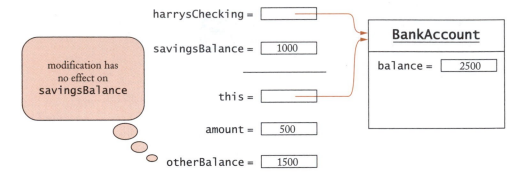

harrysChecking = [ ]

savingsBalance = [1000]

BankAccount

balance = [2500]

modification has
no effect on
savingsBalance

this = [ ]

amount = [500]

otherBalance = [1500]

Figure 3

Modifying a Numeric Parameter Has No Effect on Caller

```
        balance = balance - amount;
        otherBalance = otherBalance + amount; // won't work
    }
        . . .
}
```

This doesn't work. Let's consider a method call.

```
double savingsBalance = 1000;
harrysChecking.transfer(500, savingsBalance);
```

As the method starts, the parameter variable `otherBalance` is set to the same value as `savingsBalance`. Then the value of the `otherBalance` value is modified, but that modification had no effect on `savingsBalance`, because `otherBalance` is a separate variable (see Figure 3). When the method terminates, the `otherBalance` variable dies, and `savingsBalance` isn't increased.

Why did the example at the beginning of Section 7.4 work, where the second explicit parameter was a `BankAccount` reference? Then the parameter variable contained a copy of the object reference. Through that reference, the method is able to modify the object.

You already saw this difference between objects and primitive types in Chapter 3. As a consequence, a Java method can *never* modify numbers that are passed to it.

AT **Advanced Topic**   **7.1**

Call by Value and Call by Reference

In Java, method parameters are *copied* into the parameter variables when a method starts. Computer scientists call this call mechanism "call by value". There are some limitations to the "call by value" mechanism. As you saw in Common Error 7.1, it is not possible to implement methods that modify the contents of number variables. Other programming languages such as C++ support an alternate mechanism, called "call by reference". For example, in C++ it would be an easy matter to write a method that modifies a number, by using a so-called *reference parameter*. Here is the C++ code, for those of you who know C++:

```
// this is C++
class BankAccount
{
public:
   void transfer(double amount, double& otherBalance)
      // otherBalance is a double&, a reference to a double
   {
      balance = balance - amount;
      otherBalance = otherBalance + amount; // works in C++
   }
   . . .
};
```

You will sometimes read in Java books that "numbers are passed by value, objects are passed by reference". That is technically not quite correct. In Java, objects themselves are never passed as parameters; instead, both numbers and *object references* are copied by value. To see this clearly, let us consider another scenario. This method tries to set the otherAccount parameter to a new object:

```
public class BankAccount
{
   public void transfer(double amount,
      BankAccount otherAccount)
   {
      balance = balance - amount;
      double newBalance = other.balance + amount;
      otherAccount = new BankAccount(newBalance); // won't work
   }
}
```

In this situation, we are not trying to change the state of the object to which the parameter variable otherAccount refers; instead, we are trying to replace the object with a different one (see Figure 4). Now the parameter variable other-Account is replaced with a reference to a new account. But if you call the method with

```
harrysChecking.transfer(500, savingsAccount);
```

> In Java, a method can change the state of an object reference parameter, but it cannot replace the object reference with another.

then that change does not affect the savingsAccount variable that is supplied in the call.

As you can see, a Java method can update an object's state, but it cannot *replace* the contents of an object reference. This shows that object references are passed by value in Java.

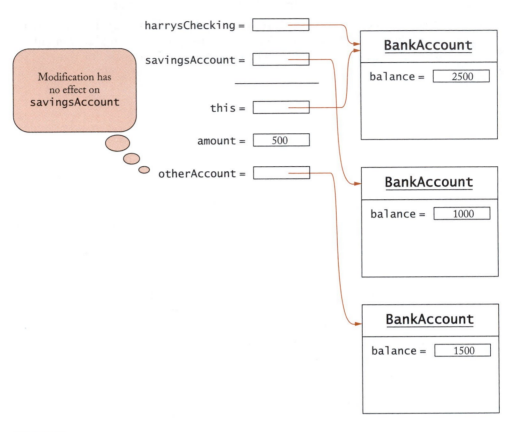

Figure 4

Modifying an Object Reference Parameter Has No Effect on the Caller

 Quality Tip   **7.3**

Don't Change the Contents of Parameter Variables

As you saw in Common Error 7.1 and Advanced Topic 7.1, a method can treat its parameter variables like any other local variables and change their contents. However, that change affects only the parameter variable within the method itself—not any values supplied in the method call. Some programmers take "advantage" of the temporary nature of the parameter variables and use them as "convenient" holders for intermediate results, as in this example:

```
public void deposit(double amount) // poor style
{
    // using the parameter variable to hold an intermediate value
    amount = balance + amount;
    balance = amount;
}
```

▼

▼

That code would produce errors if another statement in the method referred to `amount` expecting it to be the value of the parameter, and it will confuse later programmers maintaining this method. You should always treat the parameter variables as if they were constants. Don't assign new values to them. Instead, introduce a new local variable.

▼

```
public void deposit(double amount)
{
    double newBalance = balance + amount;
    balance = newBalance;
}
```

▼

7.5   Preconditions and Postconditions

> A precondition is a requirement that the caller of a method must meet. If a method is called in violation of a precondition, the method is not responsible for computing the correct result.

A *precondition* is a requirement that the caller of a method must obey. For example, the `deposit` method of the `BankAccount` class has a precondition that the amount to be deposited should not be negative. It is the responsibility of the caller never to call a method if one of its preconditions is violated. If the method is called anyway, it is not responsible for producing a correct result.

Therefore, a precondition is an important part of the method, and you must document it. Here we document the precondition that the `amount` parameter must not be negative.

```
/**
    Deposits money into this account.
    @param amount  the amount of money to deposit
    (Precondition: amount >= 0)
*/
```

Some `javadoc` extensions support a `@precondition` or `@requires` tag, but it is not a part of the standard `javadoc` program. Because the standard `javadoc` tool skips all unknown tags, we simply add the precondition to the method explanation or the appropriate `@param` tag.

Preconditions are typically stated for one of two reasons:

1. To restrict the parameters of a method
2. To require that a method is only called when it is in the appropriate *state*

For example, once a `StringTokenizer` has run out of tokens, it is no longer legal to call the `nextToken` method. Thus, a precondition for the `nextToken` methods is that the `hasMoreTokens` method returns `true`.

A method is responsible only for operating correctly when its caller has fulfilled all preconditions. The method is free to do *anything* if a precondition is not fulfilled. It would be perfectly legal if the method reformatted the hard disk every time it was called with a wrong input. Naturally, that isn't reasonable. What should a method actually do when it is called with inappropriate inputs? For example, what should `account.deposit(-1000)` do? There are two good choices.

1. A method can check for the violation and *throw an exception.* Then the method does not return to its caller; instead, control is transferred to an exception handler. If no handler is present, then the program terminates.

2. If it is too cumbersome to carry out the check, the method can simply work under the assumption that the preconditions are fulfilled. If they aren't, then any data corruption (such as a negative balance) or other failures are the caller's fault.

You'll see in Chapter 14 how to program exception handlers. Right now, we'll show you how to throw an exception to indicate that a method has been called with inappropriate parameters.

```
public double deposit(double amount)
{
   if (amount < 0)
      throw new IllegalArgumentException();
   balance = balance + amount;
}
```

When the method is called with an illegal argument, the program aborts with an error message

```
java.lang.IllegalArgumentException
        at BankAccount.deposit(BankAccount.java:14)
```

If a method is called when the object is in an inappropriate state, you can throw an `IllegalStateException` instead.

Many beginning programmers think that it isn't "nice" to abort the program. Why not simply return to the caller instead?

```
public void deposit(double amount)
{
   if (amount < 0)
      return; // not as good as throwing an exception
   balance = balance + amount;
}
```

That is legal—after all, a method can do anything if its preconditions are violated. But it is not as good as throwing an exception. If the program calling the `deposit` method has a few bugs that cause it to pass a negative amount as an input value, then the version that throws the exception will make the bugs very obvious during testing—it is hard to ignore when the program aborts. The quiet version, on the other hand, will not alert you, and you may not notice that it performs some wrong calculations as a consequence. Think of exceptions as the "tough love" approach to precondition checking.

If you test for the precondition, then you might as well throw an exception. However, sometimes the cost of testing is too high. It might slow down the method too much, or it might make it too confusing. Then you may simply go ahead and assume that the precondition is fulfilled:

```
public void deposit(double amount)
{
```

```
        // no test, for maximum efficiency
        // if this makes the balance negative, it's the caller's fault
        balance = balance + amount;
}
```

When a method is called in accordance with its preconditions, then the method promises to do its job correctly. A different kind of promise that the method makes is called a *postcondition*. There are two kinds of postconditions:

1. That the return value is computed correctly
2. That the object is in a certain state after the method call is completed

Here is a postcondition that makes a statement about the object state after the `deposit` method is called.

```
/**
    Deposits money into this account.
    (Postcondition: getBalance() >= 0)
    @param amount  the amount of money to deposit
    (Precondition: amount >= 0)
*/
```

As long as the precondition is fulfilled, this method guarantees that the balance after the deposit is not negative.

Some `javadoc` extensions support a `@postcondition` or `@ensures` tag. However, just as with preconditions, we simply add postconditions to the method explanation or the `@return` tag, because the standard `javadoc` program skips all tags that it doesn't know.

Some programmers feel that they must specify a postcondition for every method. When you use `javadoc`, however, you already specify a part of the postcondition in the `@return` tag, and you shouldn't repeat it in a postcondition.

```
// this postcondition statement is overly repetitive
/**
    Returns the current balance of this account.
    @return  the account balance
    (Postcondition: the return value equals the account balance)
*/
```

Note that we formulate pre- and postconditions only in terms of the *interface* of the class. Thus, we state the precondition of the `withdraw` method as `amount <= getBalance()`, not `amount <= balance`. After all, the caller, which needs to check the precondition, has access only to the public interface, not the private implementation.

Bertrand Meyer [1] compares preconditions and postconditions to contracts. In real life, contracts spell out the obligations of the contracting parties. For example, your mechanic may promise to fix the brakes of your car, and you promise in turn to pay a certain amount of money. If either party breaks the promise, then the other is not bound by the terms of the contract. In the same fashion, pre- and postconditions are contractual terms between a method and its caller. The method promises to fulfill the postcondition for all inputs that fulfill the precondition. The caller promises never to call the method with illegal inputs. If the caller fulfills its promise and gets a wrong answer, it can take the method to "programmer's court". If the caller doesn't fulfill its promise and something terrible happens as a consequence, it has no recourse.

▼ Ⓐ️Ⓣ️ Advanced Topic   **7.2**

Class Invariants

Advanced Topic 6.8 introduced the concept of loop invariants. A loop invariant is established when the loop is first entered, and it is preserved by all loop iterations. We then know that the loop invariant must be true when the loop exits, and we can use that information to reason about the correctness of a loop.

Class invariants fulfill a similar purpose. A class invariant is a statement about an object that is true after every constructor and that is preserved by every mutator (provided that the caller respects all preconditions). We then know that the class invariant must always be true, and we can use that information to reason about the correctness of our program.

Here is a simple example. Consider a `BankAccount` class with the following preconditions for the constructor and the mutators:

```java
public class BankAccount
{
    /**
        Constructs a bank account with a given balance.
        @param initialBalance the initial balance
        (Precondition: initialBalance >= 0)
    */
    public BankAccount(double initialBalance) { . . . }
    {
        balance = initialBalance;
    }

    /**
        Deposits money into the bank account.
        @param amount the amount to deposit
        (Precondition: amount >= 0)
    */
    public void deposit(double amount) { . . . }

    /**
        Withdraws money from the bank account.
        @param amount the amount to withdraw
        (Precondition: amount <= getBalance())
    */
    public void withdraw(double amount) { . . . }

    . . .

}
```

Now we can formulate the following invariant:

```java
getBalance() >= 0
```

To see why this invariant is true, we first check the constructor. Since the precondition of the constructor is

```
initialBalance >= 0
```

we can prove that the invariant is true after the constructor has set `balance` to `initialBalance`.

Next, check the mutators. The precondition of the `deposit` method is

```
amount >= 0
```

We can assume that the invariant condition holds before calling the method. Thus, we know that `balance >= 0` before the method executes. The laws of mathematics tell us that the sum of two nonnegative numbers is again nonnegative, so we can conclude that `balance >= 0` after the completion of the `deposit`. Thus, the `deposit` method preserves the invariant.

A similar argument shows that the `withdraw` method preserves the invariant.

Since the invariant is a property of the class, you document it with the class description:

```
/**
    A bank account has a balance that can be changed by
    deposits and withdrawals.
    (Invariant: getBalance() >= 0)
*/
public class BankAccount
{
    . . .
}
```

7.6 Static Methods

> A static method has no implicit parameter.

Sometimes you write methods that don't need an implicit parameter. Such a method is called a *static method* or a *class method*. In contrast, the methods that you wrote up to now are often called *instance methods* because they operate on a particular instance of an object. You encountered static method calls in Chapter 3. For example, the `sqrt` method in the `Math` class is a static method. When you call `Math.sqrt(x)`, you don't supply any implicit parameter. (Recall that `Math` is the name of a class, not an object.) And, of course, every application has a static `main` method (however, applets do not).

Why would you want to write a method without an implicit parameter? The most common reason is that you want to encapsulate some computations that involve only numbers. Since numbers aren't objects, you can't pass them as implicit parameters.

Here is a typical example of a static method that carries out some simple algebra. Recall from Chapter 5 that two floating-point numbers x and y are approximately equal if

$$\frac{|x - y|}{\max(|x|, |y|)} \le \varepsilon$$

where ε is a small number, typically chosen to be 10^{-14}.

However, if x or y is zero, then you need to test whether the absolute value of the other quantity is at most ε.

Of course, this computation is just complex enough that it makes a lot of sense to encapsulate it in a method. Since the parameters are numbers, the method doesn't operate on any objects at all, so we make it into a `static` method:

```java
/**
    Tests whether two floating-point numbers are
    equal, except for a roundoff error.
    @param x a floating-point number
    @param y a floating-point number
    @return true if x and y are approximately equal
*/
public static boolean approxEqual(double x, double y)
{
    final double EPSILON = 1E-14;
    if (x == 0) return Math.abs(y) <= EPSILON;
    if (y == 0) return Math.abs(x) <= EPSILON;
    return Math.abs(x - y) /
        Math.max(Math.abs(x), Math.abs(y))
        <= EPSILON;
}
```

You need to find a home for this method. You have two choices. You can simply add this method to a class whose methods need to call it. Or you can come up with a new class (similar to the `Math` class of the standard Java library) to contain this method. In this book, we will generally use the latter approach. Since this method has to do with numbers, we'll design a class `Numeric` to hold the `approxEqual` method. Here is the class:

```java
class Numeric
{
    public static boolean approxEqual(double x, double y)
    {
        . . .
    }
    // more numeric methods can be added here
}
```

When calling a static method, you supply the name of the class containing the method so that the compiler can find it. For example,

```java
double r = Math.sqrt(2);
if (Numeric.approxEqual(r * r, 2))
    System.out.println("Math.sqrt(2) squared is approximately 2");
```

Note that you do not supply an object of type `Numeric` when you call the method. Static methods have no implicit parameter—in other words, they don't have a `this` parameter.

Now we can tell you why the `main` method is static. When the program starts, there aren't any objects yet. Therefore, the *first* method in the program must be a static method.

In general, you want to minimize the use of static methods. If you find yourself using lots of static methods, then that's an indication that you may not have found the right classes to solve your problem in an object-oriented way.

You may well wonder why these methods are called `static`. The normal meaning of the word *static* ("staying fixed at one place") does not seem to have anything to do with what static methods do. Indeed, it's used by accident. Java uses the `static` keyword because C++ uses it in the same context. C++ uses `static` to denote class methods because the inventors of C++ did not want to invent another keyword. Someone noted that there was a relatively rarely used keyword, `static`, that denotes certain variables that stay in a fixed location for multiple method calls. (Java does not have this feature, nor does it need it.) It turned out that the keyword could be reused to denote class methods without confusing the compiler. The fact that it can confuse humans was apparently not a big concern. You'll just have to live with the fact that "`static` method" means "class method": a method that does not operate on an object and that has only explicit parameters.

7.7   Static Fields

Consider a slight variation of our `BankAccount` class: a bank account that has both a balance and an *account number*:

```
public class BankAccount
{
    . . .
    private double balance;
    private int accountNumber;
}
```

We want to assign account numbers sequentially. That is, we want the bank account constructor to construct the first account with number 1, the next with number 2, and so on. Therefore, we must store the last assigned account number somewhere.

It makes no sense, though, to make this value into an instance field:

```
public class BankAccount
{
    . . .
    private double balance;
    private int accountNumber;
    private int lastAssignedNumber; // NO—won't work
}
```

> A static field belongs to the class, not to any object of the class.

In that case each *instance* of the `BankAccount` class would have its own value of `lastAssignedNumber`.

Instead, we need to have a single value of `lastAssigned Number` that is the same for the entire *class*. Such a field is called a *class field* or a `static` field, because you declare it using the `static` keyword.

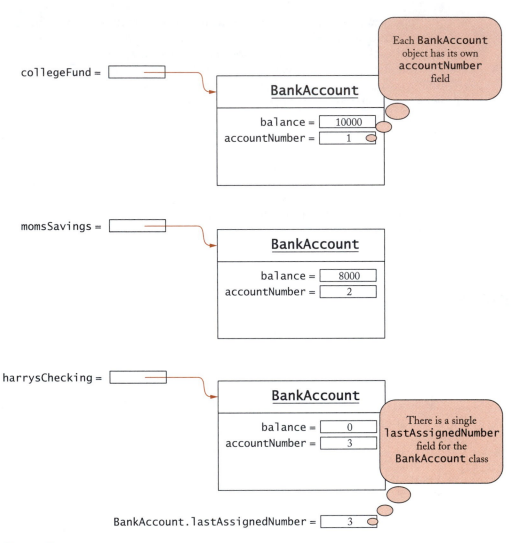

Figure 5

A Static Field and Instance Fields

```
public class BankAccount
{
    . . .
    private double balance;
    private int accountNumber;
    private static int lastAssignedNumber;
}
```

Every BankAccount object has its own balance and accountNumber instance fields, but there is only a single copy of the lastAssignedNumber variable (see Figure 5).

Every method of a class can access its static fields. Here is the constructor of the BankAccount class, which increments the last assigned number and then uses it to initialize the account number of the object to be constructed:

```
class BankAccount
{
   public BankAccount()
   {
      // generate next account number to be assigned

      lastAssignedNumber++; // updates the static field

      // assign to account number of this bank account

      accountNumber = lastAssignedNumber;
         // sets the instance field
   }
   . . .
}
```

How do you initialize static fields? You can't initialize them in the class constructor:

```
public BankAccount()
{
   lastAssignedNumber = 0; // NO—would reset to 0 for each new object
   . . .
}
```

Then the initialization would occur each time a new instance is constructed. Instead, use an explicit initializer:

```
public class BankAccount
{
   . . .
   private static lastAssignedNumber = 0;
}
```

The initialization is executed once when the class is loaded.

There are three ways to initialize a static field:

1. Do nothing. The static field is then initialized with 0 (for numbers), false (for boolean values) or null (for objects).

2. Use an explicit initializer.

3. Use a static initialization block (see Advanced Topic 7.3).

In general, static fields are considered undesirable. Methods that modify static fields have side effects, and the behavior of methods that read static fields does not simply depend on their inputs. If you call such a method twice, with the exact same inputs, it may still act differently, because the settings of the static fields are different.

In the preceding example, getting two different results from calling the BankAccount constructor twice in a row was the whole point of introducing the static lastAssignedNumber variable. However, in practical programs, static fields are rarely useful. If your program relies on a static field, you should think carefully whether you merely used that static field as a momentary convenience to "park" a value so that it can be picked up by another method. That is a bad strategy, because many other methods can also access and change that static field.

Like instance fields, static fields, when used at all, should always be declared as `private` to ensure that methods of other classes do not change their values. However, static *constants* are often declared public. For example, the `BankAccount` class may want to define a public constant value, such as

```
public class BankAccount
{
    . . .
    public static final double OVERDRAFT_FEE = 5;
}
```

Methods from any class refer to such a constant as `BankAccount.OVERDRAFT_FEE`.

It makes sense to declare constants as `static`—you wouldn't want every object of the `BankAccount` class to have its own set of variables with these constant values. It is sufficient to have one set of them for the class.

Why are class variables called `static`? As with static methods, the `static` keyword itself is just a meaningless holdover from C++. But static fields and static methods have much in common: they apply to the entire *class*, not to specific instances of the class.

Quality Tip 7.4

Do Not Abuse Static Fields

We have purposefully not covered static fields earlier in this book. They make it possible to write programs that are hard to understand and maintain. Consider the following bad example. The `Sorter` class sorts three numbers in increasing order. The `setMinMax` "helper" method sorts two numbers by setting the static fields `min` and `max` to hold the smaller and the larger values.

```
class Sorter // bad code inside
{
    public Sorter(double a, double b, double c)
    {
        setMinMax(a, b);
        if (c < min)
            smallest = c; // c is the smallest of the three
        else
        {
            smallest = min; // min is the smallest of the three
            setMinMax(c, max); // sort c and max
        }
        middle = min;
        largest = max;
    }

    public double getSmallest()
    {
```

```
            return smallest;
        }

        public double getMiddle()
        {
            return middle;
        }

        public double getLargest()
        {
            return largest;
        }

        public static void setMinMax(double a, double b)
        {
            if (a < b) { min = a; max = b; }
            else { min = b; max = a; }
        }

        private double smallest;
        private double middle;
        private double largest;

        private static double min;
        private static double max;
    }
```

The writer of this class had a problem. The `setMinMax` method computes both the smaller and the larger of its input values, but it can't return both. Therefore, the programmer chose to return neither value and instead stored them in static fields. In this example, the code will work correctly, but there is a danger. If you don't *immediately* retrieve the answers from the static fields, some other part of the program may overwrite them. When static fields are used in larger programs, they get accidentally overwritten with distressing regularity, and therefore they are best avoided.

Advanced Topic   7.3

Alternative Forms of Field Initializations

As you have seen, instance fields are initialized with a default value (0, `false`, or `null`, depending on their type). You can then set them to any desired value in a constructor, and that is the style that we prefer in this book.

However, there are two other mechanisms to specify an initial value for a field. Just as with local variables, you can specify initialization values for fields. For example,

```
public class Coin
{
    . . .
    private double value = 1;
```

```
    private String name = "Dollar";
}
```

These default values are used for *every* object that is being constructed.

There is also another, much less common, syntax. You can place one or more *initialization blocks* inside the class definition. All statements in that block are executed whenever an object is being constructed. Here is an example:

```
public class Coin
{
   . . .
   {
      value = 1;
      name = "Dollar";
   }
   private double value;
   private String name;
}
```

For static fields, you use a static initialization block:

```
public class BankAccount
{
   . . .
   private static lastAssignedNumber;

   static
   {
      lastAssignedNumber = 0;
   }
}
```

All statements in the static initialization block are executed once when the class is loaded. Initialization blocks are rarely used in practice.

When an object is constructed, the initializers and initialization blocks are executed in the order in which they appear. Then the code in the constructor is executed. Since the rules for the alternative initialization mechanisms are somewhat complex, we recommend that you simply use constructors to do the job of construction.

7.8 Scope

7.8.1 Scope of Local Variables

It sometimes happens that the same variable name is used in two methods. Consider the variables r in the following example:

```
public static double area(Rectangle rect)
{
   double r = rect.getWidth() * rect.getHeight();
```

```
        return r;
    }

    public static void main(String[] args)
    {
        Rectangle r = new Rectangle(5, 10, 20, 30);
        double a = area(r);
        . . .
    }
```

> The scope of a variable is the region of a program in which you can refer to the variable by its name.

These variables are independent from each other. You can have local variables with the same name r in different methods, just as you can have different motels with the same name "Bates Motel" in different cities.

The *scope* of a variable is the region of a program in which you can refer to the variable by its name. The scope of a local variable extends from the point of its declaration to the end of the block that encloses it. Variables declared in a `for` loop are a special case. Their scope extends to the `for` loop but not beyond.

```
    for (int i = 1; i <= years; i++)
    {
        . . .
    } // scope of i ends here
```

> In Java, you cannot have two local variables with overlapping scope.

You can never have two local variables with overlapping scope. If you try to define a second local variable within the scope of the first, then the compiler reports an error. For example, the following is an error:

```
    Rectangle r = new Rectangle(5, 10, 20, 30);
    if (x >= 0)
    {
        double r = Math.sqrt(x);
        // Error—can't declare another variable called r here
        . . .
    }
```

However, you can have local variables with identical names if their scopes do not overlap, such as

```
    if (x >= 0)
    {
        double r = Math.sqrt(-x);
        . . .
    } // scope of r ends here
    else
    {
        Rectangle r = new Rectangle(5, 10, 20, 30);
        // OK—this is a different r
        . . .
    }
```

— ## Scope of Class Members

> A qualified name is prefixed by its class name or by an object reference, such as Math.sqrt or other.balance.

Within a method of a class, you can access all fields and methods of the class by their simple name. However, if you want to use a field or method outside its class, you must *qualify* the name. You qualify a static field or method by specifying the class name, such as Math.sqrt or Math.PI. You qualify an instance field or method by specifying the object to which the field or method should be applied, such as harrysChecking.getBalance().

> An unqualified instance field or method name refers to the implicit parameter this.

Inside a method, you don't need to qualify fields or methods of their own class. Instance fields automatically refer to the implicit parameter of the method. For example, inside the transfer method

```
public void transfer(double amount, BankAccount other)
{
   balance = balance - amount; // i.e., this.balance
   other.balance = other.balance + amount;
}
```

the unqualified name balance means this.balance.

The same rule applies to methods. Thus, another implementation of the transfer method is

```
public void transfer(double amount, BankAccount other)
{
   withdraw(amount); // i.e., this.withdraw(amount);
   other.deposit(amount);
}
```

Whenever you see an instance method call without an implicit parameter, then the method is called on the this parameter. Such a method call is called a "self-call".

Similarly, you can use a static field or method of the same class without a qualifier. For example, if OVERDRAFT_FEE is a static field of the BankAccount class, then the statement

```
if (balance < 0) balance = OVERDRAFT_FEE;
```

in a BankAccount method refers to BankAccount.OVERDRAFT_FEE.

— ## Overlapping Scope

Problems arise if you have two variable names with overlapping scope. This can never occur with local variables, but the scopes of a local variable and an instance field can overlap. Here is a purposefully bad example.

```
public class Coin
{
   . . .
```

```
public void draw(Graphics2D g2)
{
    String name = "SansSerif"; // local variable
    int size = 18;
    . . .
}

private String name; // field with the same name
private double value;
}
```

> A local variable can shadow a field with the same name. You can access the shadowed field name by qualifying it with the `this` reference.

Inside the `draw` method, the variable name `name` could potentially have two meanings: the local variable or the instance field. The Java language specifies that in this situation the *local* variable wins out. It *shadows* the instance field. This sounds pretty arbitrary, but there is actually a good reason: You can still refer to the instance field as `this.name`.

```
g2.setFont(new Font(name, Font.BOLD, size));
    // accesses local variable
g2.drawString(this.name, x, y);
    // accesses field
```

Some people use this trick on purpose so that they don't have to come up with new variable names:

```
public Coin(double value, String name)
{
    this.value = value;
    this.name = name;
}
```

It isn't necessary to write code like this. You can easily change the name of the local variable to something else, such as `fontName` or `aName`. Then you, and the other readers of your code, don't have to remember that local variables shadow instance fields.

▼ ⊗ **Common Error** 7.2

Shadowing

▼

▼

Using the same name accidentally for a local variable and an instance field is a surprisingly common error. As you saw in the preceding section, the local variable then *shadows* the instance field. Even though you may have meant to access the instance field, the local variable is quietly accessed. For some reason, this problem is most common in constructors. Look at this example of a wrong constructor:

▼

```
public class Coin
{
```

```
public Coin(double aValue, String aName)
{
    value = aValue;
    String name = aName; // oops...
}

    . . .

private double value;
private String name;
}
```

The programmer declared a local variable `name` in the constructor. In all likelihood, that was just a typo—the programmer's fingers were on autopilot and typed the keyword `String`, even though the programmer all the time intended to access the instance field. Unfortunately, the compiler gives no warning in this situation and quietly sets the local variable to the value of `aName`. The instance field of the object that is being constructed is never touched, and remains `null`. Some programmers give all instance field names a special prefix to distinguish them from other variables. A common convention is to prefix all instance field names with the prefix `my`, such as `myValue` or `myName`.

Productivity Hint   7.1

Global Search and Replace

Suppose you chose an unfortunate name for a method—say `ae` instead of `approxEqual`—and you regret your choice. Of course, you can locate all occurrences of `ae` in your code and replace them manually. However, most programming editors have a command to search for the `ae`'s automatically and replace them with `approxEqual`.

You need to specify some details about the search:

- Do you want it to ignore case? That is, should `Ae` be a match? In Java you usually don't want that.

- Do you want it to match whole words only? If not, the `ae` in `maelstrom` is also a match. In Java you usually want to match whole words.

- Is this a regular-expression search? No, but regular expressions can make searches even more powerful—see Productivity Hint 7.2.

- Do you want to confirm each replace, or simply go ahead and replace all matches? I usually confirm the first three or four, and when I see that it works as expected, I give the go-ahead to replace the rest. (By the way, a *global* replace means to replace all occurrences in the document.) Good text editors can undo a global replace that has gone awry. Find out whether yours will.

- Do you want the search to go from the cursor to the rest of the program file, or should it search the currently selected text? Restricting replacement to a portion of the file can be very useful, but in this example you would want to move the cursor to the top of the file and then replace until the end of the file.

Not every editor has all these options. You should investigate what your editor offers.

Productivity Hint 7.2

Regular Expressions

Regular expressions describe character patterns. For example, numbers have a simple form. They contain one or more digits. The regular expression describing numbers is [0-9]+. The set [0-9] denotes any digit between 0 and 9, and the + means "one or more".

What good is it? Several utility programs use regular expressions to locate matching text. Also, the search commands of some programming editors understand regular expressions. The most popular program that uses regular expressions is *grep* (which stands for "generalized regular expression pattern"). You can run grep from a command prompt or from inside some compilation environments. Grep is part of the UNIX operating system, but versions are available for Windows and MacOS. It needs a regular expression and one or more files to search. When grep runs, it displays a set of lines that match the regular expression.

Suppose you want to look for all magic numbers (see Quality Tip 2.2) in a file. The command

```
grep [0-9]+ Homework.java
```

lists all lines in the file Homework.java that contain sequences of digits. That isn't terribly useful; lines with variable names x1 will be listed. OK, you want sequences of digits that do *not* immediately follow letters:

```
grep [^A-Za-z][0-9]+ Homework.java
```

The set [^A-Za-z] denotes any characters that are *not* in the ranges A ro Z and a to z. This works much better, and it shows only lines that contain actual numbers.

There are a bewildering number of symbols (sometimes called *wildcards*) with special meanings in the regular expression syntax, and unfortunately, different programs use different styles of regular expressions. It is best to consult the program documentation for details.

Advanced Topic 7.4

Calling One Constructor from Another

Consider the following Coin class. It has two constructors: a constructor with no parameters to make a dollar coin, and another constructor to supply the coin name and value.

```
public class Coin
{
    public Coin(double aValue, String aName)
    {
        value = aValue;
        name = aName;
    }

    public Coin()
    {
        this(1, "dollar");
    }
    . . .
}
```

The command this(1, "dollar"); means: Call another constructor of this class and supply the values 1 and "dollar". Such a constructor call can occur only *as the first line in another constructor.*

This syntax is a minor convenience, and we will not use it in this book. Actually, the use of the keyword this is a little confusing, because normally this denotes a reference to the implicit parameter. However, if this is followed by parentheses, it denotes a call to another constructor of *this class.*

7.9   Packages

7.9.1 — Organizing Related Classes into Packages

A Java program consists of a collection of classes. So far, most of your programs have consisted of a small number of classes.

> A package is a set of related classes.

As programs get larger, however, simply distributing the classes over multiple files isn't enough. An additional structuring mechanism is needed. In Java, packages provide this structuring mechanism. A Java package is a set of related classes. For example, the Java library consists of dozens of packages, some of which are listed in Table 1.

To put classes in a package, you must place a line

package *packagename*;

as the first instruction in the source file containing the classes. As you can see from the examples in the Java library, a package name consists of one or more identifiers separated by periods.

For example, consider the Numeric class that we introduced in this chapter. For maximum simplicity, you can include the class together with your own programs whenever you need it. However, it would be much more professional to place the class into a separate

Package	Purpose	Sample Classes
`java.lang`	Language support	`Math`
`java.util`	Utilities	`Random`
`java.io`	Input and output	`PrintStream`
`java.awt`	Abstract Windowing Toolkit	`Color`
`java.applet`	Applets	`Applet`
`java.net`	Networking	`Socket`
`java.sql`	Database access through Structured Query Language	`ResultSet`
`javax.swing`	Swing user interface	`JButton`
`omg.org.CORBA`	Common Object Request Broker Architecture for distributed objects	`ORB`

Table 1

Important Packages in the Java Library

package. That way, the classes that are specific to a particular program are clearly separated from the utility classes that you share between different programs.

Let us place the `Numeric` class into a package named `com.horstmann.bigjava`. (See Section 7.9.3 for an explanation of how to construct package names.) Each source file in that package must start with the instruction

```
package com.horstmann.bigjava;
```

For example, the `Numeric.java` file starts out as follows:

```
package com.horstmann.bigjava;

public class Numeric
{
   . . .
}
```

Not only must the package name be placed into the source file; the class file itself must be placed in a special location. We'll show you later where to place the class file.

In addition to the named packages (such as `java.util`), there is a special package, called the *default package*, which has no name. If you did not include any `package` statement at the top of your source file, its classes are placed in the default package.

> **Syntax 7.1: Package Specification**
>
> package *packageName*;
>
> **Example:**
>
> package com.horstmann.bigjava;
>
> **Purpose:**
>
> To declare that all classes in this file belong to a particular package

7.9.2 — Importing Packages

> The import directive lets you refer to a class of a package by its class name, without the package prefix.

If you want to use a class from a package, you can refer to it by its full name (package name plus class name). For example, java.awt.Color refers to the Color class in the java.awt package, and com.horstmann.bigjava.Numeric refers to the Numeric class in the com.horstmann.bigjava package:

```
java.awt.Color backgroundColor =
    new java.awt.Color(1.0, 0.7, 0.7);
```

Naturally, that is somewhat inconvenient. You can instead *import* a name with an import statement:

```
import java.awt.Color;
import com.horstmann.bigjava.Numeric;
```

Then you can refer to the classes as Color and Numeric without the package prefixes.

You can import *all classes* of a package with an import statement that ends in .*. For example, you can use the statement

```
import java.awt.*;
```

to import all classes from the java.awt package. That statement lets you refer to classes like Graphics2D or Color without a java.awt prefix. This is the most convenient method for importing classes. If a program starts with multiple imports of this form, however, it can be harder to guess to which package a class belongs. Suppose for example a program imports

```
import java.awt.*;
import java.io.*;
```

Then suppose you see a class name Image. You would not know whether the Image class is in the java.awt package or the java.io package. For that reason, we prefer to use an explicit import statement for each class, though many programmers like the convenience of importing all classes in a package.

However, you never need to import the classes in the java.lang package explicitly. That is the package containing the most basic Java classes, such as Math and Object. These classes are always available to you. In effect, an automatic import java.lang.*; statement has been placed into every source file.

Finally, you don't import the other classes in the same package. For example, when you implement the class `homework1.Test`, you don't need to import the class `homework1.Bank`. The compiler will find the class without an import statement because it is located in the same package.

⊗ Common Error 7.3

Confusing Dots

In Java, the dot symbol (.) is used as a separator in the following situations:

- Between package names (`java.util`)
- Between package and class names (`homework1.Bank`)
- Between class and inner class names (`Ellipse2D.Double`)
- Between class and instance variable names (`Math.PI`)
- Between objects and methods (`account.getBalance()`)

When you see a long chain of dot-separated names, it can be a challenge to find out which part is the package name, which part is the class name, which part is an instance variable name, and which part is a method name. Consider

```
java.lang.System.out.println(x);
```

Since the `println` is followed by an opening parenthesis, it must be a method name. Therefore, `out` must be either an object or a class with a `static println` method. (Of course, we know that `out` is an object reference of type `PrintStream`.) Again, it is not at all clear, without context, whether `System` is another object, with a public variable `out`, or a class with a `static` variable. Judging from the number of pages that the Java reference manual [1] devotes to this issue, even the compiler has trouble interpreting these dot-separated sequences of strings.

To avoid problems, it is helpful to adopt a strict coding style. If class names always start with an uppercase letter, while variable, method, and package names always start with a lowercase letter, then confusion can be avoided.

7.9.3 — Package Names

Placing related classes into a package is clearly a convenient mechanism to organize classes. However, there is a more important reason for packages: to avoid *name clashes*. In a large project, it is inevitable that two people will come up with the same name for the same concept. This even happens in the standard Java class library (which has now grown to thousands of classes). There is a class `Object` in the `java.lang` package and an interface, also called `Object`, in the `org.omg.CORBA` package. Fortunately, you never need to import both packages. If you did, then the name `Object` would be *ambiguous*.

However, thanks to the package concept, not all is lost. You can still tell the Java compiler exactly which `Object` class you need, simply by referring to them as `java.lang.Object` and `org.omg.CORBA.Object`.

> Use a domain name in reverse to construct unambiguous package names.

Of course, for the package-naming convention to work, there must be some way to ensure that package names are unique. It wouldn't be good if the car maker BMW placed all its Java code into the package `bmw`, and some other programmer (perhaps Bertha M. Walters) had the same bright idea. To avoid this problem, the inventors of Java recommend that you use a package-naming scheme that takes advantage of the uniqueness of Internet domain names.

If your company or organization has an Internet domain name, then you have an identifier that is guaranteed to be unique—the organizations who assign domain names take care of that. For example, I have a domain name `horstmann.com`, and there is nobody else on the planet with the same domain name. (I was lucky that the domain name `horstmann.com` had not been taken by anyone else when I applied. If your name is Walters, you will sadly find that someone else beat you to `walters.com`.) To get a package name, turn the domain name around, to produce a package name prefix:

```
org.omg
com.horstmann
```

Then it is up to the owner of the domain name to subdivide package names further. For example, the Object Management Group, the holder of the `omg.org` domain name, decided to use the package name `org.omg.CORBA` for the Java classes that implement their Common Object Request Broker Architecture (a mechanism for communication between objects that are distributed on different computers).

If you don't have your own domain name, you can still create a package name that has a high probability of being unique, by writing your email address backwards. For example, if Bertha Walters has an email address `walters@cs.sjsu.edu`, then she can use a package name `edu.sjsu.cs.walters` for her own classes.

Some instructors will want you to place each of your assignments into a separate package, such as `homework1`, `homework2`, and so on. The reason is again to avoid name collision. You can have two classes, `homework1.Bank` and `homework2.Bank`, with slightly different properties.

7.9.4 — How Classes Are Located

> The path of a class file must match its package name.

If the Java compiler has been properly set up on your system, and you use only the standard classes, you ordinarily need not worry about the location of class files and can safely skip this section. If you want to add your own packages, however, or if the compiler cannot locate a particular class or package, you need to understand the mechanism.

A package is located in a subdirectory that matches the package name. The parts of the name between periods represent successively nested directories. For example, the package `com.horstmann.bigjava` would be placed in a subdirectory `com/horstmann/bigjava`. If the package is to be used only in conjunction with a single program, then you can place the subdirectory inside the directory holding that program's files. For example, if you do your homework assignments in a *base directory* `/home/walters`, then you can place the class files for the `com.horstmann.bigjava` package into the directory `/home/walters/com/horstmann/bigjava`, as shown in Figure 6. (Here, we are using UNIX-style file names. Under Windows, you might use `c:\home\walters\com\horstmann\bigjava`.)

However, if you want to place your programs into many different directories, such as `/home/walters/hw1`, `/home/walters/hw2`, . . . , then you probably don't want to have lots of identical subdirectories `/home/walters/hw1/com/horstmann/bigjava`, `/home/walters/hw2/com/horstmann/bigjava`, and so on. In that case, you want to make a single directory with a name such as `/home/walters/lib/com/horstmann/bigjava`, place all class files for the package in that directory, and tell the Java compiler once and for all how to locate the class files.

You need to add the directories that might contain packages to the *class path*. In the preceding example, you add the `/home/walters/lib` directory to that class path. The details for doing this depend on your compilation environment; consult the documentation for your compiler, or your instructor. If you use the Sun Java SDK, you need to set the class path. The exact command depends on the operating system. In UNIX, the command might be

```
export CLASSPATH=/home/walters/lib:.
```

This setting places both the `/home/walters/lib` directory and the current directory `.` onto the class path.

A typical example for Windows would be

```
set CLASSPATH=c:\home\walters\lib;.
```

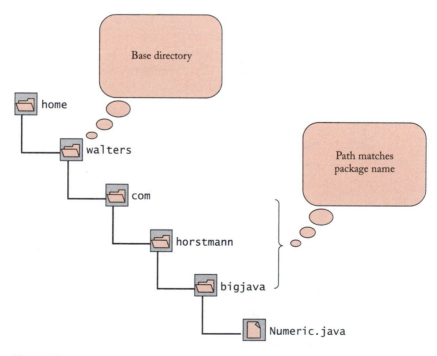

Figure 6

Base Directories and Subdirectories for Packages

Note that the class path contains the *base directories* that may contain package directories. It is a common error to place the complete package address in the class path. If the class path mistakenly contains /home/walters/lib/com/horstmann/bigjava, then the compiler will attempt to locate the com.horstmann.bigjava package in /home/walters/lib/com/horstmann/bigjava/com/horstmann/bigjava and won't find the files.

HOWTO 7.1

Programming with Packages

This HOWTO explains in detail how to place your programs into packages. For example, your instructor may ask you to place each homework assignment into a separate package. That way, you can have classes with the same name but different implementations in separate packages (such as homework1.Bank and homework2.Bank).

Step 1   Come up with a package name

Your instructor may give you a package name to use, such as homework1. Or, perhaps you want to use a package name that is unique to you only. Start with your email address, written backwards. For example, walters@cs.sjsu.edu becomes edu.sjsu.cs.walters. Then add a subpackage that describes your project or homework, such as edu.sjsu.cs.walters.homework1.

Step 2   Pick a *base directory*

The base directory is the directory that contains the directories for your various packages, for example /home/walters or c:\cs1.

Step 3   Make a subdirectory from the base directory that matches your package name

The subdirectory must be contained in your base directory. Each segment must match a segment of the package name. For example,

```
mkdir /home/bwalters/homework1
```

If you have multiple segments, build them up one by one:

```
mkdir c:\cs1\edu
mkdir c:\cs1\edu\sjsu
mkdir c:\cs1\edu\sjsu\cs
mkdir c:\cs1\edu\sjsu\cs\walters
mkdir c:\cs1\edu\sjsu\cs\walters\homework1
```

Step 4   Place your source files into the package subdirectory

For example, if your homework consists of the files Test.java and Bank.java, then you place them into

```
/home/walters/homework1/Test.java
/home/walters/homework1/Bank.java
```

or

```
c:\cs1\edu\sjsu\cs\walters\homework1\Test.java
c:\cs1\edu\sjsu\cs\walters\homework1\Bank.java
```

Step 5   Use the `package` statement in each source file

The first noncomment line of each file must be a `package` statement that lists the name of the package, such as

```
package homework1;
```

or

```
package edu.sjsu.cs.walters.homework1;
```

Step 6   Compile your source files *from the base directory*

Change to the base directory (from Step 2) to compile your files. For example,

```
cd /home/walters
javac homework1/Test.java
```

or

```
cd \cs1
javac edu\sjsu\cs\walters\homework1\Test.java
```

Note that the Java compiler needs the source *filename and not the class name. That is, you need to supply file separators (/* on UNIX, \ on Windows) and a file extension (`.java`).

Step 7   Run your program *from the base directory*

Unlike the Java compiler, the Java interpreter needs the *class name (and not a file name) of the class containing the* `main` *method.* That is, use periods as package separators, and don't use a file extension. For example,

```
cd /home/walters
java homework1.Test
```

or

```
cd \cs1
java edu.sjsu.cs.walters.homework1.Test
```

Random Fact   **7.1**

The Explosive Growth of Personal Computers

In 1971, Marcian E. "Ted" Hoff, an engineer at Intel Corporation, was working on a chip for a manufacturer of electronic calculators. He realized that it would be a better idea to develop a *general-purpose* chip that could be *programmed* to interface with the keys and display of a calculator, rather than to do yet another custom design. Thus, the *microprocessor* was born. At the time, its primary application was as a controller for calculators, washing machines, and the like. It took years for the computer industry to notice that a genuine central processing unit was now available as a single chip.

Hobbyists were the first to catch on. In 1974 the first computer *kit,* the Altair 8800, was available from MITS Electronics for about $350. The kit consisted of the microprocessor, a circuit board, a very small amount of memory, toggle switches, and a row of display lights. Purchasers had to solder and assemble it, then program it in machine language through the toggle switches. It was not a big hit.

The first big hit was the Apple II. It was a real computer with a keyboard, a monitor, and a floppy disk drive. When it was first released, users had a $3000 machine that could play Space Invaders, run a primitive bookkeeping program, or let users program it in BASIC. The original Apple II did not even support lowercase letters, making it worthless for word processing. The breakthrough came in 1979 with a new *spreadsheet* program, VisiCalc. In a spreadsheet, you enter financial data and their relationships into a grid of rows and columns (see Figure 7). Then you modify some of the data and watch in real time how the others change. For example, you can see how changing the mix of widgets in a manufacturing plant might affect estimated costs and profits. Middle managers in companies, who understood computers and were fed up with having to wait for hours or days to get their data runs back from the computing center, snapped up VisiCalc and the computer that was needed to run it. For them, the computer was a spreadsheet machine.

The next big hit was the IBM Personal Computer, ever after known as the PC. It was the first widely available personal computer that used Intel's 16-bit processor, the 8086, whose successors are still being used in personal computers today. The success of the PC was based not on any engineering breakthroughs but on the fact that it was easy to *clone.* IBM published specifications for plug-in cards, and it went one step further. It published the exact source code of the so-called BIOS (Basic Input/Output System), which controls the keyboard, monitor, ports, and disk drives and must be installed in ROM form in every PC. This allowed third-party vendors of plug-in cards to ensure that the BIOS code, and third-party extensions of it, interacted correctly with the equipment. Of course, the code itself was the property of IBM and could not be copied legally. Perhaps IBM did not foresee that functionally equivalent versions of the BIOS nevertheless could be recreated by others. Compaq, one of the first clone vendors, had fifteen engineers, who certified that they had never seen the original IBM code, write a new version that conformed precisely to the IBM specifications. Other companies did the same, and soon a variety of vendors were selling computers that ran the same software as IBM's PC but distinguished themselves by a lower price, increased portability, or better performance. In time, IBM lost its dominant position in the PC market. It is now one of many companies producing IBM PC–compatible computers.

IBM never produced an *operating system* for its PCs—that is, the software that organizes the interaction between the user and the computer, starts application programs, and manages disk storage and other resources. Instead, IBM offered customers the option of three separate operating systems. Most customers couldn't care less about the operating system. They chose the system that was able to launch most of the few applications that existed at the time. It happened to be DOS (Disk Operating System) by Microsoft. Microsoft cheerfully licensed the same operating system to

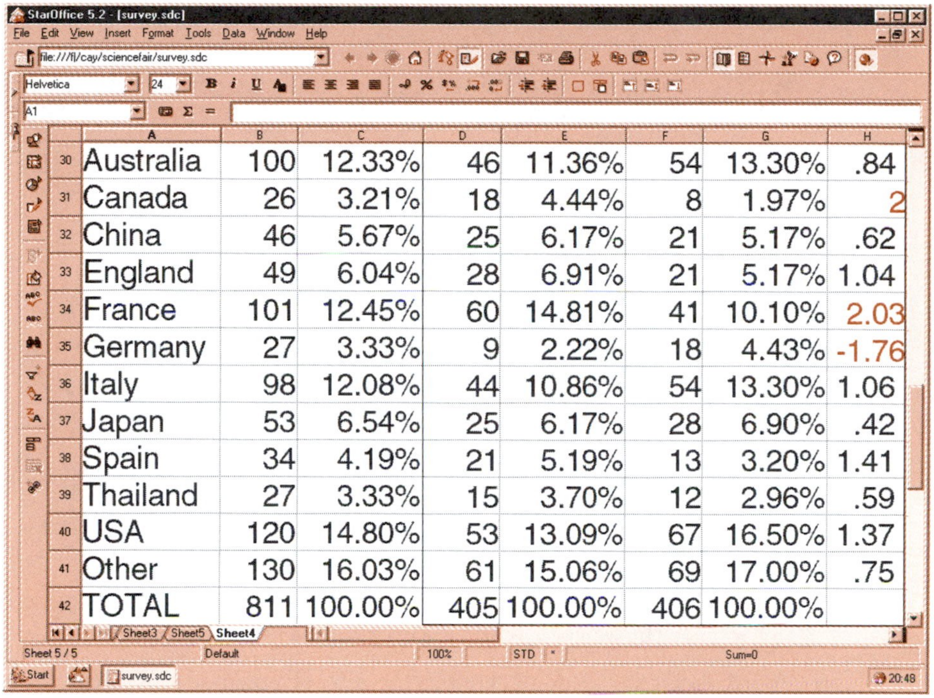

	A	B	C	D	E	F	G	H
30	Australia	100	12.33%	46	11.36%	54	13.30%	.84
31	Canada	26	3.21%	18	4.44%	8	1.97%	2
32	China	46	5.67%	25	6.17%	21	5.17%	.62
33	England	49	6.04%	28	6.91%	21	5.17%	1.04
34	France	101	12.45%	60	14.81%	41	10.10%	2.03
35	Germany	27	3.33%	9	2.22%	18	4.43%	-1.76
36	Italy	98	12.08%	44	10.86%	54	13.30%	1.06
37	Japan	53	6.54%	25	6.17%	28	6.90%	.42
38	Spain	34	4.19%	21	5.19%	13	3.20%	1.41
39	Thailand	27	3.33%	15	3.70%	12	2.96%	.59
40	USA	120	14.80%	53	13.09%	67	16.50%	1.37
41	Other	130	16.03%	61	15.06%	69	17.00%	.75
42	TOTAL	811	100.00%	405	100.00%	406	100.00%	

Figure 7

A Spreadsheet

other hardware vendors and encouraged software companies to write DOS applications. A huge number of useful application programs for PC-compatible machines was the result.

PC applications were certainly useful, but they were not easy to learn. Every vendor developed a different *user interface:* the collection of keystrokes, menu options, and settings that a user needed to master to use a software package effectively. Data exchange between applications was difficult, because each program used a different data format. The Apple Macintosh changed all that in 1984. The designers of the Macintosh had the vision to supply an intuitive user interface with the computer and to force software developers to adhere to it. It took Microsoft and PC-compatible manufacturers years to catch up.

The book [2] is highly recommended for an amusing and irreverent account of the emergence of personal computers.

At the time of this writing, it is estimated that two in three U.S. households own a personal computer and that one in two uses the Internet at least occasionally. Most personal computers are used for word processing, home finance (banking, budgeting, taxes), accessing information from CD-ROM and online sources, and entertainment. Some analysts predict that the personal computer will merge with the television set and cable network into an entertainment and *information appliance.*

CHAPTER SUMMARY

1. A class should represent a single concept from the problem domain, such as business, science, or mathematics.

2. The public interface of a class is cohesive if all of its features are related to the concept that the class represents.

3. A class depends on another class if it uses objects of that other class.

4. It is a good practice to minimize the coupling (i.e., dependency) between classes.

5. An accessor method does not change the state of its implicit parameter. A mutator method can change the state.

6. An immutable class has no mutator methods.

7. A side effect of a method is any externally observable behavior outside the implicit parameter. You should minimize side effects.

8. In Java, a method can never change parameters of primitive type.

9. In Java, a method can change the state of an object reference parameter, but it cannot replace the object reference with another.

10. A precondition is a requirement that the caller of a method must meet. If a method is called in violation of a precondition, the method is not responsible for computing the correct result.

11. If a method has been called in accordance with its preconditions, then it must ensure that its postconditions are valid.

12. A static method has no implicit parameter.

13. A static field belongs to the class, not to any object of the class.

14. The scope of a variable is the region of a program in which you can refer to the variable by its name.

15. In Java, you cannot have two local variables with overlapping scope.

16. A qualified name is prefixed by its class name or by an object reference, such as `Math.sqrt` or `other.balance`.

17. An unqualified instance field or method name refers to the implicit parameter `this`.

18. A local variable can shadow a field with the same name. You can access the shadowed field name by qualifying it with the `this` reference.

19. A package is a set of related classes.

20. The `import` directive lets you refer to a class of a package by its class name, without the package prefix.

21. Use a domain name in reverse to construct unambiguous package names.

22. The path of a class file must match its package name.

Further Reading

[1] Bertrand Meyer, *Object-Oriented Software Construction,* Prentice-Hall, 1989, chapter 7.
[2] Robert X. Cringely, *Accidental Empires,* Addison-Wesley, 1992.

CLASSES, OBJECTS, AND METHODS INTRODUCED IN THIS CHAPTER

```
java.lang.IllegalArgumentException
```

REVIEW EXERCISES

Exercise R7.1. Consider the following problem description:

> Users place coins in a vending machine and select a product by pushing a button. If the inserted coins are sufficient to cover the purchase price of the product, the product is dispensed and change is given. Otherwise, the inserted coins are returned to the user.

What classes should you use to implement it?

Exercise R7.2. Consider the following problem description:

> Employees receive their biweekly paycheck. They are paid their hourly for each hour worked; however, if they worked more than 40 hours per week, they are paid overtime at 150% of their regular wage.

What classes should you use to implement it?

Exercise R7.3. Consider the following problem description:

> Customers order products from a store. Invoices are generated to list the items and quantities ordered, payments received and amounts still due. Products are shipped to the shipping address of the customer, and invoices are sent to the billing address.

What classes should you use to implement it?

Exercise R7.4. Look at the public interface of the `System` class and discuss whether or not it is cohesive.

Exercise R7.5. Suppose an `Invoice` object contains descriptions of the products ordered, and the billing and the shipping address of the customer. Draw a UML diagram showing the dependencies between the classes `Invoice`, `Address`, `Customer`, and `Product`.

Exercise R7.6. Suppose a vending machine contains products, and users insert coins into the vending machine to purchase products. Draw a UML diagram showing the dependencies between the classes `VendingMachine`, `Coin`, and `Product`.

Exercise R7.7. On which classes does the class `Integer` in the standard library depend?

Exercise R7.8. On which classes does the class `Rectangle` in the standard library depend?

Exercise R7.9. Classify the methods of the class `StringTokenizer` as accessors and mutators.

Exercise R7.10. Classify the methods of the class `Rectangle` as accessors and mutators.

Exercise R7.11. Which of the following classes are immutable?
- `Rectangle`
- `String`
- `Random`

Exercise R7.12. Which of the following classes are immutable?
- `PrintStream`
- `Date`
- `Integer`

Exercise R7.13. What side effect, if any, do the following three methods have:

```java
public class Coin
{
    public void print()
    {
        System.out.println(name + " " + value);
    }

    public void print(PrintStream stream)
    {
        stream.println(name + " " + value);
    }

    public String toString()
    {
        return name + " " + value;
    }
    . . .
}
```

Exercise R7.14. Ideally, a method should have no side effect. Can you write a program in which no method has a side effect? Would such a program be useful?

Exercise R7.15. Write preconditions for the following methods. Do not implement the methods.
- `public static double sqrt(double x)`
- `public static String romanNumeral(int n)`
- `public static double slope(Line2D.Double a)`
- `public static String weekday(int day)`

Exercise R7.16. What preconditions do the following methods from the standard Java library have?
- `Math.sqrt`
- `Math.tan`
- `Math.log`
- `Math.exp`

- `Math.pow`
- `Math.abs`

Exercise R7.17. What preconditions do the following methods from the standard Java library have?

- `Integer.parseInt(String s)`
- `StringTokenizer.nextToken()`
- `Random.nextInt(int n)`
- `String.substring(int m, int n)`

Exercise R7.18. When a method is called with parameters that violate its precondition, it can throw an exception, or it can return to its caller. Give two examples of library methods (standard or the library methods used in this book) that return some result to their callers when called with invalid parameters, and give two examples of library methods that throw an exception.

Exercise R7.19. Consider a `Purse` class with methods

- `public void addCoin(Coin aCoin)`
- `public double getTotal()`

Give a reasonable postcondition of the `addCoin` method. What preconditions would you need so that the `Purse` class can ensure that postcondition?

Exercise R7.20. Consider the following method that is intended to swap the values of two floating-point numbers:

```java
public static void falseSwap(double a, double b)
{
   double temp = a;
   a = b;
   b = temp;
}

public static void main(String[] args)
{
   double x = 3;
   double y = 4;
   falseSwap(x, y);
   System.out.println(x + " " + y);
}
```

Why doesn't the method swap the contents of x and y?

Exercise R7.21. How *can* you write a method that swaps two floating-point numbers? *Hint:* `Point2D.Double`.

Exercise R7.22. Try compiling the following program. Explain the error message that you get.

```java
public class Exercise7_22
{
   public void print(int x)
   {
      System.out.println(x);
```

```
   }
   public static void main(String[] args)
   {
      int n = 13;
      print(13);
   }
}
```

Exercise R7.23. Look at the methods in the Integer class. Which are static? Why?

Exercise R7.24. Look at the methods in the String class (but ignore the ones that take a parameter of type char[]). Which are static? Why?

Exercise R7.25. The in and out fields of the System class are public static fields of the System class. Is that good design? If not, how could you improve on it?

Exercise R7.26. In the following class, the variable n occurs in multiple scopes. Which declarations of n are legal and which are illegal?

```
public class X
{
   public int f()
   {
      int n = 1;
      return n;
   }

   public int g(int k)
   {
      int a;
      for (int n = 1; n <= k; n++)
         a = a + n;
      return a;
   }

   public int h(int n)
   {
      int b;
      for (int n = 1; n <= 10; n++)
         b = b + n;
      return b + n;
   }

   public int k(int n)
   {
      if (n < 0)
      {
         int k = -n;
         int n = (int)(Math.sqrt(n));
         return n;
      }
      else return n;
```

```
      }

      public int m(int k)
      {
         int a;
         for (int n = 1; n <= k; n++)
            a = a + n;
         for (int n = k; n >= 1; n++)
            a = a + n;
         return a;
      }

      private int n;
}
```

Exercise R7.27. What is a qualified name? What is an unqualified name?

Exercise R7.28. When you access an unqualified name in a method, what does that access mean? Discuss both instance and static features.

Exercise R7.29. Every Java program can be rewritten to avoid `import` statements. Explain how, and rewrite IntersectionApplet.java from Chapter 4 to avoid `import` statements.

Exercise R7.30. What is the default package? Have you used it before this chapter in your programming?

Programming Exercises

Exercise P7.1. Implement the `Purse` and `Coin` classes described in Section 7.2.

Exercise P7.2. Enhance the `BankAccount` class by adding preconditions for the constructor and the `deposit` method that require the `amount` parameter to be at least zero, and a precondition for the `withdraw` method that requires `amount` to be at most the current balance. Throw exceptions if the precondition is not fulfilled.

Exercise P7.3. Write static methods

- `public static double sphereVolume(double r)`
- `public static double sphereSurface(double r)`
- `public static double cylinderVolume(double r, double h)`
- `public static double cylinderSurface(double r, double h)`
- `public static double coneVolume(double r, double h)`
- `public static double coneSurface(double r, double h)`

that compute the volume and surface area of a sphere with radius r, a cylinder with circular base with radius r and height h, and a cone with circular base with radius r and height h. Place them into an appropriate class. Then write a program that prompts the user for the values of r and h, calls the six methods, and prints the results.

Exercise P7.4. Solve the preceding exercise by implementing classes `Sphere`, `Cylinder`, and `Cone`. Which approach is more object-oriented?

Exercise P7.5. Write methods

```
public static double perimeter(Ellipse2D.Double e);
public static double area(Ellipse2D.Double e);
```

that compute the area and the perimeter of the ellipse **e**. Use these methods in an applet that prompts the user to specify an ellipse. Then display messages with the perimeter and area of the ellipse. Why does it make sense to use a static method in this case?

Exercise P7.6. Write a method

```
public static double distance(Point2D.Double p,
    Point2D.Double q)
```

that computes the distance between two points. Add the method to a suitable class. Write a test program that asks the user to enter two points. Then display the distance. Why does it make sense to use a static method in this case?

Exercise P7.7. Write a method

```
public static boolean isInside(Point2D.Double p,
    Ellipse2D.Double e)
```

that tests whether a point is inside an ellipse. Add the method to a suitable class. Write a test program that asks the user to enter a point and an ellipse. Then print whether the point is contained inside the ellipse.

Exercise P7.8. Write a method

```
public static int readInt(String prompt,
    int min, int max)
```

that displays the prompt string, reads an integer and tests whether it is between the minimum and maximum. If not, print an error message and repeat reading the input. Also, if the user cancels the input dialog, print an error message and keep reading. Add the method to an appropriate class and provide a test program.

Exercise P7.9. Write methods

- ```
  public static void drawH(Graphics2D g2,
      Point2D.Double p);
  ```
- ```
  public static void drawE(Graphics2D g2,
      Point2D.Double p);
  ```
- ```
  public static void drawL(Graphics2D g2,
      Point2D.Double p);
  ```
- ```
  public static void drawO(Graphics2D g2,
      Point2D.Double p);
  ```

that show the letters H, E, L, O on the graphics window, where the point **p** is the top left corner of the letter. Then call the methods to draw the words "HELLO" and "HOLE" on the graphics display. Draw lines and ellipses. Do not use the `drawString` method. Do not use `System.out`.

Exercise P7.10. Repeat the preceding exercise by designing classes `LetterH`, `LetterE`, `LetterL` and `LetterO`, each with a constructor that takes a `Point2D.Double` (the top left corner) and a method `draw(Graphics2D g2)`. Which solution is more object-oriented?

Figure 8

A Postal Bar Code

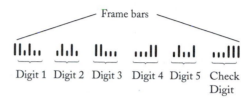

```
*************** ECRLOT ** CO57

CODE C671RTS2
JOHN DOE                              CO57
1009 FRANKLIN BLVD
SUNNYVALE      CA 95014 – 5143
```

llı..lıldlı.....llılıhlıl....llılılıllılıl.l

Figure 9

Encoding for Five-Digit Bar Codes

Frame bars

Digit 1 Digit 2 Digit 3 Digit 4 Digit 5 Check Digit

Exercise P7.11. *Postal bar codes.* For faster sorting of letters, the United States Postal Service encourages companies that send large volumes of mail to use a bar code denoting the ZIP code (see Figure 8).

The encoding scheme for a five-digit ZIP code is shown in Figure 9. There are full-height frame bars on each side. The five encoded digits are followed by a correction digit, which is computed as follows: Add up all digits, and choose the correction digit to make the sum a multiple of 10. For example, the ZIP code 95014 has sum of digits 19, so the correction digit is 1 to make the sum equal to 20.

Each digit of the ZIP code, and the correction digit, is encoded according to the following table:

	7	4	2	1	0
1	0	0	0	1	1
2	0	0	1	0	1
3	0	0	1	1	0
4	0	1	0	0	1
5	0	1	0	1	0
6	0	1	1	0	0
7	1	0	0	0	1
8	1	0	0	1	0
9	1	0	1	0	0
0	1	1	0	0	0

where 0 denotes a half bar and 1 a full bar. Note that they represent all combinations of two full and three half bars. The digit can be easily computed from the bar code using the column weights 7, 4, 2, 1, 0. For example, 01100 is $0 \cdot 7 + 1 \cdot 4 + 1 \cdot 2 + 0 \cdot 1 + 0 \cdot 0 = 6$. The only exception is 0, which would yield 11 according to the weight formula.

Write a program that asks the user for a ZIP code and prints the bar code. Use : for half bars, | for full bars. For example, 95014 becomes

```
||:|:::|:|:||::::::||:|::|:::|||
```

Use classes `BarCode` and `Digit` in your solution.

Exercise P7.12. Write a program that displays the bar code, using actual bars, on your graphic screen. In addition to the classes of the preceding exercise, use a class `Bar` with a method `void draw(Graphics2D g2)`.

Exercise P7.13. Write a program that reads in a bar code (with : denoting half bars and | denoting full bars) and prints out the ZIP code it represents. Print an error message if the bar code is not correct.

Exercise P7.14. Consider the following algorithm for computing x^n for an integer n. If $n < 0$, x^n is $1 / x^{-n}$. If n is positive and even, then $x^n = (x^{n/2})^2$. If n is positive and odd, then $x^n = x^{n-1} \cdot x$. Implement a static method `intPower(double x, int n)` that uses this algorithm. Add it to the `Numeric` class.

Exercise P7.15. Consider the `Die` class of Chapter 6. Turn the `generator` field into a static field so that all dice share a single random number generator.

Exercise P7.16. This exercise assumes that you have an email address. Write `Greeter` and `GreeterTest` classes in a package whose name is derived from your email address, as described in Section 7.9.

Exercise P7.17. Implement the `Purse` and `Coin` classes described in Section 7.2. Place them into a package called `money`. Write a test class `MoneyTest` in the default package.

Testing and Debugging

A complex program never works right the first time; it will contain errors, commonly called *bugs,* and will need to be tested. It is easier to test a program if it has been designed with testing in mind. This is a common engineering practice: On television circuit boards or in the wiring of an automobile, you will find lights and wire connectors that serve no direct purpose for the TV or car but are put in place for the repair person in case something goes wrong. In the first part of this chapter you will learn how to instrument your programs in a similar way. It is a little more work up-front, but that work is amply repaid by shortened debugging times.

In the second part of this chapter you will learn how to run the debugger to cope with programs that don't do the right thing.

CHAPTER CONTENTS

8.1 Unit Tests

Use unit tests to test classes in isolation.

The single most important testing tool is the *unit test* of a method or a set of cooperating methods.

For a unit test, the classes to be tested are compiled outside the program in which they will be used, together with a simple method called a *test harness* that feeds parameters to the methods.

Write a test harness to run a test.

The test arguments can come from one of several sources: from user input, by running through a range of values in a loop, as random values, and as values that are stored in a file or database.

In the following sections we will use a simple example for a method to test, namely an approximation algorithm to compute square roots that was known to the ancient Greeks. The algorithm, which was mentioned in Exercise P6.12, starts by guessing a value x that might be somewhat close to the desired square root $\sqrt{a}$. The initial value doesn't have to be very close; $x = a$ is a perfectly good choice. Now consider the quantities x and a / x. If $x < \sqrt{a}$, then $a / x > a / \sqrt{a} = \sqrt{a}$. Similarly, if $x > \sqrt{a}$, then $a / x < a / \sqrt{a} = \sqrt{a}$. That is, $\sqrt{a}$ lies between x and a / x. Make the *midpoint* of that interval our improved guess of the square root (see Figure 1). Therefore set $x_{new} = (x + a / x) / 2$ and repeat the procedure—that is, compute the midpoint between x_{new} and a / x_{new}. Stop when two successive approximations differ from each other by a very small amount.

This method converges very rapidly. To compute $\sqrt{100}$, only 8 steps are required:

```
Guess #1: 50.5
Guess #2: 26.24009900990099
Guess #3: 15.025530119986813
Guess #4: 10.840434673026925
Guess #5: 10.032578510960604
Guess #6: 10.000052895642693
Guess #7: 10.000000000139897
```

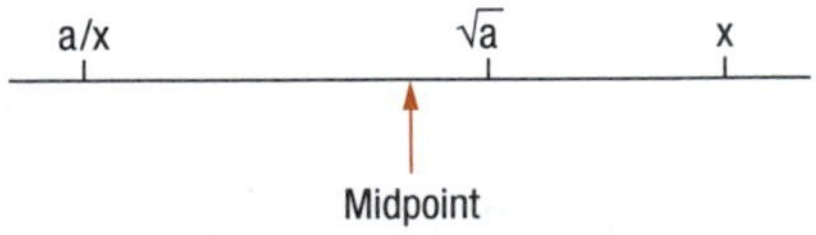

Figure 1

When Does the Needle Fall on a Line?

```
Guess #8: 10.0
Guess #9: 10.0
Guess #10: 10.0
```

Here is a class that implements the root approximation algorithm. Construct a Root-Approximator to extract a square root of a given number. The nextGuess method computes the next guess, and the getRoot method keeps calling nextGuess until two guesses are sufficiently close.

File RootApproximator.java

```
 1  /**
 2      Computes approximations to the square root of
 3      a number, using Heron's algorithm.
 4  */
 5  public class RootApproximator
 6  {
 7      /**
 8          Constructs a root approximator for a given number.
 9          @param aNumber  the number from which to extract the square root
10          (Precondition: aNumber >= 0)
11      */
12      public RootApproximator(double aNumber)
13      {
14          a = aNumber;
15          xold = 1;
16          xnew = a;
17      }
18
19      /**
20          Compute a better guess from the current guess.
21          @return  the next guess
22      */
23      public double nextGuess()
24      {
25          xold = xnew;
26          if (xold != 0)
27              xnew = (xold + a / xold) / 2;
28          return xnew;
29      }
30
31      /**
32          Compute the root by repeatedly improving the current
33          guess until two successive guesses are approximately equal.
34          @return  the computed value for the square root
35      */
36      public double getRoot()
37      {
38          while (!Numeric.approxEqual(xnew, xold))
39              nextGuess();
40          return xnew;
```

```
41      }
42
43      private double a; // the number whose square root is computed
44      private double xnew; // the current guess
45      private double xold; // the old guess
46 }
```

The guesses for $\sqrt{100}$ were computed by this test program.

File RootApproximatorTest.java

```
 1 import javax.swing.JOptionPane;
 2
 3 /**
 4     This program prints ten approximations for a square root.
 5 */
 6 public class RootApproximatorTest
 7 {
 8     public static void main(String[] args)
 9     {
10         String input
11             = JOptionPane.showInputDialog("Enter a number");
12         double x = Double.parseDouble(input);
13         RootApproximator r = new RootApproximator(x);
14         final int MAX_TRIES = 10;
15         for (int tries = 1; tries <= MAX_TRIES; tries++)
16         {
17             double y = r.nextGuess();
18             System.out.println("Guess #"
19                 + tries + ": " + y);
20         }
21         System.exit(0);
22     }
23 }
```

Does the `RootApproximator` class work correctly? Let us approach this question systematically.

If you use an environment such as BlueJ that allows you to create objects and call methods, you can easily run a few quick tests by constructing a few objects and calling methods—see Figure 2.

Alternatively, if you don't have such a development environment, it is an easy matter to write a test harness that supplies individual values for testing. Here is an example.

File RootApproximatorTest2.java

```
 1 import javax.swing.JOptionPane;
 2
 3 /**
 4     This program computes square roots of user-supplied inputs.
 5 */
 6 public class RootApproximatorTest2
```

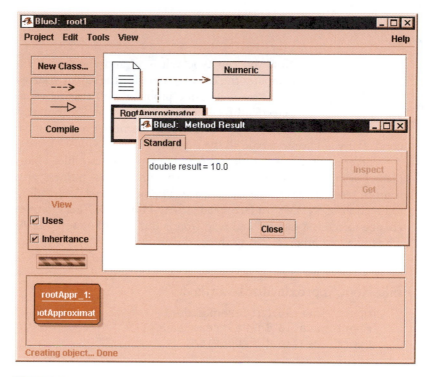

Figure 2

Testing a Class with BlueJ

```
 7  {
 8     public static void main(String[] args)
 9     {
10        boolean done = false;
11        while (!done)
12        {
13           String input = JOptionPane.showInputDialog(
14              "Enter a number, Cancel to quit");
15
16           if (input == null)
17              done = true;
18           else
19           {
20              double x = Double.parseDouble(input);
21              RootApproximator r = new RootApproximator(x);
22              double y = r.getRoot();
23
24              System.out.println("square root of " + x
25                 + " = " + y);
26           }
27        }
```

```
28        System.exit(0);
29     }
30 }
```

<table>
<tr><td>If you read test inputs from a file, you can easily repeat the test.</td></tr>
</table>

Now you can type values in and check that the `getRoot` method computes the correct values for the square root.

There is just one problem with this test approach. Suppose you detect and fix an error in your code. Of course, you will want to test the class again. The test harness program is still usable, which is good. But you have to retype all the inputs.

Therefore, it is a better idea to read the inputs from a file. That way, you can simply place the inputs into a file once and then run the test harness program whenever you want to test a new version of your code. The simplest way of reading input from a file is redirection of `System.in` (see Productivity Hint 6.1). First, you need to make a minor change to the test harness and read from a `BufferedReader` (see Advanced Topic 3.6). The following program listing shows the change.

File RootApproximatorTest3.java

```
 1 import java.io.BufferedReader;
 2 import java.io.InputStreamReader;
 3 import java.io.IOException;
 4
 5 /**
 6    This program computes square roots of inputs supplied
 7    through System.in.
 8 */
 9 public class RootApproximatorTest3
10 {
11    public static void main(String[] args)
12       throws IOException
13    {
14       BufferedReader console  = new BufferedReader(
15          new InputStreamReader(System.in));
16       boolean done = false;
17       while (!done)
18       {
19          String input = console.readLine();
20          if (input == null) done = true;
21          else
22          {
23             double x = Double.parseDouble(input);
24             RootApproximator r = new RootApproximator(x);
25             double y = r.getRoot();
26
27             System.out.println("square root of " + x
28                + " = " + y);
29          }
30       }
```

```
31     }
32  }
```

Then prepare a file with test inputs, such as this one:

```
100
20
4
1
0.25
0.01
```

Run the program like this. (Recall from Productivity Hint 6.1 that the < symbol denotes redirection of the file test.in to System.in.)

```
java RootApproximatorTest3 < test.in
```

The output is

```
square root of 100.0 = 10.0
square root of 20.0 = 4.47213595499958
square root of 4.0 = 2.0
square root of 1.0 = 1.0
square root of 0.25 = 0.5
square root of 0.01 = 0.1
```

It is also possible to generate test cases automatically. If there are few possible inputs, it is feasible to run through a representative number of them with a loop.

File RootApproximatorTest4.java

```
1  /**
2      This program computes square roots of input values
3      supplied by a loop.
4  */
5  public class RootApproximatorTest4
6  {
7     public static void main(String[] args)
8     {
9        final double MIN = 1;
10       final double MAX = 10;
11       final double INCREMENT = 0.5;
12       for (double x = MIN; x <= MAX; x = x + INCREMENT)
13       {
14          RootApproximator r = new RootApproximator(x);
15          double y = r.getRoot();
16          System.out.println("square root of " + x
17             + " = " + y);
18       }
19    }
20 }
```

The output is:

```
square root of 1.0 = 1.0
square root of 1.5 = 1.224744871391589
square root of 2.0 = 1.414213562373095
. . .
square root of 9.0 = 3.0
square root of 9.5 = 3.0822070014844885
square root of 10.0 = 3.162277660168379
```

Unfortunately, this test is restricted to only a small subset of values. To overcome that limitation, random generation of test cases can be useful:

File RootApproximatorTest5.java

```
 1  import java.util.Random;
 2
 3  /**
 4      This program computes square roots of random inputs.
 5  */
 6  public class RootApproximatorTest5
 7  {
 8     public static void main(String[] args)
 9     {
10        final double SAMPLES = 100;
11        Random generator = new Random();
12        for (int i = 1; i <= SAMPLES; i++)
13        { // generate random test value
14
15           double x = 1.0E6 * generator.nextDouble();
16           RootApproximator r = new RootApproximator(x);
17           double y = r.getRoot();
18           System.out.println("square root of " + x
19              + " = " + y);
20        }
21     }
22  }
```

A sample run looks like this:

```
square root of 298042.3906807571 = 545.932588036982
square root of 552836.0182932373 = 743.5294333738493
square root of 751687.182520626 = 866.9989518567056
square root of 872344.1056077272 = 933.9936325306116
. . .
```

Selecting good test cases is an important skill for debugging programs. Of course, you want to test your program with inputs that a typical user might supply.

You should test all program features. In the square root computation program, you should check typical test cases such as 100, 1/4, 0.01, 2, 10E12, and so on. These tests are *positive* tests. They consist of legitimate inputs, and you expect the program to handle them correctly.

> Boundary test cases are test cases that are at the boundary of acceptable inputs.

Next, you should include *boundary cases:* values that lie at the boundary of the set of acceptable inputs. For the root approximator, test what happens if the input is 0. Boundary cases are still legitimate inputs, and you expect that the program will handle them correctly—often in some trivial way or through special cases. Testing boundary cases is important, because programmers often make mistakes dealing with boundary conditions. Division by zero, extracting characters from empty strings, and accessing null pointers are common sources of errors.

Finally, gather *negative* test cases. These are inputs that you expect the program to reject. Examples are the square root of −2. However, in this case you need to be a little careful. If the precondition of a method doesn't allow an input, the method need not produce an output. In fact, if you try to compute the square root of −2 with the root approximator, the loop in the getRoot method never terminates. You can see why, by calling getNext a few times:

```
Guess #1: -0.5
Guess #2: 1.75
Guess #3: 0.3035714285714286
Guess #4: -3.142331932773109
Guess #5: -1.2529309672222557
Guess #6: 0.1716630854488237
Guess #7: -5.739532701343778
Guess #8: -2.6955361385562107
Guess #9: -0.976784358209916
Guess #10: 0.5353752385394334
```

No matter how you generate the test cases, the important point is that you test individual classes thoroughly before you put them into your program. If you have ever put together a computer or fixed a car, you probably followed a similar process. Rather than simply throwing all the parts together and hoping for the best, you probably first tested each part in isolation. It takes a little longer at the beginning, but it greatly reduces the possibility of complete and mysterious failure once the parts are put together.

8.2   Test Case Evaluation

In the last section we worried about how to get test *inputs*. Now let us consider what to do with the *outputs*. How do you know whether the output is correct?

Sometimes you can verify the output by calculating the correct values by hand. For example, for a payroll program you can compute taxes manually.

Sometimes a computation does a lot of work, and it is not practical to do the computation manually. That is the case with many approximation algorithms, which may run through dozens or hundreds of iterations before they arrive at the final answer. The square root method of Section 8.1 is an example of such an approximation.

How can you test that the square root method works correctly? You can supply test inputs for which you know the answer, such as 4 and 100, and also 1/4 and 0.01, so that you don't just restrict the inputs to integers.

Alternatively, you can write a test harness that verifies that the output values fulfill certain properties. For the square root program you can compute the square root, compute the square of the result, and verify that you obtain the original input:

File RootApproximatorTest6.java

```java
1  import java.util.Random;
2
3  /**
4     This program verifies the computation of square root values
5     by checking a mathematical property of square roots.
6  */
7  public class RootApproximatorTest6
8  {
9     public static void main(String[] args)
10    {
11       final double SAMPLES = 100;
12       int passcount = 0;
13       int failcount = 0;
14       Random generator = new Random();
15       for (int i = 1; i <= SAMPLES; i++)
16       {
17          // generate random test value
18
19          double x = 1.0E6 * generator.nextDouble();
20          RootApproximator r = new RootApproximator(x);
21          double y = r.getRoot();
22          System.out.println("square root of " + x
23             + " = " + y);
24
25          // check that test value fulfills square property
26
27          if (Numeric.approxEqual(y * y, x))
28          {
29             System.out.println("Test passed.");
30             passcount++;
31          }
32          else
33          {
34             System.out.println("Test failed.");
35             failcount++;
36          }
37       }
38       System.out.println("Pass: " + passcount);
39       System.out.println("Fail: " + failcount);
40    }
41 }
```

Finally, there may be a less efficient way of computing the same value that a method produces. You can then run a test harness that computes the method to be tested, together with the slower process, and compares the answers. For example, $\sqrt{x} = x^{1/2}$, so you can use the slower Math.pow method to generate the same value. Such a slower but reliable method is called an *oracle*. The following example program shows how to compare the result of the method to be tested with the outcome of an oracle. Alternatively, you

An oracle is a slow but reliable method to compute a result for testing purposes.

can write a separate program that writes the oracle values to a file, and then compare the results of your method against the precomputed oracle values.

File RootApproximatorTest7.java

```java
 1  import java.util.Random;
 2
 3  /**
 4      This program verifies the computation of square root values
 5      by using an oracle.
 6  */
 7  public class RootApproximatorTest7
 8  {
 9     public static void main(String[] args)
10     {
11        final double SAMPLES = 100;
12        int passcount = 0;
13        int failcount = 0;
14        Random generator = new Random();
15        for (int i = 1; i <= SAMPLES; i++)
16        {
17           // generate random test value
18
19           double x = 1.0E6 * generator.nextDouble();
20           RootApproximator r = new RootApproximator(x);
21           double y = r.getRoot();
22           System.out.println("square root of " + x
23              + " = " + y);
24
25           double oracleValue = Math.pow(x, 0.5);
26
27           // check that test value approximately equals oracle value
28
29           if (Numeric.approxEqual(y, oracleValue))
30           {
31              System.out.println("Test passed.");
32              passcount++;
33           }
34           else
35           {
36              System.out.println("Test failed.");
37              failcount++;
38           }
39        }
40        System.out.println("Pass: " + passcount);
41        System.out.println("Fail: " + failcount);
42     }
43  }
```

8.3 Regression Testing and Test Coverage

How should you collect test cases? This is easy for programs that get all their input from standard input. Just make each test case into a file—say, test1.in, test2.in, test3.in. These files contain the keystrokes that you would normally type at the keyboard when the program runs. Feed the files into the program to be tested, using redirection:

```
java Program < test1.in > test1.out
java Program < test2.in > test2.out
java Program < test3.in > test3.out
```

> A test suite is a set of tests for repeated testing.

Then study the outputs and see whether they are correct.

Keeping a test case in a file is smart, because you can then use it to test every version of the program. In fact, it is a common and useful practice to make a test file whenever you find a program bug. You can use that file to verify that your bug fix really works. Don't throw it away; feed it to the next version after that and all subsequent versions. Such a collection of test cases is called a *test suite*.

> Regression testing involves repeating previously run tests to ensure that known failures of prior versions do not appear in new versions of the software.

You will be surprised how often a bug that you fixed will reappear in a future version. This is a phenomenon known as *cycling*. Sometimes you don't quite understand the reason for a bug and apply a quick fix that appears to work. Later, you apply a different quick fix that solves a second problem but makes the first problem appear again. Of course, it is always best to think through what really causes a bug and fix the root cause instead of doing a sequence of "Band-Aid" solutions. If you don't succeed in doing that, however, at least you want to have an honest appraisal of how well the program works. By keeping all old test cases around and testing them all against every new version, you get that feedback. The process of testing against a set of past failures is called *regression testing*.

> Black-box testing describes a testing method that does not take the structure of the implementation into account.

Testing the functionality of the program without consideration of its internal structure is called *black-box testing*. That is an important part of testing, because, after all, the users of a program do not know its internal structure. If a program works perfectly on all positive inputs and fails gracefully on all negative ones, then it does its job.

> White-box testing uses information about the structure of a program.

However, it is impossible to ensure absolutely that a program will work correctly on all inputs just by supplying a finite number of test cases. As the famous computer scientist Edsger Dijkstra pointed out, testing can show only the presence of bugs—not their absence. To gain more confidence in the correctness of a program, it is useful to consider its internal structure. Testing strategies that look inside a program are called *white-box testing*. Performing unit tests of each method is a part of white-box testing.

> Test coverage is a measure of how many parts of a program have been tested.

You want to make sure that each part of your program is exercised at least once by one of your test cases. This is called *test coverage*. If some code is never executed by any of your test cases, you have no way of knowing whether that code would perform correctly if it ever were executed by user input. That means that you need to look at every if/else branch to see that each of them is reached by some test case. Many conditional branches are in the code only to take care of strange and abnormal inputs, but they still do something. It is a common phenomenon that they end up doing something incorrect, but that those faults are never discovered during testing, because nobody supplied the strange and abnormal inputs. Of course, these flaws become immediately apparent when the program is released and the first user types in a bad input and is incensed when the program crashes. A test suite should ensure that each part of the code is covered by some input.

For example, in testing the getTax method of the tax program in Chapter 5, you want to make sure that every if statement is entered for at least one test case. You should test both single and married taxpayers, with incomes in each of the three tax brackets.

It is a good idea to write the first test cases *before* the program is written completely. Designing a few test cases can give you insight into what the program should do, which is valuable for implementing it. You will also have something to throw at the program when it compiles for the first time. Of course, the initial set of test cases will be augmented as the debugging process progresses.

Modern programs can be quite challenging to test. In a program with a graphical user interface, the user can click random buttons with a mouse and supply input in random order. Programs that receive their data through a network connection need to be tested by simulating occasional network delays and failures. All this is much harder, because you cannot simply place keystrokes in a file. You need not worry about these complexities as you study this book, and there are tools to automate testing in these scenarios. The basic principles of regression testing (never throwing a test case away) and complete coverage (executing all code at least once) still hold.

▼ Productivity Hint   8.1

Batch Files and Shell Scripts

▼

If you need to perform the same tasks repeatedly on the command line, then it is worth learning about the automation features offered by your operating system.

▼

Under DOS, you use *batch files* to execute a number of commands automatically. For example, suppose you need to test a program with three inputs:

```
java Program < test1.in
java Program < test2.in
java Program < test3.in
```

▼

Then you find a bug, fix it, and run the tests again. Now you need to type the three commands once more. There has to be a better way. Under DOS, put the commands in a text file and call it test.bat:

▼

File test.bat

```
1 java Program < test1.in
2 java Program < test2.in
3 java Program < test3.in
```

Then you just type

```
test
```

and the three commands in the batch file execute automatically.

It is easy to make the batch file more useful. If you are done with Program and start working on Program2, you can of course write a batch file test2.bat, but you can do better than that. Give the test batch file a *parameter*. That is, call it with

```
test Program
```

or

```
test Program2
```

You need to change the batch file to make this work. In a batch file, %1 denotes the first string that you type after the name of the batch file, %2 the second string, and so on:

File test.bat

```
1 java %1 < test1.in
2 java %1 < test2.in
3 java %1 < test3.in
```

What if you have more than three test files? DOS batch files have a very primitive `for` loop:

File test.bat

```
1 for %%f in (test*.in) do java %1 < %%f
```

If you work in a computer lab, you will want a batch file that copies all your files onto a floppy disk when you are ready to go home. Put the following lines in a file gohome.bat:

File gohome.bat

```
1 copy *.java a:
2 copy *.txt a:
3 copy *.in a:
```

There are lots of uses for batch files, and it is well worth it to learn more about them.

Batch files are a feature of the DOS operating system, not of Java. On a UNIX system, *shell scripts* are used for the same purpose.

8.4 Program Traces, Logging, and Assertions

> A program trace consists of trace messages that show the path of execution.

Sometimes you run a program and you are not sure where it spends its time. To get a printout of the program flow, you can insert trace messages into the program, such as this one:

```
public double getTax()
{
    . . .
```

```
if (status == SINGLE)
{
   System.out.println("status is SINGLE");
      . . .
}
   . . .
```

You may also want to print out a *stack trace* that tells you how you got to this point. Use these instructions:

```
Throwable t = new Throwable();
t.printStackTrace(System.out);
```

A stack trace looks like this:

```
java.lang.Throwable
        at TaxReturn.getTax(TaxReturn.java:26)
        at TaxReturnTest.main(TaxReturnTest.java:30)
```

> A stack trace consists of a list of all pending method calls at a particular point in time.

This is very useful information—the trace message was generated inside the `getTax` method of the `TaxReturn` class (specifically, in line 26 of the `TaxReturn.java` file). That method was called from line 30 in `TaxReturnTest.java`.

However, there is a problem with trace messages. When you are done testing the program, you need to remove all print statements that produce trace messages. If you find another error, however, you need to stick the print statements back in.

To overcome this problem, you can use the `Logger` class, which allows you to turn off the trace messages. Support for logging is included in the standard Java library version 1.4 and above.

Instead of printing directly to `System.out`, use the global logger object

```
Logger logger = Logger.getLogger("global");
```

and call

```
logger.info("status is SINGLE");
```

By default, the message is printed. But if you call

```
logger.setLevel(Level.OFF);
```

all log message printing is suppressed. Thus, you can turn off the log messages when your program works fine, and you can turn them back on if you find another error.

When you are tracing execution flow, the most important events are entering and exiting a method. At the beginning of a method, print out the parameters:

```
public TaxReturn(double anIncome, int aStatus)
{
   Logger logger = Logger.getLogger("global");
   logger.info("Parameters: anIncome = " + anIncome
      + " aStatus = " + aStatus);
      . . .
}
```

At the end of a method, print out the return value:

```
public double getTax()
{
   . . .
   logger.info("Return value = " + tax);
   return tax;
}
```

To get a proper trace, you must locate *each* method exit point. Be sure to locate any `return` statements in the middle of the method.

Of course, you aren't restricted to "enter/exit" messages. You can report on progress inside a method. The `Logger` class has many other options for industrial-strength logging. You may want to check out the API documentation if you want to have more control over logging.

Program traces can be useful to analyze the behavior of a program, but they have some definite disadvantages. It can be quite time-consuming to find out which trace messages to insert. If you insert too many messages, you produce a flurry of output that is hard to analyze; if you insert too few, you may not have enough information to spot the cause of the error. If you find that a hassle, you are not alone. Most professional programmers use a *debugger*, not trace messages, to locate errors in their code. The debugger is covered in the next section.

Programs often contain implicit assumptions. For example, an interest rate should not be negative. Surely nobody would ever deposit money in an account that earns negative interest, but such a value might creep into a program due to an input or processing error. Sometimes, it is useful to check that no such error has occurred before continuing with the program. For example, before extracting the square root of a number that you know can't possibly be negative, you may want to check your assumption.

> An assertion is a logical condition in a program that you believe to be true.

An assumption that you believe to be true is called an *assertion*. An assertion test checks whether an assertion is true and terminates the program with an error report if it is not. Here is a typical assertion check:

```
public void computeIntersection()
{  . . .
   double y = r * r - (x - a) * (x - a);
   assert y >= 0;
   root = Math.sqrt(y);
   . . .
}
```

In this program excerpt, the programmer expects that the quantity y can never be negative. When the assertion is correct, no harm is done, and the program works in the normal way. If, for some reason, the assertion fails, then the programmer would rather have the program terminate than go on, compute the square root of a negative number, and cause greater harm later.

A common use for assertions is to monitor pre- and postconditions (see Section 7.5). For example, here is how you can monitor the precondition of the `deposit` method of the `Bank` class:

```
public double deposit (double amount)
{
   assert amount >= 0;
   balance = balance + amount;
}
```

Assertions are part of the Java language version 1.4 and above. To compile a program with assertions, run the Java compiler as

```
javac -source 1.4 MyProg.java
```

To execute the program with assertion checking turned on, use this command:

```
java -enableassertions MyProg
```

8.5 The Debugger

As you have undoubtedly realized by now, computer programs rarely run perfectly the first time. At times, it can be quite frustrating to find the bugs. Of course, you can insert trace messages to show the program flow as well as the values of key variables, run the program, and try to analyze the printout. If the printout does not clearly point to the problem, you may need to add and remove print commands and run the program again. That can be a time-consuming process.

> A debugger is a program that you can use to execute another program and analyze its runtime behavior.

Modern development environments contain special programs, called *debuggers*, that help you locate bugs by letting you follow the execution of a program. You can stop and restart your program and see the contents of variables whenever your program is temporarily stopped. At each stop, you have the choice of what variables to inspect and how many program steps to run until the next stop.

Some people feel that debuggers are just a tool to make programmers lazy. Admittedly some people write sloppy programs and then fix them up with the debugger, but the majority of programmers make an honest effort to write the best program they can before trying to run it through the debugger. These programmers realize that the debugger, while more convenient than print statements, is not cost-free. It does take time to set up and carry out an effective debugging session.

In actual practice, you cannot avoid using the debugger. The larger your programs get, the harder it is to debug them simply by inserting print statements. You will find that the time investment to learn about the debugger is amply repaid in your programming career.

Like compilers, debuggers vary widely from one system to another. On some systems they are quite primitive and require you to memorize a small set of arcane commands; on others they have an intuitive window interface. The screen shots in this chapter show the debugger in the Forte Community Edition development environment, presently downloadable for free from Sun Microsystems.

You will have to find out how to prepare a program for debugging and how to start the debugger on your system. If you use an integrated development environment, which contains an editor, compiler, and debugger, this step is usually very easy. You just build the program in the usual way and pick a menu command to start debugging. On some systems, you must manually build a debug version of your program and invoke the debugger.

> You can make effective use of the debugger by mastering just three concepts: breakpoints, single-stepping, and inspecting variables.

Once you have started the debugger, you can go a long way with just three debugging commands: "set breakpoint", "single step", and "inspect variable". The names and keystrokes or mouse clicks for these commands differ widely between debuggers, but all debuggers

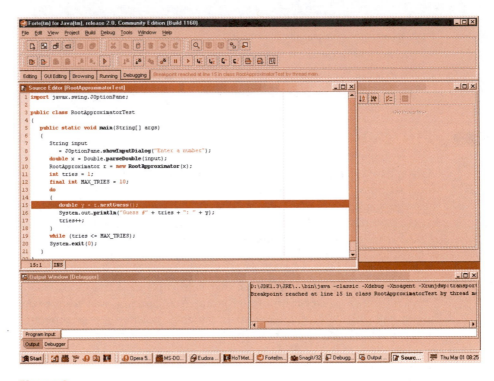

Figure 3

The Debugger Stopping at a Breakpoint

> When the debugger executes a program, the execution is suspended whenever a breakpoint is reached.

support these basic commands. You can find out how, either from the documentation or a lab manual, or by asking someone who has used the debugger before.

When you start the debugger, it runs at full speed until it reaches a *breakpoint*. Then execution stops, and the breakpoint that causes the stop is displayed (see Figure 3). You can now inspect variables and step through the program a line at a time, or continue running the program at full speed until it reaches the next breakpoint. When the program terminates, the debugger stops as well.

Breakpoints stay active until you remove them, so you should periodically clear the breakpoints that you no longer need.

Once the program has stopped, you can look at the current values of variables. Again, the method for selecting the variables differs among debuggers. Some debuggers always show you a window with the current local variables (see Figure 4). On other debuggers you issue a command such as "inspect variable" and type in or click on the variable. The debugger then displays the contents of the variable. If all variables contain what you expected, you can run the program until the next point where you want to stop.

When inspecting objects, you often need to give a command to "open up" the object, for example by clicking on a tree node. Once the object is opened up, you see its instance variables (see Figure 4).

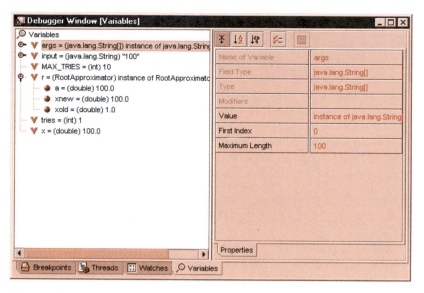

Figure 4

Inspecting Variables

> The single-step command executes the program one line at a time.

Running to a breakpoint gets you there speedily, but you don't know how the program got there. You can also step through the program a line at a time. Then you know how the program flows, but it can take a long time to step through it. The "single step" command executes the current line and stops at the next program line. Most debuggers have two "single step" commands, one called "step inside", which steps inside method calls, and one called "step over", which skips over method calls.

For example, suppose the current line is

```
String token = tokenizer.nextToken();
Word w = new Word(token);
int syllables = w.countSyllables();
System.out.println("Syllables in "
   + w.getText() + ": "
   + syllables);
```

When you "step over" method calls, you get to the next line:

```
String token = tokenizer.nextToken();
Word w = new Word(token);
int syllables = w.countSyllables();
System.out.println("Syllables in "
   + w.getText() + ": "
   + syllables);
```

However, if you "step into" method calls, you enter the first line of the `countSyllables` method.

```
public int countSyllables()
{
    int count = 0;
    int end = text.length() - 1;
}
```

You should step into a method to check whether it carries out its job correctly. You should step over a method if you know it works correctly.

Finally, when the program has completed running, the debug session is also finished. You can no longer inspect variables. To run the program again, you may be able to reset the debugger, or you may need to exit the debugging program and start over. Details depend on the particular debugger.

8.6   A Sample Debugging Session

To have a realistic example for running the debugger, we will study a Word class whose primary purpose is to count the number of syllables in a word. The class uses this rule for counting syllables:

Each *group* of adjacent vowels (a,e,i,o,u,y) counts as one syllable (for example, the "ea" in "real" contributes one syllable, but the "e..a" in "regal" count as two syllables). However, an "e" at the end of a word doesn't count as a syllable. Also, each word has at least one syllable, even if the previous rules give a count of 0.

Also, when you construct a word from a string, any characters at the beginning or the end of the string that aren't letters are stripped off. That is useful when you use a string tokenizer to break up a sentence into tokens. Tokens can still contain quotation marks and punctuation marks, and we don't want them as part of the word.

Here is the source code. There are a couple of bugs in this class.

File Word.java

```
 1 public class Word
 2 {
 3    /**
 4       Constructs a word by removing leading and trailing nonletter
 5       characters, such as punctuation marks.
 6       @param s the input string
 7    */
 8    public Word(String s)
 9    {
10       int i = 0;
11       while (i < s.length()
12             && !Character.isLetter(s.charAt(i)))
13          i++;
14       int j = s.length() - 1;
15       while (j > i
16             && !Character.isLetter(s.charAt(j)))
17          j--;
18       text = s.substring(i, j);
19    }
```

```
20
21      /**
22          Returns the text of the word, after removal of the
23          leading and trailing nonletter characters.
24          @return  the text of the word
25      */
26      public String getText()
27      {
28          return text;
29      }
30
31      /**
32          Counts the syllables in the word.
33          @return  the syllable count
34      */
35      public int countSyllables()
36      {
37          int count = 0;
38          int end = text.length() - 1;
39          if (end < 0) return 0; // the empty string has no syllables
40
41          // an e at the end of the word doesn't count as a vowel
42          char ch = Character.toLowerCase(text.charAt(end));
43          if (ch == 'e') end--;
44
45          boolean insideVowelGroup = false;
46          for (int i = 0; i <= end; i++)
47          {
48              ch = Character.toLowerCase(text.charAt(i));
49              if ("aeiouy".indexOf(ch) >= 0)
50              {
51                  // ch is a vowel
52                  if (!insideVowelGroup)
53                  {
54                      // start of new vowel group
55                      count++;
56                      insideVowelGroup = true;
57                  }
58              }
59              else
60                  insideVowelGroup = false;
61          }
62
63          // every word has at least one syllable
64          if (count == 0)
65              count = 1;
66
67          return count;
68      }
69
```

```
70    private String text;
71 }
```

Here is a simple test class. Type in one or more words into the input dialog, and the syllable counts of all words are displayed.

File WordTest.java

```
1  import java.util.StringTokenizer;
2  import javax.swing.JOptionPane;
3
4  public class WordTest
5  {
6     public static void main(String[] args)
7     {
8        String input = JOptionPane.showInputDialog(
9           "Enter a sentence");
10       StringTokenizer tokenizer =
11          new StringTokenizer(input);
12       while (tokenizer.hasMoreTokens())
13       {
14          String token = tokenizer.nextToken();
15          Word w = new Word(token);
16          int syllables = w.countSyllables();
17          System.out.println("Syllables in "
18             + token + ": "
19             + syllables);
20       }
21       System.exit(0);
22    }
23 }
```

When you run this program with an input of `hello regal real`, then the output is

```
Syllables in hello: 1
Syllables in regal: 1
Syllables in real: 1
```

That is not very promising.

First, set a breakpoint in the first line of the `countSyllables` method of the `Word` class, in line 35 of `Word.java`. Then start the program. The program will prompt you for the input. For now, just supply the input value `hello`. The program will stop at the breakpoint you just set.

First, the `countSyllables` method checks the last character of the word to see if it is a letter `'e'`. Let's just verify that this works correctly. Run the program to line 41 (see Figure 5).

Now inspect the variable `ch`. This particular debugger has a handy display of all current local and instance variables—see Figure 6. If yours doesn't, you may need to inspect `ch` manually. You can see that `ch` contains the value `'l'`. That is strange. Look at the source code. The `end` variable was set to `text.length() - 1`, the last position in the `text` string, and `ch` is the character at that position.

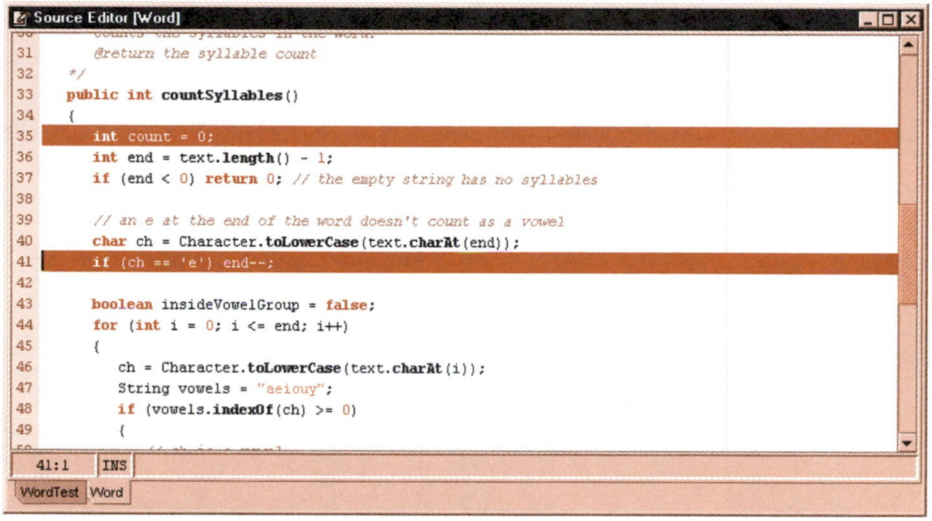

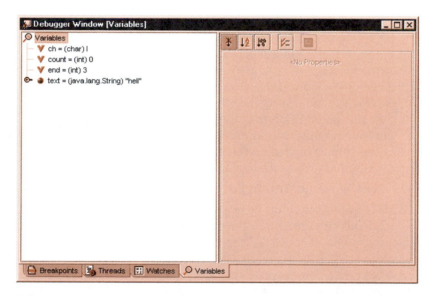

Figure 5

Debugging the countSyllables Method

Figure 6

The Current Values of the Local and Instance Variables

Looking further, you will find that end is set to 3, not 4, as you would expect. And text contains the string "hell", not "hello". Thus, it is no wonder that countSyllables returns the answer 1. We'll need to look elsewhere for the culprit. Apparently, the Word constructor contains an error.

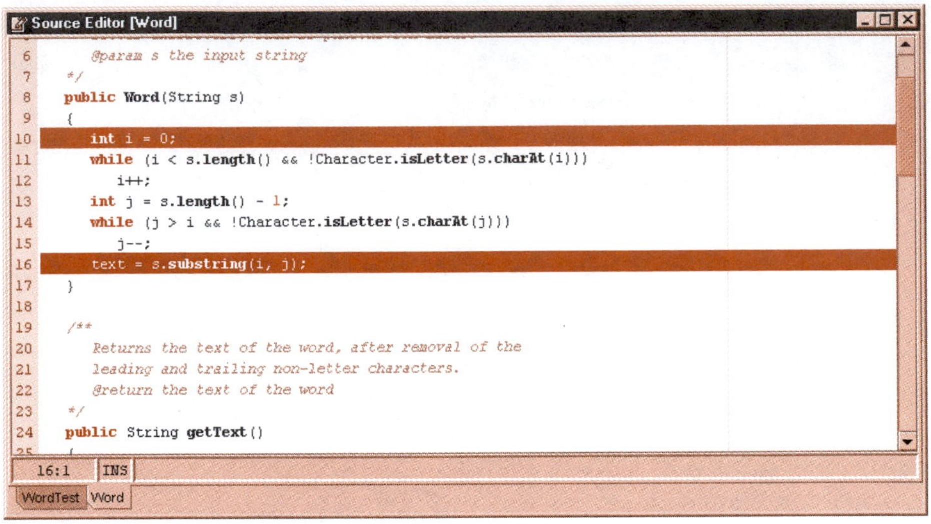

```
  Source Editor [Word]                                              _ □ X
  6       @param s the input string
  7      */
  8      public Word(String s)
  9      {
 10          int i = 0;
 11          while (i < s.length() && !Character.isLetter(s.charAt(i)))
 12              i++;
 13          int j = s.length() - 1;
 14          while (j > i && !Character.isLetter(s.charAt(j)))
 15              j--;
 16          text = s.substring(i, j);
 17      }
 18
 19      /**
 20          Returns the text of the word, after removal of the
 21          leading and trailing non-letter characters.
 22          @return the text of the word
 23      */
 24      public String getText()
 25      {
   16:1    INS
  WordTest  Word
```

Figure 7

Debugging the Word Constructor

Unfortunately, a debugger cannot go back in time. Thus, you must stop the debugger, set a breakpoint in the Word constructor, and restart the debugger. Supply the "hello" input once again. The debugger will stop at the beginning of the Word constructor. The constructor sets two variables i and j, skipping past any nonletters at the beginning and the end of the input string. Set a breakpoint past the end of the second loop (see Figure 7) so that you can inspect the values of i and j.

At this point, inspecting i and j shows that i is 0 and j is 4. That makes sense— there were no punctuation marks to skip. So why is text being set to "hell"? Recall that the substring method counts positions up to *but not including* the second parameter. Thus, the correct call should be

```
text = s.substring(i, j + 1);
```

This is a very typical "off by one" error.

Fix this error, recompile the program, and try the three test cases again. You will now get the output

```
Syllables in hello: 2
Syllables in regal: 1
Syllables in real: 1
```

That's better, but there still is a problem. Erase all breakpoints and set a breakpoint in the countSyllables method. Start the debugger and supply the input "regal". When the debugger stops at the breakpoint, start single-stepping through the lines of the method. Here is the code of the loop that counts the syllables:

```
boolean insideVowelGroup = false;
for (int i = 0; i <= end; i++)
{
```

```
ch = Character.toLowerCase(text.charAt(i));
if ("aeiouy".indexOf(ch) >= 0)
{
    // ch is a vowel
    if (!insideVowelGroup)
    {
        // start of new vowel group
        count++;
        insideVowelGroup = true;
    }
}
}
```

In the first iteration through the loop, the debugger skips the `if` statement. That makes sense, because the first letter, `'r'`, isn't a vowel. In the second iteration, the debugger enters the `if` statement, as it should, because the second letter, `'e'`, is a vowel. The `inside-VowelGroup` variable is set to `true`, and the vowel counter is incremented. In the third iteration, the `if` statement is again skipped, because the letter `'g'` is not a vowel. But in the fourth iteration, something weird happens. The letter `'a'` is a vowel, and the `if` statement is entered. But the second `if` statement is skipped, and `count` is not incremented again.

Why? The `insideVowelGroup` variable is still true, even though the first vowel group was finished when the consonant `'g'` was encountered. Reading a consonant should set `insideVowelGroup` back to `false`. This is a more subtle logic error, but not an uncommon one when designing a loop that keeps track of the processing state. To fix it, stop the debugger and add the following clause:

```
if ("aeiouy".indexOf(ch) >= 0)
{
    . . .
}
else insideVowelGroup = false;
```

Now recompile and run the test once again. The output is:

```
Syllables in hello: 2
Syllables in regal: 2
Syllables in real: 1
```

> The debugger can be used only to analyze the presence of bugs, not to show that a program is bug-free.

Is the program now free from bugs? That is not a question the debugger can answer. Remember: Testing can show only the presence of bugs, not their absence.

Random Fact 8.1

The First Bug

According to legend, the first bug was one found in 1947 in the Mark II, a huge electrome-chanical computer at Harvard University. It really was caused by a bug—a moth was trapped

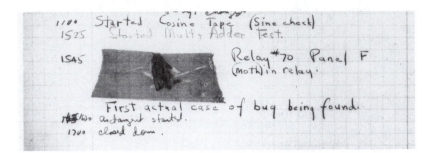

Figure 8

The "First Bug"

in a relay switch. Actually, from the note that the operator left in the log book next to the moth (see Figure 8), it appears as if the term "bug" had already been in active use at the time.

The pioneering computer scientist Maurice Wilkes wrote: "Somehow, at the Moore School and afterwards, one had always assumed there would be no particular difficulty in getting programs right. I can remember the exact instant in time at which it dawned on me that a great part of my future life would be spent finding mistakes in my own programs."

HOWTO   8.1

Debugging

Now you know about the mechanics of debugging, but all that knowledge may still leave you helpless when you fire up the debugger to look at a sick program. There are a number of strategies that you can use to recognize bugs and their causes.

Step 1   Reproduce the error

As you test your program, you notice that your program sometimes does something wrong. It gives the wrong output, it seems to print something completely random, it goes in an infinite loop, or it crashes. Find out exactly how to *reproduce* that behavior. What numbers did you enter? Where did you click with the mouse?

Run the program again; type in exactly the same answers, and click with the mouse on the same spots (or as close as you can get). Does the program exhibit the same behavior? If so, then it makes sense to fire up the debugger to study this particular problem. Debuggers are good for analyzing particular failures. They aren't terribly useful for studying a program in general.

Step 2   Simplify the error

Before you fire up the debugger, it makes sense to spend a few minutes trying to come up with a simpler input that also produces an error. Can you use shorter words or simpler numbers and still have the program misbehave? If so, use those values during your debugging session.

▼ **Step 3** Divide and conquer

Now that you have a particular failure, you want to get as close to the failure as possible. The key point of debugging is to locate the code that produces the failure. Just as with real insect pests, finding the bug can be hard, but once you find it, squashing it is usually the easy part. Suppose your program dies with a division by 0. Since there are many division operations in a typical program, it is often not feasible to set breakpoints to all of them. Instead, use a technique of *divide and conquer*. Step over the methods in `main`, but don't step inside them. Eventually, the failure will happen again. Now you know which method contains the bug: It is the last method that was called from `main` before the program died. Restart the debugger and go back to that line in `main`, then step inside that method. Repeat the process.

> Use the "divide-and-conquer" technique to locate the point of failure of a program.

Eventually, you will have pinpointed the line that contains the bad division. Maybe it is completely obvious from the code why the denominator is not correct. If not, you need to find the location where it is computed. Unfortunately, you can't go *back* in the debugger. You need to restart the program and move to the point where the denominator computation happens.

▼ **Step 4** Know what your program should do

> During debugging, compare the actual contents of variables against the values that you know they should have.

The debugger shows you what the program *does* do. You must know what the program *should* do, or you will not be able to find bugs. Before you trace through a loop, ask yourself how many iterations you *expect* the program to make. Before you inspect a variable, ask yourself what you expect to see. If you have no clue, set aside some time and think first. Have a calculator handy to make independent computations. When you know what the value should be, inspect the variable. This is the moment of truth. If the program is still on the right track, then that value is what you expected, and you must look further for the bug. If the value is different, you may be on to something. Double-check your computation. If you are sure your value is correct, find out why your program comes up with a different value.

In many cases, program bugs are the result of simple errors such as loop termination conditions that are off by 1. Quite often, however, programs make computational errors. Maybe they are supposed to add two numbers, but by accident the code was written to subtract them. Unlike your calculus instructor, programs don't make a special effort to ensure that everything is a simple integer (and neither do real-world problems). You will need to make some calculations with large integers or nasty floating-point numbers. Sometimes these calculations can be avoided if you just ask yourself, "Should this quantity be positive? Should it be larger than that value?" Then inspect variables to verify those theories.

▼ **Step 5** Look at all details

When you debug a program, you often have a theory about what the problem is. Nevertheless, keep an open mind and look around at all details. What strange messages are displayed?

Why does the program take another unexpected action? These details count. When you run a debugging session, you really are a detective who needs to look at every clue available.

If you notice another failure on the way to the problem that you are about to pin down, don't just say, "I'll come back to it later". That very failure may be the original cause for your current problem. It is better to make a note of the current problem, fix what you just found, and then return to the original mission.

Step 6 Make sure you understand each bug before you fix it

Once you find that a loop makes too many iterations, it is very tempting to apply a "Band-Aid" solution and subtract 1 from a variable so that the particular problem doesn't appear again. Such a quick fix has an overwhelming probability of creating trouble elsewhere. You really need to have a thorough understanding of how the program should be written before you apply a fix.

It does occasionally happen that you find bug after bug and apply fix after fix, and the problem just moves around. That usually is a symptom of a larger problem with the program logic. There is little you can do with the debugger. You must rethink the program design and reorganize it.

Random Fact   8.2

The Therac-25 Incidents

The Therac-25 is a computerized device to deliver radiation treatment to cancer patients (see Figure 9). Between June 1985 and January 1987, several of these machines delivered serious overdoses to at least six patients, killing some of them and seriously maiming the others.

The machines were controlled by a computer program. Bugs in the program were directly responsible for the overdoses. According to [1], the program was written by a single programmer, who had since left the manufacturing company producing the device and could not be located. None of the company employees interviewed could say anything about the educational level or qualifications of the programmer.

The investigation by the federal Food and Drug Administration (FDA) found that the program was poorly documented and that there was neither a specification document nor a formal test plan. (This should make you think. Do you have a formal test plan for your programs?)

The overdoses were caused by an amateurish design of the software that had to control different devices concurrently, namely the keyboard, the display, the printer, and of course the radiation device itself. Synchronization and data sharing between the tasks were done in an ad hoc way, even though safe multitasking techniques were known at the time. Had the programmer enjoyed a formal education that involved these techniques, or taken the effort to study the literature, a safer machine could have been built. Such a machine would have probably involved a commercial multitasking system, which might have required a more expensive computer.

The same flaws were present in the software controlling the predecessor model, the Therac-20, but that machine had hardware interlocks that mechanically prevented overdoses.

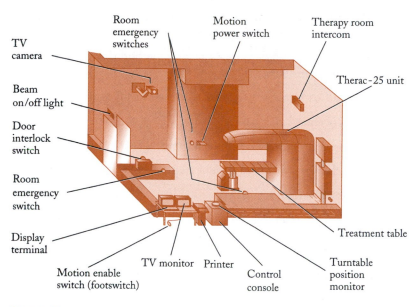

Figure 9

Typical Therac-25 Facility

The hardware safety devices were removed in the Therac-25 and replaced by checks in the software, presumably to save cost.

Frank Houston of the FDA wrote in 1985 [1]: "A significant amount of software for life-critical systems comes from small firms, especially in the medical device industry; firms that fit the profile of those resistant to or uninformed of the principles of either system safety or software engineering."

Who is to blame? The programmer? The manager who not only failed to ensure that the programmer was up to the task but also didn't insist on comprehensive testing? The hospitals that installed the device, or the FDA, for not reviewing the design process? Unfortunately, even today there are no firm standards of what constitutes a safe software design process.

CHAPTER SUMMARY

1. Use unit tests to test classes in isolation.

2. Write a test harness to run a test.

3. If you read test inputs from a file, you can easily repeat the test.

4. Boundary test cases are test cases that are at the boundary of acceptable inputs.

5. An oracle is a slow but reliable method to compute a result for testing purposes.

6. A test suite is a set of tests for repeated testing.

7. Regression testing involves repeating previously run tests to ensure that known failures of prior versions do not appear in new versions of the software.

8. Black-box testing describes a testing method that does not take the structure of the implementation into account.

9. White-box testing uses information about the structure of a program.

10. Test coverage is a measure of how many parts of a program have been tested.

11. A program trace consists of trace messages that show the path of execution.

12. A stack trace consists of a list of all pending method calls at a particular point in time.

13. An assertion is a logical condition in a program that you believe to be true.

14. A debugger is a program that you can use to execute another program and analyze its runtime behavior.

15. You can make effective use of the debugger by mastering just three concepts: breakpoints, single-stepping, and inspecting variables.

16. When the debugger executes a program, the execution is suspended whenever a breakpoint is reached.

17. The single-step command executes the program one line at a time.

18. The debugger can be used only to analyze the presence of bugs, not to show that a program is bug-free.

19. Use the "divide-and-conquer" technique to locate the point of failure of a program.

20. During debugging, compare the actual contents of variables against the values that you know they should have.

Further Reading

[1] Nancy G. Leveson and Clark S. Turner, "An Investigation of the Therac-25 Accidents," IEEE Computer, July 1993, pp. 18–41.

CLASSES, OBJECTS, AND METHODS INTRODUCED IN THIS CHAPTER

```
java.lang.Throwable
    printStackTrace
java.util.logging.Logger
    getLogger
    info
    setLevel
```

REVIEW EXERCISES

Exercise R8.1. Define the terms *unit test* and *test harness*.

Exercise R8.2. What is an oracle?

Exercise R8.3. Define the terms *regression testing* and *test suite*.

Exercise R8.4. What is the debugging phenomenon known as "cycling"? What can you do to avoid it?

Exercise R8.5. The arc sine function is the inverse of the sine function. That is, $y = \arcsin(x)$ if $x = \sin(y)$. It is defined only if $-1 \leq x \leq 1$. Suppose you need to write a Java method to compute the arc sine. List three positive test cases and one boundary test case with their expected return values, and two negative test cases.

Exercise R8.6. What is a program trace? When does it make sense to use a program trace, and when does it make more sense to use a debugger?

Exercise R8.7. Explain the differences between these debugger operations:
- Stepping into a method
- Stepping over a method

Exercise R8.8. Explain in detail how to inspect the information stored in a `Point2D.Double` object in your debugger.

Exercise R8.9. Explain in detail how to inspect the string stored in a `String` object in your debugger.

Exercise R8.10. Explain in detail how to use your debugger to inspect the balance stored in a `BankAccount` object.

Exercise R8.11. Explain the "divide-and-conquer" strategy to get close to a bug in the debugger.

Exercise R8.12. True or false:
- If a program has passed all tests in the test suite, it has no more bugs.
- If a program has a bug, that bug always shows up when running the program through the debugger.
- If all methods in a program were proven correct, then the program has no bugs.

PROGRAMMING EXERCISES

Exercise P8.1. The arc sine function is the inverse of the sine function. That is,

$$y = \arcsin(x) \text{ if } x = \sin(y)$$

where y is in radians. For example,

$$\arcsin(0) = 0$$
$$\arcsin(0.5) = \pi/6$$

$$\arcsin(\sqrt{2}/2) = \pi/4$$

$$\arcsin(\sqrt{3}/2) = \pi/3$$

$$\arcsin(1) = \pi/2$$

$$\arcsin(-1) = \pi/2$$

The arc sine is defined only for values between -1 and 1. There is a Java standard library method to compute the arc sine, but you should not use it for this exercise. Write a Java class ArcSinApproximator that computes the arc sine from its Taylor series expansion

$$\arcsin(x) = x + \frac{x^3}{3!} + \frac{3^2 \cdot x^5}{5!} + \frac{3^2 \cdot 5^2 \cdot x^7}{7!} + \frac{3^2 + 5^2 + 7^2 \cdot x^9}{9!} + \cdots$$

Hint: Don't compute the powers and factorials explicitly. Instead, compute each term from the value of the preceding term.

You should compute the sum until a new term is $< 10^{-6}$. This method will be used in subsequent exercises.

Exercise P8.2. Write a simple test harness for the ArcSinApproximator class that reads floating-point numbers from standard input and computes their arc sines, until the end of the input is reached. Then run that program and verify its outputs against the arc sine function of a scientific calculator.

Exercise P8.3. Write a test harness that automatically generates test cases for the ArcSinApproximator class, namely numbers between -1 and 1 in a step size of 0.1.

Exercise P8.4. Write a test harness that generates 10 random floating-point numbers between -1 and 1 and feeds them to ArcSinApproximator.

Exercise P8.5. Write a test harness that automatically tests the validity of the ArcSinApproximator class by verifying that

```
Math.sin(new ArcSinApproximator(x).getArcSin())
```

is approximately equal to x. Test with 100 random inputs.

Exercise P8.6. The arc sine function can be computed from the arc tangent function, according to the formula

$$\arcsin(x) = \arctan\left(x / \sqrt{1 - x^2}\right)$$

Use that expression as an *oracle* to test that your arc sine method works correctly. Test your method with 100 random inputs and verify against the oracle.

Exercise P8.7. The domain of the arc sine function is $-1 \le x \le 1$. Test your class by computing $\arcsin(1.1)$. What happens?

Exercise P8.8. Place logging messages into the loop of the arc sine method that computes the power series. Print the value of the exponent of the current term, the value of the current term, and the current approximation to the result. What trace output do you get when you compute $\arcsin(0.5)$?

Exercise P8.9. Add logging messages to the buggy Word class. Log relevant values such as instance variable values, return values, and loop counters. Run your program with the same sample inputs used for the debugging session. Are the messages informative enough to spot the bug?

Exercise P8.10. Run a test harness of the ArcSinApproximator class through the debugger. Step inside the computation of arcsin(0.5). Step through the computation until the x^7 term has been computed and added to the sum. What is the value of the current term and of the sum at this point?

Exercise P8.11. Run a test harness of the arcsin method through the debugger. Step inside the computation of arcsin(0.5). Step through the computation until the x^n term has become smaller than 10^{-6}. Then inspect n. How large is it?

Exercise P8.12. The following class has two bugs:

```java
public class RootApproximator
{
    public RootApproximator(double aNumber)
    {
        a = aNumber;
        x1 = aNumber;
    }

    public double nextGuess()
    {
        x1 = x0;
        x0 = (x1 + a / x1) / 2;
        return x1;
    }

    public double getRoot()
    {
        while (!Numeric.approxEqual(x0, x1))
            nextGuess();
        return x1;
    }

    private double a; // the number whose square root is computed
    private double x0;
    private double x1;
}
```

Create a series of test cases to flush out the bugs. Then run a debugging session to find them. What changes did you make to the class to fix the bugs?

Interfaces and Polymorphism

CHAPTER GOALS

To learn about interfaces

▶ To be able to convert between supertype and subtype references

▶ To understand the concept of polymorphism

▶ To appreciate how interfaces can be used to decouple classes

▶ To learn how to implement helper classes as inner classes

▶ To understand how inner classes access variables from the surrounding scope

▶ To implement event listeners for timer events

CHAPTER CONTENTS

9.1 Developing Reusable Solutions

Consider the `DataSet` class of Chapter 6. We used that class to compute the average and maximum of a set of input values. However, the class was suitable only for computing the average of a set of *numbers*. If we wanted to process bank accounts to find the bank account with the highest balance, we would have to modify the class, like this:

```java
public class DataSet // modified for BankAccount objects
{
   . . .
   public void add(BankAccount x)
   {
      sum = sum + x.getBalance();
      if (count == 0
            || maximum.getBalance() < x.getBalance())
         maximum = x;
      count++;
   }

   public BankAccount getMaximum()
   {
      return maximum;
   }

   private double sum;
   private BankAccount maximum;
   private int count;
}
```

Or suppose we wanted to find the coin with the highest value among a set of coins. We would need to modify the `DataSet` class again.

```java
public class DataSet // modified for Coin objects
{
   . . .
   public void add(Coin x)
   {
      sum = sum + x.getValue();
      if (count == 0
            || maximum.getValue() < x.getValue())
         maximum = x;
      count++;
   }

   public Coin getMaximum()
   {
      return maximum;
   }

   private double sum;
```

```
      private Coin maximum;
      private int count;
   }
```

Clearly, the fundamental mechanics of analyzing the data is the same in all cases, but the details of measurement differ.

Suppose that the various classes could agree on a single method `getMeasure` that obtains the measure to be used in the data analysis, such as the balance for bank accounts, value for coins, and so on. Then we could implement a single reusable `DataSet` class. The add method would look like this:

```
sum = sum + x.getMeasure();
if (count == 0 || maximum.getMeasure() < x.getMeasure())
   maximum = x;
count++;
```

What is the type of the variable x? Ideally, x should refer to any class that has a `getMeasure` method. In Java, an *interface type* expresses that concept. Here is the interface type declaration for a `Measurable` type.

```
public interface Measurable
{
   double getMeasure();
}
```

> A Java interface declares a set of methods and their signatures. Unlike a class, it provides no implementation.

The interface declaration lists all methods that the interface requires. This interface requires a single method, but in general, an interface can require multiple methods.

An interface is similar to a class, but there are several important differences:

- All methods in an interface are *abstract;* that is, they have a name, parameters, and a return type, but they don't have an implementation.

- All methods in an interface are automatically public.

- An interface does not have instance variables.

Now we can use the type `Measurable` to declare the variables x and `maximum`.

```
public class DataSet
{
   . . .

   public void add(Measurable x)
   {
      sum = sum + x.getMeasure();
      if (count == 0
            || maximum.getMeasure() < x.getMeasure())
         maximum = x;
      count++;
   }

   public Measurable getMaximum()
```

```
    {
        return maximum;
    }

    private double sum;
    private Measurable maximum;
    private int count;
}
```

> To realize an interface, a class must supply all methods that the interface requires.

This `DataSet` class is usable for analyzing objects of any class that *realizes* the `Measurable` interface. A class realizes an interface if it declares the interface in an `implements` clause, and if it implements the method or methods that the interface requires.

```
class ClassName implements Measurable
{
    public double getMeasure()
    {
        implementation
    }

    additional methods and fields
}
```

A class can realize more than one interface. Of course, the class must then define all the methods that are required by all the interfaces it realizes.

Let us modify the `BankAccount` class to realize the `Measurable` interface.

```
public class BankAccount implements Measurable
{
    public double getMeasure()
    {
        return balance;
    }
    . . .
}
```

Note that the class must declare the method as `public`, whereas the interface does not— all methods in an interface are public.

Similarly, it is an easy matter to modify the `Coin` class to realize the `Measurable` interface.

```
public class Coin implements Measurable
{
    public double getMeasure()
    {
        return value;
    }
    . . .
}
```

Now `DataSet` objects can be used to analyze collections of bank accounts or coins. Here is a test program that illustrates the fact.

File DataSetTest.java

```
 1  /**
 2      This program tests the DataSet class.
 3  */
 4  public class DataSetTest
 5  {
 6     public static void main(String[] args)
 7     {
 8
 9        DataSet bankData = new DataSet();
10
11        bankData.add(new BankAccount(0));
12        bankData.add(new BankAccount(10000));
13        bankData.add(new BankAccount(2000));
14
15        System.out.println("Average balance = "
16           + bankData.getAverage());
17        Measurable max = bankData.getMaximum();
18        System.out.println("Highest balance = "
19           + max.getMeasure());
20
21        DataSet coinData = new DataSet();
22
23        coinData.add(new Coin(0.25, "quarter"));
24        coinData.add(new Coin(0.1, "dime"));
25        coinData.add(new Coin(0.05, "nickel"));
26
27        System.out.println("Average coin value = "
28           + coinData.getAverage());
29        max = coinData.getMaximum();
30        System.out.println("Highest coin value = "
31           + max.getMeasure());
32     }
33  }
```

> Interfaces can reduce the coupling between classes.

Figure 1 shows the relationships between the classes and interfaces. In the UML notation, interfaces are tagged with a "stereotype" indicator «interface». A dotted arrow with a triangular tip denotes the realization relationship between a class and an interface. You have to look carefully at the arrow tips—a dotted line with an open v-shaped arrow tip denotes dependency.

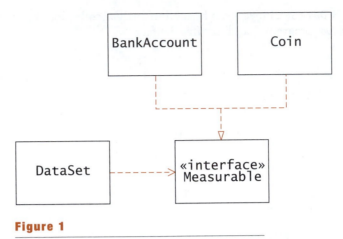

Figure 1

UML Diagram of the DataSet Class and the Classes That Realize the Measurable Interface

This diagram shows that the DataSet class depends only on the Measurable interface. It is decoupled from the BankAccount and Coin classes. This decoupling makes the DataSet class reusable. Any class that is willing to implement the Measurable interface can be used with the DataSet class.

Syntax 9.1: Defining an Interface

```
public interface InterfaceName
{
    method signatures
}
```

Example:

```
public interface Measurable
{
    double getMeasure();
}
```

Purpose:

To define an interface and its method signatures. The methods are automatically public.

Syntax 9.2: Implementing an Interface

```
public class ClassName
    implements InterfaceName, InterfaceName, ...
{
    methods
    instance variables
}
```

Example:

```
public class BankAccount
    implements Measurable
{
    // other BankAccount methods
    public double getMeasure()
    {
        // method implementation
    }
}
```

Purpose:

To define a new class that implements the methods of an
interface

▼ ⊗ **Common Error**   `9.1`

Forgetting to Define Implementing Methods as Public

▼   The methods in an interface are not declared as `public`, because they are public by
default. However, the methods in a class are not public by default—their default access
level is "package" access, which we discuss in Chapter 11. It is a common error to forget
▼   the `public` keyword when defining a method from an interface:

```
public class BankAccount implements Measurable
{
    double getMeasure() // oops—should be public
    {
        return balance;
    }
    . . .
}
```

▼   Then the compiler complains that the method has a weaker access level, namely package
access instead of public access. The remedy is to declare the method as public.

9.2 Converting between Types

Have a close look at the call

```
bankData.add(new BankAccount(10000));
```

from the test program of the preceding section. Here we pass an object of type Bank-
Account to the add method of the DataSet class. However, that
method has a parameter of type Measurable! Is it legal to convert
from the BankAccount type to the Measurable type?

> You can convert from a class type to an interface type, provided the class realizes the interface.

In Java, such a type conversion is legal. You can convert from a
class type to the type of any interface that the class realizes. For
example,

```
BankAccount account = new BankAccount(10000);
Measurable x = account; // OK
```

Alternatively, x can refer to a Coin object, provided the Coin class has been modified to
realize the Measurable interface.

```
Coin dime = new Coin(0.1, "dime");
x = dime; // also OK
```

Thus, when you have an object variable of type Measurable, you don't actually know
the exact type of the object to which x refers. All you know is that the object has a get-
Measure method.

However, you cannot convert between unrelated types:

```
x = new Rectangle(5, 10, 20, 30); // ERROR
```

That assignment is an error, because the Rectangle class doesn't realize the Measurable
interface.

Occasionally, it happens that you convert an object to an interface reference and you
need to convert it back. This happens in the getMaximum method of the DataSet class.
The DataSet stores the object with the largest measure, *as a* Measurable *reference*.

```
DataSet coinData = new DataSet();
coinData.add(new Coin(0.25, "quarter"));
coinData.add(new Coin(0.1, "dime"));
coinData.add(new Coin(0.05, "nickel"));
Measurable max = coinData.getMaximum();
```

Now what can you do with the max reference? *You* know it refers to a Coin object, but
the compiler doesn't. Thus, you cannot call the getName method:

```
String name = max.getName(); // ERROR
```

> You need a cast to convert from an interface type to a class type.

That call is an error, because the Measurable type has no getName
method.

However, as long as you are absolutely sure that max really refers
to a Coin object, you can use the *cast* notation to convert it back:

```
Coin maxCoin = (Coin)max;
String name = maxCoin.getName();
```

If you are wrong, and the object doesn't actually refer to a coin, your program will throw an exception and terminate.

This cast notation is the same notation that you saw in Chapter 3 to convert between number types. For example, if x is a floating-point number, then (int)x is the integer part of the number. The intent is similar—to convert from one type to another. However, there is one big difference between casting of number types and casting of class types. When casting number types, you *lose information*, and you use the cast to tell the compiler that you agree to the information loss. When casting object types, on the other hand, you *take a risk* of causing an exception, and you tell the compiler that you agree to that risk.

> The `instanceof` operator tests whether an object belongs to a particular type.

You saw one example of using casts in graphics programs, when you had to cast the `Graphics` object to a `Graphics2D` object. That cast is really not a sign of good programming; the library designers used the cast as a quick fix for a compatibility problem. At any rate, situations for casts occasionally arise. When they do, it is best to play it safe and test whether a cast will succeed before carrying out the cast. For that purpose, you use the `instanceof` operator. It tests whether an object belongs to a particular type. For example,

```
max instanceof Coin
```

returns `true` if the type of `max` is `Coin`, `false` if it is not. Therefore, a safe cast can be programmed as follows:

```
if (max instanceof Coin)
{
    Coin maxCoin = (Coin)max;
    ...
}
```

Syntax 9.3: The `instanceof` Operator

object `instanceof` *ClassName*

Example:

```
if (x instanceof Coin)
{
    Coin c = (Coin)x;
    ...
}
```

Purpose:

To return `true` if the *object* is an instance of *ClassName* (or one of its subclasses), and `false` otherwise

---

▼ **Advanced Topic**   **9.1**

Constants in Interfaces

Interfaces cannot have variables, but you can specify *constants*, which will be inherited by all classes that implement the interface.

For example, the `SwingConstants` interface defines various constants such as `SwingConstants.NORTH`, `SwingConstants.EAST`, and so on. Several classes implement this interface. For example, since `JLabel` implements the `SwingConstants` interface, users can refer to them as `JLabel.NORTH`, `JLabel.EAST`, and so on, when using these constants in conjunction with `JLabel` objects.

When defining a constant in an interface, you can (and should) omit the keywords `public static final`, because all variables in an interface are automatically `public static final`. For example,

```
public interface SwingConstants
{
    int NORTH = 1;
    int NORTHEAST = 2;
    int EAST = 3;
    . . .
}
```

9.3   Polymorphism

It is worth emphasizing once again that it is perfectly legal—and in fact very common—to have variables whose type is an interface, such as

```
Measurable x;
```

Just remember that the object to which x refers doesn't have type `Measurable`. In fact, *no object* has type `Measurable`. Instead, the type of the object is some class that realizes the `Measurable` interface, such as `BankAccount` or `Coin`.

Note that x can refer to objects of *different* types during its lifetime. Here the variable x first contains a reference to a bank account, later to a coin.

```
x = new BankAccount(10000); // OK
x = new Coin(0.1, "dime"); // OK
```

However, you can *never* construct an interface:

```
x = new Measurable(); // ERROR
```

Interfaces aren't classes, so you can't construct interface *objects*.

What can you do with an interface variable, given that you don't know the class of the object that it references? You can invoke the methods of the interface:

```
double m = x.getMeasure();
```

The `DataSet` class took advantage of this capability by computing the measure of the added object, without worrying exactly what kind of object was added.

Now let's think through the call to the `getMeasure` method more carefully. *Which* `getMeasure` method? The `BankAccount` and `Coin` classes provide two *different* implementations of that method. How did the correct method get called if the caller didn't even know the exact class to which x belongs?

The Java virtual machine makes a special effort to locate the correct method that belongs to the class of the actual object. That is, if x refers to a `BankAccount` object, then the `BankAccount.getMeasure` method is called. If x refers to a `Coin` object, then the `Coin.getMeasure` method is called.

That means that one method call

```
double m = x.getMeasure();
```

can call different methods depending on the momentary contents of x.

> Polymorphism denotes the principle that behavior can vary depending on the actual type of an object.

The principle that the actual type of the object determines the method to be called is called *polymorphism*. The term "polymorphism" comes from the Greek words for "many shapes". The same computation works for objects of many shapes, and adapts itself to the nature of the objects. In Java, all instance methods are polymorphic.

When you see a polymorphic method call, such as `x.getMeasure()`, there are several possible `getMeasure` methods that can be called. You have already seen another case in which the same method name can refer to different methods, namely when a method name is *overloaded:* that is, when a single class has several methods with the same name but different parameter types. For example, you can have two constructors `BankAccount()` and `BankAccount(double)`. Then the compiler selects the appropriate method when compiling the program, simply by looking at the types of the parameters:

```
account = new BankAccount();
    // compiler selects BankAccount()
account = new BankAccount(10000);
    // compiler selects BankAccount(double)
```

> Early binding of methods occurs if the compiler selects a method from several possible candidates. Late binding occurs if the method selection takes place when the program runs.

There is an important difference between polymorphism and overloading. The compiler picks an overloaded method when translating the program, before the program ever runs. This method selection is called *early binding*. However, when selecting the appropriate `getMeasure` method in a call `x.getMeasure()`, the compiler does not make any decision when translating the method. The program has to run before anyone can know what is stored in x. Therefore, the virtual machine, and not the compiler, selects the appropriate method. This method selection is called *late binding*.

9.4   Using a Strategy Interface for Improving Reusability

The interface concept that we explored up to now is a useful step towards writing reusable classes. However, as a practical matter, there are serious limitations to using the `Measurable` interface.

- You can add the `Measurable` interface only to classes under your control. If you want to process a set of `Rectangle` objects, you cannot make the `Rectangle` class realize another interface—it is a system class, which you cannot change.

- You can measure an object in only one way. If you want to analyze a set of savings accounts both by bank balance and by interest rate, you are stuck.

Therefore, let us rethink the `DataSet` class. The data set needs to be able to measure the objects that are added. When the objects are required to be of type `Measurable`, the responsibility of measuring lies with the added objects themselves, which is the cause of the limitations that we noted. It would be better if another object could carry out the measurement. Therefore, let's move the measurement method into a different interface:

```
public interface Measurer
{
    double measure(Object anObject);
}
```

The `measure` method measures an object and returns its measurement. Here we use the fact that all objects can be converted to the type `Object`, the "lowest common denominator" of all classes in Java. We will discuss the `Object` type in greater detail in Chapter 11.

The improved `DataSet` class is constructed with a `Measurer` object (that is, an object of some class that realizes the `Measurer` interface). That object is saved in a `measurer` instance variable and used to carry out the measurements, like this:

```
public void add(Object x)
{
    sum = sum + measurer.measure(x);
    if (count == 0
            || measurer.measure(maximum) < measurer.measure(x))
        maximum = x;
    count++;
}
```

You can find the complete source code for the `DataSet` class at the end of this section.

Now you can define measurers to take on any kind of measurement. For example, here is how you can measure rectangles by area. Define a class

```
class RectangleMeasurer implements Measurer
{
    public double measure(Object anObject)
    {
        Rectangle aRectangle = (Rectangle)anObject;
        double area = aRectangle.getWidth()
            * aRectangle.getHeight();
        return area;
    }
}
```

Note that the `measure` method must accept a parameter of type `Object`, even though this particular measurer just wants to measure rectangles. The method signature must match the signature of the `measure` method in the `Measurer` interface. Therefore, the `Object` parameter is cast to the `Rectangle` type:

```
Rectangle aRectangle = (Rectangle)anObject;
```

Now construct an object of the `RectangleMeasurer` class and pass it to the `DataSet` constructor.

```
Measurer m = new RectangleMeasurer();
DataSet data = new DataSet(m);
```

Next, add rectangles to the data set. The `RectangleMeasurer` object will measure them by area.

```
data.add(new Rectangle(5, 10, 20, 30));
data.add(new Rectangle(10, 20, 30, 40));
. . .
```

What would happen if you added an object of some other type, say a coin, to this data set? The `add` method does not complain—it will take any object. But when the measurer tries to convert the `Coin` reference to a `Rectangle` reference, then an exception is generated and the program terminates.

An object such as the `measurer` object of the `DataSet` class is called a *strategy* object, because it carries out a particular strategy for a computation. For a different strategy, simply use a different strategy object. For example, it is a simple matter to define a different strategy for measuring the perimeter of a rectangle.

Figure 2 shows the UML diagram of the classes and interfaces of this solution. As in Figure 1, the `DataSet` class is decoupled from the `Rectangle` class whose objects it processes. However, unlike in Figure 1, the `Rectangle` class is no longer coupled with another class. Instead, to process rectangles, you have to come up with a small "helper" class `RectangleMeasurer`.

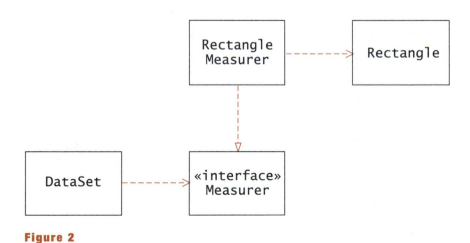

Figure 2

UML Diagram of the `DataSet` Class and the `Measurer` Interface

The `RectangleMeasurer` class is a very trivial class. Its objects don't carry any state at all. We needed this class only because the `DataSet` needs an object of some class that implements the `Measurer` interface. When you have a class that serves a very tactical purpose, such as this one, you can declare the class inside the method that needs it:

```
public static void main(String[] args)
{
    class RectangleMeasurer implements Measurer
    {
        . . .
    }

    Measurer m = new RectangleMeasurer();
    DataSet data = new DataSet(m);
    . . .
}
```

> An inner class is declared inside another class. Inner classes are commonly used for tactical classes that should not be visible elsewhere in a program.

Such a class is called an *inner class*. An inner class is any class that is defined inside another class. This arrangement signals to the reader of your program that the `RectangleMeasurer` class is not interesting beyond the scope of this method. Since an inner class inside a method is not a publicly accessible feature, you don't need to document it as thoroughly.

When you compile the source files for this program, have a look at the class files on your disk—you will find that the inner classes are stored in files with curious names, such as `DataSetTest$1$RectangleMeasurer.class`. The exact names aren't important. The point is that the compiler turns an inner class into a regular class file.

File DataSet.java

```
1  /**
2     Computes the average of a set of data values.
3  */
4  public class DataSet
5  {
6     /**
7        Constructs an empty data set with a given measurer.
8        @param aMeasurer  the measurer that is used to measure data values
9     */
10    public DataSet(Measurer aMeasurer)
11    {
12       sum = 0;
13       count = 0;
14       maximum = null;
15       measurer = aMeasurer;
```

```
16    }
17
18    /**
19       Adds a data value to the data set.
20       @param x a data value
21    */
22    public void add(Object x)
23    {
24       sum = sum + measurer.measure(x);
25       if (count == 0
26             || measurer.measure(maximum) < measurer.measure(x))
27          maximum = x;
28       count++;
29    }
30
31    /**
32       Gets the average of the added data.
33       @return the average, or 0 if no data have been added
34    */
35    public double getAverage()
36    {
37       if (count == 0) return 0;
38       else return sum / count;
39    }
40
41    /**
42       Gets the largest of the added data.
43       @return the maximum, or 0 if no data have been added
44    */
45    public Object getMaximum()
46    {
47       return maximum;
48    }
49
50    private double sum;
51    private Object maximum;
52    private int count;
53    private Measurer measurer;
54 }
```

File DataSetTest.java

```
1  import java.awt.Rectangle;
2
3  /**
4     This program demonstrates the use of a Measurer.
```

```
 5  */
 6  public class DataSetTest
 7  {
 8     public static void main(String[] args)
 9     {
10        class RectangleMeasurer implements Measurer
11        {
12           public double measure(Object anObject)
13           {
14              Rectangle aRectangle = (Rectangle)anObject;
15              double area = aRectangle.getWidth()
16                 * aRectangle.getHeight();
17              return area;
18           }
19        }
20
21        Measurer m = new RectangleMeasurer();
22
23        DataSet data = new DataSet(m);
24
25        data.add(new Rectangle(5, 10, 20, 30));
26        data.add(new Rectangle(10, 20, 30, 40));
27        data.add(new Rectangle(20, 30, 5, 10));
28
29        System.out.println("Average area = "
30           + data.getAverage());
31        Rectangle max = (Rectangle)data.getMaximum();
32        System.out.println("Maximum area = " + max);
33     }
34  }
```

File Measurer.java

```
 1  /**
 2     Describes any class whose objects can measure other objects.
 3  */
 4  public interface Measurer
 5  {
 6     /**
 7        Computes the measure of an object.
 8        @param anObject  the object to be measured
 9        @return  the measure
10     */
11     double measure(Object anObject);
12  }
```

Syntax 9.4: Inner Classes

Declared inside a method

```
class OuterClassName
{
    method signature
    {
        . . .
        class InnerClassName
        {
            methods
            fields
        }
        . . .
    }
    . . .
}
```

Declared inside the class:

```
class OuterClassName
{
    methods
    fields
    accessSpecifier class InnerClassName
    {
        methods
        fields
    }
    . . .
}
```

Example:

```
public class Test
{
    public static void main(String[] args)
    {
        class RectangleMeasurer implements Measurer
        {
            . . .
        }
        . . .
    }
}
```

Purpose:

To define an inner class whose methods have access to the same variables and methods as the outer-class methods

Advanced Topic 9.2

Anonymous Inner Classes

An entity is *anonymous* if it does not have a name. In a program, something that is only used once doesn't usually need a name. For example, you can replace

```
Coin aCoin = new Coin(0.1, "dime");
data.add(aCoin);
```

with

```
data.add(new Coin(0.1, "dime"));
```

if the coin is not used elsewhere in the same method. The object `new Coin("dime", 0.1)` is an *anonymous object*. Programmers like anonymous objects, because they don't have to go through the trouble of coming up with a name. If you have struggled with the decision whether to call a coin `c`, `dime`, or `aCoin`, you'll understand this sentiment.

Inner classes often give rise to a similar situation. After a single object of the `RectangleMeasurer` has been constructed, the class is never used again. In Java, it is possible to define *anonymous classes* if all you ever need is a single object of the class.

```java
public static void main(String[] args)
{
    Measurer m = new Measurer()
        // construct an object of anonymous class
        // class definition starts here
        {
            public double measure(Object anObject)
            {
                Rectangle aRectangle = (Rectangle)anObject;
                double area =
                    aRectangle.getWidth()
                    * aRectangle.getHeight();
                return area;
            }
        };

    DataSet data = new DataSet(m);
    . . .
}
```

This means: Construct an object of a class that implements the `Measurer` interface by defining the `measure` method as specified.

Some programmers like this style, but many newcomers find it quite bewildering. We will not cover it further in this book—you can find more information in reference [1].

9.5   Processing Timer Events

In this section we will study timer events, because the event handling uses interfaces in the same way as buttons and menus in a graphical program. However, since timers are simpler than graphical programs, we can focus on the essential mechanism without being distracted by the code for placing buttons or building menus.

Timers are also useful for programming animations (see Exercise P9.13).

> A timer generates timer events at fixed intervals.

The `Timer` class in the `javax.swing` package generates a sequence of *events*, spaced apart at even time intervals. This is useful whenever you want to have an object updated in regular intervals. For example, in an animation, you may want to update a scene 10 times per second and redisplay the image, to give the illusion of movement.

> An event listener is notified when a particular event occurs.

When a timer event occurs, the timer needs to notify some object, called the *event listener*. The designers of the `Timer` class had no idea how you would want to use the `Timer`, yet they had to specify a type for the listener object and call a specific method. They chose the `ActionListener` interface for this purpose:

```
public interface ActionListener
{
   void actionPerformed(ActionEvent event);
}
```

When you use a timer, you need to define a class that realizes the `ActionListener` interface. Place whatever action you want to occur inside the `actionPerformed` method. Construct an object of that class. Pass it to the `Timer` constructor. Finally, start the timer.

```
class MyListener implements ActionListener
{
   public void actionPerformed(ActionEvent event)
   {
      // this action will be executed at each timer event
      place listener action here
   }
}

MyListener listener = new MyListener();
Timer t = new Timer(interval, listener);
t.start();
```

Then the timer calls the `actionPerformed` method of the `listener` object every `interval` milliseconds. The `event` parameter of the `actionPerformed` method contains more detailed information about the timer event. However, in practice, many listeners ignore this parameter.

Here is a somewhat silly example program—a timer that counts down to zero.

```
10
9
. . .
```

```
2
1
0
Liftoff!
```

However, unlike a `for` loop, which would print all lines immediately, there is a one second delay between decrements.

To keep the program alive after setting up the timer, the program displays a message dialog. Click the "Ok" button to quit the program.

File TimerTest.java

```java
 1  import java.awt.event.ActionEvent;
 2  import java.awt.event.ActionListener;
 3  import javax.swing.JOptionPane;
 4  import javax.swing.Timer;
 5
 6  /**
 7      This program tests the Timer class.
 8  */
 9  public class TimerTest
10  {
11     public static void main(String[] args)
12     {
13        class CountDown implements ActionListener
14        {
15           public CountDown(int initialCount)
16           {
17              count = initialCount;
18           }
19
20           public void actionPerformed(ActionEvent event)
21           {
22              if (count >= 0)
23                 System.out.println(count);
24              if (count == 0)
25                 System.out.println("Liftoff!");
26              count--;
27           }
28
29           private int count;
30        }
31
32        CountDown listener = new CountDown(10);
33
34        final int DELAY = 1000; // milliseconds between timer ticks
35        Timer t = new Timer(DELAY, listener);
36        t.start();
37
38        JOptionPane.showMessageDialog(null, "Quit?");
39        System.exit(0);
40     }
41  }
```

The preceding example is somewhat oversimplified. Usually, the event listener needs to modify other objects in the `actionPerformed` method. That can make the design of the listener classes more complex, because they need to store instance variables to access the various objects that need to be manipulated when an event occurs. Fortunately, the Java compiler can *automatically* generate some of these variables when you use inner classes for listeners. Here is an example.

To simulate the growth of an investment, we want to add interest to a bank account once per second. The program prints the balance once a second, like this:

```
Balance = 1050.0
Balance = 1102.5
Balance = 1157.625
Balance = 1215.50625
. . .
```

Here is the `BankAccount` object:

```
public class TimerTest
{
    public static void main(String[] args)
    {
        final BankAccount account = new BankAccount(1000);
        . . .
    }

    private static final double RATE = 5;
}
```

You will see soon why the `account` variable is declared as `final`. The `actionPerformed` method of the listener class adds interest to the account and prints the new balance.

```
class InterestAdder implements ActionListener
{
    public void actionPerformed(ActionEvent event)
    {
        double interest = account.getBalance()
            * RATE / 100;
        account.deposit(interest);
        System.out.println("Balance = "
            + account.getBalance());
    }
}
```

| Methods of an inner class can access variables from the surrounding scope. |

As you can see, the `actionPerformed` method needs access to the `BankAccount` object. Of course, you can add a `BankAccount` instance variable and set it in the `InterestAdder` constructor. However, for inner classes there is a convenient shortcut. An inner class can access variables that are defined at the place of the class definition. When the `InterestAdder` definition is placed inside the `main` method, below the definition of the `account` variable, then it can access that local variable of the `main` method!

```java
public static void main(String[] args)
{
    final BankAccount account = new BankAccount(1000);

    class InterestAdder implements ActionListener
    {
        public void actionPerformed(ActionEvent event)
        {
            double interest = account.getBalance()
                * RATE / 100;
                // OK to access account
            . . .
        }
    }

    . . .
}
```

When the compiler builds the InterestAdder class, it notes that one of its methods accesses variables from the surrounding scope. It then automatically provides an instance variable inside the class and initializes it with the value from the outer variables. That's very convenient for the programmer. It significantly reduces the burden of supplying tactical helper classes. You don't actually have to think about the process that the compiler goes through when building an inner class. Simply access any variables of the surrounding scope and let the compiler worry about the details.

> Local variables that are accessed by an inner-class method must be declared as final.

There is a technical wrinkle. An inner class can access any *fields* of the surrounding scope without restrictions. But it can access *local variables* only if they are declared as final. Then there is no ambiguity about the values of local variables that the inner-class methods use. That sounds like a restriction, but it is usually not an issue in practice. Keep in mind that an object variable is final when the variable always refers to the same object. The state of the object can change, but the variable can't refer to a different object. For example, in our program, we never intended to have the account variable refer to multiple bank account objects, so there was no harm in declaring it as final.

Figure 3 shows the UML diagram of the classes and interfaces. Note how the Timer class and the BankAccount class are completely decoupled from another. Neither class knows about the other. The InterestAdder helper class forms the bridge between the two.

Here is the source code for the program.

File TimerTest.java

```java
1 import java.awt.event.ActionEvent;
2 import java.awt.event.ActionListener;
3 import javax.swing.JOptionPane;
4 import javax.swing.Timer;
5
6 /**
7    This program uses a timer to add interest to a bank
8    account once per second.
```

```
 9  */
10  public class TimerTest
11  {
12     public static void main(String[] args)
13     {
14        final BankAccount account = new BankAccount(1000);
15
16        class InterestAdder implements ActionListener
17        {
18           public void actionPerformed(ActionEvent event)
19           {
20              double interest = account.getBalance()
21                 * RATE / 100;
22              account.deposit(interest);
23              System.out.println("Balance = "
24                 + account.getBalance());
25           }
26        }
27
28        InterestAdder listener = new InterestAdder();
29
30        final int DELAY = 1000; // milliseconds between timer ticks
31        Timer t = new Timer(DELAY, listener);
32        t.start();
33
34        JOptionPane.showMessageDialog(null, "Quit?");
35        System.exit(0);
36     }
37
38     private static final double RATE = 5;
39  }
```

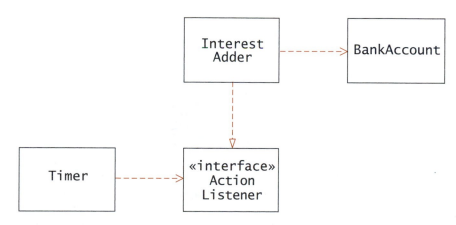

Figure 3

The Classes and Interfaces for Processing Timer Events

You have now seen how to build an event listener. This is a very common task when you program graphical user interfaces. Buttons, sliders, checkboxes, the mouse, timers, and other sources generate events. You need to attach an event listener to every event source that you want to track. For example, if your program should do something when a button is clicked, attach an event listener to the button. You will learn more about this process in the next chapter.

Common Error 9.2

Modifying the Signature in the Implementing Method

When you implement an interface, you must define each method *exactly* as it is specified in the interface. Making small changes accidentally to the parameter or return types is a common error. Here is the classical example,

```
class MyAction implements ActionListener
{
    public void actionPerformed()
    // oops ... forgot ActionEvent parameter
    {
        . . .
    }
}
```

As far as the compiler is concerned, this class has two methods:

```
public void actionPerformed(ActionEvent event)
public void actionPerformed()
```

The first method is undefined. The compiler will complain that the method is missing. However, you have to read the error message carefully and pay attention to the parameter and return types.

Random Fact 9.1

Operating Systems

Without an operating system, a computer would not be useful. Minimally, you need an operating system to locate files and to start programs. The programs that you run need services from the operating system to access devices and to interact with other programs. Operating systems on large computers need to provide more services than those on personal computers do. Here are some typical services:

- *Program loading.* Every operating system provides some way of launching application programs. The user indicates what program should be run, usually by typing the name of the program in or by clicking on an icon. The operating system locates the program code, loads it in memory, and starts it.

- *Managing files.* A storage device such as a hard disk is, electronically, simply a device capable of storing a huge sequence of zeroes and ones. It is up to the operating system to bring some structure to the storage layout and organize it into files, folders, and so on. The operating system also needs to impose some amount of security and redundancy into the file system so that a power outage does not jeopardize the contents of an entire hard disk. Some operating systems do a better job in this regard than others.

- *Virtual memory.* RAM is expensive, and few computers have enough RAM to hold all programs and their data that a user would like to run simultaneously. Most operating systems extend the available memory by storing some data on the hard disk. The application programs do not realize whether a particular data item is in memory or in the virtual memory disk storage. When a program accesses a data item that is currently not in RAM, the processor senses this and notifies the operating system. The operating system swaps the needed data from the hard disk into RAM, simultaneously swapping out a memory block of equal size that had not been accessed for some time.

- *Handling multiple users.* The operating systems of large and powerful computers allow simultaneous access by multiple users. Each user is connected to the computer through a separate terminal. The operating system authenticates users by checking that each one has a valid account and password. It gives each user a small slice of processor time, then serves the next user.

- *Multitasking.* Even if you are the sole user of a computer, you may want to run multiple applications—for example, to read your email in one window and run the Java compiler in another. The operating system is responsible for dividing processor time between the applications you are running, so that each can make progress.

- *Printing.* The operating system queues up the print requests that are sent by multiple applications. This is necessary to make sure that the printed pages do not contain a mixture of words sent simultaneously from separate programs.

- *Windows.* Many operating systems present their users with a desktop made up of multiple windows. The operating system manages the location and appearance of the window frames; the applications are responsible for the interiors.

- *Fonts.* To render text on the screen and the printer, the shapes of characters must be defined. This is especially important for programs that can display multiple type styles and sizes. Modern operating systems contain a central font repository.

- *Communicating between programs.* The operating system can facilitate the transfer of information between programs. That transfer can happen through *cut and paste*

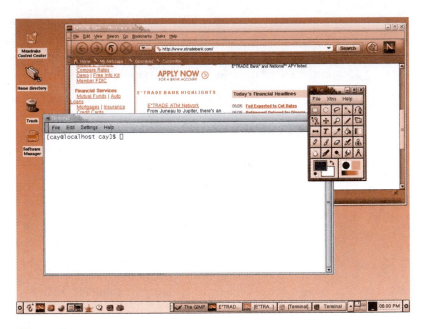

Figure 4

A Graphical Software Environment for the Linux Operating System

or *interprocess communication*. Cut and paste is a user-initiated data transfer in which the user copies data from one application into a transfer buffer (often called a "clipboard") managed by the operating system and inserts the buffer's contents into another application. Interprocess communication is initiated by applications that transfer data without direct user involvement.

- *Networking*. The operating system provides protocols and services for enabling applications to reach information on other computers attached to the network.

Today, the most popular operating systems are UNIX (and its variants such as Linux; see Figure 4), Windows, and the MacOS.

CHAPTER SUMMARY

1. A Java interface declares a set of methods and their signatures. Unlike a class, it provides no implementation.

2. To realize an interface, a class must supply all methods that the interface requires.

3. Interfaces can reduce the coupling between classes.

4. You can convert from a class type to an interface type, provided the class realizes the interface.

5. You need a cast to convert from an interface type to a class type.

6. The `instanceof` operator tests whether an object belongs to a particular type.

7. Polymorphism denotes the principle that behavior can vary depending on the actual type of an object.

8. Early binding of methods occurs if the compiler selects a method from several possible candidates. Late binding occurs if the method selection takes place when the program runs.

9. An inner class is declared inside another class. Inner classes are commonly used for tactical classes that should not be visible elsewhere in a program.

10. A timer generates timer events at fixed intervals.

11. An event listener is notified when a particular event occurs.

12. Methods of an inner class can access variables from the surrounding scope.

13. Local variables that are accessed by an inner-class method must be declared as `final`.

Further Reading

[1] Cay S. Horstmann and Gary Cornell, *Core Java Fundamentals*, 5th Edition, Prentice-Hall, 2001.

CLASSES, OBJECTS, AND METHODS INTRODUCED IN THIS CHAPTER

```
java.awt.event.ActionEvent
java.awt.event.ActionListener
    actionPerformed
javax.swing.Timer
    start
```

REVIEW EXERCISES

Exercise R9.1. Suppose C is a class that realizes the interfaces I and J. Which of the following assignments require a cast?

```
C c = . . .;
I i = . . .;
J j = . . .;
c = i; // 1
j = c; // 2
i = j; // 3
```

Exercise R9.2. Suppose C is a class that realizes the interfaces I and J. Which of the following assignments will throw an exception?

```
C c = new C();
I i = c; // 1
J j = (J)i; // 2
C d = (C)i; // 3
```

Exercise R9.3. Suppose the class Sandwich implements the Edible interface. Which of the following assignments are legal?

```
Sandwich sub = new Sandwich();
Edible e = sub; // 1
Rectangle cerealBox = new Rectangle(5, 10, 20, 30);
Edible f = cerealBox; // 2
f = (Edible)cerealBox; // 3
sub = e; // 4
sub = (Sandwich)e; // 5
sub = (Sandwich)cerealBox; // 6
```

Exercise R9.4. How does a cast such as (BankAccount)x differ from a cast of number values such as (int)x?

Exercise R9.5. The classes Rectangle2D.Double, Ellipse2D.Double, and Line2D.Double realize the Shape interface. The Graphics2D class depends on the Shape interface but not on the rectangle, ellipse, and line classes. Draw a UML diagram denoting these facts.

Exercise R9.6. Suppose r contains a reference to a new Rectangle(5, 10, 20, 30). Which of these conditions returns true? (*Hint:* Check the API documentation for the interfaces that the Rectangle class realizes.)

- r instanceof Rectangle
- r instanceof Shape
- r instanceof Point
- r instanceof Object
- r instanceof ActionListener
- r instanceof Serializable

Exercise R9.7. Classes such as Rectangle2D.Double, Ellipse2D.Double, and Line2D.Double realize the Shape interface. The Shape interface has a method

```
Rectangle getBounds()
```

that returns a rectangle completely enclosing the shape. Consider the method call:

```
Shape s = . . .;
Rectangle r = s.getBounds();
```

Explain why this is an example of polymorphism.

Exercise R9.8. In Java, a method call such as x.f() uses late binding—the exact method to be called depends on the type of the object to which x refers. Give two kinds of method calls that use early binding in Java.

Exercise R9.9. Suppose you need to process an array of employees to find the average and the highest salary. Discuss what you need to do to use the first implementation of the `DataSet` class (which processes `Measurable` objects). What do you need to do to use the second implementation? Which is easier?

Exercise R9.10. What happens if you add a `String` object to the first implementation of the `DataSet`? What happens if you add a `String` object to a `DataSet` object of the second implementation that uses a `RectangleMeasurer` class?

Exercise R9.11. How would you reorganize the test program that uses the `Rectangle-Measurer` class if you needed to make `RectangleMeasurer` into a top-level class (that is, not an inner class)?

Exercise R9.12. How would you reorganize the test program that uses the `Interest-Adder` class if you needed to make `InterestAdder` into a top-level class (that is, not an inner class)?

Exercise R9.13. What is a strategy object? Can you think of another useful strategy object for the `DataSet` class? (*Hint:* Exercise P9.8.)

Exercise R9.14. What is the difference between an event and an event listener?

Exercise P9.15. Can a `Timer` object notify multiple event listeners? If so, how? (Check the API documentation.)

Exercise R9.16. Consider this top-level and inner class. Which variables can the `f` method access?

```
public class T
{
   public void m(final int x, int y)
   {
      int a;
      final int b;

      class C implements I
      {
         public void f()
         {
            . . .
         }
      }

      final int c;
      . . .
   }

   private int t;
}
```

Exercise R9.17. What happens when an inner class tries to access a non-`final` local variable? Try it out and explain.

PROGRAMMING EXERCISES

Exercise P9.1. Have the `Die` class of Chapter 6 implement the `Measurable` interface. Generate dice, cast them, and add them to the first implementation of the `DataSet` class. Display the average.

Exercise P9.2. Define a class `Quiz` that implements the `Measurable` interface. A quiz has a score and a letter grade (such as B+). Use the first implementation of the `DataSet` class to process a collection of quizzes. Display the average score and the quiz with the highest score (both letter grade and score).

Exercise P9.3. Define a class `Person`. A person has a name and a height in centimeters. Use the second implementation of the `DataSet` class to process a collection of `Person` objects. Display the average height and the name of the tallest person.

Exercise P9.4. Modify the first implementation of the `DataSet` (the one processing `Measurable` objects) to also compute the minimum data element.

Exercise P9.5. Modify the second implementation of the `DataSet` (the one using a `Measurer` object) to also compute the minimum data element.

Exercise P9.6. Using a different `Measurer` object, process a set of `Rectangle` objects to find the rectangle with the largest perimeter.

Exercise P9.7. Enhance the `DataSet` class so that it can be used either with a `Measurer` object or for processing `Measurable` objects. *Hint:* Supply a default constructor that implements a `Measurer` that can process `Measurable` objects.

Exercise P9.8. Define an interface `Filter` as follows:

```
public interface Filter
{
   boolean accept(Object x)
}
```

Modify the second implementation of the `DataSet` class to use both a `Measurer` and a `Filter` object. Only objects that the filter accepts should be processed. Demonstrate your modification by having a data set process a collection of bank accounts, filtering out all accounts whose balance is less than $1,000.

Exercise P9.9. Use the interface

```
public interface Drawable
{
   void draw(Graphics2D g2)
}
```

Implement classes `Car` and `House` that realize this interface. The `Car` and `House` constructors should receive the position of the car or house, just as in Section 4.7.

Then write a method `randomDrawable` that randomly generates `Drawable` references. Randomly choose between a car and a house, then pick random positions. Call the method 10 times and draw all of the shapes.

Exercise P9.10. Write a method `randomShape` that randomly generates objects implementing the `Shape` interface: some mixture of rectangles, ellipses, and lines, with random positions. Call it 10 times and draw all of them.

Exercise P9.11. Write a program that uses a timer to print the current time once a second. *Hint:* The following code prints the current time:

```
Date now = new Date();
System.out.println(now);
```

The `Date` class is in the `java.util` package.

Exercise P9.12. Enhance the program that uses a timer to increment a bank account balance once per second by adding a second bank account with a balance of $2,000 and a second timer that increments it every two seconds.

Exercise P9.13. Write an applet that uses a timer to display an animation of a moving car. Ten times a second, have the `actionPerformed` method of a timer listener

- Move the car to the right by one pixel.
- Call the `repaint` method of the applet.

Exercise P9.14. Use the interface

```
public interface InputReader
{
    String readLine(String prompt) throws IOException
}
```

Define two classes, `OptionPaneReader` and `ConsoleReader`, that implement this interface. An `OptionPaneReader` reads input by displaying input dialogs. The `ConsoleReader` reads from a buffered reader attached to `System.in`.

Then define a static method

```
public Coin readCoin(InputReader reader)
```

that prompts the user for the name and value of a coin (which may be a foreign coin, not just a nickel, dime, or quarter). Demonstrate that this method can get user input both through dialog boxes and from the console window.

Exercise P9.15. Look up the definition of the standard `Comparable` interface in the API documentation. Modify the `DataSet` class to accept `Comparable` objects. With this interface, it is no longer meaningful to compute the average. The `DataSet` class should record the minimum and maximum data value. Test your modified `DataSet` class by adding a number of `String` objects. (The `String` class implements the `Comparable` interface.)

Exercise P9.16. Modify the `Coin` and `Purse` classes introduced in Chapter 3 to have them implement the `Comparable` interface.

Event Handling

CHAPTER GOALS

To understand the Java event model

▶ To install mouse and action event listeners

▶ To accept mouse and text input

▶ To display frame windows

▶ To show text output in a text area with a scroll bar

In the console applications and applets you have written so far, user input was under control of the *program*. The program asked the user for input in a specific order. For example, a program might ask the user to supply first a name, then some dollar amount. But the programs that you use every day on your computer don't work like that. In a program with a modern graphical user interface, the *user* is in control. The user can use both the mouse and the keyboard and can manipulate many parts of the user interface in any desired order. For example, the user can enter information into text fields, pull down menus, click buttons, and drag scroll bars, in any order. The program must react to the user commands, in whatever order they arrive. Having to deal with many possible inputs in random order is quite a bit harder than simply forcing the user to supply input in a fixed order.

In this chapter you will learn how to write Java programs that can react to user interface events such as keystrokes, mouse clicks, and button pushes. The Java window toolkit has a very sophisticated mechanism that allows a program to specify the events in which it is interested and which objects to notify when one of these events occurs.

10.1   Events, Event Listeners, and Event Sources

> User interface events include key presses, mouse moves, button presses, menu selections, and so on.

> You supply *event listeners* for the events about which you care. You need to implement methods for handling the event. You construct listener objects and attach them to the event sources.

> *Event source* classes report on events. When an event occurs, the event source notifies all event listeners.

> Event notifications happen in event listener classes. An event listener class implements an *event listener interface*. The interface lists all possible notifications for a particular event category.

> *Event classes* contain detailed information about various kinds of events.

Whenever the user of a graphical program types characters or uses the mouse anywhere inside one of the windows of the program, the Java window manager sends a notification to the program that an *event* has occurred. The window manager can generate huge numbers of events. For example, whenever the mouse moves a tiny interval over a window, a "mouse move" event is generated. Most programs have no interest in many of these events.

So as not to be flooded by boring events, every program must indicate which events it likes to receive. It does that by installing *event listener* objects. Furthermore, there are different *kinds* of events, such as keyboard events, mouse move events, and mouse click events. To make event listening more organized, you use different event listener classes to listen to different kinds of events.

To install a listener, you need to know the *event source*. The event source is the user interface component that generates a particular event. For example, a button is an event source for button click events; a menu item is an event source for a menu selection event; and a scrollbar is an event source for a scrollbar adjustment event.

Once you have determined the event source, you attach one or more listeners to it. Each listener is an object of a *listener class*, which you must supply. In the methods for that class, you determine what should happen whenever the particular event occurs.

Once an event occurs for which there is a listener, the event source will call the methods you supplied in the listener and supply detailed information about the event in an *event class* object.

This sounds somewhat complex, so let's run through an example. We will listen to mouse clicks in an applet. There are three classes involved:

1. *The event source.* This is the component that generates the mouse event and that manages the listeners. In our case, the event source is the applet. When the user clicks anywhere inside an applet, the applet tells the attached mouse listeners where the mouse was clicked.

2. *The listener class.* In the case of mouse clicks, this must be a class that implements the MouseListener interface. The mouse listener interface has several methods, which we will discuss below. These methods are called when the mouse button is depressed, when it is released, and so on.

3. *The event class.* In the case of mouse clicks, this is the class MouseEvent. Each listener method has a MouseEvent parameter that tells you details about the event. For example, the getX and getY methods return the *x*- and *y*-position of the mouse pointer.

> You use a *mouse listener* to capture mouse events.

The most complex part of Java event handling is to come up with the listener. A mouse listener must implement the MouseListener interface, which comprises the following five methods:

```
public interface MouseListener
{
    void mousePressed(MouseEvent event);
        // Called when a mouse button has been pressed on a component
    void mouseReleased(MouseEvent event);
        // Called when a mouse button has been released on a component
    void mouseClicked(MouseEvent event);
        // Called when the mouse has been clicked on a component
    void mouseEntered(MouseEvent event);
        // Called when the mouse enters a component
    void mouseExited(MouseEvent event);
        // Called when the mouse exits a component
}
```

Right now, we just want to "spy" on the mouse events and print them out as they occur. For that purpose, we'll implement a particular listener:

```
public class MouseSpy implements MouseListener
{
    public void mousePressed(MouseEvent event)
    {
        System.out.println("Mouse pressed. x = "
            + event.getX() + " y = " + event.getY());
    }

    public void mouseReleased(MouseEvent event)
    {
        System.out.println("Mouse released. x = "
            + event.getX() + " y = " + event.getY());
    }

    public void mouseClicked(MouseEvent event)
```

```
    {
        System.out.println("Mouse clicked. x = "
            + event.getX() + " y = " + event.getY());
    }

    public void mouseEntered(MouseEvent event)
    {
        System.out.println("Mouse entered. x = "
            + event.getX() + " y = " + event.getY());
    }

    public void mouseExited(MouseEvent event)
    {
        System.out.println("Mouse exited. x = "
            + event.getX() + " y = " + event.getY());
    }
}
```

The listener methods simply print out the cause of the event and the x- and y-positions of the mouse.

Now let's install the listener. You need to call the addMouseListener method of the event source. In our case, the event source is the applet that receives the mouse clicks. Construct a mouse spy object and pass it as the parameter to the addMouseListener method.

```
public class MouseSpyApplet extends Applet
{
    public MouseSpyApplet()
    {
        MouseSpy listener = new MouseSpy();
        addMouseListener(listener);
    }
}
```

As the applet senses mouse events, it calls the appropriate methods of the listener object. For example, when the user clicks with the mouse in the applet area, the applet calls listener.mousePressed(event1) and listener.mouseReleased(event2), where event1 and event2 are mouse event objects that describe the mouse position at the time of the mouse button press and release. If the press and release were in quick succession, the applet also calls listener.mouseClicked(event3). You can try this out by opening a console window, starting the applet viewer from that console window, clicking with the mouse in the applet, and watching the messages in the console window (see Figure 1).

10.2   Processing Mouse Input

In the preceding example, our mouse listener simply printed all mouse events to System.out. In practice, you want something more interesting to happen when the user presses the mouse. For example, suppose we want to write a program that moves a rectangle to the mouse press position.

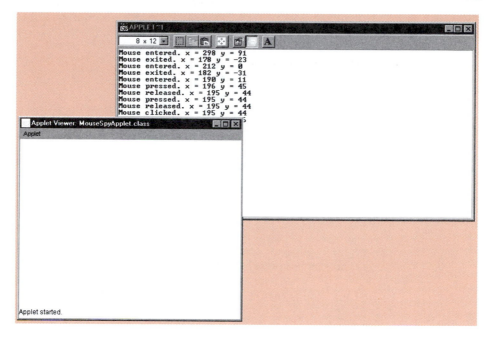

Figure 1

Spying on Mouse Events

Here is a program that draws a rectangle on the screen. The rectangle is stored as an instance variable so that we can later modify it:

```
import java.applet.Applet;
import java.awt.Graphics;
import java.awt.Graphics2D;
import java.awt.Rectangle;

public class MouseApplet extends Applet
{
   public MouseApplet()
   {
      // the rectangle that the paint method draws
      box = new Rectangle(BOX_X, BOX_Y,
         BOX_WIDTH, BOX_HEIGHT);
   }

   public void paint(Graphics g)
   {
      Graphics2D g2 = (Graphics2D)g;
```

```
        g2.draw(box);
    }

    private Rectangle box;
    private static final int BOX_X = 100;
    private static final int BOX_Y = 100;
    private static final int BOX_WIDTH = 20;
    private static final int BOX_HEIGHT = 30;
}
```

Now, let us add a mouse listener that listens to a mouse press and moves the rectangle.

```
public class MouseApplet extends Applet
{
    public MouseApplet()
    {
        . . .
        // add mouse press listener

        class MousePressListener implements MouseListener
        {
            public void mousePressed(MouseEvent event)
            {
                int x = event.getX();
                int y = event.getY();
                box.setLocation(x, y);
                repaint();
            }

            // do-nothing methods
            public void mouseReleased(MouseEvent event) {}
            public void mouseClicked(MouseEvent event) {}
            public void mouseEntered(MouseEvent event) {}
            public void mouseExited(MouseEvent event) {}
        }

        MouseListener listener = new MousePressListener();
        addMouseListener(listener);
    }
```

> You often install event listeners as *inner classes*. Recall that the inner-class methods can have access to the surrounding fields, methods, and final variables.

As you saw in Chapter 9, we define the listener class as an inner class inside the MouseApplet constructor. That gives the mousePressed the same access to fields and methods that the MouseApplet constructor enjoys.

As you can see, the mousePressed method of the inner class accesses the box field. Since the inner class has no field called box (in fact, it has no fields at all), the compiler interprets box to mean "the box field of the outer-class object that constructed this inner-class object".

When a mouse click occurs, we call `setLocation` on the rectangle object. However, that call has no effect on the screen display. The `setLocation` method merely updates the Java object that stores the rectangle's position. We need to redraw the applet. We could call the `paint` method, but then we would need a `Graphics` object, which we don't have. It is possible to get such an object, but that is actually not a good idea. You should never call `paint` directly—it can interfere with the window manager. Instead, you should *tell the applet to repaint itself* at the next convenient moment. You do that by calling the `repaint` method, which causes the `paint` method to be called, at an opportune moment, with an appropriate `Graphics` object.

> The `repaint` method causes a window to repaint itself as soon as possible.

Let us have another look at the call to `repaint` in the `mousePressed` method of the `MousePressListener` class. Of course, the inner class doesn't have a method called `repaint`. Therefore, the compiler looks in the outer applet class, where it does find a `repaint` method (which is inherited from its superclass `Component`). It invokes the method. On which object? Again, on the outer-class object that created the inner-class object—namely, the applet that constructed the listener.

Programming listener classes is somewhat involved. You may simply want to recognize and reuse the following template:

```
class MyClass
{
   public MyClass()
   {
      . . .
      class MyListener implements ListenerInterface
      {
         public void eventOccurred(EventClass event)
         {
            event action goes here
         }
      }

      MyListener listener = new MyListener();
      anEventSource.addAListener(listener);
   }
}
```

Finally, we are ready to put all the pieces together. Note how the use of inner classes makes the program easy to read—the rather specialized event listener class is placed out of the way and hidden inside the applet constructor. Furthermore, all the information about the event is kept together in one place.

Go ahead and run the program. Whenever you click the mouse on the applet, the top left corner of the rectangle moves to the mouse pointer (see Figure 2). While perhaps not the most exciting program that you have ever used, it does demonstrate how to provide mouse input to a graphical application.

Figure 2

The Mouse Applet

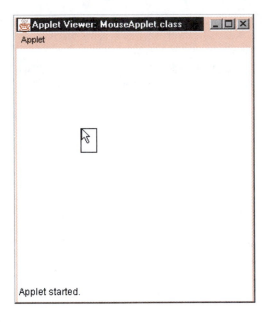

File MouseApplet.java

```
 1  import java.applet.Applet;
 2  import java.awt.Graphics;
 3  import java.awt.Graphics2D;
 4  import java.awt.Rectangle;
 5  import java.awt.event.MouseListener;
 6  import java.awt.event.MouseEvent;
 7
 8  /**
 9      This applet lets the user move a rectangle by clicking
        the mouse.
10  */
11  public class MouseApplet extends Applet
12  {
13      public MouseApplet()
14      {
15          // the rectangle that the paint method draws
16          box = new Rectangle(BOX_X, BOX_Y,
17             BOX_WIDTH, BOX_HEIGHT);
18
19          // add mouse press listener
20
21          class MousePressListener implements MouseListener
22          {
23              public void mousePressed(MouseEvent event)
24              {
25                  int x = event.getX();
26                  int y = event.getY();
```

```
27                box.setLocation(x, y);
28                repaint();
29           }
30
31           // do-nothing methods
32           public void mouseReleased(MouseEvent event) {}
33           public void mouseClicked(MouseEvent event) {}
34           public void mouseEntered(MouseEvent event) {}
35           public void mouseExited(MouseEvent event) {}
36        }
37
38        MouseListener listener = new MousePressListener();
39        addMouseListener(listener);
40     }
41
42     public void paint(Graphics g)
43     {
44        Graphics2D g2 = (Graphics2D)g;
45        g2.draw(box);
46     }
47
48     private Rectangle box;
49     private static final int BOX_X = 100;
50     private static final int BOX_Y = 100;
51     private static final int BOX_WIDTH = 20;
52     private static final int BOX_HEIGHT = 30;
53  }
```

Common Error 10.1

Forgetting to Repaint

A drawing program stores the data that are necessary to repaint the window. The `paint` method retrieves the data; generates geometric shapes such as lines, ellipses, and rectangles; and draws them. When you make a change to the data, your drawing is *not* automatically updated. You must tell the window manager that the data have changed, by calling the `repaint` method. Do not call the `paint` method directly. Only the window manager should call `paint`.

Advanced Topic 10.1

Event Adapters

In the preceding section you saw how to install a mouse listener into a mouse event source and how the listener methods are called when an event occurs. Usually, a program is not interested in all listener notifications. For example, a program may only be interested in mouse clicks and may not care that these mouse clicks are composed of "mouse pressed" and "mouse released" events. Of course, the program could supply a listener that defines all those methods in which it has no interest as "do-nothing" methods, for example:

```
class MouseClickListener implements MouseListener
{
    public void mouseClicked(MouseEvent event)
    {
        // mouse click action here
    }

    // four do-nothing methods
    public void mouseEntered(MouseEvent event) {}
    public void mouseExited(MouseEvent event) {}
    public void mousePressed(MouseEvent event) {}
    public void mouseReleased(MouseEvent event) {}
}
```

This is boring. For that reason, some friendly soul has created a `MouseAdapter` class that implements the `MouseListener` interface such that all methods do nothing. You can *extend* that class, inheriting the "do-nothing" methods and overriding just the methods that you care about, like this:

```
class MouseClickListener extends MouseAdapter
{
    public void mouseClicked(MouseEvent event)
    {
        // mouse click action here
    }
}
```

See Chapter 11 for more information on the process of extending classes.

10.3   Processing Text Input

In the preceding section you saw how to obtain input from the mouse. Let us next turn to text input. So far, your applets received text input by calling the `showInputDialog` method of the `JOptionPane` class, but that was not a very natural user interface. Most graphical programs collect text input through *text fields* (see Figure 3). In this section, you will learn how to add a control panel with text fields to an applet, and how to read what the user types into it.

In this book, we use the user interface components from the *Swing* toolkit, the most advanced user interface toolkit that Sun Microsystems has created for Java. Before the creation of Swing, Java used components in the AWT (Abstract Windowing Toolkit) for graphical applications. Both AWT and Swing components are *multiplatform*—that is, programs can run on Windows, the Macintosh, UNIX, and other platforms without modification. This behavior is often described as "write once, run anywhere". However, the toolkits achieved this goal in different ways. The AWT uses the *native* user interface

Figure 3

An Applet with a Control
Panel for Text Input

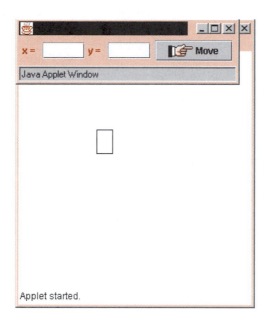

elements (buttons, text fields, menus, and so on) of the host platform. This turned out not to work very well. There are slight differences in behavior on each platform, and programmers soon began complaining that the promised "write once, run anywhere" turned out in fact to be "write once, debug everywhere". Swing takes a different approach—it *paints* the shapes for buttons, text fields, menus, and so on. That is slower but more consistent.

The Swing classes are placed in the `javax.swing` package, where the `javax` package name denotes a *standard extension* of Java. Swing was first released as a standard extension to an earlier version of Java, and it became a standard part of Java 2. For compatibility reasons, the package name was not changed from `javax` to `java`. Swing uses some parts of the AWT, such as the parts for drawing graphical shapes and handling events, so you use some classes from the `java.awt` package in Swing programs.

> Use `JTextField` components to provide space for user input. Place a `JLabel` next to each text field.

The class names for most Swing user interface components start with the letter J. For example, `JTextField` is a Swing text field. There is also a `TextField` class—the (now obsolete) AWT text field.

When you construct a text field, you need to supply the width—the approximate number of characters that you expect the user to type.

```
JTextField xField = new JTextField(5);
```

Users can type additional characters, but then a part of the contents of the field becomes invisible.

You will want to *label* each text field so that the user knows what to type into it. You need to construct a `JLabel` object for each label:

```
JLabel xLabel = new JLabel("x = ");
```

Finally, you want to give the user an opportunity to enter information into all text fields before processing it. Therefore, you also need to supply a button that the user can press to indicate that the input is ready for processing.

You construct a button by supplying a label string, an icon, or both. Here are the alternatives:

```
moveButton = new JButton("Move");
moveButton = new JButton(new ImageIcon("hand.gif"));
moveButton = new JButton("Move", new ImageIcon("hand.gif"));
```

When a button is clicked, it sends an action event. To capture it, you need to install an action listener. Here is the action listener for the Move button. The `actionPerformed` method reads the user input from the text fields, using the `getText` method of the `JTextField` class. It turns the resulting string into a number, moves the rectangle, and repaints the applet.

```
public class ButtonApplet extends Applet
{
    public ButtonApplet()
    {
        . . .
        class MoveButtonListener implements ActionListener
        {
            public void actionPerformed(ActionEvent event)
            {
                int x = Integer.parseInt(xField.getText());
                int y = Integer.parseInt(yField.getText());
                box.setLocation(x, y);
                repaint();
            }
        };
        ActionListener listener = new MoveButtonListener();
        moveButton.addActionListener(listener);
        . . .
    }
    . . .
}
```

The `actionPerformed` method accesses the `xField` and `yField` variables from the `ButtonApplet` constructor. As you saw in Chapter 9, those local variables must be declared as `final`:

```
final JTextField xField = new JTextField(5);
            final JTextField yField = new JTextField(5);;
```

The method also accesses the `box` field of the `ButtonApplet` class. Inner classes can access all fields of the surrounding class.

To finish up this program, we need to place the labels, text fields, and button into the control panel. Construct a `JPanel` object—it is a container for user interface components.

```
JPanel panel = new JPanel();
```

Then add all components into the panel.

```
panel.add(xLabel);
panel.add(xField);
panel.add(yLabel);
panel.add(yField);
panel.add(moveButton);
```

> A JFrame corresponds to a window with a border and title bar.

Finally, show the panel in its own *frame*. A frame is a window with a title bar. You set the panel as the *content pane* of the frame. The content pane is a container that holds all of the user interface components. Then you call the pack method. That method sets the size of the frame just large enough to show all components. Finally, call show to display the frame.

```
JFrame frame = new JFrame();
frame.setContentPane(panel);
frame.pack();
frame.show();
```

It is also possible to show the control panel inside the applet. You will see how in Chapter 12.

Here is the complete program.

File ButtonApplet.java

```
1  import java.applet.Applet;
2  import java.awt.Graphics;
3  import java.awt.Graphics2D;
4  import java.awt.Rectangle;
5  import java.awt.event.ActionEvent;
6  import java.awt.event.ActionListener;
7  import javax.swing.ImageIcon;
8  import javax.swing.JButton;
9  import javax.swing.JFrame;
10 import javax.swing.JLabel;
11 import javax.swing.JPanel;
12 import javax.swing.JTextField;
13
14 /**
15     This applet lets the user move a rectangle by specifying
16     the x- and y-position of the top left corner.
17 */
18 public class ButtonApplet extends Applet
19 {
20     public ButtonApplet()
21     {
22         // the rectangle that the paint method draws
23         box = new Rectangle(BOX_X, BOX_Y,
24             BOX_WIDTH, BOX_HEIGHT);
```

```
25
26        // the text fields for entering the x- and y-coordinates
27        final JTextField xField = new JTextField(5);
28        final JTextField yField = new JTextField(5);;
29
30        // the button to move the rectangle
31        JButton moveButton = new JButton("Move",
32            new ImageIcon("hand.gif"));
33
34        class MoveButtonListener implements ActionListener
35        {
36           public void actionPerformed(ActionEvent event)
37           {
38              int x = Integer.parseInt(xField.getText());
39              int y = Integer.parseInt(yField.getText());
40              box.setLocation(x, y);
41              repaint();
42           }
43        };
44
45        ActionListener listener = new MoveButtonListener();
46        moveButton.addActionListener(listener);
47
48        // the labels for labeling the text fields
49        JLabel xLabel = new JLabel("x = ");
50        JLabel yLabel = new JLabel("y = ");
51
52        // the panel for holding the user interface components
53        JPanel panel = new JPanel();
54
55        panel.add(xLabel);
56        panel.add(xField);
57        panel.add(yLabel);
58        panel.add(yField);
59        panel.add(moveButton);
60
61        // the frame for holding the component panel
62        JFrame frame = new JFrame();
63        frame.setContentPane(panel);
64        frame.pack();
65        frame.show();
66     }
67
68     public void paint(Graphics g)
69     {
70        Graphics2D g2 = (Graphics2D)g;
71        g2.draw(box);
72     }
73
74     private Rectangle box;
```

```
75    private static final int BOX_X = 100;
76    private static final int BOX_Y = 100;
77    private static final int BOX_WIDTH = 20;
78    private static final int BOX_HEIGHT = 30;
79  }
```

10.4   Multiple Buttons with Similar Behavior

Often, your program needs to process inputs from multiple buttons. Look at Figure 4—the program has four buttons to control the movement of the rectangle.

The buttons carry out similar tasks, so the code to define the buttons is very repetitive. Here is the definition of the left button:

```
JButton leftButton = new JButton("Left");

class LeftButtonListener implements ActionListener
{
   public void actionPerformed(ActionEvent event)
   {
      box.translate(-BOX_WIDTH, 0);
      repaint();
   }
};

LeftButtonListener leftListener = new ButtonListener();
leftButton.addActionListener(leftListener);
```

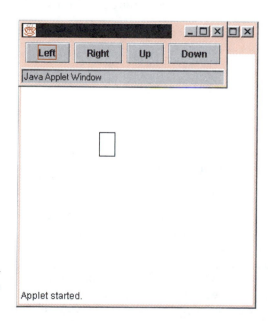

Figure 4

An Applet with Multiple Buttons

And here is the definition of the right button:

```
JButton rightButton = new JButton("Right");

class RightButtonListener implements ActionListener
{
   public void actionPerformed(ActionEvent event)
   {
      box.translate(BOX_WIDTH, 0);
      repaint();
   }
};

RightButtonListener rightListener = new ButtonListener();
rightButton.addActionListener(rightListener);

// two more to go ...
```

> Factor out similar event handlers into a separate method.

This is, of course, intensely boring. Let's factor out the common code (see Quality Tip 3.4) into a method. When we do, we find that the code differs from button to button in only these parameters:

- The button label

- The amounts by which to move the rectangle in the *x*- and *y*-directions

The method can construct any of the buttons, given the parameter values:

```
public JButton makeButton(String label,
   final int dx, final int dy)
{
   JButton button = new JButton(label);

   class ButtonListener implements ActionListener
   {
      public void actionPerformed(ActionEvent event)
      {
         box.translate(dx, dy);
         repaint();
      }
   };

   ButtonListener listener = new ButtonListener();
   button.addActionListener(listener);
   return button;
}
```

Note that the dx and dy parameters are declared as final because they are accessed in the actionPerformed method of the inner class.

We call this method four times:

```
panel.add(makeButton("Left", -BOX_WIDTH, 0));
panel.add(makeButton("Right", BOX_WIDTH, 0));
panel.add(makeButton("Up", 0, -BOX_HEIGHT));
panel.add(makeButton("Down", 0, BOX_HEIGHT));
```

Each call to the method makes a listener object of type `ButtonListener`. In other words, each button has a separate listener, but all four listener objects are instances of the same listener class. Recall from Chapter 9 that the compiler automatically turns local variables that an inner class accesses into instance fields of the inner class. That is, the four listener objects have different states for dx and dy, namely the four combinations supplied in the method calls.

Sharing a listener class among buttons with the same behavior is an effective way to reduce complexity. When you find yourself implementing multiple listener classes with essentially the same functionality, place the listener class inside a separate method.

Here is the whole program:

File ButtonApplet.java

```
 1  import java.applet.Applet;
 2  import java.awt.Graphics;
 3  import java.awt.Graphics2D;
 4  import java.awt.Rectangle;
 5  import java.awt.event.ActionEvent;
 6  import java.awt.event.ActionListener;
 7  import javax.swing.JButton;
 8  import javax.swing.JFrame;
 9  import javax.swing.JPanel;
10
11  /**
12      This applet lets the user move a rectangle by clicking
13      on buttons labeled "Left", "Right", "Up", and "Down".
14  */
15  public class ButtonApplet extends Applet
16  {
17      public ButtonApplet()
18      {
19          // the rectangle that the paint method draws
20          box = new Rectangle(BOX_X, BOX_Y,
21              BOX_WIDTH, BOX_HEIGHT);
22
23          // the panel for holding the user interface components
24          JPanel panel = new JPanel();
25
26          panel.add(makeButton("Left", -BOX_WIDTH, 0));
27          panel.add(makeButton("Right", BOX_WIDTH, 0));
28          panel.add(makeButton("Up", 0, -BOX_HEIGHT));
29          panel.add(makeButton("Down", 0, BOX_HEIGHT));
30
31          // the frame for holding the component panel
32          JFrame frame = new JFrame();
33          frame.setContentPane(panel);
34          frame.pack();
35          frame.show();
36      }
37
38      public void paint(Graphics g)
39      {
```

```
40        Graphics2D g2 = (Graphics2D)g;
41        g2.draw(box);
42    }
43
44    /**
45        Makes a button that moves the box.
46        @param label  the label to show on the button
47        @param dx  the amount by which to move the box in the x-direction
48        when the button is clicked
49        @param dy  the amount by which to move the box in the y-direction
50        when the button is clicked
51        @return  the button
52    */
53    public JButton makeButton(String label, final int dx,
54        final int dy)
55    {
56        JButton button = new JButton(label);
57
58        class ButtonListener implements ActionListener
59        {
60            public void actionPerformed(ActionEvent event)
61            {
62                box.translate(dx, dy);
63                repaint();
64            }
65        };
66
67        ButtonListener listener = new ButtonListener();
68        button.addActionListener(listener);
69        return button;
70    }
71
72    private Rectangle box;
73    private static final int BOX_X = 100;
74    private static final int BOX_Y = 100;
75    private static final int BOX_WIDTH = 20;
76    private static final int BOX_HEIGHT = 30;
77 }
```

Common Error 10.2

Forgetting to Attach a Listener

If you run your program and find that your buttons seem to be dead, double-check that you attached the button listener. The same holds for other user interface components. It is a surprisingly common error to program the listener class and the event handler action without actually attaching it to the event source.

Productivity Hint 10.1

Share Listener Classes, Not Listener Objects

You saw in the preceding section how to make a listener *class* so that each button can have its own customized listener object. You will see some programmers use another approach in which a single listener *object* is shared among buttons. Then the action-Performed method must find out which button was clicked, by calling the getSource method of the ActionEvent parameter.

```
class DirectionListener implements ActionListener
{
    public void actionPerformed(ActionEvent event)
    {
        // find the button that was clicked
        // this approach is not recommended
        Object source = event.getSource();
        if (source == leftButton)
            box.translate(-BOX_WIDTH, 0);
        else if (source == rightButton)
            box.translate(BOX_WIDTH, 0);
        else if (source == upButton)
            box.translate(0, -BOX_HEIGHT);
        else if (source == downButton)
            box.translate(0, BOX_HEIGHT);
        repaint();
    }
}
```

This solution is still quite repetitive and therefore not as good as the one we used in the preceding section, where each button had its own listener. When you find yourself calling getSource, check whether you can instead use a separate object for each event source.

Productivity Hint 10.2

Don't Use a Container as a Listener

In this book, we use inner classes for interface listeners. That approach works for many different event types, and once you master the technique, you don't have to think about it anymore. Many development environments automatically generate code with inner classes, so it is a good idea to be familiar with them.

However, some programmers bypass the event listener classes and instead turn a container (such as an applet) into a listener. Here is a typical example. The action-Performed method is added to the applet class. That is, the applet implements the ActionListener interface.

```
public class ButtonApplet extends Applet
    implements ActionListener // this approach is not recommended
{
    public ButtonApplet()
    {
        . . .
        JButton moveButton = new JButton("Move",
            new ImageIcon("hand.gif"));
        moveButton.addActionListener(this);
        . . .
    }

    public void actionPerformed(ActionEvent event)
    {
        int x = Integer.parseInt(xField.getText());
        int y = Integer.parseInt(yField.getText());
        box.setLocation(x, y);
        repaint();
    }
    . . .
    private JTextField xField;
    private JTextField yField;
}
```

Now the `actionPerformed` method is a part of the `ButtonApplet` class rather than in a separate listener class. The listener is installed as `this`.

This technique has two major flaws. First, it separates the button definition from the button action. Also, it doesn't *scale* well. If the container contains two buttons that each generate action events, then the `actionPerformed` method must investigate the event source—which is not a good idea, according to Productivity Hint 10.1.

? HOWTO   **10.1**

Handling Mouse and Action Events

Handling input from the mouse and from buttons is more challenging than processing keyboard input from the console. Follow these steps to implement the event handling code.

Step 1   Implement the *data that your program manipulates*

The data might be stored in a simple object, such as a `Rectangle` or a `Car`, or the data may be more complex, such as a collection of points.

Implement the data as instance variables of an applet, or, as you will see in Chapter 12, a panel. For example,

```
public class CarApplet
{
```

```
    . . .
    private Car myCar;
}
```

Step 2   Implement the *visual representation of the data*

A graphical program usually draws the data in a `paint` method. The `paint` method is called whenever the data need to be displayed, either because the window needs repainting or because the data have changed. For example,

```
public class CarApplet extends Applet
{
    . . .
    public void paint(Graphics g)
    {
        Graphics2D g2;
        myCar.draw(g2);
    }
    . . .
}
```

Step 3   Design a user interface for manipulating the data

So far, you have seen two user interface techniques:

- Clicking with the mouse in a window

- Clicking a button in a control panel

In Chapter 12 you will learn more about placement of buttons and other user interface components.

If you decide to use a control panel, sketch it. What text fields and buttons do you need?

Then ask yourself: How should the visual representation change when the user clicks with the mouse in the window, or when the user presses a button? What change in the data is necessary to cause that change in the visual representation?

For example, consider this simple interface for the car applet.

- When the user presses the mouse, the car is moved to the horizontal position of the mouse press. The vertical position of the car doesn't change. That means, the x-coordinate of the car is set to the x-coordinate of the mouse press.

- A control panel contains two buttons, marked "Left" and "Right". When the user clicks one of the buttons, the car moves 10 pixels to the left or right. That means, 10 is added to the x-coordinate of the car.

Step 4   Supply the user interface components

Use the following "plumbing" in the applet constructor:

```
// the panel for holding the user interface components
JPanel panel = new JPanel();

// add buttons and text fields
```

```
panel.add(. . .);
panel.add(. . .);
. . .
```

```
//  the frame for holding the component panel
JFrame frame = new JFrame();
frame.setContentPane(panel);
frame.pack();
frame.show();
```

In Chapter 12 you will see how to add user interface components to a frame.

If your program takes only mouse inputs and doesn't require any text fields or buttons, skip this step.

Step 5 Supply event handler classes

For each event that you identified in step 3, you need to add an event handler.

You use classes that implement an `ActionListener` for buttons or a `MouseListener` for mouse events. (For convenience, you may want to extend the `MouseAdapter` interface instead—see Advanced Topic 10.1.)

In the event-handling method, update the data, then call `repaint` so that the visual representation is also updated.

The most basic coding style is to supply a class for every event. For example,

```
class MousePressListener extends MouseAdapter
{
   public void mousePressed(MouseEvent event)
   {
      car.setPosition(event.getX(), car.getY());
      repaint();
   }
}
```

```
class LeftButtonListener implements ActionListener
{
   public void actionPerformed(ActionEvent event)
   {
      car.setPosition(car.getX() - 10, car.getY());
      repaint();
   }
}
class RightButtonListener implements ActionListener
{
   public void actionPerformed(ActionEvent event)
   {
      car.setPosition(car.getX() + 10, car.getY());
      car.repaint();
   }
}
```

If several events have closely related actions, you can share the same listener class and supply the varying values either in a constructor or, most concisely, as parameters of a method, like this:

```
public JButton makeMoveButton(
   String title, final int amount)
{
   class MoveButtonListener implements ActionListener
   {
      public void actionPerformed(ActionEvent event)
      {
         car.setPosition(
            car.getX() + amount, car.getY());
         car.repaint();
      }
   }
   . . .
}
```

Step 6   Make listener objects and attach them to the event sources

For mouse events, the event source is the window on which you click—usually an applet or a panel. For action events, the event source is a button or other user interface component, or a timer. You need to add a listener object to each event source, like this:

```
public class CarApplet extends Applet
{
   public CarApplet()
   {
      MousePressListener listener =
         new MousePressListener();
      addMouseListener(listener);

      JButton leftButton =
         new makeMoveButton("Left", -10);
      JButton rightButton =
         new makeMoveButton("Right", 10);
      . . .
   }
   . . .
   public JButton makeMoveButton(
      String title, final int amount)
   {
      . . .
      JButton button = new JButton(title);
      ActionListener listener = new MoveButtonListener();
      button.addActionListener(listener);
   }
}
```

10.5   Frame Windows

Up to now, all the graphical programs that you wrote have been *applets*, programs that run inside a browser or the applet viewer. You can also write regular graphical programs in Java that do not run inside another program. In this section, you will learn how to write such *graphical applications*.

> A graphical application displays one or more frame windows.

Every graphical application puts up one or more frame windows, just like the window that we used as a control panel in the preceding examples. You can put up a frame window inside the `main` method of a program:

```
public class FrameTest
{
    public static void main(String[] args)
    {
        JFrame frame = new JFrame();
        . . .
        frame.show();
    }
}
```

After you construct a frame, you should set its *default close operation*.

```
JFrame frame = new JFrame();
frame.setDefaultCloseOperation(JFrame.EXIT_ON_CLOSE);
```

When the user closes the frame, the program automatically exits. This setting is useful for very simple programs. For more complex programs, you might want to perform some shutdown actions before allowing the program to exit.

To add some interest to the frame, let's add a couple of decorative labels, one a graphic icon, the other a string of text (see Figure 5).

```
JLabel iconLabel =
    new JLabel(new ImageIcon("world.gif"));
JLabel textLabel = new JLabel("Hello, World!");
```

As in the preceding examples, add the user interface components to a panel and set that panel as the content pane of the frame.

```
JPanel panel = new JPanel();
panel.add(iconLabel);
panel.add(textLabel);
frame.setContentPane(panel);
```

Figure 5

A Frame with Two Labels

Finally, pack and show the frame:

```
frame.pack();
frame.show();
```

Here is the complete program:

File FrameTest.java

```
 1  import javax.swing.ImageIcon;
 2  import javax.swing.JFrame;
 3  import javax.swing.JLabel;
 4  import javax.swing.JPanel;
 5
 6  /**
 7      This program displays a frame with an image and a text label.
 8  */
 9  public class FrameTest
10  {
11     public static void main(String[] args)
12     {
13        JFrame frame = new JFrame();
14
15        frame.setDefaultCloseOperation(JFrame.EXIT_ON_CLOSE);
16
17        JLabel iconLabel =
18           new JLabel(new ImageIcon("world.gif"));
19        JLabel textLabel = new JLabel("Hello, World!");
20
21        JPanel panel = new JPanel();
22        panel.add(iconLabel);
23        panel.add(textLabel);
24        frame.setContentPane(panel);
25
26        frame.pack();
27        frame.show();
28     }
29  }
```

10.6   Text Components

> Use a JTextArea to show multiple lines of text.

You already saw in Section 10.3 how to construct text fields. A text field holds a single line of text. To display multiple lines of text, you use the JTextArea class.

When constructing a text area, you can specify the number of rows and columns:

```
JTextArea textArea = new JTextArea(10, 30);
```

You use the setText method to set the text of a text field or text area. The append method adds text to the end of a text area. Use newline characters to separate lines, like this:

```
textArea.append(account.getBalance() + "\n");
```

To find the current contents of a text field or text area, use the `getText` method.

If you want to use a text field or text area for display purposes only, then you can use the `setEditable` method:

```
textArea.setEditable(false);
```

> You can add scroll bars to any component with a `JScrollPane`.

Now the user can no longer edit the contents of the field, but your program can still call `setText` and `append` to change it.

You can set the font of a text component with the `setFont` method:

```
textArea.setFont(new Font(. . .));
```

To add scroll bars to a text area, use a `JScrollPane`, like this:

```
JTextArea textArea = new JTextArea(10, 30);
JScrollPane scrollPane = new JScrollPane(textArea);
frame.setContentPane(scrollPane);
```

Figure 6 shows the result.

The following sample program puts these concepts together. A user can enter numbers into the interest rate text field and then click on the "Add Interest" button (see Figure 7). The interest rate is applied, and the updated balance is appended to the text area. The text area has scroll bars and is not editable. (The scroll bars are displayed only when the text area fills up with text.)

This application is a useful prototype for a graphical user interface front end for arbitrary calculations. You can easily modify it for your own needs. Place other input components into the control panel. Change the contents of the `actionPerformed` method to carry out other calculations. Display the results in the text area.

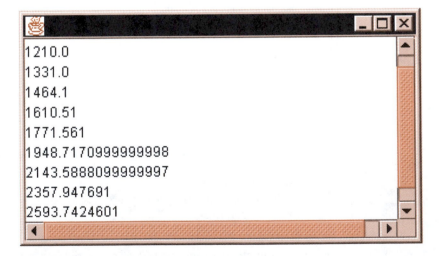

Figure 6

A Text Area with Scroll Bars

Figure 7

The Control Panel for Adding Interest to the Bank Account

File TextAreaTest.java

```
 1  import java.awt.event.ActionEvent;
 2  import java.awt.event.ActionListener;
 3  import javax.swing.JButton;
 4  import javax.swing.JFrame;
 5  import javax.swing.JLabel;
 6  import javax.swing.JPanel;
 7  import javax.swing.JScrollPane;
 8  import javax.swing.JTextArea;
 9  import javax.swing.JTextField;
10
11  /**
12      This program shows a frame with a text area that displays
13      the growth of an investment. A second frame holds a text
14      field to specify the interest rate.
15  */
16  public class TextAreaTest
17  {
18      public static void main(String[] args)
19      {
20          // the application adds interest to this bank account
21          final BankAccount account =
22              new BankAccount(INITIAL_BALANCE);
23          // the text area for displaying the results
24          final JTextArea textArea = new JTextArea(10, 30);
25          textArea.setEditable(false);
26          JScrollPane scrollPane = new JScrollPane(textArea);
27
28          // construct the frame for displaying the text area
29          JFrame frame = new JFrame();
30          frame.setDefaultCloseOperation(
31              JFrame.EXIT_ON_CLOSE);
32          frame.setContentPane(scrollPane);
33          frame.pack();
34          frame.show();
35
36          // the label and text field for entering the interest rate
37          JLabel rateLabel = new JLabel("Interest Rate: ");
38
```

```
39          final JTextField rateField = new JTextField(10);
40          rateField.setText("" + DEFAULT_RATE);
41
42          // the button to trigger the calculation
43          JButton calculateButton =
44             new JButton("Add Interest");
45
46          class CalculateListener implements ActionListener
47          {
48             public void actionPerformed(ActionEvent event)
49             {
50                double rate = Double.parseDouble(
51                   rateField.getText());
52                double interest = account.getBalance()
53                   * rate / 100;
54                account.deposit(interest);
55                textArea.append(account.getBalance() + "\n");
56             }
57          }
58
59          ActionListener listener = new CalculateListener();
60          calculateButton.addActionListener(listener);
61
62          // the control panel that holds the input components
63          JPanel controlPanel = new JPanel();
64          controlPanel.add(rateLabel);
65          controlPanel.add(rateField);
66          controlPanel.add(calculateButton);
67
68          // the frame to hold the control panel
69          JFrame controlFrame = new JFrame();
70          controlFrame.setContentPane(controlPanel);
71          controlFrame.pack();
72          controlFrame.show();
73       }
74
75       private static final double DEFAULT_RATE = 10;
76       private static final double INITIAL_BALANCE = 1000;
77    }
```

▼ ⟳ **Productivity Hint**   **10.3**

Code Reuse

Suppose you are given the task to write another graphical user interface program that reads input from a couple of text fields and displays the result of some calculations in a text area. You don't have to start from scratch. Instead, you can—and often should—*reuse* the outline of an existing program, such as the foregoing TextAreaTest program.

To reuse program code, simply make a copy of a program file and give the copy a new name. For example, you may want to copy `TextAreaTest.java` to a file `MyProg.java`. Then remove the code that is clearly specific to the old problem, but leave the outline in place. That is, keep the panel, text field, event listener, and so on. Fill in the code for your new calculations. Finally, rename classes, buttons, frame titles, and so on.

Once you understand the principles behind event listeners, frames and panels, there is no need to rethink them every time. Reusing the structure of a working program makes your work more efficient.

However, reuse by "copy and rename" is still a mechanical and somewhat error-prone approach. It is even better to package reusable program structures into a set of common classes. The inheritance mechanism lets you design classes for reuse without copy and paste. We will cover inheritance in the next chapter.

Random Fact | 10.1

Programming Languages

Many hundreds of programming languages exist today. That is actually quite surprising. The idea behind a high-level programming language is to provide a medium for programming that is independent from the instruction set of a particular processor, so that one can move programs from one computer to another without rewriting them. Moving a program from one programming language to another is a difficult process, however, and it is rarely done. Thus, it seems that there would be little use for so many programming languages.

Unlike human languages, programming languages are created with specific purposes. Some programming languages make it particularly easy to express tasks from a particular problem domain. Some languages specialize in database processing; others in "artificial intelligence" programs that try to infer new facts from a given base of knowledge; others in multimedia programming. The Pascal language was purposefully kept simple because it was designed as a teaching language. The C language was developed to be translated efficiently into fast machine code, with a minimum of housekeeping overhead. The C++ language builds on C by adding features for object-oriented programming. The Java language was designed for deploying programs across the Internet.

In the early 1970s the U.S. Department of Defense (DoD) was seriously concerned about the high cost of the software components of its weapons equipment. It was estimated that more than half of the total DoD budget was spent on the development of this *embedded-systems* software—that is, software that is embedded in some machinery, such as an airplane or missile, to control it. One of the perceived problems was the great diversity of programming languages that were used to produce that software. Many of these languages, such as TACPOL, CMS-2, SPL/1, and JOVIAL, were virtually unknown outside the defense sector.

In 1976 a committee of computer scientists and defense industry representatives was asked to evaluate existing programming languages. The committee was to determine whether any of them could be made the DoD standard for all future military programming. To nobody's surprise, the committee decided that a new language would need to be created. Contractors were then invited to submit designs for such a new language. Of 17 initial proposals, four were chosen to develop their languages. To ensure an unbiased evaluation, the languages received code names: Red (by Intermetrics), Green (by CII Honeywell Bull), Blue (by Softech), and Yellow (by SRI International). All four languages were based on Pascal. The Green language emerged as the winner in 1979. It was named Ada in honor of the world's first programmer, Ada Lovelace (see Random Fact 15.1).

The Ada language was roundly derided by academics as a typical bloated Defense Department product. Military contractors routinely sought, and obtained, exemptions from the requirement that they had to use Ada on their projects. Outside the defense industry, few companies used Ada. Perhaps that is unfair. Ada had been *designed* to be complex enough to be useful for many applications, whereas other, more popular languages, notably C++, have *grown* to be just as complex and ended up being unmanageable.

The initial version of the C language was designed about 1972. Unlike Ada, C is a simple language that lets you program "close to the machine". It is also quite unsafe. Because different compiler writers added different features, the language actually sprouted various dialects. Some programming instructions were understood by one compiler but rejected by another. Such divergence is an immense pain to a programmer who wants to move code from one computer to another, and an effort got underway to iron out the differences and come up with a standard version of C. The design process ended in 1989 with the completion of the ANSI (American National Standards Institute) Standard. In the meantime, Bjarne Stroustrup of AT&T added features of the language Simula (an object-oriented language designed for carrying out simulations) to C. The resulting language was called C++. From 1985 until today, C++ has grown by the addition of many features, and a standardization process was completed in 1998. C++ has been enormously popular because programmers can take their existing C code and move it to C++, with only minimal changes. In order to keep compatibility with existing code, every innovation in C++ had to work around the existing language constructs, yielding a language that is powerful but somewhat cumbersome to use.

In 1995, Java was designed to be conceptually simpler and more internally consistent than C++, while retaining the syntax that is familiar to millions of C and C++ programmers. The Java *language* was a great design success. It is indeed clean and simple. As for the Java *library*, you know from your own experience that it is neither.

Keep in mind that a programming language is only a part of the technology for writing programs. To be successful, a programming language needs feature-rich libraries, powerful tools, and a community of knowledgeable and enthusiastic users. Several very well-designed programming languages have withered on the vine, whereas other programming languages whose design was merely "good enough" have thrived in the marketplace.

Chapter Summary

1. User interface events include key presses, mouse moves, button presses, menu selections, and so on.

2. You supply *event listeners* for the events about which you care. You need to implement methods for handling the event. You construct listener objects and attach them to the event sources.

3. *Event source* classes report on events. When an event occurs, the event source notifies all event listeners.

4. Event notifications happen in event listener classes. An event listener class implements an *event listener interface*. The interface lists all possible notifications for a particular event category.

5. *Event classes* contain detailed information about various kinds of events.

6. You use a *mouse listener* to capture mouse events.

7. You often install event listeners as *inner classes*. Recall that the inner-class methods can have access to the surrounding fields, methods, and final variables.

8. The `repaint` method causes a window to repaint itself as soon as possible.

9. Use `JTextField` components to provide space for user input. Place a `JLabel` next to each text field.

10. Use `JButton` components for buttons. Attach an `ActionListener` to each button.

11. Use a `JPanel` container to group multiple user interface components together.

12. A `JFrame` corresponds to a window with a border and title bar.

13. Factor out similar event handlers into a separate method.

14. A graphical application displays one or more frame windows.

15. Use a `JTextArea` to show multiple lines of text.

16. You can add scroll bars to any component with a `JScrollPane`.

Further Reading

[1] Cay S. Horstmann and Gary Cornell, *Core Java 1.2 Volume 1: Fundamentals*, Prentice Hall, 1999.

CLASSES, OBJECTS, AND METHODS INTRODUCED IN THIS CHAPTER

```
java.awt.Component
    addActionListener
    addMouseListener
    repaint
java.awt.Container
    add
java.awt.Rectangle
    setLocation
java.awt.Window
    show
java.awt.event.ActionListener
    actionPerformed
java.awt.event.ActionEvent
```

```
java.awt.event.MouseEvent
   getX
   getY
java.awt.event.MouseListener
   mousePressed
javax.swing.ImageIcon
javax.swing.JButton
javax.swing.JFrame
   EXIT_ON_CLOSE
   setContentPane
   setDefaultCloseOperation
   pack
javax.swing.JLabel
javax.swing.JPanel
javax.swing.JScrollPane
javax.swing.JTextArea
   append
javax.swing.JTextField
javax.swing.text.JTextComponent
   getText
   isEditable
   setEditable
   setText
```

REVIEW EXERCISES

Exercise R10.1. What is an event object? An event source? An event listener?

Exercise R10.2. From a programmer's perspective, what is the most important difference between the user interfaces of a console application and a graphical application?

Exercise R10.3. What is the difference between an `ActionEvent` and a `MouseEvent`?

Exercise R10.4. Why does the `ActionListener` interface have only one method, whereas the `MouseListener` has five methods?

Exercise R10.5. Can a class be an event source for multiple event types?

Exercise R10.6. What information does an action event object carry? What additional information does a mouse event object carry?

Exercise R10.7. Why are we using inner classes for event listeners? If Java did not have inner classes, could we still implement event listeners? How?

Exercise R10.8. What is the difference between the `paint` and `repaint` methods?

Exercise R10.9. What is the difference between an applet and a graphical user interface application?

Exercise R10.10. What is the difference between a frame and a panel?

Exercise R10.11. What is the difference between a text field and a text area?

PROGRAMMING EXERCISES

Exercise P10.1. Reimplement the `MouseSpy` program as an application. Display the frame's mouse events in the console window.

Exercise P10.2. Implement the `MousePressListener` in the `MouseApplet` as a regular class (that is, not an inner class). *Hint:* Store a reference to the applet object in the listener, add to the listener a constructor that sets that reference, and add a public method for moving the box position to the applet.

Exercise P10.3. Write an applet that prompts the user for an integer and then draws as many rectangles at random positions as the user requested. Place a text field and a "Draw" button into an external frame.

Exercise P10.4. Write an applet that prompts the user to enter the *x*- and *y*-positions of the center and a radius. When the user clicks a "Draw" button, draw a circle with that center and radius.

Exercise P10.5. Write an applet that lets a user specify a circle by typing the radius in a text field and then clicking on the center. Note that you don't need a "Draw" button.

Exercise P10.6. Write an applet that lets a user specify a circle with two mouse presses, the first one on the center and the second on a point on the periphery. *Hint:* In the mouse press handler, you must keep track of whether you already received the center point in a previous mouse press.

Exercise P10.7. Write an applet that lets a user specify a triangle with three mouse clicks. *Hint:* In the mouse click handler, you must keep track of how many corners you already received. When the user clicks for the first time, draw a small circle to mark the position. When the user clicks for the second time, draw a line joining the two points. Finally, after the third click, draw the entire triangle.

Exercise P10.8. Write an applet that prompts the user to click on three points. Then draw a circle passing through the three points.

Exercise P10.9. Write an applet that prompts the user to click on two points. Then draw a line joining the points and write a message displaying the *slope* of the line; that is, the "rise over run" ratio. The message should be displayed at the *midpoint* of the line.

Exercise P10.10. Write an applet that prompts the user to click on two points. Then draw a line joining the points and write a message displaying the *length* of the line. The message should be displayed at the *midpoint* of the line.

Exercise P10.11. Write an applet that plots a *regression line;* that is, the line with the best fit through a collection of points. The regression line is the line with equation

$$y = \bar{y} + m(x - \bar{x}),$$

where

$$m = \frac{\sum x_i y_i - n\bar{x}\bar{y}}{\sum x_i^2 - n\bar{x}^2}$$

$\bar{x}$ is the mean of the *x*-values, and $\bar{y}$ is the mean of the *y*-values.

The user keeps clicking on points. You don't need to store the individual points, but you need to keep track of

- The count of input values
- The sum of x, y, x^2, and xy values

To draw the regression line, compute its endpoints at the left and right edges of the screen and draw a segment. Each time the user clicks on another point, you update the screen again.

Exercise P10.12. Write an applet that draws a clock face with a time that the user enters in two text fields (one for the hours, one for the minutes).

Hint: You need to find out the angles of the hour hand and the minute hand. The angle of the minute hand is easy: The minute hand travels 360 degrees in 60 minutes. The angle of the hour hand is harder; it travels 360 degrees in 12 × 60 *minutes*.

Exercise P10.13. Write an applet that asks the user to enter an integer n, and then draw an n-by-n grid on the panel. Whenever the user clicks inside one of the grid squares on the panel, color that grid square in black.

Exercise P10.14. Write an applet that asks the user for a number of sticks, and then generate a random stick chart (similar to the temperature chart in Chapter 4) with the given number of sticks.

Exercise P10.15. Write an applet that asks the user to enter data values in a text area. Then draw a stick chart showing the data values. *Hint:* Use a string tokenizer to break the text into tokens.

Exercise P10.16. Write a graphical application front end for a bank account class. Supply text fields and buttons for depositing and withdrawing money, and for displaying the current balance in a text area.

Exercise P10.17. Write a graphical application front end for a `Purse` class. Supply buttons for adding various coins, and for displaying the total amount of money in the purse. Make sure to use a single method for the event listeners for the various coin buttons.

Exercise P10.18. Write a graphical application front end for a `VendingMachine` class. Supply a text field and button for adding money and buttons for selecting products. Display messages such as "Here is your chocolate bar" or "Insufficient money" in a text area.

Exercise P10.19. Write a graphical application front end for an `Earthquake` class. Supply a text field and button for entering the strength of the earthquake. Display the earthquake description in a text area.

Exercise P10.20. Write a graphical application front end for a `DataSet` class. Supply text fields and buttons for adding values, and display the current minimum, maximum, and average in a text area.

Inheritance

11.1 An Introduction to Inheritance

> Inheritance is a method for extending existing classes by adding methods and fields.

Inheritance is a mechanism for enhancing existing, working classes. If you need to implement a new class and a class representing a more general concept is already available, then the new class can inherit from the existing class. For example, suppose you need to define a class `SavingsAccount` to model an account that pays a fixed interest rate on deposits. You already have a class `BankAccount`, and a savings account is a special case of a bank account. In this case, it makes sense to use the language construct of inheritance. Here is the syntax for the class definition:

```
class SavingsAccount extends BankAccount
{
    new methods
    new instance fields
}
```

In the `SavingsAccount` class definition you specify only new methods and instance fields. All methods and instance fields of the `BankAccount` class are *automatically inherited* by the `SavingsAccount` class. For example, the `deposit` method automatically applies to savings accounts:

```
SavingsAccount collegeFund = new SavingsAccount(10);
    // savings account with 10% interest
collegeFund.deposit(500);
    // OK to use BankAccount method with SavingsAccount object
```

> The more general class is called a superclass. The more specialized class that inherits from the superclass is called the subclass.

You have already encountered inheritance in Chapter 4, where your applets all belonged to classes that inherited from the `Applet` class.

We must introduce some more terminology here. The more general class that forms the basis for inheritance is called the *superclass*. The more specialized class that inherits from the superclass is called the *subclass*. In our example, `BankAccount` is the superclass and `SavingsAccount` is the subclass.

> Every class extends the `Object` class either directly or indirectly.

In Java, every class that does not specifically extend another class is a subclass of the class `Object`. For example, the `BankAccount` class extends the class `Object`. The `Object` class has a small number of methods that make sense for all objects, such as the `toString` method, which you can use to obtain a string that describes the state of an object.

> Inheriting from a class differs from realizing an interface: The subclass inherits behavior and state from the superclass.

Figure 1 is a class diagram showing the relationship between the three classes `Object`, `BankAccount`, and `SavingsAccount`. In a class diagram, you denote inheritance by a solid arrow with a "hollow triangle" tip that points to the superclass.

You may wonder at this point in what way inheritance differs from realizing an interface. An interface is not a class. It has *no state and no behavior*. It merely tells you which methods you should implement. A superclass has state and behavior, and the subclasses inherit them.

Figure 1

An Inheritance Diagram

One important reason for inheritance is *code reuse*. By inheriting from an existing class, you do not have to replicate the effort that went into designing and perfecting that class. For example, when implementing the SavingsAccount class, you can rely on the withdraw, deposit, and getBalance methods of the BankAccount class without touching them.

> One advantage of inheritance is code reuse.

Let us see how our savings account objects are different from BankAccount objects. We will set an interest rate in the constructor, and then we need a method to apply that interest periodically. That is, in addition to the three methods that can be applied to every account, there is an additional method addInterest. These new methods and instance fields must be defined in the subclass.

> When defining a subclass, you specify added instance fields, added methods, and changed or *overridden* methods.

```
public class SavingsAccount extends BankAccount
{
    public SavingsAccount(double rate)
    {
        constructor implementation
    }

    public void addInterest()
    {
        method implementation
    }

    private double interestRate;
}
```

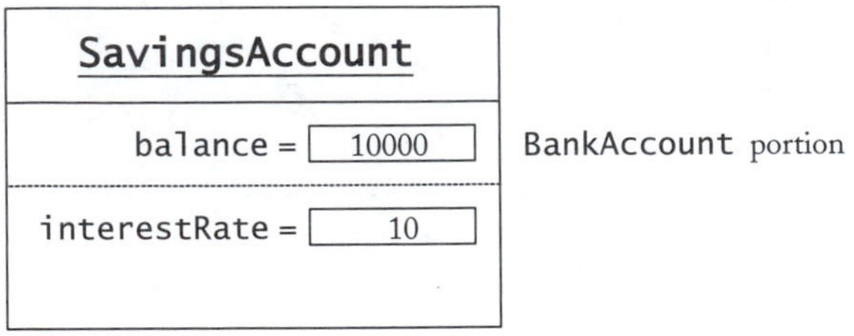

Figure 2

Layout of a Subclass Object

Figure 2 shows the layout of a SavingsAccount object. It inherits the balance instance field from the BankAccount superclass, and it gains one additional instance field: interestRate.

Next, you need to implement the new addInterest method. This method computes the interest due on the current balance and deposits that interest to the account.

```
public class SavingsAccount extends BankAccount
{
   public SavingsAccount(double rate)
   {
      interestRate = rate;
   }

   public void addInterest()
   {
      double interest = getBalance()
         * interestRate / 100;
      deposit(interest);
   }

   private double interestRate;
}
```

Note how the addInterest method calls the getBalance and deposit methods of the superclass. Because no object is specified for the calls to getBalance and deposit, the calls apply to the implicit parameter of the addInterest method. In other words, the following statements are executed:

```
double interest = this.getBalance()
   * this.interestRate / 100;
this.deposit(interest);
```

For example, if you call

```
collegeFund.addInterest();
```

then the following instructions are executed:

```
double interest = collegeFund.getBalance()
   * collegeFund.interestRate / 100;
collegeFund.deposit(interest);
```

> ### Syntax 11.1: Inheritance
>
> ```
> class SubclassName extends   SuperclassName
> {
>     methods
>     instance fields
> }
> ```
>
> ### Example:
>
> ```
> public class SavingsAccount extends BankAccount
> {
>    public SavingsAccount(double rate)
>    {
>       interestRate = rate;
>    }
>
>    public void addInterest()
>    {
>       double interest =
>          getBalance() * interestRate / 100;
>       deposit(interest);
>    }
>
>    private double interestRate;
> }
> ```
>
> ### Purpose:
>
> To define a new class that inherits from an existing class, and define the methods and instance fields that are added in the new class

Common Error   11.1

Confusing Super- and Subclasses

If you compare an object of type SavingsAccount with an object of type BankAccount, then you find that

- The keyword extends suggests that the SavingsAccount object is an extended version of a BankAccount.

- The SavingsAccount object is larger; it has an added instance field interest-Rate.

- The SavingsAccount object is more capable; it has an addInterest method.

▼   It seems a superior object in every way. So why is `SavingsAccount` called the *subclass* and `BankAccount` the *superclass*?

▼   The *super/sub* terminology comes from set theory. Look at the set of all bank accounts. Not all of them are `SavingsAccount` objects; some of them are other kinds of bank accounts. Therefore, the set of `SavingsAccount` objects is a *subset* of the set of all `BankAccount` objects, and the set of `BankAccount` objects is a *superset* of the set of

▼   `SavingsAccount` objects. The more specialized objects in the subset have richer state and more capabilities.

11.2   Inheritance Hierarchies

In the real world, you often categorize concepts into *hierarchies*. Hierarchies are frequently represented as trees, with the most general concepts at the root of the hierarchy and more specialized ones towards the branches. Figure 3 shows a typical example.

> Sets of classes can form complex inheritance hierarchies.

In Java it is equally common to group classes in complex *inheritance hierarchies*. The classes representing the most general concepts are near the root, more specialized classes towards the branches. For example, Figure 4 shows part of the hierarchy of Swing user interface components in Java.

When designing a hierarchy of classes, you ask yourself which features and behavior are common to all the classes that you are designing. Those common properties are col-

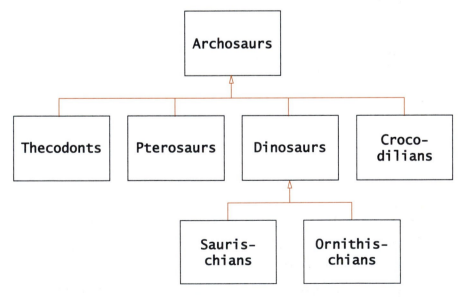

Figure 3

A Part of the Hierarchy of Ancient Reptiles

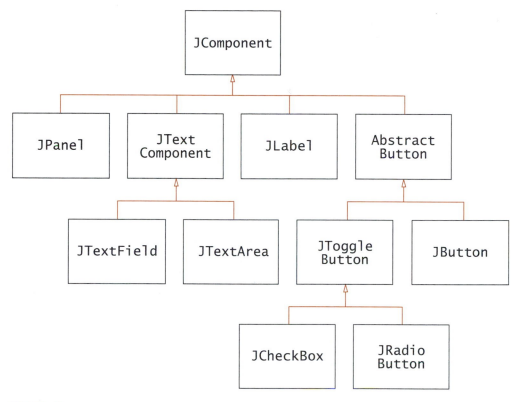

Figure 4

A Part of the Hierarchy of Swing User Interface Components

lected in a superclass. For example, all user interface components have a width and height, and the `getWidth` and `getHeight` methods of the `JComponent` class return the component's dimensions. More specialized properties can be found in subclasses. For example, buttons can have text and icon labels. The class `AbstractButton`, but not the superclass `JComponent`, has methods to set and get the button text and icon, and instance fields to store them. The individual button classes (such as `JButton`, `JRadioButton`, and `JCheckBox`) inherit these properties. In fact, the `AbstractButton` class was created to express the commonality between these buttons.

We will use a simpler example of a hierarchy in our study of inheritance concepts. Consider a bank that offers its customers the following account types:

1. The checking account has no interest, gives you a small number of free transactions per month, and charges a transaction fee for each additional transaction.

2. The savings account earns interest that compounds monthly. (In our implementation, the interest is compounded using the balance of the last day of the month, which is somewhat unrealistic. Typically, banks use either the average or the minimum daily balance. Exercise P11.1 asks you to implement this enhancement.)

Figure 5

Inheritance Hierarchy for Bank Account
Classes

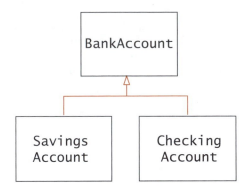

Figure 5

Inheritance Hierarchy for Bank Account
Classes

Figure 5 shows the inheritance hierarchy. Exercise P11.2 asks you to add another class to this hierarchy.

Next, let us determine the behavior of these classes. All bank accounts support the get-Balance method, which simply reports the current balance. They also support the deposit and withdraw methods, although the details of the implementation differ. For example, a checking account must keep track of the number of transactions to account for the transaction fees. A time deposit account must reject withdrawals for other than the full balance.

The checking account needs a method deductFees to deduct the monthly fees and to reset the transaction counter. The deposit and withdraw methods must be redefined to count the transactions.

The savings account needs a method addInterest to add interest.

11.3 Inheriting Instance Fields and Methods

When you form a subclass of a given class, you can specify additional instance fields and methods. In this section we will discuss this process in detail.

Let us look at methods first. When defining the methods for a subclass, there are three possibilities.

1. You can *override* methods from the superclass. If you specify a method with the same *signature* (that is, the same name and the same parameter types), it overrides the method of the same name in the superclass. Whenever the method is applied to an object of the subclass type, the overriding method, and not the original method, is executed. For example, CheckingAccount.deposit overrides BankAccount.deposit.

2. You can *inherit* methods from the superclass. If you do not explicitly override a superclass method, you automatically inherit it. The superclass method can be applied to the subclass objects. For example, the CheckingAccount class inherits the BankAccount.getBalance method.

3. You can define new methods. If you define a method that did not exist in the superclass, then the new method can be applied only to subclass objects. For example, CheckingAccount.deductFees is a new method that does not exist in the superclass BankAccount.

The situation for instance fields is quite different. You can never override instance fields. When defining instance fields for a subclass, there are only two cases:

1. You can inherit fields from the superclass. All instance fields from the superclass are automatically inherited. For example, all subclasses of the `BankAccount` class inherit the instance field `balance`.

2. You can define new fields. Any new instance fields that you define in the subclass are present only in subclass objects. For example, the subclass `SavingsAccount` defines a new instance field `interestRate`.

What happens if you define a new field with the same name as a superclass field? For example, what happens if you define another field named `balance` in the `Savings-Account` class? Then each `SavingsAccount` object has *two* instance fields of the same name. The newly defined subclass field *shadows* the superclass field. That is, the superclass field is still present, but it cannot be accessed from the `SavingsAccount` methods. Shadowing instance fields can be a source of confusion (see Common Error 11.2).

We already implemented the `BankAccount` and `SavingsAccount` classes. Now we will implement the subclass `CheckingAccount` so that you can see in detail how methods and instance fields are inherited. Recall that the `BankAccount` class has three methods and one instance field:

```
public class BankAccount
{
   public double getBalance() { . . . }
   public void deposit(double d) { . . . }
   public void withdraw(double d) { . . . }

   private double balance;
}
```

The `CheckingAccount` has an added method `deductFees` and an added instance field `transactionCount`, and it overrides the `deposit` and `withdraw` methods to increment the transaction count:

```
public class CheckingAccount extends BankAccount
{
   public void deposit(double d) { . . . }
   public void withdraw(double d) { . . . }
   public void deductFees() { . . . }

   private int transactionCount;
}
```

Each object of class `CheckingAccount` has two instance fields:

- `balance` (inherited from `BankAccount`)

- `transactionCount` (new to `CheckingAccount`)

You can apply four methods to `CheckingAccount` objects:

- `getBalance()` (inherited from `BankAccount`)

- `deposit(double)` (overrides `BankAccount` method)

- `withdraw(double)` (overrides `BankAccount` method)

- `deductFees()` (new to `CheckingAccount`)

Next, let us implement these methods. The `deposit` method increments the transaction count and deposits the money:

```
public class CheckingAccount extends BankAccount
{
   public void deposit(double amount)
   {
      transactionCount++;
      // now add amount to balance
      . . .
   }
   . . .
}
```

Now we have a problem. We can't simply add `amount` to `balance`:

```
public class CheckingAccount extends BankAccount
{
   public void deposit(double amount)
   {
      transactionCount++;
      // now add amount to balance
      balance = balance + amount; // ERROR
   }
   . . .
}
```

> A subclass has no access to private fields of its superclass.

Although every `CheckingAccount` object has a `balance` instance field, that instance field is *private* to the superclass `BankAccount`. Subclass methods have no more access rights to the private data of the superclass than any other methods. If you want to modify a private superclass field, you must use a public method of the superclass, just like everyone else.

How can we add the deposit amount to the balance, using the public interface of the `BankAccount` class? There is a perfectly good method for just that purpose—namely, the `deposit` method of the `BankAccount` class. So we have to invoke the `deposit` on some object. On which object? The checking account into which the money is deposited—that is, the implicit parameter of the `deposit` method of the `CheckingAccount` class. As you saw in Chapter 3, to invoke another method on the implicit parameter, you don't specify the parameter but just write the method name:

```
public class CheckingAccount extends BankAccount
{
    public void deposit(double amount)
    {
        transactionCount++;
        // now add amount to balance
        deposit(amount); // not complete
    }
    . . .
}
```

But this won't quite work. The compiler interprets

```
deposit(amount);
```

as

```
this.deposit(amount);
```

The `this` parameter is of type `CheckingAccount`. There is a method called `deposit` in the `CheckingAccount` class. Therefore, that method will be called—but that is just the method we are currently writing! The method will call itself over and over, and the program will die in an infinite recursion (discussed in Chapter 17).

> Use the super keyword to call a method of the superclass.

Instead, we must be more specific that we want to invoke only the *superclass's* `deposit` method. There is a special keyword `super` for this purpose:

```
public class CheckingAccount extends BankAccount
{
    public void deposit(double amount)
    {
        transactionCount++;
        // now add amount to balance
        super.deposit(amount);
    }
    . . .
}
```

This version of the `deposit` method is correct. To deposit money into a checking account, update the transaction count and then call the `deposit` method of the super-class.

The remaining methods are now straightforward.

```
public class CheckingAccount extends BankAccount
{
    . . .
    public void withdraw(double amount)
    {
        transactionCount++;
        // now subtract amount from balance
```

```
      super.withdraw(amount);
   }

   public void deductFees()
   {
      if (transactionCount > FREE_TRANSACTIONS)
      {
         double fees = TRANSACTION_FEE
            * (transactionCount - FREE_TRANSACTIONS);
         super.withdraw(fees);
      }
      transactionCount = 0;
   }
   . . .
   private static final int FREE_TRANSACTIONS = 3;
   private static final double TRANSACTION_FEE = 2.0;
}
```

Syntax 11.2: Calling a Superclass Method

super._methodName_(_parameters_);

Example:

```
public void deposit(double amount)
{
   transactionCount++;
   super.deposit(amount);
}
```

Purpose:

To call a method of the superclass instead of the
method of the current class

▼   ⊗ **Common Error**   **11.2**

Shadowing Instance Fields

▼

A subclass has no access to the private instance fields of the superclass. For example, the
methods of the CheckingAccount class cannot access the **balance** field:

▼

```
public class CheckingAccount extends BankAccount
{
   public void deposit(double amount)
   {
      transactionCount++;
```

▼

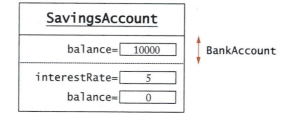

Figure 6

Shadowing Instance Fields

```
         balance = balance + amount; // ERROR
      }
      . . .
   }
```

It is a common beginner's error to "solve" this problem by adding *another* instance field with the same name.

```
   public class CheckingAccount extends BankAccount
   {
      public void deposit(double amount)
      {
         transactionCount++;
         balance = balance + amount;
      }
      . . .
      private double balance; // DON'T
      private double interestRate;
   }
```

Sure, now the `deposit` method compiles, but it doesn't update the correct balance! Such a `CheckingAccount` object has two instance fields, both named `balance` (see Figure 6). The `getBalance` method of the superclass retrieves one of them, and the `deposit` method of the subclass updates the other.

Common Error 11.3

Failing to Invoke the Superclass Method

A common error in extending the functionality of a superclass method is to forget the `super.` qualifier. For example, to withdraw money from a checking account, update the transaction count and then withdraw the amount:

```
   public void withdraw(double amount)
   {
      transactionCount++;
```

▼
```
        withdraw(amount);
        // Error—should be super.withdraw(amount)
    }
```

▼
Here withdraw(amount) refers to the withdraw method applied to the implicit parameter of the method. The implicit parameter is of type CheckingAccount, and the CheckingAccount class has a withdraw method, so that method is called. Of course,

▼
that just calls the current method all over again, which will call itself yet again, over and over, until the program runs out of memory. Instead, you must be precise which withdraw method you want to call.

▼
Another common error is to forget to call the superclass method altogether. Then the functionality of the superclass mysteriously vanishes.

11.4 Subclass Construction

Let us define a constructor to set the initial balance of a checking account.

```
public class CheckingAccount extends BankAccount
{
    public CheckingAccount(double initialBalance)
    {
        // construct superclass
        . . .
        // initialize transaction count
        transactionCount = 0;
    }
    . . .
}
```

We want to invoke the BankAccount constructor to set the balance to the initial balance. There is a special instruction to call the superclass constructor from a subclass constructor. You use the keyword **super**, followed by the construction parameters in parentheses:

```
public class CheckingAccount extends BankAccount
{
    public CheckingAccount(double initialBalance)
    {
        // construct superclass
        super(initialBalance);
        // initialize transaction count
        transactionCount = 0;
    }
    . . .
}
```

> To call the superclass constructor, you use the **super** keyword in the first statement of the subclass constructor.

When the keyword **super** is followed by a parenthesis, it indicates a call to the superclass constructor. When used in this way, the constructor call must be *the first statement of the subclass constructor*. If **super** is followed by a period and a method name, on the other hand, it indicates a call to a superclass method, as you saw in the preceding section. Such a call can be made anywhere in any subclass method. The dual use of the **super** keyword is analogous to the dual use of the **this** keyword (see Advanced Topic 7.4).

If a subclass constructor does not call the superclass constructor, the superclass is constructed with its default constructor. If the superclass does not have a default constructor, then the compiler reports an error.

For example, you can implement the **CheckingAccount** constructor without calling the superclass constructor. Then the **BankAccount** class is constructed with its default constructor, which sets the balance to zero. Of course, then the **CheckingAccount** constructor must explicitly deposit the initial balance.

Most commonly, however, subclass constructors have some parameters that they pass on to the superclass and others that they use to initialize subclass fields.

Syntax 11.3: Calling a Superclass Constructor

ClassName(parameters)
```
{
    super(parameters);
    . . .
}
```

Example:
```
public CheckingAccount(double initialBalance)
{
    super(initialBalance);
    transactionCount = 0;
}
```

Purpose:

To invoke the constructor of the superclass. Note that this statement must be the first statement of the subclass constructor.

11.5   Converting from Subclasses to Superclasses

> Subclass references can be converted to superclass references.

The class **SavingsAccount** extends the class **BankAccount**. In other words, a **SavingsAccount** object is a special case of a **BankAccount** object. Therefore, you can store a reference to a **SavingsAccount** object into an object field of type **BankAccount**. Furthermore, all object references can be stored in a variable of type **Object**.

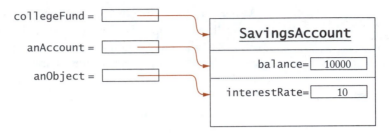

Figure 7

Variables of Different Types Refer to the Same Object

```
SavingsAccount collegeFund = new SavingsAccount(10);
BankAccount anAccount = collegeFund;
Object anObject = collegeFund;
```

Now the three object references stored in `collegeFund`, `anAccount`, and `anObject` all refer to the same object of type `SavingsAccount` (see Figure 7).

However, the object field `anAccount` knows less than the full story about the object to which it refers. Because `anAccount` is an object of type `BankAccount`, you can use the `deposit` and `withdraw` methods to change the balance of the savings account. You cannot use the `addInterest` method, though—it is not a method of the `BankAccount` superclass:

```
anAccount.deposit(1000); // OK
anAccount.addInterest();
    // No—not a method of the class to which anAccount belongs
```

And, of course, the field `anObject` knows even less. You can't even apply the `deposit` method to it—`deposit` is not a method of the `Object` class.

Conversion from a subclass type to a superclass type is very similar to the conversion from a class type to an interface type. As you saw in Chapter 9, you can convert from a class to an interface that the class realizes. For example, if `BankAccount` realizes the `Comparable` interface, then you can store a `BankAccount` object (as well as any object of a subclass of `BankAccount`) in a field of type `Comparable`.

Why would anyone *want* to know less about an object and store a reference in an object field of a superclass? This can happen if you want to reuse code that knows about the superclass but not the subclass. Here is a typical example. Consider a `transfer` method that transfers money from one account to another:

```
void transfer(double amount, BankAccount other)
{
    withdraw(amount);
    other.deposit(amount);
}
```

You can use this method to transfer money from one bank account to another:

```
BankAccount momsAccount = . . . ;
BankAccount harrysAccount = . . . ;
momsChecking.transfer(1000, harrysAccount);
```

You can *also* use the method to transfer money into a `CheckingAccount`:

```
CheckingAccount harrysChecking = . . . ;
momsAccount.transfer(1000, harrysChecking);
    // OK to pass a CheckingAccount reference to a
    // method expecting a BankAccount
```

The `transfer` method expects a reference to a `BankAccount`, and it gets a reference to the subclass `CheckingAccount`. Fortunately, rather than complaining about a type mismatch, the compiler simply copies the subclass reference `harrysChecking` to the superclass reference `other`. The `transfer` method doesn't actually know that, in this case, `other` refers to a `CheckingAccount` reference. It knows only that `other` is a `BankAccount`, and it doesn't need to know anything else. All it cares about is that the `other` object can carry out the `deposit` method.

Now let us follow the method call more precisely. *Which* `deposit` method? The `other` parameter has type `BankAccount`, so it would appear as if `BankAccount.deposit` is called. On the other hand, the `CheckingAccount` class provides its own `deposit` method that updates the transaction count. The `other` field actually refers to an object of the subclass `CheckingAccount`, so it would be appropriate if the `CheckingAccount.deposit` method were called instead.

As you already saw in Chapter 9, method calls *are always determined by the type of the actual object*, not the type of the object reference. That is, if the actual object has the type `CheckingAccount`, then the `CheckingAccount.deposit` method is called. It does not matter that the object reference is stored in a field of type `BankAccount`. Recall that this mechanism is called late binding, and that the `other` field's ability to refer to objects of multiple types with varying behavior is called polymorphism.

Why don't we store all account references in variables of type `Object`? The compiler still needs the `BankAccount` type to confirm that there are methods such as `deposit` and `withdraw`. Those methods are defined only in the `BankAccount` class, not the `Object` class.

The following program calls the polymorphic `withdraw` and `deposit` methods. You should manually calculate what the program should print for each account balance, and confirm that the correct methods have in fact been called.

File AccountTest.java

```
 1  /**
 2      This program tests the BankAccount class and
 3      its subclasses.
 4  */
 5  public class AccountTest
 6  {
 7     public static void main(String[] args)
 8     {
 9        SavingsAccount momsSavings
10           = new SavingsAccount(0.5);
11
12        CheckingAccount harrysChecking
13           = new CheckingAccount(100);
14
15        momsSavings.deposit(10000);
```

```
16
17          momsSavings.transfer(harrysChecking, 2000);
18          harrysChecking.withdraw(1500);
19          harrysChecking.withdraw(80);
20
21          momsSavings.transfer(harrysChecking, 1000);
22          harrysChecking.withdraw(400);
23
24          // simulate end of month
25          momsSavings.addInterest();
26          harrysChecking.deductFees();
27
28          System.out.println("Mom's savings balance = $"
29             + momsSavings.getBalance());
30
31          System.out.println("Harry's checking balance = $"
32             + harrysChecking.getBalance());
33       }
34   }
```

File BankAccount.java

```
 1   /**
 2       A bank account has a balance that can be changed by
 3       deposits and withdrawals.
 4   */
 5   public class BankAccount
 6   {
 7       /**
 8           Constructs a bank account with a zero balance.
 9       */
10       public BankAccount()
11       {
12          balance = 0;
13       }
14
15       /**
16           Constructs a bank account with a given balance.
17           @param initialBalance the initial balance
18       */
19       public BankAccount(double initialBalance)
20       {
21          balance = initialBalance;
22       }
23
24       /**
25           Deposits money into the bank account.
26           @param amount the amount to deposit
27       */
28       public void deposit(double amount)
29       {
30          balance = balance + amount;
```

```
31        }
32
33        /**
34            Withdraws money from the bank account.
35            @param amount  the amount to withdraw
36        */
37        public void withdraw(double amount)
38        {
39            balance = balance - amount;
40        }
41
42        /**
43            Gets the current balance of the bank account.
44            @return  the current balance
45        */
46        public double getBalance()
47        {
48            return balance;
49        }
50
51        /**
52            Transfers money from the bank account to another account.
53            @param other  the other account
54            @param amount  the amount to transfer
55        */
56        public void transfer(BankAccount other, double amount)
57        {
58            withdraw(amount);
59            other.deposit(amount);
60        }
61
62        private double balance;
63    }
```

File CheckingAccount.java

```
1    /**
2        A checking account that charges transaction fees.
3    */
4    public class CheckingAccount extends BankAccount
5    {
6        /**
7            Constructs a checking account with a given balance.
8            @param initialBalance  the initial balance
9        */
10        public CheckingAccount(int initialBalance)
11        {
12            // construct superclass
13            super(initialBalance);
14
15            // initialize transaction count
16            transactionCount = 0;
```

```
17      }
18
19      public void deposit(double amount)
20      {
21         transactionCount++;
22         // now add amount to balance
23         super.deposit(amount);
24      }
25
26      public void withdraw(double amount)
27      {
28         transactionCount++;
29         // now subtract amount from balance
30         super.withdraw(amount);
31      }
32
33      /**
34         Deducts the accumulated fees and resets the
35         transaction count.
36      */
37      public void deductFees()
38      {
39         if (transactionCount > FREE_TRANSACTIONS)
40         {
41            double fees = TRANSACTION_FEE *
42               (transactionCount - FREE_TRANSACTIONS);
43            super.withdraw(fees);
44         }
45         transactionCount = 0;
46      }
47
48      private int transactionCount;
49
50      private static final int FREE_TRANSACTIONS = 3;
51      private static final double TRANSACTION_FEE = 2.0;
52   }
```

File SavingsAccount.java

```
1   /**
2      An account that earns interest at a fixed rate.
3   */
4   public class SavingsAccount extends BankAccount
5   {
6      /**
7         Constructs a bank account with a given interest rate.
8         @param rate the interest rate
9      */
10     public SavingsAccount(double rate)
11     {
12        interestRate = rate;
13     }
```

```
14
15      /**
16          Adds the earned interest to the account balance.
17      */
18      public void addInterest()
19      {
20          double interest = getBalance()
21              * interestRate / 100;
22          deposit(interest);
23      }
24
25      private double interestRate;
26   }
```

▲T Advanced Topic   11.1

Abstract Classes

When you extend an existing class, you have the *choice* whether or not to redefine the methods of the superclass. Sometimes, it is desirable to *force* programmers to redefine a method. That happens when there is no good default for the superclass, and only the subclass programmer can know how to implement the method properly.

Here is an example. Suppose the First National Bank of Java decides that every account type must have some monthly fees. Therefore, a deductFees method should be added to the BankAccount class:

```
public class BankAccount
{
    public void deductFees() { . . . }
    . . .
}
```

But what should this method do? Of course, we could have the method do nothing. But then a programmer implementing a new subclass might simply forget to implement the deduct-Fees method, and the new account would inherit the do-nothing method of the superclass. There is a better way: namely, to declare the deductFees method as an *abstract method:*

```
public abstract void deductFees();
```

> An abstract method is a method whose implementation is not specified.

An abstract method has no implementation. This forces the implementors of subclasses to specify concrete implementations of this method. (Of course, some subclasses might decide to implement a do-nothing method, but then that is their choice—not a silently inherited default.)

You cannot construct objects of classes with abstract methods. For example, once the BankAccount class has an abstract method, the compiler will flag an attempt to create a new BankAccount() as an error. Of course, if the CheckingAccount subclass overrides the deductFees method and supplies an implementation, then you can create CheckingAccount objects.

> An abstract class is a class that cannot be instantiated.

A class for which you cannot create objects is called an *abstract class*. A class for which you can create objects is sometimes called a *concrete class*. In Java, you must declare all abstract classes with the keyword `abstract`:

```
public abstract class BankAccount
{
    public abstract void deductFees();
    . . .
}
```

A class that defines an abstract method, or that inherits an abstract method without overriding it, *must* be declared as abstract. You can also declare classes with no abstract methods as abstract. Doing so prevents programmers from creating instances of that class but allows them to create their own subclasses.

Note that you cannot construct an *object* of an abstract class, but you can still have an *object reference* whose type is an abstract class. Of course, the actual object to which it refers must be an instance of a concrete subclass:

```
BankAccount anAccount; // OK
anAccount = new BankAccount(); // Error—BankAccount is abstract
anAccount = new SavingsAccount(); // OK
anAccount = null; // OK
```

The reason for using abstract classes is to force programmers to create subclasses. By specifying certain methods as abstract, you avoid the trouble of coming up with useless default methods that others might inherit by accident.

Abstract classes differ from interfaces in an important way—they can have instance fields, and they can have some concrete methods.

Advanced Topic 11.2

Final Methods and Classes

In Advanced Topic 11.1 you saw how you can force other programmers to create subclasses of abstract classes and override abstract methods. Occasionally, you may want to do the opposite and *prevent* other programmers from creating subclasses or from overriding certain methods. In these situations, you use the `final` keyword. For example, the `String` class in the standard Java library has been declared as

```
public final class String { . . . }
```

That means that nobody can extend the `String` class. The reason is twofold. The compiler can generate more efficient method calls if it knows that it doesn't have to worry about late binding. Also, the `String` class is meant to be *immutable*—string objects can't be modified by any of their methods. Since the Java language does not enforce this, the class designers did. Nobody can create subclasses of `String`; therefore, you know that all `String` references can be copied without the risk of mutation.

▼   You can also declare individual methods as final:

▼
```
public class MyApplet extends Applet
{
    . . .
    public final boolean checkPassword(String password)
    {
        . . .
    }
}
```

▼

This way, nobody can override the `checkPassword` method with another method that
simply returns `true`.

11.6   Access Control

Java has four levels of controlling access to fields, methods, and classes:

- `public` access

- `private` access

- `protected` access (see Advanced Topic 11.3)

- Package access (the default, when no access modifier is given)

You have already used the `private` and `public` modifiers extensively. Private features
can be accessed only by the methods of their own class. Public features can be accessed
by methods of all classes. We will discuss protected access in
Advanced Topic 11.3—we will not need it in this book.

> A field or method that is not
> declared as `public`,
> `private`, or `protected`
> can be accessed by all classes
> in the same package, which is
> usually not desirable.

If you do not supply an access control modifier, then the default
is *package access*. That is, all methods of classes in the same package
can access the feature. For example, if a class is declared as `public`,
then all other classes in all packages can use it. But if a class is
declared without an access modifier, then only the other classes in
the same package can use it. Package access is a good default for
classes, but it is extremely unfortunate for fields. Instance and static
fields of classes should always be `private`. There are a few exceptions:

- Public constants (`public static final` fields) are useful and safe.

- Some objects, such as `System.out`, need to be accessible to all programs and
  therefore should be public.

- Very occasionally, several classes in a package must collaborate very closely. In that
  case, it may make sense to give some fields package access. But inner classes are
  usually a better solution—you will see examples in Chapter 19.

However, it is a common error to *forget* the keyword `private`, thereby opening up a potential security hole. For example, at the time of this writing, the `Window` class in the `java.awt` package contained the following declaration:

```
public class Window extends Container
{
    String warningString;
    . . .
}
```

The programmer was careless and didn't make the field private. There actually was no good reason to grant package access to the `warningString` field—*no other class accesses it.* It is a security risk. Packages are not closed entities—any programmer can make a new class, add it to the `java.awt` package, and gain access to the `warningString` fields of all `Window` objects! (Actually, this possibility bothered the Java implementors so much that recent versions of the class loader refuse to load classes whose package name starts with "java.". Your own packages, however, do not enjoy this protection.)

Package access for fields is very rarely useful, and most fields are given package access by accident because the programmer simply forgot the `private` keyword.

Methods should generally be `public` or `private`. Public methods are the norm. Private methods make sense for implementation-dependent tasks that should be carried out only by methods of the same class. Methods with package access can be called by any other method in the same package. That can occasionally make sense if a package consists of a small number of closely collaborating classes, but more often than not, it is simply an accident—the programmer forgot the `public` modifier. We recommend that you do not use package-visible methods.

Classes and interfaces can have public or package access. Classes that are generally useful should have public access. Classes that are used for implementation reasons should have package access. You can hide them even better by turning them into inner classes; you saw examples of inner classes in Chapter 9. There are a few examples of public inner classes, such as the familiar `Ellipse.Float` and `Ellipse.Double` classes. However, in general, inner classes should be private.

▼ ⊗ **Common Error**   **11.4**

Accidental Package Access

It is very easy to forget the `private` modifier for instance fields.

```
public class BankAccount
{
    . . .
    double balance; // Package access really intended?
}
```

Most likely, this was just an oversight. Probably the programmer never intended to grant access to this field to other classes in the same package. The compiler won't complain, of course. Much later, some other programmer may take advantage of the access privilege, either out of convenience or out of evil intent. This is a serious problem, and you must get into the habit of scanning your field declarations for missing `private` modifiers.

⊗ Common Error   11.5

Making Inherited Methods Less Accessible

If a superclass declares a method to be publicly accessible, you cannot override it to be more private. For example,

```
public class BankAccount
{
    public void withdraw(double amount) { . . . }
    . . .
}

public CheckingAccount
{
    private void withdraw(double amount) { . . . }
        // Error—subclass method cannot be more private
    . . .
}
```

The compiler does not allow this, because the increased privacy would be an *illusion*. Anyone can still call the method through a superclass reference:

```
BankAccount account = new CheckingAccount();
account.withdraw(100000); // calls CheckingAccount.withdraw
```

Because of late binding, the subclass method is called.

These errors are usually an oversight. If you forget the `public` modifier, your subclass method has package access, which is more restrictive. Simply restore the `public` modifier, and the error will go away.

Ⓐ Advanced Topic   11.3

Protected Access

> Protected features can be accessed by all subclasses and all classes in the same package.

We ran into some degree of grief when trying to implement the `deposit` method of the `CheckingAccount` class. That method needed access to the `balance` instance field of the superclass. Our remedy was to use the appropriate methods of the superclass to set the balance.

▼

▼

▼

▼

▼

▼

▼

▼

▼

Java offers another solution to this problem. The superclass can declare an instance field as *protected:*

```
public class BankAccount
{
   . . .
   protected double balance;
}
```

Protected data in an object can be accessed by the methods of the object's class and all its subclasses. For example, CheckingAccount inherits from BankAccount, so its methods can access the protected instance fields of the BankAccount class. Furthermore, protected data can be accessed by all methods of classes in the same package.

Some programmers like the protected access feature because it seems to strike a balance between absolute protection (making all fields private) and no protection at all (making all fields public). However, experience has shown that protected fields are subject to the same kind of problems as public fields. The designer of the superclass has no control over the authors of subclasses. Any of the subclass methods can corrupt the superclass data. Furthermore, classes with protected fields are hard to modify. Even if the author of the superclass would like to change the data implementation, the protected fields cannot be changed, because someone somewhere out there might have written a subclass whose code depends on them.

In Java, protected field have another drawback—they are accessible not just by subclasses but also by other classes in the same package.

It is best to leave all data private. If you want to grant access to the data only to subclass methods, consider making the *accessor* method protected.

11.7   Object: The Cosmic Superclass

In Java, every class that does not extend another class automatically extends the class Object. That is, the class Object is the direct or indirect superclass of *every* class in Java (see Figure 8).

Of course, the methods of the Object class are very general. Here are the most useful ones:

Method	Purpose
String toString()	Returns a string representation of the object
boolean equals(Object otherObject)	Tests whether the object equals another object
Object clone()	Makes a full copy of an object

It is a good idea for you to override these in your classes.

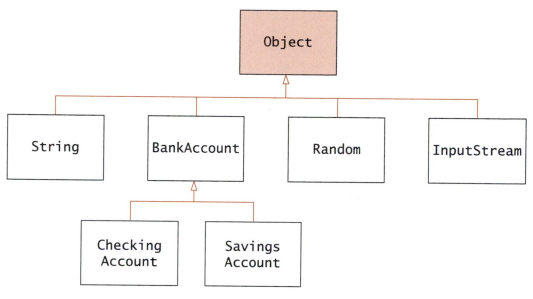

Figure 8

The Object Class Is the Superclass of Every Java Class

11.7.1 — Overriding the toString Method

> You should define the toString method to yield a string that describes the object state.

The toString method returns a string representation for each object. It is used for debugging. For example,

```
Rectangle cerealBox = new Rectangle(5, 10, 20, 30);
String s = cerealBox.toString();
/* sets s to
    "java.awt.Rectangle[x=5,y=10,width=20,height=30]"
*/
```

In fact, this toString method is called whenever you concatenate a string with an object. Consider the concatenation

```
"cerealBox=" + cerealBox;
```

On one side of the + concatenation operator is a string, but on the other side is an object reference. The Java compiler automatically invokes the toString method to turn the object into a string. Then both strings are concatenated. In this case, the result is the string

```
"cerealBox=java.awt.Rectangle[x=5,y=10,width=20,height=30]"
```

This works only if one of the objects is already a string. If you try to apply the + operator to two objects, neither of which is a string, then the compiler reports an error.

The compiler can invoke the toString method, because it knows that *every* object has a toString method: Every class extends the Object class, and that class defines toString.

As you know, numbers are also converted to strings when they are concatenated with other strings. For example,

```
int age = 18;
String s = "Harry's age is " + age;
    // sets s to "Harry's age is 18"
```

In this case, the `toString` method is not involved. Numbers are not objects, and there is no `toString` method for them. There is only a small set of primitive types, however, and the compiler knows how to convert them to strings.

Let's try the `toString` method for the `BankAccount` class:

```
BankAccount momsSavings = new BankAccount(5000);
String s = momsSavings.toString();
    // sets s to something like "BankAccount@d24606bf"
```

That's disappointing—all that's printed is the name of the class, followed by the address of the object in memory. We don't care *where* the object is in memory. We want to know what is inside the object, but, of course, the `toString` method of the `Object` class does not know what is inside our `BankAccount` class. Therefore, we have to override the method and supply our own version in the `BankAccount` class. We'll follow the same format that the `toString` method of the `Rectangle` class uses: First print the name of the class, and then the values of the instance fields inside brackets.

```
public class BankAccount
{
    . . .
    public String toString()
    {
        return "BankAccount[balance=" + balance + "]";
    }
}
```

This works better:

```
BankAccount momsSavings = new BankAccount(5000);
String s = momsSavings.toString();
    // sets s to "BankAccount[balance=5000]"
```

Productivity Hint   **11.1**

Supply `toString` in All Classes

If you have a class whose `toString()` method returns a string that describes the object state, then you can simply call `System.out.println(x)` whenever you need to inspect the current state of an object x. This works because the `println` method of the `Print-Stream` class invokes `x.toString()` when it needs to print an object. That is extremely helpful if there is an error in your program and your objects don't behave the way you think they should. You can simply insert a few print statements and peek inside the object state during the program run. Some debuggers can even invoke the `toString` method on objects that you inspect.

Sure, it is a bit more trouble to write a `toString` method when you aren't sure your program ever needs one—after all, it might just work correctly on the first try. Then again, many programs don't work on the first try. As soon as you find out that yours doesn't, consider adding those `toString` methods so that you can easily print out objects.

Advanced Topic   11.4

Inheritance and the `toString` Method

You just saw how to write a `toString` method: Form a string consisting of the class name and the names and values of the instance fields. However, if you want your `toString` method to be usable by subclasses of your class, you need to work a bit harder. Instead of hard-coding the class name, you should call the `getClass` method to obtain a *class* object, an object of the `Class` class that describes classes and their properties. Then invoke the `getName` method to get the name of the class:

```java
public String toString()
{
   return getClass().getName() + "[balance="
      + balance + "]";
}
```

Then the `toString` method prints the correct class name when you apply it to a subclass, say a SavingsAccount.

```java
SavingsAccount momsSavings = . . .;
System.out.println(momsSavings);
// prints "SavingsAccount[balance=10000]"
```

Of course, in the subclass, you should override `toString` and add the values of the subclass instance fields. Note that you must call `super.toString` to get the superclass field values—the subclass can't access them directly.

```java
public class SavingsAccount extends BankAccount
{
   public String toString()
   {
      return super.toString() +
         "[interestRate=" + interestRate + "]";
   }
}
```

Now a savings account is converted to a string such as `SavingsAccount[balance=10000][interestRate=10]`. The brackets show which fields belong to the superclass.

11.7.2 — Overriding the equals Method

> You should define the equals method to test whether two objects have equal state.

The `equals` method is called whenever you want to compare whether two objects have the same contents:

```
if (coin1.equals(coin2)) . . .
    // contents are the same—see Figure 9
```

That is different from the test with the `==` operator. That operator tests whether the two references are to the *same* object:

```
if (coin1 == coin2) . . .
    // objects are the same—see Figure 10
```

Let us implement the `equals` method for the `Coin` class. You need to override the `equals` method of the `Object` class:

```
public class Coin
{
    . . .
    public boolean equals(Object otherObject)
    {
        . . .
    }
    . . .
}
```

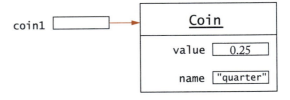

Figure 9

Two References to Equal Objects

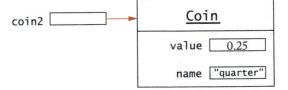

Figure 10

Two References to the Same Object

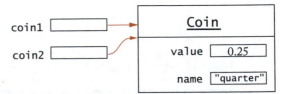

Now you have a slight problem. The `Object` class knows nothing about bank accounts, so it defines the `otherObject` parameter of the `equals` method to have the type `Object`. When redefining the method, you are not allowed to change the object signature. Cast the parameter to the class `Coin`:

```
Coin other = (Coin)otherObject;
```

Then you can compare the two coins.

```
public boolean equals(Object otherObject)
{
   Coin other = (Coin)otherObject;
   return name.equals(other.name)
      && value == other.value;
}
```

Note that you must use `equals` to compare object fields, but you use `==` to compare number fields.

▼ Ⓐⓣ Advanced Topic `11.5`

Inheritance and the `equals` Method

▼ You just saw how to write an `equals` method: Cast the `otherObject` parameter to the type of your class, and then compare the fields of the implicit parameter and the other parameter.

▼ But what if someone called `coin1.equals(x)` where `x` wasn't a `Coin` object? Then the bad cast would generate an exception, and the program would die. Therefore, you first want to test whether `otherObject` really is an instance of the `Coin` class. The easiest test would

▼ be with the `instanceof` operator. However, that test is not specific enough. It would be possible for `otherObject` to belong to some subclass of `Coin`. To rule out that possibility, you should test whether the two objects belong to the *same class*. If not, return `false`.

▼
```
if (getClass() != otherObject.getClass()) return false;
```

Moreover, the Java language specification [1] demands that the `equals` method return `false` when `otherObject` is `null`.

▼ Here is an improved version of the `equals` method that takes these two points into account:

```
public boolean equals(Object otherObject)
{
```
▼
```
   if (otherObject == null) return false;
   if (getClass() != otherObject.getClass())
      return false;

```
▼
```
   Coin other = (Coin)otherObject;
   return name.equals(other.name)
      && value == other.value;
}
```
▼ When you define `equals` in a subclass, you should first call `equals` in the superclass, like this:

▼
```
public CollectibleCoin extends Coin
{
```

```
        . . .
        public boolean equals(Object otherObject)
        {
            if (!super.equals(otherObject)) return false;

            CollectibleCoin other =
                (CollectibleCoin)otherObject;
            return year == other.year;
        }

        private int year;
}
```

11.7.3 — Overriding the clone Method

> The clone method makes a new object with the same state as an existing object.

You know that copying an object reference simply gives you two references to the same object:

```
BankAccount account1 = new BankAccount(1000);
BankAccount account2 = account1;
account2.deposit(500);
      // now both account1 and account2 have a balance of 1500
```

What can you do if you actually want to make a copy of an object? That is the purpose of the clone method. The clone method must return a *new* object that has identical state to the existing object (see Figure 11). Here is a clone method for the Bank-Account class.

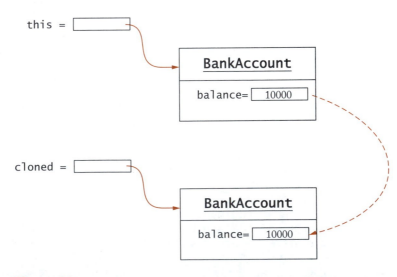

Figure 11

Cloning Objects

```
public class BankAccount
{  . . .
   public Object clone()
   {
      BankAccount cloned = new BankAccount();
      cloned.balance = balance;
      return cloned;
   }
}
```

It is more difficult to define the clone method for subclasses. See Advanced Topic 11.6 for details.

Since the clone method is defined in the Object class, it cannot know the *type* of the object to be returned. Therefore, its return type is Object. That is not a problem when implementing the clone method. But when you call the method, you must use a cast to convince the compiler that account1.clone() really has the same type as account1. Here is an example:

```
BankAccount account2 = (BankAccount)account1.clone();
```

Common Error 11.6

Forgetting to Clone

In Java, object fields contain references to objects, not actual objects. This can be convenient for giving *two names to the same object:*

```
BankAccount harrysChecking = new BankAccount();
BankAccount slushFund = harrysChecking;
   // Use Harry's checking account for the slush fund
slushFund.deposit(80000)
   // a lot of money ends up in Harry's checking account
```

However, if you don't intend two references to refer to the same object, then this is a problem. In that case, you should use the clone method:

```
BankAccount slushFund = (BankAccount)harrysChecking.clone();
```

Quality Tip 11.1

Clone Mutable Instance Fields in Accessor Methods

Consider the following class:

```
public class Customer
{
   public Customer(String aName)
```

```
    {
        name = aName;
        account = new BankAccount();
    }

    public String getName()
    {
        return name;
    }

    public BankAccount getAccount();
    {
        return account;
    }

    private String name;
    private BankAccount account;
}
```

This class looks very boring and normal, but the `getAccount` method has a curious property. It *breaks encapsulation*, because anyone can modify the object state without going through the public interface:

```
    Customer harry = new Customer("Harry Handsome");
    BankAccount account = harry.getAccount();
        // anyone can withdraw money!
    account.withdraw(100000);
```

Maybe that wasn't what the designers of the class had in mind? Maybe they wanted class users only to inspect the account? In such a situation, you should *clone* the object reference:

```
    public BankAccount getAccount();
    {
        return (BankAccount)account.clone();
    }
```

Do you also need to clone the `getName` method? No—that method returns a string, and strings are immutable. It is safe to give out a reference to an immutable object.

The rule of thumb is that a class should clone all references to mutable objects that it gives out.

Advanced Topic   11.6

Inheritance and the clone Method

You saw how to clone an object by constructing a new object with the same state:

```
    public Object clone()
    {
```

```
        BankAccount cloned = new BankAccount();
        cloned.balance = balance;
        return cloned;
    }
```

This method has an important limitation: It doesn't work for subclasses.

```
    SavingsAccount momsSavings = . . .;
    Object clonedAccount = momsSavings.clone();
```

The `clone` method constructs a new *bank account*, not a savings account!

It is better to use the `Object.clone` method to do the cloning. That method creates a new object of the same type as the original object. It also automatically copies the instance fields from the original object to the cloned object.

```
    public class BankAccount
    {  . . .
        public Object clone()
        {
            // not complete
            Object clonedAccount = super.clone();
            return clonedAccount;
        }
    }
```

However, this `Object.clone` method must be used with care. It only shifts the problem of cloning by one level; it does not completely solve it. Specifically, if an object contains a reference to another object, then the `Object.clone` method makes a copy of that object reference, not a clone of that object. Figure 12 shows how the `Object.clone` method works with a `Customer` object that has references to a `String` object and a `BankAccount` object.

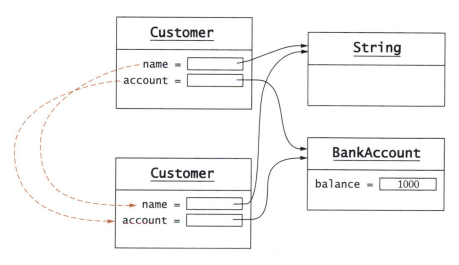

Figure 12

The `Object.clone` Method Makes a Shallow Copy

As you can see, the `Object.clone` method copies the references to the cloned `Customer` object and does not clone the objects to which they refer. Such a copy is called a *shallow copy*.

There is a reason why the `Object.clone` method does not systematically clone all subobjects. In some situations, it is unnecessary. For example, if an object contains a reference to a string, there is no harm in copying the string reference, because Java string objects can never change their contents. The `Object.clone` method does the right thing if an object contains only numbers, Boolean values, and strings. But it must be used with caution when an object contains references to other objects.

For that reason, there are two safeguards built into the `Object.clone` method to ensure that it is not used accidentally. First, the method is declared `protected` (see Advanced Topic 11.3). This prevents you from accidentally calling `x.clone()` if the class to which x belongs hasn't redefined `clone` to be public.

As a second precaution, `Object.clone` checks that the object being cloned implements the `Cloneable` interface. If not, it throws an exception. That is, the `Object.clone` method looks like this:

```
public class Object
{
   protected Object clone()
      throws CloneNotSupportedException
   {
      if (this instanceof Cloneable)
      {
         // copy the instance fields
         . . .
      }
      else
         throw new CloneNotSupportedException();
   }
}
```

Unfortunately, all that safeguarding means that the legitimate callers of `Object.clone()` pay a price—they must catch that exception *even if their class implements* `Cloneable`.

```
public class BankAccount implements Cloneable
{
   . . .
   public Object clone()
   {
      try
      {
         return super.clone();;
      }
      catch (CloneNotSupportedException e)
      {
         // can't happen because we implement Cloneable
         // but we still must catch it
         return null;
      }
```

```
            }
        }
```

If an object contains a reference to another mutable object, then you need to call `clone` for that reference. For example, suppose the `Customer` class has an instance field of class `BankAccount`. Then you can implement `Customer.clone` as follows:

```
public class Customer implements Cloneable
{
    . . .
    public Object clone()
    {
        try
        {
            Customer cloned = (Customer)super.clone();
            cloned.account = (BankAccount)account.clone();
            return cloned;
        }
        catch(CloneNotSupportedException e)
        {
            // can't ever happen because we implement Cloneable
            return null;
        }
    }

    private String name;
    private BankAccount account;
}
```

Random Fact   11.1

Scripting Languages

Suppose you work for an office where you have to help with the bookkeeping. Suppose that every sales person sends in a weekly spreadsheet with sales figures. One of your jobs is to copy and paste the individual figures into a master spreadsheet and then copy and paste the totals into a word processor document that gets emailed to several managers. This kind of repetitive work can be intensely boring. Can you automate it?

It would be a real challenge to write a Java program that can help you—you'd have to know how to read a spreadsheet file, how to format a word processor document, and how to send email.

Fortunately, many office software packages nowadays include *scripting languages*. These are programming languages that are integrated with the software for the purpose of automating repetitive tasks. The best-known of these scripting languages is Visual Basic Script, which is a part of the Microsoft Office suite. The Macintosh operating system has a language called AppleScript for the same purpose.

In addition, scripting languages are available for many other purposes. JavaScript is used for web pages. (There is no relationship between Java and JavaScript—the name JavaScript was chosen for marketing reasons.) Tcl (short for "tool control language" and pronounced "tickle") is an open source scripting language that has been ported to many platforms and is often used for scripting software test procedures. Productivity Hint 8.1 has more information about shell scripts.

Scripting languages have two features that makes them easier to use than full-fledged programming languages such as Java. First, they are *interpreted*. The interpreter program reads each line of program code and executes it immediately without compiling it first. That makes experimenting much more fun—you get immediate feedback. Also, scripting languages are usually *loosely typed*. That means, you don't have to declare the types of variables. Every variable can hold values of any type. For example, Figure 13 shows a scripting session with BeanShell, a scripting language for Java objects. The script stores frame and button objects in variables that are declared just by using them. It then sets a couple of properties and calls methods that are executed immediately—the frame pops up as soon as the line with the show command is typed. (You can download BeanShell from http://www.beanshell.org.)

In recent years, authors of computer viruses have discovered how scripting languages simplify their life. The famous "love bug" is a Visual Basic Script program that is sent as an attachment to an email. The email has an enticing subject line "I love you" and asks the recipient to click on an attachment masquerading as a love letter. In fact, the attachment is a script file that is executed when the user clicks on it. The script creates some damage on the recipient's computer and then, through the power of the scripting language, uses the Outlook email client to mail itself to all addresses found in the address book. Try programming that in Java! By the way, the person suspected of

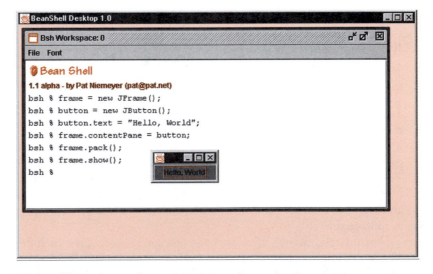

Figure 13

Writing a BeanShell Script

▼ authoring that virus was a student who had submitted a proposal to write a thesis researching how to write such programs. Perhaps not surprisingly, the proposal was rejected by the faculty.

▼ Why do we still need Java if scripting is easy and fun? Scripts often have poor error checking and are difficult to adapt to new circumstances. Scripting languages lack many of the structuring and safety mechanisms (such as classes and type checking by the compiler) that are important for building robust and scalable programs.

CHAPTER SUMMARY

1. Inheritance is a method for extending existing classes by adding methods and fields.

2. The more general class is called a superclass. The more specialized class that inherits from the superclass is called the subclass.

3. Every class extends the `Object` class either directly or indirectly.

4. Inheriting from a class differs from realizing an interface: The subclass inherits behavior and state from the superclass.

5. One advantage of inheritance is code reuse.

6. When defining a subclass, you specify added instance fields, added methods, and changed or *overridden* methods.

7. Sets of classes can form complex inheritance hierarchies.

8. A subclass has no access to private fields of its superclass.

9. Use the `super` keyword to call a method of the superclass.

10. To call the superclass constructor, you use the `super` keyword in the first statement of the subclass constructor.

11. Subclass references can be converted to superclass references.

12. An abstract method is a method whose implementation is not specified.

13. An abstract class is a class that cannot be instantiated.

14. A field or method that is not declared as `public`, `private`, or `protected` can be accessed by all classes in the same package, which is usually not desirable.

15. Protected features can be accessed by all subclasses and all classes in the same package.

16. You should define the `toString` method to yield a string that describes the object state.

17. You should define the `equals` method to test whether two objects have equal state.

18. The `clone` method makes a new object with the same state as an existing object.

Further Reading

[1] James Gosling, Bill Joy, and Guy Steele, *The Java Language Specification*, Addison-Wesley, 1996.

CLASSES, OBJECTS, AND METHODS INTRODUCED IN THIS CHAPTER

```
java.lang.Cloneable
java.lang.Comparable
    compareTo
java.lang.Object
    clone
    toString
```

REVIEW EXERCISES

Exercise R11.1. What is the balance of b after the following operations?

```
SavingsAccount b = new SavingsAccount(10);
b.deposit(5000);
b.withdraw(b.getBalance() / 2);
b.addInterest();
```

Exercise R11.2. Describe all constructors of the SavingsAccount class. List all methods that are inherited from the BankAccount class. List all methods that are added to the SavingsAccount class.

Exercise R11.3. Can you convert a superclass reference into a subclass reference? A subclass reference into a superclass reference? If so, give an example. If not, explain why.

Exercise R11.4. In the following pairs of classes, identify the superclass and the subclass:

- Employee, Manager
- Polygon, Triangle
- GraduateStudent, Student
- Person, Student
- Employee, GraduateStudent
- BankAccount, CheckingAccount
- Vehicle, Car
- Vehicle, Minivan
- Car, Minivan
- Truck, Vehicle

Exercise R11.5. Suppose the class Sub extends the class Sandwich. Which of the following assignments are legal?

```
Sandwich x = new Sandwich();
Sub y = new Sub();
x = y;
y = x;
y = new Sandwich();
x = new Sub();
```

Exercise R11.6. Draw an inheritance diagram that shows the inheritance relationships between the classes

- `Person`
- `Employee`
- `Student`
- `Instructor`
- `Classroom`
- `Object`

Exercise R11.7. In an object-oriented traffic simulation system, we have the following classes:

- `Vehicle`
- `Car`
- `Truck`
- `Sedan`
- `Coupe`
- `PickupTruck`
- `SportUtilityVehicle`
- `Minivan`
- `Bicycle`
- `Motorcycle`

Draw an inheritance diagram that shows the relationships between these classes.

Exercise R11.8. What inheritance relationships would you establish among the following classes?

- `Student`
- `Professor`
- `TeachingAssistant`
- `Employee`
- `Secretary`
- `DepartmentChair`
- `Janitor`
- `SeminarSpeaker`
- `Person`
- `Course`
- `Seminar`
- `Lecture`
- `ComputerLab`

Exercise R11.9. Which of these conditions returns `true`? Check the Java documentation for the inheritance patterns.

```
Rectangle r = new Rectangle(5, 10, 20, 30);
if (r instanceof Rectangle) . . .
if (r instanceof Point) . . .
if (r instanceof Rectangle2D.Double) . . .
if (r instanceof RectangularShape) . . .
if (r instanceof Object) . . .
if (r instanceof Shape) . . .
```

Exercise R11.10. Explain the two meanings of the `super` keyword. Explain the two meanings of the `this` keyword. How are they related?

Exercise R11.11. (Tricky.) Consider the two calls

```
public class D extends B
{
   public void f()
   {
      this.g(); // 1
   }
   public void g()
   {
      super.g(); // 2
   }
   . . .
}
```

Which of them is an example of early binding? Which of them is an example of late binding?

Exercise R11.12. Consider this program:

```
public class AccountTest
{
   public static void main(String[] args)
   {
      SavingsAccount momsSavings
         = new SavingsAccount(0.5);

      CheckingAccount harrysChecking
         = new CheckingAccount(0);

      . . .
      endOfMonth(momsSavings);
      endOfMonth(harrysChecking);
      printBalance(momsSavings);
      printBalance(harrysChecking);
   }

   public static void endOfMonth(SavingsAccount savings)
   {
      savings.addInterest();
   }

   public static void endOfMonth(CheckingAccount checking)
   {
      checking.deductFees();
   }

   public static void printBalance(BankAccount account)
   {
      System.out.println("The balance is $"
         + account.getBalance());
   }
}
```

Are the calls to the endOfMonth methods resolved by early binding or late binding? Inside the printBalance method, is the call to getBalance resolved by early binding or late binding?

Exercise R11.13. Explain the terms *shallow copy* and *deep copy*.

Exercise R11.14. What access attribute should instance fields have? What access attribute should static fields have? How about static final fields?

Exercise R11.15. What access attribute should instance methods have? Does the same hold for static methods?

Exercise R11.16. The fields System.in and System.out are static public fields. Is it possible to overwrite them? If so, how?

Exercise R11.17. Why are public fields dangerous? Are public static fields more dangerous than public instance fields?

PROGRAMMING EXERCISES

Exercise P11.1. Enhance the addInterest method of the SavingsAccount class to compute the interest on the *minimum* balance since the last call to addInterest. *Hint:* You need to modify the withdraw method as well, and you need to add an instance field to remember the minimum balance.

Exercise P11.2. Add a TimeDepositAccount class to the bank account hierarchy. The time deposit account is just like a savings account, but you promise to leave the money in the account for a particular number of months, and there is a penalty for early withdrawal. Construct the account with the interest rate and the number of months to maturity. In the addInterest method, decrement the count of months. If the count is positive during a withdrawal, charge the withdrawal penalty.

Exercise P11.3. Implement a subclass Square that extends the Rectangle class. In the constructor, accept the *x*- and *y*-positions of the *center* and the side length of the square. Call the setLocation and setSize methods of the Rectangle class. Look up these methods in the documentation for the Rectangle class. Also supply a method getArea that computes and returns the area of the square. Write a sample program that asks for the center and side length, then prints out the square (using the toString method that you inherit from Rectangle) and the area of the square.

Exercise P11.4. Implement a superclass Person. Make two classes, Student and Instructor, inherit from Person. A person has a name and a year of birth. A student has a major, and an instructor has a salary. Write the class definitions, the constructors, and the methods toString for all classes. Supply a test program that tests these classes and methods.

Exercise P11.5. Make a class Employee with a name and salary. Make a class Manager inherit from Employee. Add an instance field, named department, of type String.

Supply a method `toString` that prints the manager's name, department, and salary. Make a class `Executive` inherit from `Manager`. Supply appropriate `toString` methods for all classes. Supply a test program that tests these classes and methods.

Exercise P11.6. Write a superclass `Worker` and subclasses `HourlyWorker` and `Salaried-Worker`. Every worker has a name and a salary rate. Write a method `computePay(int hours)` that computes the weekly pay for every worker. An hourly worker gets paid the hourly wage for the actual number of hours worked, if `hours` is at most 40. If the hourly worker worked more than 40 hours, the excess is paid at time and a half. The salaried worker gets paid the hourly wage for 40 hours, no matter what the actual number of hours is. Supply a test program that uses polymorphism to test these classes and methods.

Exercise P11.7. Implement a superclass `Vehicle` and subclasses `Car` and `Truck`. A vehicle has a position on the screen. Write methods `draw` that draw cars and trucks as follows:

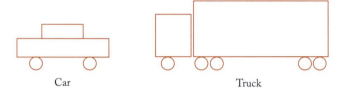

Car　　　　　　　　　　　　Truck

Then write a method `randomVehicle` that randomly generates `Vehicle` references, with an equal probability for constructing cars and trucks, with random positions. Call it 10 times and draw all of them.

Exercise P11.8. Implement the `toString`, `equals`, and `clone` methods for all three bank account classes used in this chapter.

Exercise P11.9. Implement the `toString`, `equals`, and `clone` methods for the `Coin` and `Purse` classes introduced in Chapter 3.

Exercise P11.10. Reorganize the bank account classes as follows. In the `BankAccount` class, introduce an abstract method `endOfMonth` with no implementation. Rename the `addInterest` and `deductFees` methods into `endOfMonth` in the subclasses. Which classes are now abstract and which are concrete? Write a static method `void test(BankAccount account)` that makes five random transactions, prints out the balance after each of them, and then calls `endOfMonth` and prints the balance once again. Test it with instances of all concrete account classes.

12

Graphical User Interfaces

To use inheritance to customize panels and frames

▶ To understand how user interface components are added to a container

▶ To understand the use of layout managers to arrange user interface components in a container

▶ To become familiar with common user interface components such as buttons, text components, combo boxes, and menus

▶ To build programs that handle events from user interface components

▶ To learn how to browse the Java documentation

U p to now, your graphical programs received user input from an option dialog or a mouse. The graphical applications with which you are familiar, on the other hand, have a large number of visual gadgets for information entry: buttons, scroll bars, menus, and so on. In this chapter, you will learn how to use the most common user interface components in the Java Swing user interface toolkit. However, Swing has many more components than you can master in a first course, and even the basic components have many advanced options that we cannot cover here. In fact, few programmers ever try to learn everything about a particular user interface component. It is much better to understand the concepts and to search the Java documentation for the details. This chapter walks you through one example to show you how the Java documentation is organized and how you can rely on it for your own programming.

12.1 Using Inheritance to Customize Panels

In Chapter 10 you saw how to implement applications that show results in a text area. However, those applications were not able to produce any graphical output. In this section, you will learn how to add graphics to a Java application.

Recall how you produce graphics in an applet. You extend the `Applet` class and override the `paint` method:

```
public class MyApplet extends Applet
{
    public void paint(Graphics g)
    {
        // your drawing instructions go here
        . . .
    }
    . . .
}
```

This approach does not work for frames, however. You should not directly draw onto the surface of a frame. Frames have been designed to arrange *user interface components* such as buttons, menus, and scroll bars. Drawing directly on the frame interferes with the display of the user interface components. If you want to show graphics in a frame, you draw the graphics onto a `JPanel` and add it to the frame. A `JPanel` is completely blank, and you can draw onto it what you like.

> You can draw graphical shapes on a panel by overriding the `paintComponent` method of a `JPanel` subclass.

Drawing on a panel is a bit different from drawing on an applet. You override the `paintComponent` method. There is a second important difference. When implementing your own `paintComponent` method, you *must* call the `paintComponent` method of the superclass. This gives the superclass method a chance to erase the old contents of the panel.

Here is an outline of the `paintComponent` method:

```
public class MyPanel extends JPanel
{
    public void paintComponent(Graphics g)
    {
```

```
      super.paintComponent(g);
      Graphics2D g2 = (Graphics2D)g;

      // your drawing instructions go here
         . . .
   }
}
```

Once you have called `super.paintComponent` and obtained a `Graphics2D` object, you are ready to draw graphical shapes in the usual way.

By default, panels have a size of 0 by 0 pixels. Therefore, a panel should set its *preferred size* in its constructor, like this:

```
public class MyPanel
{
   public MyPanel()
   {
      setPreferredSize(
         new Dimension(PANEL_WIDTH, PANEL_HEIGHT));
         . . .
   }
      . . .
   private static final int PANEL_WIDTH = 300;
   private static final int PANEL_HEIGHT = 300;
}
```

Recall the `MouseApplet` program from Chapter 10. That applet draws a rectangle at the position of a mouse click. Let us turn the applet into an application.

We need a panel to do the drawing. In the constructor, we set the preferred size and add a mouse listener.

```
public class RectanglePanel extends JPanel
{
   public RectanglePanel()
   {
      setPreferredSize(
         new Dimension(PANEL_WIDTH, PANEL_HEIGHT));

      // add mouse press listener
         . . .
   }

   public void paintComponent(Graphics g)
   {
      super.paintComponent(g);
      Graphics2D g2 = (Graphics2D)g;
         . . .
   }

      . . .
}
```

> A panel class that paints a drawing on the panel should store all data that it needs to repaint itself.

When implementing a panel such as the `RectanglePanel`, you need to think about minimizing the interrelationship between the component and the rest of your program. If you store information in the wrong place, you keep handing it back and forth all the time. A good rule of thumb is: *A panel should store the data that it needs to repaint itself.* In our case, the information is simple—just a rectangle. For more complex drawings, the panel needs to store the collection of all elements that are needed for recreating the drawing.

```java
public class RectanglePanel extends JPanel
{
    public RectanglePanel()
    {
        // the rectangle that the paint method draws
        box = new Rectangle(. . .);
        . . .
    }

    public void paintComponent(Graphics g)
    {
        super.paintComponent(g);
        Graphics2D g2 = (Graphics2D)g;
        g2.draw(box);
    }

    private Rectangle box;
    . . .
}
```

You will find the code for the complete class at the end of this section.

Now you need a second class to launch an application that displays this panel in a frame:

File RectangleTest.java

```java
 1  import javax.swing.JButton;
 2  import javax.swing.JFrame;
 3  import javax.swing.JLabel;
 4  import javax.swing.JPanel;
 5  import javax.swing.JTextField;
 6
 7  /**
 8      This program displays a frame containing a RectanglePanel.
 9  */
10  public class RectangleTest
11  {
12      public static void main(String[] args)
13      {
14          RectanglePanel rectPanel =
15              new RectanglePanel();
```

```
16
17          JFrame appFrame = new JFrame();
18          appFrame.setDefaultCloseOperation(
19             JFrame.EXIT_ON_CLOSE);
20          appFrame.setContentPane(rectPanel);
21          appFrame.pack();
22          appFrame.show();
23       }
24    }
```

Figure 1 shows the layout of the application. Figure 2 shows the relationships between the classes.

The result is a program that acts exactly like the MouseApplet. Because this is an application, you don't need to use the applet viewer, and you don't need to produce an HTML file.

File RectanglePanel.java

```
1  import java.awt.event.MouseEvent;
2  import java.awt.event.MouseListener;
3  import java.awt.Dimension;
4  import java.awt.Graphics;
5  import java.awt.Graphics2D;
6  import java.awt.Rectangle;
7  import javax.swing.JPanel;
8
```

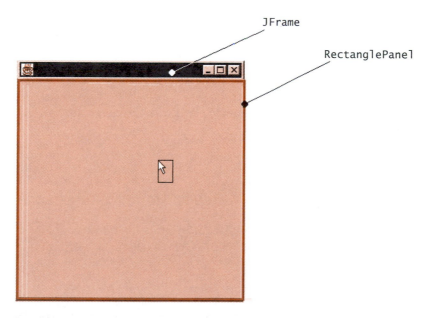

Figure 1

The Layout of the RectangleTest Application

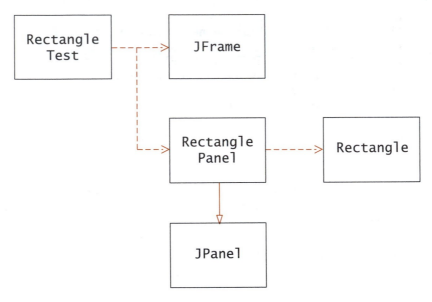

Figure 2

The Classes Used in the RectangleTest Application

```
 9  /**
10      A rectangle panel displays a rectangle that a user can
11      move by clicking the mouse.
12  */
13  public class RectanglePanel extends JPanel
14  {
15      /**
16          Constructs a rectangle panel with the rectangle at a
17          default location.
18      */
19      public RectanglePanel()
20      {
21          setPreferredSize(
22              new Dimension(PANEL_WIDTH, PANEL_HEIGHT));
23
24          // the rectangle that the paint method draws
25          box = new Rectangle(BOX_X, BOX_Y,
26              BOX_WIDTH, BOX_HEIGHT);
27
28          // add mouse press listener
29
30          class MousePressListener implements MouseListener
31          {
32              public void mousePressed(MouseEvent event)
```

```
33                {
34                    int x = event.getX();
35                    int y = event.getY();
36                    box.setLocation(x, y);
37                    repaint();
38                }
39
40                // do-nothing methods
41                public void mouseReleased(MouseEvent event) {}
42                public void mouseClicked(MouseEvent event) {}
43                public void mouseEntered(MouseEvent event) {}
44                public void mouseExited(MouseEvent event) {}
45            }
46
47        MouseListener listener = new MousePressListener();
48        addMouseListener(listener);
49    }
50
51    public void paintComponent(Graphics g)
52    {
53        super.paintComponent(g);
54        Graphics2D g2 = (Graphics2D)g;
55        g2.draw(box);
56    }
57
58    private Rectangle box;
59    private static final int BOX_X = 100;
60    private static final int BOX_Y = 100;
61    private static final int BOX_WIDTH = 20;
62    private static final int BOX_HEIGHT = 30;
63
64    private static final int PANEL_WIDTH = 300;
65    private static final int PANEL_HEIGHT = 300;
66 }
```

▼ ⊗ **Common Error**   ▶ 12.1

Overriding the paint Method of a Panel

When you implement an applet, you need to override the paint method. To draw on a panel, on the other hand, you override paintComponent. But panels also have a paint method for internal use by the Swing library. If you accidentally override that paint method, then painting of the panel will be erratic.

⊗ Common Error 12.2

Forgetting to Call the `paintComponent` Method of the Superclass

The `paintComponent` method of every subclass of a Swing component must call `super.paintComponent` in order to give the superclass `paintComponent` method a chance to draw the background, draw borders and decorations, and set the attributes of the `Graphics` object. If you forget to call `super.paintComponent`, then the background may not be erased, or your drawing instructions may show up in the wrong position.

12.2 Layout Management

> You arrange user interface components by placing them inside containers. Containers can be placed inside larger containers.

> Each container has a *layout manager* that directs the arrangement of its components.

> Three useful layout managers are the border layout, flow layout, and grid layout.

> When adding a component to a container with the border layout, specify NORTH, EAST, SOUTH, WEST, or CENTER position.

Up to now, we have simply added user interface components such as buttons and text fields into a container, such as a panel. The panel arranges the components from the left to the right. However, in many applications, you need to stack some of the components top to bottom, or have some other arrangement.

In Java, you build up user interfaces by adding components into containers such as panels. Each container has its own *layout manager*, which determines how the components are laid out.

By default, a `JPanel` uses a *flow layout*. A flow layout simply arranges its components from left to right and starts a new row when there is no more room in the current row.

Another commonly used layout manager is the *border layout*. The border layout groups the container into five areas: center, north, west, south, and east (see Figure 3). You don't usually fill all five areas at the same time.

You can set the layout manager of a panel to a border layout:

```
panel.setLayout(new BorderLayout());
```

When you add a component to a container with a border layout, you must specify the position, like this:

```
panel.add(label, BorderLayout.CENTER);
```

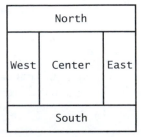

Figure 3

Border Layout Areas

> The content pane of a frame or applet has a border layout by default. A panel has a flow layout by default.

Instead of using a panel and setting its layout manager to a border layout, you can also use the default content pane of a frame—it already uses a border layout. You retrieve it with the `getContent-Pane` method:

```
frame.getContentPane().add(label, BorderLayout.CENTER);
```

> With the flow layout, the individual components stay at their preferred size. The border layout and grid layout grow components to fill the area allotted for them.

There is one important difference between the border layout and the flow layout. The border layout expands each component to fill all available space in its area. For example, Figure 4 shows how a button looks when it is placed in the South area of a border layout. In contrast, the flow layout leaves each component at its *preferred* size. That is why the buttons inside a panel stay at their natural size. Therefore, even if you have a single button, if you want to protect it from being resized, place it inside a new panel.

The *grid layout* is a third layout that is sometimes useful. The grid layout arranges components in a grid with a fixed number of rows and columns, resizing each of the components so that they all have the same size. Like the border layout, it also expands each component to fill the entire allotted area. (If that is not desirable, you need to place each component inside a panel, as described previously.) Figure 5 shows a number pad panel that uses a grid layout. To create a grid layout, you supply the number of rows and columns in the constructor. Then you add the components, row by row, left to right:

```
JPanel numberPanel = new JPanel();
numberPanel.setLayout(new GridLayout(4, 3));
numberPanel.add(button7);
numberPanel.add(button8);
numberPanel.add(button9);
numberPanel.add(button4);
. . .
```

Figure 4

Components Expanded to Fill Space in Border Layout

Figure 5

The Grid Layout

Sometimes you want to have a tabular arrangement of the components where columns have different sizes or one component spans multiple columns. A more complex layout manager called the grid bag layout can handle these situations. The grid bag layout is quite complex to use, however, and we do not cover it in this book; see, for example, [1] for more information. Using the border layout, flow layout, and grid layout, along with panels, you can create acceptable-looking layouts in nearly all situations (see, for example, Figure 6). The borders around the panels don't show up in the

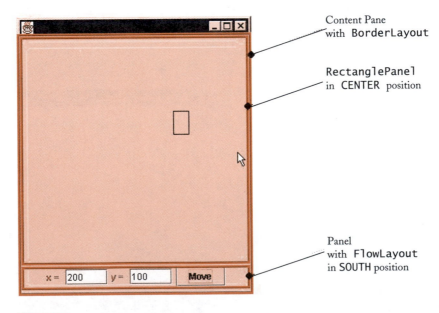

Content Pane
with `BorderLayout`

RectanglePanel
in `CENTER` position

Panel
with `FlowLayout`
in `SOUTH` position

Figure 6

Combining Layout Managers

actual frame window—they are just added to the figure to show you the extent of the containers.

If you want more control over component layout, you can check out the grid bag layout, or you can use a development environment with a layout tool that lets you place the components visually and then generates the appropriate Java code.

12.3   Using Inheritance to Customize Frames

> Define a JFrame subclass for a complex frame.

As you add more user interface components to a frame, the frame can get quite complex. You should use inheritance for a frame that contains multiple components. Here is a typical example. Let's add a control panel to set the position of a rectangle in a frame, such as in Figure 6.

Design a subclass of JFrame and add the user interface components in the constructor. If a set of user interface components gets complex, then write a separate method for building up that set. In our example, we have a separate method to build the control panel at the bottom of the frame.

```java
public class RectangleFrame extends JFrame
{
   public RectangleFrame()
   {
      // the panel that draws the rectangle
      rectPanel = new RectanglePanel();
      getContentPane().add(
         rectPanel, BorderLayout.CENTER);

      createControlPanel();

      pack();
   }

   private void createControlPanel()
   {
      // the text fields for entering the x- and y-coordinates
      final JTextField xField = new JTextField(5);
      final JTextField yField = new JTextField(5);;

      class MoveButtonListener implements ActionListener
      {
         public void actionPerformed(ActionEvent event)
         {
            int x = Integer.parseInt(xField.getText());
            int y = Integer.parseInt(yField.getText());
            rectPanel.setLocation(x, y);
         }
      };

      // create button and attach listener
```

```
      . . .

      // the panel for holding the user interface components
      JPanel controlPanel = new JPanel();

      // add components to control panel
      . . .
      getContentPane().add(
         controlPanel, BorderLayout.SOUTH);
   }

   private RectanglePanel rectPanel;
}
```

Turn any components that must be shared among these methods into instance variables of the class. For example, the rectPanel is needed both in the RectangleFrame constructor and the createControlPanel method.

Now you need a separate program class to display the frame:

```
public class RectangleTest
{
   public static void main(String[] args)
   {
      JFrame appFrame = new RectangleFrame();
      appFrame.setDefaultCloseOperation(
         JFrame.EXIT_ON_CLOSE);
      appFrame.show();
   }
}
```

There is an added complexity. The action listener of the "Move" button has no direct access to the rectangle inside the RectanglePanel. Therefore, you need to add a method to the RectanglePanel that allows others to set the rectangle location.

```
public class RectanglePanel extends JPanel
{
   public RectanglePanel()
   {
      . . .
      box = new Rectangle(. . .);
   }

   public void setLocation(int x, int y)
   {
      box.setLocation(x, y);
      repaint();
   }

   public void paintComponent(Graphics g)
   {
      super.paintComponent(g);
```

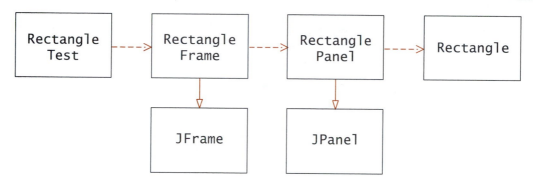

Figure 7

Classes in the Rectangle Frame Application

```
        Graphics2D g2 = (Graphics2D)g;
        g2.draw(box);
    }

    private Rectangle box;
}
```

This is very typical for a panel that displays graphics. Generally, the graphics changes through some external event. The panel class needs to supply methods to change the graphics state. These methods should apply the appropriate settings and then call repaint to trigger a redisplay of the drawing.

Figure 7 shows the classes of this application.

File RectangleTest.java

```
1  import javax.swing.JFrame;
2
3  /**
4      This program tests the RectangleFrame.
5  */
6  public class RectangleTest
7  {
8     public static void main(String[] args)
9     {
10       JFrame appFrame = new RectangleFrame();
11       appFrame.setDefaultCloseOperation(
12          JFrame.EXIT_ON_CLOSE);
13       appFrame.show();
14    }
15  }
```

File RectangleFrame.java

```
1  import java.awt.BorderLayout;
2  import java.awt.event.ActionEvent;
```

```
 3  import java.awt.event.ActionListener;
 4  import javax.swing.JButton;
 5  import javax.swing.JFrame;
 6  import javax.swing.JLabel;
 7  import javax.swing.JPanel;
 8  import javax.swing.JTextField;
 9
10  /**
11     This frame contains a panel that displays a rectangle
12     and a panel of text fields to specify the rectangle position.
13  */
14  public class RectangleFrame extends JFrame
15  {
16     /**
17        Constructs the frame.
18     */
19     public RectangleFrame()
20     {
21        // the panel that draws the rectangle
22        rectPanel = new RectanglePanel();
23
24        // add panel to content pane
25        getContentPane().add(
26           rectPanel, BorderLayout.CENTER);
27
28        createControlPanel();
29
30        pack();
31     }
32
33     /**
34        Creates the control panel with the text fields
35        at the bottom of the frame.
36     */
37     private void createControlPanel()
38     {
39        // the text fields for entering the x- and y-coordinates
40        final JTextField xField = new JTextField(5);
41        final JTextField yField = new JTextField(5);;
42
43        // the button to move the rectangle
44        JButton moveButton = new JButton("Move");
45
46        class MoveButtonListener implements ActionListener
47        {
48           public void actionPerformed(ActionEvent event)
49           {
50              int x = Integer.parseInt(xField.getText());
51              int y = Integer.parseInt(yField.getText());
52              rectPanel.setLocation(x, y);
```

```
53              }
54          };
55
56          ActionListener listener = new MoveButtonListener();
57          moveButton.addActionListener(listener);
58
59          // the labels for labeling the text fields
60          JLabel xLabel = new JLabel("x = ");
61          JLabel yLabel = new JLabel("y = ");
62
63          // the panel for holding the user interface components
64          JPanel controlPanel = new JPanel();
65
66          controlPanel.add(xLabel);
67          controlPanel.add(xField);
68          controlPanel.add(yLabel);
69          controlPanel.add(yField);
70          controlPanel.add(moveButton);
71
72          getContentPane().add(
73              controlPanel, BorderLayout.SOUTH);
74      }
75
76      private RectanglePanel rectPanel;
77 }
```

File RectanglePanel.java

```
1  import java.awt.Dimension;
2  import java.awt.Graphics;
3  import java.awt.Graphics2D;
4  import java.awt.Rectangle;
5  import javax.swing.JPanel;
6
7  /**
8      This panel displays a rectangle.
9  */
10 public class RectanglePanel extends JPanel
11 {
12      /**
13          Constructs a rectangle panel with the rectangle at a
14          default location.
15      */
16      public RectanglePanel()
17      {
18          setPreferredSize(
19              new Dimension(PANEL_WIDTH, PANEL_HEIGHT));
20          // the rectangle that the paint method draws
21          box = new Rectangle(BOX_X, BOX_Y,
22              BOX_WIDTH, BOX_HEIGHT);
```

```
23      }
24
25      /**
26         Sets the location of the rectangle and repaints the panel
27         @param x the x-coordinate of the top left corner of the rectangle
28         @param y the y-coordinate of the top left corner of the rectangle
29      */
30      public void setLocation(int x, int y)
31      {
32         box.setLocation(x, y);
33         repaint();
34      }
35
36      public void paintComponent(Graphics g)
37      {
38         super.paintComponent(g);
39         Graphics2D g2 = (Graphics2D)g;
40         g2.draw(box);
41      }
42
43      private Rectangle box;
44      private static final int BOX_X = 100;
45      private static final int BOX_Y = 100;
46      private static final int BOX_WIDTH = 20;
47      private static final int BOX_HEIGHT = 30;
48
49      private static final int PANEL_WIDTH = 300;
50      private static final int PANEL_HEIGHT = 300;
51   }
```

▼ AT Advanced Topic 12.1

Adding the main Method to the Frame Class

Have another look at the RectangleTest program. We have two classes: RectangleTest, a class with only a main method that constructs and shows the frame, and
the class RectangleFrame, which contains the frame's constructor, helper methods, and
instance variables. Some programmers prefer to combine these two classes, simply by
adding the main method to the frame class:

```
public class RectangleFrame extends JFrame
{
   public static void main(String[] args)
   {
      JFrame appFrame = new RectangleFrame();
      appFrame.setDefaultCloseOperation(
         JFrame.EXIT_ON_CLOSE);
      appFrame.show();
```

```
        }

        public RectangleFrame()
        {
            . . .
        }
            . . .
    }
```

This is a convenient shortcut that you will find in many programs, but it does muddle the responsibilities between the frame class and the program. Therefore, we do not use this approach in this book.

Advanced Topic 12.2

Converting a Frame to an Applet

If you enjoyed placing your applets onto a web page, then you will want to know how to convert a graphical application into an applet. The `javax.swing` package supplies a class `JApplet` that is very similar to a `JFrame`. Unlike a plain `Applet`, a `JApplet` also has a content pane whose default is the border layout. Therefore, laying out components in a `JApplet` works exactly the same as for a `JFrame`.

Thus, there are only a few steps to convert from a frame to an applet:

1. Drop the class with the `main` method that shows the frame.
2. Inherit from `JApplet`, not `JFrame`.
3. Remove any calls to `setSize`. You need to set the size in the applet's HTML page.
4. Remove any calls to `setTitle`. If you want to show a title, supply it in HTML around the applet tag.

Keep in mind that the visitors to your web site need a Java 2-enabled browser such as Netscape 6 or Opera. Older browsers cannot display Java 2 applets.

12.4 Choices

12.4.1 Radio Buttons

> For a small set of mutually exclusive choices, use a group of radio buttons or a combo box.

In this section you will see how to present a finite set of choices to the user. If the choices are mutually exclusive, you use a set of *radio buttons*. In a radio button set, only one button can be selected at one time. When the user selects another button in the same set, the previously selected button is automatically turned off. (These buttons are called radio buttons because they work like the station selector buttons on a car radio: If you select a new station, the old station is automatically deselected.) For example, in Figure 8, the font sizes are mutually exclusive. You can select small, medium, or large, but not a combination of them.

Figure 8

A Combo Box, Check Boxes, and Radio Buttons

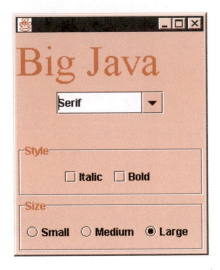

> Add radio buttons into a ButtonGroup so that only one button in the group is on at any time.

To create a set of radio buttons, you first create each button individually, and then you add all buttons of the set to a `ButtonGroup` object:

```
JRadioButton smallButton = new JRadioButton("Small");
JRadioButton mediumButton = new JRadioButton("Medium");
JRadioButton largeButton = new JRadioButton("Large");

ButtonGroup group = new ButtonGroup();
group.add(smallButton);
group.add(mediumButton);
group.add(largeButton);
```

Note that the button group does *not* place the buttons close to each other on the container. The purpose of the button group is simply to find out which buttons to turn off when one of them is turned on. It is still your job to arrange the buttons on the screen.

Your program can turn a button on or off, without the user clicking on it, by calling the `setSelected` method. If you have a reference to a button, you can call the `isSelected` method to find out whether the button is currently selected or not. For example,

```
if (largeButton.isSelected()) size = LARGE_SIZE;
```

> You can place a border around a panel to group its contents visually.

You should call `setSelected(true)` on one of the radio buttons in each radio button group before showing the container.

If you have multiple button groups in a container, it is a good idea to group them together visually. You probably use panels to build up your user interface, but the panels themselves are invisible. You can add a border to a panel to make it visible. In Figure 8, for example; the panels containing the Size radio buttons and Style check boxes have borders.

There are a large number of border types. We will show only one variation and leave it to the border enthusiasts to look up the others in the Swing documentation. The `EtchedBorder` class yields a border with a 3-D "etched" effect. You can add a border to any component, but most commonly you apply it to a panel:

```
JPanel panel = new JPanel();
panel.setBorder(new EtchedBorder());
```

If you want to add a title to the border (as in Figure 8), you need to construct a `TitledBorder`. Swing borders can be layered, similar to stream objects (discussed in Chapter 15). You make a titled border by supplying a basic border and then the title you want. Here is a typical example:

```
panel.setBorder(new TitledBorder(
    new EtchedBorder(), "Size"));
```

12.4.2 — Check Boxes

> For a binary choice, use a check box.

The choices for "Bold" and "Italic" in Figure 8 are *not* exclusive. You can choose either, both, or neither. Therefore, they are implemented as a set of separate check boxes. Radio buttons and check boxes have different visual appearances. Radio buttons are round and have a black dot when selected. Check boxes are square and have a check mark when selected. (Strictly speaking, the appearance depends on the chosen look and feel. It is possible to create a different look and feel in which check boxes have a different shape or in which they give off a particular sound when selected.)

You construct a check box by giving the name in the constructor:

```
JCheckBox italicCheckBox = new JCheckBox("Italic");
```

Do not place check boxes inside a button group.

12.4.3 — Combo Boxes

> For a large set of mutually exclusive choices, use a combo box.

If you have a large number of choices, you don't want to make a set of radio buttons, because that would take up a lot of space. Instead, you can use a *combo box*. This component is called a combo box because it is a combination of a list and a text field. The text field displays the name of the current selection. When you click on the arrow to the right of the text field of a combo box, a list of selections drops down, and you can choose one of items on the list (see Figure 9).

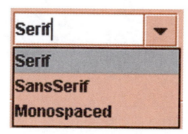

Figure 9

An Opened Combo Box

If the combol box is *editable*, you can also type in your own selection. To make a combo box editable, call the `setEditable` method.

You add strings to a combo box with the `addItem` method.

```
JComboBox facenameCombo = new JComboBox();
facenameCombo.addItem("Serif");
facenameCombo.addItem("SansSerif");
. . .
```

You get the item that the user has selected by calling the `getSelectedItem` method. However, since combo boxes can store other objects besides strings, the `getSelectedItem` method has return type `Object`. Hence you must cast the returned value back to `String`.

```
String selectedString =
    (String)facenameCombo.getSelectedItem();
```

> Radio buttons, check boxes, and combo boxes generate action events, just as buttons do.

You can select an item for the user with the `setSelectedItem` method.

Radio buttons, check boxes, and combo boxes generate an `ActionEvent` whenever the user selects an item. In the following program, we don't care which component was clicked—all components notify the same listener object. Whenever the user clicks on any one of them, we simply ask each component for its current content, using the `isSelected` and `getSelectedItem` methods. We then redraw the text sample with the new font.

Figure 10 shows how the components are arranged in the frame. Figure 11 shows the UML diagram.

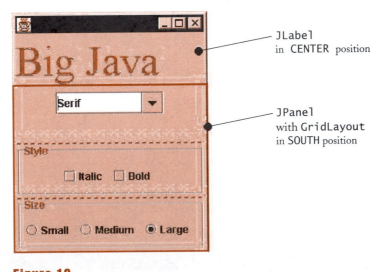

Figure 10

The Components of the `ChoiceFrame`

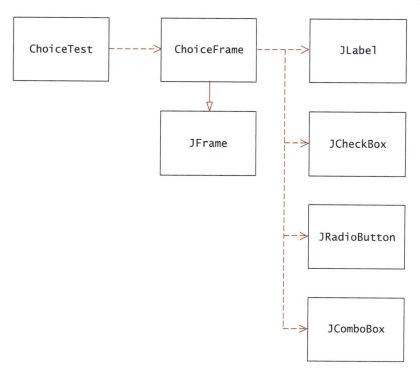

Figure 11

Classes of the ChoiceTest Program

File ChoiceTest.java

```
1  import javax.swing.JFrame;
2
3  /**
4     This program tests the ChoiceFrame.
5  */
6  public class ChoiceTest
7  {
8     public static void main(String[] args)
9     {
10       JFrame frame = new ChoiceFrame();
11       frame.setDefaultCloseOperation(
12          JFrame.EXIT_ON_CLOSE);
13       frame.show();
14    }
15 }
```

File ChoiceFrame.java

```
1  import java.awt.BorderLayout;
2  import java.awt.Container;
```

```
 3  import java.awt.Font;
 4  import java.awt.GridLayout;
 5  import java.awt.event.ActionEvent;
 6  import java.awt.event.ActionListener;
 7  import java.awt.event.WindowAdapter;
 8  import java.awt.event.WindowEvent;
 9  import javax.swing.ButtonGroup;
10  import javax.swing.JButton;
11  import javax.swing.JCheckBox;
12  import javax.swing.JComboBox;
13  import javax.swing.JFrame;
14  import javax.swing.JLabel;
15  import javax.swing.JPanel;
16  import javax.swing.JRadioButton;
17  import javax.swing.border.EtchedBorder;
18  import javax.swing.border.TitledBorder;
19
20  /**
21      This frame contains a text field and a control panel
22      to change the font of the text.
23  */
24  public class ChoiceFrame extends JFrame
25  {
26      /**
27          Constructs the frame.
28      */
29      public ChoiceFrame()
30      {
31          // construct text sample
32          sampleField = new JLabel("Big Java");
33          getContentPane().add(
34              sampleField, BorderLayout.CENTER);
35
36          // this listener is shared among all components
37          class ChoiceListener implements ActionListener
38          {
39              public void actionPerformed(ActionEvent event)
40              {
41                  setSampleFont();
42              }
43          }
44
45          listener = new ChoiceListener();
46
47          createControlPanel();
48          setSampleFont();
49          pack();
50      }
```

```
51
52      /**
53          Creates the control panel to change the font.
54      */
55      public void createControlPanel()
56      {
57          JPanel facenamePanel = createComboBox();
58          JPanel sizeGroupPanel = createCheckBoxes();
59          JPanel styleGroupPanel = createRadioButtons();
60
61          // line up component panels
62
63          JPanel controlPanel = new JPanel();
64          controlPanel.setLayout(new GridLayout(3, 1));
65          controlPanel.add(facenamePanel);
66          controlPanel.add(sizeGroupPanel);
67          controlPanel.add(styleGroupPanel);
68
69          // add panels to content pane
70
71          getContentPane().add(
72              controlPanel, BorderLayout.SOUTH);
73      }
74
75      /**
76          Creates the combo box with the font style choices.
77          @return the panel containing the combo box
78      */
79      public JPanel createComboBox()
80      {
81          facenameCombo = new JComboBox();
82          facenameCombo.addItem("Serif");
83          facenameCombo.addItem("SansSerif");
84          facenameCombo.addItem("Monospaced");
85          facenameCombo.setEditable(true);
86          facenameCombo.addActionListener(listener);
87
88          JPanel panel = new JPanel();
89          panel.add(facenameCombo);
90          return panel;
91      }
92
93      /**
94          Creates the check boxes for selecting bold and italic style.
95          @return the panel containing the check boxes
96      */
97      public JPanel createCheckBoxes()
98      {
99          italicCheckBox = new JCheckBox("Italic");
```

```
100          italicCheckBox.addActionListener(listener);
101
102          boldCheckBox = new JCheckBox("Bold");
103          boldCheckBox.addActionListener(listener);
104
105          JPanel panel = new JPanel();
106          panel.add(italicCheckBox);
107          panel.add(boldCheckBox);
108          panel.setBorder
109             (new TitledBorder(new EtchedBorder(), "Style"));
110
111          return panel;
112       }
113
114       /**
115          Creates the radio buttons to select the font size.
116          @return  the panel containing the radio buttons
117       */
118       public JPanel createRadioButtons()
119       {
120          smallButton = new JRadioButton("Small");
121          smallButton.addActionListener(listener);
122
123          mediumButton = new JRadioButton("Medium");
124          mediumButton.addActionListener(listener);
125
126          largeButton = new JRadioButton("Large");
127          largeButton.addActionListener(listener);
128          largeButton.setSelected(true);
129
130          // add radio buttons to button group
131
132          ButtonGroup group = new ButtonGroup();
133          group.add(smallButton);
134          group.add(mediumButton);
135          group.add(largeButton);
136
137          JPanel panel = new JPanel();
138          panel.add(smallButton);
139          panel.add(mediumButton);
140          panel.add(largeButton);
141          panel.setBorder
142             (new TitledBorder(new EtchedBorder(), "Size"));
143
144          return panel;
145       }
146
147       /**
```

```
148         Gets user choice for font name, style, and size.
149         and sets the font of the text sample.
150      */
151      public void setSampleFont()
152      {  // get font name
153
154         String facename
155            = (String)facenameCombo.getSelectedItem();
156
157         // get font style
158
159         int style = 0;
160         if (italicCheckBox.isSelected())
161            style = style + Font.ITALIC;
162         if (boldCheckBox.isSelected())
163            style = style + Font.BOLD;
164
165         // get font size
166
167         int size = 0;
168
169         final int SMALL_SIZE = 24;
170         final int MEDIUM_SIZE = 36;
171         final int LARGE_SIZE = 48;
172
173         if (smallButton.isSelected())
174            size = SMALL_SIZE;
175         else if (mediumButton.isSelected())
176            size = MEDIUM_SIZE;
177         else if (largeButton.isSelected())
178            size = LARGE_SIZE;
179
180         // set font of text field
181
182         sampleField.setFont(
183            new Font(facename, style, size));
184         sampleField.repaint();
185      }
186
187      private JLabel sampleField;
188      private JCheckBox italicCheckBox;
189      private JCheckBox boldCheckBox;
190      private JRadioButton smallButton;
191      private JRadioButton mediumButton;
192      private JRadioButton largeButton;
193      private JComboBox facenameCombo;
194      private ActionListener listener;
195   }
```

Layout Management

A graphical user interface is made up of components such as buttons and text fields. The Swing library uses containers and layout managers to arrange these components. This HOWTO explains how to group components into containers and how to pick the right layout managers.

Step 1 Make a sketch of your desired component layout

Draw all the buttons, labels, text fields, and borders on a sheet of paper. Graph paper works best.

Here is an example—a user interface for ordering pizza. The user interface contains

- Three radio buttons
- Two check boxes
- A label: "Your Price:"
- A text field
- A border

Size
- ● Small   ☒ Pepperoni
- ○ Medium   ☒ Anchovies
- ○ Large

Your Price: _____

Step 2 Find groupings of adjacent components with the same layout

Usually, the component arrangement is complex enough that you need to use several panels, each with its own layout manager. Start by looking at adjacent components that are arranged top to bottom or left to right. If several components are surrounded by a border, they should probably all be grouped together.

Here are the groupings from the pizza user interface:

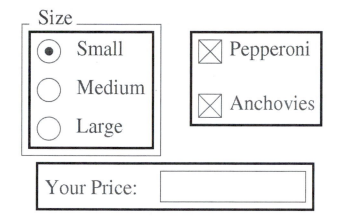

Step 3 Identify layouts for each group

When components are arranged horizontally, choose a flow layout. When components are arranged vertically, use a grid layout. The grid has as many rows as you have components, and it has one column.

In the pizza user interface example, you would choose

- A (3, 1) grid layout for the radio buttons
- A (2, 1) grid layout for the check boxes
- A flow layout for the label and text field

Step 4 Group the groups together

Look at each group as one blob, and group the blobs together into larger groups, just as you grouped the components in the preceding step. If you note one large blob surrounded by smaller blobs, you can group them together in a border layout.

You may have to repeat the grouping again if you have a very complex user interface. You are done if you have arranged all groups in a single container.

For example, the three component groups of the pizza user interface can be arranged as follows:

- A group containing the first two component groups, placed in the center of a container with a border layout
- The third component group, in the southern area of that container

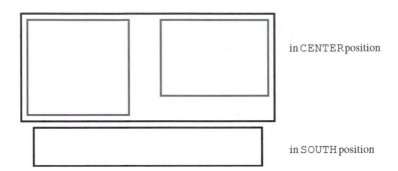

in CENTER position

in SOUTH position

In this step, you may run into a couple of complications. The group "blobs" tend to vary in size more than the individual components. If you place them inside a grid layout, the grid layout forces them all to be the same size. Also, you occasionally would like a component from one group to line up with a component from another group, but there is no way for you to communicate that intent to the layout managers.

These problems can be overcome by using more sophisticated layout managers or implementing a custom layout manager. However, those techniques are beyond the scope of this book. Sometimes, you may want to start over with step 1, using a component layout that is easier to manage. Or you can decide to live with minor imperfections of the layout. Don't worry about achieving the perfect layout—after all, you are learning programming, not user interface design.

Step 5   Write the code to generate the layout

This step is straightforward but potentially tedious, especially if you have a large number of components.

Start by constructing the components. Then construct a panel for each component group and set its layout manager if it is not a flow layout (the default for panels). Add a border to the panel if required. Finally, add the components to the panel.

Continue in this fashion until you reach the outermost container. Instead of constructing another panel, use the content pane of the surrounding JFrame or JApplet.

Of course, you also need to add event handlers to the components. That is the topic of HOWTO 10.1.

Here is an outline of the code required for the pizza user interface.

```
JPanel radioButtonPanel = new JPanel();
radioButtonPanel.setLayout(new GridLayout(3, 1));
radioButton.setBorder(new TitledBorder(
   new EtchedBorder(), "Size"));
radioButtonPanel.add(smallButton);
radioButtonPanel.add(mediumButton);
radioButtonPanel.add(largeButton);

JPanel checkBoxPanel = new JPanel();
checkBoxPanel.setLayout(new GridLayout(2, 1));
```

▼
```
checkBoxPanel.add(pepperoniButton());
checkBoxPanel.add(anchoviesButton());
```

▼
```
JPanel pricePanel = new JPanel(); // uses FlowLayout
pricePanel.add(new JLabel("Your Price:"));
pricePanel.add(priceTextField);
```

▼
```
JPanel centerPanel = new JPanel(); // uses FlowLayout
centerPanel.add(radioButtonPanel);
centerPanel.add(checkBoxPanel);
```

▼

▼
```
// use content pane as top-level container
// content pane uses BorderLayout by default
getContentPane().add(centerPanel, BorderLayout.CENTER);
getContentPane().add(pricePanel, BorderLayout.SOUTH);
```

12.5 Menus

> A frame contains a menu bar. The menu bar contains menus. A menu contains submenus and menu items.

Anyone who has ever used a graphical user interface is familiar with pull-down menus (see Figure 12). In Java it is easy to create these menus.

The container for the top-level menu items is called a *menu bar* in the Java world. First, you construct a menu bar and attach it to the frame:

```
public class MyFrame extends JFrame
{
    public MyFrame()
    {
        JMenuBar menuBar = new JMenuBar();
        setJMenuBar(menuBar);
        . . .
    }
}
```

Then you add menus to the menu bar:

```
JMenu fileMenu = new JMenu("File");
menuBar.add(fileMenu);
```

A menu is a collection of *menu items* and more menus (submenus). You add menu items and submenus with the add method:

```
JMenuItem fileNewMenuItem = new JMenuItem("New");
fileMenu.add(fileNewMenuItem);
```

> Menu items generate action events.

A menu item has no further submenus. When the user selects a menu item, the menu item sends an action event. Therefore, you want to add a listener to each menu item:

```
fileNewMenuItem.addActionListener(listener);
```

Menu bar

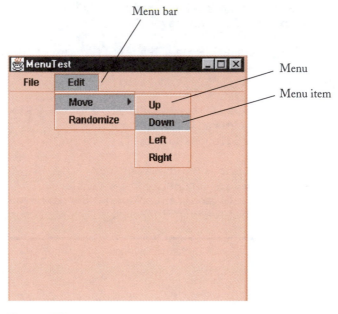

Menu

Menu item

Figure 12

Pull-Down Menus

You add action listeners only to menu items, not to menus or the menu bar. When the user clicks on a menu name and a submenu opens, no action event is sent.

The following program builds up a small but typical menu and traps the action events from the menu items. To keep the program readable, it is a good idea to use a separate method for each menu or set of related menus. Have a look at the `createMoveItem` method, which creates a menu item to move up, down, left, or right. The same action listener class takes care of the four cases, with the `dx` and `dy` values varying for each menu item.

File MenuTest.java

```java
1  import javax.swing.JFrame;
2
3  /**
4      This program tests the MenuFrame.
5  */
6  public class MenuTest
7  {
8     public static void main(String[] args)
9     {
10        JFrame frame = new MenuFrame();
11        frame.setDefaultCloseOperation(
12           JFrame.EXIT_ON_CLOSE);
13        frame.show();
14     }
15  }
```

File MenuFrame.java

```
1  import java.awt.BorderLayout;
2  import java.awt.event.ActionEvent;
3  import java.awt.event.ActionListener;
4  import java.util.Random;
5  import javax.swing.JFrame;
6  import javax.swing.JMenu;
7  import javax.swing.JMenuBar;
8  import javax.swing.JMenuItem;
9
10 /**
11     This frame has a menu with commands to set the position of
12     a rectangle.
13 */
14 class MenuFrame extends JFrame
15 {
16     /**
17         Constructs the frame.
18     */
19     public MenuFrame()
20     {
21         generator = new Random();
22
23         // add drawing panel to content pane
24
25         panel = new RectanglePanel();
26         getContentPane().add(panel, BorderLayout.CENTER);
27         pack();
28
29         // construct menu
30
31         JMenuBar menuBar = new JMenuBar();
32         setJMenuBar(menuBar);
33
34         menuBar.add(createFileMenu());
35         menuBar.add(createEditMenu());
36     }
37
38     /**
39         Creates the File menu.
40         @return the menu
41     */
42     public JMenu createFileMenu()
43     {
44         JMenu menu = new JMenu("File");
45         menu.add(createFileNewItem());
46         menu.add(createFileExitItem());
47         return menu;
48     }
49
```

```
50      /**
51          Creates the Edit menu.
52          @return the menu
53      */
54      public JMenu createEditMenu()
55      {
56          JMenu menu = new JMenu("Edit");
57          menu.add(createMoveMenu());
58          menu.add(createEditRandomizeItem());
59          return menu;
60      }
61
62      /**
63          Creates the Move submenu.
64          @return the menu
65      */
66      public JMenu createMoveMenu()
67      {
68          JMenu menu = new JMenu("Move");
69          menu.add(createMoveItem("Up", 0, -1));
70          menu.add(createMoveItem("Down", 0, 1));
71          menu.add(createMoveItem("Left", -1, 0));
72          menu.add(createMoveItem("Right", 1, 0));
73          return menu;
74      }
75
76      /**
77          Creates the File->New menu item and sets its action listener.
78          @return the menu item
79      */
80      public JMenuItem createFileNewItem()
81      {
82          JMenuItem item = new JMenuItem("New");
83          class MenuItemListener implements ActionListener
84          {
85              public void actionPerformed(ActionEvent event)
86              {
87                  panel.reset();
88              }
89          }
90          ActionListener listener = new MenuItemListener();
91          item.addActionListener(listener);
92          return item;
93      }
94
95      /**
96          Creates the File->Exit menu item and sets its action listener.
97          @return the menu item
98      */
99      public JMenuItem createFileExitItem()
```

```
100     {
101         JMenuItem item = new JMenuItem("Exit");
102         class MenuItemListener implements ActionListener
103         {
104             public void actionPerformed(ActionEvent event)
105             {
106                 System.exit(0);
107             }
108         }
109         ActionListener listener = new MenuItemListener();
110         item.addActionListener(listener);
111         return item;
112     }
113
114     /**
115         Creates a menu item to move the rectangle and sets its
116         action listener.
117         @param label  the menu label
118         @param dx  the amount by which to move the rectangle in the x-direction
119         @param dy  the amount by which to move the rectangle in the y-direction
120         @return  the menu item
121     */
122     public JMenuItem createMoveItem(String label,
123         final int dx, final int dy)
124     {
125         JMenuItem item = new JMenuItem(label);
126         class MenuItemListener implements ActionListener
127         {
128             public void actionPerformed(ActionEvent event)
129             {
130                 panel.moveRectangle(dx, dy);
131             }
132         }
133         ActionListener listener = new MenuItemListener();
134         item.addActionListener(listener);
135         return item;
136     }
137
138     /**
139         Creates the Edit->Randomize menu item and sets its action listener.
140         @return  the menu item
141     */
142     public JMenuItem createEditRandomizeItem()
143     {
144         JMenuItem item = new JMenuItem("Randomize");
145         class MenuItemListener implements ActionListener
146         {
147             public void actionPerformed(ActionEvent event)
148             {
149                 int width = panel.getWidth();
```

```
150              int height = panel.getHeight();
151              int dx = -1 + generator.nextInt(2);
152              int dy = -1 + generator.nextInt(2);
153              panel.moveRectangle(dx, dy);
154          }
155       }
156       ActionListener listener = new MenuItemListener();
157       item.addActionListener(listener);
158       return item;
159    }
160
161    private RectanglePanel panel;
162    private Random generator;
163 }
```

File RectanglePanel.java

```
1  import java.awt.Dimension;
2  import java.awt.Graphics;
3  import java.awt.Graphics2D;
4  import java.awt.Rectangle;
5  import javax.swing.JPanel;
6
7  /**
8      A panel that shows a rectangle.
9  */
10 class RectanglePanel extends JPanel
11 {
12    /**
13        Constructs a panel with the rectangle in the top left corner.
14    */
15    public RectanglePanel()
16    {
17       setPreferredSize(
18          new Dimension(PANEL_WIDTH, PANEL_HEIGHT));
19       // the rectangle that the paint method draws
20       box = new Rectangle(0, 0, BOX_WIDTH, BOX_HEIGHT);
21    }
22
23    public void paintComponent(Graphics g)
24    {
25       super.paintComponent(g);
26       Graphics2D g2 = (Graphics2D)g;
27       g2.draw(box);
28    }
29
30    /**
31        Resets the rectangle to the top left corner.
32    */
33    public void reset()
34    {
```

```
35        box.setLocation(0, 0);
36        repaint();
37    }
38
39    /**
40        Moves the rectangle and repaints it. The rectangle
41        is moved by multiples of its full width or height.
42        @param dx  the number of width units
43        @param dy  the number of height units
44    */
45    public void moveRectangle(int dx, int dy)
46    {
47        box.translate(dx * BOX_WIDTH, dy * BOX_HEIGHT);
48        repaint();
49    }
50
51    private Rectangle box;
52    private static final int BOX_WIDTH = 20;
53    private static final int BOX_HEIGHT = 30;
54    private static final int PANEL_WIDTH = 300;
55    private static final int PANEL_HEIGHT = 300;
56 }
```

12.6 Exploring the Swing Documentation

> You should learn to navigate the API documentation to find out more about user interface components.

In the preceding sections, you saw the basic properties of the most common user interface components. We purposefully omitted many options and variations to simplify the discussion. You can go a long way by using only the simplest properties of these components. If you want to implement a more sophisticated effect, you can look inside the Swing documentation. You will probably find the documentation quite intimidating at first glance, though. The purpose of this section is to show you how you can use the documentation to your advantage without becoming overwhelmed.

Recall the Color class that was introduced in Chapter 4. Every combination of red, green, and blue values represents a different color. It should be fun to mix your own colors, with a slider for the red, green, and blue values (see Figure 13).

The Swing user interface toolkit has a large set of user interface components. How do you know whether there is a slider? You can buy a book that illustrates all Swing components, such as [2]. Or you can run the sample application included in the Java Development Kit that shows off all Swing components (see Figure 14). Or you can look at the names of all of the classes that start with J and decide that JSlider may be a good candidate.

Next, you need to ask yourself a few questions:

- How do I construct a JSlider?

- How can I get notified when the user has moved it?

- How can I tell to which value the user has set it?

Figure 13

A Color Mixer

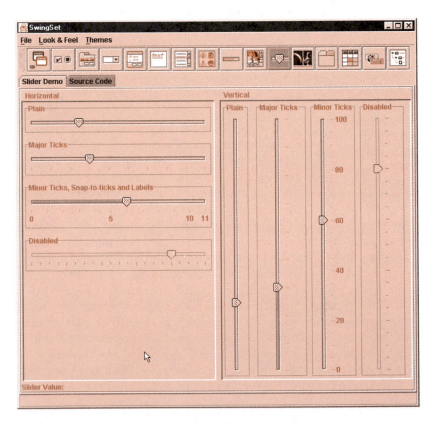

Figure 14

The Swing Set Demo

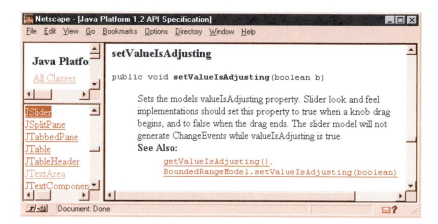

Figure 15

A Mysterious Method Description from the API Documentation

If you can answer these questions, then you can put a slider to good use. Once you achieve that, you can fritter away more time and find out how to set tick marks or otherwise enhance the visual beauty of your creation.

When you look at the documentation of the `JSlider` class, you will probably not be happy. There are over 50 methods in the `JSlider` class and over 250 inherited methods, and some of the method descriptions look downright scary, such as the one in Figure 15. Apparently some folks out there are concerned about the `valueIsAdjusting` property, whatever that may be, and the designers of this class felt it necessary to supply a method to tweak that property. Until you too feel that need, your best bet is to ignore this method. As the author of an introductory book, it pains me to tell you to ignore certain facts. But the truth of the matter is that the Java library is so large and complex that nobody understands it in its entirety, not even the designers of Java themselves. You need to develop the ability to separate fundamental concepts from ephemeral minutiae. For example, it is important that you understand the concept of event handling. Once you understand the concept, you can ask the question, "What event does the slider send when the user moves it?" But it is not important that you memorize how to set tick marks or that you know how to implement a slider with a custom look and feel.

Let us go back to our fundamental questions. In Java 2, there are six constructors for the `JSlider` class. (There may well be more by the time you read this.) You want to learn about one or two of them. You need to strike a balance somewhere between the trivial and the bizarre. Consider

```
public JSlider()
```
> Creates a horizontal slider with the range 0 to 100 and an initial value of 50

Maybe that is good enough for now, but what if you want another range or initial value? It seems too limited.

On the other side of the spectrum, there is

```
public JSlider(BoundedRangeModel brm)
```
> Creates a horizontal slider using the specified `BoundedRangeModel`

Whoa! What is that? You can click on the `BoundedRangeModel` link to get a long explanation of this class. This appears to be some internal mechanism for the Swing implementors. Let's try to avoid this constructor if we can. Looking further, we find

> public **JSlider**(int min, int max, int value)
>   Creates a horizontal slider using the specified `min`, `max`, and `value`

This sounds general enough to be useful and simple enough to be usable. You might want to stash away the fact that you can have vertical sliders as well.

Next, you want to know what events a slider generates. There is no `addActionListener` method. That makes sense. Adjusting a slider seems different from clicking a button, and Swing uses a different event type for these events. There is a method

> public void **addChangeListener**(ChangeListener l)

Click on the `ChangeListener` link to find out more about this interface. It has a single method

> void **stateChanged**(ChangeEvent e)

Apparently, that method is called whenever the user moves the slider. What is a `ChangeEvent`? Once again, click on the link, to find out that this event class has *no* methods of its own, but it inherits the `getSource` method from its superclass `EventObject`. Now we have a plan: Add a change event listener to each slider. When the slider is changed, the `stateChanged` method is called. Find out the new value of the slider. Recompute the color value and repaint the color panel. That way, the color panel is continually repainted as the user moves one of the sliders.

To compute the color value, you will still need to get the current value of the slider. Look at all the methods that start with `get`. Sure enough, you find

> public int **getValue**()
>   Returns the slider's value

Now you know everything to write the program. The program uses one new constructor, two new methods, and one event listener of a new type. Of course, now that you have "tasted blood", you may want to add those tick marks—see Exercise P12.15.

Figure 16 shows how the components are arranged in the frame. Figure 17 shows the UML diagram.

File SliderTest.java

```
 1  import javax.swing.JFrame;
 2
 3  public class SliderTest
 4  {
 5     public static void main(String[] args)
 6     {
 7        SliderFrame frame = new SliderFrame();
 8        frame.setDefaultCloseOperation(
 9           JFrame.EXIT_ON_CLOSE);
10        frame.show();
11     }
12  }
```

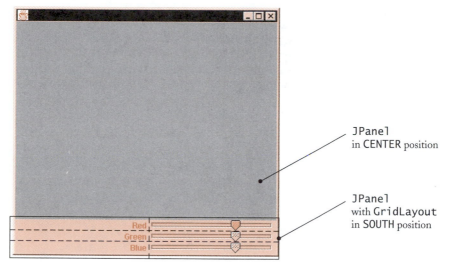

Figure 16

The Components of the SliderFrame

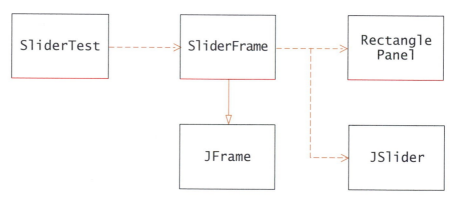

Figure 17

Classes of the SliderTest Program

File SliderFrame.java

```
1  import java.awt.BorderLayout;
2  import java.awt.Color;
3  import java.awt.Container;
4  import java.awt.Dimension;
5  import java.awt.GridLayout;
6  import java.awt.event.WindowAdapter;
7  import java.awt.event.WindowEvent;
8  import javax.swing.JFrame;
```

```
 9  import javax.swing.JLabel;
10  import javax.swing.JPanel;
11  import javax.swing.JSlider;
12  import javax.swing.SwingConstants;
13  import javax.swing.event.ChangeListener;
14  import javax.swing.event.ChangeEvent;
15
16  class SliderFrame extends JFrame
17  {
18     public SliderFrame()
19     {
20        colorPanel = new JPanel();
21        colorPanel.setPreferredSize(
22           new Dimension(PANEL_WIDTH, PANEL_HEIGHT));
23
24        getContentPane().add(colorPanel,
25           BorderLayout.CENTER);
26        createControlPanel();
27        setSampleColor();
28        pack();
29     }
30
31     public void createControlPanel()
32     {
33        class ColorListener implements ChangeListener
34        {
35           public void stateChanged(ChangeEvent event)
36           {
37              setSampleColor();
38           }
39        }
40
41        ChangeListener listener = new ColorListener();
42
43        redSlider = new JSlider(0, 100, 100);
44        redSlider.addChangeListener(listener);
45
46        greenSlider = new JSlider(0, 100, 70);
47        greenSlider.addChangeListener(listener);
48
49        blueSlider = new JSlider(0, 100, 70);
50        blueSlider.addChangeListener(listener);
51
52        JPanel controlPanel = new JPanel();
53        controlPanel.setLayout(new GridLayout(3, 2));
54
55        controlPanel.add(new JLabel("Red",
56           SwingConstants.RIGHT));
57        controlPanel.add(redSlider);
58
59        controlPanel.add(new JLabel("Green",
```

```
60              SwingConstants.RIGHT));
61          controlPanel.add(greenSlider);
62
63          controlPanel.add(new JLabel("Blue",
64              SwingConstants.RIGHT));
65          controlPanel.add(blueSlider);
66
67          getContentPane().add(controlPanel,
68              BorderLayout.SOUTH);
69      }
70
71
72      /**
73          Reads the slider values and sets the panel to
74          the selected color.
75      */
76      public void setSampleColor()
77      {   // read slider values
78
79          float red = 0.01F * redSlider.getValue();
80          float green = 0.01F * greenSlider.getValue();
81          float blue = 0.01F * blueSlider.getValue();
82
83          // set panel background to selected color
84
85          colorPanel.setBackground(
86              new Color(red, green, blue));
87          colorPanel.repaint();
88      }
89
90      private JPanel colorPanel;
91      private JSlider redSlider;
92      private JSlider greenSlider;
93      private JSlider blueSlider;
94
95      private static final int PANEL_WIDTH = 300;
96      private static final int PANEL_HEIGHT = 300;
97  }
```

▼ **Random Fact**   **12.1**

Visual Programming

Programming as you know it involves typing code into a text editor and then running it. A programmer must be familiar with the programming language to write even the simplest of programs. When programming in graphics, one must compute every screen position.

A new *visual* style of programming makes this much easier. When you use a visual programming environment, such as Visual Café or JBuilder, you use your mouse to specify

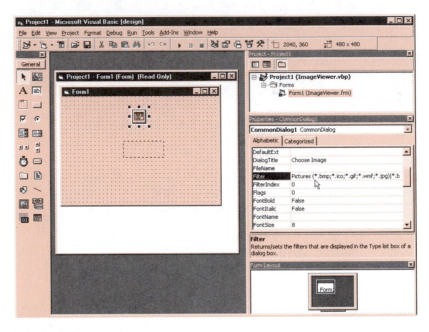

Figure 18

A Visual Programming Environment

where text, buttons, and other fields should appear on the screen (see Figure 18). You still need to do some programming. You need to write code for every event. For example, you can drag a button to its desired location, but you still need to specify what should happen when the user clicks on it.

Visual programming offers two benefits. It is much easier to lay out a screen by dragging buttons and images with the mouse than it is to compute the coordinates in a program. The visual programming environment also makes it easy to place objects with sophisticated behavior onto the screen. For example, a calendar object can show the current month's calendar, with buttons to move to the next or previous month; all of that has been preprogrammed by someone (usually the hard way, using a traditional programming language), but you can add a fully working calendar to your program simply by dragging it off a toolbar and dropping it into your program.

A prebuilt component, such as a calendar chooser, usually has a large number of *properties* that you can simply choose from a table. For example, you can simply check whether you want the calendar to be weekly or monthly. The provider of the calendar component had to work hard to include both cases in the code, but the programmer using the component does not have to care. When written in Java, these prepackaged components are called *JavaBeans*.

User interface design in a visual environment is *much* easier than writing the equivalent code in Java. In days a programmer can design an attractive user interface that would take weeks to complete by writing code. These systems are highly recommended for user interface programming.

CHAPTER SUMMARY

1. You can draw graphical shapes on a panel by overriding the `paintComponent` method of a `JPanel` subclass.

2. A panel class that paints a drawing on the panel should store all data that it needs to repaint itself.

3. You arrange user interface components by placing them inside containers. Containers can be placed inside larger containers.

4. Each container has a *layout manager* that directs the arrangement of its components.

5. Three useful layout managers are the border layout, flow layout, and grid layout.

6. When adding a component to a container with the border layout, specify the NORTH, EAST, SOUTH, WEST, or CENTER position.

7. The content pane of a frame or applet has a border layout by default. A panel has a flow layout by default.

8. With the flow layout, the individual components stay at their preferred size. The border layout and grid layout grow components to fill the area allotted for them.

9. Define a `JFrame` subclass for a complex frame.

10. For a small set of mutually exclusive choices, use a group of radio buttons or a combo box.

11. Add radio buttons into a `ButtonGroup` so that only one button in the group is on at any time.

12. You can place a border around a panel to group its contents visually.

13. For a binary choice, use a check box.

14. For a large set of mutually exclusive choices, use a combo box.

15. Radio buttons, check boxes, and combo boxes generate action events, just as buttons do.

16. A frame contains a menu bar. The menu bar contains menus. A menu contains submenus and menu items.

17. Menu items generate action events.

18. You should learn to navigate the API documentation to find out more about user interface components.

Further Reading

[1] Cay S. Horstmann and Gary Cornell, *Core Java 2 Volume 1: Fundamentals*, Prentice Hall, 2000.
[2] Kim Topley, *Core Java Foundation Classes*, Prentice Hall, 1998.

Classes, Objects, and Methods Introduced in This Chapter

```
java.awt.BorderLayout
    CENTER
    EAST
    NORTH
    SOUTH
    WEST
java.awt.Component
    setLayout
    setPreferredSize
    setSize
java.awt.FlowLayout
java.awt.GridLayout
javax.swing.AbstractButton
    addActionListener
    isSelected
    setSelected
javax.swing.ButtonGroup
    add
javax.swing.JComponent
    paintComponent
javax.swing.JFrame
    getContentPane
javax.swing.EtchedBorder
javax.swing.ImageIcon
javax.swing.JCheckBox
javax.swing.JComboBox
    addItem
    getSelectedItem
    isEditable
    setEditable
javax.swing.JComponent
    setBorder
    setFont
javax.swing.JLabel
javax.swing.JMenu
    add
javax.swing.JMenuBar
    add
javax.swing.JMenuItem
javax.swing.JRadioButton
javax.swing.JSlider
    addChangeListener
    getValue
javax.swing.border.TitledBorder
javax.swing.event.ChangeEvent
javax.swing.event.ChangeListener
    stateChanged
```

REVIEW EXERCISES

Exercise R12.1. What is the difference between the `paint` and `paintComponent` methods?

Exercise R12.2. What happens if you don't call `super.paintComponent` in a class that extends `JPanel`? Try it out with the `RectangleTest` program. Can you find out how the program misbehaves when you comment out that call?

Exercise R12.3. What happens when you paint directly on a frame? Try it out—rewrite the `RectanglePanel` application and move the `paintComponent` method directly into the `RectangleFrame` class.

Exercise R12.4. What is a layout manager? What is the advantage of a layout manager over telling the container "place this component at position (x,y)"?

Exercise R12.5. What happens when you place a single button into the CENTER area of a container that uses a border layout? Try it out, by writing a small sample program, if you aren't sure about the answer.

Exercise R12.6. What happens if you place multiple buttons into the SOUTH area? Try it out, by writing a small sample program, if you aren't sure about the answer.

Exercise R12.7. What happens when you add a button to a container that uses a border layout and omit the position? Try it out and explain.

Exercise R12.8. What happens when you try to add a component directly to a `JFrame` and not the content pane? Try it out and explain.

Exercise R12.9. The `SliderTest` program uses a grid layout manager. Explain a drawback of the grid that is apparent from Figure 16. What could you do to overcome this drawback?

Exercise R12.10. What is the difference between an `Applet` and a `JApplet`?

Exercise R12.11. Can you add icons to check boxes, radio buttons, and combo boxes? Browse the Java documentation to find out. Then write a small test program to verify your findings.

Exercise R12.12. What is the difference between radio buttons and check boxes?

Exercise R12.13. Why do you need a button group for radio buttons but not for check boxes?

Exercise R12.14. What is the difference between a menu bar, a menu, and a menu item?

Exercise R12.15. When browsing through the Java documentation for more information about sliders, we ignored the `JSlider` default constructor. Why? Would it have worked in our sample program?

Exercise R12.16. How do you construct a vertical slider? Consult the Swing documentation for an answer.

Exercise R12.17. Why doesn't a slider send out action events?

Exercise R12.18. What component would you use to show a set of choices, just as in a combo box, but so that several items are visible at the same time? Run the Swing demo app or look at a book with Swing example programs to find the answer.

Exercise R12.19. How many Swing user interface components are there? Look at the Java documentation to get an approximate answer.

Exercise R12.20. How many methods does the `JProgressBar` component have? Be sure to count inherited methods. Look at the Java documentation.

Programming Exercises

Exercise P12.1. Write an application with three buttons labeled "Red", "Green", and "Blue" that changes the background color of a panel in the center of the content pane to red, green, or blue.

Exercise P12.2. Add icons to the buttons of the preceding Exercise.

Exercise P12.3. Write a calculator application. Use a grid layout to arrange buttons for the digits and for the + – × ÷ operations. Add a text field to display the result.

Exercise P12.4. Write an application with three radio buttons labeled "Red", "Green", and "Blue" that changes the background color of a panel in the center of the content pane to red, green, or blue.

Exercise P12.5. Write an application with three check boxes labeled "Red", "Green", and "Blue" that adds a red, green, or blue component to the the background color of a panel in the center of the content pane. This application can display a total of eight color combinations.

Exercise P12.6. Write an application with a combo box containing three items labeled "Red", "Green", and "Blue" that changes the background color of a panel in the center of the content pane to red, green, or blue.

Exercise P12.7. Change the `RectangleTest` program so that the rectangle position is set by two text fields for the *x*- and *y*-positions.

Exercise P12.8. Write a program that displays a number of rectangles at random positions. Supply buttons "Fewer" and "More" that generate fewer or more random rectangles. Each time the user clicks on "Fewer", the count should be halved. Each time the user clicks on "More", the count should be doubled.

Exercise P12.9. Modify the program of the preceding exercise to replace the buttons with a slider to generate fewer or more random rectangles.

Exercise P12.10. Write an application with three labeled text fields, one each for the initial amount of a savings account, the annual interest rate, and the number of years. Add a button "Calculate" and a read-only text area to display the result, namely, the balance of the savings account after the given number of years.

Exercise P12.11. Add a bar graph to the preceding exercise that shows the balance after the end of each year.

Exercise P12.12. Write a program that contains a text area, a button "Draw Graph", and a panel that draws a bar chart of the numbers that a user typed into the text area. Use a string tokenizer to break up the text in the text area.

Exercise P12.13. Write a program that lets users design charts such as the following:

Golden Gate

Brooklyn

Delaware Memorial

Mackinac

Use appropriate components to ask for the length, label, and color, then apply them when the user clicks an "Add Bar" button.

Exercise P12.14. Write a program that lets users create pie charts. Design your own user interface.

Exercise P12.15. In the slider test program, add a set of tick marks to each slider that show the exact slider position.

Exercise P12.16. Write a graphical application front end for an `Earthquake` class. Supply a slider for entering the strength of the earthquake. Display the earthquake description in a text field that you continually update.

Array Lists and Arrays

13.1   Array Lists

Consider again the `Purse` class from Chapter 7. You can add `Coin` objects to the purse. However, the purse doesn't actually remember the individual coins that you add, only the total value. It would be more realistic if we could actually store the individual coins.

If you knew that there were always ten coins in the purse, then you could store the objects in ten fields `coin1`, `coin2`, `coin3`, . . . , `coin10`. But such a sequence of variables is not very practical to use. You would have to write quite a bit of code ten times, once for each of the variables, and you'd still not be able to model a purse that holds twenty coins. Fortunately, there is a better way of storing a collection of objects: the `ArrayList` class.

> An array list is a sequence of objects.

An *array list* is a sequence of objects. Every element of the sequence can be accessed separately. Here is how you define an array list and fill it with coins:

```
ArrayList coins = new ArrayList();
coins.add(new Coin(0.1, "dime"));
coins.add(new Coin(0.25, "quarter"));
. . .
```

> Each object in an array list has an integer position number, called the index.

To get objects out of the array list, use the `get` method and specify which position in the array list you want to access. For example, `coins.get(4)` retrieves the coin in position number 4. The position number is called the *index* of the array list element.

> When retrieving an element from an array list, you need to cast the return value of the `get` method to the element class.

However, since an `ArrayList` stores `Object` references, the return type of the `get` method is `Object`. You need to cast the returned reference to the correct class.

```
Coin aCoin = (Coin)coins.get(4);
```

For unfortunate historical reasons, the positions of array lists are numbered *starting at 0*. That is,

> Position numbers of an array range from 0 to `size()` – 1. Accessing a nonexistent position results in a bounds error.

```
coins.get(0) gets the first object
coins.get(1) gets the second object
coins.get(2) gets the third object
```

and so on.

In "ancient" times there was a technical reason why this setup was a good idea. So many programmers got used to it in C and C++ that Java follows it too. It is, however, a major source of grief for the newcomer.

If you try to access a position that does not exist, then an exception is thrown. For example, if `coins` holds ten objects, then the statement

```
Coin aCoin = (Coin)coins.get(20);
```

is a *bounds error*. To avoid bounds errors, you will want to know how many elements are in an array list. The `size` method returns the number of elements.

The most common bounds error is to use the following:

```
int i = coins.size();
aCoin = (Coin)coins.get(i);   // ERROR
```

Suppose `coins.size()` is 10. There is no element with index 10. Because the first element has index 0, the legal subscripts are 0 through 9. Thus, the call to `coins.get(10)` is a bounds error.

It is extremely common to step through *all* elements of an array list. For example, the following loop computes the total value of all coins:

```
double total = 0;
for (int i = 0; i < coins.size(); i++)
{
   Coin aCoin = (Coin)coins.get(i);
   total = total + aCoin.getValue();
}
```

Note that i is a legal index for the array list if $0 \leq$ i and i $<$ `coins.size()`.
Don't write the test as

```
for (int i = 0; i <= coins.size() - 1; i++) // DON'T
```

The condition i `<= coins.size()` - 1 means the same thing as i `< coins.size()`, but it is harder to read (see Quality Tip 6.3).

To set an array list element to a new value, use the `set` method.

```
Coin aNickel = new Coin(0.05, "nickel");
coins.set(4, aNickel);
```

This call sets position 4 of the `coins` array list to `aNickel`, overwriting whatever value was there before.

The `set` method can only overwrite existing values. To add a new object to the end of the array list, call the **add** method. You can also insert an object in the middle of an array list. The call `coins.add(i, c)` adds the object c at position i and moves all elements by one position, from the current element at position i to the last element in the array list. After each call to the **add** method, the size of the array list increases by 1 (see Figure 1).

Conversely, the call `coins.remove(i)` removes the element at position i, moves all elements after the removed element down by one position, and reduces the size of the array list by 1 (see Figure 2).

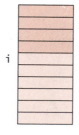
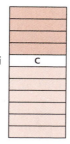

Figure 1

Adding an Element in the Middle of
an Array List

Before   After

Figure 2

Removing an Element from the Middle of an Array List

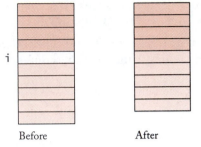

i

Before   After

Here is an implementation of the `Purse` class that uses an **array list to store the coins**. We will enhance the functionality of this class in the next section.

File Purse.java

```
1  import java.util.ArrayList;
2
3  /**
4      A purse holds a collection of coins.
5  */
6  public class Purse
7  {
8      /**
9          Constructs an empty purse.
10     */
11     public Purse()
12     {
13         coins = new ArrayList();
14     }
15
16     /**
17         Adds a coin to the purse.
18         @param aCoin the coin to add
19     */
20     public void add(Coin aCoin)
21     {
22         coins.add(aCoin);
23     }
24
25     /**
26         Get the total value of the coins in the purse.
27         @return the sum of all coin values
28     */
29     public double getTotal()
30     {
31         double total = 0;
32         for (int i = 0; i < coins.size(); i++)
33         {
34             Coin aCoin = (Coin)coins.get(i);
```

```
35            total = total + aCoin.getValue();
36        }
37        return total;
38    }
39
40    private ArrayList coins;
41 }
```

Common Error 13.1

Bounds Errors

The most common array list error is attempting to access a nonexistent position.

```
ArrayList coins = new ArrayList();
coins.add(new Coin(0.1, "dime"));
coins.add(new Coin(0.25, "quarter"));
Coin c = (Coin)coins.get(2);
// ERROR—only have positions #0 and #1
```

When the program runs, an out-of-bounds subscript generates an exception and terminates the program.

This is a great improvement over languages such as C and C++. With those languages there is no error message; instead, the program will quietly (or not so quietly) corrupt some memory. Except for very short programs, in which the problem may go unnoticed, that corruption will make the program act flaky or cause a horrible death many instructions later. These are serious errors that make C and C++ programs difficult to debug.

Common Error 13.2

Inserting Objects of the Wrong Type into an Array List

An array list is a "one size fits all" data structure. It manages a sequence of elements of type Object. As a result, you can use the add and set methods to add objects of any class into an array list. If you accidentally insert an element of the wrong type, then no error occurs until you retrieve the object.

```
coins.add(new Rectangle(5, 10, 20, 30)); // no error here
```

The call to add is technically correct—a Rectangle value can be converted to Object, and therefore it can be inserted into the array list. For that reason, the compiler will not complain. This was still a programming error, though, because the programmer's intention is that coins contain coins.

▼ The error is reported when the rectangle object is cast to the `Coin` class.

▼
```
for (int i = 0; i < coins.size(); i++)
{
    Coin aCoin = (Coin)coins.get(i); // error reported here
    total = total + aCoin.getValue();
}
```

▼

13.2 Simple Array List Algorithms

13.2.1 Finding a Value

> To find a value in an array list, check all elements until you have found a match.

Suppose you want to know whether you have a particular coin in your purse. You simply inspect each element until you find a match or reach the end of the array list. Note that the loop might fail to find an answer, namely if none of the coins match. This search process is called a *linear search* through the array list.

```
public class Purse
{
    public boolean find(Coin aCoin)
    {
        for (int i = 0; i < coins.size(); i++)
        {
            Coin c = (Coin)coins.get(i);
            if (c.equals(aCoin)) return true; // found a match
        }
        return false; // no match in the entire array list
    }
    . . .
}
```

13.2.2 Counting

> To count values in an array list, check all elements and count the matches, until you reach the end of the array list.

Suppose you want to find *how many* coins of a certain type you have. Then you must go through the entire array list and increment a counter each time you find a match.

```
public class Purse
{
    public int count(Coin aCoin)
    {
        int matches = 0;
        for (int i = 0; i < coins.size(); i++)
        {
```

```
                        Coin c = (Coin)coins.get(i);
                        if (c.equals(aCoin)) matches++; // found a match
                }
                return matches;
        }
        . . .
   }
```

13.2.3 — Finding the Maximum or Minimum

> To compute the maximum or minimum value of an array list, initialize a candidate with the starting element. Then compare the candidate with the remaining elements and update it if you find a larger or smaller value.

Suppose you want to find the coin with the largest value currently in the purse. Keep a candidate for the maximum. Visit all elements of the array. If you find an element with a larger value, then replace the candidate with that value. When you have reached the end of the array, you have found the maximum.

There is just one problem. When you visit the beginning of the array, you don't yet have a candidate for the maximum. The easiest way to overcome that is to set the candidate to the starting element of the array and start the comparison with the next element.

```
public class Purse
{
    public Coin getMaximum()
    {
        Coin max = (Coin)coins.get(0);
        for (int i = 1; i < coins.size(); i++)
        {
            Coin c = (Coin)coins.get(i);
            if (c.getValue() > max.getValue())
                max = c;
        }
        return max;
    }
    . . .
}
```

Note that the for loop starts with 1, not with 0.

Of course, this method works only if there is at least one element in the array list. It doesn't make a lot of sense to ask for the largest element of an empty collection. We can return null in that case, or else we can declare a precondition that the purse must not be empty when calling the getMaximum method. Recall from Chapter 7 that it is better to establish a reasonable precondition than to return a bogus value.

However, then the Purse class needs a method that can tell whether there are any coins in the purse—it isn't fair to set a precondition that the class user can't test. For that reason, the class at the end of this section has a method count that returns the coin count of the purse.

To compute the minimum of a data set, keep a candidate for the minimum, initialize it with the beginning data value, and replace it whenever you encounter a smaller value. At the end of the data set, you have found the minimum.

File Purse.java

```java
1  import java.util.ArrayList;
2
3  /**
4      A purse holds a collection of coins.
5  */
6  public class Purse
7  {
8     /**
9         Constructs an empty purse.
10    */
11    public Purse()
12    {
13       coins = new ArrayList();
14    }
15
16    /**
17        Adds a coin to the purse.
18        @param aCoin the coin to add
19    */
20    public void add(Coin aCoin)
21    {
22       coins.add(aCoin);
23    }
24
25    /**
26        Gets the total value of the coins in the purse.
27        @return the sum of all coin values
28    */
29    public double getTotal()
30    {
31       double total = 0;
32       for (int i = 0; i < coins.size(); i++)
33       {
34          Coin aCoin = (Coin)coins.get(i);
35          total = total + aCoin.getValue();
36       }
37       return total;
38    }
39
40    /**
41        Counts the number of coins in the purse.
42        @return the number of coins
43    */
44    public int count()
45    {
46       return coins.size();
47    }
48
49    /**
```

```
50            Tests whether the purse has a coin that matches a given coin.
51            @param aCoin the coin to match
52            @return true if there is a coin equal to aCoin
53         */
54         public boolean find(Coin aCoin)
55         {
56            for (int i = 0; i < coins.size(); i++)
57            {
58               Coin c = (Coin)coins.get(i);
59               if (c.equals(aCoin)) return true; // found a match
60            }
61            return false; // no match in the entire array list
62         }
63
64         /**
65            Counts the number of coins in the purse that match
66            a given coin.
67            @param aCoin the coin to match
68            @return the number of coins equal to aCoin
69         */
70         public int count(Coin aCoin)
71         {
72            int matches = 0;
73            for (int i = 0; i < coins.size(); i++)
74            {
75               Coin c = (Coin)coins.get(i);
76               if (c.equals(aCoin)) matches++; // found a match
77            }
78            return matches;
79         }
80
81         /**
82            Finds the coin with the largest value.
83            (Precondition: The purse is not empty)
84            @return a coin with maximum value in this purse
85         */
86         Coin getMaximum()
87         {
88            Coin max = (Coin)coins.get(0);
89            for (int i = 1; i < coins.size(); i++)
90            {
91               Coin c = (Coin)coins.get(i);
92               if (c.getValue() > max.getValue())
93                  max = c;
94            }
95            return max;
96         }
97
98         private ArrayList coins;
99      }
```

13.3 Storing Numbers in Array Lists

> To store primitive type values in an array list, you must use wrapper classes.

Because numbers are not objects in Java, you cannot directly insert them into array lists. To store sequences of integers, floating-point numbers, or `boolean` values in an array list, you must use *wrapper classes*. The classes `Integer`, `Double`, and `Boolean` wrap numbers and truth values inside objects. These wrapper objects can be stored inside array lists.

The `Double` class is a typical number wrapper. There is a constructor that makes a `Double` object out of a `double` value:

```
Double d = new Double(29.95);
```

Conversely, the `doubleValue` method retrieves the `double` value that is stored inside the `Double` object.

```
double x = d.doubleValue();
```

Here is how you can add a floating-point number into an array list. First construct a wrapper object, then add the object:

```
ArrayList data = new ArrayList();
double x = 29.95;
Double wrapper = new Double(x);
data.add(wrapper);
```

To retrieve the number, you need to cast the return value of the `get` method to `Double`, then call the `doubleValue` method:

```
Double wrapper = (Double)data.get(0);
double x = wrapper.doubleValue();
```

As you can see, using wrapper classes to store numbers in an array list is also a considerable hassle. You will see in the next section how to use arrays to store sequences of numbers.

By the way, the `Integer` and `Double` classes should look familiar. You have used their `parseInt` and `parseDouble` method many times. These static methods really have nothing to do with wrapper objects for numbers; they were just put inside these classes because it seemed to be a convenient place.

13.4 Declaring and Accessing Arrays

> An array is a fixed-length sequence of values of the same type.

An *array* is a fixed-length sequence of values of the same type, which can be an object type or a primitive type. For example, here is how you construct an array of ten `double` values:

```
new double[10]
```

In most cases you will want to store a reference to the array in a variable so that you can access it later. The type of an array variable is the element type, followed by `[]`. In this example, the type is `double[]`, because the element type is `double`. Here is the declaration of an array variable:

```
double[] data = new double[10];
```

Figure 3

An Array Reference and an Array

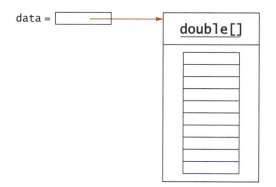

That is, `data` is a reference to an array of floating-point numbers. The call

```
new double[10]
```

creates the actual array of 10 numbers. (See Figure 3.)

Arrays differ from array lists in two aspects:

1. An array has a fixed length. In contrast, an array list starts out with length 0, grows when you add elements, and shrinks when you remove them.

2. An array has elements of a specified type, whereas an array list holds a collection of `Object` references.

When an array is first created, all values are initialized with 0 (for an array of numbers such as `int[]` or `double[]`), `false` (for a `boolean[]` array), or `null` (for an array of objects).

To change a value in the `data` array, you need to specify which position in the array you want to access. That is done with the `[]` operator, which follows the name of the array and encloses the index expression:

```
data[4] = 29.95;
```

> You access array elements with an integer index, using the notation a[i].

Now the position with index 4 of `data` is filled with the value 29.95.

To read out the data value at index 4, you simply use the expression `data[4]` as you would any variable of type `double`:

```
System.out.println("The price of this item is "
    + data[4]);
```

This is an advantage of arrays over array lists. The `[]` notation is more compact than calls to the `set` and `get` methods.

As with array lists, the positions of arrays are numbered starting at 0. That is, the legal positions for the `data` array run from `data[0]`, the first position, up to `data[9]`, the tenth position.

As with array lists, it is an error to try to access nonexistent positions.

```
int i = 10;
double x = data[i]; // ERROR
```

There is no `data[10]`. Remember, the array has length 10, so the index values range from 0 to 9. The compiler does not catch this error. Generally, it is too difficult for the compiler to follow the current contents of `data` and `i`. However, when an invalid index is detected during the execution of a program, an exception is generated and the program terminates.

Another common error is to forget to initialize the array variable:

```
double[] data; // not initialized
data[0] = 29.95;
```

<table>
<tr><td>

Use the `length` field to find the number of elements in an array.

</td><td>

When an array variable is defined, it must be initialized with an array such as `new double[10]` before any array elements can be accessed.

A Java array has an instance variable `length`, which you can access to find out the size of the array. For example, here is how you can find out the lowest price in an array of prices:

</td></tr>
</table>

```
double lowest = data[0];
for (int i = 1; i < data.length; i++)
   if (data[i] < lowest)
      lowest = data[i];
```

Note that there are *no parentheses* following `length`—it is an instance variable of the array object, not a method. However, you cannot assign a new value to this instance variable. In other words, `length` is a final public instance variable. This is quite an anomaly. Normally, Java programmers use a method to inquire about the properties of an object. You just have to remember to omit the parentheses in this case.

Using `length` is a much better idea than using a number such as 10, even if you know that the array has ten elements. If the program changes later, and there are now 20 values, then the loop automatically stays valid. This principle is another case of avoiding magic numbers, as discussed in Quality Tip 3.2.

Syntax 13.1: Array Construction

new *typeName*[*length*]

Example:

new double[10]

Purpose:

To construct an array with a given number of elements

Syntax 13.2: Array Element Access

arrayReference[*index*]

Example:

```
a[4] = 29.95;
double x = a[4];
```

Purpose:

To access an element in an array

Common Error 13.3

Uninitialized Arrays

A common error is to allocate an array reference, but not an actual array.

```
double[] data;
data[0] == 29.95; // Error—data not initialized
```

Array variables work exactly like object variables—they are only references to the actual array. To construct the actual array, you must use the new operator:

```
double[] data = new double[10];
```

Common Error 13.4

Length and Size

Unfortunately, the Java syntax for determining the number of elements in an array, an array list, and a string is not at all consistent.

Data type	Number of elements
Array	a.length
Array list	a.size()
String	a.length()

It is a common error to confuse these. You just have to remember the correct syntax for every data type.

Advanced Topic 13.1

Array Initialization

You can initialize an array by allocating it and then filling each entry:

```
int[] primes = new int[5];
primes[0] = 2;
primes[1] = 3;
primes[2] = 5;
primes[3] = 7;
primes[4] = 11;
```

▼ However, if you already know all the elements that you want to place in the array, there is an easier way. You can list all elements that you want to include in the array, enclosed in braces and separated by commas:

▼
```
int[] primes = { 2, 3, 5, 7, 11 };
```

The Java compiler counts how many elements you want to place in the array, allocates an
▼ array of the correct size, and fills it with the elements that you specify.

If you want to construct an array and pass it on to a method that expects an array parameter, you can initialize an *anonymous array* as follows:

▼
```
new int[] { 2, 3, 5, 7, 11 }
```

13.5   Copying Arrays

> An array variable stores a reference to the array. Copying the variable yields a second reference to the same array.

Array variables work just like object variables—they hold a *reference* to the actual array. If you copy the reference, you get another reference to the same array (see Figure 4):

```
double[] data = new double[10];
. . . // fill array
double[] prices = data;
```

> Use the clone method to copy the elements of an array.

If you want to make a true copy of an array, call the clone method (see Figure 5).

```
double[] prices = (double[])data.clone();
```

Note that you need to cast the return value of the clone method from the type Object to the type double[].

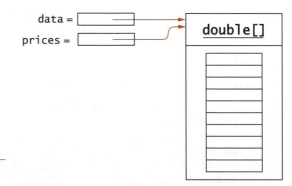

Figure 4

Two References to the Same Array

Figure 5

Cloning an Array

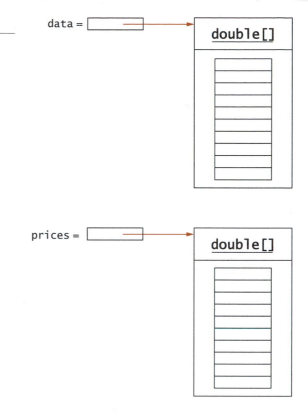

Use the
`System.arraycopy`
method to copy elements
from one array to another.

Occasionally, you need to copy elements from one array into another array. You can use the static `System.arraycopy` method for that purpose (see Figure 6):

```
System.arraycopy(from, fromStart, to, toStart, count);
```

One use for the `System.arraycopy` method is to add or remove elements in the middle of an array. To add a new element at position i into `data`, first move all elements from i onward one position up. Then insert the new value.

```
System.arraycopy(data, i, data, i + 1,
    data.length - i - 1);
data[i] = x;
```

Note that the last element in the array is lost (see Figure 7).

To remove the element at position i, copy the elements above the position downward (see Figure 8).

```
System.arraycopy(data, i + 1, data, i,
    data.length - i - 1);
```

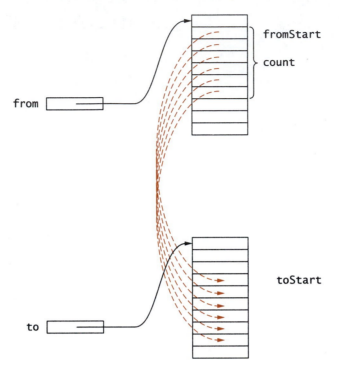

Figure 6

The System.arraycopy Method

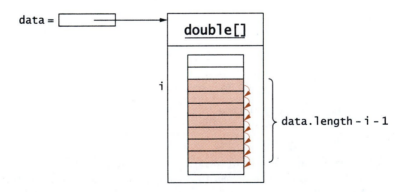

Figure 7

Inserting a New Element into an Array

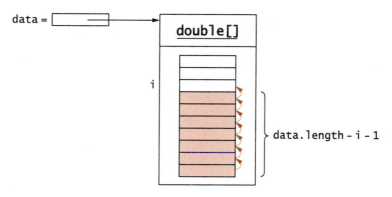

Figure 8

Removing an Element from an Array

13.6   Partially Filled Arrays

Suppose you write a program that reads a sequence of numbers into an array. How many numbers will the user enter? You can't very well ask the user to count the items for us before entering them—that is just the kind of work that the user expects the computer to do. Unfortunately, you now run into a problem. You need to set the size of the array before you know how many elements you need. Once the array size is set, it cannot be changed.

> Arrays are often *partially filled*. Then you need to remember the number of elements that you actually placed in the array.

To solve this problem, you can sometimes make an array that is guaranteed to be larger than the largest possible number of entries, and *partially fill it*. For example, you can decide that the user will never enter more than 100 data points. Then allocate an array of size 100:

```
final int DATA_LENGTH = 100;
double[] data = new double[DATA_LENGTH];
```

Then keep a *companion variable* that tells how many elements in the array are actually used. It is an excellent idea *always* to name this companion variable by adding the suffix Size to the name of the array.

```
int dataSize = 0;
```

Now data.length is the *capacity* of the array data, and dataSize is the *current size* of the array (see Figure 9). Keep adding elements into the array, incrementing the size variable each time.

```
data[dataSize] = x;
dataSize++;
```

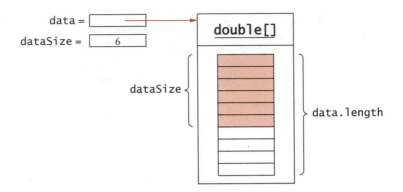

Figure 9

A Partially Filled Array

This way, `dataSize` always contains the correct element count. When inspecting the array elements, you must be careful to stop at `dataSize`, not at `data.length`:

```
for (int i = 0; i < dataSize; i++)
    sum = sum + data[i];
```

You must be careful not to overfill the array. Insert elements only if there is still room for them! If the array fills up, there are two approaches you can take. The simple way out is to refuse additional entries:

```
if (dataSize >= data.length)
    System.out.println("Sorry, the array is full.");
```

> If you run out of space in an array, you need to allocate a larger array and copy the elements into it.

Of course, refusing to accept all input is often unreasonable. Users routinely use software on larger data sets than the original developers ever imagined. Therefore, you will need to work a little harder for a realistic program. When you run out of space in an array, you can create a new, larger array; copy all elements into the new array; and then attach the new array to the old array variable.

```
if (dataSize >= data.length)
{
    // make a new array of twice the size
    double[] newData = new double[2 * data.length];
    // copy over all elements from data to newData
    System.arraycopy(data, 0, newData, 0, data.length);
    // abandon the old array and store in data
    // a reference to the new array
    data = newData;
}
```

Figure 10 shows the process.

At the end of this section, you will find an implementation of the `DataSet` class that stores an arbitrary number of elements. We test it with a program that feeds in 10,000 random numbers.

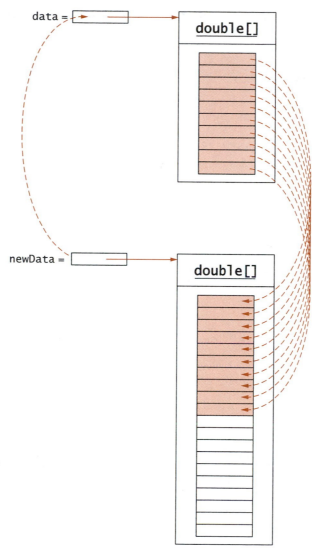

Figure 10

Growing an Array

The `ArrayList` class contains an `Object[]` array to hold a sequence of objects. When the array runs out of space, the `ArrayList` class allocates a larger array, using exactly the same technique that you just saw.

Frankly, it is a hassle to track array sizes and to grow arrays when they run out of space. If you collect *objects*, then you can avoid that hassle, simply by using an array list. You should generally use array lists to collect objects.

Fortunately, in most object-oriented programs, you collect objects, not numbers. However, when you collect numbers, you need to make a hard choice. Is it more of a hassle to track array sizes, or to use wrapper classes? An array of numbers is much more efficient than an array list of wrapper objects that contain numbers, so most programmers will choose arrays.

File DataSet.java

```
1   /**
2       This class computes the average of a set of data values.
3   */
4   public class DataSet
5   {
6       /**
7           Constructs an empty data set.
8       */
9       public DataSet()
10      {
11          final int DATA_LENGTH = 100;
12          data = new double[DATA_LENGTH];
13          dataSize = 0;
14      }
15
16      /**
17          Adds a data value to the data set.
18          @param x a data value
19      */
20      public void add(double x)
21      {
22          if (dataSize >= data.length)
23          {
24              // make a new array of twice the size
25              double[] newData = new double[2 * data.length];
26              // copy over all elements from data to newData
27              System.arraycopy(data, 0, newData, 0,
28                  data.length);
29              // abandon the old array and store in data
30              // a reference to the new array
31              data = newData;
32          }
33          data[dataSize] = x;
34          dataSize++;
35      }
36
37      /**
38          Gets the average of the added data.
39          @return the average or 0 if no data have been added
40      */
41      public double getAverage()
42      {
43          if (dataSize == 0) return 0;
44          double sum = 0;
```

```
45          for (int i = 0; i < dataSize; i++)
46              sum = sum + data[i];
47          return sum / dataSize;
48      }
49
50      private double[] data;
51      private int dataSize;
52  }
```

File DataSetTest.java

```
1  import java.util.Random;
2
3  /**
4      This program tests the DataSet class by adding 10,000 numbers
5      to the data set and computing the average.
6  */
7  public class DataSetTest
8  {
9      public static void main(String[] args)
10     {
11         Random generator = new Random();
12         DataSet data = new DataSet();
13         final int COUNT = 10000;
14         System.out.println("Adding " +
15             COUNT + " random numbers.");
16         for (int i = 0; i < COUNT; i++)
17         {
18             double x = generator.nextDouble();
19             data.add(x);
20         }
21         double average = data.getAverage();
22         System.out.println("average=" + average);
23     }
24 }
```

▼ ⊗ Common Error | 13.5

Underestimating the Size of a Data Set

Programmers commonly underestimate the amount of input data that a user will pour into an unsuspecting program. The most common problem caused by underestimating the amount of input data results from the use of fixed-sized arrays. Suppose you write a program to search for text in a file. You store each line in a string, and keep an array of strings. How big do you make the array? Surely nobody is going to challenge your program with an input that is more than 100 lines. Really? A smart grader can easily feed in the entire text of *Alice in Wonderland* or *War and Peace* (which are available on the Internet).

▼ All of a sudden, your program has to deal with tens or hundreds of thousands of lines. What will it do? Will it handle the input? Will it politely reject the excess input? Will it crash and burn?

▼ A famous article [1] analyzed how several UNIX programs reacted when they were fed large or random data sets. Sadly, about a quarter didn't do well at all, crashing or hanging without a reasonable error message. For example, in some versions of UNIX the tape backup program *tar* cannot handle file names that are longer than 100 characters, which is a pretty unreasonable limitation. Many of these shortcomings are caused by features of the C language that, unlike Java, makes it difficult to store strings of arbitrary size.

▼ **Random Fact** **13.1**

An Early Internet Worm

▼ In November 1988, a graduate student at Cornell University launched a virus program that infected about 6,000 computers connected to the Internet across the United States. Tens of thousands of computer users were unable to read their email or otherwise use their computers. All major universities and many high-tech companies were affected. (The Internet was much smaller then than it is now.)

▼ The particular kind of virus used in this attack is called a *worm*. The virus program crawled from one computer on the Internet to the next. The entire program is quite complex; its major parts are explained in [2]. However, one of the methods used in the attack is of interest here. The worm would attempt to connect to *finger*, a program in the UNIX operating system for finding information on a user who has an account on a particular computer on the network. Like many programs in UNIX, *finger* was written in the C language. C does not have array lists, only arrays, and when you construct an array in C, as in Java, you have to make up your mind how many elements you need. To store the user name to be looked up (say, `walters@cs.sjsu.edu`), the *finger* program allocated an array of 512 characters, under the assumption that nobody would ever provide such a long input. Unfortunately, C, unlike Java, does not check that an array index is less than the length of the array. If you write into an array, using an index that is too large, you simply overwrite memory locations that belong to some other objects. In some versions of the *finger* program, the programmer had been lazy and had not checked whether the array holding the input characters was large enough to hold the input. So the worm program purposefully filled the 512-character array with 536 bytes. The excess 24 bytes would overwrite a return address, which the attacker knew was stored just after the line buffer. When that function was finished, it didn't return to its caller but to code supplied by the worm. That code ran under the same super-user privileges as *finger*, allowing the worm to gain entry into the remote system.

▼ Had the programmer who wrote *finger* been more conscientious, this particular attack would not be possible. In C++ and C, all programmers must be especially careful not to overrun array boundaries.

One may well wonder what would possess a skilled programmer to spend many weeks or months to plan the antisocial act of breaking into thousands of computers and disabling them. It appears that the break-in was fully intended by the author, but the disabling of the computers was a side effect of continuous reinfection and efforts by the worm to avoid being killed. It is not clear whether the author was aware that these moves would cripple the attacked machines.

In recent years, the novelty of vandalizing other people's computers has worn off somewhat, and there are fewer jerks with programming skills who write new viruses. Other attacks by individuals with more criminal energy, whose intent has been to steal information or money, have surfaced. Reference [3] gives a very readable account of the discovery and apprehension of one such person.

Quality Tip   13.1

Make Parallel Arrays into Arrays of Objects

> Avoid parallel arrays by changing them into arrays of objects.

Programmers who are familiar with arrays but unfamiliar with object-oriented programming sometimes distribute information across separate arrays. Here is a typical example. A program needs to manage employee data, consisting of employee names and salaries. Don't store the names and salaries in separate arrays.

```
// don't do this
String[] names;
double[] salaries;
```

In such a program, related information is distributed in separate arrays. The ith *slice* (names[i] and salaries[i]) contains data that needs to be processed together. These arrays are called *parallel arrays* (Figure 11).

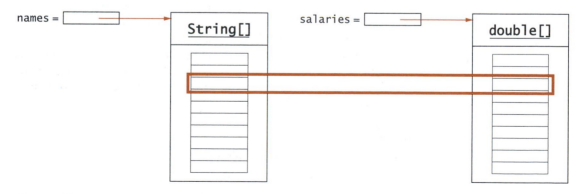

Figure 11

Avoid Parallel Arrays

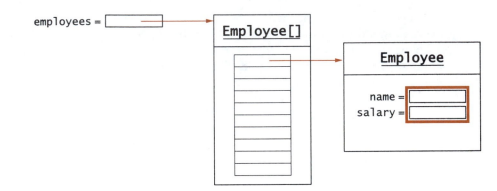

Figure 12

Reorganizing Parallel Arrays into an Array of Objects

If you find yourself using two arrays that have the same length, ask yourself whether you couldn't replace them with a single array of a class type. Look at a slice and find the *concept* that it represents. Then make the concept into a class. In our example each slice contains a name and a salary, describing an *employee*. Therefore, it is an easy matter to use a single array of objects

```
Employee[] staff;
```

(See Figure 12.) Or, even better, use an `ArrayList` of `Employee` objects.

Why is this beneficial? Think ahead. Maybe your program will change and you will need to store the job title of the employees as well. It is a simple matter to update the `Employee` class. It may well be quite complicated to add a new array and make sure that all methods that accessed the original two arrays now also correctly access the third one.

13.7   Two-Dimensional Arrays

> Two-dimensional arrays form a tabular, two-dimensional arrangement. You access elements with an index pair a[i][j].

Arrays and array lists can store linear sequences. Occasionally you want to store collections that have a two-dimensional layout. The traditional example is the tic-tac-toe board (see Figure 13).

Such an arrangement, consisting of rows and columns of values, is called a *two-dimensional array* or *matrix*. When constructing a two-dimensional array, you specify how many rows and columns you need. In this case, ask for 3 rows and 3 columns:

```
final int ROWS = 3;
final int COLUMNS = 3;
char[][] board = new char[ROWS][COLUMNS];
```

This yields a two-dimensional array with 9 elements

```
board[0][0]    board[0][1]    board[0][2]
board[1][0]    board[1][1]    board[1][2]
board[2][0]    board[2][1]    board[2][2]
```

Figure 13

A Tic-Tac-Toe Board

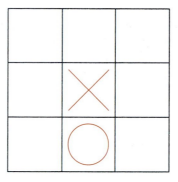

To access a particular element, specify two subscripts in separate brackets:

```
board[i][j] = 'x';
```

When filling or searching a two-dimensional array, it is common to use two nested loops. For example, this pair of loops sets all elements in the array to spaces.

```
for (int i = 0; i < ROWS; i++)
    for (int j = 0; j < COLUMNS; j++)
        board[i][j] = ' ';
```

Here is a class and a test program for playing tic-tac-toe. This class does not check whether a player has won the game. That is left as the proverbial exercise to the reader—see Exercise P13.15.

File TicTacToe.java

```
 1  /**
 2      A 3 × 3 tic-tac-toe board.
 3  */
 4  public class TicTacToe
 5  {
 6      /**
 7          Constructs an empty board.
 8      */
 9      public TicTacToe()
10      {
11          board = new char[ROWS][COLUMNS];
12
13          // fill with spaces
14          for (int i = 0; i < ROWS; i++)
15              for (int j = 0; j < COLUMNS; j++)
16                  board[i][j] = ' ';
17      }
18
```

```
19    /**
20        Sets a field in the board. The field must be unoccupied.
21        @param i  the row index
22        @param j  the column index
23        @param player  the player ('x' or 'o')
24    */
25    public void set(int i, int j, char player)
26    {
27        if (board[i][j] != ' ')
28            throw new IllegalArgumentException(
29                "Position occupied");
30        board[i][j] = player;
31    }
32
33    /**
34        Creates a string representation of the board such as
35        |x  o|
36        | x |
37        |  o|.
38        @return  the string representation
39    */
40    public String toString()
41    {
42        String r = "";
43        for (int i = 0; i < ROWS; i++)
44        {
45            r = r + "|";
46            for (int j = 0; j < COLUMNS; j++)
47                r = r + board[i][j];
48            r = r + "|\n";
49        }
50        return r;
51    }
52
53    private char[][] board;
54    private static final int ROWS = 3;
55    private static final int COLUMNS = 3;
56 }
```

File TicTacToeTest.java

```
1  import javax.swing.JOptionPane;
2
3  /**
4      This program tests the TicTacToe class by prompting the
5      user to set positions on the board and printing out the
6      result.
7  */
```

```
 8  public class TicTacToeTest
 9  {
10     public static void main(String[] args)
11     {
12        char player = 'x';
13        TicTacToe game = new TicTacToe();
14        while (true)
15        {
16           System.out.println(game); // calls game.toString()
17           String input = JOptionPane.showInputDialog(
18              "Row for " + player + " (Cancel to exit)");
19           if (input == null) System.exit(0);
20           int row = Integer.parseInt(input);
21           input = JOptionPane.showInputDialog(
22              "Column for " + player);
23           int column = Integer.parseInt(input);
24           game.set(row, column, player);
25           if (player == 'x') player = 'o';
26           else player = 'x';
27        }
28     }
29  }
```

▼ ◢◣ Advanced Topic   13.2

Two-Dimensional Arrays with Variable Row Lengths

When you declare a two-dimensional array with the command

```
int[][] a = new int[5][5];
```

then you get a 5-by-5 matrix that can store 25 elements:

```
a[0][0] a[0][1] a[0][2] a[0][3] a[0][4]
a[1][0] a[1][1] a[1][2] a[1][3] a[1][4]
a[2][0] a[2][1] a[2][2] a[2][3] a[2][4]
a[3][0] a[3][1] a[3][2] a[3][3] a[3][4]
a[4][0] a[4][1] a[4][2] a[4][3] a[4][4]
```

In this matrix, all rows have the same length. In Java it is possible to declare arrays in which the row length varies. For example, you can store an array that has triangular shape, such as this one:

```
b[0][0]
b[1][0] b[1][1]
b[2][0] b[2][1] b[2][2]
b[3][0] b[3][1] b[3][2] b[3][3]
b[4][0] b[4][1] b[4][2] b[4][3] b[4][4]
```

▼ To allocate such an array, you must work harder. First, you allocate space to hold five rows. You indicate that you will manually set each row by leaving the second array index empty:

▼
```
int[][] b = new int[5][];
```

Then you need to allocate each row separately.

▼
```
for (int i = 0; i < b.length; i++)
   b[i] = new int[i + 1];
```

▼ You can access each array element as `b[i][j]`, but you must now be careful that `j` is less than `b[i].length`.

Naturally, such "ragged" arrays are not very common.

▼

Chapter Summary

1. An array list is a sequence of objects.

2. Each object in an array list has an integer position number, called the index.

3. When retrieving an element from an array list, you need to cast the return value of the `get` method to the element class.

4. Position numbers of an array range from 0 to `size()` - 1. Accessing a nonexistent position results in a bounds error.

5. To find a value in an array list, check all elements until you have found a match.

6. To count values in an array list, check all elements and count the matches, until you reach the end of the array list.

7. To compute the maximum or minimum value of an array list, initialize a candidate with the starting element. Then compare the candidate with the remaining elements and update it if you find a larger or smaller value.

8. To store primitive type values in an array list, you must use wrapper classes.

9. An array is a fixed-length sequence of values of the same type.

10. You access array elements with an integer index, using the notation `a[i]`.

11. Use the `length` field to find the number of elements in an array.

12. An array variable stores a reference to the array. Copying the variable yields a second reference to the same array.

13. Use the `clone` method to copy the elements of an array.

14. Use the `System.arraycopy` method to copy elements from one array to another.

15. Arrays are often *partially filled*. Then you need to remember the number of elements that you actually placed in the array.

16. If you run out of space in an array, you need to allocate a larger array and copy the elements into it.

17. Avoid parallel arrays by changing them into arrays of objects.

18. Two-dimensional arrays form a tabular, two-dimensional arrangement. You access elements with an index pair a[i][j].

Further Reading

[1] Barton P. Miller, Louis Fericksen, and Bryan So, "An Empirical Study of the Reliability of Unix Utilities", *Communications of the ACM,* vol. 33, no. 12 (December 1990), pp. 32–44.
[2] Peter J. Denning, *Computers under Attack*, Addison-Wesley, 1990.
[3] Cliff Stoll, *The Cuckoo's Egg*, Doubleday, 1989.

CLASSES, OBJECTS, AND METHODS INTRODUCED IN THIS CHAPTER

```
java.lang.Boolean
    booleanValue
java.lang.Double
    doubleValue
java.lang.Integer
    intValue
java.lang.System
    arrayCopy
java.util.ArrayList
    add
    get
    remove
    set
    size
```

REVIEW EXERCISES

Exercise R13.1. What is an index? What are the bounds of an array list? What is a bounds error?

Exercise R13.2. Write a program that contains a bounds error. Run the program. What happens on your computer? How does the error message help you locate the error?

Exercise R13.3. Write Java code for a loop that simultaneously computes the maximum and minimum value of an array list. Use an array list of coins as an example.

Exercise R13.4. Write a loop that reads ten strings and inserts them into an array list. Write a second loop that prints out the strings in the opposite order from which they were entered.

Exercise R13.5. For each of the following sets of values, write code that fills an array a with the values.

- 1 2 3 4 5 6 7 8 9 10
- 0 2 4 6 8 10 12 14 16 18 20
- 1 4 9 16 25 36 49 64 81 100
- 0 0 0 0 0 0 0 0 0 0
- 1 4 9 16 9 7 4 9 11

Use a loop when appropriate.

Exercise R13.6. Write a loop that fills an array a with ten random numbers between 1 and 100. Write code (using one or more loops) to fill a with ten *different* random numbers between 1 and 100.

Exercise R13.7. What is wrong with the following loop?

```
double[] data = new double[10];
for (int i = 1; i <= 10; i++) data[i] = i * i;
```

Explain two ways of fixing the error.

Exercise R13.8. Write a program that fills an array of 20 integers with the numbers 1, 4, 9, ..., 100. Compile it and launch the debugger. After the array has been filled with three numbers, *inspect it*. What are the contents of the elements in the array beyond those that you filled?

Exercise R13.9. Give an example of

- A useful method that has an array of integers as a parameter that is not modified
- A useful method that has an array of integers as a parameter that is modified
- A useful method that has an array of integers as a return value

Just describe each method. Don't implement the methods.

Exercise R13.10. A method that has an array list as a parameter can change the contents in two ways. It can change the contents of individual array elements, or it can rearrange the elements. Describe two useful methods with ArrayList parameters that change an array list of Employee objects in each of the two ways just described.

Exercise R13.11. What are parallel arrays? Why are parallel arrays indications of poor programming? How can they be avoided?

Exercise R13.12. How do you perform the following tasks with arrays in Java?

- Test that two arrays contain the same elements in the same order.
- Copy one array to another.
- Fill an array with zeroes, overwriting all elements in it.
- Remove all elements from an array list.

Exercise R13.13. True or false?

- All elements of an array are of the same type.
- Array subscripts must be integers.
- Arrays cannot contain strings as elements.
- Arrays cannot use strings as subscripts.
- Parallel arrays must have equal length.
- Two-dimensional arrays always have the same numbers of rows and columns.
- Two parallel arrays can be replaced by a two-dimensional array.
- Elements of different columns in a two-dimensional array can have different types.
- Elements in an array list can have different types.

Exercise R13.14. True or false?

- A method cannot return a two-dimensional array.
- A method can change the length of an array parameter.
- A method can change the length of an array list that is passed as a parameter.
- An array list can hold values of any type.

PROGRAMMING EXERCISES

Exercise P13.1. Implement a class `Bank` that contains an array list of `BankAccount` objects. Support methods

```
public void addAccount(double initialBalance)
public void deposit(int account, double amount)
public void withdraw(int account, double amount)
public double getBalance(int account)
```

An account number is simply an index into the array list.

Exercise P13.2. Add a method `toString` to the `Purse` class that prints the coins in the purse in the format

```
Purse[Quarter,Dime,Nickel,Dime]
```

Exercise P13.3. Write a method `reverse` that reverses the sequence of coins in a purse. Use the `toString` method of the preceding assignment to test your code. For example, if `reverse` is called with a purse

```
Purse[Quarter,Dime,Nickel,Dime]
```

then the purse is changed to

```
Purse[Dime,Nickel,Dime,Quarter]
```

Exercise P13.4. Add a method

```
public void transfer(Purse other)
```

that transfers the contents of one purse to another. For example, if a is

```
Purse[Quarter,Dime,Nickel,Dime]
```

and b is

```
Purse[Dime,Nickel]
```

then after the call a.append(b), a is

```
Purse[Quarter,Dime,Nickel,Dime,Dime,Nickel]
```

and b is empty.

Exercise P13.5. Write an `equals` method for the `Purse` class

```
public boolean equals(Object other)
```

that checks whether the other purse has the same coins in the same order.

Exercise P13.6. Write an `equals` method for the `Purse` class

```
public boolean equals(Object other)
```

that checks whether the other purse has the same coins in *some* order. For example, the purses

```
Purse[Quarter,Dime,Nickel,Dime]
```

and

```
Purse[Nickel,Dime,Dime,Quarter]
```

should be considered equal.

You will probably need one or more helper methods.

Exercise P13.7. Implement a class `Cloud` that contains an array list of `Point2D.Double` objects. Support methods

```
public void add(Point2D.Double aPoint)
public void draw(Graphics2D g)
```

Draw each point as a tiny circle.

Write an applet that draws a cloud of 20 random points.

Exercise P13.8. Implement a class `Polygon` that contains an array list of `Point2D.Double` objects. Support methods

```
public void add(Point2D.Double aPoint)
public void draw(Graphics2D g)
```

Draw the polygon by joining adjacent points by a line, and then closing it up by joining the end and start points.

Write an applet that draws a square and a pentagon using two `Polygon` objects.

Exercise P13.9. Write methods of the `Polygon` class of the preceding exercise

```
public double perimeter()
```

and

```
public double area()
```

that compute the circumference and the area of a polygon. To compute the perimeter, compute the distance between adjacent points, and total up the distances. The area of a polygon with corners $(x_0, y_0), \ldots, (x_{n-1}, y_{n-1})$ is

$$\frac{1}{2}(x_0 y_1 + x_1 y_2 + \cdots + x_{n-1} y_0 - y_0 x_1 - y_1 x_2 - \cdots - y_{n-1} x_0)$$

As test cases, compute the perimeter and area of a rectangle and of a regular hexagon.

Exercise P13.10. Add a method that computes the *alternating sum* of all elements in the `DataSet` class of section 13.6. For example, if `alternatingSum` is called with the data

$$1 \quad 4 \quad 9 \quad 16 \quad 9 \quad 7 \quad 4 \quad 9 \quad 11$$

then it computes

$$1 - 4 + 9 - 16 + 9 - 7 + 4 - 9 + 11 = -2$$

Exercise P13.11. Write a program that produces random permutations of the numbers 1 to 10. To generate a random permutation, you need to fill an array with the numbers 1 to 10 so that no two entries of the array have the same contents. You could do it by brute force, by calling `Random.nextInt` until it produces a value that is not yet in the array. Instead, you should implement a smart method. Make a second array and fill it with the numbers 1 to 10. Then pick one of those at random, *remove it,* and append it to the permutation array. Repeat ten times. Implement a class `PermutationGenerator` with a method

```
int[] nextPermutation
```

Exercise P13.12. Write a class `Chart` with methods

```
public void add(int value)
public void draw(Graphics2D g2)
```

that displays a stick chart of the added values, similar to the chart in Section 4.10. You may assume that the values are pixel positions.

Exercise P13.13. Write a class `BarChart` with methods

```
public void add(double value)
public void draw(Graphics2D g2)
```

that displays a chart of the added values. You may assume that all values in `data` are positive. *Hint:* You must figure out the maximum of the values. Set the coordinate system so that the x-range equals the number of bars and the y-range goes from 0 to the maximum.

Exercise P13.14. Improve the `BarChart` class of the preceding exercise to work correctly when `data` contains negative values.

Exercise P13.15. Write a class `PieChart` with methods

```
public void add(double value)
public void draw(Graphics2D g2)
```

that displays a pie chart of the values in `data`. You may assume that all values in `data` are positive.

Exercise P13.16. Add a method `getWinner` to the `TicTacToe` class of Section 13.7. It should return `'x'` or `'o'` to indicate a winner, or `' '` if there is no winner yet. Recall that a winning position has three matching marks in a row, column, or diagonal.

Exercise P13.17. Write an applet that plays tic-tac-toe. Your program should draw the game board, accept mouse clicks into empty squares, change players after every successful move, and pronounce the winner.

Exercise P13.18. *Magic squares.* An $n \times n$ matrix that is filled with the numbers 1, 2, 3, ..., n^2 is a magic square if the sum of the elements in each row, in each column, and in the two diagonals is the same value. For example,

16	3	2	13
5	10	11	8
9	6	7	12
4	15	14	1

Write a program that reads in n^2 values from the keyboard and tests whether they form a magic square when arranged as a square matrix. You need to test three features:

- Did the user enter n^2 numbers for some n?
- Does each of the numbers 1, 2, ..., n^2 occur exactly once in the user input?
- When the numbers are put into a square, are the sums of the rows, columns, and diagonals equal to each other?

If the size of the input is a square, test whether all numbers between 1 and n are present. Then compute the row, column, and diagonal sums. Implement a class `Square` with methods

```
public void add(int i)
public boolean isMagic()
```

Exercise P13.19. Implement the following algorithm to construct magic n-by-n squares; it works only if n is odd. Place a 1 in the middle of the bottom row. After k has been placed in the (i, j) square, place $k + 1$ into the square to the right and down, wrapping around the borders. However, if the square to the right and down has already been filled, or if you are in the lower right corner, then you must move to the square straight up instead. Here is the 5×5 square that you get if you follow this method:

11	18	25	2	9
10	12	19	21	3
4	6	13	20	22
23	5	7	14	16
17	24	1	8	15

Write a program whose input is the number *n* and whose output is the magic square of order *n* if *n* is odd. Implement a class `MagicSquare` with a constructor that constructs the square and a `toString` method that returns a representation of the square.

Exercise P13.20. The *Game of Life* is a well-known mathematical game that gives rise to amazingly complex behavior, although it can be specified by a few simple rules. (It is not actually a game in the traditional sense, with players competing for a win.) Here are the rules. The game is played on a rectangular board. Each square can be either empty or occupied. At the beginning, you can specify empty and occupied cells in some way; then the game runs automatically. In each *generation*, the next generation is computed. A new cell is born on an empty square if it is surrounded by exactly three occupied neighbor cells. A cell dies of overcrowding if it is surrounded by four or more neighbors, and it dies of loneliness if it is surrounded by zero or one neighbors. A neighbor is an occupant of an adjacent square to the left, right, top, or bottom or in a diagonal direction. Figure 14 shows a cell and its neighbor cells.

Many configurations show interesting behavior when subjected to these rules. Figure 15 shows a *glider*, observed over five generations. Note how it moves. After four generations, it is transformed into the identical shape, but located one square to the right and below.

One of the more amazing configurations is the *glider gun*: a complex collection of cells that, after 30 moves, turns back into itself and a glider. (See Figure 16.)

Program the game to eliminate the drudgery of computing successive generations by hand. Use a two-dimensional array to store the rectangular configuration. Write a program that shows successive generations of the game. You may get extra credit if you implement an applet that lets the user add or remove cells by clicking with the mouse.

Figure 14

Neighborhood of a Cell in the Game of Life

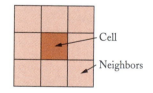

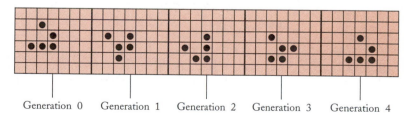

Generation 0   Generation 1   Generation 2   Generation 3   Generation 4

Figure 15

Glider

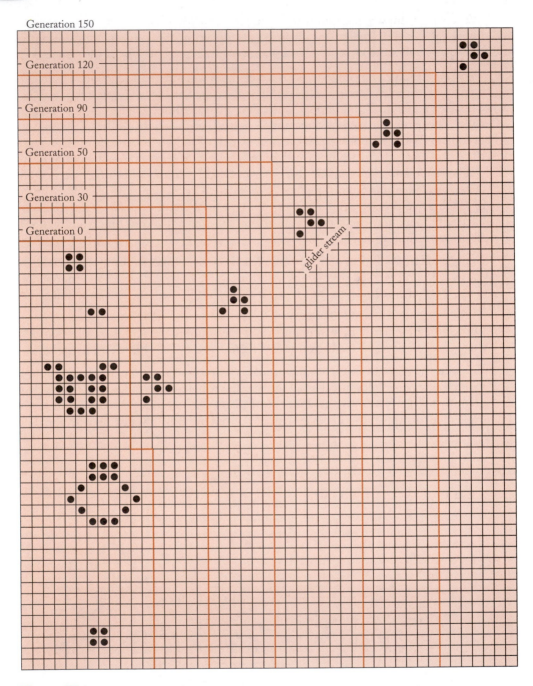

Figure 16

Glider Gun

Exception Handling

CHAPTER GOALS
To learn how to throw exceptions

CHAPTER GOALS
To learn how to throw exceptions

▶ To be able to design your own exception classes

▶ To understand the difference between checked and unchecked exceptions

▶ To learn how to catch exceptions

▶ To know when and where to catch an exception

As you probably know from your own experience, programs can fail for a variety of reasons. Bad input and programmer error are just two of many possible causes. A program should deal with failure in a predictable manner. There are two aspects to handling failure: *detection* and *recovery*. A major challenge of error handling is that the point of detection is usually decoupled from the point of recovery. For example, the get method of the ArrayList class may detect that a nonexistent element is being accessed, and the parseInt method of the Integer class may detect that the string that

it is processing can't be an integer, but neither of these methods has enough information to decide what to do about this failure. Should the user be asked to try a different operation? Should the program be aborted after saving the user's work? The logic for these actions is completely independent from the normal processing that these methods do. In Java, *exception handling* provides a flexible mechanism for passing control from the point of error detection to a competent recovery handler. This short chapter discusses the exception handling mechanism in detail and shows you how to use it appropriately in your programs.

14.1   Throwing Exceptions

When a method detects a problematic situation, what should it do? The traditional solution is that the method returns an indicator whether it succeeded or failed. For example, the `showInputDialog` method of the `JOptionPane` class returns either a string or `null` if the user canceled the dialog instead of supplying an input string. However, this approach has two problems.

1. The calling method may forget to check the return value.
2. The calling method may not be able to do anything about the failure.

If the calling method forgets to check the return value, a failure notification may go completely undetected. Then the program keeps going, processing faulty information and mysteriously failing later.

If the caller knows about the failure but it cannot do anything about it, it can fail too and let *its* caller worry about it. That would be a real hassle for the programmer, because many method calls would need to be checked for failure. Instead of programming for success,

```
x.doStuff();
```

you would always be programming for failure:

```
if (!x.doStuff()) return false;
```

That is fine when done occasionally, but if you have to check *every* method call, then your programs become very hard to read.

The exception handling mechanism has been designed to solve these two problems:

1. Exceptions can't be overlooked.
2. Exceptions can be handled by a *competent* handler—not just the caller of the failed method.

> To signal an exceptional condition, use the `throw` statement to throw an exception object.

Let us look into the details of this mechanism. When you detect an error condition, your job is really easy. You just `throw` an appropriate exception object, and you are done. For example, suppose someone tries to withdraw too much money from a bank account.

```java
public class BankAccount
{
    public void withdraw(double amount)
    {
        if (amount > balance)
            // now what?
        . . .
    }
    . . .
}
```

First look for an appropriate exception class. The Java library provides many classes to signal all sorts of exceptional conditions. Figure 1 shows the most useful ones.

Look around for an exception type that might describe your situation. How about the `IllegalStateException`? Is the bank account in an illegal state for the `withdraw` operation? Not really—some `withdraw` operations could succeed. Is the argument illegal? Indeed it is. It is just too large. Therefore, let's throw an `IllegalArgumentException`.

```java
public class BankAccount
{
    public void withdraw(double amount)
    {
        if (amount > balance)
        {
            IllegalArgumentException exception
                = new IllegalArgumentException(
                    "Amount exceeds balance");
            throw exception;
        }
        balance = balance - amount;
    }
    . . .
}
```

Actually, you don't have to store the exception object in a variable. You can just throw the object that the `new` operator returns:

```java
throw new IllegalArgumentException(
    "Amount exceeds balance");
```

> When you throw an exception, the current method terminates immediately.

When you throw an exception, the method exits immediately, just as with a `return` statement. Execution does not continue with the method's caller but with an *exception handler*. For now, we won't worry about the handling of the exception. That is the topic of Section 14.4.

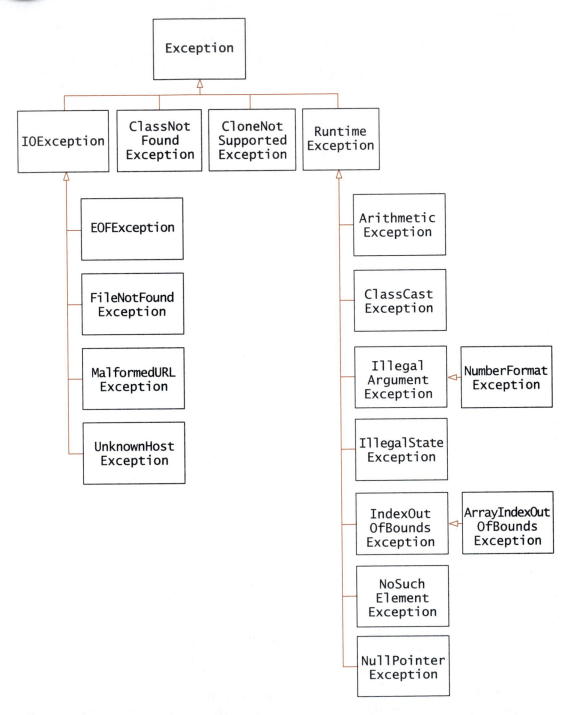

Figure 1

The Hierarchy of Exception Classes

> ### Syntax 14.1: Throwing an Exception
>
> throw *exceptionObject*;
>
> **Example:**
>
> throw new IllegalArgumentException();
>
> **Purpose:**
>
> To throw an exception and transfer control to a handler for this exception type

 **Quality Tip** **14.1**

Throw Exceptions Only in Exceptional Cases

Consider the readLine method of the BufferedReader class. It returns null at the end of the input. Why doesn't it throw an EOFException?

The designers of this method did the right thing. Every input must come to an end. In other words, the end of input is a normal condition, not an exceptional one. Whenever you read a line of input, you must be prepared to deal with the possibility that you reached the end. However, if the end of input occurs inside a data record that should be complete, then you can throw an EOFException to indicate that the input came to an *unexpected* end. This must have been caused by some exceptional event, perhaps a corrupted file.

In particular, you should *never* use exceptions as a "break statement on steroids". Don't throw an exception to exit a deeply nested loop or a set of recursive method calls. That is considered an abuse of the exception mechanism.

14.2 Checked Exceptions

> There are two kinds of exceptions:
> checked exceptions and unchecked exceptions. Unchecked exceptions extend the class RuntimeException or Error.

Java exceptions fall into two categories, called *checked* and *unchecked* exceptions. When you call a method that throws a checked exception, you *must* tell the compiler what you are going to do about the exception if it is ever thrown. For example, all subclasses of IOException are checked exceptions. On the other hand, the compiler does not require you to keep track of unchecked exceptions. Exceptions such as NumberFormatException, IllegalArgumentException, and Null-PointerException are unchecked exceptions. More generally, all exceptions that belong to subclasses of RuntimeException are unchecked, and all other subclasses of the class Exception are checked (see Figure 2). There is a second category of internal errors that are reported by throwing objects of type Error. One example is the OutOfMemoryError, which is thrown when all available

> Checked exceptions are due to external circumstances that the programmer cannot prevent. The compiler checks that your program handles these exceptions.

memory has been used up. These are fatal errors that happen rarely and are beyond your control. They too are unchecked.

Why have two kinds of exceptions? A checked exception describes a problem that is likely to occur at times, no matter how careful you are. The unchecked exceptions, on the other hand, are *your fault*. For example, an unexpected end of file can be caused by forces beyond your control, such as a disk error or a broken network connection. But you are to blame for a `NullPointerException`, because your code was wrong when it tried to use a `null` reference.

The compiler doesn't check whether you handle a `NullPointer-Exception`, because you should test your references for `null` before using them instead of installing a handler for that exception. The compiler does insist that your program be able to handle error conditions that you cannot *prevent*.

Actually, those categories aren't perfect. For example, it isn't your fault if a user enters an incorrect number, but `Integer.parseInt` throws an unchecked `NumberFormatException`.

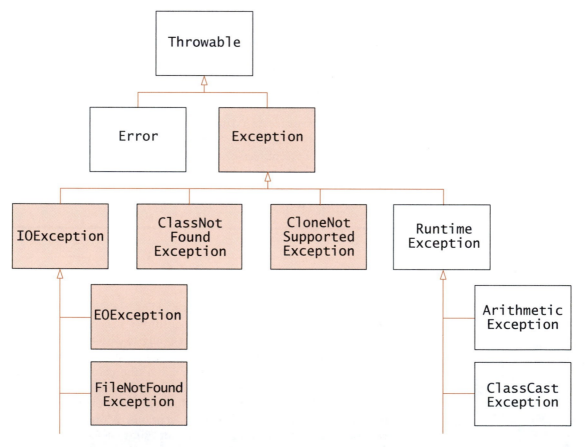

Figure 2

Checked and Unchecked Exceptions

As you can see from Figure 2, the majority of checked exceptions occur when you deal with input and output. That is a fertile ground for external failures beyond your control—a file might have been corrupted or removed, a network connection might be overloaded, a server might have crashed, and so on. Therefore, you will need to deal with checked exceptions principally when programming with files and streams.

Advanced Topic 3.6 showed you how to use a `BufferedReader` class to read console input from `System.in`. First, construct the reader object:

```
BufferedReader console = new BufferedReader(
    new InputStreamReader(System.in));
```

Then call the `readLine` method to read a line of input from the console window.

```
String input = console.readLine();
```

As you will see in greater detail in the next chapter, reading text from a file is very similar:

```
String filename = . . .;
BufferedReader reader = new BufferedReader(
    new FileReader(filename));
```

Suppose you write a method that calls the `readLine` method, which can throw an `IOException`. The `IOException` is a checked exception, so you need to tell the compiler what you are going to do about it. You have two choices. You can handle the exception in the same method that contains the call to `readLine`, using the techniques that you will see in Section 14.4. Or you can simply tell the compiler that you are aware of this exception and that you want your method to be terminated when it occurs. The method that reads input rarely knows what to do about an unexpected error, so that is usually the better option.

Here is an example of a method that reads a two-line coin description, like this:

```
0.5
half dollar
```

> Add a `throws` specifier to a method that can throw a checked exception.

The method calls `readLine` and therefore needs to declare that it might throw an `IOException`. If that happens, we want the `read` method to terminate. To declare that a method should be terminated when a checked exception occurs within it, tag the method with a `throws` specifier.

```
public class Coin
{
    public void read(BufferedReader in) throws IOException
    {
        value = Double.parseDouble(in.readLine());
        name = in.readLine();
    }
    . . .
}
```

The `throws` clause in turn signals the caller of your method that it may encounter an `IOException`. Then the caller needs to make the same decision—handle the exception, or tell its caller that the exception may be thrown. For example, consider the `read` method of a `Purse` class:

```
public class Purse
{
   public void read(BufferedReader in) throws IOException
   {
      while (. . .)
      {
         Coin c = new Coin();
         c.read(in);
         add(c);
      }
   }
   . . .
}
```

Even though the `read` method doesn't call `readLine`, it calls `Coin.read`, and that method declares that it might throw an `IOException`. Since the `Purse.read` method does not handle that exception, it too declares that it might throw it.

If your method can throw multiple checked exceptions, you separate them by commas:

```
public void read(BufferedReader in)
   throws IOException, ClassNotFoundException
```

It sounds somehow irresponsible not to handle an exception when you know that it happened. Actually, though, it is usually best not to catch an exception if you don't know how to *remedy* the situation. After all, what can you do in a low-level read method? Can you tell the user? How? By sending a message to `System.out`? You don't know whether this method is called in an applet or maybe an embedded system (such as a vending machine), where the user may never see `System.out`. And even if your users can see your error message, how do you know that they can understand English? Your class may be used to build an application for users in another country. Or can you perhaps fix up the object and keep going? How? If you set a variable to `null` or an empty string, that may just cause the program to break later, with much greater mystery.

Of course, *some* methods in the program know how to communicate with the user or take other remedial action. By allowing the exception to reach those methods, you make it possible for the exception to be processed by a *competent* handler.

Syntax 14.2: Exception Specifications

accessSpecifier returnType methodName
      (*parameterType parameterName*, . . .)
    throws *ExceptionClass*, *ExceptionClass*, . . .

Example:

```
public void read(BufferedReader in)
   throws IOException
```

Purpose:

To indicate the checked exceptions that this method can throw

---

14.3   Designing Your Own Exception Types

Sometimes none of the standard exception types describes your particular error condition well enough. In that case, you can design your own exception class. Consider a bank account. Let's report an `InsufficientFundsException` when an attempt is made to withdraw an amount from a bank account that exceeds the current balance.

```
if (amount > balance)
{
    throw new InsufficientFundsException(
        "withdrawal of " + amount +
        " exceeds balance of " + balance);
}
```

> You can design your own exception types—subclasses of `Exception` or `RuntimeException`.

Now you need to define the `InsufficientFundsException` class. Should it be a checked or an unchecked exception? Is it the fault of some external event, or is it the fault of the programmer? We take the position that the programmer could have prevented the exceptional condition—after all, it would have been an easy matter to check whether `amount <= account.getBalance()` before calling the `withdraw` method. Therefore, the exception should be an unchecked exception and extend the `RuntimeException` class or one of its subclasses.

It is customary to provide two constructors for an exception class: a default constructor and a constructor that accepts a message string describing the reason for the exception. Here is the definition of the exception class.

```
public class InsufficientFundsException
    extends RuntimeException
{
    public InsufficientFundsException()
    {
    }

    public InsufficientFundsException(String reason)
    {
        super(reason);
    }
}
```

14.4   Catching Exceptions

Every exception should be handled *somewhere* in your program. If an exception has no handler, an error message is printed, and your program terminates. That may be fine for a student program. But you would not want a professionally written program to die just because some method detected an unexpected error. Therefore, you must install exception handlers for all exceptions that your program might throw.

> In a method that is ready to handle a particular exception type, place the statements that can cause the exception inside a `try` block, and the handler inside a `catch` clause.

You install an exception handler with the `try` statement. Each `try` block contains one or more method calls that may cause an exception, and `catch` clauses for all possible exception types that the `try` block is willing to handle. Here is an example:

```
try
{
    BufferedReader in = new BufferedReader(
        new InputStreamReader(System.in));
    System.out.println("How old are you?");
    String inputLine = in.readLine();
    int age = Integer.parseInt(inputLine);
    age++;
    System.out.println("Next year, you'll be " + age);
}
catch (IOException exception)
{
    System.out.println("Input/output error "
        + exception);
}
catch (NumberFormatException exception)
{
    System.out.println("Input was not a number");
}
```

In this example, the `try` block contains six statements. Two exceptions may be thrown in this code: The `readLine` method can throw an `IOException`, and `Integer.parseInt` can throw a `NumberFormatException`. If either of these exceptions is actually thrown, then the rest of the instructions in the `try` block are skipped, and the appropriate `catch` clause is executed immediately. In that case, we inform the user of the source of the problem. (A better way of dealing with the exception would be to give the user another chance to provide a correct input—see Section 14.6 for a solution.)

When the `catch (IOException exception)` block is executed, then some method in the `try` block has failed with an `IOException`, and that exception object is stored in the variable `exception`. The `catch` clause can analyze that object to find out more details about the failure. For example, you can get a printout of the chain of method calls that lead to the exception, by calling

```
exception.printStackTrace()
```

Note that the caught object may belong to a *subclass* of `IOException` (such as `EOFException`).

Because all exceptions are subclasses of the class `Throwable`, you can catch all exceptions with a `catch (Throwable t)` clause. However, that is actually not a good idea (see Quality Tip 14.2).

It is important to remember that you should place `catch` clauses *only* in methods in which you can competently handle the particular exception type.

Syntax 14.3: General Try Block

```
try
{
    statement
    statement
    . . .
}
catch (ExceptionClass exceptionObject)
{
    statement
    statement
    . . .
}
catch (ExceptionClass exceptionObject)
{
    statement
    statement
    . . .
}
. . .
```

Example:

```
try
{
    System.out.println("What is your name?");
    String name = console.readLine();
    System.out.println("Hello, " + name + "!");
}
catch (IOException exception)
{
    exception.printStackTrace();
    System.exit(1);
}
```

Purpose:

To execute one or more statements that may generate exceptions. If an exception of a particular type occurs, then stop executing those statements and instead go to the matching `catch` clause. If no exception occurs, then skip the `catch` clauses. In all cases, execute the `finally` clause if one is present.

▼   **Quality Tip**   **14.2**

Do Not Squelch Exceptions

> It is better to declare that a method throws a checked exception than handle the exception poorly.

When you call a method that throws a checked exception, the compiler complains. In your eagerness to continue your work, it is an understandable impulse to shut the compiler up by *squelching* the exception:

```
try
{
    input = in.readLine();
    // compiler complained about IOException
}
catch (Exception e) {} // so there!
```

The do-nothing exception handler fools the compiler into thinking that the exception has been handled. In the long run, this is clearly a bad idea. Exceptions were designed to transmit problem reports to a *competent* handler. Installing an incompetent handler simply hides an error condition that could be serious.

14.5   The finally Clause

Occasionally, you need to take some action whether or not an exception is thrown. The finally construct is used to handle this situation. Here is a typical situation. Suppose a method opens a file, calls one or more methods, and then closes the file:

```
BufferedReader in;
in = new BufferedReader(new FileReader(filename));
purse.read(in);
in.close();
```

Now suppose that one of the methods before the last line throws an exception. Then the call to close is never executed! You solve this problem by placing the call to close inside a finally clause:

```
BufferedReader in = null;
try
{
    in = new BufferedReader(new FileReader(filename));
    purse.read(in);
}
finally
{
    if (in != null) in.close();
}
```

> Once a try block is entered, the statements in a finally clause are guaranteed to be executed, whether or not an exception is thrown.

In the normal case, there will be no problem. When the try block is completed, the finally clause is executed, and the file is closed. However, if an exception occurs, the finally clause is also executed before the exception is passed to its handler.

Notice that the finally clause closes the file only when in is not null. Of course, if the read method throws an exception, then in is not null. If the FileReader constructor throws an exception, however (usually because there is no file with the given name), then in has not yet been set, and you cannot close it. Also note that the in variable must be declared outside the try block so that it can be accessed in the finally clause.

Use the `finally` clause whenever you need to do some cleanup, such as closing a file, to ensure that the cleanup happens no matter how the method exits.

It is also possible to have a `finally` clause following one or more `catch` clauses. Then the code in the `finally` clause is executed whenever the `try` block is exited through any of three ways:

1. After completing the last statement of the `try` block
2. When an exception was thrown in the `try` block that is being passed to this method's caller
3. When an exception was thrown in the `try` block that was handled by one of the `catch` clauses

However, we will not use `finally` in such a complex situation in this book.

Syntax 14.4: `finally` Clause

```
try
{
    statement
    statement
    . . .
}
finally
{
    statement
    statement
    . . .
}
```

Example:

```
BufferedReader in = null;
try
{
    in = new BufferedReader(new
        FileReader(filename));
    purse.read(in);
}
finally
{
    if (in != null) in.close();
}
```

Purpose:

To execute one or more statements that may generate exceptions. If an exception of a particular type occurs, then stop executing those statements and instead go to the matching `catch` clause. If no exception occurs, then skip the `catch` clauses. In all cases, execute the `finally` clause if one is present.

A Complete Example

Let us walk through a complete example of a program with exception handling. The program asks a user for the name of a file, reads a sequence of coin descriptions from the file, adds coins to a purse, and then prints out the total of the purse.

What can go wrong? There are two principal risks.

- The file might not exist.

- The file might have data in the wrong format.

Who can detect these faults? The `FileReader` constructor will throw an exception when the file does not exist. We need to make sure that the `read` method of the `Coin` class throws an exception when it finds an error in the data format.

Who can remedy these faults? The `main` method of the `PurseTest` program interacts with the user. It should catch any exceptions and give the user another chance to enter a correct file.

Here is the `read` method of the `Coin` class.

```
public boolean read(BufferedReader in)
   throws IOException
{
   String input = in.readLine();
   if (input == null) return false;
   value = Double.parseDouble(input);
   name = in.readLine();
   if (name == null)
      throw new EOFException("Coin name expected");
   return true;
}
```

The method passes along all exceptions of type `IOException` that `readLine` may throw. Furthermore, when the method encounters an unexpected end of file, it reports it as an `EOFException`.

Note that the method differentiates between an *expected* end of file and an *unexpected* end of file. All files must come to an end. The method is prepared for the case that the end of the file has been reached before the *start* of a record. In that case, the method simply returns `false`. However, if the file ends in the *middle* of a record, then the method throws an exception.

Now let us put this method to use. The following `read` method of the `Purse` class reads coin records and adds them into a purse. It is completely unconcerned with any exceptions. If there is a problem with the input file, it simply passes the exception to its caller.

```
public void read(BufferedReader in)
   throws IOException
{
   boolean done = false;
   while (!done)
```

```
    {
        Coin c = new Coin();
        if (c.read(in))
            add(c);
        else
            done = true;
    }
}
```

Next, here is the `readFile` method of the `Purse` class that opens the file and invokes the method you just saw. Note how the `finally` clause ensures that the file is closed even when an exception occurs.

```
public void readFile(String filename)
    throws IOException
{
    BufferedReader in = null;
    try
    {
        in = new BufferedReader(
            new FileReader(filename));
        read(in);
    }
    finally
    {
        if (in != null) in.close();
    }
}
```

To complete the program, let's implement the user interaction in the `main` method. We ask the user for a file name, read the file, and print the total value of the coins. If there is a problem, we report the nature of the problem. The program is not terminated, and the user has a chance to open a different file.

```
boolean done = false;
String filename
    = JOptionPane.showInputDialog("Enter file name");

while (!done)
{
    try
    {
        Purse myPurse = new Purse();
        myPurse.readFile(filename);
        System.out.println("total="
            + myPurse.getTotal());
        done = true;
    }
    catch (IOException exception)
    {
        System.out.println("Input/output error "
            + exception);
```

```
        }
        catch (NumberFormatException exception)
        {
            exception.printStackTrace();
        }

        if (!done)
        {
            filename = JOptionPane.showInputDialog(
                "Try another file:");
            if (filename == null) done = true;
        }
    }
```

Let us look at a specific scenario.

1. `PurseTest.main` calls `Purse.readFile`.

2. `Purse.readFile` calls `Purse.read`.

3. `Purse.read` calls `Coin.read`.

4. `Coin.read` throws an `EOFException`.

5. `Coin.read` has no handler for the exception and terminates immediately.

6. `Purse.read` has no handler for the exception and terminates immediately.

7. `Purse.readFile` has no handler for the exception and terminates immediately after executing the `finally` clause and closing the file.

8. `PurseTest.main` has a handler for an `IOException`, a superclass of `EOFException`. That handler prints a message to the user. Afterwards, the user is given another chance to enter a file name. Note that the statement printing the purse total has been skipped.

This example shows the separation between error detection (in the `Coin.read` method) and error handling (in the `main` method). In between the two are the `Purse.read` and `Purse.readFile` methods, which just pass exceptions along.

File PurseTest.java

```
 1  import javax.swing.JOptionPane;
 2  import java.io.IOException;
 3
 4  /**
 5      This program prompts the user to enter a file name
 6      with coin values. A Purse object is filled with
 7      the coins specified in the file. In case of an exception,
 8      the user can choose another file.
 9  */
10  public class PurseTest
11  {
12      public static void main(String[] args)
13      {
14          boolean done = false;
```

```
15          String filename
16              = JOptionPane.showInputDialog(
17                  "Enter file name");
18
19          while (!done)
20          {
21              try
22              {
23                  Purse myPurse = new Purse();
24                  myPurse.readFile(filename);
25                  System.out.println("total="
26                      + myPurse.getTotal());
27                  done = true;
28              }
29              catch (IOException exception)
30              {
31                  System.out.println("Input/output error "
32                      + exception);
33              }
34              catch (NumberFormatException exception)
35              {
36                  exception.printStackTrace();
37              }
38
39              if (!done)
40              {
41                  filename = JOptionPane.showInputDialog(
42                      "Try another file:");
43                  if (filename == null) done = true;
44              }
45          }
46          System.exit(0);
47      }
48 }
```

File Purse.java

```
1 import java.io.BufferedReader;
2 import java.io.FileReader;
3 import java.io.IOException;
4
5 /**
6     A purse computes the total of a collection of coins.
7 */
8 public class Purse
9 {
10     /**
11         Constructs an empty purse.
12     */
13     public Purse()
14     {
```

```
15          total = 0;
16       }
17
18       /**
19          Reads a file with coin descriptions and adds the coins
20          to the purse.
21          @param filename the name of the file
22       */
23       public void readFile(String filename)
24          throws IOException
25       {
26          BufferedReader in = null;
27          try
28          {
29             in = new BufferedReader(
30                new FileReader(filename));
31             read(in);
32          }
33          finally
34          {
35             if (in != null) in.close();
36          }
37       }
38
39       /**
40          Reads a file with coin descriptions and adds the coins
41          to the purse.
42          @param in the buffered reader for reading the input
43       */
44       public void read(BufferedReader in)
45          throws IOException
46       {
47          boolean done = false;
48          while (!done)
49          {
50             Coin c = new Coin();
51             if (c.read(in))
52                add(c);
53             else
54                done = true;
55          }
56       }
57
58       /**
59          Adds a coin to the purse.
60          @param aCoin the coin to add
61       */
62       public void add(Coin aCoin)
63       {
64          total = total + aCoin.getValue();
```

```
65        }
66
67        /**
68            Gets the total value of the coins in the purse.
69            @return the sum of all coin values
70        */
71        public double getTotal()
72        {
73            return total;
74        }
75
76        private double total;
77 }
```

File Coin.java

```
 1 import java.io.BufferedReader;
 2 import java.io.EOFException;
 3 import java.io.IOException;
 4
 5 /**
 6     A coin with a monetary value.
 7 */
 8 public class Coin
 9 {
10     /**
11         Constructs a default coin.
12         Use the read method to fill in the value and name
13     */
14     public Coin()
15     {
16         value = 0;
17         name = "";
18     }
19
20     /**
21         Constructs a coin.
22         @param aValue the monetary value of the coin
23         @param aName the name of the coin
24     */
25     public Coin(double aValue, String aName)
26     {
27         value = aValue;
28         name = aName;
29     }
30
31     /**
32         Reads a coin value and name.
33         @param in the reader
34         @return true if the data were read,
```

```
35          false if the end of the stream was reached
36       */
37       public boolean read(BufferedReader in)
38          throws IOException
39       {
40          String input = in.readLine();
41          if (input == null) return false;
42          value = Double.parseDouble(input);
43          name = in.readLine();
44          if (name == null)
45             throw new EOFException("Coin name expected");
46          return true;
47       }
48
49       /**
50          Gets the coin value.
51          @return the value
52       */
53       public double getValue()
54       {
55          return value;
56       }
57
58       /**
59          Gets the coin name.
60          @return the name
61       */
62       public String getName()
63       {
64          return name;
65       }
66
67       private double value;
68       private String name;
69    }
```

Random Fact 14.1

The Ariane Rocket Incident

The European Space Agency, Europe's counterpart to NASA, had developed a rocket model called Ariane that it had successfully used several times to launch satellites and scientific experiments into space. However, when a new version, the Ariane 5, was launched on June 4, 1996, from ESA's launch site in Kourou, French Guiana, the rocket veered off course about 40 seconds after liftoff. Flying at an angle of more than 20 degrees, rather than straight up, exerted such an aerodynamic force that the boosters separated, which triggered the automatic self-destruction mechanism. The rocket blew itself up.

Figure 3

The Explosion of the Ariane Rocket

The ultimate cause of this accident was an unhandled exception! The rocket contained two identical devices (called inertial reference systems) that processed flight data from measuring devices and turned the data into information about the rocket position. The onboard computer used the position information for controlling the boosters. The same inertial reference systems and computer software had worked fine on the Ariane 4 predecessor.

However, due to design changes of the rocket, one of the sensors measured a larger acceleration force than had been encountered in the Ariane 4. That value, expressed as a floating-point value, was stored in a 16-bit integer (like a `short` variable in Java). Unlike Java, the Ada language, used for the device software, generates an exception if a floating-point number is too large to be converted to an integer. Unfortunately, the programmers of the device had decided that this situation would never happen and didn't provide an exception handler.

When the overflow did happen, the exception was triggered and, since there was no handler, the device shut itself off. The onboard computer sensed the failure and switched over to the backup device. However, that device had shut itself off for exactly the same reason, something that the designers of the rocket had not expected. They figured that the devices might fail for mechanical reasons, and the chances of two devices having the same mechanical failure was considered remote. At that point, the rocket was without reliable position information and went off course.

Perhaps it would have been better if the software hadn't been so thorough? If it had ignored the overflow, the device wouldn't have been shut off. It would have just computed bad data. But then the device would have reported wrong position data, which could have been just as fatal. Instead, a correct implementation should have caught overflow exceptions and come up with some strategy to recompute the flight data. Clearly, giving up was not a reasonable option in this context.

The advantage of the exception-handling mechanism is that it makes these issues explicit to programmers—something to think about when you curse the Java compiler for complaining about uncaught exceptions.

CHAPTER SUMMARY

1. To signal an exceptional condition, use the `throw` statement to throw an exception object.

2. When you throw an exception, the current method terminates immediately.

3. There are two kinds of exceptions: checked exceptions and unchecked exceptions. Unchecked exceptions extend the class `RuntimeException` or `Error`.

4. Checked exceptions are due to external circumstances that the programmer cannot prevent. The compiler checks that your program handles these exceptions.

5. Add a `throws` specifier to a method that can throw a checked exception.

6. You can design your own exception types—subclasses of `Exception` or `Runtime-Exception`.

7. In a method that is ready to handle a particular exception type, place the statements that can cause the exception inside a `try` block, and the handler inside a `catch` clause.

8. It is better to declare that a method throws a checked exception than to handle the exception poorly.

9. Once a `try` block is entered, the statements in a `finally` clause are guaranteed to be executed, whether or not an exception is thrown.

Classes, Objects, and Methods Introduced in This Chapter

```
java.io.EOFException
java.io.FileNotFoundException
java.lang.IllegalStateException
java.lang.NullPointerException
java.lang.NumberFormatException
java.lang.RuntimeException
```

Review Exercises

Exercise R14.1. What is the difference between throwing and catching an exception?

Exercise R14.2. What is a checked exception? What is an unchecked exception? Is a `NullPointerException` checked or unchecked? Which exceptions do you need to declare with the `throws` keyword?

Exercise R14.3. Why don't you need to declare that your method might throw a `NullPointerException`?

Exercise R14.4. When your program executes a `throw` statement, which statement is executed next?

Exercise R14.5. What happens if an exception does not have a matching `catch` clause?

Exercise R14.6. What can your program do with the exception object that a `catch` clause receives?

Exercise R14.7. Is the type of the exception object always the same as the type declared in the `catch` clause that catches it?

Exercise R14.8. What kind of objects can you throw? Can you throw a string? An integer?

Exercise R14.9. What is the purpose of the `finally` clause? Give an example of how it can be used.

Exercise R14.10. What happens when an exception is thrown, the code of a `finally` clause executes, and that code throws an exception of a different kind than the original one? Which one is caught by a surrounding `catch` clause? Write a sample program to try it out.

PROGRAMMING EXERCISES

Exercise P14.1. Modify the `BankAccount` class to throw an `IllegalArgumentException` when the account is constructed with a negative balance, when a negative amount is deposited, or when an amount that is not between 0 and the current balance is withdrawn. Write a test program that causes all three exceptions to occur and that catches them all.

Exercise P14.2. Repeat the preceding exercise, but throw exceptions of three exception types that you define yourself.

Exercise P14.3. Write a program that asks the user to input a set of coin values and names. When the user enters a coin value that is not a number, give the user a second chance to enter the value. After two chances, quit the program. Add all correctly specified coins to a purse, and print its total value when the user is done entering data. Use a `JOptionPane` to prompt for the input.

Exercise P14.4. Repeat the preceding problem, but give the user as many chances as necessary to enter a correct coin value. Quit the program only when the user cancels an input dialog.

Exercise P14.5. Define a class `ConsoleReader` with a method

```
String readLine(String prompt) { . . . }
```

that throws no exception. The `ConsoleReader` reads from a buffered reader attached to `System.in`. You need to catch the `IOException` that the `readLine` method may throw. Return a `null` in that case. Write a test program that tests the class.

Exercise P14.6. Enhance the class from the preceding problem to include two additional methods.

```
int readInt(String prompt)
double readDouble(String prompt)
```

As long as the conversion from the string to a number throws a `NumberFormatException`, repeat the prompt and give the user another chance to enter a correct value. Write a test program that tests the class.

Exercise P14.7. Repeat the preceding exercise, except read the input from a `JOptionPane`.

Exercise P14.8. You can read the contents of a text file with this sequence of commands.

```
String filename = "myfile.txt";
BufferedReader reader =
   new BufferedReader(new FileReader(filename));
```

```
boolean done = false;
while (!done)
{
    String input = reader.readLine();
    if (input == null) done = true;
    else do something with input
}
```

Design a class `TextFileReader` whose constructor receives the name of a file and whose `readLine` method returns the next line of input from the text file or `null` if the end of the file has been reached. Don't have these methods catch any exceptions, but use `throws` specifiers to report the exceptions that may occur. You may need to consult the API documentation for the exceptions. Be sure to close the file when any exception occurs. Write a test program that tests your class.

Exercise P14.9. You can read the contents of a web page with this sequence of commands.

```
String address = "http://java.sun.com/index.html";
URL u = new URL(address);
URLConnection connection = u.openConnection(u);
InputStream in = connection.getInputStream();
BufferedReader reader =
    new BufferedReader(new InputStreamReader(in));
boolean done = false;
while (!done)
{
    String input = reader.readLine();
    if (input == null) done = true;
    else do something with input
}
```

Design a class `WebPageReader`, whose constructor receives an address string and whose `readLine` method returns the next line of input from the web page or `null` if the end of the page has been reached. Don't have these methods catch any exceptions, but use `throws` specifiers to report the exceptions that may occur. You may need to consult the API documentation for the exceptions. Write a test program that tests your class.

Exercise P14.10. Design a class `Bank` that contains a number of bank accounts. Each account has an account number and a current balance. Add an `accountNumber` field to the `BankAccount` class. Store the bank accounts in an array list. Write a `readFile` method of the `Bank` class for reading a file with the format

```
accountNumber1  balance1
accountNumber2  balance2
. . .
```

Follow the design of the sample program in Section 14.6 and implement `read` methods for the `Bank` and `BankAccount` classes. Write a sample program to read in a file with bank accounts. Afterwards, print the account with the highest balance. If the file is not properly formatted, give the user another chance to select another file.

Streams

▶ To become familiar with the concepts of text and binary formats

▶ To be able to read and write objects using serialization

▶ To be able to process the command line

▶ To learn about encryption

▶ To understand when to use sequential and random file access

All of the programs we have discussed until now read their input from the keyboard and mouse and displayed their output on the screen. For console programs, you can read from a file or write to a file by using redirection (see Productivity Hint 6.1). That method for accessing files is useful but still limited. In this chapter you will learn how to write Java programs that interact with disk files and other sources of bytes and characters.

15.1 Streams, Readers, and Writers

There are two fundamentally different ways to store data: in *text* or *binary* format. In text format, data items are represented in human-readable form, as a sequence of *characters*. For example, the integer 12,345 is stored as the sequence of five characters:

```
'1' '2' '3' '4' '5'
```

In binary form, data items are represented in *bytes*. A byte is composed of 8 bits and can denote one of 256 values. For example, in binary format, the integer 12,345 is stored as a sequence of four *bytes:*

```
0 0 48 57
```

> Streams access sequences of bytes. Readers and writers access sequences of characters.

(because 12,345 = 48 · 256 + 57).

If you store information in text form, as a sequence of characters, you need to use the `Reader` and `Writer` class and their subclasses to process input and output. If you store information in binary form, as a sequence of bytes, you use the `InputStream` and `OutputStream` classes and their subclasses.

> Use `FileReader`, `FileWriter`, `FileInputStream`, and `FileOutputStream` classes to read and write disk files.

Text input and output are more convenient for humans, because it is easier to produce input (just use a text editor) and it is easier to check that output is correct (just look at the output file in an editor). However, binary storage is more compact and more efficient.

To read text data from a disk file, you create a `FileReader` object:

```
FileReader reader =
    new FileReader("input.txt");
```

To read binary data from a disk file, you create a `FileInputStream` object instead:

```
FileInputStream inputStream =
    new FileInputStream("input.dat");
```

Similarly, you use `FileWriter` and `FileOutputStream` objects to write data to a disk file in text or binary form:

```
FileWriter writer = new FileWriter("output.txt");
FileOutputStream outputStream =
   new FileOutputStream("output.dat");
```

All these classes are defined in the `java.io` package.

> The read method returns an integer, either −1, at the end of the file, or another value, which you need to cast to a char or byte.

The `Reader` class has a method, `read`, to read a single character at a time. (The `FileReader` class overrides this method to obtain the characters from a disk file.) However, the `read` method actually returns an `int` so that it can signal either that a character has been read or that the end of input has been reached. At the end of input, `read` returns −1. Otherwise it returns the character (as an integer between 0 and 65,535). You should test the return value and, if it is not −1, cast it to a char:

```
Reader reader = . . .;
int next = reader.read();
char c;
if (next != -1)
   c = (char)next;
```

The `InputStream` class also has a method, `read`, to read a single byte. The method also returns an `int`, namely either the byte that was input (as an integer between 0 and 255) or the integer −1 if the end of the input stream has been reached. You should test the return value and, if it is not −1, cast it to a `byte`:

```
InputStream in = . . .;
int next = in.read();
byte b;
if (next != -1)
   b = (byte)next;
```

> You must close all files that you no longer need.

Similarly, the `Writer` and `FileOutputStream` classes have a `write` method to write a single character or byte.

When you are done reading or writing from a file or reader, you should call the `close` method. This is particularly important when writing to a file. Only when you close it can you be assured that all changes are committed to the disk file. For example,

```
writer.close();
```

> Basic streams, readers, and writers can process only individual bytes or characters. You need to combine them with other classes to process lines of text or entire objects.

These basic methods are the only input and output methods that the file input and output classes provide. The Java stream package is built on the principle that each class should have a very focused responsibility. The job of a `FileInputStream` is to interact with files. Its job is to *get* bytes, not to analyze them. If you want to read numbers, strings, or other objects, you have to combine the class with other classes whose responsibility is to group individual bytes or characters together into numbers, strings, and objects. You will see those classes later in this chapter.

Common Error 15.1

Backslashes in File Names

When you specify a file name as a constant string, and the name contains backslash characters (as in a Windows filename), you must supply each backslash *twice:*

```
in = new FileReader("c:\\homework\\input.dat");
```

Recall that a single backslash inside quoted strings is an *escape character* that is combined with another character to form a special meaning, such as \n for a newline character. The \\ combination denotes a single backslash.

When a user supplies a file name to a program, however, the user should not type the backslash twice.

Common Error 15.2

Negative byte Values

In Java, the byte type is a *signed* type. There are 256 values of the byte type, from −128 to 127. The starting bit of the byte is the *sign bit*. If it is on, the number is negative. In converting an integer into a byte, only the least significant byte of the integer is taken, and the remaining bytes are ignored. The result can be negative even if the integer is positive. For example,

```
int n = 233; // binary 00000000 00000000 00000000 11101001
byte b = (byte)n; // binary 11101001, sign bit is on
if (b == n) . . . // not true! b is negative, n is positive
```

When the byte is converted back to an integer, then the result is still negative. In particular, it is *different* from the original.

Here is an even trickier case. Consider this test:

```
int next = in.read();
byte b = (byte)next;
if (b == 'é') . . .
```

This test is *never* true, *even if* next was equal to the Unicode value for the 'é' character. That Unicode value happens to be 233, but a single byte is always a value between −128 and 127. American readers won't be too concerned, because all characters and symbols used in American English have Unicode values in the "safe" range between 1 and 127, but international programmers who use characters with Unicode values between 128 and 255 find this a source of continual frustration.

15.2   Reading and Writing Text Files

> When writing text files, use the `PrintWriter` class and the `print`/`println` methods.

In the previous section, you saw how to write data to a text file. You construct a `FileWriter` object from the file name:

```
FileWriter writer = new FileWriter("output.txt");
```

Now you can send your output to the file, a character at a time, by calling the `write` method.

Of course, you don't have the output available a character at a time. You have the output in the form of numbers or strings. For that reason, you need another class whose task it is to break up numbers and strings into individual characters and send them to a writer. That class is called a `PrintWriter`. You construct a `Print-Writer` from any `Writer` object:

```
PrintWriter out = new PrintWriter(writer);
```

Now you can use the familiar `print` and `println` methods to print numbers, objects, and strings:

```
out.println(29.95);
out.println(new Rectangle(5, 10, 15, 25));
out.println("Hello, World!");
```

The `print` and `println` methods convert numbers to their decimal string representations and use the `toString` method to convert objects to strings; break up the strings into individual characters; and give each character to the `FileWriter` object through its `write` method. The `FileWriter` then sends them off to a file, a network connection, or some other destination.

> When reading text files, use the `BufferedReader` class and the `readLine` method.

Reading text files is unfortunately much less convenient. The Java library supplies no classes to read numbers directly. The best you can do is use the `BufferedReader` class, which has a `readLine` method that lets you read a line at a time. The `readLine` method keeps calling the `read` method of the reader object that you supplied in the constructor, until it has collected an entire input line. Then it returns that line. When all input has been consumed, the `readLine` method returns `null`.

After reading a line of input, you can use the `Integer.parseInt` and `Double.parseDouble` methods to convert the strings you find in the input to numbers.

```
FileReader reader = new FileReader("input.txt");
BufferedReader in = new BufferedReader(reader);
String inputLine = in.readLine();
double x = Double.parseDouble(inputLine);
```

If there are several items in a single input line, you can use the `StringTokenizer` class to break up the input line into multiple strings.

15.3   File Dialogs

> The `JFileChooser` dialog lets users select a file by navigating through directories.

In this section we show you how you can have a user supply a file name through a file dialog such as the one shown in Figure 1. The `JFileChooser` class implements a file dialog for the Swing user interface toolkit.

The `JFileChooser` class relies on another class, `File`, which describes disk files and directories. For example,

```
File inputFile = new File("input.txt");
```

> A `File` object describes a file or directory.

describes the file `input.txt` in the current directory. The `File` class has methods to delete or rename the file. The file does not actually have to exist—you may want to pass the `File` object to an output stream or writer so that the file can be created. The `exists` method returns `true` if the file already exists.

> You can pass a `File` object to the constructor of a file reader, writer, or stream.

You cannot directly use a `File` object for reading or writing. You still need to construct a file reader, writer, or stream from the `File` object. Simply pass the `File` object in the constructor.

```
FileReader in = new FileReader(inputFile);
```

The `JFileChooser` class has many options to fine-tune the display of the dialog, but in its most basic form it is quite simple: Construct a file chooser object; then call the `showOpenDialog` or `showSaveDialog` method. Both methods show the same dialog, but the button for selecting a file is labeled "Open" or "Save", depending on which method you call. For better placement of the dialog on the screen, you can specify the user interface component over which to pop up the dialog. If you don't care where the dialog pops up, you can simply pass `null`. These methods return either `JFileChooser.APPROVE_OPTION`, if the user has chosen a file, or `JFileChooser.CANCEL_OPTION`, if the user canceled the selection. If a file was chosen,

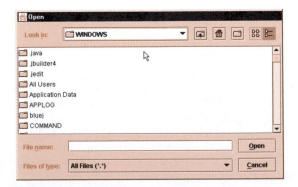

Figure 1

A `JFileChooser` Dialog

then you call the `getSelectedFile` method to obtain a `File` object that describes the file. Here is a complete example:

```
JFileChooser chooser = new JFileChooser();
FileReader in = null;
if (chooser.showOpenDialog(null)
    == JFileChooser.APPROVE_OPTION)
{
    File selectedFile = chooser.getSelectedFile();
    in = new FileReader(selectedFile);
}
```

15.4 An Encryption Program

Let us write a program that *encrypts* a file—that is, scrambles it so that it is unreadable except to those who know the decryption method and the secret keyword. Ignoring over 2000 years of progress in the field of encryption, we will use a method familiar to Julius Caesar. The person performing any encryption chooses an *encryption key;* here the key is a number between 1 and 25 that indicates the shift to be used in encrypting each letter. For example, if the key is 3, replace A with D, B with E, and so on (see Figure 2).

To decrypt, simply use the negative of the encryption key. For example, to decrypt the message of Figure 2, use a key of −3.

In this program we process binary data—we read each byte separately, encrypt it, and write the encrypted byte.

```
int next = in.read();
if (next == -1)
    done = true;
else
{
    byte b = (byte)next;
    byte c = encrypt(b);
    out.write(c);
}
```

In a more complex encryption program, you would read a block of bytes, encrypt the block, and write it out.

Because the program reads binary data, it uses streams, not readers and writers.

Here is the program. We put the `JFileChooserDialog` class to work to ask the user to specify the input and output files. Try out the program on a file of your choice. You will find that the encrypted file is unreadable. In fact, because the newline characters are

Figure 2

The Caesar Cipher

Plain text

Encrypted text

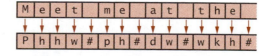

transformed, you may not be able to read the encrypted file in a text editor. To decrypt, simply run the program again and supply the negative of the encryption key.

Program Encryptor.java

```
 1  import java.io.File;
 2  import java.io.FileInputStream;
 3  import java.io.FileOutputStream;
 4  import java.io.InputStream;
 5  import java.io.OutputStream;
 6  import java.io.IOException;
 7
 8  /**
 9      An encryptor encrypts files using the Caesar cipher.
10      For decryption, use an encryptor whose key is the
11      negative of the encryption key.
12  */
13  public class Encryptor
14  {
15      /**
16          Constructs an encryptor.
17          @param aKey the encryption key
18      */
19      public Encryptor(int aKey)
20      {
21          key = aKey;
22      }
23
24      /**
25          Encrypts the contents of a file.
26          @param inFile the input file
27          @param outFile the output file
28      */
29      public void encryptFile(File inFile, File outFile)
30          throws IOException
31      {
32          InputStream in = null;
33          OutputStream out = null;
34
35          try
36          {
37              in = new FileInputStream(inFile);
38              out = new FileOutputStream(outFile);
39              encryptStream(in, out);
40          }
41          finally
42          {
43              if (in != null) in.close();
44              if (out != null) out.close();
45          }
```

```
46        }
47
48        /**
49            Encrypts the contents of a stream.
50            @param in the input stream
51            @param out the output stream
52        */
53        public void encryptStream(InputStream in,
54            OutputStream out)
55            throws IOException
56        {
57            boolean done = false;
58            while (!done)
59            {
60                int next = in.read();
61                if (next == -1) done = true;
62                else
63                {
64                    byte b = (byte)next;
65                    byte c = encrypt(b);
66                    out.write(c);
67                }
68            }
69        }
70
71        /**
72            Encrypts a byte.
73            @param b the byte to encrypt
74            @return the encrypted byte
75        */
76        public byte encrypt(byte b)
77        {
78            return (byte)(b + key);
79        }
80
81        private int key;
82 }
```

Program EncryptorTest.java

```
1  import java.io.File;
2  import java.io.IOException;
3  import javax.swing.JFileChooser;
4  import javax.swing.JOptionPane;
5
6  /**
7      A program to test the Caesar cipher encryptor.
8  */
9  public class EncryptorTest
10 {
```

```
11    public static void main(String[] args)
12    {
13       try
14       {
15          JFileChooser chooser = new JFileChooser();
16          if (chooser.showOpenDialog(null)
17             != JFileChooser.APPROVE_OPTION)
18             System.exit(0);
19
20          File inFile = chooser.getSelectedFile();
21          if (chooser.showSaveDialog(null)
22             != JFileChooser.APPROVE_OPTION)
23             System.exit(0);
24          File outFile = chooser.getSelectedFile();
25          String input =
26             JOptionPane.showInputDialog("Key");
27          int key = Integer.parseInt(input);
28          Encryptor crypt = new Encryptor(key);
29          crypt.encryptFile(inFile, outFile);
30       }
31       catch (NumberFormatException exception)
32       {
33          System.out.println("Key must be an integer: "
34             + exception);
35       }
36       catch (IOException exception)
37       {
38          System.out.println("Error processing file: "
39             + exception);
40       }
41       System.exit(0);
42    }
43 }
```

Random Fact

15.1

Encryption Algorithms

The exercises at the end of this chapter give a few algorithms to encrypt text. Don't actually use any of those methods to send secret messages to your lover. Any skilled cryptographer can *break* these schemes in a very short time—that is, reconstruct the original text without knowing the secret keyword.

In 1978 Ron Rivest, Adi Shamir, and Leonard Adleman introduced an encryption method that is much more powerful. The method is called RSA encryption, after the last names of its inventors. The exact scheme is too complicated to present here, but it is not actually difficult to follow. You can find the details in [2].

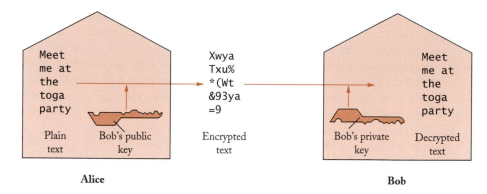

Alice   **Bob**

Figure 3

Public Key Encryption

RSA is a remarkable encryption method. There are two keys: a public key and a private key. (See Figure 3.) You can print the public key on your business card (or in your email signature block) and give it to anyone. Then anyone can send you messages that only you can decrypt. Even though everyone else knows the public key, and even if they intercept all the messages coming to you, they cannot break the scheme and actually read the messages. In 1994, hundreds of researchers, collaborating over the Internet, cracked an RSA message encrypted with a 129-digit key. Messages encrypted with a key of 230 digits or more are expected to be secure.

The inventors of the algorithm obtained a *patent* for it. That means that for a period of 20 years, anyone using it had to seek a license from the inventors. They have given permission for most noncommercial usage, but companies that implemented RSA in a product that they sold had to get the patent holder's permission and pay substantial royalties. The RSA patent expired on September 20, 2000, so you are now free to use the algorithm without restriction.

A patent is a deal that society makes with an inventor. For a period of 20 years after the filing date, the inventor has an exclusive right for its commercialization, may collect royalties from others wishing to manufacture the invention, and may even stop competitors from marketing it altogether. In return, the inventor must publish the invention, so that others may learn from it, and must relinquish all claim to it after the protection period ends. The presumption is that in the absence of patent law, inventors would be reluctant to go through the trouble of inventing, or they would try to cloak their techniques to prevent others from copying their devices.

What do you think? Are patents a fair deal? Unquestionably, some companies have chosen not to implement RSA, and instead chose a less capable method, because they could not or would not pay the royalties. Thus, it seems that the patent may have hindered, rather than advanced, commerce. Had there not been patent protection, would the inventors have published the method anyway, thereby giving the benefit for society without the cost of the 20-year monopoly? In this case, the answer is probably yes; the inventors were academic researchers, who live on salaries rather than sales receipts and are usually rewarded for their discoveries by a boost in their reputation and careers.

Would their followers have been as active in discovering (and patenting) improvements? There is no way of knowing, of course.

Further, is an algorithm even patentable in the first place? Or is it a mathematical fact that belongs to nobody? The patent office did take the latter attitude for a long time. The RSA inventors and many others described their inventions in terms of imaginary electronic devices, rather than algorithms, to circumvent that restriction. Nowadays, the patent office will award software patents.

There is another fascinating aspect to the RSA story. A programmer named Phil Zimmermann developed a program called PGP (for *Pretty Good Privacy*) [3]. PGP implements RSA. That is, you can have it generate a pair of public and private keys, publish the public key, receive encrypted messages from others who use their copy of PGP and your public key, and decrypt them with your private key. Even though the encryption can be performed on any personal computer, decryption is not feasible even with the most powerful computers. You can get a copy of PGP from `http://web.mit.edu/network/pgp.html`. As long as it is for personal use, there is no charge, courtesy of Phil Zimmermann and the folks at MIT and RSA.

The existence of PGP bothers the government to no end. They worry that criminals use the package to correspond by email and that the police cannot tap those "conversations". Foreign governments can send communications that the National Security Agency (the premier electronic spy organization of the United States) cannot decipher. In the 1990s, the U.S. government unsuccessfully attempted to standardize on a different encryption scheme, called *Skipjack*, to which government organizations hold a decryption key that—of course—they promise not to use without a court order. There have been serious proposals to make it illegal to use any other encryption method in the United States. At one time, the government considered charging Mr. Zimmermann with breaching another law that forbids the unauthorized export of munitions as a crime and defines cryptographic technology as "munitions". They made the argument that, even though Mr. Zimmermann never exported the program, he should have known that it would immediately spread through the Internet when he released it in the United States.

What do you think? Will criminals and terrorists be harder to detect and convict once encryption of email and phone conversations is widely available? Should the government therefore have a backdoor key to any legal encryption method? Or is this a gross violation of our civil liberties? Is it even possible to put the genie back into the bottle at this time?

15.5   Command Line Arguments

Depending on the operating system and Java development system used, there are different methods of starting a program—for example, by selecting "Run" in the compilation environment, by clicking on an icon, or by typing the name of the program at a prompt in a terminal or shell window. The latter method is called "invoking the program from the command line". When you use this method, you must of course type the name of the program, but you can also type in additional information that the program can use.

These additional strings are called *command line arguments*. For example, if you start a program with the command line

```
java MyProgram -d file.txt
```

then the program receives two command line arguments: the strings "-d" and "file.txt". It is entirely up to the program what to do with these strings. It is customary to interpret strings starting with a - as options and other strings as file names.

Only application programs receive command line arguments; you cannot pass a command line to an applet. (The corresponding mechanism for applets is the HTML param tag; see Advanced Topic 4.3.)

Command line arguments are placed in the args parameter of the main method:

```
class MyProgram
{
   public static void main(String[] args)
   {
      . . .
   }
}
```

Now you finally know the use of the args array that you have seen in so many programs. In our example, args contains the two strings

args[0]	"-d"
args[1]	"file.txt"

To put command line processing to work, let us write a driver for the Encryptor class that reads the file names and encryption key from the command line rather than prompting the user. The program takes the following command line arguments:

- An optional -d flag to indicate decryption instead of encryption
- An optional encryption key, specified with a -k flag
- The input file name
- The output file name

If no key is specified, then 3 is used. For example,

```
java Crypt input.txt encrypt.txt
```

encrypts the file input.txt with a key of 3 and places the result into encrypt.txt. On the other hand,

```
java Crypt -d -k11 encrypt.txt output.txt
```

decrypts the file encrypt.txt with a key of 11 and places the result into output.txt.

What is better for the user? A graphical user interface with file chooser dialogs, or a command-line interface where files need to be specified on the command line? For a casual and infrequent user, the graphical user interface is much better. The user interface guides the user along and makes it possible to navigate the application without much knowledge. But for a frequent user, graphical user interfaces have a major drawback— they are hard to automate. If you need to process hundreds of files every day, you could spend all your time typing file names into file chooser dialogs. But it is not difficult to call a program multiple times automatically with different command-line arguments. Productivity Hint 8.1 discusses how to use shell scripts (also called batch files) for this purpose.

Here is the front end for the encryption program. Combine it with the `Encryptor` class of the preceding section.

File Crypt.java

```java
 1  import java.io.File;
 2  import java.io.IOException;
 3
 4  /**
 5      A program to run the Caesar cipher encryptor with
 6      command line arguments.
 7  */
 8  public class Crypt
 9  {
10     public static void main(String[] args)
11     {
12        boolean decrypt = false;
13        int key = DEFAULT_KEY;
14        File inFile = null;
15        File outFile = null;
16
17        if (args.length < 2 || args.length > 4) usage();
18
19        try
20        {
21           for (int i = 0; i < args.length; i++)
22           {
23              if (args[i].charAt(0) == '-')
24              {
25                 // it is a command line option
26                 char option = args[i].charAt(1);
27                 if (option == 'd')
28                    decrypt = true;
29                 else if (option == 'k')
30                    key = Integer.parseInt(
31                       args[i].substring(2));
32              }
33              else
34              {
35                 // it is a file name
36                 if (inFile == null)
37                    inFile = new File(args[i]);
38                 else if (outFile == null)
```

```
39                        outFile = new File(args[i]);
40                    else usage();
41                }
42            }
43            if (decrypt) key = -key;
44            Encryptor crypt = new Encryptor(key);
45            crypt.encryptFile(inFile, outFile);
46        }
47        catch (NumberFormatException exception)
48        {
49            System.out.println("Key must be an integer: "
50                + exception);
51        }
52        catch (IOException exception)
53        {
54            System.out.println("Error processing file: "
55                + exception);
56        }
57    }
58
59    /**
60        Prints a message describing proper usage and exits.
61    */
62    public static void usage()
63    {
64        System.out.println(
65            "Usage: java Crypt [-d] [-kn] infile outfile");
66        System.exit(1);
67    }
68
69    public static final int DEFAULT_KEY = 3;
70 }
```

15.6   Object Streams

> Use object streams to save and restore all instance fields of an object automatically.

In the sample program of Section 14.6, you read `Coin` objects by processing strings that describe the coin data. To save a set of coins in the same format, you would need to write code to break up coin objects into strings and numbers. Actually, in Java, there is an easier way. The `ObjectOutputStream` class can save entire objects out to disk, and the `ObjectInputStream` class can read them back in. Objects are saved in binary format; hence, you use streams and not writers.

For example, you can write a `Coin` object to a file as follows:

```
Coin c = . . .;
ObjectOutputStream out = new ObjectOutputStream
    (new FileOutputStream("coins.dat"));
out.writeObject(c);
```

The object output stream automatically saves all instance variables of the object to the stream. When reading the object back in, you use the `readObject` method of the `ObjectInputStream` class. That method returns an `Object` reference, so you need to remember the types of the objects that you saved and use a cast:

```
ObjectInputStream in = new ObjectInputStream
   (new FileInputStream("coins.dat"));
Coin c = (Coin)in.readObject();
```

The `readObject` method can throw a `ClassCastException`—it is a checked exception, so you need to catch or declare it.

You can do even better than that, though. You can store a whole bunch of objects in an array list or array, or inside another object, and then save that object:

```
ArrayList a = new ArrayList();
// now add many Coin objects into a
out.writeObject(a);
```

With one instruction, you can save the array list and *all the objects that it references*. You can read all of them back with one instruction:

```
ArrayList a = (ArrayList)in.readObject();
```

Of course, if the `Purse` class contains an `ArrayList` of coins, then you can simply save and restore the `Purse` object. Then its array list, and all the `Coin` objects that it contains, are automatically saved and restored as well. The sample program at the end of this section uses this approach.

> Objects saved to an object stream must belong to classes that implement the `Serializable` interface.

This is a truly amazing capability that is highly recommended (see Productivity Hint 15.1).

To place objects of a particular class into an object stream, the class must implement the `Serializable` interface. That interface has no methods, so there is no effort involved in implementing it:

```
class Coin implements Serializable
{
   . . .
}
```

The process of saving objects to a stream is called *serialization* because each object is assigned a serial number on the stream. If the same object is saved twice, only the serial number is written out the second time. When the objects are read back in, duplicate serial numbers are restored as references to the same object.

Why don't all classes implement `Serializable`? For security reasons, some programmers may not want to serialize classes with confidential contents. Once a class is serializable, anyone can write its objects to disk and analyze the disk file. There are also some classes that contain values that are meaningless once a program exits, such as operating-system-specific font descriptors. These values should not be serialized.

Here is a sample program that puts serialization to work. The `Coin` and `Purse` classes are identical to those of Chapter 13, except that they both implement the `Serializable` interface. Run the program several times. Whenever the program exits, it saves the `Purse` object (and all coin objects that the purse contains) into a file `purse.dat`. When the program starts again, the file is loaded, and your additional coins are added. However, if the file is missing (either because the program is running for the first time, or because the file was erased), then the program starts with a new purse.

File PurseTest.java

```
1  import java.io.File;
2  import java.io.IOException;
3  import java.io.FileInputStream;
4  import java.io.FileOutputStream;
5  import java.io.ObjectInputStream;
6  import java.io.ObjectOutputStream;
7  import javax.swing.JOptionPane;
8
9  /**
10     This program tests serialization of a Purse object.
11     If a file with serialized purse data exists, then it is
12     loaded. Otherwise the program starts with a new purse.
13     More coins are added to the purse. Then the purse data
14     are saved.
15  */
16  public class PurseTest
17  {
18     public static void main(String[] args)
19        throws IOException, ClassNotFoundException
20     {
21        Purse myPurse;
22
23        File f = new File("purse.dat");
24        if (f.exists())
25        {
26           ObjectInputStream in = new ObjectInputStream
27              (new FileInputStream(f));
28           myPurse = (Purse)in.readObject();
29           in.close();
30        }
31        else myPurse = new Purse();
32
33        // add coins to the purse
34        myPurse.add(new Coin(NICKEL_VALUE, "nickel"));
35        myPurse.add(new Coin(DIME_VALUE, "dime"));
36        myPurse.add(new Coin(QUARTER_VALUE, "quarter"));
37
38        double totalValue = myPurse.getTotal();
39        System.out.println("The total is " + totalValue);
40
41        ObjectOutputStream out = new ObjectOutputStream
42           (new FileOutputStream(f));
43        out.writeObject(myPurse);
44        out.close();
```

```
45       }
46
47       private static double NICKEL_VALUE = 0.05;
48       private static double DIME_VALUE = 0.1;
49       private static double QUARTER_VALUE = 0.25;
50  }
```

▼ Productivity Hint 15.1

Use Object Streams

Object streams have a huge advantage over other data file formats. You don't have to come up with a way of breaking objects up into numbers and strings when writing a file. You don't have to come up with a way of combining numbers and strings back into objects when reading a file. The serialization mechanism takes care of this automatically. You simply write and read objects. For this to work, you need to have each of your classes implement the `Serializable` interface, which is trivial to do.

To save your data to disk, it is best to put them all into one large object (such as an array list or an object that describes your entire program state) and save that object. When you need to read the data back, read that object back in. It is easier for you to retrieve data from an object than it is to search for them in a file.

▼ Advanced Topic 15.1

Serializing Geometric Objects

Many classes in the standard library are serializable—after all, it is a simple matter for class designers to add `implements Serializable` to their classes. Unfortunately, the geometry classes `Point2D.Double`, `Rectangle2D.Double`, `Ellipse2D.Double`, and `Line2D.Double` are not. There is no good reason for this. It was just an oversight.

The `Point` and `Rectangle` classes are serializable. If you can get by with integer coordinates, then you may want to use them instead of `Point2D.Double` and `Rectangle2D.Double`.

If you have classes with instance fields that are not serializable, you have to work a bit harder to make serialization work. Follow these steps.

First, mark the nonserializable instance fields with the keyword `transient`:

```
public class Car implements Serializable
{
   . . .
   private Rectangle body; // ok, Rectangle is serializable
   private transient Ellipse2D.Double frontTire;
   private transient Ellipse2D.Double rearTire;
}
```

▼   Then add two methods to save and restore the transient fields explicitly, like this:

```
private void writeObject(ObjectOutputStream out)
    throws IOException
{
    out.defaultWriteObject();

    out.writeDouble(frontTire.getX());
    out.writeDouble(frontTire.getY());
    out.writeDouble(frontTire.getWidth());
    out.writeDouble(frontTire.getHeight());

    out.writeDouble(rearTire.getX());
    out.writeDouble(rearTire.getY());
    out.writeDouble(rearTire.getWidth());
    out.writeDouble(rearTire.getHeight());
}

private void readObject(ObjectInputStream in)
    throws IOException, ClassNotFoundException
{
    in.defaultReadObject();

    double x = in.readDouble();
    double y = in.readDouble();
    double width = in.readDouble();
    double height = in.readDouble();
    frontTire = new Ellipse2D.Double(x, y, width, height);

    x = in.readDouble();
    y = in.readDouble();
    width = in.readDouble();
    height = in.readDouble();
    rearTire = new Ellipse2D.Double(x, y, width, height);
}
```

These special methods *must* be private, and they must call `defaultWriteObject`/
`defaultReadObject` before saving and restoring the additional information.

15.7   Random Access

Consider a file that contains a set of bank accounts. We want to change the balances of
some of the accounts. Of course, we can read all account data into an array list, update
the information that has changed, and save the data out again. If the data set in the file is
very large, we may end up doing a lot of reading and writing just to update a handful of
records. It would be better if we could locate the changed information in the file and just
replace it.

> In sequential file access, a file is processed a byte at a time. Random access allows access at arbitrary locations in the file, without first reading the bytes preceding the access location.

This is quite different from the file access you have programmed up to now. In the past, you read from a file, starting at the beginning and reading the entire contents until you reached the end. That access pattern is called *sequential access*. Now we would like to access specific locations in a file and change just those locations. This access pattern is called random access (see Figure 4). There is nothing "random" about random access—the term just means that you can read and modify any byte stored at any location in the file.

Only disk files support random access; the System.in and System.out streams, which are attached to the keyboard and the terminal window, do not. Each disk file has a special *file pointer* position. Normally, the file pointer is at the end of the file, and any output is appended to the end. However, if you move the file pointer to the middle of the file and write to the file, the output overwrites what is already there. The next read command starts reading input at the file pointer location. You can move the file pointer just beyond the last byte currently in the file but no further.

In Java, you use a RandomAccessFile object to access a file and move a file pointer. To open a random-access file, you supply a file name and a string to specify the *open mode*. You can open a file either for reading only ("r") or for reading and writing ("rw"). For example, the following command opens the file accounts.dat for both reading and writing:

```
RandomAccessFile f =
    new RandomAccessFile("bank.dat", "rw");
```

The method call

```
f.seek(n);
```

moves the file pointer to byte n counted from the beginning of the file. To find out the current position of the file pointer (counted from the beginning of the file), use

```
n = f.getFilePointer();
```

> A file pointer is a position in a random-access file. Because files can be very large, the file pointer is of type long.

Because files can be very large, the file pointer values are long integers. To find out the number of bytes in a file, use the length method:

```
long fileLength = f.length();
```

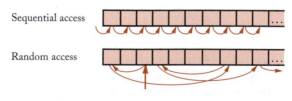

Figure 4

Sequential and Random Access

In the example program at the end of this section, we use a random-access file to store a set of savings accounts, each of which has a current balance and an interest rate. The test program lets you pick a random account and add the interest.

If you want to manipulate a data set in a file, you have to pay special attention to the formatting of the data. Suppose you just store the data as text. Say the balance is $950, and the interest rate is 10%.

    950 10

If the balance is increased by 10% or $95, the new price has more digits. Suppose you place the file pointer to the first character of the old value.

    950 10

If you now simply write out the new value, the result is

    104510

That is not working too well. The update is overwriting the space that separates the fields.

In order to be able to update a file, you must give each field a *fixed* size that is sufficiently large. As a result, every record in the file has the same size. That has another advantage: It is then easy to skip quickly to, say, the 50th record, without having to read the first 49 records in. Just set the file pointer to 50 × the record size.

When storing numbers in a file with fixed record sizes, it is easier to store them in binary format, rather than text format. For that reason, the `RandomAccessFile` class stores binary data. The `readInt` and `writeInt` methods read and write integers as four-byte quantities. The `readDouble` and `writeDouble` methods process double-precision floating-point numbers as eight-byte quantities.

```
double x = f.readDouble();
f.writeDouble(x);
```

If we save the balance and interest rate as `double` values, then each savings account record consists of 16 bytes: 8 bytes for each double-precision value.

Now that we have determined the file layout, we can implement our random-access file methods. In the program at the end of this section, we use a `BankData` class to translate between the random-access file format and savings account objects. The `size` method determines the total number of accounts by dividing the file length by the size of a record.

```
public int size() throws IOException
{
    return (int)(file.length() / RECORD_SIZE);
}
```

To read the nth account in the file, the `read` method positions the file pointer to the offset n * `RECORD_SIZE`, then reads the data, and constructs a savings account object:

```
public SavingsAccount read(int n)
    throws IOException
```

```
   {
      file.seek(n * RECORD_SIZE);
      double balance = file.readDouble();
      double interestRate = file.readDouble();
      SavingsAccount account =
         new SavingsAccount(interestRate);
      account.deposit(balance);
      return account;
   }
```

Writing an account works the same way:

```
   public void write(int n, SavingsAccount account)
      throws IOException
   {
      file.seek(n * RECORD_SIZE);
      file.writeDouble(account.getBalance());
      file.writeDouble(account.getInterestRate());
   }
```

The test program asks the user to enter the position of the account that should be updated and the amount of the deposit or withdrawal. The user can also add new accounts to the database.

Program BankDataTest.java

```
 1  import java.io.IOException;
 2  import java.io.RandomAccessFile;
 3  import javax.swing.JOptionPane;
 4
 5  /**
 6      This program tests random access. You can access existing
 7      accounts and add interest, or create new accounts. The
 8      accounts are saved in a random-access file.
 9  */
10  public class BankDataTest
11  {
12     public static void main(String[] args)
13        throws IOException
14     {
15        BankData data = new BankData();
16        try
17        {
18           data.open("bank.dat");
19
20           boolean done = false;
21           while (!done)
22           {
23              String input = JOptionPane.showInputDialog(
24                 "Account number or " + data.size()
25                 + " for new account");
26              if (input == null) done = true;
```

```
27                  else
28                  {
29                      int pos = Integer.parseInt(input);
30
31                      if (0 <= pos && pos < data.size())
32                      // add interest
33                      {
34                          SavingsAccount account =
35                              data.read(pos);
36                          System.out.println("balance="
37                              + account.getBalance()
38                              + ",interest rate="
39                              + account.getInterestRate());
40                          account.addInterest();
41                          data.write(pos, account);
42                      }
43                      else // add account
44                      {
45                          input = JOptionPane.showInputDialog(
46                              "Balance");
47                          double balance =
48                              Double.parseDouble(input);
49                          input = JOptionPane.showInputDialog(
50                              "Interest Rate");
51                          double interestRate =
52                              Double.parseDouble(input);
53                          SavingsAccount account
54                              = new SavingsAccount(interestRate);
55                          account.deposit(balance);
56                          data.write(data.size(), account);
57                      }
58                  }
59              }
60          }
61          finally
62          {
63              data.close();
64              System.exit(0);
65          }
66      }
67 }
```

Program BankData.java

```
1 import java.io.IOException;
2 import java.io.RandomAccessFile;
3
4 /**
5    This class is a conduit to a random-access file
6    containing savings account data.
7 */
```

```
 8  public class BankData
 9  {
10      /**
11          Constructs a BankData object that is not associated
12          with a file.
13      */
14      public BankData()
15      {
16          file = null;
17      }
18
19      /**
20          Opens the data file.
21          @param filename the name of the file containing savings
22          account information
23      */
24      public void open(String filename)
25          throws IOException
26      {
27          if (file != null) file.close();
28          file = new RandomAccessFile(filename, "rw");;
29      }
30
31      /**
32          Gets the number of accounts in the file.
33          @return the number of accounts
34      */
35      public int size()
36          throws IOException
37      {
38          return (int)(file.length() / RECORD_SIZE);
39      }
40
41      /**
42          Closes the data file.
43      */
44      public void close()
45          throws IOException
46      {
47          if (file != null) file.close();
48          file = null;
49      }
50
51      /**
52          Reads a savings account record.
53          @param n the index of the account in the data file
54          @return a savings account object initialized with the file data
55      */
56      public SavingsAccount read(int n)
57          throws IOException
58      {
59          file.seek(n * RECORD_SIZE);
```

```
60        double balance = file.readDouble();
61        double interestRate = file.readDouble();
62        SavingsAccount account =
63           new SavingsAccount(interestRate);
64        account.deposit(balance);
65        return account;
66     }
67
68     /**
69        Writes a savings account record to the data file.
70        @param n the index of the account in the data file
71        @param account the account to write
72     */
73     public void write(int n, SavingsAccount account)
74        throws IOException
75     {
76        file.seek(n * RECORD_SIZE);
77        file.writeDouble(account.getBalance());
78        file.writeDouble(account.getInterestRate());
79     }
80
81     private RandomAccessFile file;
82
83     public static final int DOUBLE_SIZE = 8;
84     public static final int RECORD_SIZE
85        = 2 * DOUBLE_SIZE;
86  }
```

? HOWTO   15.1

Using Files and Streams

Suppose your program needs to process data in files. This HOWTO walks you through the steps that are involved.

Step 1   Select a data format

The most important question you need to ask yourself concerns the format to use for saving your data.

- Does your program need to save and restore objects? Then use object streams.

- Does your program manipulate text, such as a plain text files? Then use readers and writers.

- Does your program manipulate binary data, such as image files or encrypted data? Then use binary streams.

We don't discuss random-access files here since they are not commonly needed for student projects.

Step 2   If you use object streams, make your classes implement the `Serializable` interface

Simply go through your classes and tag them with `implements Serializable`. You don't need to add any additional methods.

Also go to the online API documentation to check that the library classes that you are using implement the `Serializable` interface. Fortunately, many of them do. In particular, `String` and `ArrayList` are serializable.

If your classes use geometric objects (such as `Point2D.Double`, `Rectangle2D.Double`, and so on), then you have to work harder, because those classes are unfortunately not serializable—see Advanced Topic 15.1.

Step 3a   Use object streams if you are processing objects

Now simply put all the objects you want to save into a class (or an array or array list—but why not make another class containing that?).

Saving all program data is a trivial operation:

```
ProgramData data = . . .;
ObjectOutputStream out = new ObjectOutputStream
   (new FileOutputStream("program.dat"));
out.writeObject(data);
out.close();
```

Similarly, to restore the program data, you use an `ObjectInputStream` and call

```
ProgramData data = (ProgramData)in.readObject();
```

The `readObject` method can throw a `ClassNotFoundException`. You must catch or declare that exception.

Step 3b   Use readers and writers if you are processing text

You need to turn the file input stream into a buffered reader:

```
BufferedReader in = new BufferedReader(
   new FileReader("input.txt"));
```

Now you can read the input a line at a time:

```
boolean done = false;
while (!done)
{
   String input = in.readLine();
   if (input == null)
      done = true;
   else
   {
      process input
   }
}
```

Of course, you need to use `Integer.parseInt` and `Double.parseDouble` to read any numbers in the text file. But wait—if you have numbers in the text file, are you converting numbers and strings into objects? If so, you should probably use object streams instead.

▼   To write output, turn the file output stream into a `PrintWriter`:

```
PrintWriter out = new PrintWriter(
    new FileWriter("output.txt"));
```

▼   Then use the familiar `print` and `println` methods:

```
out.println(text);
```

▼   **Step 3c** Use streams if you are processing bytes

▼   Use this loop to process input a byte at a time:

```
BufferedReader in = new BufferedReader(
    new FileReader("input.txt"));
```

▼   Now you can read the input a byte at a time:

```
InputStream in = new FileInputStream("input.bin");
boolean done = false;
while (!done)
{
    int next = in.read();
    if (next = -1)
        done = true;
    else
    {
        byte b = (byte)next;
        process input
    }
}
in.close();
```

▼   Similarly, write the output a byte at a time:

```
OutputStream out = new FileOutputStream("output.bin");
. . .
byte b = . . .;
out.write(b);
. . .
out.close();
```

▼   You want to use binary streams only if you are ready to process the input a byte at a time. This makes sense for encryption/decryption or processing the pixels in an image. In other situations, binary streams are not appropriate.

CHAPTER SUMMARY

1. Streams access sequences of bytes. Readers and writers access sequences of characters.

2. Use `FileReader`, `FileWriter`, `FileInputStream`, and `FileOutputStream` classes to read and write disk files.

3. The `read` method returns an integer, either −1, at the end of the file, or another value, which you need to cast to a `char` or `byte`.

4. You must close all files that you no longer need.

5. Basic streams, readers, and writers can process only individual bytes or characters. You need to combine them with other classes to process lines of text or entire objects.

6. When writing text files, use the `PrintWriter` class and the `print`/`println` methods.

7. When reading text files, use the `BufferedReader` class and the `readLine` method.

8. The `JFileChooser` dialog lets users select a file by navigating through directories.

9. A `File` object describes a file or directory.

10. You can pass a `File` object to the constructor of a file reader, writer, or stream.

11. When you launch a program from the command line, you can specify arguments after the program name. The program can access these strings by processing the `args` parameter of the `main` method.

12. Use object streams to save and restore all instance fields of an object automatically.

13. Objects saved to an object stream must belong to classes that implement the `Serializable` interface.

14. In sequential file access, a file is processed a byte at a time. Random access allows access at arbitrary locations in the file, without first reading the bytes preceding the access location.

15. A file pointer is a position in a random-access file. Because files can be very large, the file pointer is of type `long`.

Further Reading

[1] Bruce Schneier, *Applied Cryptography,* John Wiley & Sons, 1994.
[2] Phillip R. Zimmermann, *The Official PGP User's Guide,* MIT Press, 1995.
[3] David F. Linowes, *Privacy in America,* University of Illinois Press, 1989.
[4] Abraham Sinkov, *Elementary Cryptanalysis,* Mathematical Association of America, 1966.

CLASSES, OBJECTS, AND METHODS INTRODUCED IN THIS CHAPTER

```
java.io.EOFException
java.io.File
    exists
java.io.FileInputStream
java.io.FileNotFoundException
```

```
java.io.FileOutputStream
java.io.FileReader
java.io.FileWriter
java.io.InputStream
    read
    close
java.io.ObjectInputStream
    readObject
java.io.ObjectOutputStream
    writeObject
java.io.OutputStream
    write
    close
java.io.PrintWriter
    print
    println
java.io.RandomAccessFile
    getFilePointer
    length
    readChar
    readDouble
    readInt
    seek
    writeChar
    writeChars
    writeDouble
    writeInt
java.io.Reader
    read
    close
java.io.Writer
    write
    close
java.lang.Serializable
javax.swing.JFileChooser
    getSelectedFile
    showOpenDialog
    showSaveDialog
```

REVIEW EXERCISES

Exercise R15.1. What is the difference between a stream and a reader?

Exercise R15.2. How can you open a file for both reading and writing in Java?

Exercise R15.3. What happens if you try to write to a file reader? What happens if you try to write to a random-access file that you opened only for reading? Try it out if you don't know.

Exercise R15.4. What happens if you try to open a file for reading that doesn't exist? What happens if you try to open a file for writing that doesn't exist?

Exercise R15.5. What happens if you try to open a file for writing, but the file or device is write-protected (sometimes called read-only)? Try it out with a short test program.

Exercise R15.6. How do you open a file whose name contains a backslash, like c:\temp\output.dat?

Exercise R15.7. How can you break the Caesar cipher? That is, how can you read a document that was encrypted with the Caesar cipher, even though you don't know the key?

Exercise R15.8. What is a command line? How can a program read its command line arguments?

Exercise R15.9. Give two examples of programs on your computer that read arguments from the command line.

Exercise R15.10. If a program Woozle is started with the command

```
java Woozle -DNAME=Piglet -I\eeyore -v heff.txt a.txt lump.txt
```

what are the values of args[0], args[1], and so on?

Exercise R15.11. What happens if you try to save in an object stream an object that is not serializable? Try it out and report your results.

Exercise R15.12. Of the classes that you encountered in this book, which implement the Serializable interface?

Exercise R15.13. Why is it better to save an entire ArrayList to an object stream instead of programming a loop that writes each element?

Exercise R15.14. What is the difference between sequential access and random access?

Exercise R15.15. What is the file pointer in a file? How do you move it? How do you tell the current position? Why is it a long integer?

Exercise R15.16. How do you move the file pointer to the first byte of a file? To the last byte? To the exact middle of the file?

Exercise R15.17. What happens if you try to move the file pointer past the end of a file? Can you move the file pointer of System.in? Try it out and report your results.

PROGRAMMING EXERCISES

Exercise P15.1. Write a program that asks the user for a file name and prints the number of characters, words, and lines in that file. Then the program asks for the name of the next file. When the user enters a file that doesn't exist (such as the empty string), the program exits.

Exercise P15.2. *Random monoalphabet cipher.* The Caesar cipher, which shifts all letters by a fixed amount, is ridiculously easy to crack—just try out all 25 possible keys. Here is a better idea. For the key, don't use numbers but words. Suppose the key word is FEATHER. Then first remove duplicate letters, yielding FEATHR, and append the other letters of the alphabet in reverse order: Now encrypt the letters as follows:

A	B	C	D	E	F	G	H	I	J	K	L	M	N	O	P	Q	R	S	T	U	V	W	X	Y	Z
F	E	A	T	H	R	Z	Y	X	W	V	U	S	Q	P	O	N	M	L	K	J	I	G	D	C	B

Write a program that encrypts or decrypts a file using this cipher. For example,

```
java Crypt -d -kFEATHER encrypt.txt output.txt
```

decrypts a file using the keyword FEATHER. It is an error not to supply a keyword.

Exercise P15.3. *Letter frequencies.* If you encrypt a file using the cipher of the preceding exercise, it will have all of its letters jumbled up, and it doesn't look as if there was any hope of decrypting it without knowing the keyword. Guessing the keyword seems hopeless too. There are just too many possible keywords. However, someone who is trained in decryption will be able to break this cipher in no time at all. The average letter frequencies of English letters are well known. The most common letter is E, which occurs about 13% of the time. Here are the average frequencies of the letters (see [5]).

A	8%	N	8%
B	<1%	O	7%
C	3%	P	3%
D	4%	Q	<1%
E	13%	R	8%
F	3%	S	6%
G	2%	T	9%
H	4%	U	3%
I	7%	V	1%
J	<1%	W	2%
K	<1%	X	<1%
L	4%	Y	2%
M	3%	Z	<1%

Write a program that reads an input file and prints the letter frequencies in that file. Such a tool will help a code breaker. If the most frequent letters in an encrypted file are H and K, then there is an excellent chance that they are the encryptions of E and T.

Exercise P15.4. *Vigenère cipher.* The trouble with a monoalphabetic cipher is that it can be easily broken by frequency analysis. The so-called Vigenère cipher overcomes this problem by encoding a letter into one of several cipher letters, depending on its position in the input document. Choose a keyword, for example TIGER. Then encode the first letter of the input text like this:

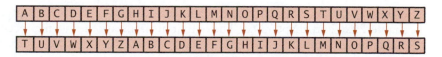

A	B	C	D	E	F	G	H	I	J	K	L	M	N	O	P	Q	R	S	T	U	V	W	X	Y	Z
T	U	V	W	X	Y	Z	A	B	C	D	E	F	G	H	I	J	K	L	M	N	O	P	Q	R	S

That is, the encoded alphabet is just the regular alphabet shifted to start at T, the first letter of the keyword TIGER. The second letter is encrypted according to the map

A	B	C	D	E	F	G	H	I	J	K	L	M	N	O	P	Q	R	S	T	U	V	W	X	Y	Z
I	J	K	L	M	N	O	P	Q	R	S	T	U	V	W	X	Y	Z	A	B	C	D	E	F	G	H

The third, fourth, and fifth letters in the input text are encrypted using the alphabet sequences beginning with characters G, E, and R, and so on. Because the key is only five letters long, the sixth letter of the input text is encrypted in the same way as the first.

Write a program that encrypts or decrypts an input text according to this cipher.

Exercise P15.5. *Playfair cipher.* Another way of thwarting a simple letter frequency analysis of an encrypted text is to encrypt *pairs* of letters together. A simple scheme to do this is the Playfair cipher. You pick a keyword and remove duplicate letters from it. Then you fill the keyword, and the remaining letters of the alphabet, into a 5 × 5 square. (Since there are only 25 squares, I and J are considered the same letter.) Here is such an arrangement with the keyword PLAYFAIR:

```
P L A Y F
I R B C D
E G H K M
N O Q S T
U V W X Z
```

To encrypt a letter pair, say AT, look at the rectangle with corners A and T:

```
P L A Y F
I R B C D
E G H K M
N O Q S T
U V W X Z
```

The encoding of this pair is formed by looking at the other two corners of the rectangle—in this case, FQ. If both letters happen to be in the same row or column, such as GO, simply swap the two letters. Decryption is done in the same way.

Write a program that encrypts or decrypts an input text according to this cipher.

Exercise P15.6. Write a program CopyFile that copies one file to another. The file names are specified on the command line. For example,

```
java CopyFile report.txt report.sav
```

Exercise P15.7. Write a program that *concatenates* the contents of several files into one file. For example,

```
java CatFiles chapter1.txt chapter2.txt chapter3.txt book.txt
```

makes a long file, book.txt, that contains the contents of the files chapter1.txt, chapter2.txt, and chapter3.txt. The output file is always the last file specified on the command line.

Exercise P15.8. Write a program `Find` that searches all files specified on the command line and prints out all lines containing a keyword. For example, if you call

```
java Find Buff report.txt address.txt Homework.java
```

then the program might print

```
report.txt: Buffet style lunch will be available at the
address.txt: Buffet, Warren|11801 Trenton Court|Dallas|TX
address.txt: Walters, Winnie|59 Timothy Circle|Buffalo|MI
Homework.java: BufferedReader in;
```

The keyword is always the first command line argument.

Exercise P15.9. Write a program that checks the spelling of all words in a file. It should read each word of a file and check whether it is contained in a word list. A word list is available on most UNIX systems in the file /usr/dict/words. (If you don't have access to a UNIX system, your instructor should be able to get you a copy.) The program should print out all words that it cannot find in the word list.

Exercise P15.10. Write a program that opens a file for reading and writing, and replaces each line with its reverse. For example, if you run

```
java Reverse Hello.java
```

then the contents of Hello.java are changed to

```
olleH ssalc cilbup
)sgra ][gnirtS(niam diov citats cilbup  {
;"n\\!dlroW, olleH" = gniteerg gnirtS  {
;)gniteerg(tnirp.tuo.metsyS
}
}
```

Of course, if you run `Reverse` twice on the same file, you get back the original file.

Exercise P15.11. Write a program that reads a file from standard input and rewrites the file to standard output, replacing all tab characters '\t' with the *appropriate* number of spaces. Make the distance between tab columns a constant and set it to 3, the value we use in this book for Java programs. Then expand tabs to the number of spaces necessary to move to the next tab column. *That may be less than three spaces.* For example, consider the line containing "\t|\t||\t|". The first tab is changed to three spaces, the second to two spaces, and the third to one space.

Exercise P15.12. Reimplement the `BankData` class of Section 15.6 by storing all savings accounts in an `ArrayList` and by using serialization. Change only the implementation of the class, not the public interface.

Exercise P15.13. Write a graphical application in which the user clicks on a panel to add car shapes at the mouse click location. The shapes are stored in an array list. When the user selects File→Save from the menu, save the selection of shapes in a file. When the user selects File→Open, load in a file. Use serialization.

Exercise P15.14. The program in Section 15.6 only locates one bank account and adds interest. Add an option to the program that adds interest to all bank accounts.

Exercise P15.15. Implement a graphical user interface for the program in Section 15.6.

System Design

CHAPTER GOALS

To learn about the software life cycle

▶ To learn how to discover new classes and methods

▶ To understand the use of CRC cards for class discovery

▶ To be able to identify inheritance, aggregation, and dependency relationships between classes

▶ To master the use of UML class diagrams to describe class relationships

▶ To learn how to use object-oriented design to build complex programs

To implement a software system successfully, be it as simple as your next homework project or as complex as the next air traffic monitoring system, some amount of planning, design, and testing is required. In fact, for larger projects, the amount of time spent on planning is much higher than the amount of time spent on programming and testing.

If you find that most of your homework time is spent in front of the computer, keying code in and fixing bugs, you are probably spending more time on your homework than you should. You could cut down your total time by spending more on the planning and design phase. This chapter tells you how to approach these tasks in a systematic manner.

16.1 The Software Life Cycle

> The life cycle of software encompasses all activities from initial analysis until obsolescence.

> A formal process for software development describes phases of the development process and gives guidelines for how to carry out the phases.

In this section we will discuss the *software life cycle:* the activities that take place between the time a software program is first conceived and the time it is finally retired.

A software project usually starts because some customer has some problem and is willing to pay money to have it solved. The Department of Defense, the customer of many programming projects, was an early proponent of a *formal process* for software development. A formal process identifies and describes different phases and gives guidelines how to carry out the phases and when to move from one phase to the next.

Many software engineers break the development process down into the following five phases:

- Analysis

- Design

- Implementation

- Testing

- Deployment

In the *analysis* phase, you decide *what* the project is supposed to accomplish; you do not think about *how* the program will accomplish its tasks. The output of the analysis phase is a *requirements document*, which describes in complete detail what the program will be able to do once it is completed. Part of this requirements document can be a user manual that tells how the user will operate the program to derive the promised benefits. Another part sets performance criteria—how many inputs the program must be able to handle in what time, or what its maximum memory and disk storage requirements are.

In the *design* phase, you develop a plan for how you will implement the system. You discover the structures that underlie the problem to be solved. When you use object-oriented design, you decide what classes you need and what their most important methods are. The output of this phase is a description of the classes and methods, with diagrams that show the relationships among the classes.

In the *implementation* phase, you write and compile program code to implement the classes and methods that were discovered in the design phase. The output of this phase is the completed program.

In the *testing* phase, you run tests to verify that the program works correctly. The output of this phase is a report describing the tests that you carried out and their results.

> The waterfall model of software development describes a sequential process of analysis, design, implementation, testing, and deployment.

In the *deployment* phase, the users of the program install it and use it for its intended purpose.

When formal development processes were first established in the early 1970s, software engineers had a very simple visual model of these phases. They postulated that one phase would run to completion, its output would spill over to the next phase, and the next phase would begin. This model is called the *waterfall model* of software development (see Figure 1).

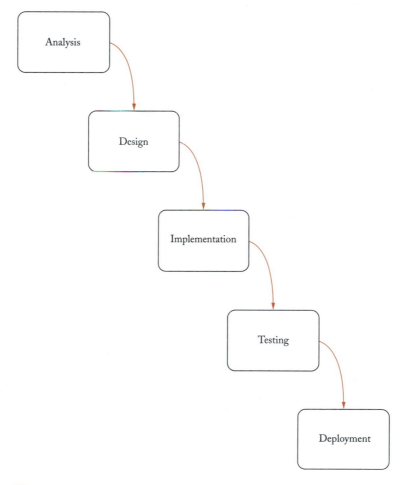

Figure 1

The Waterfall Model

In an ideal world the waterfall model has a lot of appeal: You figure out what to do; then you figure out how to do it; then you do it; then you verify that you did it right; then you hand the product to the customer. When rigidly applied, though, the waterfall model simply did not work. It was very difficult to come up with a perfect requirement specification. It was quite common to discover in the design phase that the requirements were not consistent or that a small change in the requirements would lead to a system that was both easier to design and more useful for the customer, but the analysis phase was over, so the designers had no choice—they had to take the existing requirements, errors and all. This problem would repeat itself during implementation. The designers may have thought they knew how to solve the problem as efficiently as possible, but when the design was actually implemented, it turned out that the resulting program was not as fast as the designers had thought. The next transition is one with which you are surely familiar. When the program was handed to the quality assurance department for testing, many bugs were found that would best be fixed by reimplementing, or maybe even redesigning, the program, but the waterfall model did not allow for this. Finally, when the customers received the finished product, they were often not at all happy with it. Even though the customers typically were very involved in the analysis phase, often they themselves were not sure exactly what they needed. After all, it can be very difficult to describe how you want to use a product that you have never seen before. But when the customers started using the program, they began to realize what they would have liked. Of course, then it was too late, and they had to live with what they got.

> The spiral model of software development describes an iterative process in which design and implementation are repeated.

Having some level of iteration is clearly necessary. There simply must be a mechanism to deal with errors from the preceding phase. The *spiral model*, proposed by Barry Boehm in 1988, breaks the development process down into multiple phases (see Figure 2). Early phases focus on

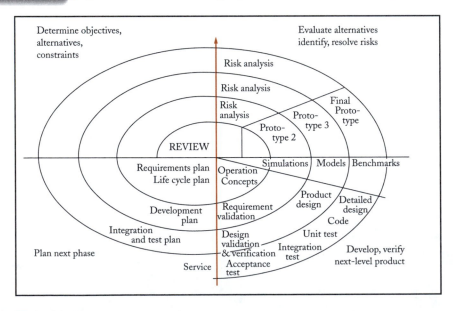

Figure 2

The Spiral Model

the construction of *prototypes*. A prototype is a small system that shows some aspects of the final system. Because prototypes model only a part of a system and do not need to withstand customer abuse, they can be implemented quickly. It is common to build a *user interface prototype* that shows the user interface in action. This gives customers an early chance to become more familiar with the system and to suggest improvements before the analysis is complete. Other prototypes can be built to validate interfaces with external systems, to test performance, and so on. Lessons learned from the development of one prototype can be applied to the next iteration of the spiral.

By building in repeated trials and feedback, a development process that follows the spiral model has a greater chance of delivering a satisfactory system. However, there is also a danger. If engineers believe that they don't have to do a good job because they can always do another iteration, then there will be many iterations, and the process will take a very long time to complete.

> Extreme Programming is a development methodology that strives for simplicity by removing formal structure and focusing on best practices.

Figure 3 (from [1]) shows activity levels in the "Rational Unified Process", a development process methodology by the inventors of UML. You can see that this is a complex process involving multiple iterations.

Even complex development processes with many iterations have not always met with success. In 1999, Kent Beck published an influential book [2] on *Extreme Programming*, a development methodology that strives for simplicity by cutting out most of the formal trappings of a traditional development methodology and instead focusing on a set of *practices:*

- *Realistic planning:* Customers are to make business decisions, programmers are to make technical decisions. Update the plan when it conflicts with reality.

- *Small releases:* Release a useful system quickly, then release updates on a very short cycle.

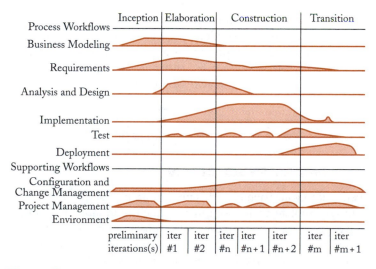

Figure 3

Activity Levels in the Rational Unified Process Methodology

- *Metaphor:* All programmers should have a simple shared story that explains the system under development.

- *Simplicity:* Design everything to be as simple as possible instead of preparing for future complexity.

- *Testing:* Both programmers and customers are to write test cases. The system is continuously tested.

- *Refactoring:* Programmers are to restructure the system continuously to improve the code and eliminate duplication.

- *Pair programming:* Put programmers together in pairs, and require each pair to write code on a single computer.

- *Collective ownership:* All programmers are to have permission to change all code as it becomes necessary.

- *Continuous integration:* Whenever a task is completed, build the entire system and test it.

- *40-hour week:* Don't cover up unrealistic schedules with bursts of heroic effort.

- *On-site customer:* An actual customer of the system is to be accessible to team members at all times.

- *Coding standards:* Programmers are to follow standards that emphasize self-documenting code.

Many of these practices are common-sense. Others, such as the pair programming requirement, are surprising. Beck claims that the value of the Extreme Programming approach lies in the synergy of these practices—the sum is bigger than the parts.

In your first programming course, you will not yet develop systems that are so complex that you need a full-fledged methodology to solve your homework problems. This introduction to the development process should, however, show you that successful software development involves more than just coding. In the remainder of this chapter we will have a closer look at the *design phase* of the software development process.

▼ Random Fact 16.1

Programmer Productivity

If you talk to your friends in this programming class, you will find that some of them consistently complete their assignments much more quickly than others. Perhaps they have more experience. However, even when programmers with the same education and experience are compared, wide variations in competence are routinely observed and measured. It is not uncommon to have the best programmer in a team be five to ten times as productive as the worst, using any of a number of reasonable measures of productivity [3].

That is a staggering range of performance among trained professionals. In a marathon race, the best runner will not run five to ten times faster than the slowest one. Software product managers are acutely aware of these disparities. The obvious solution is, of

▼ course, to hire only the best programmers, but even in recent periods of economic slow-down the demand for good programmers has greatly outstripped the supply.

▼ Fortunately for all of us, joining the rank of the best is not necessarily a question of raw intellectual power. Good judgment, experience, broad knowledge, attention to detail, and superior planning are at least as important as mental brilliance. These skills can be acquired by individuals who are genuinely interested in improving themselves.

▼ Even the most gifted programmer can deal with only a finite number of details in a given time period. Suppose a programmer can implement and debug one method every two hours, or one hundred methods per month. (This is a generous estimate. Few pro-

▼ grammers are this productive.) If a task requires 10,000 methods (which is typical for a medium-sized program), then a single programmer would need 100 months to complete the job. Such a project is sometimes expressed as a "100-man-month" project. But as

▼ Fred Brooks explains in his famous book [4], the concept of "man-month" is a myth. One cannot trade months for programmers. One hundred programmers cannot finish the task in one month. In fact, 10 programmers probably couldn't finish it in 10 months. First of

▼ all, the 10 programmers need to learn about the project before they can get productive. Whenever there is a problem with a particular method, both the author and its users need to meet and discuss it, taking time away from all of them. A bug in one method may have

▼ other programmers twiddling their thumbs until it is fixed.

It is difficult to estimate these inevitable delays. They are one reason why software is often released later than originally promised. What is a manager to do when the delays

▼ mount? As Brooks points out, adding more personnel will make a late project even later, because the productive people have to stop working and train the newcomers.

▼ You will experience these problems when you work on your first team project with other students. Be prepared for a major drop in productivity, and be sure to set ample time aside for team communications.

There is, however, no alternative to teamwork. Most important and worthwhile

▼ projects transcend the ability of one single individual. Learning to function well in a team is as important for your education as it is to become a competent programmer.

16.2   Discovering Classes

> In object-oriented design, you discover classes, determine the responsibilities of classes, and describe the relationships between classes.

In the design phase of software development, your task is to discover structures that make it possible to implement a set of tasks on a computer. When you use the object-oriented design process, you carry out the following tasks:

1. Discover classes.
2. Determine the responsibilities of each class.
3. Describe the relationships between the classes.

A class represents some useful concept. You have seen classes for concrete entities such as bank accounts, ellipses, and products. Other classes represent abstract concepts such as streams and

INVOICE

Sam's Small Appliances
100 Main Street
Anytown, CA 98765

Item	Qty	Price	Total
Toaster	3	$29.95	$89.85
Hair Dryer	1	$24.95	$24.95
Car Vacuum	2	$19.99	$39.98

AMOUNT DUE: $154.78

Figure 4

An Invoice

windows. A simple rule for finding classes is to look for *nouns* in the task description. For example, suppose your job is to print an invoice such as the one in Figure 4. Obvious classes that come to mind are `Invoice`, `Item`, and `Customer`. It is a good idea to keep a list of *candidate classes* on a whiteboard or a sheet of paper. As you brainstorm, simply put all ideas for classes onto the list. You can always cross out the ones that weren't useful after all.

Once a set of classes has been identified, you need to define the behavior for each class. That is, you need to find out what methods each object needs to carry out to solve the programming problem. A simple rule for finding these methods is to look for *verbs* in the task description, and then match the verbs to the appropriate objects. For example, in the invoice program, some class needs to compute the amount due. Now you need to figure out *which class* is responsible for this method. Do customers compute what they owe? Do invoices total up the amount due? Do the items total themselves up? The best choice is to make "compute amount due" the responsibility of the `Invoice` class.

An excellent way to carry out this task is the so-called *CRC* card method. "CRC" stands for "classes", "responsibilities", "collaborators", and in its simplest form, the method works as follows. Use an index card for each *class* (see Figure 5). As you think about verbs in the task description that indicate methods, you pick the card of the class that

A CRC card describes a class, its responsibilities, and its collaborating classes.

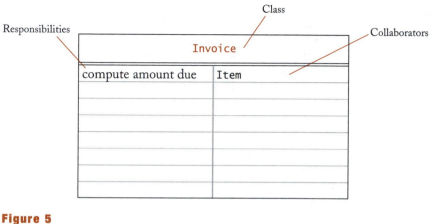

Figure 5

A CRC Card

you think should be responsible, and write that *responsibility* onto the card. For each responsibility, you record which other classes are needed to fulfill it. Those classes are the *collaborators*.

For example, suppose you decide that an invoice should compute the amount due. Then you write "compute amount due" on the left-hand side of an index card with the title `Invoice`.

If a class can carry out that responsibility all by itself, you do nothing further. But if the class needs the help of other classes, you write the names of these collaborators on the right-hand side of the card.

To compute the total, the invoice needs to ask each item about its total price. Therefore, the `Item` class is a collaborator.

This is a good time to look up the index card for the `Item` class. Does it have a "get total price" method? If not, add one:

How do you know that you are on the right track? For each responsibility, ask yourself how it can actually be done, using just the responsibilities written on the various cards. Many people find it helpful to group the cards on a table so that the collaborators are close to each other, and to simulate tasks by moving a token (such as a coin) from one card to the next to indicate which object is currently active.

Keep in mind that the responsibilities that you list on the CRC card are on a *high level*. Sometimes a single responsibility may need two or more Java methods for carrying it out. Some researchers say that a CRC card should have no more than three distinct responsibilities.

The CRC card method is informal on purpose, so that you can be creative and discover classes and their properties. Once you find that you have settled on a good set of classes, you will want to know how they are related to each other. Can you find classes with common properties, so that some responsibilities can be taken care of by a common superclass? Can you organize classes into clusters that are independent of each other? Finding class relationships and documenting them with diagrams is the topic of the next section.

16.3 Relationships between Classes

When designing a program, it is useful to document the relationships between classes. This helps you in a number of ways. For example, if you find classes with common behavior, you can save effort by placing the common behavior into a superclass. If you know that some classes are *not* related to each other, you can assign different programmers to implement each of them, without worrying that one of them has to wait for the other.

You have seen the inheritance relationship between classes many times in this book. Inheritance is a very important relationship between classes, but, as it turns out, it is not the only useful relationship, and it can be overused.

Inheritance is a relationship between a more general class (the superclass) and a more specialized class (the subclass). This relationship is often described as the *is-a* relationship. Every truck is a vehicle. Every savings account is a bank account. Every circle is an ellipse (with equal width and height).

> Inheritance (the "is-a" relationship) is sometimes inappropriately used when the "has-a" relationship would be more appropriate.

Inheritance is sometimes abused, however. For example, consider a `Tire` class that describes a car tire. Should the class `Tire` be a subclass of a class `Circle`? It sounds convenient. There are probably quite a few useful methods in the `Circle` class—for example, the `Tire` class may inherit methods that compute the radius, perimeter, and center point. All that should come in handy when drawing tire shapes. Yet though it may be convenient for the programmer, this arrangement makes no sense conceptually. It isn't true that every tire is a circle. Tires are car parts, whereas circles are geometric objects.

There is a relationship between tires and circles, though. A tire *has* a circle as its boundary. Java lets us model that relationship, too. Use an instance variable:

```java
class Tire
{
   . . .
   private String rating;
   private Circle boundary;
}
```

The technical term for this relationship is *association*. Each `Tire` object is associated with a `Circle` object.

Here is another example. Every car *is a* vehicle. Every car *has a* tire (in fact, it has four or, if you count the spare, five). Thus, you would use inheritance from `Vehicle` and use association of `Tire` objects:

```java
class Car extends Vehicle
{
   . . .
   private Tire[] tires;
}
```

In this book, we use the UML notation for class diagrams. You have already seen many examples of the UML notation for inheritance—an arrow with an open triangle

A class is associated with another class if you can navigate from its objects to objects of the other class, usually by following object references.

Dependency is another name for the "uses" relationship.

pointing to the superclass. In the UML notation, association is denoted by a solid line with an open arrow tip. Figure 6 shows a class diagram with an inheritance and an association relationship.

A class is associated with another if you can *navigate* from objects of one class to objects of the other class. For example, given a Car object, you can navigate to the Tire objects, simply by accessing the tires instance field. When a class has an instance field whose type is another class, then the two classes are associated.

The association relationship is related to the *dependency* relationship, which you saw in Chapter 7. Recall that a class depends on another if one of its methods *uses* an object of the other class in some way.

For example, all of our applet classes depend on the Graphics class, because they receive a Graphics object in the paint method and then use it to draw various shapes. The console applications depend on the System class, because they use the static variable System.out.

Association is a stronger form of dependency. If a class is associated with another, it also depends on the other class.

However, the converse is not true. If a class is associated with another, objects of the class can locate objects of the associated class, usually because they store references to those objects. If a class depends on another, it comes in contact with objects of the other class in some way, not necessarily through navigation. For example, an applet depends on the Graphics class, but it is not associated with the Graphics class. Given an applet object, you can't navigate to a Graphics object. You have to wait for the paint method to pass a Graphics object as a parameter.

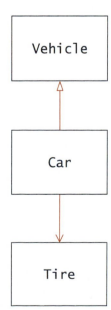

Figure 6

UML Notation for Inheritance and Association

> You need to be able to distinguish the UML notations for inheritance, realization, association, and dependency.

As you saw in Chapter 7, the UML notation for dependency is a dashed line with an open arrow that points to the dependent class.

The arrows in the UML notation can get confusing. Table 1 shows a summary of the four UML relationship symbols that we use in this book.

Relationship	Symbol	Line style	Arrow tip
Inheritance	——————▷	Solid	Closed
Realization	– – – – –▷	Dotted	Closed
Association	——————›	Solid	Open
Dependency	– – – – –›	Dotted	Open

🄰🅃 Advanced Topic   16.1

Attributes and Methods in UML Diagrams

Sometimes it is useful to indicate class *attributes* and *methods* in a class diagram. An *attribute* is an externally observable property that objects of a class have. For example, `name` and `price` would be attributes of the `Product` class. Usually, attributes correspond to instance variables. But they don't have to—a class may have a different way of organizing its data. Consider the ellipse class from the Java library. Conceptually, it has attributes `center`, `width`, and `height`, but it doesn't actually store the center of the ellipse. Instead, it stores the top left corner and computes the center from it.

You can indicate attributes and methods in a class diagram by dividing a class rectangle into three compartments, with the class name in the top, attributes in the middle, and methods in the bottom (see Figure 7). You need not list *all* attributes and methods in a particular diagram. Just list the ones that are helpful to understand whatever point you are making with a particular diagram.

Also, don't list as an attribute what you also draw as an association. If you denote by association the fact that a `Car` has `Tire` objects, don't add an attribute `tires`.

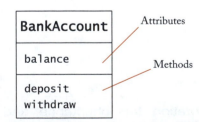

Figure 7

Attributes and Methods in a Class Diagram

Advanced Topic   16.2

Association, Aggregation, and Composition

The association relationship is the most complex relationship in the UML notation. It is also the least standardized. As you read other books and see class diagrams produced by fellow programmers, you may encounter quite a few different flavors of the association relationship.

The association relationship that we use in this book is called a *directed* association. It implies that you can navigate from one class to another, but not the other way around. For example, given a `Car` object, you can navigate to `Tire` objects. But if you have a `Tire` object, then there is no indication to which car it belongs.

Of course, a `Tire` object may contain a reference back to the `Car` object so that you can navigate from the tire back to the car to which it belongs. Then the association is *bidirectional*. For cars and tires, this is an unlikely implementation. But consider the example of `Person` and `Company` objects. The company may keep a list of people working for it, and each person object may keep a reference to the current employer.

According to the UML standard, a bidirectional association is drawn as a solid line with *no* arrow tips. (See Figure 8 for this and other variations of the association notation.) But some designers interpret an association without arrow tips as an "undecided" association, where it is not yet known in which direction the navigation can happen.

Some designers like to add *adornments* to the association relationships. An association can have a name, roles, or multiplicities. A name describes the nature of the relationship. Role adornments express specific roles that the associated classes have toward each other. Multiplicities state how many objects can be reached when navigating the association relationship. The example in Figure 8 expresses the fact that every tire is associated with 0 or 1 car, whereas every car must have 4 or more tires.

Aggregation is a stronger form of association. A class aggregates another if there is a "whole-part" relationship between the classes. For example, the `Company` class aggregates the `Person` class because a company (the "whole") is made up from people (the "parts"), namely its employees and contractors. But a `BankAccount` class does not aggregate a `Person` class, even though it may be possible to navigate from a bank customer object to a person object—the owner of the account. Conceptually, a person is not a part of the bank account.

Composition is an even stronger form of aggregation that denotes that a "part" can belong to only one "whole" at a given point in time. For example, a tire can be in only one car at a time, but a person can work for two companies at the same time.

Frankly, the differences between association, aggregation, and composition are confusing, even to experienced designers. If you find the distinctions helpful, by all means use them. But don't spend time pondering subtle differences between these concepts. From the practical point of view of a Java programmer, it is useful to know when one class stores a reference to another class. Directed associations accurately describe this phenomenon.

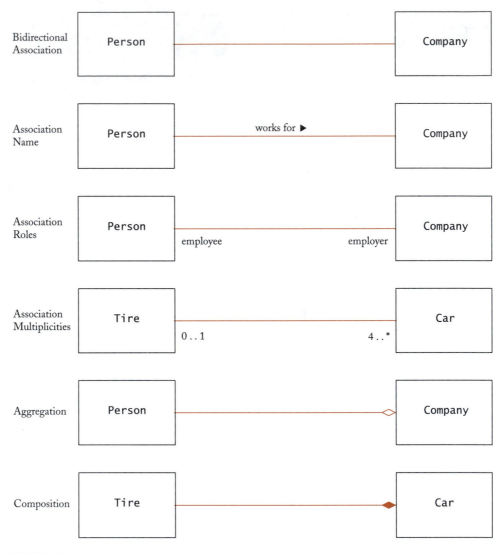

Figure 8

Variations of the Association Notation

? HOWTO **16.1**

CRC Cards and UML Diagrams

Before writing code for a complex problem, you need to design a solution. The methodology introduced in this chapter suggests that you follow a design process that is composed of the following tasks:

1. Discover classes.
2. Determine the responsibilities of each class.
3. Describe the relationships between the classes.

CRC cards and UML diagrams help you discover and record this information.

Step 1 Discover classes

Highlight the nouns in the problem description. Make a list of the nouns. Cross out those that don't seem reasonable candidates for classes.

Step 2 Discover responsibilities

Make a list of the major tasks that your system needs to fulfill. From those tasks, pick one that is not trivial and that is intuitive to you. Find a class that is responsible for carrying out that task. Make an index card and write the name and the task on it. Now ask yourself how an object of the class can carry out the task. It probably needs help from other objects. Then make CRC cards for the classes to which those objects belong and write the responsibilities on them.

Don't be afraid to cross out, move, split, or merge responsibilities. Rip up cards if they become too messy. This is an informal process.

You are done when you have walked through all major tasks and satisfied yourself that they can all be solved with the classes and responsibilities that you discovered.

Step 3 Discover relationships

Make a class diagram that shows the relationships between all the classes that you discovered.

Start with inheritance—the "is-a" relationship between classes. Is any class a specialization of another? If so, draw inheritance arrows. Keep in mind that many designs, especially for simple programs, don't use inheritance extensively.

The "collaborators" column of the CRC cards tell you which classes use another. Draw usage arrows for the collaborators on the CRC cards.

For each of the dependency relationships, ask yourself: How does the object locate its collaborator? Does it navigate to it directly because it stores a reference? Does it ask another object to locate the collaborator? Is the collaborator passed as a parameter to a method? Only in the first case is the collaborating class an associated class. In those cases, draw association arrows.

16.4   Example: Printing an Invoice

In this chapter, we discuss a five-part development process that is recommended for you to follow:

1. Gather requirements.
2. Use CRC cards to find classes, responsibilities, and collaborators.
3. Use UML diagrams to record class relationships.

4. Use `javadoc` to document method behavior.

5. Implement your program.

This process is particularly well suited for beginning programmers. There isn't a lot of notation to learn. The class diagrams are simple to draw. The deliverables of the design phase are obviously useful for the implementation phase—you simply take the source files and start adding the method code. Of course, as your projects get more complex, you will want to learn more about formal design methods. There are many techniques to describe object scenarios, call sequencing, the large-scale structure of programs, and so on, that are very beneficial even for relatively simple projects. The book [1] gives a good overview of these techniques.

In this section, we will walk through the object-oriented design technique with a very simple example. In this case, the methodology will certainly feel overblown, but it is a good introduction to the mechanics of each step. You will then be better prepared for the more complex example that follows.

16.4.1 — Requirements

The task of this program is to print out an *invoice*. An invoice describes the charges for a set of products in certain quantities. (We omit complexities such as dates, taxes, and invoice and customer numbers.) The program simply prints the billing address, all line items, and the amount due. Each line item contains the description and unit price of a product, the quantity ordered, and the total price.

```
                I N V O I C E

Sam's Small Appliances
100 Main Street
Anytown, CA 98765

Description                    Price  Qty  Total
Toaster                        29.95   3   89.85
Hair dryer                     24.95   1   24.95
Car vacuum                     19.99   2   39.98

AMOUNT DUE: $154.78
```

Also, in the interest of simplicity, we do not provide a user interface. We just supply a test program that adds items to the invoice and then prints it.

16.4.2 — CRC Cards

First, you need to discover classes. Classes correspond to nouns in the problem description. In this problem, it is pretty obvious what the nouns are:

```
Invoice
Address
Item
Product
Description
Price
Quantity
Total
Amount Due
```

(Of course, `Toaster` doesn't count—it is the description of an `Item` object and therefore a data value, not the name of a class.)

The product description and price are fields of the `Product` class. What about the quantity? The quantity is not an attribute of a `Product`. Just as in the printed invoice, let's have a class `Item` that records the product and the quantity (such as "3 toasters").

The total and amount due are computed—not stored anywhere. Thus, they don't lead to classes.

After this process of elimination, we are left with four candidates for classes:

```
Invoice
Address
Item
Product
```

Each of them represents a useful concept, so let's make them all into classes.

The purpose of the program is to print an invoice. However, the `Invoice` class won't necessarily know whether to display the output in `System.out`, in a text area, or in a file. Therefore, let's relax the task slightly and make the invoice responsible for *formatting* the invoice. The result is a string (containing multiple lines) that can be printed out or displayed. Record that responsibility in a CRC card:

Invoice
format the invoice

How does an invoice format itself? It must format the billing address, format all items, and then add the amount due. How can the invoice format an address? It can't— that really is the responsibility of the `Address` class. This leads to a second CRC card:

Address
format the address

Similarly, formatting of an item is the responsibility of the `Item` class.

The `format` method of the `Invoice` class calls the `format` methods of the `Address` and `Item` classes. Whenever a method uses another class, you list that other class as a collaborator. In other words, `Address` and `Item` are collaborators of `Invoice`:

Invoice	
format the invoice	Address
	Item

When formatting the invoice, the invoice also needs to compute the total amount due. To obtain that amount, it must ask each item about the total price of the item.

How does an item obtain that total? It must ask the product for the unit price, and then multiply it by the quantity. That is, the `Product` class must reveal the unit price, and it is a collaborator of the `Item` class.

Product	
get description	
get unit price	

Item	
format the item	Product
get total price	

Finally, the invoice must be populated with products and quantities, so that it makes sense to format the result. That too is a responsibility of the `Invoice` class.

Invoice	
format the invoice	Address
add a product and quantity	Item
	Product

We now have a set of CRC cards that completes the CRC card process.

16.4.3 — UML Diagrams

You get the dependency relationships from the collaboration column in the CRC cards. Each class depends on the classes with which it collaborates. In our example, the `Invoice` class collaborates with the `Address`, `Item`, and `Product` classes. The `Item` class collaborates with the `Product` class.

Now ask yourself which of these dependencies are actually associations. How does an invoice know about the address, item, and product objects with which it collaborates? An invoice object must hold references to the address and the items when it formats the invoice. But an invoice object need not hold a reference to a product object when adding a product. The product is turned into an item, and then it is the item's responsibility to hold a reference to it.

Therefore, the `Invoice` class is associated with the `Address` class and the `Item` class. The `Item` class is associated with the `Product` class. However, you cannot directly navigate from an invoice to a product. An invoice doesn't store products directly—they are stored in the `Item` objects.

There is no inheritance in this example.

Figure 9 shows the class relationships that we discovered.

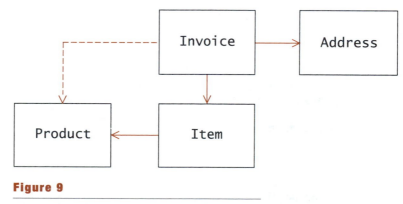

Figure 9

The Relationships between the Invoice Classes

16.4.4 — Method Documentation

> You can use `javadoc` documentation comments (with the bodies of the methods left blank) to record formally the behavior of the classes that you discovered.

The final step of the design phase is to write the documentation of the discovered classes and methods. Simply write a Java source file for each class, write the method comments for those methods that you have discovered, and leave the bodies of the methods blank.

```java
/**
    Describes an invoice for a set of purchased products.
*/
public class Invoice
{
    /**
        Adds a charge for a product to this invoice.
        @param aProduct the product that the customer ordered
        @param quantity the quantity of the product
    */
    public void add(Product aProduct, int quantity)
    {
    }

    /**
        Formats the invoice.
        @return the formatted invoice
    */
    public String format()
    {
    }
}


/**
    Describes a quantity of an article to purchase and its price.
*/
public class Item
{
    /**
        Computes the total cost of this item.
        @return the total price
    */
    public double getTotalPrice()
    {
    }

    /**
        Formats this item.
        @return a formatted string of this item
```

```java
    */
    public String format()
    {
    }
}


/**
    Describes a product with a description and a price.
*/
public class Product
{
    /**
        Gets the product description.
        @return the description
    */
    public String getDescription()
    {
    }

    /**
        Gets the product price.
        @return the unit price
    */
    public double getPrice()
    {
    }
}


/**
    Describes a mailing address.
*/
public class Address
{
    /**
        Formats the address.
        @return the address as a string with 3 lines
    */
    public String format()
    {
    }
}
```

Then run the `javadoc` program to obtain a prettily formatted version of your documentation in HTML format (see Figure 10).

This approach for documenting your classes has a number of advantages. You can share the HTML documentation with others if you work in a team. You use a format that is immediately useful—Java source files that you can carry into the implementation phase. And, most importantly, you supply the comments of the key methods—a task that less prepared programmers leave for later, and then often neglect for lack of time.

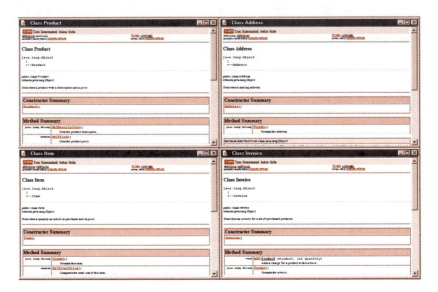

Figure 10

The Class Documentation in the HTML Format

16.4.5— Implementation

Finally, you are ready to implement the classes.

You already have the method signatures and comments from the previous step. Now look at the UML diagram to add instance variables. Associated classes yield instance variables. Start with the `Invoice` class. An invoice is associated with `Address` and `Item`. Every invoice has one billing address, but it can have many items. To store multiple `Item` objects, you can use an array list. Now you have the instance variables of the `Invoice` class:

```
public class Invoice
{
   . . .
   private Customer theCustomer;
   private Vector items;
}
```

As you can see from the UML diagram, the `Item` class is associated with a product. Also, you need to store the product quantity. That leads to the following instance variables:

```
public class Item
{
   . . .
   private Product theProduct;
   private int quantity;
}
```

The methods themselves are now very easy. Here is a typical example. You already know what the `getTotalPrice` method of the `Item` class needs to do—get the unit price of the product and multiply it with the quantity.

```
/**
    Computes the total cost of this item.
    @return the total price
*/
public double getTotalPrice()
{
    return theProduct.getPrice() * quantity;
}
```

We will not discuss the other methods in detail—they are equally straightforward. Finally, you need to supply constructors, another routine task.

Here is the entire program. It is a good practice to go through it in detail and match up the classes and methods against the CRC cards and UML diagram.

File InvoiceTest.java

```
 1 import java.util.Vector;
 2
 3 /**
 4     This program tests the invoice classes by printing
 5     a sample invoice.
 6 */
 7 public class InvoiceTest
 8 {
 9     public static void main(String[] args)
10     {
11         Address samsAddress = new Address(
12             "Sam's Small Appliances", "100 Main Street",
13             "Anytown", "CA", "98765");
14
15         Invoice samsInvoice = new Invoice(samsAddress);
16         samsInvoice.add(new Product("Toaster", 29.95), 3);
17         samsInvoice.add(
18             new Product("Hair dryer", 24.95), 1);
19         samsInvoice.add(
20             new Product("Car vacuum", 19.99), 2);
21
22         System.out.println(samsInvoice.format());
23     }
24 }
```

File Invoice.java

```
 1 import java.util.ArrayList;
 2
 3 /**
 4     Describes an invoice for a set of purchased products.
 5 */
 6 class Invoice
 7 {
 8     /**
 9         Constructs an invoice.
```

```java
10          @param anAddress the billing address
11       */
12       public Invoice(Address anAddress)
13       {
14          items = new ArrayList();
15          billingAddress = anAddress;
16       }
17
18       /**
19          Adds a charge for a product to this invoice.
20          @param aProduct the product that the customer ordered
21          @param quantity the quantity of the product
22       */
23       public void add(Product aProduct, int quantity)
24       {
25          Item anItem = new Item(aProduct, quantity);
26          items.add(anItem);
27       }
28
29       /**
30          Formats the invoice.
31          @return the formatted invoice
32       */
33       public String format()
34       {
35          String r =
36             "                    I N V O I C E\n\n"
37             + billingAddress.format()
38             + "\n\nDescription                Price  "
39             + "Qty  Total\n";
40          for (int i = 0; i < items.size(); i++)
41          {
42             Item nextItem = (Item)items.get(i);
43             r = r + nextItem.format() + "\n";
44          }
45
46          r = r + "\nAMOUNT DUE: $" + getAmountDue();
47
48          return r;
49       }
50
51       /**
52          Computes the total amount due.
53          @return the amount due
54       */
55       public double getAmountDue()
56       {
57          double amountDue = 0;
58          for (int i = 0; i < items.size(); i++)
59          {
60             Item nextItem = (Item)items.get(i);
61             amountDue = amountDue
```

```
62                        + nextItem.getTotalPrice();
63            }
64            return amountDue;
65        }
66
67        private Address billingAddress;
68        private ArrayList items;
69  }
```

File Item.java

```
1   /**
2       Describes a quantity of an article to purchase and its price.
3   */
4   class Item
5   {
6       /**
7           Constructs an item from the product and quantity.
8           @param aProduct  the product
9           @param aQuantity  the item quantity
10       */
11       public Item(Product aProduct, int aQuantity)
12       {
13           theProduct = aProduct;
14           quantity = aQuantity;
15       }
16
17       /**
18           Computes the total cost of this item.
19           @return  the total price
20       */
21       public double getTotalPrice()
22       {
23           return theProduct.getPrice() * quantity;
24       }
25
26       /**
27           Formats this item.
28           @return  a formatted string of this item
29       */
30       public String format()
31       {
32           final int COLUMN_WIDTH = 30;
33           String description = theProduct.getDescription();
34
35           String r = description;
36
37           // pad with spaces to fill column
38
39           int pad = COLUMN_WIDTH - description.length();
40           for (int i = 1; i <= pad; i++)
```

```
41              r = r + " ";
42
43          r = r + theProduct.getPrice()
44              + "    " + quantity
45              + "    " + getTotalPrice();
46
47          return r;
48      }
49
50      private int quantity;
51      private Product theProduct;
52 }
```

File Product.java

```
1  /**
2      Describes a product with a description and a price.
3  */
4  class Product
5  {
6      /**
7          Constructs a product from a description and a price.
8          @param aDescription  the product description
9          @param aPrice  the product price
10     */
11     public Product(String aDescription, double aPrice)
12     {
13         description = aDescription;
14         price = aPrice;
15     }
16
17     /**
18         Gets the product description.
19         @return  the description
20     */
21     public String getDescription()
22     {
23         return description;
24     }
25
26     /**
27         Gets the product price.
28         @return  the unit price
29     */
30     public double getPrice()
31     {
32         return price;
33     }
34
35     private String description;
36     private double price;
37 }
```

File Address.java

```java
1  /**
2      Describes a mailing address.
3  */
4  class Address
5  {
6     /**
7         Constructs a mailing address.
8         @param aName the recipient name
9         @param aStreet the street
10        @param aCity the city
11        @param aState the 2-letter state code
12        @param aZip the ZIP postal code
13     */
14     public Address(String aName, String aStreet,
15        String aCity, String aState, String aZip)
16     {
17        name = aName;
18        street = aStreet;
19        city = aCity;
20        state = aState;
21        zip = aZip;
22     }
23
24     /**
25        Formats the address.
26        @return the address as a string with 3 lines
27     */
28     public String format()
29     {
30        return name + "\n" + street + "\n"
31           + city + ", " + state + " " + zip;
32     }
33
34     private String name;
35     private String street;
36     private String city;
37     private String state;
38     private String zip;
39  }
```

16.5   Example: An Automatic Teller Machine

16.5.1 Requirements

The purpose of this project is to design a simulation of an automatic teller machine (ATM). The ATM has a keypad to enter numbers, a display to show messages, and a set of buttons, labeled A, B, and C, whose function depends on the state of the machine (see Figure 11).

The ATM is used by the customers of a bank. Each customer has two accounts: a checking account and a savings account. Each customer also has a customer number and a personal identification number (PIN). Both are required to gain access to the accounts. (In a real ATM, the customer number would be recorded on the magnetic strip of the ATM card. In this simulation, the customer will need to type it in.) With the ATM, customers can select an account (checking or savings). The balance of the selected account is displayed. Then the customer can deposit and withdraw money. This process is repeated until the customer chooses to exit.

Specifically, the user interaction is as follows. When the ATM starts up, it expects a user to enter a customer number. The display shows the following message:

```
Enter customer number
A = OK
```

The user enters the customer number on the keypad and presses the A button. The display message changes to

```
Enter PIN
A = OK
```

Next, the user enters the PIN and presses the A button again. If the customer number and ID match those of one of the customers in the bank, then the customer can proceed. If not, the user is again prompted to enter the customer number.

If the customer has been authorized to use the system, then the display message changes to

```
Select Account
A = Checking
B = Savings
C = Exit
```

If the user presses the C button, the ATM reverts to its original state and asks the next user to enter a customer number.

If the user presses the A or B button, the ATM remembers the selected account, and the display message changes to

```
Balance = balance of selected account
Enter amount and select transaction
A = Withdraw
B = Deposit
C = Cancel
```

If the user presses the A or B button, the value entered in the keypad is withdrawn from or deposited into the selected account. (This is just a simulation, so no money is dis-

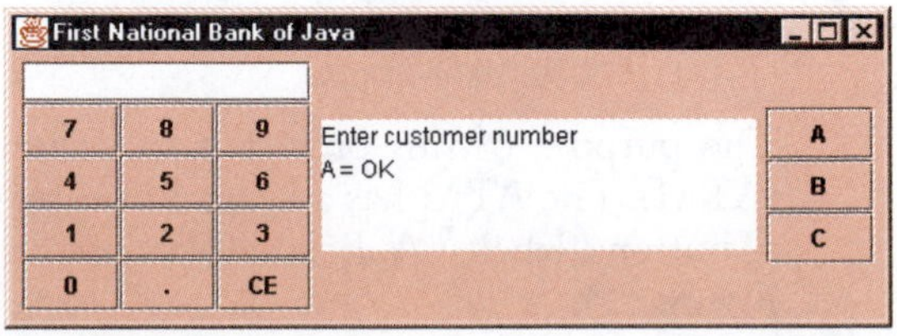

Figure 11

User Interface of the Automatic Teller Machine

pensed and no deposit is accepted.) Afterwards, the ATM reverts to the preceding state, allowing the user to select another account or to exit.

If the user presses the C button, the ATM reverts to the preceding state without executing any transaction.

Since this is a simulation, the ATM does not actually communicate with a bank. It simply loads a set of customer numbers and PINs from a file. All accounts are initialized with a zero balance.

16.5.2 — CRC Cards

We will again follow the recipe of Section 16.2 and show how to discover classes, responsibilities, and relationships and how to obtain a detailed design for the ATM program.

Recall that the first rule for finding classes is "Look for nouns in the problem description". Here is a list of the nouns:

```
ATM
User
Keypad
Display
Display message
Button
State
Bank account
Checking account
Savings account
Customer
Customer number
PIN
Bank
```

Of course, not all of these nouns will become names of classes, and we may yet discover the need for classes that aren't in this list, but it is a good start.

Let's start simply with a noncontroversial choice. A `Keypad` sounds like an excellent idea for a class. A keypad is a component with buttons and a text field that lets the user type in a value. What can we do with a keypad? There is one essential method: get the value the user entered. (Of course, the keypad will end up using one or more internal methods to track the button clicks, but we are not concerned with such an implementation detail now.) Here is the CRC card for the `Keypad` class:

Keypad	
get value	

On the other hand, there is already a good class for the display, namely `JTextArea`. Thus we won't need to create a separate `Display` class. Similarly, there is no need for a class to encapsulate display messages—we will just use strings. Also, we will use the existing `JButton` class for buttons.

Users and customers represent the same concept in this program. Let's use a class `Customer`. A customer has two bank accounts, and a customer object must be able to tell us the accounts. A customer also has a customer number and a PIN. We can, of course, require that a customer object give us the customer number and the PIN. But perhaps that isn't so secure. Instead, let us simply require that a customer object, when given a customer number and a PIN, will tell us whether it matches its own information or not.

Customer
get accounts
match number and PIN

A bank contains a collection of customers. When a user walks up to the ATM and enters a customer number and PIN, it is the job of the bank to find the matching customer. How can the bank do this? It needs to check for each customer whether its customer number and PIN match. Thus, it needs to call the `match number and PIN` method of the `Customer` class that we just discovered. Because the `find customer` method calls a `Customer` method, it collaborates with the `Customer` class. We record that fact in the right-hand column of the CRC card.

Bank	
find customer	Customer
read customers	

When the simulation starts up, the bank must also be able to read a collection of customers and PINs.

The `BankAccount` class is our familiar class, with methods to get the balance and to deposit and withdraw money:

In this program there is nothing that distinguishes checking accounts from savings accounts. The ATM does not add interest or deduct fees. Therefore, we decide not to implement separate subclasses for checking and savings accounts.

Finally, we are left with the ATM class itself. An important notion of the ATM is the state. Whenever the state changes, the display needs to be updated, and the meaning of the buttons changes. There are four states:

1. START: Enter customer ID
2. PIN: Enter PIN
3. ACCOUNT: Select account
4. TRANSACT: Select transaction

To understand how to move from one state to the next, it is useful to draw a *state diagram* (Figure 12). The UML notation has standardized shapes for state diagrams. Draw states

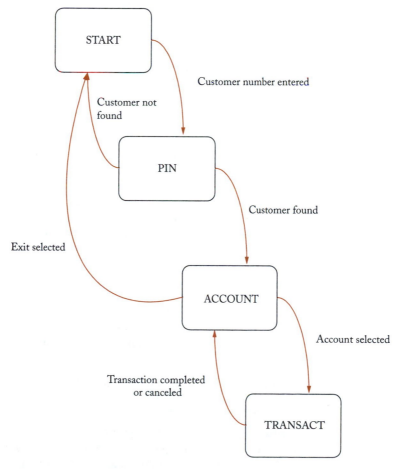

Figure 12

State Diagram for the ATM Class

as rectangles with rounded corners. Draw state changes as arrows, with labels that indicate the reason for the change.

We will implement a `setState` method that sets the system to a new state and updates the display.

The user must type a valid customer number and PIN. Then the ATM can ask the bank to find the customer. This calls for a `select customer` method. It collaborates with the bank, asking the bank for the customer that matches the customer number and PIN. Next, there must be a `select account` method that asks the current customer for the checking or savings account. Finally, the deposit and withdraw methods carry out the selected transaction on the current account.

ATM	
set state	Customer
select customer	Bank
select account	BankAccount
execute transaction	Keypad

Of course, discovering these classes and methods was not as neat and orderly as it appears from this discussion. When I designed these classes for this book, it took me several trials and tearing up of cards to come up with a satisfactory design. It is also important to remember that there is seldom one best design.

This design has several advantages. The classes describe clear concepts. The methods are sufficient to implement all necessary tasks. (I mentally walked through every ATM usage scenario to verify that.) There are not too many collaboration dependencies between the classes. Thus, I was satisfied with this design and proceeded to the next step.

16.5.3 — UML Diagram

Figure 13 shows the relationship between these classes. There are two examples of inheritance. The keypad is a panel. The ATM is a frame.

To draw the dependencies, use the "collaborator" columns from the CRC cards. Looking at those columns, you find that the dependencies are as follows:

- ATM uses `KeyPad`, `Bank`, `Customer`, and `BankAccount`.

- Bank uses `Customer`.

It is easy to see the association relationships. Given a bank, we can navigate to its customers. Given a customer, we can navigate to its bank accounts. The ATM can navigate to the keypad, the bank, the current customer, and the current bank account.

In this case, it turns out that all of the collaboration relationships are associations, so there are no additional dependency relationships to draw.

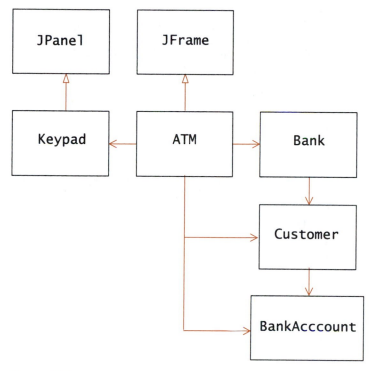

Figure 13

Relationships between the ATM Classes

The class diagram is a good tool to visualize dependencies. Look at the `Keypad` class. It is completely independent from the rest of the ATM system—you could take out the `Keypad` class and use it in another application. Also, the `Bank`, `BankAccount`, and `Customer` classes, although dependent on each other, don't know anything about the ATM class. That makes sense—you can have banks without ATMs. As you can see, when you analyze relationships, you look for the absence of relationships just as much as for their presence.

16.5.4 — Method Documentation

Now you are ready for the final step of the design phase: to document the classes and methods that you discovered. Here is the documentation for the ATM class:

```
public class ATM
{
    /**
        Gets PIN from keypad, finds customer in bank.
        If found sets state to ACCOUNT, else to START
    */
    public void selectCustomer()
    {
    }
```

```
/**
    Sets current account to checking or savings.
    Sets state to TRANSACT.
    @param account one of CHECKING_ACCOUNT
        or SAVINGS_ACCOUNT
*/
public void selectAccount(int account)
{
}


/**
    Withdraws amount typed in keypad from current account.
    Sets state to ACCOUNT
*/
public void withdraw()
{
}

/**
    Deposits amount typed in keypad to current account.
    Sets state to ACCOUNT
*/
public void deposit()
{
}

/**
    Sets state and updates display message.
    @param state the next state
*/
public void setState(int newState)
{
}
}
```

Then run the `javadoc` utility to turn this documentation into HTML format.

For conciseness, we omit the documentation of the other classes.

16.5.5— Implementation

Finally, the time has come to implement the ATM simulator. You will find that the implementation phase is very straightforward and should take *much less time than the design phase.*

A good strategy for implementing the classes is to go "bottom-up". Start with the classes that don't depend on others, such as `Keypad` and `BankAccount`. Then implement a class such as `Customer` that depends only on the `BankAccount` class. This "bottom-up" approach allows you to test your classes individually. You will find the implementations of these classes at the end of this section.

The most complex class is the `ATM` class. In order to implement the methods, you need to define the necessary instance variables. From the class diagram, you can tell that the ATM has a keypad and a bank object. They become instance variables of the class:

```
class ATM
{  . . .
   private Bank theBank;
   private Keypad pad;
   . . .
}
```

From the description of the ATM states, it is clear that we require additional instance variables to store the current state, customer, and bank account.

```
class ATM
{  . . .
   private int state;
   private Customer currentCustomer;
   private BankAccount currentAccount;

}
```

Most methods are very straightforward to implement. Consider the `withdraw` method. From the design documentation, we have the description

```
/**
    Withdraws amount typed in keypad from current account.
    Sets state to ACCOUNT
*/
```

This description can be almost literally translated to Java instructions:

```
public void withdraw()
{
   currentAccount.withdraw(pad.getValue());
   setState(ACCOUNT_STATE);
}
```

Much of the remaining complexity in the ATM program results from the user interface. The ATM constructor has many statements to lay out components, and there are three button handlers that laboriously call the various ATM methods, depending on the state. This code is lengthy but straightforward.

We won't go through a method-by-method description of the ATM program. You should take some time and compare the actual implementation against the CRC cards and the UML diagram.

File ATMSimulation.java

```
 1 import javax.swing.JFrame;
 2
 3 /**
 4     A simulation of an automatic teller machine.
 5 */
 6 public class ATMSimulation
 7 {
 8    public static void main(String[] args)
 9    {
10       JFrame frame = new ATM();
```

```
11        frame.setTitle("First National Bank of Java");
12        frame.setDefaultCloseOperation(
13           JFrame.EXIT_ON_CLOSE);
14        frame.pack();
15        frame.show();
16     }
17  }
```

File ATM.java

```
1  import java.awt.Container;
2  import java.awt.FlowLayout;
3  import java.awt.GridLayout;
4  import java.awt.event.ActionEvent;
5  import java.awt.event.ActionListener;
6  import java.awt.event.WindowEvent;
7  import java.awt.event.WindowAdapter;
8  import java.io.IOException;
9  import javax.swing.JButton;
10 import javax.swing.JFrame;
11 import javax.swing.JOptionPane;
12 import javax.swing.JPanel;
13 import javax.swing.JTextArea;
14
15 /**
16     A frame displaying the components of an ATM.
17 */
18 class ATM extends JFrame
19 {
20     /**
21         Constructs the user interface of the ATM application.
22     */
23     public ATM()
24     {
25        // initialize bank and customers
26
27        theBank = new Bank();
28        try
29        {
30           theBank.readCustomers("customers.txt");
31        }
32        catch(IOException e)
33        {
34           JOptionPane.showMessageDialog(null,
35              "Error opening accounts file.");
36        }
37
38        // construct components
39
40        pad = new KeyPad();
```

```
41
42          display = new JTextArea(4, 20);
43
44          aButton = new JButton("  A  ");
45          aButton.addActionListener(new AButtonListener());
46
47          bButton = new JButton("  B  ");
48          bButton.addActionListener(new BButtonListener());
49
50          cButton = new JButton("  C  ");
51          cButton.addActionListener(new CButtonListener());
52
53          // add components to content pane
54
55          JPanel buttonPanel = new JPanel();
56          buttonPanel.setLayout(new GridLayout(3, 1));
57          buttonPanel.add(aButton);
58          buttonPanel.add(bButton);
59          buttonPanel.add(cButton);
60
61          Container contentPane = getContentPane();
62          contentPane.setLayout(new FlowLayout());
63          contentPane.add(pad);
64          contentPane.add(display);
65          contentPane.add(buttonPanel);
66
67          setState(START_STATE);
68       }
69
70       /**
71          Sets the current customer number to the keypad value
72          and sets state to PIN.
73       */
74       public void setCustomerNumber()
75       {
76          customerNumber = (int)pad.getValue();
77          setState(PIN_STATE);
78       }
79
80       /**
81          Gets PIN from keypad, finds customer in bank.
82          If found, sets state to ACCOUNT, else to START.
83       */
84       public void selectCustomer()
85       {
86          int pin = (int)pad.getValue();
87          currentCustomer = theBank.findCustomer(
88             customerNumber, pin);
89          if (currentCustomer == null)
90             setState(START_STATE);
```

```
91        else
92           setState(ACCOUNT_STATE);
93     }
94
95     /**
96        Sets current account to checking or savings. Sets
97        state to TRANSACT.
98        @param account one of CHECKING_ACCOUNT
99           or SAVINGS_ACCOUNT
100    */
101    public void selectAccount(int account)
102    {
103       if (account == CHECKING_ACCOUNT)
104          currentAccount =
105             currentCustomer.getCheckingAccount();
106       else
107          currentAccount =
108             currentCustomer.getSavingsAccount();
109       setState(TRANSACT_STATE);
110    }
111
112    /**
113       Withdraws amount typed in keypad from current account.
114       Sets state to ACCOUNT.
115    */
116    public void withdraw()
117    {
118       currentAccount.withdraw(pad.getValue());
119       setState(ACCOUNT_STATE);
120    }
121
122    /**
123       Deposits amount typed in keypad to current account.
124       Sets state to ACCOUNT.
125    */
126    public void deposit()
127    {
128       currentAccount.deposit(pad.getValue());
129       setState(ACCOUNT_STATE);
130    }
131
132    /**
133       Sets state and updates display message.
134       @param state the next state
135    */
136    public void setState(int newState)
137    {
138       state = newState;
139       pad.clear();
140       if (state == START_STATE)
```

```
141              display.setText(
142                 "Enter customer number\nA = OK");
143        else if (state == PIN_STATE)
144           display.setText("Enter PIN\nA = OK");
145        else if (state == ACCOUNT_STATE)
146           display.setText("Select Account\n"
147              + "A = Checking\nB = Savings\nC = Exit");
148        else if (state == TRANSACT_STATE)
149           display.setText("Balance = "
150              + currentAccount.getBalance()
151              + "\nEnter amount and select transaction\n"
152              + "A = Withdraw\nB = Deposit\nC = Cancel");
153     }
154
155     private class AButtonListener
156        implements ActionListener
157     {
158        public void actionPerformed(ActionEvent event)
159        {
160           if (state == START_STATE)
161              setCustomerNumber();
162           else if (state == PIN_STATE)
163              selectCustomer();
164           else if (state == ACCOUNT_STATE)
165              selectAccount(CHECKING_ACCOUNT);
166           else if (state == TRANSACT_STATE)
167              withdraw();
168        }
169     }
170
171     private class BButtonListener
172        implements ActionListener
173     {
174        public void actionPerformed(ActionEvent event)
175        {
176           if (state == ACCOUNT_STATE)
177              selectAccount(SAVINGS_ACCOUNT);
178           else if (state == TRANSACT_STATE)
179              deposit();
180        }
181     }
182
183     private class CButtonListener
184        implements ActionListener
185     {
186        public void actionPerformed(ActionEvent event)
187        {
188           if (state == ACCOUNT_STATE)
189              setState(START_STATE);
190           else if (state == TRANSACT_STATE)
```

```
191                    setState(ACCOUNT_STATE);
192         }
193      }
194
195    private int state;
196    private int customerNumber;
197    private Customer currentCustomer;
198    private BankAccount currentAccount;
199    private Bank theBank;
200
201    private JButton aButton;
202    private JButton bButton;
203    private JButton cButton;
204
205    private KeyPad pad;
206    private JTextArea display;
207
208    private static final int START_STATE = 1;
209    private static final int PIN_STATE = 2;
210    private static final int ACCOUNT_STATE = 3;
211    private static final int TRANSACT_STATE = 4;
212
213    private static final int CHECKING_ACCOUNT = 1;
214    private static final int SAVINGS_ACCOUNT = 2;
215 }
```

File KeyPad.java

```
 1 import java.awt.BorderLayout;
 2 import java.awt.GridLayout;
 3 import java.awt.event.ActionEvent;
 4 import java.awt.event.ActionListener;
 5 import javax.swing.JButton;
 6 import javax.swing.JPanel;
 7 import javax.swing.JTextField;
 8
 9 /**
10     A component that lets the user enter a number, using
11     a button pad labeled with digits.
12 */
13 public class KeyPad extends JPanel
14 {
15    /**
16        Constructs the keypad panel.
17    */
18    public KeyPad()
19    {
20       setLayout(new BorderLayout());
21
22       // add display field
23
```

```
24          display = new JTextField();
25          add(display, "North");
26
27          // make button panel
28
29          buttonPanel = new JPanel();
30          buttonPanel.setLayout(new GridLayout(4, 3));
31
32          // add digit buttons
33
34          addButton("7");
35          addButton("8");
36          addButton("9");
37          addButton("4");
38          addButton("5");
39          addButton("6");
40          addButton("1");
41          addButton("2");
42          addButton("3");
43          addButton("0");
44          addButton(".");
45
46          // add clear entry button
47
48          clearButton = new JButton("CE");
49          buttonPanel.add(clearButton);
50
51          class ClearButtonListener implements ActionListener
52          {
53             public void actionPerformed(ActionEvent event)
54             {
55                display.setText("");
56             }
57          }
58          ActionListener listener =
59             new ClearButtonListener();
60
61          clearButton.addActionListener(new
62             ClearButtonListener());
63
64          add(buttonPanel, "Center");
65       }
66
67       /**
68          Adds a button to the button panel.
69          @param label  the button label
70       */
71       private void addButton(final String label)
72       {
73          class DigitButtonListener implements ActionListener
```

```
74        {
75            public void actionPerformed(ActionEvent event)
76            {
77
78                // don't add two decimal points
79                if (label.equals(".")
80                    && display.getText().indexOf(".") != -1)
81                    return;
82
83                // append label text to button
84                display.setText(display.getText() + label);
85            }
86        }
87
88        JButton button = new JButton(label);
89        buttonPanel.add(button);
90        ActionListener listener =
91            new DigitButtonListener();
92        button.addActionListener(listener);
93    }
94
95    /**
96        Gets the value that the user entered.
97        @return the value in the text field of the keypad
98    */
99    public double getValue()
100    {
101        return Double.parseDouble(display.getText());
102    }
103
104    /**
105        Clears the display.
106    */
107    public void clear()
108    {
109        display.setText("");
110    }
111
112    private JPanel buttonPanel;
113    private JButton clearButton;
114    private JTextField display;
115 }
```

File Bank.java

```
1 import java.io.BufferedReader;
2 import java.io.FileReader;
3 import java.io.IOException;
4 import java.util.ArrayList;
5 import java.util.StringTokenizer;
6
```

```
 7  /**
 8      A bank contains customers with bank accounts.
 9  */
10  public class Bank
11  {
12      /**
13          Constructs a bank with no customers.
14      */
15      public Bank()
16      {
17          customers = new ArrayList();
18      }
19
20      /**
21          Reads the customer numbers and PINs
22          and initializes the bank accounts.
23          @param filename the name of the customer file
24      */
25      public void readCustomers(String filename)
26          throws IOException
27      {
28          BufferedReader in = new BufferedReader
29              (new FileReader(filename));
30          boolean done = false;
31          while (!done)
32          {
33              String inputLine = in.readLine();
34              if (inputLine == null) done = true;
35              else
36              {
37                  StringTokenizer tokenizer
38                      = new StringTokenizer(inputLine);
39                  int number
40                      = Integer.parseInt(tokenizer.nextToken());
41                  int pin
42                      = Integer.parseInt(tokenizer.nextToken());
43
44                  Customer c = new Customer(number, pin);
45                  addCustomer(c);
46              }
47          }
48          in.close();
49      }
50
51      /**
52          Adds a customer to the bank.
53          @param c the customer to add
54      */
55      public void addCustomer(Customer c)
56      {
```

```
57        customers.add(c);
58     }
59
60     /**
61        Finds a customer in the bank.
62        @param aNumber a customer number
63        @param aPin a personal identification number
64        @return the matching customer, or null if no customer
65        matches
66     */
67     public Customer findCustomer(int aNumber, int aPin)
68     {
69        for (int i = 0; i < customers.size(); i++)
70        {
71           Customer c = (Customer)customers.get(i);
72           if (c.match(aNumber, aPin))
73              return c;
74        }
75        return null;
76     }
77
78     private ArrayList customers;
79  }
```

File Customer.java

```
1  /**
2     A bank customer with a checking and savings account.
3  */
4  public class Customer
5  {
6     /**
7        Constructs a customer with a given number and PIN.
8        @param aNumber the customer number
9        @param aPin the personal identification number
10    */
11    public Customer(int aNumber, int aPin)
12    {
13       customerNumber = aNumber;
14       pin = aPin;
15       checkingAccount = new BankAccount();
16       savingsAccount = new BankAccount();
17    }
18
19    /**
20       Tests whether this customer matches a customer number
21       and PIN.
22       @param aNumber a customer number
23       @param aPin a personal identification number
24       @return true if the customer number and PIN match
```

```
25      */
26      public boolean match(int aNumber, int aPin)
27      {
28          return customerNumber == aNumber && pin == aPin;
29      }
30
31      /**
32          Gets the checking account of this customer.
33          @return  the checking account
34      */
35      public BankAccount getCheckingAccount()
36      {
37          return checkingAccount;
38      }
39
40      /**
41          Gets the savings account of this customer.
42          @return  the checking account
43      */
44      public BankAccount getSavingsAccount()
45      {
46          return savingsAccount;
47      }
48
49      private int customerNumber;
50      private int pin;
51      private BankAccount checkingAccount;
52      private BankAccount savingsAccount;
53  }
```

In this chapter, you learned a *systematic* approach for building a relatively complex program. However, object-oriented design is definitely not a spectator sport. To really learn how to design and implement programs, you have to gain experience by repeating this process with your own projects. It is quite possible that you don't immediately home in on a good solution and that you need to go back and reorganize your classes and responsibilities. That is normal and only to be expected. The purpose of the object-oriented design process is to spot these problems in the design phase, when they are still easy to rectify, instead of in the implementation phase, when massive reorganization is more difficult and time-consuming.

▼ **Random Fact**   16.2

▼

▼ **Computing—Art or Science?**

There has been a long discussion whether the discipline of computing is a science or not. We call the field "computer science", but that doesn't mean much. Except possibly for librarians and sociologists, few people believe that library science and social science are scientific endeavors.

A scientific discipline aims to discover certain fundamental principles dictated by the laws of nature. It operates on the *scientific method:* by posing hypotheses and testing them with experiments that are repeatable by other workers in the field. For example, a physicist may have a theory on the makeup of nuclear particles and attempt to confirm or refute that theory by running experiments in a particle collider. If an experiment cannot be confirmed, such as the "cold fusion" research in the early 1990s, then the theory dies a quick death.

Some programmers indeed run experiments. They try out various methods of computing certain results or of configuring computer systems, and measure the differences in performance. However, their aim is not to discover laws of nature.

Some computer scientists discover fundamental principles. One class of fundamental results, for instance, states that it is impossible to write certain kinds of computer programs, no matter how powerful the computing equipment is. For example, it is impossible to write a program that takes as its input any two Java program files and as its output prints whether or not these two programs always compute the same results. Such a program would be very handy for grading student homework, but nobody, no matter how clever, will ever be able to write one that works for all input files. However, the majority of computer scientists are not researching the limits of computation.

Some people view programming as an *art* or *craft*. A programmer who writes elegant code that is easy to understand and runs with optimum efficiency can indeed be considered a good craftsman. Calling it an art is perhaps far-fetched, because an art object requires an audience to appreciate it, whereas the program code is generally hidden from the program user.

Others call computing an *engineering discipline*. Just as mechanical engineering is based on the fundamental mathematical principles of statics, computing has certain mathematical foundations. There is more to mechanical engineering than mathematics, though, such as knowledge of materials and of project planning. The same is true for computing.

In one somewhat worrisome aspect, computing does not have the same standing as other engineering disciplines. There is little agreement as to what constitutes professional conduct in the computer field. Unlike the scientist, whose main responsibility is the search for truth, the engineer must strive to satisfy the conflicting demands of quality, safety, and economy. Engineering disciplines have professional organizations that hold their members to standards of conduct. The computer field is so new that in many cases we simply don't know the correct method for achieving certain tasks. That makes it difficult to set professional standards.

What do you think? From your limited experience, do you consider the discipline of computing an art, a craft, a science, or an engineering activity?

Chapter Summary

1. The life cycle of software encompasses all activities from initial analysis until obsolescence.

2. A formal process for software development describes phases of the development process and gives guidelines for how to carry out the phases.

3. The waterfall model of software development describes a sequential process of analysis, design, implementation, testing, and deployment.

4. The spiral model of software development describes an iterative process in which design and implementation are repeated.

5. Extreme Programming is a development methodology that strives for simplicity by removing formal structure and focusing on best practices.

6. In object-oriented design, you discover classes, determine the responsibilities of classes, and describe the relationships between classes.

7. A CRC card describes a class, its responsibilities, and its collaborating classes.

8. Inheritance (the "is-a" relationship) is sometimes inappropriately used when the "has-a" relationship would be more appropriate.

9. A class is associated with another class if you can navigate from its objects to objects of the other class, usually by following object references.

10. Dependency is another name for the "uses" relationship.

11. You need to be able to distinguish the UML notations for inheritance, realization, association, and dependency.

12. You can use `javadoc` documentation comments (with the bodies of the methods left blank) to record formally the behavior of the classes that you discovered.

Further Reading

[1] Grady Booch, James Rumbaugh, and Ivar Jacobson, *The Unified Modeling Language User Guide*, Addison-Wesley, 1999.
[2] Kent Beck, *Extreme Programming Explained*, Addison-Wesley, 1999.
[3] F. Brooks, *The Mythical Man-Month*, Addison-Wesley, 1975.
[4] W. H. Sackmann, W. J. Erikson, and E. E. Grant, "Exploratory Experimental Studies Comparing Online and Offline Programming Performance", *Communications of the ACM, vol. 11, no. 1* (January 1968), pp. 3–11.

REVIEW EXERCISES

Exercise R16.1. What is the software life cycle?

Exercise R16.2. Explain the process of object-oriented design that this chapter recommends for student use.

Exercise R16.3. Give a rule of thumb for how to find classes when designing a program.

Exercise R16.4. Give a rule of thumb for how to find methods when designing a program.

Exercise R16.5. After discovering a method, why is it important to identify the object that is *responsible* for carrying out the action?

Exercise R16.6. What relationship is appropriate between the following classes: aggregation, inheritance, or neither?

- University–Student
- Student–TeachingAssistant
- Student–Freshman
- Student–Professor
- Car–Door
- Truck–Vehicle
- Traffic–TrafficSign
- TrafficSign–Color

Exercise R16.7. Every BMW is a car. Should a class BMW inherit from the class Car? BMW is a car manufacturer. Does that mean that the class BMW should inherit from the class CarManufacturer?

Exercise R16.8. Some books on object-oriented programming recommend deriving the class Circle from the class Point. Then the Circle class inherits the setLocation method from the Point superclass. Explain why the setLocation method need not be redefined in the subclass. Why is it nevertheless not a good idea to have Circle inherit from Point? Conversely, would deriving Point from Circle fulfill the "is-a" rule? Would it be a good idea?

Exercise R16.9. Write CRC cards for the Coin and Purse classes of Chapter 3.

Exercise R16.10. Write CRC cards for the bank account classes in Chapter 9.

Exercise R16.11. Draw a UML diagram for the Coin and Purse classes of Chapters 3 and 13.

Exercise R16.12. Draw a UML diagram for the classes in the ChoiceTest program in Chapter 12. Use associations when appropriate.

Exercise R16.13. A file contains a set of records describing countries. Each record consists of the name of the country, its population, and its area. Suppose your task is to write a program that reads in such a file and prints

- The country with the largest area
- The country with the largest population
- The country with the largest population density (people per square kilometer)

Think through the problems that you need to solve. What classes and methods will you need? Produce a set of CRC cards, a UML diagram, and a set of javadoc comments.

Exercise R16.14. Discover classes and methods for generating a student report card that lists all classes, grades, and the grade point average for a semester. Produce a set of CRC cards, a UML diagram, and a set of javadoc comments.

Programming Exercises

Exercise P16.1. Enhance the invoice-printing program by providing for two kinds of line items: One kind describes products that are purchased in certain numerical quantities (such as "3 toasters"), another describes a fixed charge (such as "shipping: $5.00"). *Hint:* Use inheritance. Produce a UML diagram of your modified implementation.

Exercise P16.2. The invoice-printing program is somewhat unrealistic because the formatting of the `Item` objects won't lead to good visual results when the prices and quantities have varying numbers of digits. Enhance the `format` method in two ways: Accept an `int[]` array of column widths as a parameter. Use the `Number-Format` class to format the currency values.

Exercise P16.3. The invoice-printing program has an unfortunate flaw—it mixes "business logic", the computation of total charges, and "presentation", the visual appearance of the invoice. To appreciate this flaw, imagine the changes that would be necessary to draw the invoice in HTML for presentation on the web. Reimplement the program, using a separate `InvoiceFormatter` class to format the invoice. That is, the `Invoice` and `Item` methods are no longer responsible for formatting. However, they will acquire other responsibilities, because the `InvoiceFormatter` class needs to query them for the values that it requires.

Exercise P16.4. Implement a program to teach your baby sister to *read the clock*. In the game, present an analog clock such as the one in Figure 14. Generate random times and display the clock. Accept guesses from the player. Reward the player for correct guesses. After two incorrect guesses, display the correct answer and make a new random time. Implement several levels of play. In level 1, only show full hours. In level 2, show quarter hours. In level 3, show five-minute multiples, and in level 4, show any number of minutes. After a player has achieved five correct guesses at one level, advance to the next level.

Exercise P16.5. Write a program that implements a different game, to teach arithmetic to your younger brother. The program tests addition and subtraction. In level 1 it tests only addition of numbers less than 10 whose sum is less than 10. In level 2 it tests addition of arbitrary one-digit numbers. In level 3 it tests subtraction of one-digit numbers with a nonnegative difference. Generate random problems and get the player input. The player gets up to two tries per problem. Advance from one level to the next when the player has achieved a score of five points. Your user interface can be text-based or graphical.

Figure 14

An Analog Clock

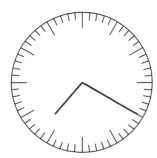

Exercise P16.6. Write a bumper car game with the following rules. Bumper cars are located in grid points (x, y), where x and y are integers between -10 and 10. A bumper car starts moving in a random direction, either left, right, up, or down. If it reaches a boundary (that is, x or y is 10 or -10), then it reverses direction. If it is about to bump into another bumper car, it reverses direction. Supply a user interface to add bumper cars, and to run the simulation. Use at least four classes in your program.

Exercise P16.7. Write a program that can be used to design a suburban scene, with houses, streets, and cars. Users can add houses and cars of various colors to a street. Design a user interface that firms up the requirements, discover classes and methods, provide UML diagrams, and implement your program.

Exercise P16.8. Design a simple email messaging system. A message has a recipient, a sender, and a message text. A mailbox can store messages. Supply a number of mailboxes for different users and a user interface for users to log in, send messages to other users, read their own messages, and log out. Your user interface can be text-based or graphical. Follow the design process that was described in this chapter.

Exercise P16.9. Write a program that simulates a vending machine. Products can be purchased by inserting the correct number of coins into the machine. A user selects a product from a list of available products, adds coins, and either gets the product or gets the coins returned if insufficient money was supplied or if the product is sold out. Products can be restocked and money removed by an operator. Follow the design process that was described in this chapter.

Exercise P16.10. Write a program to design an appointment calendar. An appointment includes the starting time, ending time, and a description; for example,

```
Dentist 2001/10/1 17:30 18:30
CS1 class 2001/10/2 08:30 10:00
```

Supply a user interface to add appointments, remove canceled appointments, and print out a list of appointments for a particular day. Your user interface can be text-based or graphical. Follow the design process that was described in this chapter.

Exercise P16.11. *Airline seating.* Write a program that assigns seats on an airplane. Assume the airplane has 20 seats in first class (5 rows of 4 seats each, separated by an aisle) and 180 seats in economy class (30 rows of 6 seats each, separated by an aisle). Your program should take three commands: add passengers, show seating, and quit. When passengers are added, ask for the class (first or economy), the number of passengers traveling together (1 or 2 in first class; 1 to 3 in economy), and the seating preference (aisle or window in first class; aisle, center, or window in economy). Then try to find a match and assign the seats. If no match exists, print a message. Your user interface can be text-based or graphical. Follow the design process that was described in this chapter.

Exercise P16.12. Write a simple graphics editor that allows users to add a mixture of shapes (ellipses, rectangles, lines, and text in different colors) to a panel. Supply commands to load and save the picture. For simplicity, you may use a single text size, and you don't have to fill any shapes. Design a user interface, discover classes, supply a UML diagram, and implement your program.

Exercise P16.13. Write a tic-tac-toe game that lets a human player play against the computer. Your program will play many turns against a human opponent, and it will learn. When it is the computer's turn, the computer randomly selects an empty field, except that it won't ever choose a losing combination. For that purpose, your program must keep an array of losing combinations. Whenever the human wins, the immediately preceding combination is stored as losing. For example, suppose that x = computer and o = human. Suppose the current combination is

```
 O | X | X
---+---+---
   | O |
---+---+---
   |   |
```

Now it is the human's turn, who will of course choose

```
 O | X | X
---+---+---
   | O |
---+---+---
   |   | O
```

The computer should then remember the preceding combination

```
 O | X | X
---+---+---
   | O |
---+---+---
   |   |
```

as a losing combination. As a result, the computer will never again choose that combination from

```
 O | X |
---+---+---
   | O |
---+---+---
   |   |
```

or

```
 O |   | X
---+---+---
   | O |
---+---+---
   |   |
```

Discover classes and supply a UML diagram before you begin to program. *Hint:* Make a class `Combination` that contains an `int[][]` array. Each element in that two-dimensional array is `EMPTY`, `FILLED_X`, or `FILLED_O`. Write an `equals` method that tests whether two combinations are identical.

Recursion

The method of recursion is a powerful technique to break up complex computational problems into simpler ones. The term "recursion" refers to the fact that the same computation recurs, or occurs repeatedly, as the problem is solved. Recursion is often the most natural way of thinking about a problem, and there are some computations that are very difficult to perform without recursion. This chapter shows you both simple and complex examples of recursion and teaches you how to "think recursively".

17.1 Triangle Numbers

In this example, we will look at triangle shapes such as the ones from Section 6.3. We'd like to compute the area of a triangle of width n, assuming that each [] square has area 1. This value is sometimes called the nth *triangle number*. For example, as you can tell from looking at

```
[]
[][]
[][][]
```

the third triangle number is 6.

You may know that there is a very simple formula to compute these numbers, but you should pretend for now that you don't know about it. The ultimate purpose of this section is not to compute triangle numbers, but to learn about the concept of recursion in a simple situation.

Here is the outline of the class that we will develop:

```java
public class Triangle
{
    public Triangle(int aWidth)
    {
        width = aWidth;
    }

    public int getArea()
    {
        . . .
    }

    private int width;
}
```

If the width of the triangle is 1, then the triangle consists of a single square, and its area is 1. Let's take care of this case first.

```java
public int getArea()
{
    if (width == 1) return 1;
    . . .
}
```

To deal with the general case, consider this picture.

```
[]
[][]
[][][]
[][][][]
```

Suppose we knew the area of the smaller, colored triangle. Then we could easily compute the area of the larger triangle as

```
smallerArea + width
```

How can we get the smaller area? Let's just make a smaller triangle and ask it!

```
Triangle smallerTriangle = new Triangle(width - 1);
int smallerArea = smallerTriangle.getArea();
```

Now we can complete the `getArea` method:

```
public int getArea()
{
    if (width == 1) return 1;
    Triangle smallerTriangle = new Triangle(width - 1);
    int smallerArea = smallerTriangle.getArea();
    return smallerArea + width;
}
```

> A recursive computation solves a problem by using the solution of the same problem with simpler inputs.

Here is an illustration of what happens when we compute the area of a triangle of width 4.

- The `getArea` method makes a smaller triangle of width 3.
    - It calls `getArea` on that triangle.
        - That method makes a smaller triangle of width 2.
            - It calls `getArea` on that triangle.
                - That method makes a smaller triangle of width 1.
                - It calls `getArea` on that triangle.
                    - That method returns 1.
                - The method returns `smallerArea + width` = 1 + 2 = 3.
            - The method returns `smallerArea + width` = 3 + 3 = 6.
    - The method returns `smallerArea + width` = 6 + 4 = 10.

This solution has one remarkable aspect. To solve the area problem for a triangle of a given width, we use the fact that we can solve the same problem for a lesser width. This is called a *recursive* solution.

The call pattern of a recursive method looks complicated, and the key to the successful design of a recursive method is *not to think about it*. Instead, look at the `area` method one more time and notice how utterly reasonable it is. If the width is 1, then of course the area is 1. The next part is just as reasonable. Compute the area of the smaller triangle *and don't think about why that works*. Then the area of the larger triangle is clearly the sum of the smaller area and the width.

There are two key requirements to make sure that the recursion is successful:

- Every recursive call must simplify the computation in some way.

- There must be special cases to handle the simplest computations directly.

The `getArea` method calls itself again with smaller and smaller width values. Eventually the width must reach 1, and there is a special case for computing the area of a triangle with width 1. Thus, the `getArea` method always succeeds.

> For a recursion to terminate, there must be special cases for the simplest inputs.

Actually, you have to be careful. What happens when you call the area of a triangle with width −1? It computes the area of a triangle with width −2, which computes the area of a triangle with width −3, and so on. To avoid this, the `getArea` method should return 0 if the width is <= 0.

Recursion is not really necessary to compute the triangle numbers. The area of a triangle equals the sum

```
1 + 2 + 3 + . . . + width
```

Of course, we can program a simple loop:

```
double area = 0;
for (int i = 1; i <= width; i++)
   area = area + i;
```

Many simple recursions can be computed as loops. However, loop equivalents for more complex recursions—such as the one in our next example—can be complex.

Actually, in this case, you don't even need a loop to compute the answer. The sum of the first *n* integers can be computed as

$$1 + 2 + \cdots + n = n \times (n + 1) / 2$$

Thus, the area equals

```
width * (width + 1) / 2
```

Therefore, neither recursion nor a loop are required to solve this problem. The recursive solution is intended as a "warm-up" for the next section.

File Triangle.java

```
 1  /**
 2      A triangular shape composed of stacked unit squares like this:
 3      []
 4      [][]
 5      [][][]
 6      . . .
 7  */
 8  public class Triangle
 9  {
```

```
10    /**
11        Constructs a triangular shape.
12        @param aWidth the width (and height) of the triangle
13    */
14    public Triangle(int aWidth)
15    {
16        width = aWidth;
17    }
18
19    /**
20        Computes the area of the triangle.
21        @return the area
22    */
23    public int getArea()
24    {
25        if (width <= 0) return 0;
26        if (width == 1) return 1;
27        Triangle smallerTriangle = new Triangle(width - 1);
28        int smallerArea = smallerTriangle.getArea();
29        return smallerArea + width;
30    }
31
32    private int width;
33 }
```

File TriangleTest.java

```
1  import javax.swing.JOptionPane;
2
3  public class TriangleTest
4  {
5      public static void main(String[] args)
6      {
7          String input =
8              JOptionPane.showInputDialog("Enter width");
9          int width = Integer.parseInt(input);
10         Triangle t = new Triangle(width);
11         int area = t.getArea();
12         System.out.println("Area = " + area);
13     }
14 }
```

⊗ Common Error   17.1

Infinite Recursion

A common programming error is an infinite recursion: a method calling itself over and over with no end in sight. The computer needs some amount of memory for bookkeeping for each call. After some number of calls, all memory that is available for this purpose is exhausted. Your program shuts down and reports a "stack fault".

▼

▼

Infinite recursion happens either because the parameter values don't get simpler or because a special terminating case is missing. For example, suppose the `getArea` method computes the area of a triangle with width 0. If it wasn't for the special test, the method would have constructed triangles with −1, −2, −3, and so on.

17.2　Permutations

We will now turn to a more complex example of recursion that would be difficult to program with a simple loop. We will design a class that lists all *permutations* of a string. A permutation is simply a rearrangement of the letters. For example, the string `"eat"` has six permutations (including the original string itself):

```
"eat"
"eta"
"aet"
"ate"
"tea"
"tae"
```

Our `PermutationGenerator` class will have a public interface that is similar to the `StringTokenizer` class.

```
class PermutationGenerator
{
    public PermutationGenerator(String s) { . . . }
    public String nextPermutation() { . . . }
    public boolean hasMorePermutations() { . . . }
}
```

Here is the test program that prints out all permutations of the string `"eat"`:

File PermutationGeneratorTest.java

```
1  /**
2      This program tests the permutation generator.
3  */
4  public class PermutationGeneratorTest
5  {
6     public static void main(String[] args)
7     {
8        PermutationGenerator generator
9           = new PermutationGenerator("eat");
10       while (generator.hasMorePermutations())
11          System.out.println(generator.nextPermutation());
12    }
13 }
```

Now we need an idea how to generate the permutations recursively. Consider the string `"eat"` and let's simplify the problem. First, we'll generate all permutations that start with the letter `'e'`, then those that start with `'a'`, and finally those that start with `'t'`. How do we generate the permutations that start with `'e'`? We need to know the permutations of the substring `"at"`. But that's the same problem—to generate all permutations—with a simpler input, namely the shorter string `"at"`. Thus, we can use recursion. Make another `PermutationGenerator` object that generates the permutations of the substring `"at"`. That generator will produce

```
"at"
"ta"
```

For each permutation of that substring, prepend the letter `'e'` to get the permutations of `"eat"` that start with `'e'`, namely

```
"eat"
"eta"
```

Now let's turn our attention to the permutations of `"eat"` that start with `'a'`. We need to create a permutation generator that produces the permutations of the remaining letters, `"et"`. That generator will produce:

```
"et"
"te"
```

We add the letter `'a'` to the front of the strings and obtain

```
"aet"
"ate"
```

We generate the permutations that start with `'t'` in the same way.

That's the idea. To carry it out, we have to implement the `nextPermutation` method, which gets just one permutation, not all permutations at once. To do that, the `PermutationGenerator` needs to remember the *state* of the permutation computation. Each call to `nextPermutation` produces a new permutation and advances the state so that the next call to `nextPermutation` can pick up where the current call left off.

Clearly, an important part of the state is the character that we currently put in front. We'll call the position of that character `current`. As we generate more permutations, `current` moves from 0 to `word.length() - 1`, where `word` is the word whose letters we permute.

We also need to store the permutation generator of the substring. Let's call it `tailGenerator`. Now we are ready to compute the next permutation. Simply ask `tailGenerator` what *its* next permutation is, and then return

```
word.charAt(current) + tailGenerator.nextPermutation()
```

For the most part, that will work just fine. However, there is one special case. When the tail generator runs out of permutations, we have exhausted all permutations that start with the current letter. Then we need to

- Increment the current position.

- Compute the tail string that contains all letters except for the current one.

- Make a new permutation generator for the tail string.

When are we done? When `current` has reached `word.length()`. Here is the next-Permutation method:

```java
public String nextPermutation()
{
   . . .

   String r = word.charAt(current)
      + tailGenerator.nextPermutation();

   if (!tailGenerator.hasMorePermutations())
   {
      current++;
      if (current < word.length())
      {
         String tailString =
            word.substring(0, current)
                  + word.substring(current + 1);
         tailGenerator =
            new PermutationGenerator(tailString);
      }
   }

   return r;
}
```

The `hasMorePermutations` method simply checks whether `current` has moved past the end of the word:

```java
public boolean hasMorePermutations()
{   return current < word.length();   }
```

The permutation generation algorithm is recursive—it uses the fact that we can generate the permutations of shorter words. When does the recursion stop? We need to build in a stopping point, as a special case to handle words of length 1. A word of length 1 has a single permutation, namely itself. The `nextPermutation` method needs to recognize that as a special case, and not generate permutations of the (empty) tail. Here is the added code to handle a word of length 1.

```java
public String nextPermutation()
{
   if (word.length() == 1)
   {
      current++;
      return word;
   }
   . . .
}
```

By advancing `current`, we make sure that `hasMorePermutations` returns `false` after `nextPermutations` has been called once.

Here is the complete `PermutationGenerator` class.

File PermutationGenerator.java

```
1  /**
2      This class generates permutations of a word.
3  */
4  class PermutationGenerator
5  {
6      /**
7          Constructs a permutation generator.
8          @param aWord  the word to permute
9      */
10     public PermutationGenerator(String aWord)
11     {
12        word = aWord;
13        current = 0;
14        if (s.length() > 1)
15           tailGenerator =
16              new PermutationGenerator(word.substring(1));
17     }
18
19     /**
20         Computes the next permutation of the word.
21         @return  the next permutation
22     */
23     public String nextPermutation()
24     {
25        if (word.length() == 1)
26        {
27           current++;
28           return word;
29        }
30
31        String r = word.charAt(current)
32           + tailGenerator.nextPermutation();
33
34        if (!tailGenerator.hasMorePermutations())
35        {
36           current++;
37           if (current < word.length())
38           {
39              String tailString =
40                 word.substring(0, current)
41                    + word.substring(current + 1);
42              tailGenerator =
43                 new PermutationGenerator(tailString);
44           }
45        }
46
47        return r;
48     }
```

```
49
50    /**
51        Tests whether there are more permutations.
52        @return true if more permutations are available
53    */
54    public boolean hasMorePermutations()
55    {
56        return current < word.length();
57    }
58
59    private String word;
60    private int current;
61    private PermutationGenerator tailGenerator;
62 }
```

Compare the `PermutationGenerator` and `Triangle` classes. Both of them work on the same principle. When they work on a more complex input, they generate another object of the same class that works on a simpler input. Then they combine the work of that object with their own work to deliver the results for the more complex input. There really is no particular complexity behind that process as long as you think about the solution on that level only. However, behind the scenes, the object with the simpler input creates yet another object that works on even simpler input, which creates yet another, and so on, until one object's input is so simple that it can compute the results without further help. It is interesting to think about that process, but it can also be confusing. What's important is that you can focus on the one level that matters—putting a solution together from the slightly simpler problem, ignoring the fact that it also uses recursion to get its results.

▼ ⊗ **Common Error**   **17.2**

Tracing through Recursive Methods

Debugging a recursive method can be somewhat challenging. When you set a breakpoint in a recursive method, the program stops as soon as that program line is encountered in *any call to the recursive method.* Suppose you want to debug the recursive `getArea` method of the `Triangle` class. Debug the `TriangleTest` program with an input of 4. Run until the beginning of the `getArea` method (Figure 1). Inspect the `width` instance variable. It is 4.

Remove the breakpoint and now run until the statement `return smallerArea + width;`. When you inspect `width` again, its value is 2! That makes no sense. There was no instruction that changed the value of `width`! Is that a bug with the debugger?

No. The program stopped in the first *recursive* call to `getArea` that reached the `return` statement. If you are confused, look at the *call stack* (Figure 2). You will see that three calls to `getArea` are pending.

You can debug recursive methods with the debugger. You just need to be particularly careful, and watch the call stack to understand in which nested call you currently are.

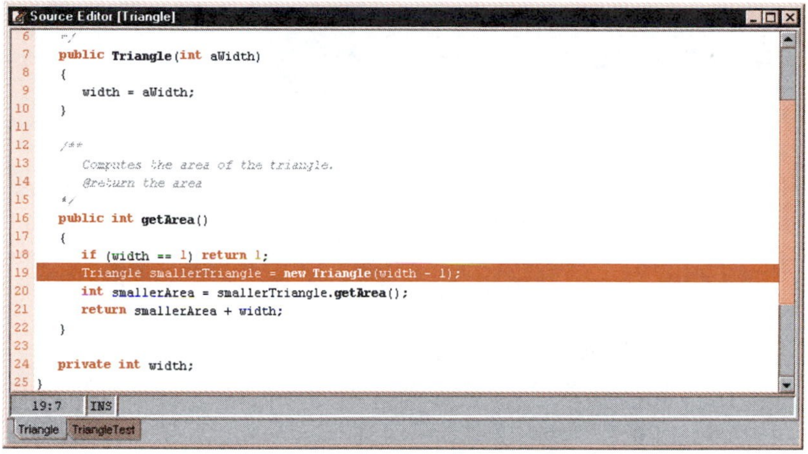

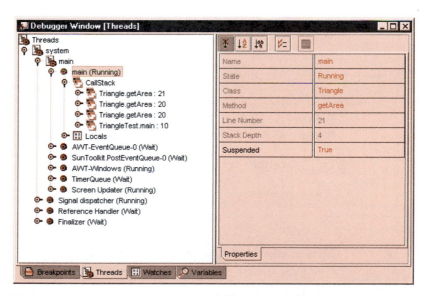

Figure 1

Debugging a Recursive Method

Figure 2

Call Stack Display

Thinking Recursively

To solve a problem recursively requires a different mindset than to solve it by programming loops. In fact, it helps if you are, or pretend to be, a bit lazy and like others to do most of the work for you. If you need to solve a complex problem, pretend that "someone else" will do most of the heavy lifting and solve the problem for all simpler inputs. Then you only need to figure out how you can turn the solutions with simpler inputs into a solution for the whole problem.

To illustrate the method of recursion, let us consider the following problem. We want to test whether a sentence is a *palindrome*—a string that is equal to itself when you reverse all characters. Typical examples of palindromes are

- A man, a plan, a canal—Panama!

- Go hang a salami, I'm a lasagna hog

and, of course, the oldest palindrome of all:

- Madam, I'm Adam

When testing for a palindrome, match upper-and lowercase letters, and ignore all spaces and punctuation marks.

We want to implement the `isPalindrome` method in the following class:

```
public class Sentence
{
   /**
      Constructs a sentence.
      @param aText a string containing all characters of the sentence.
   */
   public Sentence(String aText)
   {
      text = aText;
   }

   /**
      Tests whether this sentence is a palindrome.
      @return true if this sentence is a palindrome, false otherwise
   */
   public isPalindrome()
   {
      . . .
   }

   private String text;
}
```

Step 1   Consider various ways for simplify inputs

In your mind, fix a particular input or set of inputs for the problem that you want to solve.

Think how you can simplify the inputs in such a way that the same problem can be applied to the simpler input.

When you consider simpler inputs, you may want to remove just a little bit from the original input—maybe remove one or two characters from a string, or remove a small portion of a geometric shape. But sometimes it is more useful to cut the input in half and then see what it means to solve the problem for both halves.

In the palindrome test problem, the input is the string that we need to test. How can you simplify the input? Here are several possibilities:

- Remove the first character.

- Remove the last character.

- Remove both the first and the last character.

- Remove a character from the middle.

- Cut the string into two halves.

These simpler inputs are all potential inputs for the palindrome test.

Step 2   Combine solutions with simpler inputs to a solution of the original problem

In your mind, consider the solutions of your problem for the simpler inputs that you have discovered in Step 1. Don't worry *how* those solutions are obtained. Simply have faith that the solutions are readily available. Just say to yourself: These are simpler inputs, so someone else will solve the problem for me.

Now think how you can turn the solution for the simpler inputs into a solution for the input that you are currently thinking about. Maybe you need to add a small quantity, related to the quantity that you lopped off to arrive at the simpler input. Maybe you cut the original input in two halves and have solutions for both halves. Then you may need to add both solutions to arrive at a solution for the whole.

Consider the methods for simplifying the inputs for the palindrome test. Cutting the string in half doesn't seem a good idea. If you cut

```
"Madam, I'm Adam"
```

in half, you get two strings:

```
"Madam, I"
```

and

```
"'m Adam"
```

Neither of them is a palindrome. Cutting the input in half and testing whether the halves are palindromes seems a dead end.

The most promising simplification is to remove the first *and* last characters.

Removing the M at the front and the m at the back yields

```
"adam, I'm Ada"
```

Suppose you can verify that the shorter string is a palindrome. Then *of course* the original string is a palindrome—we put the same letter in the front and the back. That's extremely promising. A word is a palindrome if

- The first and last letters match (ignoring letter case)

and

- The word obtained by removing the first and last letters is a palindrome.

Again, don't worry how the test works for the shorter string. It just works.

There is one other case to consider. What if the first or last letter of the word is not a letter? For example, the string

```
"A man, a plan, a canal, Panama!"
```

ends in a '!' character, which does not match the 'A' in the front. But we should ignore nonletters when testing for palindromes. Thus, when the last character is not a letter but the first character is a letter, it doesn't make sense to remove both the first and the last characters. That's not a problem. Remove just the last character. If the shorter string is a palindrome, then it stays a palindrome when you attach a nonletter.

The same argument applies if the first character is not a letter. Now we have a complete set of cases.

- If the first and last character are both letters, then check whether they match. If so, remove both and test the shorter string.

- Otherwise, if the last character isn't a letter, remove it and test the shorter string.

- Otherwise, the first character isn't a letter. Remove it and test the shorter string.

In all three cases, you can use the solution to the simpler problem to arrive at a solution to your problem.

Step 3 Find solutions to the simplest inputs

A recursive computation keeps simplifying its inputs. Eventually it arrives at very simple inputs. To make sure that the recursion comes to a stop, you must deal with the simplest inputs separately. Come up with special solutions for them. That is usually very easy.

However, sometimes you get into philosphical questions dealing with *degenerate* inputs: empty strings, shapes with no area, and so on. Then you may want to investigate a slightly larger input that gets reduced to such a trivial input and see what value you should attach to the degenerate inputs so that the simpler value, when used according to the rules you discovered in Step 2, yields the correct answer.

Let's look at the simplest strings for the palindrome test:

- Strings with two characters

- Strings with a single character

- The empty string

We don't have to come up with a special solution for strings with two characters. Step 2 still applies to those strings—either or both of the characters are removed. But we do need to worry about strings of length 0 and 1. In those cases, Step 2 can't apply. There aren't two characters to remove.

A string with a single character, such as `"I"`, is a palindrome. It doesn't matter whether or not the character is a letter. The string `"!"` is also a palindrome.

The empty string is a palindrome—it's the same string when you read it backwards. If you find that too artificial, consider a string `"mm"`. According to the rule discovered in Step 2, this string is a palindrome if the first and last character of that string match and the remainder—that is, the empty string—is also a palindrome. Therefore, it makes sense to consider the empty string a palindrome.

Thus, all strings of length 0 or 1 are palindromes.

Step 4 Implement the solution by combining the simple cases and the reduction step

Now you are ready to implement the solution. Make separate cases for the simple inputs that you considered in Step 3. If the input isn't one of the simplest cases, then implement the logic you discovered in Step 2.

Here is the `isPalindrome` method.

```java
public boolean isPalindrome()
{
    // separate case for shortest strings
    if (text.length() <= 1) return true;

    // get first and last character, converted to lowercase
    char first = Character.toLowerCase(text.charAt(0));
    char last = Character.toLowerCase(
        text.charAt(text.length() - 1));

    if (Character.isLetter(first)
        && Character.isLetter(last))
    {
        // both are letters
        if (first == last)
        {
            // remove both first and last character
            Sentence shorter = new Sentence(
                text.substring(1, text.length() - 2));
            return shorter.isPalindrome();
        }
        else
            return false;
    }
    else if (!Character.isLetter(last))
    {
        // remove last character
        Sentence shorter = new Sentence(
            text.substring(1, text.length() - 1));
```

```
▼           return shorter.isPalindrome();
        }
        else
▼       {
            // remove first character
            Sentence shorter = new Sentence(
               text.substring(0, text.length() - 1));
▼           return shorter.isPalindrome();
        }
    }
▼
```

17.3 Recursive Helper Methods

> Sometimes it is easier to find a recursive solution if you make a slight change to the original problem.

Sometimes it is easier to find a recursive solution if you change the original problem slightly. Then the original problem can be solved by calling a recursive helper method.

Here is a typical example. Consider the palindrome test of HOWTO 17.1. It is a bit inefficient to construct new `Sentence` objects in every step. Now consider the following change in the problem. Rather than testing whether the entire sentence is a palindrome, let's check whether a substring is a palindrome:

```
/** Tests whether a substring of the sentence is a palindrome.
    @param start the index of the first character of the substring
    @param end the index of the last character of the substring
    @return true if the substring is a palindrome
*/
boolean isPalindrome(int start, int end)
```

This method turns out to be even easier to implement than the original test. In the recursive calls, simply adjust the `start` and `end` parameters to skip over matching letter pairs and characters that are not letters. There is no need to construct new `Sentence` objects to represent the shorter strings.

```
public boolean isPalindrome(int start, int end)
{
    // separate case for substrings of length 0 and 1
    if (start >= end) return true;

    // get first and last character, converted to lowercase
    char first = Character.toLowerCase(
       text.charAt(start));
    char last = Character.toLowerCase(text.charAt(end));

    if (Character.isLetter(first)
       && Character.isLetter(last))
```

```
   {
      if (first == last)
      {
         // test substring that doesn't contain the matching letters
         return isPalindrome(start + 1, end - 1);
      }
      else
         return false;
   }
   else if (!Character.isLetter(last))
   {
      // test substring that doesn't contain the last character
      return isPalindrome(start, end - 1);
   }
   else
   {
      // test substring that doesn't contain the first character
      return isPalindrome(start + 1, end);
   }
}
```

You should still supply a method to solve the whole problem—the user of your method shouldn't have to know about the trick with the substring positions. Simply call the helper method with positions that test the entire string:

```
public boolean isPalindrome()
{
   return isPalindrome(0, text.length() - 1);
}
```

Note that this call is *not* a recursive method. The `isPalindrome()` method calls a different method, `isPalindrome(int, int)`. The latter method is recursive.

Use the technique of recursive helper methods whenever it is easier to solve a recursive problem that is slightly different from the original problem.

17.4   Mutual Recursions

> In a mutual recursion, a set of cooperating methods calls each other repeatedly.

In the preceding examples, a method called itself to solve a simpler problem. Sometimes, a set of cooperating methods calls each other in a recursive fashion. In this section, we will explore a typical situation of such a mutual recursion.

We will develop a program that can compute the values of arithmetic expressions such as

```
3 + 4 * 5
(3 + 4) * 5
1 - (2 - (3 - (4 - 5)))
```

Computing such an expression is complicated by the fact that * and / bind more strongly than + and -, and that parentheses can be used to group subexpressions.

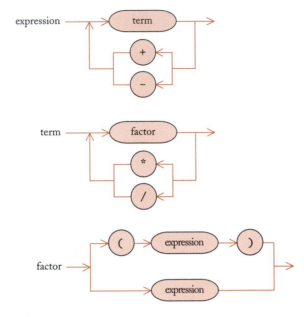

Syntax Diagrams for Evaluating an Expression

Figure 3 shows a set of *syntax diagrams* that describes the syntax of these expressions. An expression is either a term, or a sum or difference of terms. A term is either a factor, or a product or quotient of factors. Finally, a factor is either a number or an expression enclosed in parentheses.

Figure 4 shows how the expressions 3 + 4 * 5 and (3 + 4) * 5 are derived from the syntax diagram.

Why do the syntax diagrams help us compute the value of the tree? If you look at the syntax trees, you will see that they accurately represent which operations should be carried out first. In the first tree, 4 and 5 should be multiplied, and then the result should be added to 3. In the second tree, 3 and 4 should be added, and the result should be multiplied with 5.

At the end of this section, you will find the implementation of the `Evaluator` class, which evaluates these expressions. The `Evaluator` makes use of an `ExpressionTokenizer` class, which breaks up an input string into tokens—numbers, operators, and parentheses. When you call `nextToken`, the next input token is returned as a string. However, unlike the `StringTokenizer`, we supply another method, `peekToken`, which lets you see the next token without consuming it. To see why this method is necessary, consider the syntax diagram of the factor type. If the next token is a `"*"` or `"/"`, you want to continue adding and subtracting terms. But if the next token is another character, such as a `"+"` or `"-"`, you want to stop without actually consuming it, so that the token can be considered later.

To compute the value of an expression, we implement three methods: `getExpression-Value`, `getTermValue`, and `getFactorValue`. The `getExpressionValue` method first

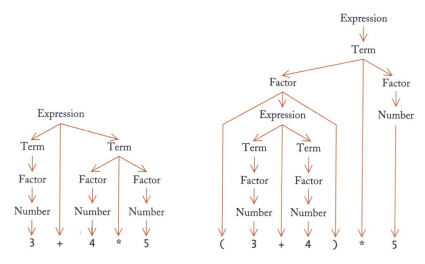

Figure 4

Syntax Trees for Two Expressions

calls `getTermValue` to get the value of the first term of the expression. Then it checks whether the next input token is one of + or -. If so, it calls `getTermValue` again and adds or subtracts it.

```
public int getExpressionValue()
{
   int value = getTermValue();
   boolean done = false;
   while (!done)
   {
      String next = tokenizer.peekToken();
      if ("+".equals(next) || "-".equals(next))
      {
         tokenizer.nextToken();
         int value2 = getTermValue();
         if ("+".equals(next)) value = value + value2;
         else value = value - value2;
      }
      else done = true;
   }
   return value;
}
```

The `getTermValue` method calls `getFactorValue` in the same way, multiplying or dividing the factor values.

Finally, the `getFactorValue` method checks whether the next input is a number, or whether it begins with a (token. In the first case, the value is simply the value of the number. However, in the second case, the `getFactorValue` method makes a recursive call to `getExpressionValue`. Thus, the three methods are mutually recursive.

```
public int getFactorValue()
{
   int value;
   String next = tokenizer.peekToken();
   if ("(".equals(next))
   {
      tokenizer.nextToken();
      value = getExpressionValue();
      next = tokenizer.nextToken(); // read ")"
   }
   else
      value = Integer.parseInt(tokenizer.nextToken());
   return value;
}
```

As always with a recursive solution, you need to ensure that the recursion terminates. In this situation, that is easy to see. If getExpressionValue calls itself, the second call works on a shorter subexpression than the original expression. At each recursive call, at least some of the tokens of the input string are consumed, so eventually the recursion must come to an end.

File Evaluator.java

```
1  /**
2      A class that can compute the value of an arithmetic expression.
3  */
4  public class Evaluator
5  {
6     /**
7         Constructs an evaluator.
8         @param anExpression a string containing the expression
9         to be evaluated
10     */
11     public Evaluator(String anExpression)
12     {
13        tokenizer = new ExpressionTokenizer(anExpression);
14     }
15
16     /**
17         Evaluates the expression.
18         @return the value of the expression
19     */
20     public int getExpressionValue()
21     {
22        int value = getTermValue();
23        boolean done = false;
24        while (!done)
25        {
26           String next = tokenizer.peekToken();
27           if ("+".equals(next) || "-".equals(next))
28           {
29              tokenizer.nextToken();
30              int value2 = getTermValue();
```

```
31                       if ("+".equals(next)) value = value + value2;
32                       else value = value - value2;
33                   }
34                   else done = true;
35               }
36           return value;
37       }
38
39       /**
40           Evaluates the next term found in the expression.
41           @return the value of the term
42       */
43       public int getTermValue()
44       {
45           int value = getFactorValue();
46           boolean done = false;
47           while (!done)
48           {
49               String next = tokenizer.peekToken();
50               if ("*".equals(next) || "/".equals(next))
51               {
52                   tokenizer.nextToken();
53                   int value2 = getFactorValue();
54                   if ("*".equals(next)) value = value * value2;
55                   else value = value / value2;
56               }
57               else done = true;
58           }
59           return value;
60       }
61
62       /**
63           Evaluates the next factor found in the expression.
64           @return the value of the factor
65       */
66       public int getFactorValue()
67       {
68           int value;
69           String next = tokenizer.peekToken();
70           if ("(".equals(next))
71           {
72               tokenizer.nextToken();
73               value = getExpressionValue();
74               next = tokenizer.nextToken(); // read ")"
75           }
76           else
77               value = Integer.parseInt(tokenizer.nextToken());
78           return value;
79       }
80
81       private ExpressionTokenizer tokenizer;
82   }
```

File ExpressionTokenizer.java

```
1  /**
2     This class breaks up a string describing an expression
3     into tokens: numbers, parentheses, and operators.
4  */
5  public class ExpressionTokenizer
6  {
7     /**
8        Constructs a tokenizer.
9        @param anInput  the string to tokenize
10    */
11    public ExpressionTokenizer(String anInput)
12    {
13       input = anInput;
14       start = 0;
15       end = 0;
16       nextToken();
17    }
18
19    /**
20       Peeks at the next token without consuming it.
21       @return  the next token or null if there are no more tokens
22    */
23    public String peekToken()
24    {
25       if (start >= input.length()) return null;
26       else return input.substring(start, end);
27    }
28
29    /**
30       Gets the next token and moves the tokenizer to the
31       following token.
32       @return  the next token or null if there are no more tokens
33    */
34    public String nextToken()
35    {
36       String r = peekToken();
37       start = end;
38       if (start >= input.length()) return r;
39       if (Character.isDigit(input.charAt(start)))
40       {
41          end = start + 1;
42          while (end < input.length()
43             && Character.isDigit(input.charAt(end)))
44             end++;
45       }
46       else
47          end = start + 1;
48       return r;
49    }
50
51    private String input;
```

```
52      private int start;
53      private int end;
54  }
```

File EvaluatorTest.java

```
 1  import javax.swing.JOptionPane;
 2
 3  /**
 4      This program tests the expression evaluator.
 5  */
 6  public class EvaluatorTest
 7  {
 8      public static void main(String[] args)
 9      {
10          String input = JOptionPane.showInputDialog(
11              "Enter an expression:");
12          Evaluator e = new Evaluator(input);
13          int value = e.getExpressionValue();
14          System.out.println(input + "=" + value);
15          System.exit(0);
16      }
17  }
```

17.5   The Efficiency of Recursion

As you have seen in this chapter, recursion can be a powerful tool to implement complex algorithms. On the other hand, recursion can lead to algorithms that perform poorly. In this section, we will analyze the question of when recursion is beneficial and when it is inefficient.

Consider the Fibonacci sequence introduced in Chapter 5: a sequence of numbers defined by the equation

$$f_1 = 1$$

$$f_2 = 1$$

$$f_n = f_{n-1} + f_{n-2}$$

That is, each value of the sequence is the sum of the two preceding values. The first ten terms of the sequence are

$$1, 1, 2, 3, 5, 8, 13, 21, 34, 55$$

It is easy to extend this sequence indefinitely. Just keep appending the sum of the last two values of the sequence. For example, the next entry is $34 + 55 = 89$.

We would like to write a function that computes f_n for any value of n. Suppose we translate the definition directly into a recursive method:

File FibTest.java

```
 1  import javax.swing.JOptionPane;
 2
 3  /**
```

```
 4      This program computes Fibonacci numbers using a recursive
 5      method.
 6  */
 7  public class FibTest
 8  {
 9     public static void main(String[] args)
10     {
11        String input = JOptionPane.showInputDialog(
12           "Enter n: ");
13        int n = Integer.parseInt(input);
14
15        for (int i = 1; i <= n; i++)
16        {
17           int f = fib(i);
18           System.out.println("fib(" + i + ") = " + f);
19        }
20        System.exit(0);
21     }
22
23     /**
24        Computes a Fibonacci number.
25        @param n an integer
26        @return  the nth Fibonacci number
27     */
28     public static int fib(int n)
29     {
30        if (n <= 2) return 1;
31        else return fib(n - 1) + fib(n - 2);
32     }
33  }
```

That is certainly simple, and the method will work correctly. But watch the output closely as you run the test program. The first few calls to the fib method are quite fast. For larger values, though, the program pauses an amazingly long time between outputs.

That makes no sense. Armed with pencil, paper, and a pocket calculator you could calculate these numbers pretty quickly, so it shouldn't take the computer anywhere near that long.

To find out the problem, let us insert trace messages into the method:

File FibTrace.java

```
 1  import javax.swing.JOptionPane;
 2
 3  /**
 4     This program prints trace messages that show how often the
 5     recursive method for computing Fibonacci numbers calls itself.
 6  */
 7  public class FibTrace
 8  {
 9     public static void main(String[] args)
10     {
11        String input = JOptionPane.showInputDialog(
12           "Enter n: ");
13        int n = Integer.parseInt(input);
```

```
14
15        int f = fib(n);
16
17        System.out.println("fib(" + n + ") = " + f);
18        System.exit(0);
19     }
20
21     /**
22        Computes a Fibonacci number.
23        @param n an integer
24        @return the nth Fibonacci number
25     */
26     public static int fib(int n)
27     {
28        System.out.println("Entering fib: n = " + n);
29        int f;
30        if (n <= 2) f = 1;
31        else f = fib(n - 1) + fib(n - 2);
32        System.out.println("Exiting fib: n = " + n
33          + " return value = " + f);
34        return f;
35     }
36 }
```

Following is the trace for computing fib(5). Figure 5 shows the call tree

```
Entering fib: n = 6
Entering fib: n = 5
Entering fib: n = 4
Entering fib: n = 3
Entering fib: n = 2
Exiting fib: n = 2 return value = 1
```

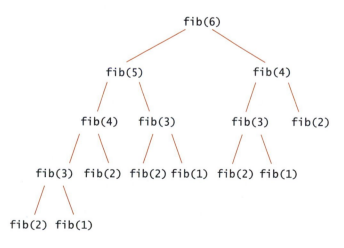

Figure 5

Call Pattern of the Recursive fib Method

```
Entering fib: n = 1
Exiting fib: n = 1 return value = 1
Exiting fib: n = 3 return value = 2
Entering fib: n = 2
Exiting fib: n = 2 return value = 1
Exiting fib: n = 4 return value = 3
Entering fib: n = 3
Entering fib: n = 2
Exiting fib: n = 2 return value = 1
Entering fib: n = 1
Exiting fib: n = 1 return value = 1
Exiting fib: n = 3 return value = 2
Exiting fib: n = 5 return value = 5
Entering fib: n = 4
Entering fib: n = 3
Entering fib: n = 2
Exiting fib: n = 2 return value = 1
Entering fib: n = 1
Exiting fib: n = 1 return value = 1
Exiting fib: n = 3 return value = 2
Entering fib: n = 2
Exiting fib: n = 2 return value = 1
Exiting fib: n = 4 return value = 3
Exiting fib: n = 6 return value = 8
```

Now it is becoming apparent why the method takes so long. It is computing the same values over and over. For example, the computation of fib(6) calls fib(4) twice and fib(3) three times. That is very different from the computation we would do with pencil and paper. There we would just write down the values as they were computed and add up the last two to get the next one until we reached the desired entry; no sequence value would ever be computed twice.

If we imitate the pencil-and-paper process, then we get the following program.

File FibLoop.java

```
 1  import javax.swing.JOptionPane;
 2
 3  /**
 4      This program computes Fibonacci numbers using an iterative method.
 5  */
 6  public class FibLoop
 7  {
 8      public static void main(String[] args)
 9      {
10          String input = JOptionPane.showInputDialog(
11              "Enter n: ");
12          int n = Integer.parseInt(input);
13
14          for (int i = 1; i <= n; i++)
15          {
16              double f = fib(i);
17              System.out.println("fib(" + i + ") = " + f);
```

```
18          }
19          System.exit(0);
20      }
21
22      /**
23          Computes a Fibonacci number.
24          @param n  an integer
25          @return  the nth Fibonacci number
26      */
27      public static double fib(int n)
28      {
29          if (n <= 2) return 1;
30          double fold = 1;
31          double fold2 = 1;
32          double fnew = 1;
33          for (int i = 3; i <= n; i++)
34          {
35              fnew = fold + fold2;
36              fold2 = fold;
37              fold = fnew;
38          }
39          return fnew;
40      }
41  }
```

This method runs *much* faster than the recursive version.

In this example of the `fib` method, the recursive solution was easy to program because it exactly followed the mathematical definition, but it ran far more slowly than the iterative solution, because it computed many intermediate results multiple times.

Can you always speed up a recursive solution by changing it into a loop? Frequently, the iterative and recursive solution have essentially the same performance. For example, here is an iterative solution for the palindrome test.

```
public boolean isPalindrome()
{
    int start = 0;
    int end = text.length() - 1;
    while (start < end)
    {
        char first = Character.toLowerCase(
            text.charAt(start));
        char last = Character.toLowerCase(text.charAt(end));

        if (Character.isLetter(first)
            && Character.isLetter(last))
        {
            // both are letters
            if (first == last)
            {
                start++;
                end--;
            }
        }
```

```
        else
            return false;
        if (!Character.isLetter(last))
            end--;
        if (!Character.isLetter(first))
            start++;
    }
    return true;
}
```

This solution keeps two index variables: `start` and `end`. The first index starts at the beginning of the string and is advanced whenever a letter has been matched or a nonletter has been ignored. The second index starts at the end of the string and moves towards the beginning. When the two index variables meet, then the iteration stops.

> Occasionally, a recursive solution runs much slower than its iterative counterpart. However, in most cases, the recursive solution is only slightly slower.

Both the iteration and the recursion run at about the same speed. If a palindrome has n characters, the iteration executes the loop between $n/2$ and n times, depending on how many of the characters are letters, since one or both index variables are moved in each step. Similarly, the recursive solution calls itself between $n/2$ and n times, because one or two characters are removed in each step.

In such a situation, the iterative solution tends to be a bit faster, because each recursive method call takes a certain amount of processor time. In principle, it is possible for a smart compiler to avoid recursive method calls if they follow simple patterns, but most compilers don't do that. From that point of view, an iterative solution is preferable.

> In many cases a recursive solution is easier to understand and implement correctly than an iterative solution.

There are quite a few problems that are dramatically easier to solve recursively than iteratively. For example, it is not at all obvious how you can come up with a nonrecursive solution for the permutation generator. As Exercise P17.11 shows, it is possible to avoid the recursion, but the resulting solution is quite complex (and no faster).

Often, recursive solutions are easier to understand and implement correctly than their iterative counterparts. There is a certain elegance and economy of thought to recursive solutions that makes them more appealing. As the computer scientist (and creator of the GhostScript interpreter for the PostScript graphics description language) L. Peter Deutsch put it: "To iterate is human, to recurse divine."

▼ **Random Fact** **17.1**

The Limits of Computation

Have you ever wondered how your instructor or grader makes sure your programming homework is correct? In all likelihood, they look at your solution and perhaps run it with some test inputs. But usually they have a correct solution available. That suggests that there might be an easier way. Perhaps they could feed your program and their correct program into a program comparator, a computer program that analyzes both programs and determines whether they both compute the same results. Of course, your solution and the program that is known to be correct need not be identical—what matters is that they produce the same output when given the same input.

How could such a program comparator work? Well, the Java compiler knows how to read a program and make sense of the classes, methods, and statements. So it seems plausible that someone could, with some effort, write a program that reads two Java programs, analyzes what they do, and determines whether they solve the same task. Of course, such a program would be very attractive to instructors, because it could automate the grading process. Thus, even though no such program exists today, it might be tempting to try to develop one and sell it to universities around the world.

However, before you start raising venture capital for such an effort, you should know that theoretical computer scientists have proven that it is impossible to develop such a program, *no matter how hard you try*.

There are quite a few of these unsolvable problems. The first one, called the *halting problem*, was discovered by the British researcher Alan Turing in 1936 (see Figure 6). Because his research occurred before the first actual computer was constructed, Turing had to devise a theoretical device, the *Turing machine*, to explain how computers could work. The Turing machine consists of a long magnetic tape, a read/write head, and a program that has numbered instructions of the form: "If the current symbol under the head is *x*, then replace it with *y*, move the head one unit left or right, and continue with instruction *n*" (see Figure 7). Interestingly enough, with just these instructions, you can program just as much as with Java, even though it is incredibly tedious to do so. Theoretical computer scientists like Turing machines because they can be described using nothing more than the laws of mathematics.

Figure 6

Alan Turing

Instruction number	If tape symbol is	Replace with	Then move head	Then go to instruction
1	0	2	right	2
1	1	1	left	4
2	0	0	right	2
2	1	1	right	2
2	B	0	left	3
3	0	0	left	3
3	1	1	left	3
3	2	2	right	1
4	1	1	right	5
4	2	0	left	4

Program

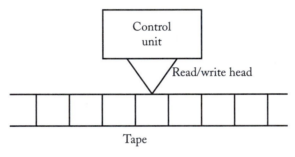

Figure 7

A Turing Machine

Expressed in terms of Java, the halting problem states: "It is impossible to write a program with two inputs, namely the source code of an arbitrary Java program P and a string I, and that decides whether the program P, when executed with the input I, will halt without getting into an infinite loop". Of course, for some kinds of programs and inputs, it is possible to decide whether the programs halt with the given input. The halting problem asserts that it is impossible to come up with a single decision-making algorithm that works with all programs and inputs. Note that you can't simply run the program P on the input I to settle this question. If the program runs for 1,000 days, you don't know that the program is in an infinite loop. Maybe you just have to wait another day for it to stop.

Such a "halt checker", if it could be written, might also be useful for grading homework. An instructor could use it to screen student submissions to see if they get into an infinite loop with a particular input, and then not check them any further. However, as Turing demonstrated, such a program cannot be written. His argument is ingenious and quite simple.

Suppose a "halt checker" program existed. Let's call it H. From H, we will develop another program, the "killer" program K. K does the following computation. Its input is a string containing the source code for a program R. It then applies the halting checker on the input program R and the input string R. That is, it checks whether the program R halts if its input is its own source code. It sounds bizarre to feed a program to itself, but it isn't impossible. For example, the Java compiler is written in Java, and you can use it to

▼ compile itself. Or, as a simpler example, you can use the word count program from Chapter 6 to count the words in its own source code.

▼ When *K* gets the answer from *H* that *R* halts when applied to itself, it is programmed to enter an infinite loop. Otherwise *K* exits. In Java, the program might look like this:

```
public class Killer
{
    public static void main(String[] args)
    {
        String r = read program input;
        HaltChecker checker = new HaltChecker();
        if (checker.check(r, r))
            while (true) { } // infinite loop
        else
            return;
    }
}
```

Now ask yourself: What does the halt checker answer when asked whether *K* halts when given *K* as the input? Maybe it finds out that *K* gets into an infinite loop with such an input. But wait, that can't be right. That would mean that `checker.check(r, r)` returns `false` when r is the program code of *K*. As you can plainly see, in that case, the `killer` method returns, so *K* didn't get into an infinite loop. That shows that *K* must halt when analyzing itself, so `checker.check(r, r)` should return `true`. But then the `killer` method doesn't terminate—it goes into an infinite loop. That shows that it is logically impossible to implement a program that can check whether *every* program halts on a particular input.

It is sobering to know that there are *limits* to computing. There are problems that no computer program, no matter how ingenious, can answer.

Theoretical computer scientists are working on other research involving the nature of computation. One important question that remains unsettled to this day deals with problems that in practice are very time-consuming to solve. It may be that these problems are intrinsically hard, in which case it would be pointless to try to look for better algorithms. Such theoretical research can have important practical applications. For example, right now, nobody knows whether the most common encryptions schemes used today could be broken by discovering a new algorithm (see Random Fact 15.1 for more information on encryption algorithms). Knowing that no fast algorithms exist for breaking a particular code could make us feel more comfortable about the security of encryption.

CHAPTER SUMMARY

1. A recursive computation solves a problem by using the solution of the same problem with simpler inputs.

2. For a recursion to terminate, there must be special cases for the simplest inputs.

3. Sometimes it is easier to find a recursive solution if you make a slight change to the original problem.

4. In a mutual recursion, a set of cooperating methods calls each other repeatedly.

5. Occasionally, a recursive solution runs much slower than its iterative counterpart. However, in most cases, the recursive solution is only slightly slower.

6. In many cases, a recursive solution is easier to understand and implement correctly than an iterative solution.

REVIEW EXERCISES

Exercise R17.1. Define the terms

- Recursion
- Iteration
- Infinite recursion
- Indirect recursion

Exercise R17.2. Outline, but do not implement, a recursive solution for finding the smallest value in an array.

Exercise R17.3. Outline, but do not implement, a recursive solution for sorting an array of numbers. *Hint:* First find the smallest value in the array.

Exercise R17.4. Outline, but do not implement, a recursive solution for generating all subsets of the set $\{1, 2, \ldots, n\}$.

Exercise R17.5. Exercise P17.11 shows an iterative way of generating all permutations of the sequence $(0, 1, \ldots, n - 1)$. Explain why the algorithm produces the right result.

Exercise R17.6. Write a recursive definition of x^n, where $n \geq 0$, similar to the recursive definition of the Fibonacci numbers. *Hint:* How do you compute x^n from x^{n-1}? How does the recursion terminate?

Exercise R17.7. Write a recursive definition of $n! = 1 \times 2 \times \cdots \times n$, similar to the recursive definition of the Fibonacci numbers.

Exercise R17.8. Find out how often the recursive version of `fib` calls itself. Keep a static variable `fibCount` and increment it once in every call of `fib`. What is the relationship between `fib(n)` and `fibCount`?

Exercise R17.9. How many moves are required in the "Towers of Hanoi" problem of Exercise P17.12 to move n disks? *Hint:* As explained in the exercises,

moves(1) = 1

moves(n) = 2 · moves(n − 1) + 1

PROGRAMMING EXERCISES

Exercise P17.1. Write a recursive method `void reverse()` that reverses a sentence. For example:

```
Sentence greeting = new Sentence("Hello!");
greeting.reverse();
System.out.println(greeting.getText());
```

prints the string "!olleH". Implement a recursive solution by removing the first character, reversing a sentence consisting of the remaining text, and combining the two.

Exercise P17.2. Redo Exercise P17.1 with a recursive helper method that reverses a substring of the message text.

Exercise P17.3. Implement the `reverse` method of Exercise P17.1 as an iteration.

Exercise P17.4. Use recursion to implement a method `boolean find(String t)` that tests whether a string is contained in a sentence:

```
Sentence s = new Sentence("Mississippi!");
boolean b = s.find("sip"); // returns true
```

Hint: If the text starts with the string you want to match, then you are done. If not, consider the sentence that you obtain by removing the first character.

Exercise P17.5. Use recursion to implement a method `int indexOf(String t)` that returns the starting position of the first substring of the text that matches t. Return −1 if t is not a substring of s. For example,

```
Sentence s = new Sentence("Mississippi!");
int n = s.find("sip"); // returns 6
```

Hint: This is a bit trickier than the preceding problem, because you need to keep track of how far the match is from the beginning of the sentence. Make that value a parameter of a helper method.

Exercise P17.6. Using recursion, find the largest element in an array.

```
public class DataSet
{
    public DataSet(int[] anArray) { . . . }
    public int getMaximum() { . . . }
    . . .
}
```

Hint: Find the largest element in the subset containing all but the last element. Then compare that maximum to the value of the last element.

Exercise P17.7. Using recursion, compute the sum of all values in an array.

```
public class DataSet
{
    public DataSet(int[] anArray) { . . . }
    public int getSum() { . . . }
    . . .
}
```

Exercise P17.8. Using recursion, compute the area of a polygon. Cut off a triangle and use the fact that a triangle with corners (x_1, y_1), (x_2, y_2), (x_3, y_3) has area

$$(x_1y_2 + x_2y_3 + x_3y_1 - y_1x_2 - y_2x_3 - y_3x_1) / 2$$

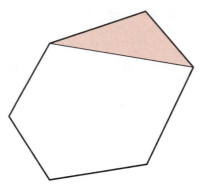

Exercise P17.9. Implement a `SubStringGenerator` that generates all substrings of a string. For example, the substrings of the string `"rum"` are the seven strings

"r", "ru", "rum", "u", "um", "m", ""

Hint: First enumerate all substrings that start with the first character. There are *n* of them if the string has length *n*. Then enumerate the substrings of the string that you obtain by removing the first character.

Exercise P17.10. Implement a `SubSetGenerator` that generates all subsets of characters of a string. For example, the subsets of characters of the string `"rum"` are the eight strings

"rum", "ru", "rm", "r", "um", "u", "m", ""

Note that the subsets don't have to be substrings—for example, `"rm"` isn't a substring of `"rum"`.

Exercise P17.11. The following class generates all permutations of the numbers 0, 1, 2, ..., *n* − 1, without using recursion.

```java
public class NumberPermutationGenerator
{
    public NumberPermutationGenerator(int n)
    {
        a = new int[n];
        done = false;
        for (int i = 0; i < n; i++) a[i] = i;
    }

    public void nextPermutation()
    {
        if (a.length <= 1) return;

        for (int i = a.length - 1; i > 0; i--)
        {
            if (a[i - 1] < a[i])
            {
                int j = a.length - 1;
                while (a[i - 1] > a[j]) j--;
                swap(i - 1, j);
                reverse(i, a.length - 1);
```

```
                    return;
               }
          }
     }

     public boolean hasMorePermutations()
     {
          if (a.length <= 1) return false;
          for (int i = a.length - 1; i > 0; i--)
          {
               if (a[i - 1] < a[i]) return true;
          }
          return false;
     }

     public void swap(int i, int j)
     {
          int temp = a[i];
          a[i] = a[j];
          a[j] = temp;
     }

     public void reverse(int i, int j)
     {
          while (i < j) { swap(i, j); i++; j--; }
     }
     . . .
     private int[] a;
}
```

The algorithm uses the fact that the set to be permuted consists of distinct numbers. Thus, you cannot use the same algorithm to compute the permutations of the characters in a string. You can, however, use this class to get all permutations of the character positions and then compute a string whose ith character is word.charAt(a[i]). Use this approach to reimplement the PermutationGenerator without recursion.

Exercise P17.12. *Towers of Hanoi.* This is a well-known puzzle. A stack of disks of decreasing size is to be transported from the leftmost peg to the rightmost peg. The middle peg can be used as a temporary storage. (See Figure 8.) One disk can be moved at one time, from any peg to any other peg. You can place smaller disks only on top of larger ones, not the other way around.

Write a program that prints the moves necessary to solve the puzzle for *n* disks. (Ask the user for *n* at the beginning of the program.) Print moves in the form

```
Move disk from peg 1 to peg 3
```

Hint: Implement a class DiskMover. The constructor takes

- The source peg from which to move the disks (1, 2, or 3)
- The target peg to which to move the disks (1, 2, or 3)
- The number of disks to move

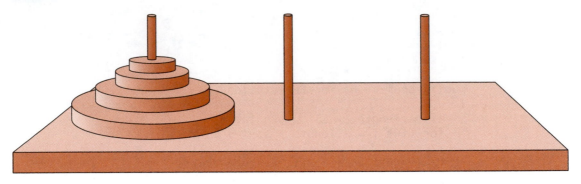

Figure 8

Towers of Hanoi

A disk mover that moves a single disk from one peg to another simply has a `nextMove` method that returns a string

`Move disk from peg` *source* `to peg` *target*

A disk mover with more than disk to move must work harder. It needs another `Disk-Mover` to help it. In the constructor, construct a `DiskMover(source, other, disks - 1)` where `other` is the peg other than `from` and `target`.

The `nextMove` asks that disk mover for its next move until it is done. The effect is to move the first `disks - 1` disks to the other peg. Then the `nextMove` method issues a command to move a disk from the `from` peg to the `to` peg. Finally, it constructs another disk mover `DiskMover(other, target, disks - 1)` that generates the moves that move the disks from the other peg to the target peg.

Hint: It helps to keep track of the state of the disk mover:

- `BEFORE_LARGEST`: The helper mover moves the smaller pile to the other peg.
- `LARGEST`: Move the largest disk from the source to the destination.
- `AFTER_LARGEST`: The helper mover moves the smaller pile from the other peg to the target.
- `DONE`: All moves are done.

Test your program as follows:

```
DiskMover mover = new DiskMover(1, 3, n);
while (mover.hasMoreMoves())
    System.out.println(mover.nextMove());
```

Exercise P17.13. Implement a graphical version of the Towers of Hanoi program. Every time the user clicks on a button labeled "Next", draw the next move.

Chapter 18

Sorting and Searching

To study the several sorting and searching algorithms

▶ To appreciate that algorithms for the same task can differ widely in performance

▶ To understand the big-Oh notation

▶ To learn how to estimate and compare the performance of algorithms

▶ To learn how to measure the running time of a program

One of the most common tasks in data processing is sorting. For example, a collection of employees needs to be printed out in alphabetical order or sorted by salary. We will study several sorting methods in this chapter and compare their performance. This is by no means an exhaustive treatment on the subject of sorting. You will likely revisit this topic at a later time in your computer science studies. Reference [1] gives a good overview of the many sorting methods available.

Once a sequence of objects is sorted, one can locate individual objects rapidly. We will study the *binary search* algorithm, which carries out this fast lookup.

18.1   Selection Sort

To keep the examples simple, we will discuss how to sort an array of integers before going on to sorting strings or employee data. Consider the following array a:

| 11 | 9 | 17 | 5 | 12 |

> The selection sort algorithm sorts an array by repeatedly finding the smallest element of the unsorted tail region and moving it to the front.

An obvious first step is to find the smallest element. In this case the smallest element is 5, stored in a[3]. We should move the 5 to the beginning of the array. Of course, there is already an element stored in a[0], namely 11. Therefore we cannot simply move a[3] into a[0] without moving the 11 somewhere else. We don't yet know where the 11 should end up, but we know for certain that it should not be in a[0]. We simply get it out of the way by *swapping* it with a[3].

Now the first element is in the correct place. In the foregoing figure, the color indicates the portion of the array that is already sorted from the unsorted remainder.

Next we take the minimum of the remaining entries a[1] . . . a[4]. That minimum value, 9, is already in the correct place. We don't need to do anything in this case and can simply extend the sorted area by one to the right:

| 5 | 9 | 17 | 11 | 12 |

We repeat the process. The minimum value of the unsorted region is 11, which needs to be swapped with the first value of the unsorted region, 17:

Now the unsorted region is only two elements long, but we keep to the same successful strategy. The minimum value is 12, and we swap it with the first value, 17.

That leaves us with an unprocessed region of length 1, but of course a region of length 1 is always sorted. We are done.

Let us program this algorithm. For this program as well as the other programs in this chapter, we will use two utility methods—one to generate an array with random entries, and the other to print the values of an array—which we pack up in a class `ArrayUtil` so that we don't have to repeat them for every code example.

This algorithm will sort any array of integers. If speed were not an issue for us, or if there simply were no better sorting method available, we could stop the discussion of sorting right here. As the next section shows, however, this algorithm, while entirely correct, shows disappointing performance when run on a large data set.

Exercise R18.13 discusses insertion sort, another simple (and equally inefficient) sorting algorithm.

File SelectionSorter.java

```
1   /**
2       This class sorts an array, using the selection sort
3       algorithm.
4   */
5   public class SelectionSorter
6   {
7       /**
8           Constructs a selection sorter.
9           @param anArray  the array to sort
10      */
11      public SelectionSorter(int[] anArray)
12      {
13          a = anArray;
14      }
15
16      /**
17          Sorts the array managed by this selection sorter.
18      */
19      public void sort()
20      {
21          for (int i = 0; i < a.length - 1; i++)
22          {
23              int minPos = minimumPosition(i);
24              swap(minPos, i);
25          }
26      }
27
28      /**
29          Finds the smallest element in a tail range of the array.
30          @param from  the first position in a to compare
31          @return  the position of the smallest element in the
32              range a[from]...a[a.length - 1]
33      */
34      private int minimumPosition(int from)
35      {
36          int minPos = from;
37          for (int i = from + 1; i < a.length; i++)
```

```
38            if (a[i] < a[minPos]) minPos = i;
39         return minPos;
40      }
41
42      /**
43         Swaps two entries of the array.
44         @param i  the first position to swap
45         @param j  the second position to swap
46      */
47      private void swap(int i, int j)
48      {
49         int temp = a[i];
50         a[i] = a[j];
51         a[j] = temp;
52      }
53
54      private int[] a;
55   }
56   File SelectionSortTest.java
57   /**
58      This program tests the selection sort algorithm by
59      sorting an array that is filled with random numbers.
60   */
61   public class SelectionSortTest
62   {
63      public static void main(String[] args)
64      {
65         int[] a = ArrayUtil.randomIntArray(20, 100);
66         ArrayUtil.print(a);
67
68         SelectionSorter sorter = new SelectionSorter(a);
69         sorter.sort();
70
71         ArrayUtil.print(a);
72      }
73   }
```

File ArrayUtil.java

```
1   import java.util.Random;
2
3   /**
4      This class contains utility methods for array
5      manipulation.
6   */
7   public class ArrayUtil
8   {
9      /**
10        Creates an array filled with random values.
11        @param length  the length of the array
12        @param n  the number of possible random values
```

```
13            @return an array filled with length numbers between
14                0 and n-1
15     */
16     public static int[] randomIntArray(int length, int n)
17     {  int[] a = new int[length];
18        Random generator = new Random();
19
20        for (int i = 0; i < a.length; i++)
21           a[i] = generator.nextInt(n);
22
23        return a;
24     }
25
26     /**
27        Prints all elements in an array.
28        @param a the array to print
29     */
30     public static void print(int[] a)
31     {
32        for (int i = 0; i < a.length; i++)
33           System.out.print(a[i] + " ");
34        System.out.println();
35     }
36 }
```

18.2   Profiling the Selection Sort Algorithm

To measure the performance of a program, you could simply run it and measure how long it takes by using a stopwatch. However, most of our programs run very quickly, and it is not easy to time them accurately in this way. Furthermore, when a program does take a noticeable time to run, a certain amount of that time may simply be used for loading the program from disk into memory (for which we should not penalize it) or for screen output (whose speed depends on the computer model, even for computers with identical CPUs). We will instead create a StopWatch class. This class works just like a real stopwatch. You can start it, stop it, and read out the elapsed time. The class uses the System.current-TimeMillis method, which returns the milliseconds that have elapsed since midnight at the start of January 1, 1970. Of course, you don't care about the absolute number of seconds since this historical moment, but the *difference* of two such counts gives us the number of milliseconds of a time interval. Here is the code for the StopWatch class:

File StopWatch.java

```
1 /**
2     A stopwatch accumulates time when it is running. You can
3     repeatedly start and stop the stopwatch. You can use a
4     stopwatch to measure the running time of a program.
5 */
6 public class StopWatch
7 {
```

```
 8    /**
 9        Constructs a stopwatch that is in the stopped state
10        and has no time accumulated.
11    */
12    public StopWatch()
13    {
14        reset();
15    }
16
17    /**
18        Starts the stopwatch. Time starts accumulating now.
19    */
20    public void start()
21    {
22        if (isRunning) return;
23        isRunning = true;
24        startTime = System.currentTimeMillis();
25    }
26
27    /**
28        Stops the stopwatch. Time stops accumulating and is
29        is added to the elapsed time.
30    */
31    public void stop()
32    {
33        if (!isRunning) return;
34        isRunning = false;
35        long endTime = System.currentTimeMillis();
36        elapsedTime = elapsedTime + endTime - startTime;
37    }
38
39    /**
40        Returns the total elapsed time.
41        @return  the total elapsed time
42    */
43    public long getElapsedTime()
44    {
45        if (isRunning)
46        {
47            long endTime = System.currentTimeMillis();
48            elapsedTime = elapsedTime + endTime - startTime;
49            startTime = endTime;
50        }
51        return elapsedTime;
52    }
53
54    /**
55        Stops the watch and resets the elapsed time to 0.
56    */
57    public void reset()
```

```
58    {
59        elapsedTime = 0;
60        isRunning = false;
61    }
62
63    private long elapsedTime;
64    private long startTime;
65    private boolean isRunning;
66 }
```

Here is how we will use the stopwatch to measure the performance of the sorting algorithm:

File SelectionSortTimer.java

```
1  import javax.swing.JOptionPane;
2
3  /**
4      This program measures how long it takes to sort an
5      array of a user-specified size with the selection
6      sort algorithm.
7  */
8  public class SelectionSortTimer
9  {
10     public static void main(String[] args)
11     {
12        String input = JOptionPane.showInputDialog(
13           "Enter array size:");
14        int n = Integer.parseInt(input);
15
16        // construct random array
17
18        int[] a = ArrayUtil.randomIntArray(n, 100);
19        SelectionSorter sorter = new SelectionSorter(a);
20
21        // use stopwatch to time selection sort
22
23        StopWatch timer = new StopWatch();
24
25        timer.start();
26        sorter.sort();
27        timer.stop();
28
29        System.out.println("Elapsed time: "
30           + timer.getElapsedTime() + " milliseconds");
31        System.exit(0);
32     }
33 }
```

By starting to measure the time just before sorting, and stopping the stopwatch just afterwards, you don't count the time it takes to initialize the array or the time during which the program waits for the user to type in n.

Figure 1

Time Taken by Selection
Sort

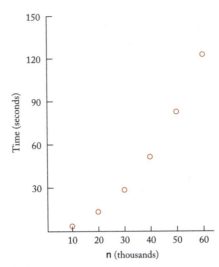

Here are the results of some sample runs:

n	Milliseconds
10,000	3,460
20,000	13,240
30,000	28,290
40,000	51,520
50,000	82,670
60,000	121,820

These measurements were obtained with a Pentium processor with a clock speed of
166 MHz, with 96MB of memory, and running Windows 98. On another computer the
actual numbers will look different, but the relationship between the numbers will be the
same. Figure 1 shows a plot of the measurements. As you can see, doubling the size of
the data set more than doubles the time needed to sort it.

18.3 Analyzing the Performance of the Selection Sort Algorithm

Let us count the number of operations that the program must carry out to sort an array by
the selection sort algorithm. We don't actually know how many machine operations are
generated for each Java instruction or which of those instructions are more time-consuming
than others, but we can make a simplification. We will simply count how often an array element is *visited*. Each visit requires about the same amount of work by other operations, such
as incrementing subscripts and comparing values.

Let n be size of the array. First, we must find the smallest of n numbers. To achieve that, we must visit n array elements. Then we swap the elements, which takes 2 visits. (You may argue that there is a certain probability that we don't need to swap the values. That is true, and one can refine the computation to reflect that observation. As we will soon see, doing so would not affect the overall conclusion.) In the next step, we need to visit only $n - 1$ elements to find the minimum. In the following step, $n - 2$ elements are visited to find the minimum. The last step visits two elements to find the minimum. Each step requires 2 visits to swap the elements. Therefore, the total number of visits is

$$n + 2 + (n - 1) + 2 + \cdots + 2 + 2$$
$$= n + (n - 1) + \cdots + 2 + (n - 1) \cdot 2$$
$$= 2 + \cdots + (n - 1) + n + (n - 1) \cdot 2$$
$$= \frac{n \cdot (n + 1)}{2} - 1 + (n - 1) \cdot 2$$

because

$$1 + 2 + \cdots + (n - 1) + n = \frac{n \cdot (n + 1)}{2}$$

After multiplying out and collecting terms of n, we find that the number of visits is

$$\tfrac{1}{2} \cdot n^2 + \tfrac{1}{2} \cdot n - 3$$

We obtain a quadratic equation in n. That explains why the graph of Figure 1 looks approximately like a parabola.

Now let us simplify the analysis further. When you plug in a large value for n (for example, 1000 or 2000), then $\tfrac{1}{2} \cdot n^2$ is 500,000 or 2,000,000. The lower term, $\tfrac{5}{2} \cdot n - 3$, doesn't contribute much at all; it is just 2497 or 4997, a drop in the bucket compared to the hundreds of thousands or even millions of comparisons specified by the $\tfrac{1}{2} \cdot n^2$ term. We will just ignore these lower-level terms. Next, we will ignore the constant factor $\tfrac{1}{2}$. We are not interested in the actual count of visits for a single n. We want to compare the ratios of counts for different values of n. For example, we can say that sorting an array of 2000 numbers requires 4 times as many visits as sorting an array of 1000 numbers:

$$\frac{\tfrac{1}{2} \cdot 2000^2}{\tfrac{1}{2} \cdot 1000^2} = 4$$

> Computer scientists use the big-Oh notation $f(n) = O(g(n))$ to express that the function f grows no faster than the function g.

The factor cancels out in comparisons of this kind. We will simply say, "The number of visits is of order n^2". That way, we can easily see that the number of comparisons increases fourfold when the size of the array doubles: $(2n)^2 = 4n^2$.

To indicate that the number of visits is of order n^2, computer scientists often use *big-Oh notation:* The number of visits is $O(n^2)$. This is a convenient shorthand.

In general, the expression $f(n) = O(g(n))$ means that f grows no faster than g, or, more formally, that for all n larger than some threshold, the ratio $f(n)/g(n) \le C$ for some constant value C. The function g is usually chosen to be very simple, such as n^2 in our example.

To turn an exact expression like

$$\tfrac{1}{2} \cdot n^2 + \tfrac{5}{2} \cdot n - 3$$

into big-Oh notation, simply locate the fastest-growing term, n^2, and ignore its constant coefficient, no matter how large or small it may be.

We observed before that the actual number of machine operations, and the actual number of microseconds that the computer spends on them, is approximately proportional to the number of element visits. Maybe there are about 10 machine operations (increments, comparisons, memory loads and stores) for every element visit. The number of machine operations is then approximately $10 \cdot \frac{1}{2} \cdot n^2$. Again, we aren't interested in the coefficient, so we can say that the number of machine operations, and hence the time spent on the sorting, is of the order of n^2 or $O(n^2)$.

> Selection sort is an $O(n^2)$ algorithm. Doubling the data set means a fourfold increase in processing time.

The sad fact remains that doubling the size of the array causes a fourfold increase in the time required for sorting it with selection sort. When the size of the array increases by a factor of 100, the sorting time increases by a factor of 10,000. To sort an array of a million entries (for example, to create a telephone directory) takes 10,000 times as long as sorting 10,000 entries. If 10,000 entries can be sorted in 3.5 seconds (as in our example), then a million entries require over 9 hours. That is a problem. We will see in the next section how one can dramatically improve the performance of the sorting process by choosing a more sophisticated algorithm.

18.4   Merge Sort

Suppose we have an array of 10 integers. Let us engage in a bit of wishful thinking and hope that the first half of the array is already perfectly sorted, and the second half is too, like this:

Now it is an easy matter to *merge* the two sorted arrays into a sorted array, simply by taking a new element from either the first or the second subarray, choosing the smaller of the elements each time:

In fact, you probably performed this merging before when you and a friend had to sort a pile of papers. You and the friend split up the pile in the middle, each of you sorted your half, and then you merged the results together.

That is all good and well, but it doesn't seem to solve the problem for the computer. It still has to sort the first and the second half of the array, because it can't very well ask a few buddies to pitch in. As it turns out, though, if the computer keeps dividing the array into smaller and smaller subarrays, sorting each half and merging them back together, it carries out dramatically fewer steps than the selection sort requires.

> The merge sort algorithm sorts an array by cutting the array in half, recursively sorting each half, and then merging the sorted halves.

Let us write a `MergeSorter` class that implements this idea. When the `MergeSorter` sorts an array, it makes two arrays, each half the size of the original, and sorts them recursively. Then it merges the two sorted arrays together:

```
public void sort()
{
    if (a.length <= 1) return;
    int[] first = new int[a.length / 2];
    int[] second = new int[a.length - first.length];
    System.arraycopy(a, 0, first, 0, first.length);
    System.arraycopy(a,
        first.length, second, 0, second.length);
    MergeSorter firstSorter = new MergeSorter(first);
    MergeSorter secondSorter = new MergeSorter(second);
    firstSorter.sort();
    secondSorter.sort();
    merge(first, second);
}
```

The `merge` method is tedious but quite straightforward. You will find it in the code at the end of this section.

File MergeSorter.java

```
 1  /**
 2      This class sorts an array, using the merge sort algorithm.
 3  */
 4  public class MergeSorter
 5  {
 6      /**
 7          Constructs a merge sorter.
 8          @param anArray the array to sort
 9      */
10      public MergeSorter(int[] anArray)
11      {
12          a = anArray;
13      }
14
15      /**
16          Sorts the array managed by this merge sorter.
17      */
18      public void sort()
19      {
20          if (a.length <= 1) return;
21          int[] first = new int[a.length / 2];
22          int[] second = new int[a.length - first.length];
```

```
23          System.arraycopy(a, 0, first, 0, first.length);
24          System.arraycopy(a,
25             first.length, second, 0, second.length);
26          MergeSorter firstSorter = new MergeSorter(first);
27          MergeSorter secondSorter = new MergeSorter(second);
28          firstSorter.sort();
29          secondSorter.sort();
30          merge(first, second);
31       }
32
33       /**
34          Merges two sorted arrays into the array to be sorted by this
35          merge sorter.
36          @param first the first sorted array
37          @param second the second sorted array
38       */
39       private void merge(int[] first, int[] second)
40       {
41          // merge both halves into the temporary array
42
43          int iFirst = 0;
44             // next element to consider in the first array
45          int iSecond = 0;
46             // next element to consider in the second array
47          int j = 0;
48             // next open position in a
49
50          // as long as neither i1 nor i2 past the end, move
51          // the smaller element into a
52          while (iFirst < first.length
53             && iSecond < second.length)
54          {
55             if (first[iFirst] < second[iSecond])
56             {
57                a[j] = first[iFirst];
58                iFirst++;
59             }
60             else
61             {
62                a[j] = second[iSecond];
63                iSecond++;
64             }
65             j++;
66          }
67
68          // Note that only one of the two while loops
69          // below is executed.
70
71          // Copy any remaining entries of the first array.
72          System.arraycopy(first,
73             iFirst, a, j, first.length - iFirst);
74
```

```
75          // Copy any remaining entries of the second half.
76          System.arraycopy(second,
77             iSecond, a, j, second.length - iSecond);
78       }
79
80    private int[] a;
81 }
```

File MergeSortTest.java

```
1  /**
2     This program tests the merge sort algorithm by
3     sorting an array that is filled with random numbers.
4  */
5  public class MergeSortTest
6  {
7     public static void main(String[] args)
8     {
9        int[] a = ArrayUtil.randomIntArray(20, 100);
10       ArrayUtil.print(a);
11       MergeSorter sorter = new MergeSorter(a);
12       sorter.sort();
13       ArrayUtil.print(a);
14    }
15 }
```

18.5   Analyzing the Merge Sort Algorithm

The merge sort algorithm looks a lot more complicated than the selection sort algorithm, and it appears that it may well take much longer to carry out these repeated subdivisions. However, the timing results for merge sort look much better than those for selection sort:

n	Merge sort (milliseconds)	Selection sort (milliseconds)
10,000	110	3,460
20,000	160	13,240
30,000	220	28,290
40,000	280	51,520
50,000	360	82,670
60,000	450	121,820

Figure 2 shows a graph comparing both sets of performance data. That is a tremendous improvement. To understand why, let us estimate the number of array element visits that are required to sort an array with the merge sort algorithm. First, let us tackle the merge process that happens after the first and second half have been sorted.

Figure 2

Merge Sort Timing (Rectangles) versus Selection Sort (Circles)

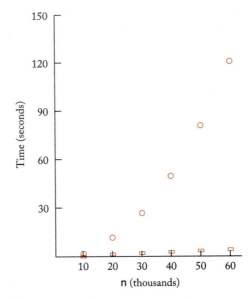

Each step in the merge process adds one more element to **a**. That element may come from **first** or **second**, and in most cases the elements from the two halves must be compared to see which one to take. Let us count that as 3 visits (one for **a** and one each for **first** and **second**) per element, or $3n$ visits total, where n denotes the length of **a**. Moreover, at the beginning, we had to copy from **a** to **first** and **second**, yielding another $2n$ visits, for a total of $5n$.

If we let $T(n)$ denote the number of visits required to sort a range of n elements through the merge sort process, then we obtain

$$T(n) = T\left(\frac{n}{2}\right) + T\left(\frac{n}{2}\right) + 5n$$

because sorting each half takes $T(n/2)$ visits. Actually, if n is not even, then we have one subarray of size $(n - 1)/2$ and one of size $(n + 1)/2$. Although it turns out that this detail does not affect the outcome of the computation, we will nevertheless assume for now that n is a power of 2, say $n = 2^m$. That way, all subarrays can be evenly divided into two parts.

Unfortunately, the formula

$$T(n) = 2T\left(\frac{n}{2}\right) + 5n$$

does not clearly tell us the relationship between n and $T(n)$. To understand the relationship, let us evaluate $T(n/2)$, using the same formula:

$$T\left(\frac{n}{2}\right) = 2T\left(\frac{n}{4}\right) + 5\frac{n}{2}$$

Therefore

$$T(n) = 2 \times 2T\left(\frac{n}{4}\right) + 5n + 5n$$

Let us do that again:

$$T\left(\frac{n}{4}\right) = 2T\left(\frac{n}{8}\right) + 5\frac{n}{4}$$

hence

$$T(n) = 2 \times 2 \times 2T\left(\frac{n}{8}\right) + 5n + 5n$$

This generalizes from 2, 4, 8, to arbitrary powers of 2:

$$T(n) = 2^k T\left(\frac{n}{2^k}\right) + 5nk$$

Recall that we assume that $n = 2^m$; hence, for $k = m$,

$$T(n) = 2^m T\left(\frac{n}{2^m}\right) + 5nk$$

$$= nT(1) + 5nm$$

$$= n + 5n \log_2(n)$$

Because $n = 2^m$, we have $m = \log_2(n)$.

To establish the growth order, we drop the lower-order term n and are left with $5n \log_2(n)$. We drop the constant factor 5. It is also customary to drop the base of the logarithm, because all logarithms are related by a constant factor. For example,

$$\log_2(x) = \log_{10}(x) / \log_{10}(2) \approx \log_{10}(x) \times 3.32193$$

> Merge sort is an $O(n \log (n))$ algorithm. The $n \log (n)$ function grows much more slowly than n^2.

Hence we say that merge sort is an $O(n \log(n))$ algorithm.

Is the $O(n \log(n))$ merge sort algorithm better than an $O(n^2)$ selection sort algorithm? You bet it is. Recall that it took $100^2 = 10,000$ times as long to sort a million records as it took to sort 10,000 records with the $O(n^2)$ algorithm. With the $O(n \log(n))$ algorithm, the ratio is

$$\frac{1,000,000 \log(1,000,000)}{10,000 \log(10,000)} = 100 \cdot \left(\frac{6}{4}\right) = 150$$

Suppose for the moment that merge sort takes the same time as selection sort to sort an array of 10,000 integers, that is, 3.5 seconds on the test machine. (Actually, it is much faster than that.) Then it would take about 3.5×150 seconds, or about 9 minutes, to sort a million integers. Contrast that with selection sort, which would take over 9 hours for the same task. As you can see, even if it takes you nine hours to learn about a better algorithm, that can be time well spent.

> The `Arrays` class implements a sorting method that you should use for your Java programs.

In this chapter we have barely begun to scratch the surface of this interesting topic. There are many sorting algorithms, some with even better performance than the merge sort algorithm, and the analysis of these algorithms can be quite challenging. If you are a computer science major, you will revisit these important issues in a later computer science class.

However, when you write Java programs, you don't have to implement your own sorting algorithm. The `Arrays` class contains static `sort` methods to sort arrays of integers and floating-point numbers. For example, you can sort an array of integers simply as

```
int[] a = . . .;
Arrays.sort(a);
```

That **sort** method uses the Quicksort algorithm—see Advanced Topic 18.1 for more information about that algorithm.

Random Fact   18.1

The First Programmer

Before pocket calculators and personal computers existed, navigators and engineers used mechanical adding machines, slide rules, and tables of logarithms and trigonometric functions to speed up computations. Unfortunately, the tables—whose values had to be computed by hand—were notoriously inaccurate. The mathematician Charles Babbage (1791–1871) had the insight that if a machine could be constructed that produced printed tables automatically, both calculation and typesetting errors could be avoided. Babbage set out to develop a machine for this purpose, which he called a *Difference Engine* because it used successive differences to compute polynomials. For example, consider the function $f(x) = x^3$. Write down the values for $f(1)$, $f(2)$, $f(3)$, and so on. Then take the *differences* between successive values:

```
  1
        7
  8
        19
 27
        37
 64
        61
125
        91
216
```

Repeat the process, taking the difference of successive values in the second column, and then repeat once again:

```
  1
        7
  8          12
        19          6
 27          18
        37          6
 64          24
        61          6
125          30
        91
216
```

Now the differences are constant. You can retrieve the function values by a pattern of additions—you need to know the values at the fringe of the pattern and the constant difference. This method was very attractive, because mechanical addition machines had been known for some time. They consisted of cog wheels, with ten cogs per wheel, to represent digits, and mechanisms to handle the carry from one digit to the next. Mechanical multiplication machines, on the other hand, were fragile and unreliable. Babbage built a successful prototype of the Difference Engine (see Figure 3) and, with his own money and government grants, proceeded to build the table-printing machine. However, because of funding problems and the difficulty of building the machine to the required precision, it was never completed.

While working on the Difference Engine, Babbage conceived of a much grander vision that he called the *Analytical Engine*. The Difference Engine was designed to carry out a limited set of computations—it was no smarter than a pocket calculator is today. But Babbage realized that such a machine could be made *programmable* by storing programs as well as data. The internal storage of the Analytical Engine was to consist of

Figure 3

Babbage's Difference Engine

1,000 registers of 50 decimal digits each. Programs and constants were to be stored on punched cards—a technique that was at that time commonly used on looms for weaving patterned fabrics.

Ada Augusta, Countess of Lovelace (1815–1852), the only child of Lord Byron, was a friend and sponsor of Charles Babbage. Ada Lovelace was one of the first people to realize the potential of such a machine, not just for computing mathematical tables but for processing data that were not numbers. She is considered by many the world's first programmer. The Ada programming language, a language developed for use in U.S. Department of Defense projects (see Random Fact 10.1), was named in her honor.

Advanced Topic   18.1

The Quicksort Algorithm

Quicksort is a commonly used algorithm that has the advantage over merge sort that no temporary arrays are required to sort and merge the partial results.

The quicksort algorithm, like merge sort, is based on the strategy of divide and conquer. To sort a range a[from] . . . a[to] of the array a, first rearrange the elements in the range so that no element in the range a[from] . . . a[p] is larger than any element in the range a[p + 1] . . . a[to]. This step is called *partitioning* the range.

For example, suppose we start with a range

| 5 | 3 | 2 | 6 | 4 | 1 | 3 | 7 |

Here is a partitioning of the range. Note that the partitions aren't yet sorted.

| 3 | 3 | 2 | 1 | 4 | | 6 | 5 | 7 |

You'll see later how to obtain such a partition. In the next step, sort each partition, by recursively applying the same algorithm on the two partitions. That sorts the entire range, because the largest element in the first partition is at most as large as the smallest element in the second partition.

| 1 | 2 | 3 | 3 | 4 | | 5 | 6 | 7 |

Quicksort is implemented recursively as follows:

```
public void sort(int from, int to)
{
   if (from >= to) return;
   int p = partition(from, to);
   sort(from, p);
   sort(p + 1, to);
}
```

Let us return to the problem of partitioning a range. Pick an element from the range and call it the *pivot*. There are several variations of the quicksort algorithm. In the simplest one, we'll pick the first element of the range, a[from], as the pivot.

Figure 4

Partitioning a Range

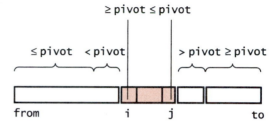

Figure 5

Extending the Partitions

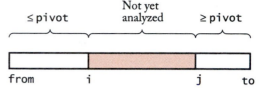

Now form two regions a[from] . . . a[i], consisting of values at most as large as the pivot and a[j] . . . a[to], consisting of values at least as large as the pivot. The region a[i + 1] . . . a[j - 1] consists of values that haven't been analyzed yet. (See Figure 4.) At the beginning, both the left and right areas are empty; that is, i = from - 1 and j = to + 1.

Then keep incrementing i while a[i] < pivot and keep decrementing j while a[j] > pivot. Figure 5 shows i and j when that process stops.

Now swap the values in positions i and j, increasing both areas once more. Keep going while i < j. Here is the code for the partition method:

```
private int partition(int from, int to)
{
   int pivot = a[from];
   int i = from - 1;
   int j = to + 1;
   while (i < j)
   {
      i++; while (a[i] < pivot) i++;
      j--; while (a[j] > pivot) j--;
      if (i < j) swap(i, j);
   }
   return j;
}
```

On average, the quicksort algorithm is an $O(n \log(n))$ algorithm. Because it is simpler, it runs faster than merge sort in most cases. There is just one unfortunate aspect to the quicksort algorithm. Its *worst-case* runtime behavior is $O(n^2)$. Moreover, if the pivot element is chosen as the first element of the region, that worst-case behavior occurs when the input set is already sorted—a common situation in practice. By selecting the pivot element more cleverly, we can make it extremely unlikely for the worst-case behavior to occur. Such "tuned" quicksort algorithms are commonly used, because their performance

▼

is generally excellent. For example, as was mentioned, the `sort` method in the `Arrays` class uses a quicksort algorithm.

18.6   ## Searching

Suppose you need to find the telephone number of your friend. You look up his name in the telephone book, and naturally you can find it quickly, because the telephone book is sorted alphabetically. Quite possibly, you may never have thought how important it is that the telephone book is sorted. To see that, think of the following problem: Suppose you have a telephone number and you must know to what party it belongs. You could of course call that number, but suppose nobody picks up on the other end. You could look through the telephone book, a number at a time, until you find the number. That would obviously be a tremendous amount of work, and you would have to be desperate to attempt that.

> A linear search examines all values in an array until it finds a match or reaches the end.

This thought experiment shows the difference between a search through an unsorted data set and a search through a sorted data set. The following two sections will analyze the difference formally.

If you want to find a number in a sequence of values that occur in arbitrary order, there is nothing you can do to speed up the search. You must simply look through all elements until you have found a match or until you reach the end. This is called a *linear* or *sequential search*.

> A linear search locates a value in an array in $O(n)$ steps.

How long does a linear search take? If we assume that the element v is present in the array a, then the average search visits $n/2$ elements, where n is the length of the array. If it is not present, then all n elements must be inspected to verify the absence. Either way, a linear search is an $O(n)$ algorithm.

Here is a class that performs linear searches through an array a of integers. When searching for the value v, the `search` method returns the first index of the match, or −1 if v does not occur in a.

File LinearSearcher.java

```
1   /**
2       A class for executing linear searches through an array.
3   */
4   public class LinearSearcher
5   {
6       /**
7           Constructs the LinearSearcher.
8           @param anArray  an array of integers
9       */
10      public LinearSearcher(int[] anArray)
11      {
12          a = anArray;
13      }
```

```
14
15    /**
16        Finds a value in an array, using the linear search algorithm.
17        @param v the value to search
18        @return the index at which the value occurs, or -1
19            if it does not occur in the array
20    */
21    public int search(int v)
22    {
23        for (int i = 0; i < a.length; i++)
24        {
25            if (a[i] == v)
26                return i;
27        }
28        return -1;
29    }
30
31    private int[] a;
32 }
```

File LinearSearchTest.java

```
1  import javax.swing.JOptionPane;
2
3  /**
4      This program tests the linear search algorithm.
5  */
6  public class LinearSearchTest
7  {
8      public static void main(String[] args)
9      {
10         // construct random array
11
12         int[] a = ArrayUtil.randomIntArray(20, 100);
13         ArrayUtil.print(a);
14         LinearSearcher searcher = new LinearSearcher(a);
15
16         boolean done = false;
17         while (!done)
18         {
19             String input = JOptionPane.showInputDialog(
20                 "Enter number to search for, "
21                 + "Cancel to quit:");
22             if (input == null)
23                 done = true;
24             else
25             {
26                 int n = Integer.parseInt(input);
27                 int pos = searcher.search(n);
28                 System.out.println(
```

```
29                    "Found in position " + pos);
30             }
31         }
32         System.exit(0);
33     }
34 }
```

18.7 Binary Search

Now let us search an item in a data sequence that had been previously sorted. Of course, we could still do a linear search, but it turns out we can do much better than that.

Consider the following example: The data set is

a[0]	a[1]	a[2]	a[3]	a[4]	a[5]	a[6]	a[7]
14	43	76	100	115	290	400	511

We would like to see whether the value 123 is in the data set. Let's narrow our search by finding whether the value is in the first or second half of the array. The last point in the first half of the data set, a[3], is 100, which is smaller than the value we are looking for. Hence, we should look in the second half of the array for a match, that is, in the sequence

a[4]	a[5]	a[6]	a[7]
115	290	400	411

Now the last value of the first half of this sequence is 290; hence, the value must be located in the sequence

a[4]	a[5]
115	290

The last value of the first half of this very short sequence is 115, which is smaller than the value that we are searching, so we must look in the second half:

a[5]
290

> A binary search locates a value in a sorted array by determining whether the value occurs in the first or second half, then repeating the search in one of the halves.

It is trivial to see that we don't have a match, because 123 ≠ 290. If we wanted to insert 123 into the sequence, we would need to insert it just before a[5].

This search process is called a *binary search*, because we cut the size of the search in half in each step. That cutting in half works only because we know that the sequence of values is sorted.

The following class implements binary searches in a sorted array of integers. The search method returns the position of the match if the search succeeds, or −1 if v is not found in a:

File BinarySearcher.java

```
1 /**
2     A class for executing binary searches through an array.
3 */
```

```
 4  public class BinarySearcher
 5  {
 6     /**
 7        Constructs a BinarySearcher.
 8        @param anArray a sorted array of integers
 9     */
10     public BinarySearcher(int[] anArray)
11     {
12        a = anArray;
13     }
14
15     /**
16        Finds a value in a sorted array, using the binary
17        search algorithm.
18        @param v the value to search
19        @return the index at which the value occurs, or −1
20        if it does not occur in the array
21     */
22     public int search(int v)
23     {
24        int low = 0;
25        int high = a.length - 1;
26        while (low <= high)
27        {
28           int mid = (low + high) / 2;
29           int diff = a[mid] - v;
30
31           if (diff == 0) // a[mid] == v
32              return mid;
33           else if (diff < 0) // a[mid] < v
34              low = mid + 1;
35           else
36              high = mid - 1;
37        }
38        return -1;
39     }
40
41     private int[] a;
42  }
```

Let us determine the number of visits of array elements required to carry out a search. We can use the same technique as in the analysis of merge sort. Since we look at the middle element, which counts as one comparison, and then search either the left or the right subarray, we have

$$T(n) = T\left(\frac{n}{2}\right) + 1$$

Using the same equation,

$$T\left(\frac{n}{2}\right) = T\left(\frac{n}{4}\right) + 1$$

By plugging this result into the original equation, we get

$$T(n) = T\left(\frac{n}{4}\right) + 2$$

That generalizes to

$$T(n) = T\left(\frac{n}{2^k}\right) + k$$

As in the analysis of merge sort, we make the simplifying assumption that n is a power of 2, $n = 2^m$, where $m = \log_2(n)$. Then we obtain

$$T(n) = 1 + \log_2(n)$$

Therefore, binary search is an $O(\log(n))$ algorithm.

> A binary search locates a value in an array in $O(\log(n))$ steps.

That result makes intuitive sense. Suppose that n is 100. Then after each search, the size of the search range is cut in half, to 50, 25, 12, 6, 3, and 1. After seven comparisons we are done. This agrees with our formula, since $\log_2(100) \approx 6.64386$, and indeed the next larger power of 2 is $2^7 = 128$.

Since a binary search is so much faster than a linear search, is it worthwhile to sort an array first and then use a binary search? It depends. If you search the array only once, then it is more efficient to pay for an $O(n)$ linear search than for an $O(n \log(n))$ sort and an $O(\log(n))$ binary search. But if you will be making many searches in the same array, then sorting it is definitely worthwhile.

The `Arrays` class contains a static `binarySearch` method that implements the binary search algorithm, but with a useful enhancement. If a value is not found in the array, then the returned value is not -1, but $-k - 1$, where k is the position before which the element should be inserted. For example,

```
int[] a = { 1, 4, 9 };
int v = 7;
int pos = Arrays.binarySearch(a, v);
   // returns -3; v should be inserted before position 2
```

18.8   Searching and Sorting Real Data

In this chapter we have studied how to search and sort arrays of integers. Of course, in real programming there is rarely a need to search through a collection of integers. However, it is easy to modify these techniques to search through real data.

The `Arrays` class contains methods for sorting and searching collections of objects. You can sort objects of any class that implements the `Comparable` interface. That interface has a single method:

```
public interface Comparable
{
   int compareTo(Object otherObject);
}
```

The call

```
a.compareTo(b)
```

must return a negative number if a should come before b, 0 if a and b are the same, and a positive number otherwise.

Several classes in the standard Java library, such as the `String` and `Date` classes, implement the `Comparable` interface.

You can implement the `Comparable` interface for your own classes as well. For example, to sort a collection of bank accounts, the `BankAccount` class would need to implement this interface and define a `compareTo` method:

```java
public class BankAccount
{
   . . .
   public int compareTo(Object otherObject)
   {
      BankAccount other = (BankAccount)other;
      if (balance < other.balance) return -1;
      if (balance == other.balance) return 0;
      return 1;
   }
   . . .
}
```

When you implement the `compareTo` method of the `Comparable` interface, you must make sure that the method defines a *total ordering relationship*, with the following three properties:

- *Antisymmetric:* sign(x.compareTo(y)) = −sign(y.compareTo(x))

- *Reflexive:* x.compareTo(x) = 0

- *Transitive:* If x.compareTo(y) ≤ 0 and y.compareTo(z) ≤ 0, then x.compareTo(z)≤ 0

> The `Arrays` class contains a sort method that can sort arrays of objects that implement the `Comparable` interface.

The `Arrays` class implements both sorting and binary search for arrays of objects that implement the `Comparable` interface. Thus, you can easily sort and search arrays of strings. If you are willing to implement the `Comparable` interface in your own classes, then you can also sort and search arrays of objects.

```java
BankAccount[] accounts = . . .;
Arrays.sort(accounts);
```

> The `Arrays` class contains another sort method that requires a `Comparator` object. That method can sort arrays of arbitrary objects.

However, sometimes it is impossible for you to modify a class so that it implements the `Comparable` interface. If you don't own the class, or if you already implemented the `Comparable` interface but you want to sort the objects in a different way, then you need to use an alternate approach. Define a class that realizes the *strategy interface* `Comparator`.

```
public interface Comparator
{
   public int compare(
      Object firstObject, Object secondObject);
}
```

If `comp` is a comparator object, then the call

```
comp.compare(a, b)
```

must return a negative number if `a` should come before `b`, 0 if `a` and `b` are the same, and a positive number otherwise.

For example, here is a `Comparator` class for coins:

```
public class CoinComparator implements Comparator
{
   public int compare(
      Object firstObject, Object secondObject)
   {
      Coin first = (Coin)firstObject;
      Coin second = (Coin)secondObject;
      if (first.getValue() < second.getValue())
         return -1;
      if (first.getValue() == second.getValue())
         return 0;
      return 1;
   }
}
```

Then you can sort an array of coins like this:

```
Coin[] a = . . .;
Comparator comp = new CoinComparator();
Arrays.sort(a, comp);
```

> The `Collections` class contains `sort` methods that can sort array lists.

The `Coin` class does not have to implement the `Comparable` interface.

Finally, the `Collections` class contains static `sort` and `binarySearch` methods that work with `ArrayList` collections.

```
ArrayList coins = new ArrayList();
// add coins
. . .
Comparator comp = new CoinComparator();
Collections.sort(coins, comp);
```

This `sort` method uses the merge sort algorithm. The example at the end of this section shows a `Purse` class whose `toString` method sorts the coins in the purse by increasing value.

As a practical matter, you should use the sorting and searching methods in the `Arrays` and `Collections` classes and not those that you write yourself. The library algorithms have been fully debugged and optimized. Thus, the primary purpose of this chapter was not to teach you how to implement practical sorting and searching algorithms.

Instead, you have learned something more important, namely that different algorithms can vary widely in performance, and that it is worthwhile to learn more about the design and analysis of algorithms.

File Purse.java

```
1  import javax.swing.JOptionPane;
2
3  /**
4     This class tests the Purse class by prompting the
5     user to add coins into a purse and printing the
6     purse contents, sorted by coin value.
7  */
8  public class PurseTest
9  {
10    public static void main(String[] args)
11    {
12       double NICKEL_VALUE = 0.05;
13       double DIME_VALUE = 0.1;
14       double QUARTER_VALUE = 0.25;
15
16       Purse myPurse = new Purse();
17
18       boolean done = false;
19       while (!done)
20       {
21          String input = JOptionPane.showInputDialog(
22                "Enter coin name or Cancel");
23          if (input == null)
24             done = true;
25          else
26          {
27             double value = 0;
28             if (input.equals("nickel"))
29                value = NICKEL_VALUE;
30             else if (input.equals("dime"))
31                value = DIME_VALUE;
32             else if (input.equals("quarter"))
33                value = QUARTER_VALUE;
34             if (value != 0)
35             {
36                Coin c = new Coin(value, input);
37                myPurse.add(c);
38                System.out.println(
39                   "The contents of the purse is "
40                   + myPurse);
41             }
42          }
43       }
```

```
44        System.exit(0);
45    }
46 }
```

CHAPTER SUMMARY

1. The selection sort algorithm sorts an array by repeatedly finding the smallest element of the unsorted tail region and moving it to the front.

2. Computer scientists use the big-Oh notation $f(n) = O(g(n))$ to express that the function f grows no faster than the function g.

3. Selection sort is an $O(n^2)$ algorithm. Doubling the data set means a fourfold increase in processing time.

4. The merge sort algorithm sorts an array by cutting the array in half, recursively sorting each half, and then merging the sorted halves.

5. Merge sort is an $O(n \log(n))$ algorithm. The $n \log(n)$ function grows much more slowly than n^2.

6. The `Arrays` class implements a sorting method that you should use for your Java programs.

7. A linear search examines all values in an array until it finds a match or reaches the end.

8. A linear search locates a value in an array in $O(n)$ steps.

9. A binary search locates a value in a sorted array by determining whether the value occurs in the first or second half, then repeating the search in one of the halves.

10. A binary search locates a value in an array in $O(\log(n))$ steps.

11. The `Arrays` class contains a `sort` method that can sort arrays of objects that implement the `Comparable` interface.

12. The `Arrays` class contains another `sort` method that requires a `Comparator` object. That method can sort arrays of arbitrary objects.

13. The `Collections` class contains `sort` methods that can sort array lists.

Further Reading

[1] Michael T. Goodrich and Roberto Tamassia: *Data Structures and Algorithms in Java*, John Wiley & Sons, 1998.

CLASSES, OBJECTS, AND METHODS INTRODUCED IN THIS CHAPTER

```
java.lang.Comparable
    compareTo
java.lang.System
```

```
    currentTimeMillis
java.util.Arrays
    binarySearch
    sort
java.util.Collections
    binarySearch
    sort
java.util.Comparator
    compare
```

REVIEW EXERCISES

Exercise R18.1. *Checking against off-by-1 errors.* When writing the selection sort algorithm of Section 18.1, a programmer must make the usual choices of < against <=, a.length against a.length - 1, and from against from + 1. This is a fertile ground for off-by-1 errors. Conduct code walkthroughs of the algorithm with arrays of length 0, 1, 2, and 3 and check carefully that all index values are correct.

Exercise R18.2. What is the difference between searching and sorting?

Exercise R18.3. For the following expressions, what is the order of the growth of each?

$$n^2 + 2n + 1$$
$$n^{10} + 9n^9 + 20n^8 + 145n^7$$
$$(n + 1)^4$$
$$(n^2 + n)^2$$
$$n + 0.001n^3$$
$$n^3 - 1000n^2 + 10^9$$
$$n + \log(n)$$
$$n^2 + n \log(n)$$
$$2^n + n^2$$
$$\frac{n^3 + 2n}{n^2 + 0.75}$$

Exercise R18.4. We determined that the actual number of visits in the selection sort algorithm is

$$T(n) = \tfrac{1}{2}n^2 + \tfrac{5}{2}n - 3$$

We then characterized this method as having $O(n^2)$ growth. Compute the actual ratios

$$T(2000)/T(1000)$$
$$T(4000)/T(1000)$$
$$T(10000)/T(1000)$$

and compare them with

$$f(2000)/f(1000)$$
$$f(4000)/f(1000)$$
$$f(10000)/f(1000)$$

where $f(n) = n^2$.

Exercise R18.5. Suppose algorithm A takes 5 seconds to handle a data set of 1000 records. If the algorithm A is an $O(n)$ algorithm, how long will it take to handle a data set of 2000 records? Of 10,000 records?

Exercise R18.6. Suppose an algorithm takes 5 seconds to handle a data set of 1,000 records. Fill in the following table, which shows the approximate growth of the execution times depending on the complexity of the algorithm.

	$O(n)$	$O(n^2)$	$O(n^3)$	$O(n \log n)$	$O(2^n)$
1000	5	5	5	5	5
2000					
3000		45			
10000					

For example, since $3000^2/1000^2 = 9$, the algorithm would take 9 times as long, or 45 seconds, to handle a data set of 3000 records.

Exercise R18.7. Sort the following growth rates from slowest growth to fastest growth.

$O(n)$
$O(n^3)$
$O(n^n)$
$O(\log(n))$
$O(n^2 \log(n))$
$O(1)$
$O(n \log(n))$
$O(2^n)$
$O(\sqrt{n})$
$O(n\sqrt{n})$
$O(n^{\log(n)})$

Exercise R18.8. What is the growth rate of the standard algorithm to find the minimum value of an array? Of finding both the minimum and the maximum?

Exercise R18.9. What is the growth rate of the following method?

```
public static int count(int[] a, int c)
{
```

```
        int i;
        int count = 0;

        for (i = 0; i < a.length; i++)
        {
            if (a[i] == c) count++;
        }
        return count;
    }
```

Exercise R18.10. Your task is to remove all duplicates from an array. For example, if the array has the values

> 4 7 11 4 9 5 11 7 3 5

then the array should be changed to

> 4 7 11 9 5 3

Here is a simple algorithm. Look at a[i]. Count how many times it occurs in a. If the count is larger than 1, remove it. What is the growth rate of the time required for this algorithm?

Exercise R18.11. Consider the following algorithm to remove all duplicates from an array. Sort the array. For each element in the array, look at its next neighbor to decide whether it is present more than once. If so, remove it. Is this a faster algorithm than the one in the preceding exercise?

Exercise R18.12. Develop a fast algorithm for removing duplicates from an array if the resulting array must have the same ordering as the original array.

Exercise R18.13. *Insertion sort.* Consider the following sorting algorithm. To sort a, make a second array b of the same size. Then insert elements from a into b, keeping b in sorted order. Whenever you insert an element a[i] into the sorted range b[0] . . . b[i - 1], compare all elements until you find an element b[j] > a[i]. Then move the subrange b[j] . . . b[i - 1] by one position and insert a[i] into position j.

Is this an efficient algorithm? Estimate the number of array element visits in the sorting process. Assume that on average half of the elements of b need to be moved to insert a new element.

Exercise R18.14. Consider the following speedup of the insertion sort algorithm of the preceding exercise. For each element, call the binary search method of Exercise P18.7 to determine where it needs to be inserted. Does this speedup have a significant impact on the efficiency of the algorithm?

PROGRAMMING EXERCISES

Exercise P18.1. Modify the selection sort algorithm to sort an array of integers in descending order.

Exercise P18.2. Modify the selection sort algorithm to sort an array of coins by their value.

Exercise P18.3. Write a program that generates the table of sample runs of the selection sort times automatically. The program should ask for the smallest and largest value of n and the number of measurements and then make all sample runs.

Exercise P18.4. Modify the merge sort algorithm to sort an array of strings in lexicographic order.

Exercise P18.5. Write a telephone lookup program. Read a data set of 1000 names and telephone numbers from a file that contains the numbers in random order. Handle lookups by name and also reverse lookups by phone number. Use a binary search for both lookups.

Exercise P18.6. Implement the insertion sort algorithm described in Exercise R18.13.

Exercise P18.7. Modify the Purse class at the end of Section 18.8 so that the toString method lists the coins with the most valuable ones first.

Exercise P18.8. Consider the binary search algorithm in Section 18.7. If no match is found, the search method returns −1. Modify the method so that if a is not found, the method returns $-k - 1$, where k is the position before which the element should be inserted.

Exercise P18.9. Use the modification of the binary search method of the preceding exercise to sort an array as described in Exercise R18.14. Implement this algorithm and measure its performance.

Exercise P18.10. Implement the sort method of the merge sort algorithm without recursion, where the length of the array is a power of 2. First merge adjacent regions of size 1, then adjacent regions of size 2, then adjacent regions of size 4, and so on.

Exercise P18.11. Implement the sort method of the merge sort algorithm without recursion, where the length of the array is an arbitrary number. Keep merging adjacent regions whose size is a power of 2, and pay special attention to the last area whose size is less.

Exercise P18.12. Give a *graphical animation* of selection sort as follows: Fill an array with a set of random numbers between 1 and 100. Draw each array element as a stick, as in Figure 6. Whenever the algorithm changes the array, display an option pane and wait for the user to click OK, then call the repaint method.

Exercise P18.13. Write a graphical animation of merge sort.

Exercise P18.14. Write a graphical animation of binary search. Highlight the currently inspected element and the current values of from and to.

Exercise P18.15. Supply a class Person that implements the Comparable interface. Compare persons by their names. Ask the user to input ten names and generate ten Person objects. Using the compareTo method, determine the first and last person among them and print them.

Exercise P18.16. Sort an array list of strings by increasing *length*. *Hint:* Supply a Comparator.

Figure 6

Graphical Animation

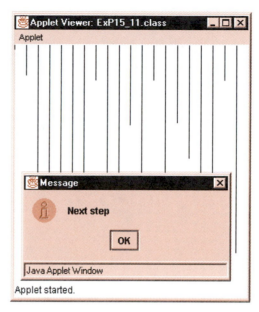

Exercise P18.17. Sort an array list of strings by increasing length, so that strings of the same length are sorted lexicographically. *Hint:* Supply a `Comparator`.

Exercise P18.18. Write a program that keeps an appointment book. Make a class `Appointment` that stores a description of the appointment, the appointment day, the starting time, and the ending time. Your program should keep the appointments in a sorted vector. Users can add appointments and print out all appointments for a given day. When a new appointment is added, use binary search to find where it should be inserted in the vector. Do not add it if it conflicts with another appointment.

An Introduction to Data Structures

CHAPTER GOALS

To learn how to use linked lists provided in the standard library

▶ To be able to use iterators to traverse linked lists

▶ To understand the implementation of linked lists

▶ To distinguish between abstract and concrete data types

▶ To know the efficiency of fundamental operations of lists and arrays

▶ To become familiar with the stack and queue types

Up to this point, we used ArrayList objects as a "one size fits all" mechanism for collecting objects. However, computer scientists have developed many different data structures that have varying performance tradeoffs. In this chapter, you will learn about the linked list, a data structure lets you add and remove elements efficiently, without moving any existing elements. You will also learn about the distinction between concrete and abstract data types. An abstract type spells out what fundamental operations should be supported efficiently, but it leaves the implementation unspecified. The stack and queue types, introduced at the end of this chapter, are examples of abstract types.

19.1   Using Linked Lists

Imagine a program that maintains an array of employee objects, sorted by the last names of the employees. When a new employee is hired, an object needs to be inserted into the array. Unless the company happened to hire employees in dictionary order, the new object probably needs to be inserted somewhere near the middle of the array. Then all objects following the new hire must be moved toward the end.

Conversely, if an employee leaves the company, the object must be removed, and the hole in the sequence needs to be closed up by moving all employee objects that come after it. Moving a large number of values can involve a substantial amount of computer time. We would like to discover a method that minimizes this cost.

> A linked list consists of a number of links, each of which has a reference to the next link.

> Adding and removing elements in the middle of a linked list is efficient.

To minimize movement of values, let us change the structure of the storage. Rather than storing the object references in an array, let us break up the array into a sequence of *links*. Each link stores an element and a reference to the next link in the sequence (see Figure 1). Such a data structure is called a *linked list*.

When you insert a new element into a linked list, only the neighboring link references need to be updated. The same is true when you remove an element.

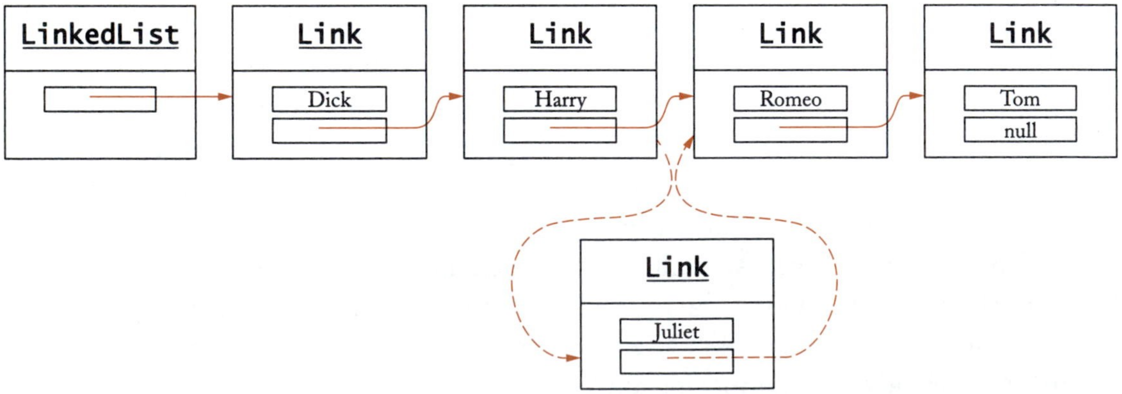

Figure 1

Inserting an Element Into a Linked List

Visiting the elements of a linked list in sequential order is efficient, but random access is not.

What's the catch? Linked lists allow speedy insertion and removal, but *element access* is slow. To locate the fifth element, you have to traverse the first four. This is a problem if you need to access the elements in random order. But if you mostly visit all elements in sequence (for example, to display or print the elements), the lack of random access is not a problem. You use linked lists when you are concerned about the efficiency of inserting or removing elements and you don't need element access in random order.

The Java library provides a linked-list class. In this section you will learn how to use this class. In the next section you will peek under the hood and see how some of its key methods are implemented.

The `LinkedList` class in the `java.util` package implements linked lists. This linked list remembers both the first and the last link in the list. You have easy access to both ends of the list with the methods

```
void addFirst(Object obj)
void addLast(Object obj)
Object getFirst()
Object getLast()
Object removeFirst()
Object removeLast()
```

How do you add and remove elements in the middle of the list? The list will not give you references to the links. If you had direct access to them and somehow messed them up, you would break the linked list. As you will see in the next section, where you implement some of the linked list operations yourself, keeping all links intact is not trivial.

You use a list iterator to access elements inside a linked list.

For your protection, the Java library supplies a `ListIterator` type. A list iterator encapsulates a position anywhere inside the linked list (see Figure 2).

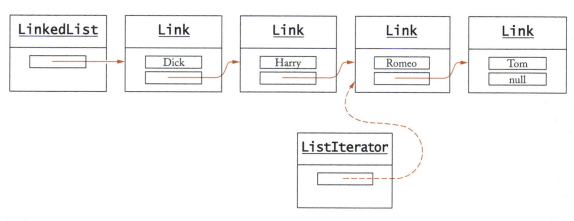

Figure 2

A List Iterator

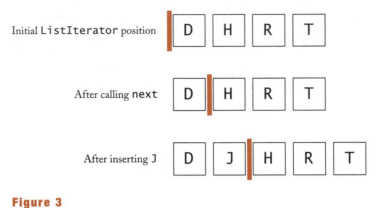

Initial `ListIterator` position

After calling `next`

After inserting J

Figure 3

A Conceptual View of the List Iterator

Conceptually, you should think of the iterator as pointing between two links, just as the cursor in a word processor points between two characters (see Figure 3). In the conceptual view, think of each link element as being like a letter in a word processor, and think of the iterator as being like the blinking cursor between letters.

You obtain a list iterator with the `listIterator` method of the `LinkedList` class:

```
LinkedList list = . . .;
ListIterator iterator = list.listIterator();
```

Initially, the iterator points before the first element. You can move the iterator position with the `next` method:

```
iterator.next();
```

The `next` method throws a `NoSuchElementException` if you are already past the end of the list. You should always call the method `hasNext` before calling `next`—it returns `true` if there is a next element.

```
if (iterator.hasNext())
   iterator.next();
```

The `next` method returns the object of the link that it is passing. Therefore, you can traverse all elements in a linked list with the following loop:

```
while (iterator.hasNext())
{
   Object obj = iterator.next();
   do something with obj
}
```

Actually, the links of the `LinkedList` class store two links: one to the next element and one to the previous one. Such a list is called a *doubly linked list*. You can use the `previous` and `hasPrevious` methods of the iterator class to move the list position backwards.

The **add** method adds an object after the iterator, and then moves the iterator position past the new element.

```
iterator.add("Juliet");
```

You can visualize insertion to be like typing text in a word processor. Each character is inserted after the cursor, and then the cursor moves past the inserted character (see Figure 3). Most people never pay much attention to this—you may want to try it out and watch carefully how your word processor inserts characters.

The **remove** method removes and returns the object that was returned by the last call to **next** or **previous**. For example, the following loop removes all objects that fulfill a certain condition:

```
while (iterator.hasNext())
{
   Object obj = iterator.next();
   if (obj fulfills condition)
      iterator.remove();
}
```

You have to be careful when calling **remove**. It can be called only once after calling **next** or **previous**, and you cannot call it immediately after a call to **add**. If you call the method improperly, it throws an **IllegalStateException**.

Here is a sample program that inserts elements into a list and then iterates through the list, adding and removing elements. Finally, the entire list is printed. The comments indicate the iterator position.

File ListTest.java

```
 1  import java.util.LinkedList;
 2  import java.util.ListIterator;
 3
 4  /**
 5     A program that demonstrates the LinkedList class.
 6  */
 7  public class ListTest
 8  {
 9     public static void main(String[] args)
10     {
11        LinkedList staff = new LinkedList();
12        staff.addLast("Dick");
13        staff.addLast("Harry");
14        staff.addLast("Romeo");
15        staff.addLast("Tom");
16
17        // | in the comments indicates the iterator position
18
19        ListIterator iterator =
20           staff.listIterator(); // |DHRT
21        iterator.next(); // D|HRT
22        iterator.next(); // DH|RT
```

```
23
24          // add more elements after second element
25
26          iterator.add("Juliet"); // DHJ|RT
27          iterator.add("Nina"); // DHJN|RT
28
29          iterator.next(); // DHJNR|T
30
31          // remove last traversed element
32
33          iterator.remove(); // DHJN|T
34
35          // print all elements
36
37          iterator = staff.listIterator();
38          while (iterator.hasNext())
39             System.out.println(iterator.next());
40       }
41 }
```

19.2 Implementing Linked Lists

In the last section you saw how to use the linked list class that is supplied by the Java library. In this section, we will look at the implementation of a simplified version of this class. This shows you how the list operations manipulate the links as the list is modified.

To keep this sample code simple, we will not implement all methods of the linked-list class. We will implement only a singly linked list, and the list class will supply direct access only to the first list element, not the last one. The result will be a fully functional list class that shows how the links are updated in the add and remove operations and how the iterator traverses the list.

A Link object stores an object and a reference to the next link. Because the methods of both the linked list class and the iterator class have frequent access to the Link instance variables, we do not make the instance variables private. Instead, we make Link a private inner class of the LinkedList class. Since none of the list methods returns a Link object, it is safe to leave the instance variables public.

```
class LinkedList
{  . . .
   private class Link
   {
      public Object data;
      public Link next;
   }
}
```

The LinkedList class holds a reference first to the first link (or null, if the list is completely empty).

```
class LinkedList
{
    public LinkedList()
    {
        first = null;
    }

    public Object getFirst()
    {
        if (first == null)
            throw new NoSuchElementException();
        return first.data;
    }


    . . .
    private Link first;
}
```

Now let us turn to the `addFirst` method (see Figure 4). When a new link is added to the list, it becomes the head of the list, and the link that was the old list head becomes its next link:

```
class LinkedList
{   . . .
    public void addFirst(Object obj)
    {
        Link newLink = new Link();
        newLink.data = obj;
        newLink.next = first;
        first = newLink;
    }
    . . .
}
```

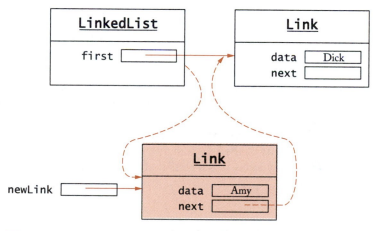

Figure 4

Adding a Link to the Head of a Linked List

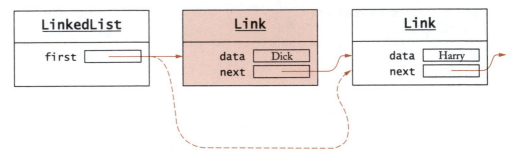

Figure 5

Removing the First Link from a Linked List

Removing the first element of the list works as follows. The data of the first link are saved and later returned as the method result. The successor of the first link becomes the first link of the shorter list (see Figure 5). Then there are no further references to the old link, and the garbage collector will eventually recycle it.

```
class LinkedList
{   . . .
    public Object removeFirst()
    {
        if (first == null)
            throw new NoSuchElementException();
        Object obj = first.data;
        first = first.next;
        return obj;
    }
    . . .
}
```

Next, let us turn to the iterator class. The `ListIterator` interface in the standard library defines nine methods. We omit four of them (the methods that move the iterator backwards and the methods that report an integer index of the iterator).

The `LinkedList` class defines a private inner class `LinkedListIterator`, which implements the simplified `ListIterator` interface. Because `LinkedListIterator` is an inner class, it has access to the private features of the `LinkedList` class—in particular, the `first` field and the private `Link` class.

Note that clients of the `LinkedList` class don't actually know the name of the iterator class. They only know it is a class that implements the `ListIterator` interface.

```
class LinkedList
{
    . . .
    public ListIterator listIterator()
    {
        return new LinkedListIterator();
```

```
      }

      private class LinkedListIterator
      {
         public LinkedListIterator()
         {
            position = null;
            previous = null;
         }

         . . .
         private Link position;
         private Link previous;
      }
      . . .
   }
```

Each iterator object has a reference `position` to the last visited link. We also store a reference to the last link before that. We will need that reference to adjust the links properly in the `remove` operation.

The `next` method is simple. The `position` reference is advanced to `position.next`, and the old position is remembered in `previous`. There is a special case, however—if the iterator points before the first element of the list, then the old `position` is `null`, and `position` must be set to `first`.

```
   private class LinkedListIterator
      implements ListIterator
   {
      . . .
      public Object next()
      {
         if (!hasNext())
            throw new NoSuchElementException();
         previous = position; // remember for remove

         if (position == null)
            position = first;
         else
            position = position.next;

         return position.data;
      }
      . . .
   }
```

The `next` method is supposed to be called only when the iterator is not yet at the end of the list. The iterator is at the end if the list is empty (that is, `first == null`) or if there is no element after the current position (`position.next == null`).

```
   private class LinkedListIterator
      implements ListIterator
```

```
    {
        . . .
        public boolean hasNext()
        {
            if (position == null)
                return first != null;
            else
                return position.next != null;
        }
        . . .
    }
```

> Implementing operations that modify a linked list is challenging—you need to make sure that you update all link references correctly.

Removing the last visited link is more involved. If the element to be removed is the first element, we just call `removeFirst`. Otherwise, an element in the middle of the list must be removed, and the link preceding it needs to have its `next` reference updated to skip the removed element (see Figure 6). If the `previous` reference is `null`, then this call to `remove` does not immediately follow a call to `next`, and we throw an `IllegalStateException`.

According to the definition of the `remove` method, it is illegal to call `remove` twice in a row. Therefore, the `remove` method sets the `previous` reference to `null`.

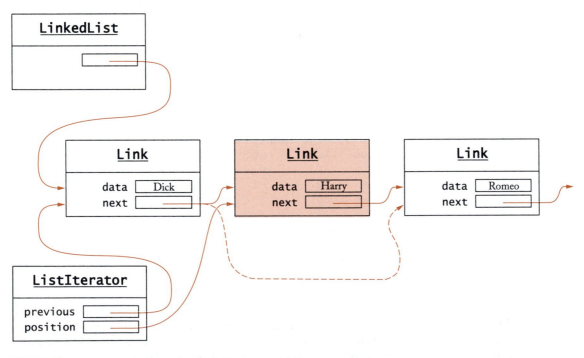

Figure 6

Removing a Link from the Middle of a Linked List

```
private class LinkedListIterator
   implements ListIterator
{  . . .
   public void remove()
   {
      if (position == first)
      {
         removeFirst();
         position = first;
      }
      else
      {
         if (previous == null)
            throw new IllegalStateException();
         previous.next = position.next;
         position = previous;
      }
      previous = null;
   }
   . . .
}
```

The set method changes the data stored in the previously visited element. Its implementation is straightforward because our linked lists can be traversed in only one direction. The linked-list implementation of the standard library must keep track of whether the last iterator movement was forward or backward. For that reason, the standard library forbids a call to the set method following an add or remove method. We do not enforce that restriction.

```
public void set(Object obj)
{
   if (position == null)
      throw new NoSuchElementException();
   position.data = obj;
}
```

Finally, the most complex operation is the addition of a link. You insert the new link after the current position, and set the successor of the new link to the successor of the current position (see Figure 7).

```
private class LinkedListIterator
   implements ListIterator
{  . . .
   public void add(Object obj)
   {
      if (position == null)
      {
         addFirst(obj);
         position = first;
      }
      else
```

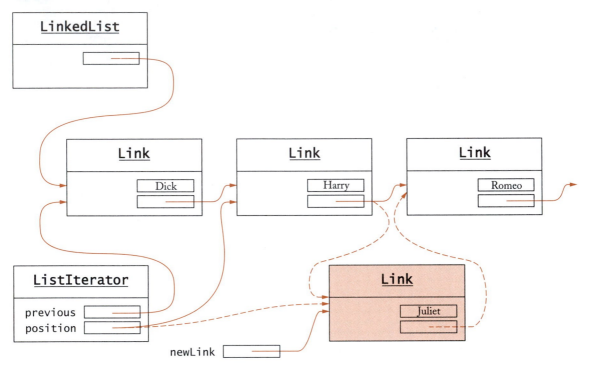

Figure 7

Adding a Link to the Middle of a Linked List

```
      {
          Link newLink = new Link();
          newLink.data = obj;
          newLink.next = position.next;
          position.next = newLink;
          position = newLink;
      }
      previous = null;
   }
   . . .
}
```

At the end of this section is the complete implementation of our `LinkedList` class. You can test it with the test program of the preceding section.

You now know how to use the `LinkedList` class in the Java library, and you have had a peek "under the hood" to see how linked lists are implemented.

File LinkedList.java

```
1  import java.util.NoSuchElementException;
2
3  /**
```

```
 4      A linked list is a sequence of links with efficient
 5      element insertion and removal. This class
 6      contains a subset of the methods of the standard
 7      java.util.LinkedList class.
 8  */
 9  public class LinkedList
10  {
11      /**
12          Constructs an empty linked list.
13      */
14      public LinkedList()
15      {
16          first = null;
17      }
18
19      /**
20          Returns the first element in the linked list.
21          @return  the first element in the linked list
22      */
23      public Object getFirst()
24      {
25          if (first == null)
26              throw new NoSuchElementException();
27          return first.data;
28      }
29
30      /**
31          Removes the first element in the linked list.
32          @return  the removed element
33      */
34      public Object removeFirst()
35      {
36          if (first == null)
37              throw new NoSuchElementException();
38          Object obj = first.data;
39          first = first.next;
40          return obj;
41      }
42
43      /**
44          Adds an element to the front of the linked list.
45          @param obj  the object to add
46      */
47      public void addFirst(Object obj)
48      {
49          Link newLink = new Link();
50          newLink.data = obj;
51          newLink.next = first;
52          first = newLink;
53      }
```

```
54
55      /**
56          Returns an iterator for iterating through this list.
57          @return an iterator for iterating through this list
58      */
59      public ListIterator listIterator()
60      {
61          return new LinkedListIterator();
62      }
63
64      private Link first;
65
66      private class Link
67      {
68          public Object data;
69          public Link next;
70      }
71
72      private class LinkedListIterator
73          implements ListIterator
74      {
75          /**
76              Constructs an iterator that points to the front
77              of the linked list.
78          */
79          public LinkedListIterator()
80          {
81              position = null;
82              previous = null;
83          }
84
85          /**
86              Moves the iterator past the next element.
87              @return the traversed element
88          */
89          public Object next()
90          {
91              if (!hasNext())
92                  throw new NoSuchElementException();
93              previous = position; // remember for remove
94
95              if (position == null)
96                  position = first;
97              else
98                  position = position.next;
99
100             return position.data;
101         }
102
103         /**
```

```
104                 Tests whether there is an element after the iterator
105                 position.
106                 @return true if there is an element after the iterator
107                 position
108             */
109             public boolean hasNext()
110             {
111                 if (position == null)
112                     return first != null;
113                 else
114                     return position.next != null;
115             }
116
117             /**
118                 Adds an element before the iterator position
119                 and moves the iterator past the inserted element.
120                 @param obj the object to add
121             */
122             public void add(Object obj)
123             {
124                 if (position == null)
125                 {
126                     addFirst(obj);
127                     position = first;
128                 }
129                 else
130                 {
131                     Link newLink = new Link();
132                     newLink.data = obj;
133                     newLink.next = position.next;
134                     position.next = newLink;
135                     position = newLink;
136                 }
137                 previous = null;
138             }
139
140             /**
141                 Removes the last traversed element. This method may
142                 be called only after a call to the next() method.
143             */
144             public void remove()
145             {
146                 if (position == first)
147                 {
148                     removeFirst();
149                     position = first;
150                 }
151                 else
152                 {
153                     if (previous == null)
```

```
154                     throw new IllegalStateException();
155                 previous.next = position.next;
156                 position = previous;
157             }
158             previous = null;
159         }
160
161         /**
162             Sets the last traversed element to a different
163             value.
164             @param obj the object to set
165         */
166         public void set(Object obj)
167         {
168             if (position == null)
169                 throw new NoSuchElementException();
170             position.data = obj;
171         }
172
173         private Link position;
174         private Link previous;
175     }
176 }
```

File ListIterator.java

```
1  import java.util.NoSuchElementException;
2
3  /**
4      A list iterator allows access to a position in a linked list.
5      This interface contains a subset of the methods of the
6      standard java.util.ListIterator interface. The methods for
7      backward traversal are not included.
8  */
9  public interface ListIterator
10 {
11     /**
12         Moves the iterator past the next element.
13         @return the traversed element
14     */
15     Object next();
16
17     /**
18         Tests whether there is an element after the iterator position.
19         @return true if there is an element after the iterator
20         position
21     */
22     boolean hasNext();
23
24     /**
```

```
25              Adds an element before the iterator position
26              and moves the iterator past the inserted element.
27              @param obj  the object to add
28      */
29      void add(Object obj);
30
31      /**
32              Removes the last traversed element. This method may
33              be called only after a call to the next() method.
34      */
35      void remove();
36
37      /**
38              Sets the last traversed element to a different value.
39              @param obj  the object to set
40      */
41      void set(Object obj);
42  }
```

Advanced Topic   19.1

Static Inner Classes

You first saw the use of inner classes for event handlers. Inner classes are useful in that context, because their methods have the privilege of accessing private data members of outer-class objects. The same is true for the LinkedListIterator inner class in the sample code for this section. The iterator needs to access the first instance variable of its linked list.

However, the Link inner class has no need to access the outer class. In fact, it has no methods. Thus, there is no need to store a reference to the outer list class with each Link object. To suppress the outer-class reference, you can declare the inner class as static:

```
class LinkedList
{
   . . .
   private static class Link
   {
      . . .
   }
}
```

The purpose of the keyword static in this context is to indicate that the inner-class objects do not depend on the outer-class objects that generate them. In particular, the methods of a static inner class cannot access the outer-class instance variables. Declaring the inner class static is efficient, because its objects do not store an outer-class reference.

19.3 Abstract and Concrete Data Types

> An abstract data type defines the fundamental operations on the data but does not specify an implementation.

> An abstract list is an ordered sequence of items that can be traversed sequentially and that allows for insertion and removal of elements at any position.

> An abstract array is an ordered sequence of items with random access by specifying an integer index.

There are two ways of looking at a linked list. One way is to think of the concrete implementation of such a list, with its link nodes that have references to data items and to their successor nodes (see Figure 8).

On the other hand, you can think of the *abstract* concept of the linked list. In the abstract, a linked list is an ordered sequence of data items that can be traversed with an iterator (see Figure 9).

Similarly, there are two ways of looking at an array list. Of course, an array list has a concrete implementation: a partially filled array of object references (see Figure 10). But you don't usually think about the concrete implementation when using an array list. You take the abstract point of view. An array list is an ordered sequence of data items, each of which can be accessed by an integer index (see Figure 11).

The concrete implementations of a linked list and an array list are quite different. The abstractions, on the other hand, seem to be similar at first glance. To see the difference, consider the public interfaces, stripped down to their minimal essentials.

An array list allows *random access* to all elements. You specify an integer index, and you can get or set the corresponding element.

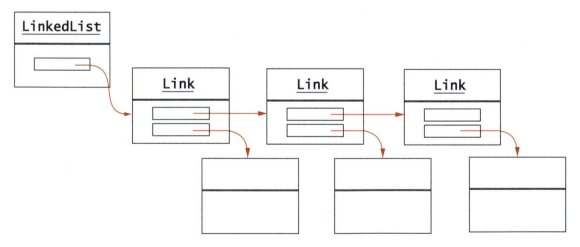

Figure 8

A Concrete View of a Linked List

Figure 9

An Abstract View of a Linked List

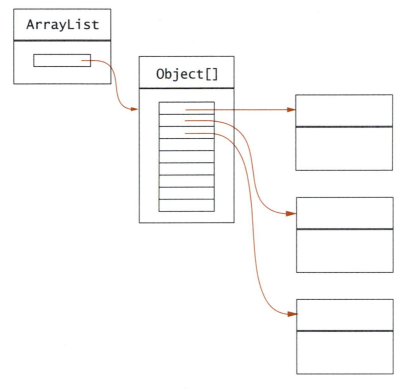

Figure 10

A Concrete View of an Array List

Figure 11

An Abstract View of an Array List

```
public class ArrayList
{
    public Object get(int index) { . . . }
    public void set(int index, Object value) { . . . }
    . . .
}
```

With a linked list, on the other hand, element access is a bit more complex. A linked list allows sequential access. You need to ask the linked list for an iterator. Using that iterator, you can easily traverse the list elements one at a time. But if you want to go to a particular element, say the 100th one, you first have to skip all elements before it.

```
public class LinkedList
{
   public ListIterator listIterator() { . . . }
   . . .
}

public interface ListIterator
{
   Object next();
   boolean hasNext();
   void add(Object value);
   void remove();
   void set(Object value);
   . . .
}
```

Here we show only the *fundamental* operations on array lists and linked lists. Other operations can be composed from these fundamental operations. For example, you can add or remove an element in an array list by moving all elements beyond the insertion or removal index, calling `get` and `set` multiple times.

Of course, the `ArrayList` class has methods to add and remove elements in the middle, even if they are slow. Conversely, the `LinkedList` class has `get` and `set` methods that let you access any element in the linked list, albeit very inefficiently, by performing repeated sequential accesses.

In fact, the term `ArrayList` signifies that its implementors wanted to combine the interfaces of an array and a list. Somewhat confusingly, both the `ArrayList` and the `LinkedList` class implement an interface called `List` that defines operations both for random access and for sequential access.

That terminology is not in common use outside the Java library. Instead, let us adopt a more traditional terminology. We will call the abstract types *array* and *list*. The Java library provides concrete implementations `ArrayList` and `LinkedList` for these abstract types. Other concrete implementations are possible in other libraries. In fact, Java arrays (`Object[]`) are another implementation of the abstract array type.

To understand an abstract data type completely, you need to know not just its fundamental operations but also their relative efficiency.

In a linked list, an element can be added or removed in constant time (assuming that the iterator is already in the right position). A fixed number of link references need to be modified to add or remove a link, regardless of the size of the list. Using the big-Oh notation, an operation that requires a bounded amount of time, regardless of the total number of elements in the structure, is denoted as $O(1)$. Random access in an array list also takes $O(1)$ time.

Adding or removing an arbitrary element in an array takes $O(n)$ time, where n is the size of the array list, because on average $n/2$ elements need to be moved. Random access in a linked list takes $O(n)$ time because on average $n/2$ elements need to be skipped.

Table 1 shows this information for arrays and lists.

Table 1

Efficiency of Operations for Arrays and Lists

Operation	Array	List
Random access	$O(1)$	$O(n)$
Linear traversal step	$O(1)$	$O(1)$
Add/remove an element	$O(n)$	$O(1)$

Why consider abstract types at all? If you implement a particular algorithm, you can tell what operations you need to carry out on the data structures that your algorithm manipulates. You can then determine the abstract type that supports those operations efficiently.

For example, suppose you have a sorted collection of items and you want to locate items using the binary search algorithm (see Section 18.7). That algorithm makes a random access to the middle of the collection, followed by other random accesses. Thus, fast random access is essential for the algorithm to work correctly. Once you know that an array supports fast random access and a linked list does not, you then look for concrete implementations of the abstract array type. You won't be fooled into using a `LinkedList`, even though the `LinkedList` class actually provides `get` and `set` methods.

In the next section and in Chapter 20, you will see additional examples of abstract data types.

19.4 Stacks and Queues

> A stack is a collection of items with "last in first out" retrieval.

In this section we will consider two common abstract data types that allow insertion and removal of items at the ends only, not in the middle. A *stack* lets you insert and remove elements at only one end, traditionally called the *top* of the stack. To visualize a stack, think of a stack of books (see Figure 12).

New items can be added to the top of the stack. Items are removed at the top of the stack as well. Therefore, they are removed in the order that is opposite from the order in

Figure 12

A Stack of Books

which they have been added, called *last in, first out* or *LIFO* order. For example, if you add items A, B, and C and then remove them, you obtain C, B, and A. Traditionally, the addition and removal operations are called `push` and `pop`.

There is a `Stack` class in the Java library that implements the abstract stack type and the `push` and `pop` operations. The following sample code shows how to use that class.

```
Stack s = new Stack();
s.push("A");
s.push("B");
s.push("C");
// the following loop prints C, B, and A
while (s.size() > 0)
    System.out.println(s.pop());
```

The `Stack` class in the Java library uses an `Object[]` array to implement a stack. Exercise P19.8 shows how to use a linked list instead.

A *queue* is similar to a stack, except that you add items to one end of the queue (the *tail*) and remove them from the other end of the queue (the *head*). To visualize a queue, simply think of people lining up (see Figure 13). People join the tail of the queue and wait until they have reached the head of the queue. Queues store items in a *first in, first out* or *FIFO* fashion. Items are removed in the same order in which they have been added.

> A queue is a collection of items with "first in first out" retrieval.

There are many uses of queues in computer science. For example, the Java graphical user interface system keeps an event queue of all events, such as mouse and keyboard events. The events are inserted into the queue whenever the operating system notifies the application of the event. Another thread of control removes them from the queue and passes them to the appropriate

Figure 13

A Queue

event listeners. Another example is a print queue. A printer may be accessed by several applications, perhaps running on different computers. If each of the applications tried to access the printer at the same time, the printout would be garbled. Instead, each application places all bytes that need to be sent to the printer into a file and inserts that file into the print queue. When the printer is done printing one file, it retrieves the next one from the queue. Therefore, print jobs are printed using the "first in, first out" rule, which is a fair arrangement for users of the shared printer.

There is no implementation of a queue in the standard Java library; however, it is a simple matter to create your own.

```java
public class Queue
{
    /**
        Constructs an empty queue.
    */
    public Queue()
    {
        list = new LinkedList();
    }

    /**
        Adds an item to the tail of the queue.
        @param x the item to add
    */
    public void add(Object x)
    {
        list.addLast(x);
    }

    /**
        Removes an item from the head of the queue.
        @return the removed item
    */
    public Object remove()
    {
        return list.removeFirst();
    }

    /**
        Gets the number of items in the queue.
        @return the size
    */
    int size()
    {
        return list.size();
    }

    private LinkedList list;
}
```

You would definitely not want to use the **add** and `remove` methods of an array to implement a queue. Removing the first element of an array is inefficient—all other elements must be moved towards the beginning. However, Exercise P19.9 shows you how to implement a queue efficiently as a "circular" array, in which all elements stay at the position at which they were inserted, but the index values that denote the head and tail of the queue change when elements are added and removed.

In this chapter, you have seen the two most fundamental abstract data types, arrays and lists, and their concrete implementations. You also learned about the stack and queue types. Reference [1] discusses additional data types that require more sophisticated implementation techniques.

Random Fact   19.1

Standardization

You encounter the benefits of standardization every day. When you buy a light bulb, you can be assured that it fits the socket without having to measure the socket at home and the light bulb in the store. In fact, you may have experienced how painful the lack of standards can be if you have ever purchased a flashlight with nonstandard bulbs. Replacement bulbs for such a flashlight can be difficult and expensive to obtain.

Programmers have a similar desire for standardization. Consider the important goal of platform independence for Java programs. After you compile a Java program into class files, you can execute the class files on any computer that has a Java virtual machine. For this to work, the behavior of the virtual machine has to be strictly defined. If virtual machines don't all behave exactly the same way, then the slogan of "write once, run anywhere" turns into "write once, debug everywhere". In order for multiple implementors to create compatible virtual machines, the virtual machine needed to be *standardized*. That is, someone needed to create a definition of the virtual machine and its expected behavior.

Who creates standards? Some of the most successful standards have been created by volunteer groups such as the Internet Engineering Task Force (IETF) and the World Wide Web Consortium (W3C). You can find the Requests for Comment (RFC) that standardize many of the Internet protocols at the IETF site, http://www.ietf.org/rfc.html. For example, RFC 822 standardizes the format of email, and RFC 2616 defines the Hypertext Transmission Protocol (HTTP) that is used to serve web pages to browsers. The W3C standardizes the Hypertext Markup Language (HTML), the format for web pages—see http://www.w3c.org. These standards have been instrumental in the creation of the World Wide Web as an open platform that is not controlled by any one company.

Many programming languages, such as C++ and Scheme, have been standardized by independent standards organizations such as the American National Standards Institute (ANSI) and the International Organization for Standardization, called ISO for short (not an acronym; see http://www.iso.ch/iso/en/aboutiso/introduction/whatisISO.html). ANSI and ISO are associations of industry professionals who develop standards for everything from car tires and credit card shapes to programming languages.

▼ The process of standardizing the C++ language turned out to be very painstaking and time-consuming, and the standards organization followed a rigorous process to ensure fairness and to avoid being influenced by companies with vested interests.

▼ When a company invents a new technology, it has an interest in its invention becoming a standard, so that other vendors produce tools that work with the invention and thus increase its likelihood of success. On the other hand, by handing over the invention to a standards committee, especially one that insists on a fair process, the company may lose control over the standard. For that reason, Sun Microsystems, the inventor of Java, never agreed to have a third-party organization standardize the Java language. They run their own standardization process, involving other companies but refusing to relinquish control. Another unfortunate but common tactic is to create a weak standard. For example, Netscape and Microsoft chose the European Computer Manufacturers Association (ECMA) to standardize the JavaScript language (see Random Fact 11.1). ECMA was willing to settle for something less than truly useful, standardizing the behavior of the core language and just a few of its libraries. Since most useful JavaScript programs need to use more libraries than those defined in the standard, programmers still go through a lot of tedious trial and error to write JavaScript code that runs identically on Netscape's and Microsoft's browsers.

▼ Often, competing standards are developed by different coalitions of vendors. For example, at the time of this writing, hardware vendors are in disagreement whether to use the IEEE 1394 (also called "FireWire" or iLink) or High-Speed USB for connecting external devices to computers. As Grace Hopper, the famous computer science pioneer, observed: "The great thing about standards is that there are so many to choose from".

▼ Of course, many important pieces of technology aren't standardized at all. Consider the Windows operating system. Although Windows is often called a de-facto standard, it really is no standard at all. Nobody has ever attempted to define formally what the Windows operating system should do. The behavior changes at the whim of its vendor. That suits Microsoft just fine, because it makes it impossible for a third party to create its own version of Windows.

▼ As a computer professional, there will be many times in your career when you need to make a decision whether to support a particular standard. Consider a simple example. In this chapter, we use the `LinkedList` class from the standard Java library. However, many computer scientists dislike this class because the interface muddies the distinction between abstract lists and arrays, and the iterators are clumsy to use. Should you use the `LinkedList` class in your own code, or should you implement a better list? If you do the former, you have to deal with an implementation that is less than optimal. If you do the latter, other programmers may have a hard time understanding your code because they aren't familiar with your list class.

CHAPTER SUMMARY

1. A linked list consists of a number of links, each of which has a reference to the next link.

2. Adding and removing elements in the middle of a linked list is efficient.

3. Visiting the elements of a linked list in sequential order is efficient, but random access is not.

4. You use a list iterator to access elements inside a linked list.

5. Implementing operations that modify a linked list is challenging—you need to make sure that you update all link references correctly.

6. An abstract data type defines the fundamental operations on the data but does not specify an implementation.

7. An abstract list is an ordered sequence of items that can be traversed sequentially and that allows for insertion and removal of elements at any position.

8. An abstract array is an ordered sequence of items with random access by specifying an integer index.

9. A stack is a collection of items with "last in first out" retrieval.

10. A queue is a collection of items with "first in first out" retrieval.

Further Reading

[1] Michael T. Goodrich and Roberto Tamassia: *Data Structures and Algorithms in Java,* John Wiley & Sons, 1998.

CLASSES, OBJECTS, AND METHODS INTRODUCED IN THIS CHAPTER

```
java.util.AbstractList
    listIterator
java.util.LinkedList
    addFirst
    addLast
    getFirst
    getLast
    removeFirst
    removeLast
java.util.ListIterator
    add
    hasNext
    hasPrevious
    next
    previous
    remove
    set
```

REVIEW EXERCISES

Exercise R19.1. Explain what the following code prints. Draw pictures of the linked list after each step. Just draw the forward links, as in Figure 1.

```
LinkedList staff = new LinkedList();
staff.addFirst("Harry");
```

```
staff.addFirst("Dick");
staff.addFirst("Tom");
System.out.println(staff.removeFirst());
System.out.println(staff.removeFirst());
System.out.println(staff.removeFirst());
```

Exercise R19.2. Explain what the following code prints. Draw pictures of the linked list after each step. Just draw the forward links, as in Figure 1.

```
LinkedList staff = new LinkedList();
staff.addFirst("Harry");
staff.addFirst("Dick");
staff.addFirst("Tom");
System.out.println(staff.removeLast());
System.out.println(staff.removeFirst());
System.out.println(staff.removeLast());
```

Exercise P19.3. Explain what the following code prints. Draw pictures of the linked list after each step. Just draw the forward links, as in Figure 1.

```
LinkedList staff = new LinkedList();
staff.addFirst("Harry");
staff.addLast("Dick");
staff.addFirst("Tom");
System.out.println(staff.removeLast());
System.out.println(staff.removeFirst());
System.out.println(staff.removeLast());
```

Exercise R19.4. Explain what the following code prints. Draw pictures of the linked list and the iterator position after each step.

```
LinkedList staff = new LinkedList();
ListIterator iterator = staff.listIterator();
iterator.add("Tom");
iterator.add("Dick");
iterator.add("Harry");
iterator = staff.listIterator();
if (iterator.next().equals("Tom"))
    iterator.remove();
while (iterator.hasNext())
    System.out.println(iterator.next());
```

Exercise R19.5. Explain what the following code prints. Draw pictures of the linked list and the iterator position after each step.

```
LinkedList staff = new LinkedList();
ListIterator iterator = staff.listIterator();
iterator.add("Tom");
iterator.add("Dick");
iterator.add("Harry");
iterator = staff.listIterator();
iterator.next();
iterator.next();
```

```
iterator.add("Romeo");
iterator.next();
iterator.add("Juliet");
iterator = staff.listIterator();
iterator.next();
iterator.remove();
while (iterator.hasNext())
    System.out.println(iterator.next());
```

Exercise R19.6. The linked-list class in the Java library supports operations `addLast` and `removeLast`. To carry out these operations efficiently, the `LinkedList` class has an added reference `last` to the last node in the linked list. Draw a "before/after" diagram of the changes of the links in a linked list under the `addLast` and `removeLast` methods.

Exercise R19.7. The linked-list class in the Java library supports bidirectional iterators. To go backward efficiently, each `Link` has an added reference, `previous`, to the predecessor node in the linked list. Draw a "before/after" diagram of the changes of the links in a linked list under the `addFirst` and `removeFirst` methods that shows how the `previous` links need to be updated.

Exercise R19.8. What advantages do lists have over arrays? What disadvantages do they have?

Exercise R19.9. Suppose you needed to organize a collection of telephone numbers for a company division. There are currently about 6,000 employees, and you know that the phone switch can handle at most 10,000 phone numbers. You expect several hundred lookups against the collection every day. Would you use an array or a list to store the information?

Exercise R19.10. Suppose you needed to keep a collection of appointments. Would you use a list or an array of `Appointment` objects?

Exercise R19.11. Suppose you write a program that models a card deck. Cards are taken from the top of the deck and given out to players. As cards are returned to the deck, they are placed on the bottom of the deck. Would you store the cards in a stack or a queue?

Exercise R19.12. Suppose the strings "A" ... "Z" are pushed onto a stack. Then they are popped off the stack and pushed onto a second stack. Finally, they are all popped off the second stack and printed. In which order are the strings printed?

Programming Exercises

Exercise P19.1. Using just the public interface of the linked-list class, write a method

```
public static void downsize(LinkedList staff)
```

that removes every other employee from a linked list.

Exercise P19.2. Using just the public interface of the linked-list class, write a method

```
public static void reverse(LinkedList staff)
```

that reverses the entries in a linked list.

Exercise P19.3. Add a method `reverse()` to our implementation of the `LinkedList` class that reverses the links in a list. Implement this method by directly rerouting the links, not by using an iterator.

Exercise P19.4. Write a method `draw` to display a linked list graphically. Draw each element of the list as a box, and indicate the links with arrows.

Exercise P19.5. Add a method `size()` to our implementation of the `LinkedList` class that computes the number of elements in the list, by following links and counting the elements until the end of the list is reached.

Exercise P19.6. Add a `currentSize` field to our implementation of the `LinkedList` class. Modify the add and remove methods of both the linked list and the list iterator to update the `currentSize` field so that it always contains the correct size. Change the `size()` method of the preceding exercise so that it simply returns the value of this instance variable.

Exercise P19.7. Write a class `Polynomial` that stores a polynomial such as

$$p(x) = 5x^{10} + 9x^7 - x - 10$$

Store it as a linked list of terms. A term contains the coefficient and the power of x. For example, you would store $p(x)$ as

$(5, 10), (9, 7), (-1, 1), (-10, 0)$

Supply methods to add, multiply, and print polynomials. For example, the polynomial p can be constructed as

```
Polynomial p = new Polynomial();
p.addTerm(-10, 0);
p.addTerm(-1, 1);
p.addTerm(9, 7);
p.addTerm(5, 10);
```

Then compute $p(x) \times p(x)$.

```
Polynomial q = p.multiply(p);
q.print();
```

Exercise P19.8. Implement a `Stack` class by using a linked list to store the elements.

Exercise P19.9. Implement a queue as a *circular array* as follows: Use two index variables `head` and `tail` that contain the index of the next element to be removed and the next element to be added. After an element is removed or added, the index is incremented (see Figure 14).

Figure 14

Adding and Removing Queue Elements

Figure 15

A Queue Element Set That Wraps
Around the End of the Array

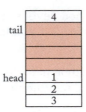

After a while, the `tail` element will reach the top of the array. Then it "wraps around" and starts again at 0—see Figure 15. For that reason, the array is called "circular".

```
public class CircularArrayQueue
{
    public CircularArrayQueue(int capacity) { . . . }
    public void add(Object x) { . . . }
    public Object remove() { . . . }
    public int getLength() { . . . }
    private int head;
    private int tail;
    private int length;
    private Object[] elements;
}
```

This implementation supplies a *bounded* queue—it can eventually fill up. See the next exercise on how to remove that limitation.

Exercise P19.10. The queue in the preceding exercise can fill up if more elements are added than the array can hold. Improve the implementation as follows. When the array fills up, allocate a larger array, copy the values to the larger array and assign it to the `elements` instance variable. *Hint:* You can't just copy the elements into the same position of the new array. Move the head element to position 0 instead.

Java Language Coding Guidelines

Introduction

This coding style guide is a simplified version of one that has been used with good success both in industrial practice and for college courses.

A style guide is a set of mandatory requirements for layout and formatting. Uniform style makes it easier for you to read code from your instructor and classmates. You will really appreciate that advantage if you do a team project. It is also easier for your instructor and your grader to grasp the essence of your programs quickly.

A style guide makes you a more productive programmer because it *reduces gratuitous choice*. If you don't have to make choices about trivial matters, you can spend your energy on the solution of real problems.

In these guidelines, several constructs are plainly outlawed. That doesn't mean that programmers using them are evil or incompetent. It does mean that the constructs are not essential and can be expressed just as well or even better with other language constructs.

If you already have programming experience, in Java or another language, you may be initially uncomfortable at giving up some fond habits. However, it is a sign of professionalism to set aside personal preferences in minor matters and to compromise for the benefit of your group.

These guidelines are necessarily somewhat dull. They also mention features that you may not yet have seen in class. Here are the most important highlights:

- Tabs are set every three spaces.

- Variable and method names are lowercase, with occasional upperCase characters in the middle.

- Class names start with an Uppercase letter.

- Constant names are UPPERCASE, with an occasional UNDER_SCORE.

- There are spaces after keywords and surrounding binary operators.

- Braces must line up horizontally or vertically.

- No magic numbers may be used.

- Every method, except for `main` and overridden library methods, must have a comment.

- At most 30 lines of code may be used per method.

- No `continue` or `break` is allowed.

- All non-`final` variables must be private.

Note to the instructor: Of course, many programmers and organizations have strong feelings about coding style. If this style guide is incompatible with your own preferences or with local custom, please feel free to modify it. For that purpose, this coding style guide is available in electronic form from the author.

Source Files

Each Java program is a collection of one or more source files. The executable program is obtained by compiling these files. Organize the material in each file as follows:

- `package` statement, if appropriate

- `import` statements

- A comment explaining the purpose of this file

- A `public` class

- Other classes, if appropriate

The comment explaining the purpose of this file should be in the format recognized by the `javadoc` utility. Start with a `/**`, and use the `@author` and `@version` tags:

```
/**
    COPYRIGHT (C) 1997 Harry Hacker. All Rights Reserved.
    Classes to manipulate widgets.
    Solves CS101 homework assignment #3
    @author  Harry Hacker
```

```
    @version 1.01 1997-02-15
*/
```

Classes

Each class should be preceded by a class comment explaining the purpose of the class.

First list all public features, then all private features.

Within the public and private sections, use the following order:

1. Constructors
2. Instance methods
3. Static methods
4. Instance fields
5. Static fields
6. Inner classes

Leave a blank line after every method.

All non-`final` variables must be private. (However, instance variables of a `private` inner class may be public.) Methods and final variables can be either public or private, as appropriate.

All features must be tagged `public` or `private`. Do not use the default visibility (that is, package visibility) or the `protected` attribute.

Avoid static variables (except `final` ones) whenever possible. In the rare instance that you need static variables, you are permitted one static variable per class.

Methods

Every method (except for `main`) starts with a comment in `javadoc` format.

```
/**
    Convert calendar date into Julian day.
    Note: This algorithm is from Press et al., Numerical Recipes
    in C, 2nd ed., Cambridge University Press, 1992.
    @param day  day of the date to be converted
    @param month  month of the date to be converted
    @param year  year of the date to be converted
    @return  the Julian day number that begins at noon of the
    given calendar date.
*/
public static int dat2jul(int day, int month, int year)
{
    . . .
}
```

Methods must have at most 30 lines of code. The method signature, comments, blank lines, and lines containing only braces are not included in this count. This rule forces you to break up complex computations into separate methods.

Variables and Constants

Do not define all variables at the beginning of a block:

```
{
    double xold;
    double xnew; // Don't
    boolean more;
    . . .
}
```

Define each variable just before it is used for the first time:

```
{
    . . .
    double xold = Integer.parseInt(input);
    boolean more = false;
    while (more)
    {
        double xnew = (xold + a / xold) / 2; // OK
        . . .
    }
    . . .
}
```

Do not define two variables on the same line:

```
int dimes = 0, nickels = 0; // Don't
```

Instead, use two separate definitions:

```
int dimes = 0; // OK
int nickels = 0;
```

In Java, constants must be defined with the keyword `final`. If the constant is used by multiple methods, declare it as `static final`. It is a good idea to define static final variables as `private` if no other class has an interest in them.

Do not use *magic numbers!* A magic number is a numeric constant embedded in code, without a constant definition. Any number except −1, 0, 1, and 2 is considered magic:

```
if (p.getX() < 300) // Don't
```

Use `final` variables instead:

```
final double WINDOW_WIDTH = 300;
. . .
if (p.getX() < WINDOW_WIDTH) // OK
```

Even the most reasonable cosmic constant is going to change one day. You think there are 365 days per year? Your customers on Mars are going to be pretty unhappy about your silly prejudice. Make a constant

```
public static final int DAYS_PER_YEAR = 365;
```

so that you can easily produce a Martian version without trying to find all the 365s, 364s, 366s, 367s, and so on, in your code.

When declaring array variables, group the [] with the type, not the variable.

```
int[] values; // OK
int values[]; // Ugh—this is an ugly holdover from C
```

Control Flow

The if Statement

Avoid the "if ... if ... else" trap. The code

```
if ( ... )
   if ( ... ) ...;
else ...;
```

will not do what the indentation level suggests, and it can take hours to find such a bug. Always use an extra pair of { ... } when dealing with "if ... if ... else":

```
if ( ... )
{
   if ( ... ) ...;
} // {...} are necessary
else ...;

if ( ... )
{
   if ( ... ) ...;
   else ...;
} // {...} not necessary, but they keep you out of trouble
```

The for Statement

Use for loops only when a variable runs from somewhere to somewhere with some constant increment/decrement:

```
for (int i = 0; i < a.length; i++)
   System.out.println(a[i]);
```

Do not use the for loop for weird constructs such as

```
for (a = a / 2; count < ITERATIONS;
   System.out.println(xnew))
   // Don't
```

Make such a loop into a while loop. That way, the sequence of instructions is much clearer.

```
a = a / 2;
while (count < ITERATIONS) // OK
{  . . .
   System.out.println(xnew);
}
```

Nonlinear Control Flow

Avoid the `switch` statement, because it is easy to fall through accidentally to an unwanted case. Use `if`/`else` instead.

Avoid the `break` or `continue` statements. Use another `boolean` variable to control the execution flow.

Exceptions

Do not tag a method with an overly general exception specification:

```
Widget readWidget(Reader in)
    throws Exception // Bad
```

Instead, specifically declare any checked exceptions that your method may throw:

```
Widget readWidget(Reader in)
    throws IOException, MalformedWidgetException // Good
```

Do not "squelch" exceptions:

```
try
{
    double price = in.readDouble();
}
catch (Exception e)
{} // Bad
```

Beginners often make this mistake "to keep the compiler happy". If the current method is not appropriate for handling the exception, simply use a `throws` specification and let one of its callers handle it.

Lexical Issues

Naming Convention

The following rules specify when to use upper- and lowercase letters in identifier names.

- All variable and method names and all data fields of classes are in lowercase (maybe with an occasional upperCase in the middle); for example, `firstPlayer`.

- All constants are in uppercase (maybe with an occasional UNDER_SCORE); for example, `CLOCK_RADIUS`.

- All class and interface names start with uppercase and are followed by lower-case letters (maybe with an occasional UpperCase letter); for example, `BankTeller`.

Names must be reasonably long and descriptive. Use `firstPlayer` instead of `fp`. No drppng f vwls. Local variables that are fairly routine can be short (`ch`, `i`) as long as they are really just boring holders for an input character, a loop counter, and so on. Also, do not use `ctr`, `c`, `cntr`, `cnt`, `c2` for variables in your method. Surely these variables all have specific purposes and can be named to remind the reader of them (for example, `current`, `next`, `previous`, `result`, ...).

Indentation and White Space

Use tab stops every three columns. That means you will need to change the tab stop setting in your editor!

Use blank lines freely to separate parts of a method that are logically distinct.

Use a blank space around every binary operator:

```
x1 = (-b - Math.sqrt(b * b - 4 * a * c)) / (2 * a);
// Good

x1=(-b-Math.sqrt(b*b-4*a*c))/(2*a);
// Bad
```

Leave a blank space after (and not before) each comma or semicolon. Do not leave a space before or after a parenthesis or bracket in an expression. Leave spaces around the (. . .) part of an `if`, `while`, `for`, or `catch` statement.

```
if (x == 0) y = 0;

f(a, b[i]);
```

Every line must fit on 80 columns. If you must break a statement, add an indentation level for the continuation:

```
a[n] = .................................... . .
   + ...............;
```

Start the indented line with an operator (if possible).

If the condition in an `if` or `while` statement must be broken, be sure to brace the body in, *even if it consists of only one statement:*

```
if ( ...............................................
   && .................
   || .......... )
{
   . . .
}
```

If it weren't for the braces, it would be hard to separate the continuation of the condition visually from the statement to be executed.

Braces

Opening and closing braces must line up, either horizontally or vertically:

```
while (i < n) { System.out.println(a[i]); i++; }

while (i < n)
{
```

```
        System.out.println(a[i]);
        i++;
    }
```

Some programmers don't line up vertical braces but place the { behind the keyword:

```
    while (i < n) { // DON'T
        System.out.println(a[i]);
        i++;
    }
```

Doing so makes it hard to check that the braces match.

Unstable Layout

Some programmers take great pride in lining up certain columns in their code:

```
    firstRecord = other.firstRecord;
    lastRecord  = other.lastRecord;
    cutoff      = other.cutoff;
```

This is undeniably neat, but the layout is not *stable* under change. A new variable name that is longer than the preallotted number of columns requires that you move *all* entries around:

```
    firstRecord = other.firstRecord;
    lastRecord  = other.lastRecord;
    cutoff      = other.cutoff;
    marginalFudgeFactor = other.marginalFudgeFactor;
```

This is just the kind of trap that makes you decide to use a short variable name like `mff` instead.

Do not use // comments for comments that extend for more than two lines. You don't want to have to move the // around when you edit the comment.

```
    // comment—don't do this
    // more comment
    // more comment
```

Use /* . . . */ comments instead. When using /* . . . */ comments, don't "beautify" them with additional asterisks:

```
    /* comment—don't do this
     * more comment
     * more comment
     */
```

It looks neat, but it is a major disincentive to update the comment. Some people have text editors that lay out comments. But even if you do, you don't know whether the next person who maintains your code has such an editor.

Instead, format long comments like this:

```
    /*
        comment
        more comment
```

```
        more comment
    */
```

or this:

```
    /*
    comment
    more comment
    more comment
    */
```

These comments are easier to maintain as your program changes. If you have to choose between pretty but unmaintained comments and ugly comments that are up to date, truth wins over beauty.

A2

The Java Library

This appendix lists all classes and methods from the standard Java library that are used in this book.

In the following inheritance diagram, superclasses that are not used in this book are shown in parentheses. Some classes implement interfaces not covered in this book; they are omitted. Classes are sorted first by package, then alphabetically within a package.

```
java.awt.Shape
java.awt.Stroke
java.lang.Cloneable
java.lang.Object
    java.awt.BasicStroke implements Stroke
    java.awt.Color implements Serializable
    java.awt.Component implements Serializable
        java.awt.Container
            javax.swing.JComponent
                javax.swing.AbstractButton
                    javax.swing.JButton
                    javax.swing.JMenuItem
                        javax.swing.JMenu
                    (javax.swing.JToggleButton)
                        javax.swing.JCheckBox
                        javax.swing.JRadioButton
                javax.swing.JComboBox
                javax.swing.JFileChooser
                javax.swing.JMenuBar
                javax.swing.JPanel
                javax.swing.JOptionPane
                javax.swing.JSlider
                javax.swing.text.JTextComponent
                    javax.swing.JTextArea
                    javax.swing.JTextField
```

```
            (java.awt.Panel)
             java.applet.Applet
                javax.swing.JApplet
          java.awt.Window
            java.awt.Frame
              javax.swing.JFrame
    java.awt.FlowLayout implements Serializable
    java.awt.Font implements Serializable
    java.awt.Graphics
       java.awt.Graphics2D;
    java.awt.GridLayout implements Serializable
    java.awt.event.MouseAdapter implements MouseListener
    java.awt.event.WindowAdapter
       implements WindowListener
    java.awt.font.FontRenderContext
    java.awt.font.TextLayout implements Cloneable
    java.awt.geom.Line2D
       implements Cloneable, Shape
       java.awt.geom.Line2D.Double
    java.awt.geom.Point2D implements Cloneable
       java.awt.geom.Point2D.Double
    java.awt.geom.RectangularShape
       implements Cloneable, Shape
      (java.awt.geom.Rectangle2D)
          java.awt.Rectangle implements Serializable
          java.awt.Rectangle2D.Double
       java.awt.geom.Ellipse2D
          java.awt.geom.Ellipse2D.Double
    java.io.File implements Comparable, Serializable
    java.io.InputStream
       java.io.FileInputStream
       java.io.ObjectInputStream
    java.io.OutputStream
       java.io.FileOutputStream
       java.io.ObjectOutputStream
    java.io.RandomAccessFile
    java.io.Reader
       java.io.BufferedReader
       java.io.InputStreamReader
          java.io.FileReader
    java.io.Writer
       java.io.PrintWriter
      (java.io.OutputStreamWriter)
          java.io.FileWriter
    java.lang.Boolean implements Serializable
    java.lang.Math
  (java.lang.Number implements Serializable)
       java.math.BigDecimal implements Comparable
       java.math.BigInteger implements Comparable
       java.lang.Double implements Comparable
```

```
           java.lang.Float implements Comparable
           java.lang.Integer implements Comparable
        java.lang.String implements Comparable, Serializable
        java.lang.System
        java.lang.Throwable
           java.lang.Error
           java.lang.Exception
              java.lang.CloneNotSupportedException
              java.io.IOException
                 java.io.EOFException
                 java.io.FileNotFoundException
              java.lang.RuntimeException
                 java.lang.IllegalArgumentException
                    java.lang.NumberFormatException
                 java.lang.NullPointerException
      (java.text.Format implements Cloneable, Serializable)
        java.text.DateFormat
        java.text.NumberFormat
      (java.util.AbstractCollection)
        java.util.AbstractList
           (java.util.AbstractSequentialList)
              java.util.LinkedList
           java.util.ArrayList
              implements Cloneable, List, Serializable
      java.util.logging.Level implements Serializable
      java.util.logging.Logger
      java.util.Arrays
      java.util.EventObject implements Serializable
        (java.awt.AWTEvent)
           java.awt.event.ActionEvent
           (java.awt.event.ComponentEvent)
              java.awt.event.InputEvent
                 java.awt.event.MouseEvent
              java.awt.event.WindowEvent
        javax.swing.event.ChangeEvent
      java.util.Random implements Serializable
      java.util.StringTokenizer
      javax.swing.ButtonGroup implements Serializable
      javax.swing.ImageIcon implements Serializable
      javax.swing.Timer implements Serializable
      (javax.swing.border.AbstractBorder
           implements Serializable)
           javax.swing.border.EtchedBorder
           javax.swing.border.TitledBorder
  java.lang.Serializable
  java.util.Collection
     java.util.List
  java.util.EventListener
     java.awt.event.ActionListener
     java.awt.event.MouseListener
```

```
java.awt.event.WindowListener
javax.swing.event.ChangeListener
java.util.Iterator
java.util.ListIterator
```

In the following descriptions, the phrase "this object" ("this component", "this container", and so forth) means the object (component, container, and so forth) on which the method is invoked (the implicit parameter, `this`).

Package `java.applet`

Class `java.applet.Applet`

- `void destroy()`

   This method is called when the applet is about to be terminated, after the last call to `stop`.

- `void init()`

   This method is called when the applet has been loaded, before the first call to `start`. Applets override this method to carry out applet-specific initialization and to read applet parameters.

- `void start()`

   This method is called after the `init` method and each time the applet is revisited.

- `void stop()`

   This method is called whenever the user has stopped watching this applet.

Package `java.awt`

Class `java.awt.BasicStroke`

- `BasicStroke(float width)`

   This constructs a stroke object that draws lines of a given width.

   Parameters:

        `width`—The stroke width

Class `java.awt.BorderLayout`

- `BorderLayout()`

   This constructs a border layout. A border layout has five regions for adding components, called `"North"`, `"East"`, `"South"`, `"West"`and `"Center"`.

- `static final int CENTER`

   This value identifies the center position of a border layout.

- `static final int EAST`

  This value identifies the east position of a border layout.

- `static final int NORTH`

  This value identifies the north position of a border layout.

- `static final int SOUTH`

  This value identifies the south position of a border layout.

- `static final int WEST`

  This value identifies the west position of a border layout.

Class `java.awt.Color`

- `Color(float red, float green, float blue)`

  This creates a color with the specified red, green, and blue values between `0.0F` and `1.0F`.

  Parameters:

  > `red`—The red component
  >
  > `green`—The green component
  >
  > `blue`—The blue component

Class `java.awt.Component`

- `int getHeight()`

  This method gets the height of this component.

  Returns: The height in pixels.

- `int getWidth()`

  This method gets the width of this component.

  Returns: The width in pixels.

- `void repaint()`

  This method repaints this component by scheduling a call to the `paint` method.

- `void setPreferredSize(int width, int height)`

  This method sets the preferred size for this component.

  Parameters:

  > `width`—The preferred width
  >
  > `height`—The preferred height

Class `java.awt.Container`

- `void add(Component c)`
- `void add(Component c, Object position)`

These methods add a component to the end of this container. If a position is given, the layout manager is called to position the component.

Parameters:

> `c`—The component to be added
>
> `position`—An object expressing position information for the layout manager

- `void paint(Graphics g)`

This method is called when the surface of the container needs to be repainted.

Parameters:

> `g`—The graphics context

- `void setLayout(LayoutManager manager)`

This method sets the layout manager for this container.

Parameters:

> `manager`—A layout manager

- `void setSize(int width, int height)`

This method changes the size of this container.

Parameters:

> `width`—The new width
>
> `height`—The new height

Class `java.awt.FlowLayout`

- `FlowLayout()`

This constructs a new flow layout. A flow layout places as many components as possible in a row, without changing their size, and starts new rows when necessary.

Class `java.awt.Font`

- `Font(String name, int style, int size)`

This constructs a font object from the specified name, style, and point size.

Parameters:

> `name`—The font name, either a font face name or a logical font name, which must be one of `"Dialog"`, `"DialogInput"`, `"Monospaced"`, `"Serif"`, or `"SansSerif"`

> style—One of Font.PLAIN, Font.ITALIC, Font.BOLD, or Font.ITALIC
> +Font.BOLD
>
> size—The point size of the font

- Rectangle2D getStringBounds(String s, FontRenderContext context)

This method measures the size of a string.

Parameters:

> s—The string to measure
>
> context—The font render context to use for measuring

Returns: A rectangle enclosing the string, whose basepoint is positioned at (0, 0).

Class java.awt.Frame

- void setTitle(String title)

This method sets the frame title.

Parameters:

> title—The title to be displayed in the border of the frame

Class java.awt.Graphics

- void setColor(Color c)

This method sets the current color. From now on, all graphics operations use this color.

Parameters:

> c—The new drawing color

- void setFont(Font font)

This method sets the current font. From now on, all text operations use this font.

Parameters:

> font–The font

Class java.awt.Graphics2D

- void draw(Shape s)

> This method draws the outline of the given shape. Many classes—among
> them Rectangle and Line2D.Double—implement the Shape interface.

Parameters:

> s—The shape to be drawn

- void drawString(String s, int x, int y)
- void drawString(String s, float x, float y)

These methods draw a string in the current font.

Parameters:

> s—The string to draw
>
> x,y—The basepoint of the first character in the string

- **void fill(Shape s)**

This method draws the given shape and fills it with the current color.

Parameters:

> s—The shape to be filled

- **FontRenderContext getFontRenderContext()**

This method gets the font render context, an object that is used for measuring and drawing fonts.

Returns: The font render context.

- **void setStroke(Stroke s)**

This method sets the current stroke for drawing lines and curves.

Parameters:

> s—The stroke to use

Class java.awt.GridLayout

- **GridLayout(int rows, int cols)**

This constructor creates a grid layout with the specified number of rows and columns. The components in a grid layout are arranged in a grid with equal widths and heights. One, but not both, of rows and cols can be zero, in which case any number of objects can be placed in a row or in a column, respectively.

Parameters:

> rows—The number of rows in the grid
>
> cols—The number of columns in the grid

Class java.awt.Rectangle

- **Rectangle()**

This constructs a rectangle whose top left corner is at (0, 0) and whose width and height are both zero.

- **Rectangle(int x,int y,int width,int height)**

This constructs a rectangle with given top left corner and size.

Parameters:

> x,y—The upper left corner
>
> width—The width
>
> height—The height

- Rectangle intersection(Rectangle other)

  This method computes the intersection of this rectangle with the specified rectangle.

  Parameters:

  > other—A rectangle

  Returns: The largest rectangle contained in both this and other.

- void setLocation(int x, int y)

  This method moves this rectangle to a new location.

  Parameters:

  > x,y—The new top left corner

- void setSize(int width, int height)

  This method changes the size of this rectangle.

  Parameters:

  > width—The new width

  > height—The new height

- void translate(int dx, int dy)

  This method moves this rectangle.

  Parameters:

  > dx—The distance to move along the *x*-axis

  > dy—The distance to move along the *y*-axis

- Rectangle union(Rectangle other)

  This method computes the union of this rectangle with the specified rectangle. This is not the set-theoretic union but the smallest rectangle that contains both this and other.

  Parameters:

  > other—A rectangle

  Returns: The smallest rectangle containing both this and other.

Interface java.awt.Shape

The Shape interface describes shapes that can be drawn and filled by a Graphics2D object.

Class java.awt.Window

- void addWindowListener(WindowListener listener)

  This method adds a window listener. The window listener is notified whenever a window event originates from this window.

Parameters:

> `listener`—The window listener to be added

- `void pack()`

This method lays out the components in the window to occupy as little space as possible, and sizes the window to enclose the components.

- `void show()`

This method makes the window visible and brings it to the front.

Package `java.awt.event`

Class `java.awt.event.ActionEvent`

- `String getActionCommand()`

This method returns a string describing this action event, such as the label of the button or menu that caused it. These strings are subject to change, so you should generally not use them to identify the event source.

Returns: The action command string.

Interface `java.awt.event.ActionListener`

- `void actionPerformed(ActionEvent e)`

The event source calls this method when an action occurs.

Class `java.awt.event.MouseAdapter`

- `void mouseClicked(MouseEvent e)`

This method is called when the mouse has been clicked (that is, pressed and released in quick succession).

- `void mousePressed(MouseEvent e)`

This method is called when a mouse button has been pressed.

- `void mouseReleased(MouseEvent e)`

This method is called when a mouse button has been released.

Class `java.awt.event.MouseEvent`

- `int getX()`

This method returns the horizontal position of the mouse as of the time the event occurred.

Returns: The *x*-position of the mouse.

- `int getY()`

This method returns the vertical position of the mouse as of the time the event occurred.

Returns: The *y*-position of the mouse.

Interface `java.awt.event.MouseListener`

- `void mouseClicked(MouseEvent e)`

  This method is called when the mouse has been clicked (that is, pressed and released in quick succession).

- `void mousePressed(MouseEvent e)`

  This method is called when a mouse button has been pressed.

- `void mouseReleased(MouseEvent e)`

  This method is called when a mouse button has been released.

Class `java.awt.event.WindowAdapter`

- `void windowClosing(WindowEvent e)`

  This method is called when a window is in the process of being closed. Override this method if you want to exit the program when the window is closed.

Interface `java.awt.event.WindowListener`

- `void windowClosing(WindowEvent e)`

  This method is called when a window is in the process of being closed. Override this method if you want to exit the program when the window is closed.

Package `java.awt.font`

Class `java.awt.font.FontRenderContext`

A font render context is an object that is used for measuring and drawing fonts. It is obtained by the `getFontRenderContext()` method of the `java.awt.Graphics2D` class and used by the `java.awt.font.TextLayout` constructor.

Class `java.awt.font.TextLayout`

- `TextLayout(String s, Font f, FontRenderContext context)`

  This constructs a text layout to measure and draw a string in a particular font.

  Parameters:

  > s—The string to lay out

  > f—The font to use

  > context—The font render context of the output device

- `float getAdvance()`

  This method gets the total width of the string laid out by this `TextLayout` object.

  Returns: The advance (width in pixels) of the string.

- `float getAscent()`

This method gets the height above the base line of the string laid out by this Text-Layout object.

Returns: The ascent of the string in pixels.

- `float getDescent()`

This method gets the depth below the base line of the string laid out by this Text-Layout object.

Returns: The descent of the string in pixels.

- `float getLeading()`

This method gets the distance between two lines in the font used by this Text-Layout object.

Returns: The leading of the font in pixels.

Package `java.awt.geom`

Class `java.awt.geom.Ellipse2D.Double`

- `Ellipse2D.Double(double x, double y, double w, double h)`

This constructs an ellipse from the specified coordinates.

Parameters:

      x,y—The top left corner of the bounding rectangle

      w—The width of the bounding rectangle

      h—The height of the bounding rectangle

Class `java.awt.geom.Line2D`

- `double getX1()`
- `double getX2()`
- `double getY1()`
- `double getY2()`

These methods get the requested coordinate of an endpoint of this line.

Returns: The x- or y-coordinate of the first or second endpoint.

- `void setLine(double x1, double y1, double x2, double y2)`

This methods sets the endpoints of this line.

Parameters:

      x1,y1—A new endpoint of this line

      x2,y2—The other new endpoint

Class `java.awt.geom.Line2D.Double`

- `Line2D.Double(double x1, double y1, double x2, double y2)`

  This constructs a line from the specified coordinates.

  Parameters:

  > `x1, y1`—One endpoint of the line
  >
  > `x2, y2`—The other endpoint

- `Line2D.Double(Point2D p1, Point2D p2)`

  This constructs a line from the two endpoints.

  Parameters:

  > `p1, p2`—The endpoints of the line

Class `java.awt.geom.Point2D`

- `double getX()`
- `double getY()`

  These methods get the requested coordinates of this point.

  Returns: The *x*- or *y*-coordinate of this point.

- `void setLocation(double x, double y)`

  This method sets the *x*- and *y*-coordinates of this point.

  Parameters:

  > `x,y`—The new location of this point

Class `java.awt.geom.Point2D.Double`

- `Point2D.Double(double x, double y)`

  This constructs a point with the specified coordinates.

  Parameters:

  > `x,y`—The coordinates of the point

Class `java.awt.geom.Rectangle2D.Double`

- `Rectangle2D.Double(double x, double y, double w, double h)`

  This constructs a rectangle.

  Parameters:

  > `x, y`—The upper left corner
  >
  > `w`—The width
  >
  > `h`—The height

Class `java.awt.geom.RectangularShape`

- `int getHeight()`
- `int getWidth()`

These methods get the height or width of the bounding rectangle of this rectangular shape.

Returns: The height or width, respectively.

- `double getCenterX()`
- `double getCenterY()`
- `double getMaxX()`
- `double getMaxY()`
- `double getMinX()`
- `double getMinY()`

These methods get the requested coordinate value of the corners or center of the bounding rectangle of this shape.

Returns: The minimum, center, or maximum *x*- and *y*-coordinates.

- `void setFrame(double x, double y, double w, double h)`

This method sets the bounding rectangle of this rectangular shape.

Parameters:

      `x, y`—The upper left corner

      `w`—The width

      `h`—The height

- `void setFrameFromDiagonal(double x1, double y1, double x2, double y2)`

This method sets the bounding rectangle of this rectangular shape.

Parameters:

      `x1, y1`—A corner point

      `x2, y2`—The diametrically opposite corner point

Package `java.io`

Class `java.io.BufferedReader`

- `BufferedReader(Reader in)`

This constructs a buffered reader, an object that stores characters in a buffer for more efficient reading.

Parameters:

in—A reader

- `String readLine()`

This method reads a line of input from this buffered reader.

Returns: The input line, or `null` if the end of input has been reached.

Class `java.io.EOFException`

- `EOFException(String message)`

This constructs an "end of file" exception object.

Parameters:

`message`—The detail message

Class `java.io.File`

This class describes a disk file or directory. Objects of this class are returned by the `getSelectedFile()` method of the `javax.swing.JFileChooser` class.

Class `java.io.FileInputStream`

- `FileInputStream(File f)`

This constructs a file input stream and opens the chosen file. If the file cannot be opened for reading, a `FileNotFoundException` is thrown.

Parameters:

`f`—The file to be opened for reading

- `FileInputStream(String name)`

This constructs a file input stream and opens the named file. If the file cannot be opened for reading, a `FileNotFoundException` is thrown.

Parameters:

`name`—The name of the file to be opened for reading

Class `java.io.FileNotFoundException`

This exception is thrown when a file could not be opened.

Class `java.io.FileOutputStream`

- `FileOutputStream(File f)`

This constructs a file output stream and opens the chosen file. If the file cannot be opened for writing, a `FileNotFoundException` is thrown.

Parameters:

`f`—The file to be opened for writing

- `FileOutputStream(String name)`

This constructs a file output stream and opens the named file. If the file cannot be opened for writing, a `FileNotFoundException` is thrown.

Parameters:

> name—The name of the file to be opened for writing

Class `java.io.FileReader`

- `FileReader(File f)`

This constructs a file reader and opens the chosen file. If the file cannot be opened for reading, a `FileNotFoundException` is thrown.

Parameters:

> f—The file to be opened for reading

- `FileReader(String name)`

This constructs a file reader and opens the named file. If the file cannot be opened for reading, a `FileNotFoundException` is thrown.

Parameters:

> name—The name of the file to be opened for reading

Class `java.io.FileWriter`

- `FileWriter(File f)`

This constructs a file writer and opens the chosen file. If the file cannot be opened for writing, a `FileNotFoundException` is thrown.

Parameters:

> f—The file to be opened for writing

- `FileWriter(String name)`

This constructs a file writer and opens the named file. If the file cannot be opened for writing, a `FileNotFoundException` is thrown.

Parameters:

> name—The name of the file to be opened for writing

Class `java.io.InputStream`

- `void close()`

This method closes this input stream (such as a `FileInputStream`) and releases any system resources associated with the stream.

- `int read()`

This method reads the next byte of data from this input stream.

Returns: The next byte of data, or −1 if the end of the stream is reached.

Class `java.io.InputStreamReader`

- `InputStreamReader(InputStream in)`

  This constructs a reader from a specified input stream.

  Parameters:

    `in`—The stream to read from

Class `java.io.IOException`

This type of exception is thrown when an input/output error is encountered.

Class `java.io.ObjectInputStream`

- `ObjectInputStream(InputStream in)`

  This constructs an object input stream.

  Parameters:

    `in`—The stream to read from

- `Object readObject()`

  This method reads the next object from this object input stream.

  Returns: The next object.

Class `java.io.ObjectOutputStream`

- `ObjectOutputStream(OutputStream out)`

  This constructs an object output stream.

  Parameters:

    `out`—The stream to write to

- `Object writeObject(Object obj)`

  This method writes the next object to this object output stream.

  Parameters:

    `obj`—The object to write

Class `java.io.OutputStream`

- `void close()`

  This method closes this output stream (such as a `FileOutputStream`) and releases any system resources associated with this stream. A closed stream cannot perform output operations and cannot be reopened.

- `void write(int b)`

  This method writes the lowest byte of `b` to this output stream.

  Parameters:

    `b`—The integer whose lowest byte is written

Class `java.io.PrintStream`

- `void print(int x)`
- `void print(double x)`
- `void print(Object x)`
- `void print(String x)`
- `void println()`
- `void println(int x)`
- `void println(double x)`
- `void println(Object x)`
- `void println(String x)`

These methods print a value to this print stream. The `println` methods print a newline after the value. Objects are printed by converting them to strings with their `toString` methods.

Parameters:

x—The value to be printed

Class `java.io.PrintWriter`

- `PrintWriter(Writer out)`

This constructs a print writer from a specified writer (such as a `FileWriter`).

Parameters:

out—The writer to write output to

- `void print(int x)`
- `void print(double x)`
- `void print(Object x)`
- `void print(String x)`
- `void println()`
- `void println(int x)`
- `void println(double x)`
- `void println(Object x)`
- `void println(String x)`

These methods print a value to this print writer. The `println` methods print a newline after the value. Objects are printed by converting them to strings with their `toString` methods.

Parameters:

x—The value to be printed

Class `java.io.RandomAccessFile`

- `RandomAccessFile(String name, String mode)`

    This method opens a named random access file for reading or read/write access.

    Parameters:

    > name—The file name

    > mode—"r" for reading or "rw" for read/write access

- `long getFilePointer()`

    This method gets the current position in this file.

    Returns: The current position for reading and writing.

- `long length()`

    This method gets the length of this file.

    Returns: The file length.

- `char readChar()`
- `double readDouble()`
- `int readInt()`

    These methods read a value from the current position in this file.

    Returns: The value that was read from the file.

- `void seek(long position)`

    This method sets the position for reading and writing in this file.

    Parameters:

    > position—The new position

- `void writeChar(int x)`
- `void writeChars(String x)`
- `void writeDouble(double x)`
- `void writeInt(int x)`

    These methods write a value to the current position in this file.

    Parameters:

    > x—The value to be written

Class `java.io.Reader`

- `int read()`

    This method reads the next character from this reader (such as a `FileReader`).

    Returns: The next character, or −1 if the end of the input is reached.

Interface `java.io.Serializable`

A class must implement this interface to enable its objects to be written to object streams.

Class `java.io.Writer`

- `void write(int b)`

  This method writes the lowest two bytes of b to this writer (such as a `FileWriter`).

  Parameters:

  > b—The integer whose lowest two bytes are written

Package `java.lang`

Class `java.lang.Boolean`

- `Boolean(boolean value)`

  This constructs a wrapper object for a `boolean` value.

  Parameters:

  > value—The value to store in this object

- `boolean booleanValue()`

  This method returns the `boolean` value stored in this `Boolean` object.

  Returns: The Boolean value of this object.

Interface `java.lang.Cloneable`

> A class implements this interface to indicate that the `Object.clone` method is allowed to make a shallow copy of its instance variables.

Class `java.lang.CloneNotSupportedException`

> This exception is thrown when a program tries to use `Object.clone` to make a shallow copy of an object of a class that does not implement the `Cloneable` interface.

Interface `java.lang.Comparable`

- `int compareTo(Object other)`

  This method compares this object with the `other` object.

  Parameters:

  > other—The object to be compared

  Returns: A negative integer if this object is less than the other, zero if they are equal, or a positive integer otherwise.

Class `java.lang.Double`

- `Double(double value)`

  This constructs a wrapper object for a double-precision floating-point number.

Parameters:

> `value`—The value to store in this object

- `double doubleValue()`

This method returns the floating-point value stored in this `Double` wrapper object.

Returns: The value stored in the object.

- `static double parseDouble(String s)`

This method returns the floating-point number that the string represents. If the string cannot be interpreted as a number, a `NumberFormatException` is thrown.

Parameters:

> `s`—The string to be parsed

Returns: The value represented by the string parameter.

- `static String toString(double x)`

This method converts a number to a string representation.

Parameters:

> `x`—The number to be converted

Returns: The string representing the number parameter.

Class `java.lang.Error`

This is the superclass for all unchecked system errors.

Class `java.lang.Float`

- `static float parseFloat(String s)`

This method returns the single-precision floating-point number that the string represents. If the string cannot be interpreted as such a number, a `NumberFormat-Exception` is thrown.

Parameters:

> `s`—The string to be parsed

Returns: The value represented by the string parameter.

Class `java.lang.IllegalArgumentException`

- `IllegalArgumentException()`

This constructs an `IllegalArgumentException` with no detail message.

Class `java.lang.Integer`

- `Integer(int value)`

This constructs a wrapper object for an integer.

Parameters:

> value—The value to store in this object.

- `int intValue()`

This method returns the integer value stored in this wrapper object.

Returns: The value stored in the object.

- `static int parseInt(String s)`

This method returns the integer that the string represents. If the string cannot be interpreted as an integer, a `NumberFormatException` is thrown.

Parameters:

> s—The string to be parsed

Returns: The value represented by the string parameter.

- `static Integer parseInt(String s,int base)`

This method returns the integer value that the string represents in a given number system. If the string cannot be interpreted as an integer, a `NumberFormat-Exception` is thrown.

Parameters:

> s—The string to be parsed
>
> base—The base of the number system (such as 2 or 16)

Returns: The value represented by the string parameter.

- `static String toString(int i)`
- `static String toString(int i, int base)`

This method creates a string representation of an integer in a given number system. If no base is given, a decimal representation is created.

Parameters:

> i—An integer number
>
> base—The base of the number system (such as 2 or 16)

Returns: A string representation of the number parameter in the specified number system.

- `static final int MAX_VALUE`

This constant is the largest value of type `int`.

- `static final int MIN_VALUE`

This constant is the smallest (negative) value of type `int`.

Class `java.lang.Math`

- `static double abs(double x)`

This method returns the absolute value $|x|$.

Parameters:

x—A floating-point value

Returns: The absolute value of the parameter.

- `static double acos(double x)`

This method returns the angle with the given cosine, $\cos^{-1} x \in [0, \pi]$.

Parameters:

x—A floating-point value between −1 and 1

Returns: The arc cosine of the parameter, in radians.

- `static double asin(double x)`

This method returns the angle with the given sine, $\sin^{-1} x \in [-\pi/2, \pi/2]$.

Parameters:

x—A floating-point value between −1 and 1

Returns: The arc sine of the parameter, in radians.

- `static double atan(double x)`

This method returns the angle with the given tangent, $\tan^{-1} x \, (-\pi/2, \pi/2)$.

Parameters:

x—A floating-point value

Returns: The arc tangent of the parameter, in radians.

- `static double atan2(double y, double x)`

This method returns the arc tangent, $\tan^{-1}(y/x) \in (-\pi, \pi)$. If x can equal zero, or if it is necessary to distinguish "northwest" from "southeast" and "northeast" from "southwest", use this method instead of `atan(y/x)`.

Parameters:

y,x—Two floating-point values

Returns: The angle, in radians, between the points (0, 0) and (x, y).

- `static double ceil(double x)`

This method returns the smallest integer $\leq x$ (as a `double`).

Parameters:

x—A floating-point value

Returns: The "ceiling integer" of the parameter.

- `static double cos(double radians)`

This method returns the cosine of an angle given in radians.

Parameters:

>   radians—An angle, in radians

Returns: The cosine of the parameter.

- `static double exp(double x)`

This method returns the value e^x, where e is the base of the natural logarithms.

Parameters:

>   x—A floating-point value

Returns: e^x.

- `static double floor(double x)`

This method returns the largest integer $\geq x$ (as a `double`).

Parameters:

>   x—A floating-point value

Returns: The "floor integer" of the parameter.

- `static double log(double x)`

This method returns the natural (base e) logarithm of x, ln x.

Parameters:

>   x—A number greater than 0.0

Returns: The natural logarithm of the parameter.

- `static double pow(double x, double y)`

This method returns the value x^y ($x > 0$, or $x = 0$ and $y > 0$, or $x < 0$ and y is an integer).

Parameters:

>   x,y—Two floating-point values

Returns: The value of the first parameter raised to the power of the second parameter.

- `static long round(double x)`

This method returns the closest `long` integer to the parameter.

Parameters:

>   x—A floating-point value

Returns: The value of the parameter rounded to the nearest `long` value.

- `static double sin(double radians)`

This method returns the sine of an angle given in radians.

Parameters:

> radians—An angle, in radians

Returns: The sine of the parameter.

- `static double sqrt(double x)`

  This method returns the square root of x, $\sqrt{x}$.

  Parameters:

  > x—A nonnegative floating-point value

  Returns: The square root of the parameter.

- `static double tan(double radians)`

  This method returns the tangent of an angle given in radians.

  Parameters:

  > radians—An angle, in radians

  Returns: The tangent of the parameter.

- `static double toDegrees(double radian)`

  This method converts radians to degrees.

  Parameters:

  > radians—An angle, in radians

  Returns: The angle in degrees.

- `static double toRadians(double degrees)`

  This methods converts degrees to radians.

  Parameters:

  > degrees—An angle, in degrees

  Returns: The angle in radians.

- `static final double E`

  This constant is the value of e, the base of the natural logarithms.

- `static final double PI`

  This constant is the value of π.

Class `java.lang.NullPointerException`

This exception is thrown when a program tries to use an object through a `null` reference.

Class `java.lang.NumberFormatException`

This exception is thrown when a program tries to parse the numerical value of a string that is not a number.

Class `java.lang.Object`

- `protected Object clone()`

  This method constructs and returns a shallow copy of this object whose instance variables are copies of the instance variables of this object. If an instance variable of the object is an object reference itself, only the reference is copied, not the object itself. However, if the class does not implement the `Cloneable` interface, a `CloneNotSupportedException` is thrown. Subclasses should redefine this method to make a deep copy.

  Returns: A copy of this object.

- `boolean equals(Object other)`

  This method tests whether `this` and the other object are equal. This method tests only whether the object references are to the same object. Subclasses should redefine this method to compare the instance variables.

  Parameters:

  > `other`—The object with which to compare

  Returns: `true` if the objects are equal, `false` otherwise.

- `String toString()`

  This method returns a string representation of this object. This method produces only the class name and locations of the objects. Subclasses should redefine this method to print the instance variables.

  Returns: A string describing this object.

Class `java.lang.RuntimeException`

This is the superclass for all unchecked exceptions.

Class `java.lang.String`

- `int compareTo(String other)`

  This method compares this string and the other string lexicographically.

  Parameters:

  > `other`—The other string to be compared

  Returns: A value less than 0 if this string is lexicographically less than the other, 0 if the strings are equal, and a value greater than 0 otherwise.

- `boolean equals(String other)`

- `boolean equalsIgnoreCase(String other)`

  These methods test whether two strings are equal, or whether they are equal when letter case is ignored.

Parameters:

> other—The other string to be compared

Returns: true if the strings are equal.

- int length()

This method returns the length of this string.

Returns: The count of characters in this string.

- String substring(int begin)
- String substring(int begin, int pastEnd)

These methods return a new string that is a substring of this string, made up of all characters starting at position begin and up to either position pastEnd - 1 is given, or the end of the string.

Parameters:

> begin—The beginning index, inclusive
> pastEnd—The ending index, exclusive

Returns: The specified substring.

- String toLowerCase()

This method returns a new string that consists of all characters in this string converted to lowercase.

Returns: A string with all characters of this string converted to lowercase.

- String toUpperCase()

This method returns a new string that consists of all characters in this string converted to uppercase.

Returns: A string with all characters of this string converted to uppercase.

Class java.lang.System

- static void arraycopy(Object from, int fromStart, Object to, int toStart, int count)

This method copies values from one array to the other. (The array parameters are of type Object because you can convert an array of numbers to an Object but not to an Object[].)

Parameters:

> from—The source array
> fromStart—Start position in the source array
> to—The destination array
> toStart—Start position in the destination data
> count—The number of array elements to be copied

- `static long currentTimeMillis()`

  This method returns the difference, measured in milliseconds, between the current time and midnight, Universal Time, January 1, 1970.

  Returns: The current time in milliseconds.

- `static void exit(int status)`

  This method terminates the program.

  Parameters:

  > `status`—exit status. A nonzero status code indicates abnormal termination.

- `static final InputStream in`

  This object is the "standard input" stream. Reading from this stream typically reads keyboard input.

- `static final PrintStream out`

  This object is the "standard output" stream. Printing to this stream typically sends output to the console window.

Class `java.lang.Throwable`

This is the superclass of exceptions and errors.

- `Throwable()`

  This constructs a `Throwable` with no detail message.

- `void printStackTrace()`

  This method prints a stack trace to the "standard error" stream. The stack trace contains a printout of this object and of all calls that were pending at the time it was created.

Package `java.math`

Class `java.math.BigDecimal`

- `BigDecimal(String value)`

  This constructs an arbitrary-precision floating-point number from the digits in the given string.

  Parameters:

  > `value`—A string representing the floating-point number

- `BigDecimal add(BigDecimal other)`
- `BigDecimal subtract(BigDecimal other)`
- `BigDecimal multiply(BigDecimal other)`
- `BigDecimal divide(BigDecimal other, int roundingMode)`

These methods return a `BigDecimal` whose value is the sum, difference, product, or quotient of this number and the other.

Parameters:

     `other`—The other number

     `roundingMode`—The rounding mode to apply to division (use `BigDecimal-.ROUND_HALF_EVEN` for general-purpose calculations)

Returns: The result of the arithmetic operation.

Class `java.math.BigInteger`

- `BigInteger(String value)`

This method constructs an arbitrary-precision integer from the digits in the given string.

Parameters:

     `value`—A string representing an arbitrary-precision integer

- `BigInteger add(BigInteger other)`
- `BigInteger subtract(BigInteger other)`
- `BigInteger multiply(BigInteger other)`
- `BigInteger divide(BigInteger other)`
- `BigInteger mod(BigInteger other)`

These methods return a `BigInteger` whose value is the sum, difference, product, quotient, or remainder of this number and the other.

Parameters:

     `other`—The other number

Returns: The result of the arithmetic operation.

Package `java.text`

Class `java.text.NumberFormat`

- `String format(double x)`

This method formats a number according to the formatting rules of this object.

Parameters:

     `x`—The number to format

Returns: A string representing `x`.

- `static NumberFormat getCurrencyInstance()`

This method returns a currency formatter, which formats numbers with a currency symbol and a fixed number of fractional digits.

- static NumberFormat getNumberInstance()

This method returns a number formatter, which formats numbers with decimal separators and a user-selectable number of fractional digits.

- void setMaximumFractionDigits(int digits)

This method sets the maximum number of fraction digits used when formatting numbers. Numbers will be rounded if they have more digits.

Parameters:

> digits—The maximum number of to digits to use

- void setMinimumFractionDigits(int digits)

This method sets the minimum number of fraction digits used when formatting numbers. Formatted numbers are padded with trailing zeroes if they have fewer digits.

Parameters:

> digits—The minimum number of digits to use

Package java.util

Class java.util.ArrayList

- ArrayList()

This constructs an empty array list.

- boolean add(Object element)

This method appends an element to the end of this array list.

Parameters:

> element—The element to add

Returns: true. (This method returns a value because it overrides a method in the List interface.)

- void add(int index, Object element)

This method inserts an element into this array list.

Parameters:

> index—Insert position
>
> element—The element to insert

- void copyInto(Object[] array)

This method copies the components of this array list into an array. The array must be big enough to hold all the objects in this array list.

Parameters:

> `array`—The array into which the components get copied

- `Object get(int index)`

This method gets the element at the specified position in this array list.

Parameters:

> `index`—Position of the element to return

Returns: The requested element.

- `Object remove(int index)`

This method removes the element at the specified position in this array list and returns it.

Parameters:

> `index`—Position of the element to remove

Returns: The removed element.

- `Object set(int index, Object element)`

This method replaces the element at a specified position in this array list.

Parameters:

> `index`—Position of element to replace
>
> `element`—Element to be stored at the specified position

Returns: The element previously at the specified position.

- `int size()`

This method returns the number of elements in this array list.

Returns: The number of elements in this array list.

Class `java.util.Arrays`

- `static int binarySearch(Object[] a, Object key)`

This method searches the specified array for the specified object using the binary search algorithm. The array elements must implement the `Comparable` interface. The array must be sorted in ascending order.

Parameters:

> `a`—The array to be searched
>
> `key`—The value to be searched for

Returns: The position of the search key, if it is contained in the list; otherwise, −*index* − 1, where *index* is the position where the element may be inserted.

- `static void sort(Object[] a)`

This method sorts the specified array of objects into ascending order. Its elements must implement the `Comparable` interface.

Parameters:

> a—The array to be sorted

Interface `java.util.Collection`

- `boolean add(Object element)`

This method adds an element to this collection.

Parameters:

> element—The element to add

Returns: `true` if adding the element changes the collection.

- `boolean contains(Object element)`

This method tests whether an element is present in this collection.

Parameters:

> element—The element to find

Returns: `true` if the element is contained in the collection.

- `Iterator iterator()`

This method returns an iterator that can be used to traverse the elements of this collection.

Returns: An object of a class implementing the `Iterator` interface.

- `boolean remove(Object element)`

This method removes an element from this collection.

Parameters:

> element—The element to remove

Returns: `true` if removing the element changes the collection.

- `int size()`

This method returns the number of elements in this collection.

Returns: The number of elements in this collection.

Class `java.util.EventObject`

- `Object getSource()`

This method returns a reference to the object on which this event initially occurred.

Returns: The source of this event.

Interface `java.util.Iterator`

- `boolean hasNext()`

  This method checks whether the iterator is past the end of the list.

  Returns: `true` if the iterator is not yet past the end of the list.

- `Object next()`

  This method moves the iterator over the next element in the linked list. This method throws an exception if the iterator is past the end of the list.

  Returns: The object that was just skipped over.

- `void remove()`

  This method removes the element that was returned by the last call to **next** or **previous**. This method throws an exception if there was an **add** or **remove** operation after the last call to **next** or **previous**.

Interface `java.util.List`

- `ListIterator listIterator()`

  This method gets an iterator to visit the elements in this list.

  Returns: An iterator that points before the first element in this list.

Interface `java.util.ListIterator`

Objects implementing this interface are created by the `listIterator` methods of list classes.

- `void add(Object element)`

  This method adds an element after the iterator position and moves the iterator after the new element.

  Parameters:

     `element`—The element to be added

- `boolean hasPrevious()`

  This method checks whether the iterator is before the first element of the list.

  Returns: `true` if the iterator is not before the first element of the list.

- `Object previous()`

  This method moves the iterator over the previous element in the linked list. This method throws an exception if the iterator is before the first element of the list.

  Returns: The object that was just skipped over.

Class `java.util.LinkedList`

- `void addFirst(Object element)`
- `void addLast(Object element)`

  These methods add an element before the first or after the last element in this list.

Parameters:

> element—The element to be added

- Object getFirst()
- Object getLast()

These methods return a reference to the specified element from this list.

Returns: The first or last element.

- Object removeFirst()
- Object removeLast()

These methods remove the specified element from this list.

Returns: A reference to the removed element.

Class java.util.Random

- Random()

This constructs a new random number generator.

- double nextDouble()

This method returns the next pseudorandom, uniformly distributed floating-point number between 0.0 (inclusive) and 1.0 (exclusive) from this random number generator's sequence.

Returns: The next pseudorandom floating-point number.

- int nextInt(int n)

This method returns the next pseudorandom, uniformly distributed integer between 0 (inclusive) and the specified value (exclusive) drawn from this random number generator's sequence.

Parameters:

> n—Number of values to draw from

Returns: The next pseudorandom integer.

Class java.util.StringTokenizer

- StringTokenizer(String s)

This constructs a string tokenizer that breaks the specified string into tokens. Tokens are delimited by white space.

Parameters:

> s—The string to break up into tokens

- int countTokens()

This method counts the number of tokens in the string being processed by this tokenizer.

Returns: The token count.

```
boolean hasMoreTokens()
```

This method checks whether all tokens in the string being processed by this tokenizer have been skipped over by `nextToken()`.

Returns: `true` if more tokens are available.

- `String nextToken()`

This method skips over and returns the next token in the string being processed by this tokenizer.

Returns: A string containing the token that was just skipped over.

Package `java.util.logging`

Class `java.util.logging.Level`

- `static final int ALL`

This value indicates logging of all messages.

- `static final int INFO`

This value indicates informational logging.

- `static final int NONE`

This value indicates logging of no messages.

Class `java.util.logging.Logger`

- `static Logger getLogger(String id)`

This method gets the logger for a given ID. Use the ID `"global"` to get the default global logger.

Parameters:

> `id`—the logger ID such as `"global"` or `"com.mycompany.mymodule"`

Returns: The logger with the given ID.

- `void info(String message)`

This method logs an informational message.

Parameters:

> `message`—The message to log

- `void setLevel(Level aLevel)`

This method sets the logging level. Logging messages with a lesser severity than the current level are ignored.

Parameters:

> `aLevel`—The minimum level for logging messages

Package `javax.swing`

Class `javax.swing.AbstractButton`

- `void addActionListener(ActionListener listener)`

  This method adds an action listener to the button.

  Parameters:

  > `listener`—The action listener to be added

- `boolean isSelected()`

  This method returns the selection state of the button.

  Returns: `true` if the button is selected.

- `void setSelected(boolean state)`

  This method sets the selection state of the button. This method updates the button but does not trigger an action event.

  Parameters:

  > `state`—`true` to select, `false` to deselect

Class `javax.swing.ButtonGroup`

- `void add(AbstractButton button)`

  This method adds the button to the group.

  Parameters:

  > `button`—The button to add

Class `javax.swing.ImageIcon`

- `ImageIcon(String filename)`

  This constructs an image icon from the specified graphics file.

  Parameters:

  > `filename`—A string specifying a file name

Class `javax.swing.JApplet`

- `Container getContentPane()`

  This method returns the content pane of this applet.

  Returns: The content pane.

Class `javax.swing.JCheckBox`

- `JCheckBox(String text)`

This constructs a check box, having the given text, initially deselected. (Use the `set-Selected()` method to make the box selected; see the `javax.swing.Abstract-Button` class.)

Parameters:

> `text`—The text displayed next to the check box

Class `javax.swing.JComboBox`

- `JComboBox()`

This constructs a combo box with no items.

- `void addItem(Object item)`

This method adds an item to the item list of this combo box.

Parameters:

> `item`–The item to add

- `Object getSelectedItem()`

This method gets the currently selected item of this combo box.

Returns: The currently selected item.

- `boolean isEditable()`

This method checks whether the combo box is editable. An editable combo box allows the user to type into the text field of the combo box.

Returns: `true` if the combo box is editable.

- `void setEditable(boolean state)`

This method is used to make the combo box editable or not.

Parameters:

> `state`—`true` to make editable, `false` to disable editing

Class `javax.swing.JComponent`

- `protected void paintComponent(Graphics g)`

Override this method to paint the surface of a component. Your method needs to call `super.paintComponent(g)`.

Parameters:

> `g`—The graphics context used for drawing

- `void setBorder(Border b)`

This method sets the border of this component.

Parameters:

> `b`—The border to surround this component

- `void setFont(Font f)`

Sets the font used for the text in this component.

Parameters:

> f—A font

Class `javax.swing.JFileChooser`

- `JFileChooser()`

This constructs a file chooser.

- `File getSelectedFile()`

This method gets the selected file from this file chooser.

Returns: The selected file.

- `int showOpenDialog(Component parent)`

This method displays an "Open File" file chooser dialog.

Parameters:

> parent—The parent component or `null`

Returns: The return state of this file chooser after it has been closed by the user: either `APPROVE_OPTION` or `CANCEL_OPTION`. If `APPROVE_OPTION` is returned, call `getSelectedFile()` on this file chooser to get the file.

- `int showSaveDialog(Component parent)`

This method displays a "Save File" file chooser dialog.

Parameters:

> parent—The parent component or `null`

Returns: The return state of the file chooser after it has been closed by the user: either `APPROVE_OPTION` or `CANCEL_OPTION`.

Class `javax.swing.JFrame`

- `static final int EXIT_ON_CLOSE`

This value indicates that when the user closes this frame, the application is to exit.

- `Container getContentPane()`

This method returns the content pane of this frame.

Returns: The content pane.

- `void setContentPane(Container pane)`

This method sets the content pane of this frame to a new container.

Parameters:

> pane—The new content pane

- void setDefaultCloseOperation(int operation)

This method sets the default action for closing the frame.

Parameters:

> operation–The desired close operation. Choose among
> DO_NOTHING_ON_CLOSE, HIDE_ON_CLOSE (the default),
> DISPOSE_ON_CLOSE, or EXIT_ON_CLOSE

- void setJMenuBar(JMenuBar mb)

This method sets the menu bar for this frame.

Parameters:

> mb—The menu bar. If mb is null, then the current menu bar is removed.

Class javax.swing.JLabel

- JLabel(String text,int alignment)

This container creates a JLabel instance with the specified text and horizontal alignment.

Parameters:

> text—The label text to be displayed by the label
>
> alignment—One of SwingConstants.LEFT, SwingConstants.CENTER, or SwingConstants.RIGHT

Class javax.swing.JMenu

- JMenu()

This constructs a menu with no items.

- JMenuItem add(JMenuItem menuItem)

This method appends a menu item to the end of this menu.

Parameters:

> menuItem—The menu item to be added

Returns: The menu item that was added.

Class javax.swing.JMenuBar

- JMenuBar()

This constructs a menu bar with no menus.

- JMenu add(JMenu menu)

This method appends a menu to the end of this menu bar.

Parameters:

> menu—The menu to be added

Returns: The menu that was added.

Class `javax.swing.JMenuItem`

- `JMenuItem(String text)`

This constructs a menu item.

Parameters:

> text—The text to appear in the menu item

Class `javax.swing.JOptionPane`

- `static String showInputDialog(Object prompt)`

This method brings up a modal input dialog, which displays a prompt and waits for the user to enter an input in a text field, preventing the user from doing anything else in this program.

Parameters:

> prompt—The prompt to display

Returns: The string that the user typed.

- `static void showMessageDialog(Component parent,Object message)`

This method brings up a confirmation dialog that displays a message and waits for the user to confirm it.

Parameters:

> parent—The parent component or `null`
>
> message—The message to display

Class `javax.swing.JPanel`

This class is a component without decorations. It can be used as an invisible container for other components. A subclass can implement its own `paintComponent` method.

Class `javax.swing.JRadioButton`

- `JRadioButton(String text)`

This constructs a radio button having the given text that is initially deselected. (Use the `setSelected()` method to select it; see the `javax.swing.Abstract-Button` class.)

Parameters:

> text—The string displayed next to the radio button

Class `javax.swing.JSlider`

- `JSlider(int min,int max,int value)`

This constructor creates a horizontal slider using the specified minimum, maximum, and value.

Parameters:

> `min`—The smallest possible slider value
>
> `max`—The largest possible slider value
>
> `value`—The initial value of the slider

- `void addChangeListener(ChangeListener listener)`

This method adds a change listener to the slider.

Parameters:

> `listener`—The change listener to add

- `int getValue()`

This method returns the slider's value.

Returns: The current value of the slider.

Class `javax.swing.JTextArea`

- `JTextArea()`

This constructs an empty text area.

- `JTextArea(int columns)`

This constructs an empty text area with the specified number of rows and columns.

Parameters:

> `rows`—The number of rows
>
> `columns`—The number of columns

Class `javax.swing.JTextField`

- `JTextField()`

This constructs an empty text field.

- `JTextField(int columns)`

This constructs an empty text field with the specified number of columns.

Parameters:

> `columns`—The number of columns

- `void addActionListener(ActionListener listener)`

This method adds an action listener to be notified when the user hits the Enter key in this text field.

Parameters:

> `listener`—The action listener

Class `javax.swing.Timer`

- `Timer(int millis, ActionListener listener)`

  This constructor constructs a timer that notifies an action listener whenever a time interval has elapsed.

  Parameters:

  > `millis`—The number of milliseconds between timer notifications
  >
  > `listener`—The object to be notified when the time inverval has elapsed

- `void start()`

  This method starts the timer. Once the timer has started, it begins notifiying its listener.

- `void stop()`

  This method stops the timer. Once the timer has stopped, it no longer notifies its listener.

Package `javax.swing.border`

Class `javax.swing.border.EtchedBorder`

- `EtchedBorder()`

  This constructor creates a lowered etched border.

Class `javax.swing.border.TitledBorder`

- `TitledBorder(Border b,String title)`

  This constructor creates a titled border that adds a title to a given border.

  Parameters:

  > `b`—The border to which the title is added
  >
  > `title`—The title the border should display

Package `javax.swing.event`

Class `javax.swing.event.ChangeEvent`

A slider emits change events when it is adjusted.

Class `javax.swing.event.ChangeListener`

- `void stateChanged(ChangeEvent e)`

  This event is called when the event source has changed its state.

Parameters:

> e—A change event

Package `javax.swing.text`

Class `javax.swing.text.JTextComponent`

- `String getText()`

  This method returns the text contained in this text component.

  Returns: The text.

- `boolean isEditable()`

  This method checks whether this text component is editable.

  Returns: `true` if the component is editable.

- `void setEditable(boolean state)`

  This method is used to make this text component editable or not.

  Parameters:

  > state—`true` to make editable, `false` to disable editing

- `void setText(String text)`

  This method sets the text of this text component to the specified text. If the text is empty, the old text is deleted.

  Parameters:

  > text—The new text to be set

A3

The Basic Latin and Latin-1 Subsets of Unicode

Char.	Code	Dec.	Char.	Code	Dec.	Char.	Code	Dec.
			0	'\u0030'	48	@	'\u0040'	64
!	'\u0021'	33	1	'\u0031'	49	A	'\u0041'	65
"	'\u0022'	34	2	'\u0032'	50	B	'\u0042'	66
#	'\u0023'	35	3	'\u0033'	51	C	'\u0043'	67
$	'\u0024'	36	4	'\u0034'	52	D	'\u0044'	68
%	'\u0025'	37	5	'\u0035'	53	E	'\u0045'	69
&	'\u0026'	38	6	'\u0036'	54	F	'\u0046'	70
'	'\u0027'	39	7	'\u0037'	55	G	'\u0047'	71
(	'\u0028'	40	8	'\u0038'	56	H	'\u0048'	72
)	'\u0029'	41	9	'\u0039'	57	I	'\u0049'	73
*	'\u002A'	42	:	'\u003A'	58	J	'\u004A'	74
+	'\u002B'	43	;	'\u003B'	59	K	'\u004B'	75
,	'\u002C'	44	<	'\u003C'	60	L	'\u004C'	76
–	'\u002D'	45	=	'\u003D'	61	M	'\u004D'	77
.	'\u002E'	46	>	'\u003E'	62	N	'\u004E'	78
/	'\u002F'	47	?	'\u003F'	63	O	'\u004F'	79

Table 1

The Basic Latin (ASCII) Subset of Unicode (*continues*)

Char.	Code	Dec.	Char.	Code	Dec.	Char.	Code	Dec.
P	'\u0050'	80	`	'\u0060'	96	p	'\u0070'	112
Q	'\u0051'	81	a	'\u0061'	97	q	'\u0071'	113
R	'\u0052'	82	b	'\u0062'	98	r	'\u0072'	114
S	'\u0053'	83	c	'\u0063'	99	s	'\u0073'	115
T	'\u0054'	84	d	'\u0064'	100	t	'\u0074'	116
U	'\u0055'	85	e	'\u0065'	101	u	'\u0075'	117
V	'\u0056'	86	f	'\u0066'	102	v	'\u0076'	118
W	'\u0057'	87	g	'\u0067'	103	w	'\u0077'	119
X	'\u0058'	88	h	'\u0068'	104	x	'\u0078'	120
Y	'\u0059'	89	i	'\u0069'	105	y	'\u0079'	121
Z	'\u005A'	90	j	'\u006A'	106	z	'\u007A'	122
[	'\u005B'	91	k	'\u006B'	107	{	'\u007B'	123
\	'\u005C'	92	l	'\u006C'	108	|	'\u007C'	124
]	'\u005D'	93	m	'\u006D'	109	}	'\u007D'	125
^	'\u005E'	94	n	'\u006E'	110	~	'\u007E'	126
_	'\u005F'	95	o	'\u006F'	111			

Table 1 (*continued*)

The Basic Latin (ASCII) Subset of Unicode

Table 2

Selected Control Characters

Char.	Code	Dec.
Space	' '	32
Newline	'\n'	10
Return	'\r'	13
Tab	'\t'	9

Char.	Code	Dec.	Char.	Code	Dec.	Char.	Code	Dec.
			À	'\u00C0'	192	à	'\u00E0'	224
¡	'\u00A1'	161	Á	'\u00C1'	193	á	'\u00E1'	225
¢	'\u00A2'	162	Â	'\u00C2'	194	â	'\u00E2'	226
£	'\u00A3'	163	Ã	'\u00C3'	195	ã	'\u00E3'	227
¤	'\u00A4'	164	Ä	'\u00C4'	196	ä	'\u00E4'	228
¥	'\u00A5'	165	Å	'\u00C5'	197	å	'\u00E5'	229
¦	'\u00A6'	166	Æ	'\u00C6'	198	æ	'\u00E6'	230
§	'\u00A7'	167	Ç	'\u00C7'	199	ç	'\u00E7'	231
¨	'\u00A8'	168	È	'\u00C8'	200	è	'\u00E8'	232
©	'\u00A9'	169	É	'\u00C9'	201	é	'\u00E9'	233
ª	'\u00AA'	170	Ê	'\u00CA'	202	ê	'\u00EA'	234
«	'\u00AB'	171	Ë	'\u00CB'	203	ë	'\u00EB'	235
¬	'\u00AC'	172	Ì	'\u00CC'	204	ì	'\u00EC'	236
	'\u00AD'	173	Í	'\u00CD'	205	í	'\u00ED'	237
®	'\u00AE'	174	Î	'\u00CE'	206	î	'\u00EE'	238
¯	'\u00AF'	175	Ï	'\u00CF'	207	ï	'\u00EF'	239
°	'\u00B0'	176	Ð	'\u00D0'	208	ð	'\u00F0'	240
±	'\u00B1'	177	Ñ	'\u00D1'	209	ñ	'\u00F1'	241
²	'\u00B2'	178	Ò	'\u00D2'	210	ò	'\u00F2'	242
³	'\u00B3'	179	Ó	'\u00D3'	211	ó	'\u00F3'	243
´	'\u00B4'	180	Ô	'\u00D4'	212	ô	'\u00F4'	244
µ	'\u00B5'	181	Õ	'\u00D5'	213	õ	'\u00F5'	245
¶	'\u00B6'	182	Ö	'\u00D6'	214	ö	'\u00F6'	246
·	'\u00B7'	183	×	'\u00D7'	215	÷	'\u00F7'	247
¸	'\u00B8'	184	Ø	'\u00D8'	216	ø	'\u00F8'	248
¹	'\u00B9'	185	Ù	'\u00D9'	217	ù	'\u00F9'	249
º	'\u00BA'	186	Ú	'\u00DA'	218	ú	'\u00FA'	250
»	'\u00BB'	187	Û	'\u00DB'	219	û	'\u00FB'	251
¼	'\u00BC'	188	Ü	'\u00DC'	220	ü	'\u00FC'	252
½	'\u00BD'	189	Ý	'\u00DD'	221	ý	'\u00FD'	253
¾	'\u00BE'	190	Þ	'\u00DE'	222	þ	'\u00FE'	254
¿	'\u00BF'	191	ß	'\u00DF'	223	ÿ	'\u00FF'	255

Table 3

The Latin-1 Subset of Unicode

Glossary

Abstract array An ordered sequence of items that can be efficiently accessed at random through an integer index.

Abstract class A class that cannot be instantiated.

Abstraction The process of finding the essential feature set for a building block of a program such as a class.

Abstract list An ordered sequence of items that can be traversed sequentially and that allows for efficient insertion and removal of elements at any position.

Abstract method A method with a name, parameter types, and return type but without an implementation.

Accessor method A method that accesses an object but does not change it.

Actual parameter The expression supplied for a formal parameter of a method by the caller.

ADT (abstract data type) A specification of the fundamental operations that characterize a data type, without supplying an implementation.

Aggregation The "has-a" relationship between classes.

Algorithm An unambiguous, executable, and terminating specification of a way to solve a problem.

API (application programming interface) A code library for building programs.

Applet A graphical Java program that executes inside a web browser or applet viewer.

Argument An actual parameter in a method call, or one of the values combined by an operator.

Array A collection of values of the same type stored in contiguous memory locations, each of which can be accessed by an integer index.

Array list A Java class that implements a dynamically growing array of objects.

Assertion A claim that a certain condition holds in a particular program location.

Assignment Placing a new value into a variable.

Association A relationship between classes in which one can navigate from objects of one class to objects of the other class, usually by following object references.

Balanced tree A tree in which *each* subtree has the property that the number of descendants to the left is approximately the same as the number of descendants to the right.

Big-Oh notation The notation $g(n) = O(f(n))$, which denotes that the function g grows at a rate that is bounded by the growth rate of the function f with respect to n. For example, $10n^2 + 100n - 1000 = O(n^2)$.

Binary file A file in which values are stored in their binary representation and cannot be read as text.

Binary operator An operator that takes two arguments, for example $+$ in $x + y$.

Binary search A fast algorithm to find a value in a sorted array. It narrows the search down to half of the array in every step.

Binary search tree A binary tree in which *each* subtree has the property that all left descendants are smaller than the value stored in the root, and all right descendants are larger.

Binary tree A tree in which each node has at most two child nodes.

Bit Binary digit; the smallest unit of information, having two possible values: 0 and 1. A data element consisting of n bits has 2^n possible values.

Black-box testing Testing a method without knowing its implementation.

Block A group of statements bracketed by {}.

Boolean operator → **Logical operator**

Boolean type A type with two possible values: `true` and `false`.

Border layout A layout management scheme in which components are placed into the center or one of the four borders of their container.

Boundary test case A test case involving values that are at the outer boundary of the set of legal values. For example, if a function is expected to work for all nonnegative integers, then 0 is a boundary test case.

Bounds error Trying to access an array element that is outside the legal range.

Breakpoint A point in a program, specified in a debugger, at which it stops executing the program and lets the user inspect the program state.

break statement A statement that terminates a loop or `switch` statement.

Buffer A temporary storage location for holding values that have been produced (for example, characters typed by the user) and are waiting to be consumed (for example, read a line at a time).

Buffered input Input that is gathered in batches, for example, a line at a time.

Byte A number made up of eight bits. Essentially all currently manufactured computers use a byte as the smallest unit of storage in memory.

Bytecode Instructions for the Java virtual machine.

Call by reference A method call mechanism in which the method receives the location in memory of a variable supplied as an actual parameter. Call by reference enables a method to change the contents of the original variable so that the change remains in effect after the method returns.

Call by value A method call mechanism in which the method receives a copy of the contents of a variable supplied as an actual parameter. Java uses only call by value. If a parameter variable's type is a class, its value is an object reference, so the method can alter that object but cannot make the parameter variable refer to a different object.

Call stack The ordered set of all methods that currently have been called but not yet terminated, starting with the current method and ending with `main`.

Case-sensitive Distinguishing upper- and lowercase characters.

Cast Explicitly converting a value from one type to a different type. For example, the cast from a floating-point number `x` to an integer is expressed in Java by the cast notation `(int)x`.

catch clause A part of a `try` block that is executed when a matching exception is thrown by any statement in the `try` block.

Check box A user interface component that can be used for a binary selection.

Checked exception An exception that the compiler checks. All checked exceptions must be declared or caught.

Class A programmer-defined data type.

Cloning Making a copy of an object whose state can be modified independently of the original object.

Cohesion A class is cohesive if its features support a single abstraction.

Combo box A user interface component that combines a text field with a drop-down list of selections.

Command line The line the user types to start a program in DOS or UNIX or a command window in Windows. It consists of the program name followed by any necessary arguments.

Comment An explanation to help the human reader understand a section of a program; ignored by the compiler.

Compiler A program that translates code in a high-level language (such as Java) to machine instructions (such as bytecode for the Java virtual machine).

Compile-time error An error that is detected when a program is compiled.

Component → **User interface component**

Compound statement A statement such as `if` or `while` that is made up of several parts such as a condition and a body.

Concatenation Placing one string after another to form a new string.

Console program A Java program that does not have a graphical window. A console program reads input from the keyboard and writes output to the terminal screen.

Constant A value that cannot be changed by a program. In Java, constants are defined with the keyword `final`.

Construction Setting a newly allocated object to an initial state.

Constructor A method that initializes a newly instantiated object.

Container A user interface component that can hold other components and present them together to the user. Also, a data structure, such as a list, that can hold a collection of objects and present them individually to a program.

Content pane The part of a Swing frame that holds the user interface components of the frame.

Coupling The degree to which classes are related to each other by dependency.

CPU (Central Processing Unit) The part of a computer that executes the machine instructions.

CRC card An index card representing a class, listing its responsibilities and its collaborating classes.

Debugger A program that lets a user run another program one or a few steps at a time, stop execution, and inspect the variables in order to analyze it for bugs.

Default constructor A constructor that is invoked with no parameters.

Dependency The "uses" relationship between classes, in which one class needs services provided by another class.

Dictionary ordering → **Lexicographic ordering**

Directory A structure on a disk that can hold files or other directories; also called a folder.

Documentation comment A comment in a source file that can be automatically extracted into the program documentation by a program such as javadoc.

Dot notation The notation *object*.*method*(*parameters*) or *object*.*field* used to invoke a method or access a field.

Doubly linked list A linked list in which each link has a reference to both its predecessor and successor links.

Early binding Choosing at compile time among several methods with the same name but different parameter types.

Encapsulation The hiding of implementation details.

End of file The condition that is true when all characters of a file have been read. Note that there is no special "end of file character". When composing a file on the keyboard, you may need to type a special character to tell the operating system to end the file, but that character is not part of the file.

Escape character A character in text that is not taken literally but has a special meaning when combined with the character or characters that follow it. The \ character is an escape character in Java strings.

Event class A class that contains information about an event, such as its source.

Event adapter A class that implements an event listener interface by defining all methods to do nothing.

Event listener An object that is notified by an event source when an event occurs.

Event source An object that can notify other classes of events.

Exception A class that signals a condition that prevents the program from continuing normally. When such a condition occurs, an object of the exception class is thrown.

Exception handler A sequence of statements that is given control when an exception of a particular type has been thrown and caught.

Explicit parameter A parameter of a method other than the object on which the method is invoked.

Expression A syntactical construct that is made up of constants, variables, method calls, and operators combining them.

Extension The last part of a file name, which specifies the file type. For example, the extension .java denotes a Java file.

Extreme Programming A development methodology that strives for simplicity, by removing formal structure and focusing on best practices.

Fibonacci numbers The sequence of numbers 1, 1, 2, 3, 5, 8, 13, …, in which every term is the sum of its two predecessors.

File A sequence of bytes that is stored on disk.

File pointer The position within a random-access file of the next byte to be read or written. It can be moved so as to access any byte in the file.

finally clause A part of a `try` block that is executed no matter how the `try` block is exited.

Floating-point number A number that can have a fractional part.

Flow layout A layout management scheme in which components are laid out left to right.

Flushing a stream Sending all characters that are still held in a buffer to its destination.

Folder → **Directory**

Font A set of character shapes in a particular style and size.

Formal parameter A variable in a method definition; it is initialized with an actual parameter value when the method is called.

Frame A window with a border and a title bar.

Garbage collection Automatic reclamation of memory occupied by objects that are no longer referenced.

goto statement A statement that transfers control to some other statement, which is tagged with a label. Java does not have a `goto` statement.

Graphics context A class through which a programmer can cause shapes to appear on a window or off-screen bitmap.

grep The "generalized regular expression pattern" search program, useful for finding all strings matching a pattern in a set of files.

Grid layout A layout management scheme in which components are placed into a two-dimensional grid.

GUI (graphical user interface) A user interface in which the user supplies inputs through graphical components such as buttons, menus, and text fields.

HTML (Hypertext Markup Language) The language in which web pages are described.

IDE (integrated development environment) A programming environment that includes an editor, compiler, and debugger.

Immutable class A class without a mutator method.

Implementing an interface → **Realizing an interface**

Implicit parameter The object on which a method is invoked. For example, in the call `x.f(y)`, the object `x` is the implicit parameter of the method `f`.

Inheritance The "is-a" relationship between a more general superclass and a more specialized subclass.

Initialization Setting a variable to a well-defined value when it is created.

Inner class A class that is defined inside another class.

Instance method A method with an implicit parameter; that is, a method that is invoked on an instance of a class.

Instance of a class An object whose type is that class.

Instance field A variable defined in a class for which every object of the class has its own value.

Instantiation of a class Constructing an object of that class.

Integer A number that cannot have a fractional part.

Integer division Taking the quotient of two integers, discarding the remainder. In Java the / symbol denotes integer division if both arguments are integers. For example, 11/4 is 2, not 2.75.

Interface A type with no instance variables and only abstract methods and constants.

Internet A worldwide collection of networks, routing equipment, and computers using a common set of protocols that define how participants interact with each other.

Interpreter A program that reads a set of codes and carries out the commands specified by them. The Java virtual machine is an interpreter that reads and executes Java bytecode.

Iterator An object that can inspect all elements in a container such as a linked list.

javadoc The documentation generator in the Java SDK. It extracts documentation comments from Java source files and produces a set of linked HTML files.

Late binding Choosing at run time among several methods with the same name invoked on objects belonging to subclasses of the same superclass.

Layout manager A class that arranges user interface components inside a container.

Lexicographic ordering Ordering strings in the same order as in a dictionary, by skipping all matching characters and comparing the first nonmatching characters of both strings. For example, "orbit" comes before "orchid" in lexicographic ordering. Note that in Java, unlike a dictionary, the ordering is case-sensitive: Z comes before a.

Library A set of precompiled classes that can be included into programs.

Linear search Searching a container (such as an array or list) for an object by inspecting each element in turn.

Linked list A data structure that can hold an arbitrary number of objects, each of which is stored in a link object, which contains a pointer to the next link.

Local variable A variable whose scope is a block.

Logging Sending messages that trace the progress of a program to a file or window.

Logical operator An operator that can be applied to Boolean values. Java has three logical operators: &&, ||, and !.

Logic error An error in a syntactically correct program that causes it to act differently from its specification.

Loop A sequence of instructions that is executed repeatedly.

Loop and a half A loop whose termination decision is neither at the beginning nor at the end.

Loop invariant A statement about the program state that is preserved when the statements in the loop are executed once.

Machine code Instructions that can be executed directly by the CPU.

Magic number A number that appears in a program without explanation.

main method The method that is first called when a Java application executes.

Merge sort A sorting algorithm that first sorts two halves of a data structure and then merges the sorted subarrays together.

Method A sequence of statements that has a name, may have formal parameters, and may return a value. A method can be invoked any number of times, with different values for its parameters.

Method signature The name of a method and the types of its parameters.

Mutator method A method that changes the state of an object.

Mutual recursion Cooperating methods that call each other.

Name clash Accidentally using the same name to denote two program features in a way that cannot be resolved by the compiler.

Negative test case A test case that is expected to fail. For example, when testing a root-finding program, an attempt to compute the square root of −1 is a negative test case.

Nested block A block that is contained inside another block.

Newline The '\n' character, which indicates the end of a line.

new operator An operator that allocates new objects.

Null reference A reference that does not refer to any object.

Object A value of a class type.

Object-oriented design Designing a program by discovering objects, their properties, and their relationships.

Object reference A value that denotes the location of an object in memory. In Java, a variable whose type is a class contains a reference to an object of that class.

Off-by-one error A common programming error in which a value is one larger or smaller than it should be.

Opening a file Preparing a file for reading or writing.

Operating system The software that launches application programs and provides services (such as a file system) for those programs.

Operator A symbol denoting a mathematical or logical operation, such as + or &&.

Operator associativity The rule that governs in which order operators of the same precedence are executed. For example, in Java the - operator is left-associative because a - b - c is interpreted as (a - b) - c, and = is right-associative because a = b = c is interpreted as a = (b = c).

Operator precedence The rule that governs which operator is evaluated first. For example, in Java the && operator has a higher precedence than the || operator. Hence a || b && c is interpreted as a || (b && c).

Oracle A program that predicts how another program should behave.

Overloading Giving more than one meaning to a method name.

Overriding Redefining a method in a subclass.

Package A collection of related classes. The import statement is used to access one or more classes in a package.

Panel A user interface component with no visual appearance. It can be used to group other components, or as the superclass of a component that defines a method for painting.

Parallel arrays Arrays of the same length, in which corresponding elements are logically related.

Parameter An item of information that is specified to a method when the method is called. For example, in the call `System.out.println("Hello,World!")`, the parameters are the implicit parameter `System.out` and the explicit parameter `"Hello,World!"`.

Parameter passing Specifying expressions to be actual parameter values for a method when it is called.

Partially filled array An array that is not filled to capacity, together with a companion variable that indicates the number of elements actually stored.

Polymorphism Selecting a method among several methods that have the same name on the basis of the actual types of the implicit parameters.

Positive test case A test case that a method is expected to handle correctly.

Postfix operator A unary operator that is written after its argument.

Precondition A condition that must be true when a method is called if the method is to work correctly.

Predicate method A method that returns a Boolean value.

Prefix operator A unary operator that is written before its argument.

Primitive type In Java, a number type or `boolean`.

Private feature A feature that is accessible only by methods of the same class or an inner class.

Project A collection of source files and their dependencies.

Prompt A string that tells the user to provide input.

Protected feature A feature that is accessible by a class, its inner classes, its subclasses, and the other classes in the same package.

Public feature A feature that is accessible by all classes.

Qualified name A name that is made unambiguous because it starts with the package name.

Queue A collection of items with "first in, first out" retrieval.

Quicksort A generally fast sorting algorithm that picks an element, called the pivot, partitions the sequence into the elements smaller than the pivot and those larger than the pivot, and then recursively sorts the subsequences.

Radio button A user interface component that can be used for selecting one of several options.

RAM (random-access memory) Electronic circuits in a computer that can store code and data of running programs.

Random access The ability to access any value directly without having to read the values preceding it.

Reader In the Java input/output library, a class from which to read characters.

Realizing an interface Implementing a class that defines all methods specified in the interface.

Recursive method A method that can call itself with simpler values. It must handle the simplest values without calling itself.

Redirection Linking the input or output of a program to a file instead of the keyboard or display.

Reference → **Object reference**

Regression testing Keeping old test cases and testing every revision of a program against them.

Regular expression A string that defines a set of matching strings according to their content. Each part of a regular expression can be a specific required character; one of a set of permitted characters such as `[abc]`, which can be a range such as `[a-z]`; any character not in a set of forbidden characters, such as `[^0-9]`; a repetition of one or more matches, such as `[0-9]+`, or zero or more, such as `[ACGT]*`; one of a set of alternatives, such as `and|et|und`; or various other possibilities. For example, `"[A-Za-z]*[0-9]+"` matches `"Cloud9"` or `"007"` but not `"Jack"`.

Relational database A data repository that stores information in tables and retrieves data as the result of queries that are formulated in terms of table relationships.

Reserved word A word that has a special meaning in a programming language and therefore cannot be used as a name by the programmer.

Return value The value returned by a method through a `return` statement.

Roundoff error An error introduced by the fact that the computer can store only a finite number of digits of a floating-point number.

Run-time error → **Logic error**

Run-time stack The data structure that stores the local variables of all called methods as a program runs.

Scope The part of a program in which a variable is defined.

SDK (Software Development Kit) A collection of tools for developing software.

Selection sort A sorting algorithm in which the smallest element is repeatedly found and removed until no elements remain.

Sentinel A value in input that is not to be used as an actual input value but to signal the end of input.

Sequential access Accessing values one after another without skipping over any of them.

Serialization The process of saving an object, and all the objects that it references, to a stream.

Shadowing Hiding a variable by defining another one with the same name.

Shell A part of an operating system in which the user types command lines to execute programs and manipulate files.

Shell script A file that contains commands for running programs and manipulating files. Typing the name of the shell script file on the command line causes those commands to be executed.

Side effect An effect of a method other than returning a value.

Signature → **Method signature**

Simple statement A statement consisting only of an expression.

Single-stepping Executing a program in the debugger one statement at a time.

Software life cycle All activites related to the creation and maintenance of the software from initial analysis until obselescence.

Source file A file containing instructions in a programming language such as Java.

Spiral model An iterative process model of software development in which design and implementation are repeated.

Stack A data structure with "last in, first out" retrieval. Elements can be added and removed only at one position, called the top of the stack.

Stack trace A printout of the call stack, listing all currently pending method calls.

Statement A syntactical unit in a program. In Java a statement is either a simple statement, a compound statement, or a block.

Static method A method with no implicit parameter.

Static field A variable defined in a class that has only one value for the whole class, which can be accessed and changed by any method of that class.

Stream An abstraction for a sequence of bytes from which data can be read or to which data can be written.

String A sequence of characters.

Stub A method with no or minimal functionality.

Subclass A class that inherits variables and methods from a superclass but adds instance variables, adds methods, or redefines methods.

Superclass A general class from which a more specialized class (a subclass) inherits.

Swing A Java toolkit for implementing graphical user interfaces.

Syntax Rules that define how to form instructions in a particular programming language.

Syntax error An instruction that does not follow the programming language rules and is rejected by the compiler.

Tab character The '\t' character, which advances the next character on the line to the next one of a set of fixed positions known as tab stops.

Ternary operator An operator with three arguments. Java has one ternary operator, `a ? b : c`.

Test coverage The instructions of a program that are executed in a set of test cases.

Test harness A program that calls a function that needs to be tested, supplying parameters and analyzing the function's return value.

Test suite A set of test cases for a program.

Text field A user interface component that allows a user to provide text input.

Text file A file in which values are stored in their text representation.

Thread A program unit that is executed independently of other parts of the program.

Throwing an exception Indicating an abnormal condition by terminating the normal control flow of a program and transferring control to a matching `catch` clause.

`throws` specifier Indicates the types of the checked exceptions that a method may throw.

Token A sequence of consecutive characters from an input source that belongs together for the purpose of analyzing the input. For example, a token can be a sequence of characters other than white space.

Trace message A message that is printed during a program run for debugging purposes.

`try` block A block of statements that contains exception processing clauses. A `try` block contains at least one `catch` or `finally` clause.

Turing machine A very simple model of computation that is used in theoretical computer science to explore computability of problems.

Two-dimensional array A tabular arrangement of elements in which an element is specified by a row and a column index.

Unary operator An operator with one argument.

Unchecked exception An exception that the compiler doesn't check.

Unicode A standard code that assigns code values consisting of two bytes to characters used in scripts around the world. Java stores all characters as their Unicode values.

Uninitialized variable A variable that has not been set to a particular value. In Java, using an uninitialized local variable is a syntax error.

Unit test A test of a method by itself, isolated from the remainder of the program.

URL (Uniform Resource Locator) A pointer to an information resource (such as a web page or an image) on the World Wide Web.

User interface component A building block for a graphical user interface, such as a button or a text field. User interface components are used to present information to the user and allow the user to enter information to the program.

Variable A symbol in a program that identifies a storage location that can hold different values.

Virtual machine A program that simulates a CPU that can be implemented efficiently on a variety of actual machines. A given program in Java bytecode can be executed by any Java virtual machine, regardless of which CPU is used to run the virtual machine itself.

Visual programming Programming by arranging graphical elements on a form, setting program behavior by selecting properties for these elements, and writing only a small amount of "glue" code linking them.

void keyword A keyword indicating no type or an unknown type.

Watch window A window in a debugger that shows the current values of selected variables.

Waterfall model A sequential process model of software development, consisting of analysis, design, implementation, testing, and deployment.

White-box testing Testing functions taking their implementations into account, in contrast to black-box testing; for example, by selecting boundary test cases and ensuring that all branches of the code are covered by some test case.

White space Any sequence of only space, tab, and newline characters.

Writer In the Java input/output library, a class to which characters are to be sent.

Index*

Photo Credits